COMMENTARY ON
ISAIAH

COMMENTARY ON
ISAIAH

HARRY BULTEMA

KREGEL PUBLICATIONS
Grand Rapids, Michigan 49501

Cover Design: Don Ellens

Library of Congress Cataloging-in-Publication Data

Bultema, Harry, (1884-1952).
    Commentary on Isaiah.

    Translation of: Practische Commentaar op Jesaja.
    1. Bible. O.T. Isaiah—Commentaries. I. Bible. O.T. Isaiah. English. 1981. II. Title.

BS1515.B8413   1981   224'.107   81-11795
                                            CIP
ISBN   0-8254-2261-2   (pbk.)

2 3 4 5 6 Printing/Year 95 94 93 92 91

Printed in the United States of America

CONTENTS

FOREWORD

It was in the year 1923 when my father expressed heartfelt gratitude to Almighty God for allowing him, in the midst of pressing cares and activities, to publish his popular exposition of Isaiah.

Pressing cares? Yes! Four years earlier, in 1919, he had been led to leave his large denominational pastorate. Why? Because he had delved deeply into the storehouse of God's grace and taken a stand for the sublime truth of the premillennial return of Christ. It was a truth he fervently loved and about which he preached with power. His prolific pen also etched this blessed truth in numerous volumes that he authored.

One of those volumes was this practical commentary on Isaiah. It was published in the Dutch language, as were most of his writings.

For over fifty years, the truth of this book was locked in that language; very few could read it. How often my father, and members of our family, longed to get this volume translated and published in English. This was not realized in his lifetime for in 1952 he was ushered into the presence of his blessed Lord, whom he loved, served and longed to see.

Now, fifty-nine years after the last edition, we are privileged to publish this practical Commentary on Isaiah in the English language. Through thoughtful urging and help of Dale DeWitt, Professor at Grace Bible College, we were led to Cornelius Lambregtse, who very ably translated this book from the Dutch language into English.

With much joy, I express my warm gratitude to Professor Dale DeWitt, Cornelius Lambregtse, Herbert Birchenough, Pastor and Mrs. Ernest Green, Mrs. Jacob Molenkamp, my brother, John Bultema, and others who worked on this book in any way, for their invaluable help and encouragement in getting this volume published. I am also deeply grateful to Kregel Publications for their assistance in publishing this book.

The name Isaiah means *Salvation is of the Lord.* What a blessed truth! By God's matchless, marvelous grace, we can know, *even now,* His wonderful salvation in and through the once-for-all sacrifice of our Savior, Jesus Christ, on the cross of Calvary.

In a future sense also, *Salvation is of the Lord.* My father looked and longed for the coming of the Lord in his day. The truth of Christ's coming was the watermark of his ministry.

The truth concerning Christ's coming to set up the long awaited Kingdom on earth is precious, indeed. But, even before that event, *at any moment,* our wonderful Savior will come to snatch away believers in Him.

It is our earnest prayer that many will be led to the *Salvation of the Lord* and that believers will be led to love, look and long for His blessed return through reading this book.

Daniel C. Bultema

* * * * * * * * * *

"For our conversation is in heaven; from whence also we look for the Savior, the Lord Jesus Christ: Who shall change our vile body, that it may be fashioned like unto his glorious body, according to the working whereby he is able to subdue all things unto himself," Philippians 3:20, 21.

INTRODUCTION

ISAIAH 1-39

INTRODUCTION: ISAIAH 1-39

I. ISAIAH

1. His Name

The name Isaiah means *Salvation is of the Lord,* and this indicates the fundamental thought of his entire prophecy. The word is related to the name Jesus and literally means *Jehovah saves from oppression and gives deliverance.* The idea of salvation is the principle one in the Bible and hence is embodied in numerous names in Scripture. Thus, the name of Isaiah was very common in Israel. No less than seven persons in Scripture are called by that name: one of the sons of Jeduthun, a descendant of Eliezer; the son of Moses; a Benjamite; a grandson of Zerubbabel; one of the exiles who returned with Ezra from Babylon; one of the Levites who was invited to come by Ezra; and finally our great prophet. To distinguish him from these people with the same name, our famous prophet is called "the son of Amoz." Because the Greek and Latin translators translated the original *Amoz* by *Amos,* some were of the opinion, as was Hieronymus, that this man was the same person as Amos, and that Isaiah, the major prophet, was therefore the son of the minor prophet, but the original name contradicts this thought. According to the Rabbinical tradition this Amoz was a brother of King Amaziah, but proof of this is lacking.

2. His Place of Residence

Isaiah lived and worked in Jerusalem (cf. 7:3; 22:1, 15; 37:2, 21; 38:5; 39:3). His call to repentance was mostly directed to the frivolous and proud inhabitants of Jerusalem. We find him here during the Syro-Ephraimitic War and also during the invasions of Sennacherib, many years later. There he received his call to be a prophet in the year of the death of

King Uzziah. Jerusalem was the city of the royal residence and at the same time the religious center. It was the focal point of culture, but as often is the case in history, at the same time the cesspool of every wickedness. In its streets Isaiah saw the stately chariots of the proud princes and courtiers, the refined and sensuous ladies in their luxurious attire and makeup, walking and mincing, and with wanton eyes casting seductive looks at men. It was also in Jerusalem that Isaiah saw the feasts and banquets at which wine flowed so freely that the participants, the spiritual leaders of the people, wallowed dead drunk in their own vomit and excrement. That was culture! The culture of the holy city! Here Isaiah heard the crying of the widows and orphans on account of their rich oppressors; the wailing of the poor who were dragged off by their rich creditors. It was also in this city that he saw the haughty people, who also sacrificed in the temple, slinking under the heavy shade trees in parks and squares to pay homage to the idols. Upon hearing and seeing all this, his eyes blazed and his words bristled in holy anger.

3. His Family

Isaiah was married. His wife is called a *prophetess* (8:3). This must not be taken as though she were a prophetess in an official sense or possessed the gift of prophecy, but it does convey the idea that by her marital relationship with the prophet she was very closely involved in his work and fought along with him. Hence in this respect Isaiah had a totally different life than Jeremiah who was explicitly forbidden to take a wife (Jer. 16:2) and from whose manner of life it was clearly evident that he lacked the support of a woman and was unmarried. The prophet Isaiah was the father of at least two sons. Some even think of three, but there is no certainty about a third one. His elder son bore the symbolic name of Shear-jashub, that is to say, *A Remnant Returns,* and the second the name of *Haste-Plunder-Fast-Spoil.* The prophet himself says of these sons, "Behold, I and the children whom the Lord hath given me are for signs and for wonders in Israel." In Hebrews 2:13 these words are applied to the Lord Jesus and the children whom He leads to glory. Although our prophet was hated, as were all true prophets, as a peevish spoilsport and was mocked by the drunk prophets and priests, he nevertheless seems to have gathered a small circle of faithful followers around him. At least that is the impression we get from the otherwise very difficult sixteenth verse of the eighth chapter.

4. His Character

Already in early antiquity Isaiah was called the great prophet, not only on account of his work and word but also because of his character. He was a man of royal spirit, no matter from which angle he is considered. Nevertheless this great one in the kingdom of God has been frequently attacked by higher criticism. He was accused of being narrow-minded and vengeful with regard to Babylon and other foreign nations as well as Judah's foreign policy. In the headings and notations of the Leyden Translation are many examples of this to be found. We see Isaiah, not only as a prophet but also as a man, as a sharply outlined figure, a noble personality and a fearless warrior. There is no imaginable talent of head and heart which he does not possess. Dr. J. J. P. Valeton says correctly of him: "Everything that comprises the excellence of the various prophets is as it were combined in him." He has the courage of a Daniel, the sensitivity of a Jeremiah, the pathos of a Hosea, and the raging anger of an Amos; and moreover he leaves all of them far behind in the unique art of holy mockery. His courage is of such a nature that he never, not even for a moment, shows himself to be weak or timid. He addresses the princes as *rulers of Sodom;* he orally denudes the sensuous women for their shameful nakedness; and he flings a sixfold woe at the heads of six classes of evildoers. When everyone's heart was trembling and Jerusalem was seized by panic, he mocked at the raging enemies, calling them "two tails of smoking firebrands." Proud Shebna has to hear from him that he will be tossed away like a ball. He warns against the policy of the Egyptian greats, and he does not fear a boasting Rabshakeh like everyone else. Nevertheless he also knew pity and his heart cried out on account of Moab (15:5; 16:9, 11). Indeed, his sensitive heart sympathized with the fall of Babylon (21:4, 10; see also 22:4).

5. His End

Nothing is recorded about either the year of his birth or about the manner of his death. He must have been quite old, for we know with certainty that he prophesied for forty-six long years. Jotham and Ahaz both reigned for sixteen years, which gives a total of thirty-two years. And we know that Hezekiah became sick in the fourteenth year of his reign, so that we can be sure of at least forty-six years of prophetic activity. There is, however, a strong Judeo-Christian tradition that holds that Isaiah also outlived Hezekiah and was sawn asunder by his successor Manasseh with a wooden saw after the prophet had hidden himself in a hollow tree from the angry king. Origen bases this on chapter three, verses six to twelve. Justin Martyr in a debate with Trypho the Jew accused the Jews that they had sawn Isaiah into pieces with a wooden saw. In a very old story, entitled *The Vision of Isaiah* or *The Ascension of Isaiah,* this is recounted in great detail. Many Jews and Christians accepted this tradition. Rome honors Isaiah as martyr and saint on the 6th of July and the Greek Orthodox Church on May 9. The old Roman *Book of Martyrs* notes for the 6th of July: "In Judea the commemoration of St. Isaiah, the prophet, who during the reign of King Manasseh was cut into two and died." With De Buck, however, we say, "Isaiah was not the kind of man to take flight." But we also think that we can say with Klosterman, "On the basis of this strong tradition, one thing can be safely assumed, namely, that Isaiah died during the reign of Manasseh." If this is so, then he prophesied for at least sixty-one years.

6. Isaiah as Poet

The poetic talent of Isaiah can be no better indicated than in the well-known triad by Da Costa:

> Feeling, imagination, courage,
> Fused into one irresistible power;
> Molten into a red-hot mass,
> And sent forth by the heart
> On wings of melody,
> Behold, the gift of poetry!

According to Da Costa, with Isaiah "the gift of poetry"

was also "connected with holy prophecy," indeed, was totally fused with it. Moreover, his feeling was not of the soft, weak, pitiful kind, but a

> Feeling that suddenly awakens
> At every impression from on high,
> That grows, shares, burns and blazes
> With ever increasing power.

Since he had heard the cherubim cry about the threefold holiness and the earth-shaking glory of the Lord, he himself was able to pour out his soul in the most soul-stirring songs. Isaiah possesses an incomparable mastery of language. There is the greatest diversity of songs — the lyrical, elegiacal and the epical element is represented in his style. He sings in every kind of tone — the commanding, berating, lamenting, bewailing and jubilating. He lets us hear the rumble of thunder, the roaring of the lion, the war cry of on-marching armies, the screaming of fugitives, the crackle of flames, the rattle of chariots, the clanging of armor, the roar of the seas, and the din of earthquakes. Van Hamelveld, Van Der Palm, Jonckbloet, and Ridderbos all have rendered a beautiful poetic translation of our poet.

There are no poetic images and figures he has not used. Proverb and Metaphor, rhyme and epigram, soul-searching question and dialog, antithesis, alliteration, hyperbole, parable, wordplay, irony, and parallelism — all of these are found in their most perfect form in Isaiah. The Church Father, Jerome, wrote, "It is not possible that a translation into any other language can preserve the flower of his style undamaged." Van Der Palm writes in the Preface of his beautiful translation, "If the language of ecstasy had been totally foreign to me, I would never have ventured a translation of a poet like Isaiah!" And Van Hamelveld writes in his Preface, "As a poet Isaiah possesses the greatest eminence." Dillmann says that every single word of Isaiah is correct and hits the target. C. L. Robinson calls him "a perfect artist in words." Ten Kate calls him a poetic artist and compares him to Moses, David, and Nahum. Driver writes, "Isaiah's poetical genius is superb." The famous orator Edmund Burke had the custom of reading Isaiah before he gave a speech in Parliament. Indeed, as far as poetic genius and poetic output are concerned, there is no room for diverging opinion, and the praise of all authorities is here unanimously high. His vocabulary is richer than that of any other writer of sacred Scriptures and his usage of synonyms of related words is unique. Ezekiel used only 1,535 words, Jeremiah 1,653, the Psalmist 2,170, while Isaiah uses 2,186 words. In this respect, he leaves all of them far behind. Indeed might Da Costa sing of him:

> Thou Prince, thou angelic Isaiah!
> Awesome interpreter of God's counsel!
> Who, as a herald of vengeance, but also of the Messiah,
> Spreadest terror as well as hope among the people;
> And who repeatest in thy song for the earth
> The Holy, holy, holy of the angels
> With which their choirs greet God in His throne,
> While safely hiding in the shadow of wings
> From the fire of His reflection!
> Thou, holy one, art the true poet,
> Thy language is soul in soul's melody!

7. Isaiah as Orator

Closely related to his poetic genius is his talent as an orator. The Church Father, Jerome, compared him to Demosthenes. Of all fine talents, that of oratory is the highest. It is not the gift of singing but of speaking that God wants to use in the dissemination of salvation in Christ (Mark 16:15, 16). The gift of speech, therefore, has had greater influence on people throughout the course of history than the gift of singing beautifully. Well then, also as an orator Isaiah stands on the highest rung of the ladder and leaves all orators of fame far behind. One may freely read a dozen collections of the best and most famous orations in the world, and one will have to agree that in comparison with the brilliant and glittering words of the son of Amoz, they are no more than dry, spiritless speeches.

Just listen to these powerful words as a sample of his eloquence:

> Enter into the rock, and hide thee in the dust, for fear of the Lord, and for the glory of his majesty.
> The lofty looks of man shall be humbled, and the haughtiness of men shall be bowed down, and the Lord alone shall be exalted in that day.

For the day of the Lord of hosts shall be upon every one that is proud and lofty, and upon every one that is lifted up; and he shall be brought low:
And upon all the cedars of Lebanon, that are high and lifted up, and upon all the oaks of Bashan, and upon all the high mountains, and upon all the hills that are lifted up,
And upon every high tower, and upon every fenced wall,
And upon all the ships of Tarshish, and upon all pleasant pictures.
And the loftiness of man shall be bowed down, and the haughtiness of men shall be made low: and the Lord alone shall be exalted in that day.

This eloquence is unique in its kind. He ever casts his entire righteous soul into his words. All his courage, his power, his sense of justice, his anger and his compassion with the oppressed are used in service of his eloquence. His deep feelings and rich imagination, as well as his great vocabulary, make him extremely vivacious. He always places the concrete before the abstract. In 41:19 he mentions no less than seven kinds of trees. He can enumerate the names of the various pieces of finery and ornaments of women in one breath for so long, in such minutiae that it had to create the impression of devastating mockery. When he leads his audience into the workshop of the maker of idols, he is able to describe everything in detail; we see the woodcutter, the carpenter, the smith and the goldsmith at their trades. We even see the chips fly and hear the noise of soldering. A lifeless creation simply does not exist for him. Mountains, woods, rivers — everything lives and coexists with man. The little words *behold* and *hear* appear often. With him we find the oratorical effect in frequent repetition and climax. "Babylon is fallen, is fallen!" (21:9); "Watchman, what of the night? Watchman, what of the night?" (v. 11). "Fadeth away , . . . fadeth away" (24:4). "My leanness, my leanness" (24:16). "Precept upon precept, precept upon precept" (28:13). "To Ariel, to Ariel" (29:1). "Comfort ye, comfort ye" (40:1); "Lift up , . . . lift it up" (40:9). "I, even I" (43:11). "For mine own sake, even for mine own sake" (48:11); "I, even I" (v. 15). "I, even I" (51:12). "Awake, awake" (51:9,17). "Depart ye, depart ye" (52:11). "Peace, peace" (57:19). "According . . . accordingly" (59:18). "Go through, go through" (62:10); "cast up, cast up" (v. 10);

"Behold . . . behold" (v. 11). "Behold me, behold me" (65:1). "Behold, my servants , . . . behold, my servants" (65:13). These are not only the repetitions in the same words, but so-called parallelism, specifically synonym and culmulative parallelism, very often express the same thought in related words. A frequent example of this form is "Sing , . . . break forth into singing , . . . cry aloud." Professor Berkhof in his hermeneutical manual says of parallelism, "It is the fruit of a deeply touched heart and deep sensitivity in connection with the passion of the Oriental, who prefers to use short sentences." By not taking this parallelism into account many exegetes and preachers have become victims of misinterpretation.

8. Isaiah as Writer

Not only has Isaiah written this extensive prophecy, but he has also written two biographies of the Kings Uzziah and Hezekiah. In II Chronicles 26:22 we read, "Now the rest of the acts of Uzziah, first and last, did Isaiah the prophet, the son of Amoz write." According to II Chronicles 32:32, Isaiah wrote also such a biography of King Hezekiah. The one on Uzziah has become lost, but most exegetes believe – and we are of the same opinion – that we have at least a summary of the second biography in II Kings 18:13 - 20:19 and in Isaiah 36 - 39. This shows us that our prophet was not exclusively concerned with the future, but with the past as well. In other words, he was also a chronicler, an historian. Besides, from his long prophecy, it is quite obvious that he had a great knowledge of the history of Israel. He speaks of Creation, Paradise, the Flood, Noah, Sodom, Abraham, the exodus from Egypt, the wanderings in the wilderness, the entry into Canaan, the wars of Joshua, Gideon, David, etc. Among Isaiah's activities as a writer was also the fact that he wrote some very important things on a tablet or plate (or, as we would say, a placard), and held these up in clearly legible writing to the people as a warning or admonition. Examples of that are found in 8:1 and 30:8. His most important writing, however, is in the book that carries his name. If this were printed in booklet form, it would be about twenty pages less than the book of Jeremiah and even a little less than the book of Ezekiel. As far as the quality — the essential contents — is concerned he is second to none. We reject the statement by those critics who state, without proof, that there is a lack of coherence in his book. There may not be a chronological order in it, but there certainly is a topical order. Concerning the unity of the book of Isaiah, we will say more in the introduction to the second part.

II. ISAIAH AS PROPHET

Just as Samson's power resided in his being a Nazarite, so Isaiah's power did not reside in his natural and spiritual talents of mind and heart, but particularly in the fact that he was a *prophet.* Hence it is necessary that we briefly consider this. All peoples in the dark ages of antiquity had their soothsayers who pretended to be able to lift the heavy curtain hiding the future, but only the small nation of the Jews had its prophets who, in the name of the Lord, shed the light of grace in dark times. A prophet is a man of God who goes forth with a mandate from the Lord and as an interpreter of the Lord's will. The word *nabi',* the most common name for a prophet, is most likely derived from a root word meaning *bubble up.* under the pressure of a higher inspiration. Hence, a prophet is a man out of whom *bubbles up* the thought and will of the Lord upon prior divine revelation. And, since the prophets were emissaries of a holy God and were sent to an extremely sinful people, they frequently found themselves compelled to use condemnatory language regarding the wickedness of the people. They were Israel's guardians, especially of the theocracy and the kings who, as humble vicars of God, were called to govern in Jerusalem. If the prophets were faithful to their calling, they had to berate without respect of persons all who publicly departed from Jehovah's will. They were the sheep dogs who were to keep a watchful eye just as much on Israel's shepherds, the king and the princes and priests, as on the Lord's flock. This Isaiah did very faithfully for many years.

Isaiah was in the fullest sense of the word a man of God, i.e., a man who stood in a very special relationship to God.

Although we may be sure that he was extremely gifted, far-seeing, judicious, wise, and God-fearing, he, nevertheless, would not on account of all these assets have been able to speak as he did, if the Lord had not frequently made His will known to him by way of a revelation. He could not have passed on the Word of God if he had not first received it. Hence the Lord spoke to him in the three most common manners of divine revelation.

At his calling as a prophet he received a magnificent vision, which dominated his entire life and all his labors, namely, the vision of the coming Christ, who fills the whole world with His glory and who causes the heavens to resound with His holiness and glory. As is evident from 30:10, he himself was occasionally called a seer by his contemporaries. Thus, this old appellation (I Sam. 9:9) was still in use in his day.

A second manner of revelation was powerful seizure as in 8:11. We must undoubtedly think of God's Spirit coming powerfully upon him, which also Ezekiel calls *God's hand* being upon him. In a manner inexplicable to us the men of God were seized and irresistibly urged and compelled to speak or act. Then the Word of the Lord became as a fire in their bones. Although Isaiah mentions such an occasion only once, we may assume that this happened more often to him.

Finally, direct speaking was the third manner in which Jehovah revealed Himself to the prophet. In 22:14, he says that Jehovah Sabaoth revealed Himself in his *ears,* from which we may conclude that he heard the audible voice of the Lord with his ears. See also 8:11; 20:2; 22:14. Speaking from mouth to mouth, as a friend to a friend, was the noblest form of revelation, in which Moses shared more than anyone else. But it seems that the royal Isaiah shared in this incomparable privilege quite often as well. This method belongs to the *divers manners* in which God revealed Himself to the fathers according to Hebrews 1:1. Let this suffice as far as the reception of God's revelation is concerned. Let's now consider briefly his reproduction of the revelation received.

Just as the prophet received the revelation of truth in three forms, he passed it on in three main forms. First of all he passed it on by oral prophetic preaching and teaching. We can safely assume that Isaiah frequently acted as an open-air preacher. As a preacher of penitence he admonished the gaily mincing ladies and gentlemen to repent by pointing to the inescapable judgments. He also made known the truth by symbolic actions. According to 20:2, 3, he was for three long years a sign and wonder by walking barefoot and naked to show Judah, which put its trust in Egypt, that the Egyptians would be carried off barefoot and naked as captured slaves by the Assyrians. Instances such as mentioned in 7:3; 8:1-3, and 30:7 may be considered symbolic acts as well. Not only by his words but also by his name and children, he was a sign to Israel.

And in the third place, Isaiah passed on the truth he received by revelation by writing for posterity. Since we have already considered him as a writer, we need not go further into this.

In the book of Ecclesiasticus, Jesus Ben Sirach says of Isaiah: "Isaiah, a great man trustworthy in his vision . . . . In the power of the Spirit he saw the last things, he comforted the mourners of Zion, he revealed the future to the end of time, and hidden things long before they happened." It is exactly this last statement that is a thorn in the flesh of the critics, who do not believe in the miracle of foretelling. Isaiah mentioned *Koresh,* i.e., Cyrus the Great, by name two centuries before he appeared. He foretold the rise of the Babylonian empire as well as its fall. He saw and depicted the sacking of Babylon by Cyrus in the brightest of colors almost two centuries before this took place, and it happened just in that way. He saw the banquet on the memorable night of Babylon's fall, and Daniel five is simply the literal fulfillment of 21:5. He mentions the nations that would conquer Babylon, 21:2; the name of the general, 44:28; 45:1, the manner in which this would take place, 21:2-7; 44:27, and he describes repeatedly Babylon's destruction, 13:19; 14:20-30. Thus he saw, guided and enlightened by the Spirit of the Lord, powerful nations "rise, shine, and sink," but just as clearly he saw that the people of the promise would never be exterminated, no matter how they would be vexed, but would at last obtain world dominion under their Messiah. Repeatedly, he pictured this glorious future in the most brilliant colors. And one day these pictures will be just as surely fulfilled as were the pictures of Babylon's fall.

III. ISAIAH'S TIME

In the strictest sense of the word, Isaiah was not a child of his time, although at the same time it is an undeniable fact that his labors were to a large extent determined by his time. For that reason it is necessary that we briefly look at the political, religious, and moral situation of his time.

1. The Political Situation

His was the time of the rise of world powers.

First Assyria and Egypt fought for supremacy, and then in the final years of Isaiah, Assyria and Babylon did. The Assyrian kings Tiglath-pileser, Shalmaneser, Sargon, Sennacherib, Esarhaddon, and Ashurbanipal were powerful and ambitious rulers, bent on military glory and conquest and who in varying degrees acted according to the present-day principle of "might is right." Thus, the smaller nations were the victims. They had to live by the grace of Assyria. The small states in and around Palestine in the time of the prophet experienced this in a most grievous way. In his beautiful rectorial speech on Sennacherib, Dr. C. Van Gelderen pictured the unbridled appetite for world dominion in those days.

Israel's first painful contact with this world power was in the days of the ghastly murderer, Menahem, of the kingdom of the ten tribes. We read in II Kings 15:19, 20 that by way of punishment:

Pul, the king of Assyria, came against the land, and Menahem gave Pul a thousand talents of silver, that his hand might be with him to conform the kingdom in his hand. And Menahem exacted the money of Israel, even of all the mighty men of wealth, of each man fifty shekels of silver, to give to the king of Assyria. So the king of Assyria turned back, and stayed not there in the land.

Thus, we see that it was the selfish politics of a murderer that kindled the first covetous desire in the predatory nation of Assyria for the possession of God's covenant people. A few years later, during the final year of Uzziah, hence in the year when Isaiah received his mandate, Tiglath-pileser invaded the northern kingdom. We read of it in II Kings 15:29, "In the days of Pekah, king of Israel, came Tiglath-pileser, king of Assyria, and took Ijon, and Abel-beth-maachah, and Janoah, and Kedesh, and Hazor, and Gilead, and Galilee, all the land of Naphtali, and carried them captive to Assyria." This sad history is alluded to in 8:22 and 9:1-5. It was this same Pekah who destroyed Ahaz's army, killed 120,000 and carried 200,000 captive to Samaria. Isaiah one is a probable reference to this. And it was also this Pekah who aligned himself with Rezin of Syria with the satanic object to exterminate the house of David. We must view chapter seven in this light. But the murderer, Pekah, was in turn murdered by Hoshea. At his accession to the throne he was of course a vassal of Assyria, as were his predecessors. It seems, however, that Assyria did not quite trust matters in Samaria. At least we read in II Kings 17:3, 4:

> Against him came up Shalmaneser king of Assyria; and Hoshea became his servant, and gave him presents. And the king of Assyria found conspiracy in Hoshea: for he had sent messengers to So king of Egypt, and brought no present to the king of Assyria, as he had done year by year: therefore the king of Assyria shut him up, and bound him in prison.

After that we read of the three year siege of Samaria by Shalmaneser and Israel's exile to Assyria. According to the commonly accepted chronology, this was in 722 B.C.

> And it came to pass in the fourth year of king Hezekiah, which was the seventh year of Hoshea son of Elah king of Israel, that Shalmaneser king of Assyria came up against Samaria, and besieged it. And at the end of three years they took it: even in the sixth year of Hezekiah, that is the ninth year of Hoshea king of Israel, Samaria was taken. And the king of Assyria did carry away Israel unto Assyria, and put them in Halah and in Habor by the river of Gozan, and in the cities of Medes" (II Kings 18:9-11; cf. II Kings 17:5, 6).

The following are mentioned as the causes of Israel's exile: disobedience to the voice of the Lord, transgression of His covenant, ingratitude for God's blessings, idolatry and image-worship, pursuing the heathen abominations, covering up their wickedness and rejecting the word of the prophets (see II Kings 18:12 and 17:7-23). We read in these passages the striking words:

> Therefore the Lord was very angry with Israel, and removed them out of his sight: *there was none left but the tribe of Judah only.* Also Judah kept not the commandments of the Lord their God, but walked in the statutes of Israel which they made" (II Kings 17:18-19).

When reading Isaiah we do well to keep all these things in mind. Also for Judah, the axe lay at the foot of the tree. Many of Isaiah's pronouncements were made under the pressure of the tremendous events during which a sister nation was vexed, besieged, and carried away. Samaria was only about thirty-five to forty miles away from Jerusalem. So if people climbed on their roofs in the cities of Judah and in Jerusalem, they could see the big campfires of the enemy burn and a while later even see the sister capital go up in flames (see Isaiah 22:1). Seen in this light, it is very understandable that Isaiah warned the frivolous people of Judah and Jerusalem most seriously. But, it is not understandable that Judah, seeing the vehement wrath of God upon Israel, did not start living more modestly and decently, but rather like a wildly running horse heading for its destruction.

We have seen how the selfish, murderous politics of the ten tribes played into the hands of the Assyrian empire, but, closely considered, the situation in Judah was not any different. It was during the oppressive time of the Syro-Ephraimitic war against Judah that Ahaz, contrary to all Isaiah's warnings, sent messengers to Tiglath-pileser, saying,

> I am thy servant and thy son: come up, and save me out of the hand of the king of Syria, and out of the hand of the king of Israel, which rise up against me" (II Kings 16:7).

He had given the treasures of the temple and the palace to

the messengers as a present for the king of Assyria. Upon this despicable plea of Ahaz, Tiglath-pileser indeed advanced to Damascus, captured it, took its inhabitants to Kir, and killed Rezin. Nevertheless Ahaz, even though he paid his respects to his lord ever so obsequiously at Damascus, did not get what he wanted, for we read that Tiglath-pileser *distressed* him, *strengthened* him not, and *helped* him not (II Chron. 28:20, 21).

But there was at least one person in all of foolish Judah who, guided by divine light, recognized the futility of these politics, and that one man was Isaiah. He realized that such politics were bound to carry Judah sooner or later to the Abyss, and he was not mistaken, as the final outcome proved. The Assyrian beast of prey had received a tender piece of meat from Ahaz, and that whetted its appetite. Hence, when the ambitious and rapacious Sennacherib ascended the throne of Assyria, he soon marched upon Judah with a mighty army. For had not Hezekiah, the son of Ahaz, refused further obedience to him also? Again we find many allusions to this march of the mighty Sennacherib in Isaiah.

Chapter thirty-seven describes how wonderfully the Lord saved the city from his claws. But even this miraculous rescue occasioned a twofold hapless result. In the first place, many of the frivolous people now got the mistaken idea that Jerusalem, in contrast to Samaria and other cities, was invincible and untouchable on account of the temple and its worship. Less than a century later, this was obviously the general attitude, as is clear from the prophecies of Jeremiah. In the second place, the result of the defeat of Sennacharib before the walls of Jerusalem was that Babylon, which was growing in strength and was also vying for world dominion, sent its messengers with congratulations and presents to the God-fearing Hezekiah with the woeful result that the king fell victim to pride and was told in the name of the Lord that all his treasures and his sons would be carried away to Babylon. Hence, the victory became, as so often was the case later on, the occasion of a complete downfall. To those who do not walk in the ways of the Lord all victories are occasions to become proud; and pride, according to Solomon, "goeth before destruction, and a haughty spirit before a fall."

2. The Religious Situation

Needless to say, we are taking the word "religious" in a broad sense, so that it also includes the general religious life. Hence, it means not only the spiritual life, but also Judah's total relationship to the first table of the law.

First, it must be pointed out that Judah had experienced a half-century of great outward prosperity under the prosperous rule of Uzziah. During his long reign this king had applied himself with heart and soul to fostering the external and internal prosperity and fortification of his country and people, and the Lord blessed his efforts with success. For we read of him, *". . . he was marvelously helped."* But toward the end of his life, as an old man, he committed the greatest foolishness of his life by wishing to be priest as well as king. Scripture ascribes this pointedly to the pride of his heart, as later with Hezekiah: ". . . his heart was lifted up to his destruction: for he transgressed against the Lord his God." This was a very bad example for the entire nation. Moreover, throughout the ages it has been manifest that outward prosperity is very bad for true religious life. Those legs are strong indeed that can support prosperity, and experience teaches again and again that in days of great prosperity man's legs are too weak to support it and him. This became all too evident in the days of Uzziah. When we read the books of Isaiah's contemporaries (Hosea, Micah, and Amos, as well as many statements by Isaiah) it becomes sufficiently clear that the religious situation was far from sound. See, besides the first three chapters of Isaiah, Hosea 4:15; 6:11; 12:1; Amos 5:5; 8:14; and Micah 2 and 3.

But outright brazen public wickedness was not committed, however, until the reign of the good-for-nothing Ahaz who disgraced the throne of Judah from about 741 - 726 B.C. By his foolishness and abominations, he nearly brought his nation to complete ruin. He was totally a heathen and as much superstitious as he was unbelieving. He led his people in the worship of Baal and Molech and even burned his own sons in the fire in the valley of the son of Hinnom. The severe punishments with which God visited him did not bring him to repentance, but rather, made him even more foolish and turned him into a hypocrite and set his feet on the hapless path of the Assyrian politics. He went from bad to worse and turned from one evil to another. He removed the altar of burnt offerings of Solomon from the temple and replaced it by an altar of a Syrian idol. He stole the treasures of the temple, destroyed its vessels, and finally closed the house of the Lord and declared that the worship of Jehovah was abolished, whereupon the country was covered with abominable images of idols. It was obviously his intent to heathenize all of Judah and Jerusalem. The most remarkable aspect was, no doubt, that his people acquiesced, with the exception of Micah, Amos, and Isaiah! These men of God put the trumpet of penitence to their lips and their trumpet made no uncertain sound. And, no doubt, there were many God-fearing people left, the silent ones in the land, who must have bewailed these conditions. They did not come to the fore but rather hid themselves in fear.

It was inevitable that this religious breakdown went hand in hand with the greatest moral collapse. It is useful to look briefly at this.

3. The Moral Situation

We wish to emphasize here that Isaiah's time was very much like our own and that Judah had the same problems we have in our own evil day. If, in our day, we hear about alliances and federations for the sake of obtaining power, the same was true in Isaiah's time as the cry was heard for alliance and federation. But, the Lord warned His servant against it (8:12). The Lord's people ought to be federated only with the Lord. With Him, they are stronger than Satan, sin, and the world. If *spiritism* is one of the ruinous signs of the times today, at that time too they spoke to the dead in spiritist séances (2:6; 8:19). If today the people perish from *ignorance* as a result of religionless education, at that time, too, they were dumber than oxen and asses in matters divine (1:2-4). If today Queen *Fashion* rules with an iron scepter, she did at that time too (3:16-26). If today the *children* lord it over many parents and teachers, this was in Isaiah's day a phenomenon (3:4, 5). If we now experience *feminism* and dominion by women, 3:12 points to something similar. If today thousands of so-called *leaders* of the people are deceivers, the prophet complained about the same thing (3:12). If we today complain about *Mammon service* and *monopolies,* the man of God pronounced a woe upon them, too (5:8). If we still battle *alcoholism,* in spite of prohibition or no prohibition, Isaiah did the same without prohibition (5:11, 22). If present-day *culture* is by and large filthy and obscene, at that time it was extremely beastly (28:7-10). If we complain about the *social abuses* and injustices, Isaiah frequently raised his powerful voice against them (see chapters 5, 10 and 28). If today we see a God-insulting unconcern in the face of the seriousness of the times, it was present then, too (3:16-23; 5:19; 28:1-10). If the scorners of the Word of God now fill the so-called Christian world, Isaiah, in his day, frequently threatened them with God's judgment. And, finally, if today we observe a pride that precedes a fall, it is extensively depicted in 2:10-22. Pride and haughtiness preceded a miserable fall then, too.

When studying Isaiah we must keep in mind that life in his day was in every respect totally decadent. It is true that for a while it seemed that through the powerful reformation of Hezekiah a turn for the better was at hand. Outwardly, very many things improved but at the same time it caused hypocrisy to increase. It was due to no fault of the well-intentioned Hezekiah, since many people partook in the worship of the Lord with a heathenized heart. He attacked idolatry at the root and exterminated everything that might remind his subjects of it. Yet, the root of idolatry, lodged as it is in the idolatrous heart, was beyond his reach. At any rate, we must not think that the idolatrous people of Ahaz were suddenly changed into an upright and God-fearing people. That would be psychologically and religiously inexplicable. Then, too, many of Isaiah's statements would be inexplicable if we were to accept such a change. In spite of the good intentions and reformations of Hezekiah, there remained in large segments of the population an ungodly and idolatrous tendency. His rulers belonged to the part that favored an alliance with Egypt.

IV. THE MAIN THEMES OF THE BOOK OF ISAIAH

1. The Name Isaiah

Isaiah's name is a brief summary of his entire prophetic preaching: *Salvation is of the Lord,* or, briefer yet, *Jehovah is salvation.* He himself says in 8:18 that he, as well as his children, were as signs and wonders in Israel. The basic idea of his entire message was that the secret of everyone's blessing for time and eternity was found in Israel's God, Jehovah. He kept insisting on maintaining this in the face of all the powers of hell. He did so in different ways, it is true, but that was what it always came down to. In a beautiful play on words of which there are many in the original, he says to Ahaz, "If you will not believe, you will not receive!" (7:9). But when the hypocritical Ahaz, under a pious pretense, refuses to ask for a sign, then his word becomes like the thunder that from the distance comes rolling across the mountains. There is none among the holy writers of the Old Covenant — unless it is David — who has presented the way of salvation so often and so clearly as Isaiah. That is the reason why, since ages past, he has justly carried the name of "the evangelist" among the prophets. St. Augustine, shortly after his conversion, asked Ambrose which book he advised him to read, upon which the grey-headed bishop answered, "Isaiah!"

2. The Name Shear-jashub

This is the name of the eldest son of the prophet, and it, too, was a sign in Israel (7:3; 8:18). This remarkable name can be translated as *a remnant will return* or *a remnant will repent.* No doubt, we have to combine the two meanings. Verb *shub,* present here, means "to return physically" and also "to *turn around* spiritually," hence, *to convert.* This word appears from 800 - 1000 times in the Old Testament and often implies Israel's future return and conversion. The prophet could not have given his son a name that was richer in meaning. This name presupposes three ideas: the judgment upon the Lord's people, the carrying away into exile, and the remaining (i.e. after the judgment) of a small remnant. On the other hand, this meaningful name expresses that Israel will not, in its entirety, become apostate or exterminated but, on the contrary, will some day return to Jehovah and to Palestine. Further on we shall have plenty of opportunity to show that the ideas of judgment and glory on Judah and all of Israel appear many times in the message of Isaiah. Of the ten spies only two were faithful and all of Israel died off in the desert except for those two. During Elijah's apostate time there were seven thousand people in Israel who had not bowed the knees unto Baal. It seems that according to 6:13 and Amos 5:3 only one-tenth of Israel will return and according to Ezekiel 5 and Zechariah 13:8, 9, one-third will remain. See also Nehemiah 11:20 and Romans 9:27; 11:5.

3. Maher-shalal-hash-baz

Prophetically, this name is not as far-reaching as the previous one but had a more local and immediate significance for Samaria. It was that soon the enemy would advance and *speed to the spoil, hasten to the prey* obtained in his victory over Samaria. What Assyria had done to Samaria would one day also happen to Judah and Jerusalem. This name was of sufficient significance to be written clearly in a roll for the public. As we intend shortly to consider specifically Isaiah's message of judgment on the great day of the Lord, we can for the time being let the subject of this name rest.

4. The Name HOLY ONE OF ISRAEL

Isaiah uses this name again and again when referring to Jehovah, and it is peculiarly his. This name appears very often in his book and only six times outside of it (Jer. 50:29; 51:5; Ezek. 39:7; and Ps. 71:22; 78:41, 89:18). This name runs like a golden thread through his entire prophecy, proving thereby the unity of the book, in the first part as well as in the second. See: 1:4; 5:19, 24; 10:17, 20; 12:6; 17:7; 29:19, 23; 30:11, 12, 15; 31:1; 37:23; 41:14, 16, 20; 43:3, 14, 15; 45:11; 47:4; 48:17; 49:7; 54:5; 55:5 and 60:9, 14.

This raises a twofold question: To *whom* is he referring? And *what* does he mean by this name? After a careful study of this name in all these places we have not the slightest doubt but that our Lord Jesus is meant by it. He is constantly indicated and further defined as the One who created and formed Israel and who one day shall deliver, protect, and glorify it as the Savior. Moreover, many exegetes have correctly noted that in this name we find the echo of the song of the seraphim, which the prophet as a young man had heard at his consecration to his office. That was a doxology on the threefold holiness and glory of God. At that time he saw Christ, sitting on the throne of His glory, as one day He will fill the whole earth with His glory. See the brief explanation Jesus Himself gives of this vision in John 12:41. Christ is to be found in every chapter of Isaiah. *What* does the prophet mean by this name? It is not what Schultz and others took it to mean, *dedicated to Israel,* but rather the Lord's absolute fullness of being. He is immaculately pure and beautiful. Oetinger correctly writes: "Holiness is hidden glory and glory revealed holiness." At His coming the beauty of His holiness will be revealed (Ps. 50:1-6).

This perfect, pure, glorious Deliverer is Israel's possession on the basis of the covenant of grace, and it is Israel's duty to accept Him by faith. That is why He is called the Holy One of *Israel.* He gave Himself to Israel and wills that Israel give itself to Him.

This *Holy One of Israel* is to Isaiah the absolute sovereign God who, as the living God, is contrasted with the dead (8:19), who rules Israel and all the nations, and exalts the one and humbles the other. The prophet constantly presents Him as a true man with human members. He can sit, stand up, ride, become angry, dwell, look, and when He speaks or lifts up His arm, there is thunder, lightning, hail, storm, and man is seized by fear and dismay. These things are often interpreted as anthropomorphisms and anthropopathisms, but here that is not necessary at all, for we are dealing with a glorious actuality. In these cases, the prophet sees the Christ who took on a real body from the virgin Mary and who, as the true man, will return to judge the world in righteousness. Hence, it is truly noteworthy that the attributes eternal, unchangeable, and omnipresent are virtually never applied to the Holy One of Israel. Of course, that does not at all mean that He is not God, but that the emphasis is put just as much, if not more, on His true humanity as on His divinity. Closely connected with His holiness, however, is His righteousness. *Righteousness, peace, and knowledge of the truth are ever the* main characteristics of the glorious kingdom of peace He will found when He comes as *Jehovah Sabaoth.* This name does not refer to Him as the commander of Israel's armies, nor as the Lord of the stars, but specifically as the Lord of the angels who will come with Him to judge and to gather the saints.

5. The Covenantal Relationship Between God and Israel.

Israel stands in a totally unique relationship to God. In the covenant of grace, God has accepted Israel as His wife. That is why He is repeatedly called *Israel's God and Husband* in the rich meaning of Israel's Covenant God (17:6; 21:17; 29:23; 37:21; 54:5). He is called the God of Ahaz (7:11), of David (38:5) and of Isaiah (7:13). On the other hand, Israel is the people of the Lord (1:3; 5:25; 10:24; 40:1; 47:6; and numerous other places). Israel is the Lord's vineyard (5:1-7); Canaan is His land (11:9; 14:25); Jerusalem is His city (29:1; 30:19). It is there that He *dwells* (8:18), and there He will dwell again some day (12:6; 30:29; 31:9). At times, however, He is also presented as the *Father* of Israel (1:2; 63:8, 16).

The masters of criticism do not see this close covenant relationship between Jehovah and Israel. Usually, they consider it no more than presumption and pride on the part of Israel and its prophets — narrow-minded particularism. And when Isaiah in the second part of his prophecy points to the salvation that one day shall blossom forth through a restored Israel, it is called the universalism of a great unknown person who presumably lived during the time of the exile. As far as we are concerned, however, this covenant relationship is not a fallacy on the part of the prophet, but the wise ordering of the election of the grace of God. The Lord, as the sovereign Creator, has formed Israel for Himself so that this people should show forth His praise (43:21). He is sovereign in all He does, also in His elective work. So He, Himself, says to Israel, "I have loved thee" (43:4). Whoever dares to call this narrow-minded particularism finds fault with the Holy One in His sovereign ordinances. He is the Potter and we are the clay, O man!

6. The Day of the Lord

The designation *day of the Lord* is a common expression in the prophets. It appears for the first time in Isaiah in 2:12, "For the day of the Lord of hosts shall be upon every one that is proud and lofty, and upon every one that is lifted up; and he shall be brought low." The description in this chapter is one of the most extensive ones of this illustrious and terrible day. Wherever we find the expression "the day of the Lord," it always refers to the day in which the Lord comes against Satan and all satanic powers. Already, in the Middle Ages, this day was sung of as the *diesirae,* i.e. the day of wrath. At that time, however, the thought prevailed — and is still widely held — that the believers had to fear that day too, so that many upright, God-fearing people sigh when contemplating it. But they will, in the words of the Heidelberg Catechism, "never enter the judgment of God," since Christ took their curse upon Him and bore the wrath of God for them. Christ is coming to take them up to Himself before that terrible day of destruction dawns. Christ is coming *for* them first to make that day possible, while His coming *with* them makes that day a reality. Read and reread Revelation 19, and I Corinthians 1:7; Philippians 3:20; 21; I Thessalonians 1:10; II Timothy 4:8; Titus 2:13; Hebrews 9:28; II Thessalonians 3:5; and James 5:7,8.

Since we have said little about the name Maher-shalal-hash-baz in 8:1-3, by which was already given a hint and warning regarding the *day of the Lord* to all of Israel both by the public written announcement and by the name of Isaiah's son, and since the concept of the *day of the Lord* and the description of the destruction on that day keep recurring, it is necessary to go into this a little further.

A. The Name

Usually the day of judgment upon Israel and the nations is called *the day of the Lord,* but Isaiah often uses also the expression *in that day.* The expression *in the last days* of 2:2 points to the same time of judgment and glory as well. That is the only time this expression, which, according to the Rabbinic tradition, refers to the Messianic rule, appears in

Isaiah. He usually speaks of the *day of the Lord,* or simply *that day* (2:12; 7:18; 10:3; 13:6, 9; 22:5; 34:8). In 61:2 and 63:4 he calls it the *day of vengeance.* This day is called the day of the *Lord* in contrast to the day of man and because only the Lord Jesus Christ will be great in that day. The *day of Christ,* of which only the New Testament speaks, is very much to be distinguished from it as being full of the glory of His bridal congregation. Needless to say that chronologically they run almost parallel.

B. The Duration

The day of the Lord is not a day of twelve hours, as was generally thought in times past, but obviously the long period of a thousand years when Christ shall judge and rule, and the morning and evening of which are determined by the terrible judgments of the destruction of the wicked and the purging of all of creation (cf. I Cor. 15:23-28). The Old Testament nowhere indicates its precise length of time. It even pleased the Lord not to reveal this truth until the end of the first century, when all the apostles except John had gone the way of all flesh. Not until Revelation 20 are we told six times that this period will be a thousand years.

C. The Judge

Christ shall be the Judge and for that purpose first arises from His seat and appears unto judgment (2:10, 21; 19:1; 29:6; 30:18; 33:10). Twelve times Scripture says that Christ is now sitting at the right hand of God, and in the Orient an accusation or judgment was made only while standing. Hence, the expression, "The men of Nineveh shall *rise up* in the judgment with this generation, and shall condemn it." When Stephen saw the Lord Jesus *standing,* he knew that He was ready to sentence those who stoned him as well as to take him to Himself. The Lord emphatically declares regarding the time before the judgment, "I will take my rest, and I will consider in my dwelling place . . ." (18:4). After taking His rest and considering the nations during the times of the Gentiles, the Lord will arise and scatter His enemies far and wide. The prophet gives us the most glorious descriptions of the Lord's coming in 2:10-22; 4:2-6; 6:1-5; 10:33, 34;

11:3-5; 13:3-11; 19:1; 24:19-23; 25:5-12; 26:20, 21; etc. He will come to wreak vengeance upon those who scorned Him and His people. That is why the *day of vengeance* and the *year of His redeemed* are so closely connected. All judgment has been given to Him and He is fully capable of executing it, for He is omniscient and absolutely just. His perfect ability to judge is presented in brief and powerful outlines in 11:2-5 and 63:3-6. In a variety of bold imagery His judging is presented as hail, forest fire, storm, earthquake, pestilence, hewing down giant trees of the woods, harvesting, winnowing, a swarm of grasshoppers, the breaking of an earthen vessel, the gobbling up of an early fruit, famine, etc. We call it imagery, but one day all these things shall become actual reality.

D. The Double Aspect

The *day of the Lord* is a day of judgment for the wicked and of blessing for the believers. This is clearly indicated in 3:10, 11, where we read, "Say ye to the righteous, that it shall be well with him: for they shall eat the fruit of their doings. Woe unto the wicked! it shall be ill with him: for the reward of his hands shall be given him." Just as the prophetic preaching had to present the weal and the woe, so, too, shall this day reveal both. It will be burning as an oven for all the wicked and basking as the sun with healing in his wings for those who fear the Lord (Mal. 4:1, 2). So, too, does Isaiah constantly juxtapose the hailstorm upon the wicked and the unspeakable happiness of those who love Him in that day (32:19, 20). The wicked are recompensed according to the punishing righteousness of God, and the faithful remnant of Israel according to His rewarding righteousness. The fashion crazy women will be robbed of all the things with which they committed fornication — of their ornaments as well as of their men (3:17-25; 4:1). Those who always cried for more will be robbed of all their possessions, while those who lived excessively will be subjected to hunger and thirst (5:13). That day is the day of righteous recompense, but since at the Lord's return there will be found a class of wicked people and a class of praying people in Israel, the recompense must of necessity be twofold. Moreover, this double aspect is demanded by the truth that God shall render to every man according to his work. There are both evil and good works.

7. The Triumph of the Lord in the Kingdom of Peace

After the judgment follows the Kingdom of God that will be established for Israel. This is the continuous teaching of Isaiah as well as of the entire Scripture. Proof for this is found in almost every chapter of the prophet. After having depicted the sins and the ensuing judgment, the seer in 1:26-28 briefly sketches the great glory which will dawn after the judgment. The city, which was as a harlot (v. 21), is now called a *city of righteousness* and receives new counselors and judges. By the severe justice of the Lord, Zion shall be redeemed with judgment and its returning exiles with righteousness. Sin, judgment, glory – this triad again and again occurs in closest connection in this prophet. In 2:1-5, we see the same thing again. These verses are not speaking of the glorious state of the Church in the last days, but of Israel. It is emphatically stated that the prophet saw this glorious vision concerning *Judah and Jerusalem.* And according to the Savior's word, in the last days of this dispensation it will be the same situation as in the days of Noah and Lot, which alone precludes a glorious state of the Church. From verse four, it is obvious that the glory of which these verses speak will dawn only after the Lord Jesus has done justice among the nations and has removed all militarism and wars. After the judgment in chapter three on the wanton ladies of Jerusalem, Christ, who at His first coming had neither beauty nor comeliness, shall be *beautiful* and *glorious* for the God-fearing remnant of Israel, and Israel itself will have great glory as well (4:2-6).

After Christ has killed the *wicked one,* i.e., the antichrist, with the breath of His nostrils, the kingdom of peace will be ushered in, as this is described in the most brilliant colors in the following verses. Chapter thirteen mentions the judgment on Babylon as the personification of the entire religious and, at the same time, anti-christian world power. A basis and reason for this judgment is given: "For the Lord will have mercy on Jacob, and will yet choose Israel, and set them in their own land, and the strangers shall be joined with them, and they shall cleave to the house of Jacob." Then, it is stated how Israel will have dominion over its former oppressors and will enjoy perfect rest and peace, while also the whole earth will be at rest and break forth into singing on account of the fall of the world powers and Satan (14:1-17). According to 18:7 a present will be brought to Jehovah after He has poured out His terrible judgment on His enemies. See further chapter 25, 32:1-8, chapter 35, and other places, especially in the second part, and then we shall be convinced, if we believe these words of the prophet, that rest and peace on earth are not brought about by the Church but *by the most terrible judgments, which Christ at His second coming shall pour out on the earth.* Before the glorious new day can dawn, a mighty enemy must first be vanquished (9:3; 11:4; 14:4, 5; 27:1; 40:10; 49:25; 54:16).

Then Christ, as the true theocratic King, shall reign over restored Israel and the entire earth. He will rule from Mount Zion and Jerusalem in the presence of His ancients in glory (24:23). His law and word will go forth from Jerusalem unto the ends of the earth (2:3). He fills Zion with justice and righteousness and causes His people to taste joy, indeed joy upon joy (9:3, 29:19). He heals Israel's wounds inflicted upon them by the judgment (30:26) and protects Jerusalem as a mother bird protects her nest (31:4, 5). He removes all dimness and makes everything light (9:1). He even causes the sun to shine with a sevenfold brightness. Every burden and yoke that weighed His people down He will remove (9:4; 10:27; 14:25). Only the memory of it will stay alive (33:18). Not only the wounds of His afflicted people are healed, but He heals them of all their afflictions, such as blindness, deafness, stammering, being crippled, etc. (29:18; 32:4; 33:23). No inhabitant of the holy city will ever be sick again, since all iniquity has been forgiven.

There will never be idolatry and image-worship again. With utmost disdain and holy horror, they have smashed and thrown away their images (2:18, 20; 30:22; 31:7). They put their trust only in Christ 10:20; 11:9; 17:7). Wicked governments, of which there were so many in Isaiah's day, no longer exist. The rulers, under the blessed reign of Christ, govern in righteousness and judgment (1:26; 32:1; 33:17).

Jehova-Jesus alone is Law-giver, Judge, and King. Now Jerusalem is safe and at peace and needs not, as in Isaiah's day to think of outward means of defense. Not even storms, rain, and burning sunshine can hit the city any more, since He is Israel's glory and beauty (4:4-6).

Satan gone, Israel restored, Christ present — these are the three glorious facts of salvation that comprise the essence of the kingdom of peace, from which flow the most blessed results. The curse will be lifted from the earth when the second Adam with His majesty presents Himself here below. By His Spirit, He imbues and sanctifies all of nature (32:15-20; 35:1, 2, 6-9). Now earth enjoys its greatest fruitfulness (29:17; 30:25).

Nature fell together with the first Adam but will be restored by the second Adam. This is the simple principle that applies here. Even the cruel fighting and disturbances in the animal kingdom cease (11:6-8; 65:25). Carefully compare Romans 8:19-22 with these texts.

During this golden age of Christ's reign, the nations will be converted. First Israel is saved, united, and exalted, and after that and through them, the nations will be, also. Jerusalem will be the seat and focal point of this glorious period of peace; nevertheless, it will encompass the ends of the earth and the most distant peoples. Then, the promise of Genesis 12:3 will be truly fulfilled for the first time. Of this restored Israel it is said, "And the Gentiles shall come to thy light, and kings to the brightness of thy rising" (60:3). Everything is destroyed — the big armies, strong fortifications, and the murderous arms (2:3; 24:3-23; 31:8, 9). The nations join converted Israel, for now the name Jacob, for centuries a derision and scorn, has become a name of honor (44:5). "The earth shall be full of the knowledge of the Lord, as the waters cover the sea" (11:9). From the rising of the sun to its setting, the people shall fear the Lord (59:19). In bold imagery, the prophet lets the Gentile princes lay themselves on the Lord's altar like rams (60:7). And no longer will the Japhethites rule the world — as had been the case until then — but now the Semites and Hamites will rule (19:18-25).

Needless to say, this glorious period has never appeared in

the past, neither does it exist now, nor is it ever to be expected in this dispensation of Satan and sin. There are many Christians who are doing the latter, but they are deceiving themselves, as with this expectation they diametrically oppose the words of our Lord Jesus Christ. In eternity, these glorious promises of God cannot be fulfilled either, for then we end up with all kinds of absurdities and then many results of sin must still continue even when God is all and in all. Hence, no other way is left than either to deny these promises, or to spiritualize them in such a manner that nothing is left of them, *or* to accept a separate dispensation for their fulfillment. Only when accepting the latter can we obtain a reasonable explanation for these glorious promises of God. And we need not accept this separate dispensation, before eternity, by way of a working hypothesis, but we may safely *accept* it on the basis of God's Word, for the New Testament speaks again and again of the new *aeon* or dispensation. Presently, however, let us get acquainted with the mighty words of the prophet, which at the same time are the infallible Word of the Lord.

ISAIAH 1

The Title of the Book

> 1. The vision of Isaiah the son of Amoz, which he saw concerning Judah and Jerusalem in the days of Uzziah, Jotham, Ahaz, and Hezekiah, kings of Judah.

This first verse is the title of the entire book. It speaks of four matters in this book that we know under the name of Isaiah the author, the contents, the topics and the period of the prophecy of Isaiah. In II Chronicles 32:32, this book is also called the *vision* of Isaiah. This word gives us a hint as to the manner in which this book came about. The prophet did not just sit down and, on the basis of his religious and moral concepts, send a well-written book into the world. At God's command, he wrote what the Lord had first shown him. He passes on only the truth he received from above — and this truly separates him essentially from the false prophets who did not receive revelations from God but merely spoke from the imagination of the thoughts, which is only evil continually. The word *vision* is related to. the word *seer,* which is frequently used of the prophets (I Chron. 21:9; 29:29; II Chron. 9:29; 12:15; 19:2; 29:25; 33:18, 19). Although many scholars have tried to make a distinction between the names *man of God, prophet, seer, viewer (beholder),* there is on the basis of the facts no real distinction. The prophet Shemaiah is both called *man of God* (II Chron. 11:2) and *prophet* (II Chron. 12:5), while Iddo is called *seer* (II Chron. 12:15) as well as *prophet,* Hanani *seer* (II Chron. 16:7, 10) as well as *viewer* (II Chron. 19:2). So also the concept *vision* is the same as the concepts *prophecy* and the *words of the Lord.* Hence, we must not conclude from this word that Isaiah saw only visions, for the facts prove something entirely different.

Further, on this introductory verse of Isaiah, we wish to remember the advice of Luther:

> Let all those who desire to read and understand the prophet Isaiah profitably not despise — unless they know something better — my advice and counsel: Do not overlook the title or the beginning of the book, but think about it for a while until you understand it well, for the title of this prophecy is like a marginal note and a light that illuminates the entire book. By this I do not mean that you should read the names of the kings correctly, but that you take and read the second book of the Kings and of the Chronicles, especially that which was said and took place during the reign of these kings.

Every person who desires to study especially the first part of Isaiah will be wise to follow this good advice of the Reformer, for many of Isaiah's statements have indubitably a historical background. Even though his eye was fixed on the faraway day of the coming of the Lord nevertheless, the words which he spoke on behalf of the Lord are often rooted in the events of his own day.

Unsuccessful Upbringing

> 2. Hear, O Heavens, and give ear, O earth: for the LORD hath spoken, I have nourished and brought up children, and they have rebelled against me.

Nothing in human life is more tragic than an unsuccessful upbringing. This holds true in a double sense for the godly upbringing of God-fearing parents. We only have to think of the sons of Jacob, Aaron, Eli, Samuel and David. But we may speak of an impenetrable mystery when we read that God has brought up children whose upbringing apparently has failed. Thus it is that we hear the Lord lament, here as elsewhere, about His children. Many questions arise in our minds regarding this mystery, but out of holy respect for His exalted majesty we will suppress them. That it, nevertheless, must be viewed as a dreadful fact is apparent from the solemn invocation of heaven and earth. Moses does the same thing at the beginning of his glorious song (Deut. 32:1). In it, too, Israel's sins in the past, present, and future are described. And after seven centuries the prophet invokes here the unchanged witnesses of heaven and earth again to listen to the Lord's lament and to be amazed at the hardness of Israel. For the Lord had adopted Israel as His first-born son. But what the people as a whole had done in a collective sense, the individual children of Israel had dared to do as well; they had turned their proud backs upon their merciful Father and Pedagogue. Of course, we must not take the word *children* here in a regenerative but in a covenantal sense. Israel stood in a very close covenant relationship to God, and this relationship is frequently expressed as that of a man to his wife or of a father to his child (Deut. 4:6; 14:1; 32:5, 13, 14, 16-19; Jer. 2:2, 3; Hos. 11:1). The citizens of Israel are called *brethren* (I Chron. 13:2; II Chron. 11:4; 28:10, 11; 35:5). The covenant idea is predominant with all the prophets and also with Isaiah. For that reason God is very often called the *God of the fathers* in Scripture. In Chronicles, this term is found as often as thirty times.

The expression *nourished* points to the fact that God formed Israel and delivered her from Egypt and slavery, led her through the desert and into Canaan, and made her into a great nation under David and Solomon. The words *brought up* indicate that God made Israel the first-born among the nations, indeed a priestly kingdom (Exod. 19:6). But *"they have rebelled against me"* is the plaintive conclusion. Regarding sin, Scripture has a wealth of expressions of which the most frequently occurring are: forsaking Jehovah, doing evil in God's sight, sinning, acting foolishly, acting wickedly, departing from God, wandering away, trespassing against Him, playing the harlot and provoking God. Sin is always directed against the personal God who revealed Himself to Israel. "They have transgressed *against Me.*" The transgression of His law is a transgression against Him. If God were to reveal Himself today, would He not utter the same complaint against His people?

Oxen and Asses

3. The ox knoweth his owner, and the ass his master's crib, but Israel doth not know, my people doth not consider.

Isaiah knows the secret of using striking and original similes as no other. This is one of the main characteristics of his style. Because of this, his style is characterized by a rich vocabulary, vividness, and power. The comparison he uses in this verse is known to everyone who reads the Bible. An ox is one of the least intelligent animals but he knows his owner. When he is hungry he walks up to him, lowing, to make his need known, and asking for food. But that is not what Israel does. She quiets the hunger of her heart with Baals and Ashtaroths. Israel demonstrates no knowledge of Jehovah, who has just been presented as her own Father. Comparing His people with an ass serves to strengthen this alarming idea. Usually an ass is considered the dumbest and most stubborn animal. In earliest antiquity, the ass was a useful domesticated animal in the Orient and together with the camel the means of transportation, par excellence. The Oriental ass, however, is bigger and better looking than the Occidental one. The warm climate of the Orient suits him better than the cold, wet climate of the West. Although it is said that the ass in the East is not as stupid as ours, it is nevertheless clear that he is mentioned here with the ox as one of the dumbest animals. Nevertheless, he shows evidence of knowledge, obedience, and even attachment to his master. Even when far from home, he loves his stable and knows exactly how to find it again.

This was not the case with Israel. The people had no knowledge of Jehovah and of the blessings of His covenant. They had some external and historical knowledge, but not the knowledge of love that seeks and serves the Lord. The Lord Jesus said of His sheep, "I am the good shepherd, and know my sheep, and am known of mine." This knowledge of love, Israel lacked completely. She did not seek the Lord, but left Him, to go whoring after other gods. Irrational animals put them to shame.

By bit and bridle, guided by man's skillful hand,
Are kept in check the beasts that do not understand.

The reins of the law of the Lord, made powerless by the flesh, did not keep Israel from unbridled sensuality and frowardness.

Woe Upon a Sevenfold Sin

> 4. Ah sinful nation, a people laden with iniquity, a seed of evildoers, children that are corrupters: they have forsaken the LORD, they have provoked the Holy One of Israel unto anger, they are gone away backward.

The prophet is extremely fond of the number seven. He does not mention it very often, but he does give many descriptions containing seven main features. We shall have many opportunities to call attention to examples of this. We shall also see that the number seven is not the number of perfection but of completeness, whether in a positive or a negative sense, and that it is usually divided into two parts, one of four and one of three. This is also the case in this verse. First, he describes in four powerful phrases the sinful life and evil mentality of Israel; then in three more the wicked deeds of Israel in regard to its walk, word, and will are enumerated.

According to Exodus 19:6, Israel was to be a holy nation, but instead it was a *sinful* nation. The word *goi* is used here, which was usually reserved for the Gentile nations outside Israel. The word for *sin* points to missing the goal. By unbelief and disobedience, Israel had already missed the goal for many centuries. Instead of being a holy covenant people that was closely related to its God, she became like the heathen nations in her sin and misery, a *people laden with iniquity,* as he goes on to say. Her iniquities weighed Israel down like a heavy load. All the miseries she had to bear from the world powers were altogether the result of her iniquities. No man and no people ever sin cheaply! Whoever commits evil will be severely punished. Evil always calls for punishment, and whoever forsakes God, the fountain of all good things, will have to face grief upon grief.

The prophet with his rich vocabulary calls them a *seed of evildoers.* This sinful people, originally the seed of Abraham and ever boasting of being that, became, by her iniquities, a generation of vipers and children of the devil (Matt. 3:7; John 8:33, 44). That is how terribly sin corrupts and degenerates man! *Children that are corrupters.* The degenerated children who, according to verse two, have forsaken their Father have thereby corrupted themselves and others and, as corrupters, they are headed for eternal corruption. As soon as the son in the well-known parable left the house of his father, he started to corrupt himself by squandering his possessions and health with harlots. In Revelation 11:18, the wicked are called those who *destroy the earth.*

With three forceful strokes Israel is finally depicted in her wicked manner of life. By mentioning the seven aspects of the people's wickedness, the prophet, moved by the Holy Spirit, has given a complete presentation of the sins of the people. He continues to compare Israel's condition with that of a mortally sick person; no healing could be expected any more, because the horrible cancer of sin had affected the entire body of the state from the top of the head to the sole of the foot. Hence, we read these striking words in II Chronicles 36:16, ". . . the wrath of the Lord arose against his people, *till there was no remedy.*" Concerning the name *Holy One of Israel,* see the Introduction, p. 22. This name appears twelve times in Chapters 1 - 39 and seventeen times in Chapters 40 - 66.

Incurable Sickness from the Foot to the Head

5. Why should ye be stricken any more? ye will revolt and more: the whole head is sick, and the whole heart faint.

6. From the sole of the foot even unto the head there is no soundness in it; but wounds, and bruises, and putrifying sores: they have not been closed, neither bound up, neither mollified with ointment.

God had sent terrible calamities upon Israel in the days when Isaiah spoke these words. It cannot be determined with certainty which judgments the prophet had in mind. Most commentators think of the heavy blows the country sustained in the days of Ahaz. It seems to us that this is most likely the case. This degenerated criminal did not take these divine blows to heart, however. On the contrary, we read specifically of him that the more he was visited the more he trespassed against the Lord (II Chron. 28:22). Verse five apparently alludes to this. The people had refused to accept the Fatherly chastisement. One of the most terrible aspects of discipline is when a recalcitrant son remains untouched under the rod of his father. Not only does he resist it, but stiffens his neck and hardens his heart against it. That was Judah's attitude in the days of Ahaz. The Lord complains about this through Jeremiah, saying, "In vain have I smitten your children; they received no correction" (Jer. 2:30). And he continues, ". . . thou hast stricken them, but they have not grieved; thou hast consumed them, but they have refused to receive correction: they have made their faces harder than a rock; they have refused to return" (Jer. 5:3). Hence, the chastisements no longer softened them, rather they hardened them. The visitations, which were meant to make them see the error of their ways, caused them to rebell all the more and evoked revulsion and apostasy. There are some who translate *why* by *where: Where should ye be stricken any more?* The implication of the question is then that there was no part of the body left that had not become sick because of the blows already received. This idea, as such, is wholly true but we see no reason to depart from the usual translation. The prophet, then, describes the moral sickness as well as the national chaos of the people, resulting from their guilt and punishment in the image of a person who suffers from head to toe with a repulsive ailment. The illness is described as one that affects the entire body. Both head and heart are affected by it, both the government and the people. Hence, the sickness is incurable and leaves no hope for healing. Worse still, there is no physician to press the pus from the abscesses or to bind and mollify the wounds. From early times in the Orient, olive oil and figs were two common remedies. As in Judah, there was no balm in Gilead, nor a physician, to recover the health of the sick one.

This seems also to be the case with the deplorable condition of the so-called Christian nations today. There is no doubt about it any more — the nations are decayed from the sole of the foot to the crown of the head. There is not a single law or measure any more that can bring improvement. With all their agitation and activities, the nations get themselves deeper and deeper into disarrangement. There is only One who now can cause the sun of salvation to rise upon the weary nations. That one is Jesus Christ.

The Desolation in Judah

7. Your country is desolate, your cities are burned with fire: your land, strangers devour it in your presence, and it is desolate, as overthrown by strangers.

What the prophet has just presented in the image of a repulsive sickness, he now depicts in a few forceful strokes of reality. The fruitful land, once given by God to His people, had been destroyed by invading armies. The cities had been burned to ashes, as is usually the case in a war. The foreign invaders had destroyed the harvest before the eyes of the people. Surely, the people in those days were no worse than the civilized nations of today. In spite of all the cries about advancement, they have not progressed for the better but rather regressed for the worst. One observation that should certainly be noted at the beginning of our exegesis is that the reader must be aware of the specifically prophetical and, in general, Oriental style in expressions such as "Your country is desolate." This must not be taken in an absolute literal sense but rather as a hyperbole for the destruction brought about by the invading armies. When we read: *your cities are burned,* it does not mean that not a single little town was left. Another example is the expression in verse 15: "your hands are full of blood," which of course does not mean that they were praying with unwashed and blood-covered hands. In the same way, David says that he made his bed to swim, and watered his couch with tears. Of John the Baptist, it is said that all of Judea and Jerusalem went out to him; which, again, must not be taken in a strictly literal and matter-of-fact sense.

The Remnant from the Judgment

> 8. And the daughter of Zion is left as a cottage in a vineyard, as a lodge in a garden of cucumbers, as a besieged city.
> 9. Except the LORD of hosts had left unto us a very small remnant, we should have been as Sodom, and we should have been like unto Gomorrah.

We shall meet the idea of a *remnant* again and again in Isaiah. On this, see the Introduction, p. 19. We shall say more about this in chapter four; it will be sufficient to simply point out here the imagery used for indicating the remnant. In the larger vineyards in those days, there were watchmen who had to guard against thieves and wild animals. They built shacks to protect them from the heat of the day and the cold and dampness of the night. Now the *daughter of Zion,* i.e., Jerusalem, had been left like such a shack amidst the general destruction. Since cities are generally sought, admired, and proud, Jerusalem as the royal residential city and the city of the temple is usually compared to a beautiful virgin. Now, however, with all those burnt cities and villages round about, Jerusalem was a spectacle of loneliness and forsakenness. The harvest had been gathered but the cottage had been left. What a striking simile of silent loneliness! Jerusalem is as a besieged city. The word *as* warns us not to think of the siege by Sennacherib. Isaiah does not want to ascribe the sparing of the city to the virtue of its inhabitants, but only to the saving grace of God. God could have let it perish like Sodom.

Address to the Rulers and People of Jerusalem

> 10. Hear the word of the LORD, ye rulers of Sodom; give ear unto the law of our God, ye people of Gomorrah.
> 11. To what purpose is the multitude of your sacrifices unto me? saith the LORD: I am full of the burnt-offerings of rams, and the fat of fed beasts; and I delight not in the blood of bullocks, or of lambs, or of he goats.

Fear was simply unknown to Isaiah. More than once we notice that Jeremiah was weak at times, but Isaiah *never,* unless it be that one time when he faced the glory of the

Messiah and cried out, *Woe is me! for I am undone.*
Compared to God only, he was small and weak, but
compared to people he always stood his ground and knew no
fear. In the beautiful apostrophe of verse ten we see an
example of his lion-like courage. Would it not have taken
courage to address the proud rulers of Jerusalem as *rulers of
Sodom* and its no less haughty inhabitants as *people of
Gomorrah?* In the estimation of the people these cities were
registered in black charcoal. Still, this address is peculiarly
Isaianic not only because of the courage it reflects but also
on account of its form. He has in a few words expressed a
terrible reality. For that reason everyone understood him
perfectly and knew that he wished to indicate that although
Jehovah had spared them in the time of war, they were just
as filthy as Sodom and Gomorrah, and deserved to be
overturned just as much as these cities. The famous Professor
Van Der Palm correctly writes that today we do not have
anything in our literature that approximates this crushing
courage of Isaiah. The fact that he mentions the rulers first
shows they were primarily responsible for the lamentable
situation. Their corruption was so immense that the huge
quantity and fatness of their sacrifices were not able to wash
it away, not even all the blood of rams and bullocks.

Religion That God Loathes

12. When ye come to appear before me, who hath required
this at your hand, to tread my courts?
13. Bring no more vain oblations; incense is an abomination
unto me; the new moons and sabbaths, the calling of assemblies, I
cannot away with; it is iniquity, even the solemn meeting.
14. Your new moons and your appointed feasts my soul
hateth: they are a trouble unto me; I am weary to bear them.
15. And when ye spread forth your hands, I will hide mine
eyes from you: yea, when ye make many prayers, I will not hear:
your hands are full of blood.

No statement is more superficial and unfounded than
saying that the worship service in the Old Testament was not
concerned with the attitude of the heart. God has never
instituted a merely external worship service that does not

involve the heart. Every sacrifice was supposed to express the grateful attitude of the heart. Already by then, God had required feeling of the heart and truth in the inward parts. The book of Chronicles, which gives a blueprint for the theocracy in Israel, demands, in the first place, piety on the part of the kings. David is presented as the type and example of a true king. Abijah and Josiah walked in the ways of their father David. Ahaz did *not*, Hezekiah *did*, as their father David had done (II Chron. 28:2; 29:2). In the form of technical terms and stereotype expressions, we constantly read of the kings' doing or not doing the following: seeking Jehovah, asking, following, serving, acknowledging and walking before Him, in His statutes, laws and ways. The bold statement by the Leyden professor Eerdmans, "It is a well-known fact that Old Testament ethics is not concerned with the attitude of the heart," has been sufficiently refuted by the Groningen professors, Wildeboer and Bleeker. We can safely say that this flippant statement is refuted by the entire Old Testament and especially by this section. The seat of piety is, according to the Old Testament as well as the New, the heart and its attitude; hence, the definition of piety *as the heart being perfect toward Him* (I Chron. 29:18; II Chron. 16:9). On the other hand, the seat of sin is also in the heart and not merely in man's outward behavior.

Equally foolish is the assertion by some critics that Isaiah and the other prophets were not favorably inclined toward the sacrificial worship of the shed blood of goats and bulls. It is true that they frequently uttered harsh words against mere formalism, which was satisfied with the mere bringing of the required animals according to the law while the heart remained far from God and the feet walked in the ways of unrighteousness. Examples are recorded in Hosea 6:6, Amos 5:21-24 and Micah 6:6-8. But then, one might on the basis of the statement in James 1:26, 27, with just as much justification, assert that James was an antinomian, as asserted from texts like these that the prophets were unfavorably inclined towards the service of sacrifices. By using this language, they only defended serving Jehovah with an upright heart. All the prophets were deeply convinced that God desires truth in the inward parts and that the object of His instituting the legal sacrifices was not the outward forms but the piety of men's hearts. Sacrifices were pleasing to Him only when they were an expression of the love and gratitude, praise and adoration of the heart. This is a principle of religious life that has never ceased and never will. We, today, may add that all church going, baptizing, celebrating the Lord's Supper, paying our financial support mean nothing at all, indeed are stench in God's nostrils, if they are performed without love in the heart. The same holds true for the most eloquent confession. No matter how good and excellent it may be of and by itself, it can never make up for a lack of love in the heart for the Savior. The church at Ephesus was in many respects an excellent church, but the Lord Jesus considered it as *fallen,* since its erstwhile, heartfelt love had turned cold.

In the last days of this dispensation there will be many who have the form of godliness but deny the power thereof, notwithstanding the fact that God hates the form without the power. That is formalism, hypocrisy, and Phariseeism. And, that was the situation in Isaiah's time. The word *tread,* in verse twelve, actually means *trample down.* Like the people of Sodom and Gomorrah, the people of Judah lived a life of false peace and wantonness, of avarice and abomination. Yet, at the same time, they wanted to remain religious and therefore kept up the forms of religion. They absolutely did not *walk* before God according to the demand of the covenant, but they still did *appear* before Him. Hence, we do not marvel that God loathed their sacrifices, their incense, and their appointed feasts. He calls them *in vain,* an *abomination.* He *cannot away with them, hates* them; they are a *trouble* unto Him; He is *weary* of them, and he does not want to see or hear the prayers of these blood-polluted people. He demands that appearance and reality go hand in hand.

Religion God Demands

16. Wash you, make you clean; put away the evil of your doings from before mine eyes; cease to do evil;

17. Learn to do well; seek judgment, relieve the oppressed, judge the fatherless, plead for the widow.

18. Come now, and let us reason together, saith the LORD: though your sins be as scarlet, they shall be as white as snow; though they be red like crimson, they shall be as wool.

The hands of those who prayed and brought sacrifices were polluted with the blood of the innocent. Referring to this, the Lord cries out to them: *Wash you, make you clean!* Israel might complain that God did not answer their prayers (59:2-3; Jer. 11:14; Lam. 3:44; Ps. 80:4), but the prayer of the wicked is an abomination to God. According to Exodus 30:19-21, the priests had to wash themselves before serving in the sanctuary, lest they die. Alluding to this, it is said that those who pray and bring sacrifices must wash and purify themselves. First, they had to wash their hands in innocency (Ps. 26:6, 73:13) before approaching God. James the Just also cries out, "Draw nigh to God, and he will draw nigh to you," but at the same time he adds, *"Cleanse your hands!"*.

Two matters are then mentioned in verse sixteen, which Israel must put away, while verse seventeen mentions five things that must be sought and practiced positively. Although generally speaking Israel's ethics were stated negatively, we cannot simply state that they were exclusively so, for they definitely had a positive character as well. The wicked are not only admonished to break unconditionally with evil in every form, but also at the same time to do *well, seek the judgment* of God and man, and *relieve* the oppressed. As examples of the oppressed, the orphan and the widow are mentioned. In His law God had especially spread His hand protectively over widows, orphans, and the poor (Exod. 22:22-25; Deut. 10:18; Ps. 68:5), but in Isaiah's day Judah had trampled these ordinances under foot.

"Come now," the LORD calls kindly and urgently, after first having pointed out to Judah the right preconditions for communion with Himself. We must keep in mind, however, that this is not said to sinners who know absolutely nothing of God and His service, but to the people of the LORD who stood in a covenant relationship with Him. There have been preachers who, on the basis of this injunction, have foolishly presented it in such a way that a sinner must first improve himself before he may draw nigh to God. But that is not only

contrary to the doctrine of free grace, but also to verse eighteen itself. According to this verse, there are no abominable sins that can keep a sinner away from God or which cannot be forgiven. Whoever comes to Christ will in no wise be cast out. Also, "Just as I am, without one plea" applies here. We must never forget that God is speaking here to very religious though hypocritical people. They could not, as long as they continued in their abominations, receive an answer to their prayers or the favor of God. There first had to be a breaking with sin and an improvement of their lives. Otherwise, their outward religious form meant nothing. But even so, God still wanted to deal with this hypocritical people. He wanted to *reason* with this people, to talk together and come to a right conclusion. He wanted to point out their sin, guilt and punishment, as well as His infinite mercy to them though their sins were as scarlet. This red color is mentioned with an allusion to the innocent blood that had been shed. Scarlet was an indelible color, which was made of the purple mollusk. The red heifer and the red ashes were, according to Numbers 19:2, 6, 9, a reference to sin, also. But, God wanted to make sin white by the red blood of His Lamb, as white as freshly fallen show and as undyed wool. Judah, however, did not accept the invitation.

Willing or Unwilling and Rebellious?

19. If ye be willing and obedient, ye shall eat the good of the land:
20. But if ye refuse and rebel, ye shall be devoured with the sword: for the mouth of the LORD hath spoken it.

After His kind invitation, the LORD puts before Judah what the result will be of the willing acceptance of His urgent request or of its rejection. *Willing* refers to obediently coming to the Lord to be cleansed by Him, for He alone could make their scarlet abominations white as snow. The gracious result of the willing submission to Jehovah would be that they would eat the good of Canaan. We must not overlook the fact that the Lord was not speaking of heaven or glory, but of Canaan. We may speak to a thousand Jews about the glory of heaven and not one will be touched by it, for an orthodox Jew has little interest in heaven. But start painting the glorious promised blessings in Canaan, and he is all ears. How can this remarkable phenomenon, known to all missionaries to the Jews, be explained? Only on the basis of God's ordering. According to His holy counsel and promise, Israel is the people of the earth, whose citizenship, unlike ours, is not in heaven but in Canaan. By being *obedient,* Israel would receive the richest blessings *in its country.* The Church sings about this continuously, but as a rule believes or understands very little of it. They sing lustily, "Had My people but willingly obeyed Me," followed by "Then I would have fed you with wheat and honey." However, the promise is given here to Judah. And the woe, is juxtaposed to the weal in a play on words of which Isaiah is a master.

Over against *eating the good* he puts *being devoured by the sword.* The Hebrews often presented the sword as a voracious animal of prey that devoured many. They spoke of "the mouth of the sword" and "being eaten and devoured by the sword," language which refers to the devastations of wars. Mention is made of the *mouth of the Lord,* which has spoken these promises and threats. He surely will fulfill His words according to whether Israel will listen or not. Already, in the books of Moses, God had referred to this (Lev. 26:25; Deut. 32:41, 42). The Assyrians and Babylonians might come with their sword, but ultimately and in essence it was the Lord's sword of vengeance that struck Israel.

Isaiah's Song of Lamentation Over Jerusalem

21. How is the faithful city become an harlot! It was full of judgment; righteousness lodged in it; but now murderers.

22. Thy silver is become dross, thy wine mixed with water:

23. Thy princes are rebellious, and companions of thieves: every one loveth gifts, and followeth after rewards: they judge not the fatherless, neither doth the cause of the widow come unto them.

Isaiah was a man not only of great intellect and stedfast will, but also of deep feeling. His language and style reveal this clearly. Although we firmly believe in the verbal inspiration of all Scripture, we nevertheless strongly emphasize the organic character of this inspiration and maintain that the characteristics of the holy authors, and particularly of Isaiah, can be detected in their style, since it reflects them most beautifully. It can be concluded from Isaiah's style that he was not as oversensitive a man as Jeremiah, but at the same time that his innermost feelings were not devoid of a fine and deep sensitivity. Here, he breaks out in a stirring song of lamentation over the apostasy of his beloved city, just as was done in antiquity at the funeral of a beloved departed one. With great longing, he looks back to the days of David and Solomon and even to the time after the irreparable schism between north and south when the city became a safe place for the Levite refugees from the northern tribes. Then, the city was faithful to God and His covenant. But, alas, later it broke the marriage bond with Jehovah and became a harlot! The prophet does not call her a fallen woman, but a *whore*. The difference is obvious. A woman can unexpectedly and suddenly be overtaken by temptation and for the rest still be an honorable woman, who regrets and bewails her fall with many tears. But still she can be much bolder than her sister who never fell. A *whore,* on the other hand, does not fall just once but deliberately walks in the ways of adultery and throws herself at not just one man but every man. That is what happened to Israel according to the soul-stirring lament of Isaiah. According to the word of prophecy, this will happen also to the Church (Rev. 17 and 18). Already today, the Church does not look much better than a filthy woman.

In earlier days, Jerusalem was full of *judgment* and *righteousness* lodged in it. Righteousness did not just pass through it like a stranger, but it *lodged* in it and had a permanent seat of honor there. The concepts *justice* and *righteousness* are often joined in the poetic style of Scripture to indicate the reign and kingdom of the Messiah. Taken together, these concepts express the true relationship between men and God and between men and fellow men. But when the prophet looks at the capital city of the land now, his heart breaks on account of the swift deterioration. All relationships of justice and righteousness are broken. Judgment and righteousness have left their lodging place and all manner of unrighteousness has taken their place. *Murderers* have a permanent home in Jerusalem. What in earlier times was like *silver* has now turned to slag, totally worthless *dross.* The *wine* has been diluted with water. The Lord Jesus made water into wine; sinners make wine into water.

In verse twenty-three, the prophet identifies the people he is referring to with the words *silver* and *wine.* It is the proud and rebellious princes who always were the vanguard at violating justice and corrupting politics. They should have been the most eminent, the spiritual leaders; they were rather the most ignominious criminals. In powerful strokes Isaiah depicts them as *rebellious, companions of thieves, lovers of gifts and followers after rewards,* i.e., they offered their services to those who paid the most, while they had not the least concern for the poor who had nothing to pay. Among the latter are specifically mentioned the *orphans* and *widows.* In this light it is well to read verse seventeen again. Also verse five, for in it we see that the head and the heart of the body of the state were sick indeed.

Judgment and Restoration

24. Therefore saith the Lord, the LORD of hosts, the mighty One of Israel, Ah, I will ease me of mine adversaries, and avenge me of mine enemies:
25. And I will turn my hand upon thee, and purely purge away thy dross, and take away all thy tin:
26. And I will restore thy judges as at the first, and thy counsellors as at the beginning: afterward thou shalt be called, The city of righteousness, the faithful city.
27. Zion shall be redeemed with judgment, and her converts with righteousness.

After the prophet's lamentation the Lord Himself starts speaking again. In a terrible manner the Lord announces the judgment upon this wicked troop of murderers. It is terrible for three reasons. First of all because of the three divine names that are used here to indicate His awesome power. The first name, *Jehovah,* points to Him as the great Judge before whom Israel had to appear three times each year (Exod.

23:17, 34:23). The rebellious troop trampled down His courts as hypocrites and murderers, but He will put a stop to that forever. The name *Jehovah Sabaoth* describes Him as the Warrior who has all the angels as mighty soldiers at His disposal in the battle against the wicked. This is God's battle name and as a rule it signifies little good when He uses it in reference to His people, as is the case here. It usually implies that He considers and deals with His people as His enemies. The third name used here is *mighty One of Israel*. This name also points to His irresistible power. It is possible that these three names are a faint reference to the holy Trinity, but the main object of their use is to indicate the dreadfulness of the judgment that awaits the wicked. Secondly, it is a terrible thing for the wicked because the Lord calls them here His *adversaries* and *enemies*. He considers His erstwhile beloved people, who were His spouse, His bitterest enemies. We see in Him the dreadful anger of injured and rejected love. Thirdly, the Lord indicates that it is a sweet and comforting thought to vent His anger on His haters. Must we not call it a terrible thing when the vengeance of the Lord upon His covenant people becomes sweet to Him? To us it is a comforting thought, however, that with God there is only a *day* of vengeance but a *year* of the redeemed (61:2; 63:4).

In His wrath, He, nevertheless, is mindful of His mercy, according to verse 25. This verse is the transition from the judgment to the restoration of the people. His judgment is always a *crisis,* a separation between darkness and light, between sin and grace. Like the fire of the goldsmith, He will make a separation between the dross and the noble metal. With the fan in His hand He will make a separation between chaff and wheat. As silver is purged in the crucible and in the fire is purified by the use of potassium hydroxide, so God will purge Israel. This comparison has both a light and dark side. The fire of the smelter leaves him with the pure metal, the fire of judgment leaves a cleansed city and a pure people. The object of judgment on Israel is never complete destruction but always the separation of the dross from the silver. "Thou removest the wicked from the earth like dross." After Jerusalem has been purged, the Lord will restore it completely and give back its *judges* as at the first when the city was still the *faithful city* (v. 21). The city also receives new *counsellors,* in short, a new government. We know who this will be: our Lord Jesus Christ and His apostles, who will sit on twelve thrones, judging and governing the twelve tribes of Israel in the great day of restoration.

And, after the judgment, Jerusalem will be called the *city of righteousness.* As every reader of the Bible knows, a *name* and the *giving of a name* play a significant role in Scripture. This is especially the case of Isaiah. The phrase, "his (her) name shall be called," or something similar, appears in Isaiah, as well as in the other prophets frequently (7:14; 8:3; 9:6; 35:8; 45:3, 4; 48:1; 61:3; 62:2, 12). The city of prophet-killers will, after the return of the Lord, be indeed a city of righteousness and of faithfulness to God, which will radiate its justice, peace and holiness to the four corners of the earth. Here the name covers what it is and reveals its nature. *Jehovah-zidkenu,* the Lord our Righteousness (Jer. 23:6), will manifest His glory there as in no other place on earth.

Once more, however, it is reiterated that *Zion,* i.e. Jerusalem, shall be redeemed with judgment. Here the word judgment has the meaning of deciding, rendering the verdict. Not until after the day of great tribulation will salvation dawn for Israel. This is what Isaiah continuously teaches. *Her converts* are the Jews returning from present-day exile. It must be obvious that this cannot be said of the Church, but very appropriately said of dispersed Jews. These dispersed Jews will also be visited with the severe chastisement of the inviolate justice of God. However, this judgment will not mean annihilation for them but purification. According to Zechariah 13:8, two of the three parts of the land will be destroyed. Verse twenty-eight alludes to this dreadful fact. The wicked people will turn to *ashes, chaff, dross* and *stubble.* These images, which indicate total worthlessness, are used again and again with reference to the wicked who will be cut off.

The Destruction of the Wicked

28. And the destruction of the transgressors and of the sinners

shall be together, and they that forsake the LORD shall be consumed.

29. For they shall be ashamed of the oaks which ye have desired, and ye shall be confounded for the gardens that ye have chosen.

30. For ye shall be as an oak whose leaf fadeth, and as a garden that hath no water.

31. And the strong shall be as tow, and the maker of it as a spark, and they shall both burn together, and none shall quench them.

The wicked are referred to with three different words. At the time of judgment, they shall be ashamed and confounded on account of the *oaks*. It seems that the abominable idolatry with Baal and Ashtaroth, which was accompanied by all manner of repulsive immorality, was preferably committed in oak woods. At least the name *(oak) trees of righteousness* in 61:3 hints at this. This name is obviously contrasted with the oak trees mentioned here. Finally, the prophet depicts the wicked in two beautiful images of a dying *oak* tree and of a *garden* that has no water. He is adept in saying very much in simple natural images. He indicates that idolatry was the cause of the degenerating condition of the people in the days of Ahaz. A green, fruit-bearing tree was the standard image of a God-fearing and blessed man in Israel (Ps. 1). The *strong,* which is here the collective name for the mighty ones among them, shall be as coarse *tow* and their wicked deeds as a spark that ignites this coarsely chopped flax and makes it go up in flames; no one will be able to quench the fire. Sinners, together with their works, will be consumed. Their sinful deeds were the spark that consumed themselves. The imagery is very striking and meaningful; by his sin the sinner ignites the fire of hell. He ignites it, but he cannot quench it.

ISAIAH 2

The Kingdom of Peace

1. The word that Isaiah the son of Amoz saw concerning Judah and Jerusalem.

2. And it shall come to pass in the last days, that the mountain of the LORD'S house shall be established in the top of the mountains, and shall be exalted above the hills; and all nations shall flow unto it.

3. And many people shall go and say, Come ye, and let us go up to the mountain of the LORD, to the house of the God of Jacob; and he will teach us of his ways, and we will walk in his paths: for out of Zion shall go forth the law, and the word of the Lord from Jerusalem.

4. And he shall judge among the nations, and shall rebuke many people: and they shall beat their swords into plowshares, and their spears into pruninghooks: nation shall not lift up sword against nation, neither shall they learn war any more.

These words are also found in Micah 4:1-3. Much has been written about the authorship of these words. There are four possibilities, so the opinions can be reduced to the same number. (1) The most general opinion today is that a later collator derived these words from Micah. It is said that these words appear in Micah in a very fitting context and these, as a promise, are contrasted with the threat of Zion's complete destruction. (2) According to others, this prophecy originates with Isaiah, and Micah borrowed it from the great prophet. The solemn introduction presented here and the fact that the Holy Spirit, the true Author, placed it in the canon for Micah, point in this direction. (3) According to many critics, both Isaiah and Micah borrowed these words from a source not known to us. Not a single logical argument can be adduced in defense of this idea, however. (4) Finally, it can be argued that because of their great import these same words were revealed twice to two different prophets on two different occasions. Thus, there is no basis for assuming a slavish borrowing from an unnamed source; but the words are original with both prophets. To us, this idea is the most acceptable. Once we have accepted the miracle of inspiration, there is not a single reason why the Holy Spirit could not have communicated the same prophecy twice — once to Isaiah in the days of Ahaz, and once to Micah in the days of Hezekiah.

Let us now focus our attention on the glorious contents of these words. The introduction contains a refutation of the ideas expressed under (1) and (3). Isaiah *saw* this *word*. That is a remarkable expression, for human words are not *seen* but *heard!* This expression, which we meet frequently in the prophets, points up the unique character of prophetic inspiration. The Lord not only spoke with an audible voice to the prophets, but also showed them the future so that they could see the most glorious vistas. For that reason, the prophets were called "seers." Not a single author has succeeded in explaining *how* this communication, which on the Lord's side was objective and on the prophet's subjective, took place. We are faced here with a divine miracle which *cannot be understood* by the mind, but *can only be grasped* by faith. The prophet saw this vision *concerning Judah and Jerusalem.* This indication should have been sufficient for all exegetes to keep them from applying it to the Church or heaven, as has been done most of the time. Calvin says, "This concerns a scene of the restoration of God's Church — a matter of the utmost significance." This entirely contradicts the opening words *concerning Judah and Jerusalem.* Moreover, the gates of hell will never prevail against the Church, so that it is not necessary for her to be restored. But, such willful exegesis is the result of the hapless identification of Israel with the Church, a heresy that more than anything else has led to the breakdown of the historic churches. The famous Lutheran theologian Luthardt writes on Romans eleven as follows:

We have to view the teaching concerning Israel's future in Romans eleven as a heritage which the Apostles left us Christians among the Gentiles; it is because the Holy Spirit foresaw and wished to warn us against the false identification of the Gentile-Christian Church with Israel, which originated so early, dominates the view of the Roman Church and its expectation, and which also penetrated the Lutheran Church.

And Scofield, the well-known Bible scholar, writes concerning this in his *Correspondence Course,*

> It may safely be said that the Judaizing of the Church has done more to hinder her progress, pervert her mission and destroy her spirituality than all the other causes combined. Instead of pursuing her appointed path of separation, persecution, world-hatred, poverty, and non-resistance, she has used Jewish Scripture to justify her in lowering her purpose to the civilization of the world, and acquisition of wealth, the use of an imposing ritual, and the erection of magnificent cathedrals.

In all of Scripture there is not a semblance or shadow of justification for the identification of Israel as a nation with the Church as the body of Christ. In the New Testament the word *Israel* appears seventy times, but it must always be taken in its literal historical meaning. This is also the opinion of men such as Dr. James Brooks, Dr. Wilkinson, Dr. McCaul, Dr. Eadie, and others. Dr. Eadie says of this name (Israel) that Paul "never gives the grand old theocratic name to any but the chosen people." In refutation of this position, Galatians 3:28 is sometimes quoted. But, if this text proves that a believing Jew ceases to be a Jew, then the same verse must prove that a slave who believes in Christ ceases to be a slave, and that a believing man and woman change their sexes. The word *Jew* appears about two hundred times and always refers to a *Jew* in distinction from a *Gentile.* The word *Jerusalem* appears more than 140 times, and unless it is further designated by the concepts *new, heavenly,* or *from above,* which happens only in a few instances, it always means the capital of Palestine. Not only in preaching and the Church, but even in mission to the Jews this foolish mixing of Israel and the Church has bad results. In Luther's life, it can be seen that this identification makes mission among the Jews almost impossible. When we start with it, such mission becomes very unsuccessful on account of it.

At one time, the Rev. Renkema, writing in the *Noord Hollandsche Kerkbode,* even objected to continue to speak of *mission among Israel.* He writes;

> With the coming of the New Testament, the Jewish people have ceased to be God's people in a special sense, as was the case in olden times. 'The Vineyard' has been taken away from them and has been given to the believers among the Gentiles. To say it differently, the Church of Christ, the community of believers, is the Israel of the New Testament dispensation."

The Apostle Paul lived under the new dispensation, but he had no difficulty writing, "Brethren, my heart's desire and prayer to God for Israel is, that they might be saved" (Rom. 10:1). But all similar foolishness in teaching and practice is the natural result of positing that Israel and the Church are one and the same thing. Here, however, this identification, or rather confusion, is moreover at variance with the preceding and following contexts. All exegetes agree that in the preceding and following threats *Judah and Jerusalem* are the targets. Is it not extremely unfair then to assign the wickedness and punishments to the Jews, and the promises in between to the Church?

But the objection to our taking these words literally is that if you insist on taking them to apply to physical Israel, you then come to the most absurd conclusions. Then, you will have to accept that all the mountains of the world will be piled on top of each other and that little Mount Zion will be set on top of that pile. We are fully acquainted with this argument. It shows that it does not take into account the character of prophetic language nor the difference between a literal and a foolish inflexible literal explanation of Scripture. The latter would in this case be indeed absurd. But literal interpretation has always insisted and advocated taking the words in their natural and obvious meaning, *unless this would lead to obvious absurdities.* This method of exegesis does not defend ignoring the rich imagery of the prophets. No right-minded person wishes to promote such lunacy. That had better be left to such sects as the Mormons, the House of David and the Flying Rollers. There is no figure of speech or thought that is not found in Isaiah, and every exegete ought to have an eye for this. In the symbolism of the prophets, Mount *Zion* always stands for the theocratic kingdom of Israel, while the great and high mountains stand for the proud kingdoms of the world (Ps. 68:16, 17; Dan. 2:35; Rev. 13:1; 17:9-11). This is the case here also.

In continuation of what was said in Isaiah 1:25-27, it is said here that the theocratic kingdom of Israel will one day be at the head of all the kingdoms of the world. *At the head* is here the only correct translation, and not *in the top. It shall come to pass,* i.e., it shall become history *in the last days.* Actually, the Hebrew says *at the last end of the days.* The old Rabbinic tradition explained this expression as referring to the Messianic time, the time when the Messiah would reign on earth. That is the only correct interpretation, for wherever we come across this phrase, it always refers to the great end-time (Gen. 49:1; Num. 24:14; Deut. 4:30; 31:29; Jer. 48:47; 49:39; Ezek. 38:8, 16; Dan. 2:28; Hos. 3:5; Mic. 4:1). The expression is also found in the New Testament, but there it refers to the last days of this dispensation (II Tim. 3:1; James 5:3; II Pet. 3:3). The term *day of the Lord,* which we meet in Isaiah 2:12, refers chronologically to about the same time as *the last days* except that this expression refers more to the dreadful judgment that must precede the bliss of the *last days.*

The Kingdom of the great King of Israel will, in contrast to the other kingdoms, be *established* at the head of the nations. This agrees with what Daniel says of the Messianic Kingdom: it will never be destroyed and will not be left to other people, but will stand forever (Dan. 2:44). If we take the mountains to mean the large kingdoms, then we can properly take the hills to mean the smaller nations. The future Kingdom of Peace will be exalted above them. The honor and glory above all nations will be manifested by the fact that *all nations* — all the nations outside of Israel — will flow unto it. Whereas the nations are represented as mountains, the peoples are represented as *streams* that will flow unto the Kingdom of Peace founded in Israel. We shall come across the conversion of the nations in connection with Israel's restoration again and again in Isaiah, especially in the second part.

We need not take the phrase *many people* in a more restricted sense than *all nations,* for elsewhere it appears, as it does here, in the widest sense (52:15; Zech. 2:11). Nevertheless, on the basis of 66:19, we know that there will be a difference of knowledge among the various nations during the Kingdom of Peace. At least at the start of this Kingdom, there will be nations, according to this verse, which have not learned of the Savior's return and glory. It is equally to be expected that not all nations that have been spared from the judgment will immediately urge each other with the same enthusiasm to serve Jehovah-Jesus. To say the least, it is a very weak explanation which Calvin gives when he says of this appeal by the nations, "The believers will one day be so desirous of visiting the Holy Land that they will urge their like-minded brethren to do the same." This text simply does not speak of the various believers but of *many people.* Nor does it speak of a desire to see Palestine but of going up to the house of the God of Jacob. The temple, which is so extensively described by Ezekiel, will then be a house of prayer for all people (Isa. 56:7).

After Christ has returned on the clouds of heaven unto judgment and to establish His glorious Kingdom on the ruins of this old world and to cause it to shine in incomparable glory, the nations will be irresistibly drawn to it and exhort each other to seek to obtain the glory and blessings of Israel's Messiah. They will wish to *learn* of His ways and to *walk* in His paths. What a contrast to the raging of the nations as we still see it today. Jerusalem will then be the greatest capital of the world, the resident city of King Messiah, and the seat and glittering center of truth and glory. From there, the Lord Jesus will give His commands and make known His new revelations to the world. By *law (torah)* we do not merely understand the Mosaic law, but also the law of the Kingdom as enunciated in Matthew five to seven. In that day, the injunctions given in these laws will all be adhered to and of them, too, not a jot or tittle will fall to the ground. Then, Israel will exalt, "The Lord is our Judge, the Lord is our Law-Giver, the Lord is our King!" Then, the Word of the Lord will be the law for Israel and all the nations and it will be strictly observed. It may safely be assumed that then the

Lord Jesus will reveal new truths that are presently hidden. This is quite clearly indicated in Joel 2:28.

This glorious new life will not dawn along the lines of a gradual development, but only after the most horrifying judgments. The Lord will first *judge* and *rebuke* among the dechristianized and antichristian nations, according to the first part of verse four. This verse clearly teaches that only after and by this judgment does the Kingdom of Peace come about; the nations will dwell in safety as during the time of Solomon (I Kings 4:25). The tools of war will be turned into tools of peace. But before this takes place, Joel 3:10 tells us, the opposite will first take place. And then there will be true peace; it will not be just an armed peace, but absolute peace. The nations will not even forge any weapons any more nor learn warfare. All military science, which today has reached such terrifying proportions, will then belong to a dark past. Then, He who is greater than Solomon will give the nations lasting peace.

Full of Wealth and Wantonness

5. O house of Jacob, come ye, and let us walk in the light of the LORD.

6. Therefore thou hast forsaken thy people the house of Jacob, because they be replenished from the east, and are soothsayers like the Philistines, and they please themselves in the children of strangers.

7. Their land also is full of silver and gold, neither is there any end of their treasures; their land is also full of horses, neither is there any end of their chariots:

8. Their land is also full of idols; they worship the work of their own hands, that which their own fingers have made.

9. And the mean man boweth down, and the great man humbleth himself: therefore forgive them not.

The prophet here turns from the imperishable majesty of the Kingdom of Peace to the exceeding wickedness of his days. When he sees how the future nations will invite each other to the Messianic bliss, and looks at the wickedness of his contemporaries, he discovers a sad contrast. Full of grief he cries, "O house of Jacob, come ye, and let us walk in the light of the Lord." The Word of the Lord, which Israel knew, was a light unto Israel, but she refused to walk in that light.

She loved the darkness more than the light, since her works were evil. She had forsaken God and in righteous judgment God had forsaken her. The principle of righteous retribution frequently occurs in the prophets.

Isaiah continues to describe the sins of his people as *overflowing* wickedness. They are full of the sins committed by the pagans of the East. West of Judah lived the Philistines. Judah had even adopted their *soothsaying,* literally, *cloud-making.* Undoubtedly this refers to astrology. The Philistines were extremely superstitious and now the Jews are accused of having adopted their superstitions. They are shown to have *pleasure* in the *children of strangers,* i.e., everything that comes from strange countries. According to the original, they received all the strange pagan practices with clapping of hands. In this respect, Judah resembled the Dutch people of more than a century ago, when they were enamored by all that came out of France; those who favored the French revolution were welcomed with a happy clapping of hands.

It was all the more serious for the Jews to do so since, according to the law, they were not to have any intimate traffic with foreign nations. As a result of the land and sea trade under Uzziah and Jotham, the country had become very rich. This prosperity led to wealth, wantonness and worldly-mindedness. The strong wording of verse seven points to enormous wealth and endless treasures. The country was full of gold, but the people were very cold and bold towards their God. With their gold they bought war horses and chariots. Horsemen and chariots were supposed to protect the accumulated treasures. The people should not fear, for the nation can manage without Him. They committed the accursed sin of making flesh their arm. They made beautiful idols of gold and silver, before which they all knelt, from the poorest and most insignificant to the richest and most prominent.

Thus, the wickedness of Judah and Jerusalem was fourfold: they were filled with superstitious rituals, treasures, militarism and heathen idolatry. But, the Lord is not an idle spectator of evil. He saw their abominable walk. He would not let all these things pass by unpunished. He might keep silent for a while, but there would come an end to His long-suffering and then His anger would be kindled. The prophet was fully conscious of this and therefore cries out in a sudden turn of speech, quite common in his lively style, ". . . therefore forgive them not!" The second part of this chapter says that no forgiveness follows these abominations, but only dreadful judgment.

The Judgment on Haughtiness

10. Enter into the rock, and hide thee in the dust, for fear of the LORD, and for the glory of his majesty.

11. The lofty looks of man shall be humbled, and the haughtiness of men shall be bowed down, and the LORD alone shall be exalted in that day.

12. For the day of the LORD of hosts shall be upon every one that is proud and lofty, and upon every one that is lifted up; and he shall be brought low:

13. And upon all the cedars of Lebanon, that are high and lifted up, and upon all the oaks of Bashan,

14. And upon all the high mountains, and upon all the hills that are lifted up,

15. And upon every high tower, and upon every fenced wall,

16. And upon all the ships of Tarshish, and upon all pleasant pictures.

17. And the loftiness of man shall be bowed down, and the haughtiness of men shall be made low: and the LORD alone shall be exalted in that day.

18. And the idols he shall utterly abolish.

I Kings 2:46 states, "And the kingdom was established in the hand of Solomon." When we ask the question how his kingdom was established, then the context gives the answer and tells us that his kingdom of peace was established by judgment upon the wicked. It will not be different in the future with respect to the Kingdom of Peace of our Lord Jesus Christ. It too shall be established, and that by means of a judgment as is described in these verses (Isa. 9:6).

In times of war, mountain caves and clefts in rocks were hiding places for the fearful refugees and displaced persons. Alluding to this, the prophet cries in his lofty eloquence, "Enter into the rock, and hide thee in the dust." The words *fear* and *glory* point to Christ's awesome and majestic appearance in the day of His coming. Among the main arguments of an orator are description and enumeration, and we find both here in rare power and beauty. The eloquence here is unique and incomparable; indeed crushing. *The Lord alone shall be exalted in that day* is the main theme. And since the Lord Jesus − for·He and none other is meant here − will only be exalted; all the haughtiness and pride of men must be pulled down and humbled to the depths of hell.

To express the completeness of the judgment, the prophet indicates the haughty people and their proud cultural achievements in seven distichs. By the cedars of Lebanon and the *oaks* of Bashan are to be understood the proud kings and generals such as Rabshakeh; by *mountains* and *hills* the big and small kingdoms. The *high tower* and *fenced wall* represent all fortified and well-defended cities, while the *ships of Tarshish* and the *pleasant pictures* represent all world trade and culture. Religious man may be very proud of a Christless culture, but here we see that it will be destroyed in the day of Christ. The main topic and, at the same time, the basic theme of this powerful prophecy is repeated at the end. Today there is nowhere room for the Man of Sorrows. Therefore, in that day, He will succeed in securing His rightful place by crushing all His adversaries. He will rise up in all His magnitude and majesty as the King of kings and the Lord of lords on the ruins of an overthrown culture.

In holy irony it is finally stated that the *idols* are totally destroyed. After such lofty eloquence this statement seems laconic and dry. Isaiah has no equal in his mastery of the art of irony and holy mockery. With regard to the abominable idolatry, he is inexhaustible. Irony is a witty, pointed, pithy and even somewhat barbed manner of speaking. In Scripture, however, irony is never profane, but always holy in its intent to present sin as absurd, ridiculous and despicable.

Hiding in Holes and Caves Because of the Appearance of Christ

19. And they shall go into the holes of the rocks, and into the caves of the earth, for fear of the LORD, and for the glory of his majesty, when he ariseth to shake terribly the earth.

The summons of Isaiah in verse ten will be literally fulfilled in the future. Both Hosea and the Apostle John have pointed this out (Hos. 10:8; Rev. 6:15, 16). For everyone not covered by the blood of the Lamb, the wrath of the Lamb will be so unspeakably terrible that they will not know where to hide. Compare with this the description in Revelation eight and nine. The Great Tribulation will be terrible and defies all description. Men will seek death as something greatly desirable, but it will mysteriously flee from them. Suicide will be an unobtainable luxury. Men will wish the shaking mountains to crush them; they will pray for it to happen, they will beg them, scream at them, but it will all be in vain. No sinner shall escape God's certain wrath, when He shall strike him in his sinful path. The Lord shall *arise*, equipped as a warrior, to *shake terribly the earth*. Now, He is still willing to save the sinner, to fill him with eternal, divine happiness; but then it will be His goal to fill all those who rejected Him with eternal terror. Then, He will laugh at their calamity and mock when their fear comes. For that reason today, He still cries, "Kiss the Son, lest He be angry!" (Psalm 2:12).

Idolatry Abolished

20. In that day a man shall cast his idols of silver, and his idols of gold, which they made each one for himself to worship, to the moles and to the bats;
21. To go into the clefts of the rocks, and into the tops of the ragged rocks, for fear of the LORD, and for the glory of his majesty, when he ariseth to shake terribly the earth.
22. Cease ye from man, whose breath is in his nostrils: for wherein is he to be accounted of?

Verse nine says that God cannot and will not forgive systematic idolatry; in verse eighteen the prophet mocks that every one of the idols will be utterly destroyed. He points out that in that day man, far from receiving help from his idols, will instead throw them away to the moles and the bats. The prophet pictures terrified refugees who seek a hiding place in the holes and clefts of the rocks, but will not take their gods with them. Usually, when going on a trip they took small images. But then they will throw them disdainfully away. Moles and bats hide in dark places and are repulsive animals that are afraid of light. The meaning is clear. The erstwhile, esteemed and venerated idols end up with the most despised animals; their worshippers in their desperation sling them away as totally worthless. This is a horrible representation both of the worshipped and the worshipping. If the description of the judgment already frightens us, what will the actuality be one day? The object of the almost literal repetition of verse nineteen in twenty-one is to drive home the gruesome reality of the judgment. Frivolous man in his intoxication with sensual pleasures does not always hear the voice of the Lord. The Lord warns once again, since He has no pleasure in the death of the wicked; He rather desires that the wicked turn from his way and live. The intent of the last verse is to warn against putting any trust in man. For such trust is vain, as man in all his pride and with all his proud cultural achievements is futility and vanity personified. If God takes away his breath, he dies, and returns to dust (Ps. 104:29). Do not esteem man, for his entire being depends on the breath in his nostrils; adore God who made him and one day will judge him.

ISAIAH 3

The Country in Shambles

> 1. For, behold, the Lord, the LORD of hosts, doth take away from Jerusalem and Judah the stay and the staff, the whole stay of bread, and the whole stay of water,
> 2. The mighty man, and the man of war, the judge, and the prophet, and the prudent, and the ancient,
> 3. The captain of fifty, and the honourable man, and the counsellor, and the cunning artificer, and the eloquent orator.

In chapter three Isaiah again displays all his holy eloquence and rich vocabulary. He enumerates the nation's twelve supporting pillars, which will be snatched away by God's anger, causing the country to end up in total disarray. Bread and water are the chief means of support of a people. Just as an old man leans on his stick and a shepherd on his staff, so a people leans for its natural sustenance on bread and water; hence, the expression *the stay of bread and the stay of water* shows that there will be famine. Already the law of Moses (Lev. 26 and Deut. 28) contained the threat of a terrible famine upon disobedience. From the history of the destruction of Samaria and Jerusalem, we know that these threatenings of the Lord were literally fulfilled. The Lord will take further away from Judah, by the sword or by exile into foreign countries or by both at the same time, *the mighty man and the man of war.* These two supporting pillars represent the entire army in which people normally put their trust for the defense of the country. The *judge* and the *prophet* represent the civil and spiritual rulers. The *prudent* and the *ancient* represent wise counselors. The others mentioned here indicate the leaders of the nation. At that time, it was customary for the conquerors to carry away captive the leaders of the people to their own countries. This served a twofold purpose. First, this colonial system prevented the danger of an uprising; and second, such a choice group of colonists could reclaim fruitful but as yet wild areas for their conquerors. The kings of Assyria and Babylon applied this system to Israel and Judah, as the books of Kings and Chronicles tell us.

"Woe to Thee, O land, When Thy King is a Child"

> 4. And I will give children to be their princes, and babes shall rule over them.
> 5. And the people shall be oppressed, every one by another, and every one by his neighbour: the child shall behave himself proudly against the ancient, and the base against the honourable.

The proverb by Solomon, quoted above may aptly describe these verses. The preceding verses said that Judah would be robbed of its best rulers; but here the prophet predicts on behalf of the Lord that young and inexperienced leaders would take their places. Inexperienced young men and even children will have authority over the people. The word *king* is intentionally avoided here, but most likely the prophet alludes to Manasseh who at the death of his father Hezekiah was only twelve years old. As a result of misrule by rash young men, the confusion will increase. The people will be *oppressed*, pressured, straightened and vexed. This will be the first result with the second being that civil war will ensue. They will not only be attacked from without but also fly at each other's throat. Thirdly, it will be a time of bolshevism. All authority, obedience, and submissiveness will disappear. The aged and the honorable citizens will be disrespected, while young hotheads and rabble will rule the roost. Today, we are experiencing the fulfillment of these words!

Disruption and Despair During Anarchy

> 6. When a man shall take hold of his brother of the house of his father, saying, Thou hast clothing, be thou our ruler, and let this ruin be under thy hand:
> 7. In that day shall he swear, saying, I will not be an healer;

for in my house is neither bread nor clothing: make me not a
ruler of the people.

By introducing a symbolic act and a lively dialog, the
prophet in a few words sketches the hopeless confusion
resulting from the departure from God and His service.
Brother means fellow citizen and the *house of his father* his
country and people. The situation is depicted as so desolate
that no one will accept the reins of government any more. No
one considers it possible to save the collapsed body of state.
Yet the people realize that there must be a government and
they do their utmost to find someone willing to provide
leadership. In this general poverty there is still someone who
has a piece of *clothing,* i.e., some standing and property. "Be
thou our ruler!" they beseech him, "let this *ruin* be under
thy hand."

The attempts at obtaining a ruler are totally in vain. He
who was offered the highest government post solemnly
declines. He even lifts his hand up to swear and exclaims, "I
will not be a healer!" He considers the country as bleeding
from a thousand wounds and totally incurable. He feels
himself to be as a physician called to a patient who can no
more be healed and whose condition is totally hopeless. As a
further reason for his refusal, he adds that he himself
together with the rest are victims of the general misery of
hunger and poverty; there is no food or clothing in his house,
either, cf. 1:5, 6.

All the Misery the People's Own Fault

8. For Jerusalem is ruined, and Judah is fallen: because their
tongue and their doings are against the LORD, to provoke the
eyes of his glory.
9. The shew of their countenance doth witness against them;
and they declare their sin as Sodom, they hide it not. Woe unto
their soul! for they have rewarded evil unto themselves.

Here is indicated in a prophetic perfect tense — as though
it was already an accomplished fact — the reason for the
wretched condition of the people. Jerusalem has run into and
stumbled over the stumbling stone. Judah has fallen because

its speaking and action provoke Jehovah; His anger blazes from His all-seeing and holy eyes. Instead of living uprightly before His countenance, as demanded by the original covenant conditions, they committed the most horrible abominations before Him. The brazen countenance of the wicked is contrasted with the holy countenance of God in which the God-fearing find their life. Their sensual faces are witnesses against them. Their wantonness and adultery are written on their faces. They have shaken off all sense of shame. After Adam had sinned, he hid himself, but these people refuse to be ashamed. They live and speak like the Sodomites. Their glory is in their shame. When the jailer wanted to take his own life, Paul cried, "Do thyself no harm!" Isaiah cries, "Woe unto their souls!" They are engaged in murdering their soul and their own people. How great is the folly of sin!

Weal and Woe

10. Say ye to the righteous, that it shall be well with him: for they shall eat the fruit of their doings.
11. Woe unto the wicked! it shall be ill with him: for the reward of his hands shall be given him.

Even in a situation similar to that of Sodom, God remembers the righteous as He did in the time of Lot. At the Lord's command, Isaiah must tell the righteous man, representing all the righteous people in general, that it will be well with them in the way of obedience. Like Lot in the days of old, the God-fearing people in the future will not be struck by the judgments and doomed to destruction. According to God's rewarding justice, they will eat the fruits of their good works. What man sows, *that* he will reap. This law of the Kingdom is valid through all the ages. On this abiding law the whole doctrine of the reward of grace is based as well as the doctrine of punishment. Even the adversities of the righteous, which are often man, redound to his well-being, his true spiritual prosperity. All the paths of the Lord are to him mercy and truth; all things work together for good. Jacob may lament that all his bitter experiences are against him, but exactly the opposite is true; they are rather for him. "Who can harm you," Peter says to his fellow believers," if ye be followers of that which is good?" Strictly speaking, nothing or no one can harm a child of God, for the mercilessness of life is God's mercy to him; his adversities are God's opportunities to purify him spiritually.

Totally different, however, is the situation for him who loves evil, and who is called *wicked* here. The Dutch word for *wicked* here is *goddeloze,* meaning *godless,* someone who is *loose* or separated from God; who has not yet been bound to and united with God by the Mediator. This expresses well the idea of the Hebrew word, *rasha.* The same law of righteousness also holds true for him, but in the opposite sense. He too will have to eat the fruit of his hands, not as the recompense of reward, but of wrath. A century later, Jeremiah called the attention of his contemporaries to the same irrevocable law of the Lord, which no one can escape and to which everyone's conscience must say yea and amen: "Thine own wickedness shall correct thee, and thy backslidings shall reprove thee" (Jer. 2:19). Hence, God punishes not only *because of* sin, but also *through* sin. The crimes themselves become the fire that will consume them. All the prosperity of the wicked is adversity. Their eyes may stand out with fatness, but they are fattened for the day of slaughter (Jas. 5:5). They are reserved unto fire against the day of judgment (II Pet. 3:7). Israel then, Christendom now, must be acquainted with this unalterable law of rewarding and punishing, the law of retribution. With regret it must be said that "the preaching of the Word" has all too often neglected to point this out. There is a lamentable ignorance concerning the glorious doctrine of the reward of grace, which God has attached to the performing of good works. The same is true of the punishment of wickedness. Even though it may be true, as some say, that Isaiah is quoting here a pair of old proverbs, they nevertheless represent a truth which never becomes obsolete. At the same time our preaching should never omit the two classes of people mentioned.

Feminism

12. As for my people, children are their oppressors, and

women rule over them. O my people, they which lead thee cause
thee to err, and destroy the way of thy paths.

The heart of the Jews was just as wicked as the heart of all
of us; Judah's sins are an example and prelude of the sins
which will be found in the whole world toward the end time.
We find in this chapter lawlessness, unruliness and confusion.
We are experiencing these very things in our own dark days
but on a much larger scale. This verse speaks of government
being in the hands of children and women who are making
rapid advances in our day. We see no necessity to depart from
the literal meaning of this verse, because under the last kings
of Judah women and children were in charge of the matters
of business in the country most of the time. It is equally true
that the last kings of Judah were spineless, effeminate men
and not entirely unlike old women and children. The
populace generally remained attached to its unworthy leaders
and blindly followed them in their evil ways. The books of
Kings and Chronicles give ample evidence of this. Hence the
prophet at the Lord's command cries out in holy indignation,
"O my people, they which lead thee cause thee to err!" It is
good to be obedient, even to hard masters, but woe unto us if
we slavishly follow others into their evil ways, like Judah did.
We need to be seriously warned against it as Isaiah does here.
If the leaders had heard of it, they would have easily accused
him of resistance to the government. But this knight without
fear or fault is by no means deterred. He presents the leaders
as wild animals who devour the paths of justice making it
impossible for the people to find them. Judgment will strike
these leaders!

The Lord Comes to Judge the Unfaithful Leaders

13. The LORD standeth up to plead, and standeth to judge
the people.
14. The LORD will enter into judgment with the ancients of
his people, and the princes thereof: for ye have eaten up the
vineyard; the spoil of the poor is in your houses.
15. What mean ye that ye beat my people to pieces, and grind
the faces of the poor? saith the Lord GOD of hosts.

By a solemn announcement of judgment, the prophet assures that Jehovah is preparing Himself to come in judgment on the unfaithful leaders. All prophecies similar to those in verse thirteen should be taken literally and not as imagery or personification. The Lord Jesus is presently *sitting* at the right hand of God to indicate that He is resting after the labor of His soul. Just as He rested after creation, so does He rest after recreation. He is *sitting* to indicate His perfect and completed sacrifice. The high priest in the old days was not allowed to sit down, but had to perform his priestly duties while standing. In the day of His coming, however, He will stand up to do battle. Stephen and John did not see Him sitting, but *standing* as in the day of His coming. The leaders are called *ancients* and *princes*. The prophet compares them with vermin that have eaten the *vineyard* of Israel bare (5:1-7). They have plundered and emptied the houses of the wretched, carrying off the loot to their own palaces. They crushed the poor under foot and mistreated them as slaves. *They grind the faces of the poor* — a strong expression that indicates that the poverty and despair could be read from the faces of the poor as a result of their oppression. The Lord Himself asks what has come over them to treat His poor and miserable people so cruelly.

Description of the Judgment on the Fine Ladies

16. Moreover the LORD saith, Because the daughters of Zion are haughty, and walk with stretched forth necks and wanton eyes, walking and mincing as they go, and making a tinkling with their feet:

17. Therefore the Lord will smite with a scab the crown of the head of the daughters of Zion, and the LORD will discover their secret parts.

18. In that day the Lord will take away the bravery of their tinkling ornaments about their feet, and their cauls, and their round tires like the moon,

19. The chains, and the bracelets, and the mufflers,

20. The bonnets, and the ornaments of the legs, and the headbands, and the tablets, and the earrings,

21. The rings, and nose jewels,

22. The changeable suits of apparel, and the mantles, and the wimples, and the crisping pins,

23. The glasses, and the fine linen, and the hoods, and the vails.

After having depicted the judgment on the wicked leaders, who had become seducers and oppressors of the people, this remarkable section now describes the judgment on Judah's daughters. We get the impression here that these women exercised a fateful influence on the leaders. Once again, we can see that the same is happening today! This section proves once more what a sharp observer and literary artist the prophet was. Not without a hint of irony, in which he excels so well, he describes in the minutest detail the trappings of the wanton women of Jerusalem.

It has been said that today we need another Isaiah in view of the ever increasing mania for the goddess of fashion; but Paris, London, Berlin and New York could care less what a new Isaiah would say; they care no more than Jerusalem did in the day of the first Isaiah. Isaiah himself would also say, "What is needed is not Isaiah but Jehovah!" It must not escape our attention that it was not merely Isaiah who saw and condemned all this, but Jehovah Himself who sees the ways of men and in the day of judgment will pronounce His irrevocable verdict on the minutest details. He even pays attention to *the tinkling ornaments about the feet.* His anger burns and smokes against everything that, although not sinful in itself, is used in the service of a frivolity that laughs at the seriousness of life and leads to the wasting of His time and the talents He gave.

Is this not also the case with regard to most of our present day culture? To be sure, there are many things that in themselves are absolutely not sinful. But man in his pride uses them only for himself, is wholly taken up with them and forgets the Giver of all good and perfect gifts. This is why God admonishes His people to lay aside every weight and the sin which so easily besets them. But most believers are like the daughters of Zion whom Isaiah condemns; they go through life with many unnecessary burdens and superfluous luxury which corrupt the heart.

As far as the words for these articles of adornment are concerned, it is difficult to give the correct meaning of many of them. The most famous commentary that has ever been written on these verses is by N.W. Schroder, who at an early age published a learned and greatly praised commentary in

Latin; it is still followed by most exegetes. We shall briefly call attention to the most important matters. The prophet sees the proud and frivolous damsels mincing in the streets of Jerusalem. According to the original, they put black makeup on their eyes. The Orientals were very fond of big eyes with black circles around them. Quite frequently they tore the eyelids further apart for that purpose and smeared a heavy paste on them. They did not powder the entire face as the women do today since they wore a veil before their faces. They pranced past the seer with short, measured steps. In order to do so more evenly, they wore small silver or gold chains around the ankles. These foot chains made a tinkling sound. The prophet naturally reminds us of the mincing walk and the open and sometimes tinkling footwear of today's women. In fact, this whole section shows that mankind is exactly the same today as in Isaiah's time. Essentially, the fair sex still entertains the same follies as then.

In verse seventeen the seer calls out to the tinkling, coquetting women who pass him with minced steps that the Lord will make their *scalp scabby*. God would bring baldness in place of wavy flowing hair and would reveal their secret parts as the result of an unclean sickness. The latter expression is often taken in a symbolic sense as the dismantling of the city walls and fortifications. But here it must be taken literally as a cruel shame inflicted upon these frivolous women. *The bravery of the tinkling ornaments about the feet* refers again to the *tinkling shoe buckles,* as the Jew Izak Leeser renders this expression. *Cauls* are hair nets, and *round tires like the moon* are moon-shaped pendants. The word translated *chains* is rendered *perfume boxes* in Dutch *(scent bottles* in other translations) and is derived from the verb *to drip*. We prefer to think here of a fragrant fluid, or balsam boxes. The *mufflers* (Dutch has *glistening clothing)* seems to refer to beautiful veils. The second word in verse twenty again indicates the tinkling foot chains; *headbands* mean ornamental sashes. *Tablets* again refers to scent boxes or bottles. Then three kinds of rings are mentioned: *earrings, finger rings,* and *nose rings* (v. 20b, 21). Today there are still tribes who think nose rings are beautiful. Verse twenty-two should read: expensive dresses, mantles, cloaks and purses. The word *glasses* (v. 23) indicates a transparent dress that reveals the body. Here again it looks like Isaiah was thinking of the lascivious women of our day. *Fine linen* refers to expensive underclothing. Undoubtedly the words refers to fine shirts of flax. By *hoods* is meant turbans, consisting of a wide strip of cloth wound around the head. At last the prophet has come to the end of the finery of the Jerusalem women. It is as though with this enumeration of three groups of seven he wishes to express the fullness of unrighteousness. By enumerating all these things piece by piece he not only ridicules their lasciviousness and pride, but he also wishes, as is evident from what follows, to depict the stark contrast between their present frivolity and future misery. He indicates this in seven contrasts.

The Wretchedness That Shall Descend Upon the Daughters of Zion

> 24. And it shall come to pass, that instead of sweet smell there shall be stink; and instead of a girdle a rent; and instead of well set hair baldness; and instead of a stomacher a girding of sackcloth; and burning instead of beauty.
> 25. Thy men shall fall by the sword, and thy mighty in the war.
> 26. And her gates shall lament and mourn; and she being desolate shall sit upon the ground.

Instead of the sweet smell of spices, there will be the stench of wounds and pus. These lewd damsels will be beaten and mistreated as captured slaves; instead of a gorgeous girdle there will be a rope, a noose, with which the captured ladies will be bound. The word is also translated by *rent, ripped rags of blue welts*. Their waving hair will be cut off as a sign of captivity and slavery. Instead of the beautiful flowing dress they will don sackcloth as a sign of mourning. The word *burning* does not refer to a sun-burned, tan face, but the burnt mark of a branding iron on the hand or forehead of slaves. They will lose their men by the sword of war; and their mighty, in whom they put their trust, will fall on the battlefield. In that day there will be general mourning and grief in the gates of Jerusalem and Judah. Every one of the haughty daughters of Zion will then sit down on the earth, robbed and bereft, lonely and forsaken. Then, they will no longer walk with minced tinkling steps to beguile the men; but rather, totally crushed they will bewail the men who are no longer there since they have fallen in battle. Actually, the first verse of the next chapter belongs to this chapter. This entire description by Isaiah is one eloquent and deeply gripping sermon against the disastrous results of allowing oneself to be ruled by the goddess of fashion.

ISAIAH 4

Seven Women Taking Hold of One Man

1. And in that day seven women shall take hold of one man, saying, We will eat our own bread and wear our own apparel: only let us be called by thy name, to take away our reproach.

The chapter division here is most unfortunate. It is evident that this verse belongs to the condemnatory speech given to the wanton women in the preceding chapter. There they were told that they would lose all their fashion and trappings in the judgments of the Lord. Here they are depicted as being desperate on account of the shortage of men. The country is depopulated; the young men and the mighty warriors, the bloom of the nation, have fallen in battle. We must keep in mind that it was a disgrace for a Jewish woman to die without having been married and having had children. There are many references in Scripture hinting at this idea. What a long discourse on the depopulation of the country and the resulting perplexity of the women could not have done, the prophet does with one stroke of his pen by depicting a curious scene of seven lovesick women who all together seize one man with the plea to be their husband. They make it as easy for him as possible, for even though the law demanded that a man must buy and take care of his wife (Exod. 21:10; 22:16; Deut. 22:28; I Sam. 18:20-22), they do not require this of him. On the contrary, they promise that they will take care of their own clothing and food. All they desperately want is to be his wife, so that they will have a name and protector. The number seven does not indicate completeness here, but incompleteness. It is used here as well as elsewhere in both a negative and a positive sense. There is no record of an exact fulfillment of this statement. The time reference *in that day* points to the time of Israel's great tribulation, when her Messiah will return in glory.

The Branch of the Lord the Only Adornment for Israel

> 2. In that day shall the branch of the LORD be beautiful and glorious, and the fruit of the earth shall be excellent and comely for them that are escaped of Israel.

The *branch of the Lord* is not Hezekiah, nor in general the blessings of the Messiah, but Messiah Himself. He is also called *Branch* in Jeremiah 23:5; 33:15; Zechariah 3:8; 6:12. Calvin contests the Messianic interpretation here and takes the expressions *Branch* and *fruit of the earth* together; he explains them to mean an unprecedented manifestation of divine grace. But the five words used here to express the glory of this Branch point obviously to the unique majesty of the Redeemer at His return to His people Israel. At His first coming, there was neither form nor comeliness that Israel should have desired Him. After His return, He will not only be beautiful and glorious but also Israel's beauty and glory. Obviously, the prophet points to these glorious attributes of King Messiah in contrast to the whorish adornments he enumerated in the preceding chapter. Only after we have lost the adornment of our good works does God adorn us with His holy adornment of the robe of righteousness and the garments of salvation in which we will be led to the King. The name *fruit of the earth* also refers to Christ. The first name indicates Him as the Son of God, who has branched forth from Jehovah. The second name refers to Him as the true man who has come forth from mankind; He has become one with mankind for the benefit of mankind.

The Chosen Remnant

> 3. And it shall come to pass, that he that is left in Zion, and he that remaineth in Jerusalem, shall be called holy, even every one that is written among the living in Jerusalem:
> 4. When the Lord shall have washed away the filth of the daughters of Zion, and shall have purged the blood of Jerusalem

from the midst thereof by the spirit of judgment, and by the spirit of burning.

The word *remnant* is rich in meaning. It presupposes and encompasses the ideas of sin, judgment, election, grace and glory. Four words in the text point this out: *escaped, left, remaineth* and *written among the living.* As we shall meet this concept again and again in Isaiah, it may be useful to pay special attention to it. The prophet speaks of a remnant from Israel and the nations in a fourfold sense.

First of all, there is a remnant of Israel from its past history. Regardless how great the apostasy was, the Lord always retained a remnant, which was the channel through which He caused the blessings of His covenant to flow to Israel. In Ahab's day, there was apostasy and judgment but Elijah and the seven thousand who had not bowed the knees to Baal were the chosen remnant. In Isaiah's day, the whole head of the nation was sick and the entire heart faint, but he and his family were the center of the remnant that remained faithful to the God of the covenant. The days of Jeremiah and the seventy years of exile were dark times; Jeremiah and his private secretary, Ezekiel, and Daniel and his three friends were part of the little flock that was saved in the judgments. After the exile we find such a remnant mentioned in Malachi 3:16 and 4:2, which in the midst of a general apostasy remained faithful to its God, feared the name of the Lord and continued to hope upon His name.

Secondly, there is always a remnant according to the election of grace during Israel's partial and temporary hardening and blindness of today. The Apostle Paul points this out in Romans eleven. Every era in Israel's history has such a remnant. Today, this remnant is greater than in any other period since the days of the Apostles.

Thirdly, the word *remnant* is used for the nations that remain after their judgment (Acts 15:17).

Fourthly, the word *remnant* is used time and again in connection with Israel's restoration. In the day of Jacob's calamity, according to Zechariah, two of the three parts of Israel will be cut off. Suppose there will then be fifteen million Jews, as there are now, then ten million would be exterminated and five million spared. Those five million would be the chosen remnant whose names are recorded in the book of life. Scripture frequently speaks of people's names being written in the book of life (Exod. 32:32; Ps. 69:28; Dan. 12:1; Luke 10:20; Rev. 20:12). So the fact that *all Israel* will one day be saved must not be taken to mean that every individual Jew will one day be saved. All the leaves, the branches, the twigs, and even the entire top may be hewn off a tree, but the tree, as such, remains. This is what will happen with Israel. The greater part of the people will be exterminated, but the people as a people will be saved in the remnant. The third part, the remnant, will be called *holy*. It will be separated from all its former uncleanness and be wholly consecrated to the Lord (Zech. 13:9; 14:20, 21). This will not take place, however, until after the process of purification in The Great Tribulation. The filth and blood-guiltiness of the city of prophet-killers will be purged by water and fire. Verse four clearly tells us that the Holy Spirit will be active in that fearful day of calamity. He is not only the good Spirit who renews the sinner, but also the Spirit of judgment and of burning.

The Fulfillment of the Pillar of Cloud and the Pillar of Fire

> 5. And the LORD will create upon every dwelling place of mount Zion, and upon her assemblies, a cloud and smoke by day, and the shining of a flaming fire by night: for upon all the glory shall be a defence.
> 6. And there shall be a tabernacle for a shadow in the daytime from the heat, and for a place of refuge, and for a covert from storm and from rain.

After the judgment of The Great Tribulation, Israel will obtain great glory. First, however, the wicked must be destroyed and the remnant must be purged as gold and silver are refined (Zech. 13:9). The pillar of cloud during the day and the pillar of fire during the night were for Israel in the desert the sign of God's presence, care, guidance and protection. It is highly improbable that Israel in the future will see these manifestations again as in the past. It is far more probable that here the fulfillment of those signs is described — Christ Himself will then be present as the glorious King of Israel. Verse six refers to the tabernacle which was a spiritual comfort to Israel in the desert. Perhaps the word *tabernacle* refers to the new temple of the Kingdom of Peace, which shall be called a *house of prayer unto all nations* (Isa. 56:7; Mk. 11:17). At any rate, this word refers to the glorious protection and consolation which will be afforded Israel under the blessed reign of Christ.

ISAIAH 5

The Song of the Vineyard

1. Now will I sing to my wellbeloved a song of my beloved touching his vineyard. My wellbeloved hath a vineyard in a very fruitful hill:

2. And he fenced it, and gathered out the stones thereof, and planted it with the choicest vine and built a tower in the midst of it, and also made a winepress therein: and he looked that it should bring forth grapes, and it brought forth wild grapes.

The *Song of the Vineyard* is a parable that was possibly recited with the accompaniment of song and music as a sort of folk song in the hearing of the people. The prophets used several means to draw the attention of the people in order to make the message of the Lord more impressive and unforgettable. It is, however, not merely a folk tune or love song, such as the troubadours in the Middle Ages sang to the people. Here we are dealing with a divine and deeply tragic song. We must take the word *Wellbeloved* to mean the Father and *Beloved* to refer to Christ. It can be considered a rule that we meet the Christ in nearly every chapter of Isaiah, and the name *Beloved* is also given Him in the Song of Solomon. Is not this name entirely fitting for the Son of God's love (Matt. 3:17; Col. 1:13)?

The meaning of the vineyard is unmistakably given in verse seven: all of Israel and Judah. It is said of this vineyard:

(1) It is planted on a *fruitful hill* or, literally, a *horn of fatness.* This refers to Canaan, the land flowing with milk and honey. The frequent droughts and famines and floods were not due to the rich land but to Israel's sin.

(2) The Lord *fenced* this vineyard. This refers to the wall of partition by His law, by which Israel was separated from all surrounding nations.

(3) God *gathered out the stones* in this vineyard. This took place by the removal of the heathen, who were like hard stones and would have impaired the growth of the Lord's people, as the few remaining ones so often did.

(4) God planted this vineyard with *choicest vines.* He did not plant Canaan with a heathen nation but with a covenant nation that knew Him (cf. Jer. 2:21).

(5) God built a *tower* in His vineyard. In the mountain vineyards there were watchtowers to protect the vineyards from thieves and wild animals. This refers to Israel's prophets, priests and kings.

(6) He built a *winepress* in it, i.e., a big hollow stone that was cemented in the ground, in which the grapes were trodden and the juices gathered. This beautiful parable is worked out in the finest detail. It is appropriate to identify the winepress with the temple.

After having bestowed so much care on His vineyard, the Owner could expect much fruit. No more improvement could be made and no more care given than had already been done. The Husbandman had done everything He could. Verse six shows that He also kept His vineyard clean and that He pruned it. Hence, the complaint about that vineyard is justified. After having *looked* long, year in and year out, for grapes, finally there appeared grapes, but they were bad. Hence, the vineyard was not completely unfruitful, but the fruit was bad fruit. It has been thought that the text refers to the wolfsbane, a poisonous weed which grows very fast, sucking up the fruitful moisture from the ground, blocking the sunlight with its shadow and so choking out the good vegetation. We are dealing here with something worse than unfruitfulness. The New Testament also speaks of a faith that brings forth fruit, but the fruit is *dead works,* which pollute the air like a cadaver. The wolfsbane, or wild vine (II Kings 4:39), does bear beautiful berries, but they are bitter, foul-smelling and poisonous in nature. This is a precise description of the self-willed and false religion of the unfaithful covenant people. How pitiful is the Lord's complaint after all His care! Heaven and earth may well be astounded and amazed, as in Isa. 1:2 over the unsuccessful upbringing of the Lord's people. It is deeply sad when

God-fearing parents must complain about their bad children, but how much sadder it is when the Almighty speaks so pathetically about His disappointing vineyard! It is evident that in this complaint of the Lord about His unfaithful people there lies a great and inexplicable mystery. Is it not the Lord Himself who must give the increase together with the planting and weeding? We shall not find fault with the doings of the Almighty, for His works are great and majestic. The text casts all the blame exclusively on Israel.-

The Judges of the Vineyard

> 3. And now, O inhabitants of Jerusalem, and men of Judah, judge, I pray you, betwixt me and my vineyard.
> 4. What could have been done more to my vineyard, that I have not done in it? wherefore, when I looked that it should bring forth grapes, brought it forth wild grapes?

The Owner of the vineyard is speaking. He summons the people of Judah and Jerusalem to pronounce judgment themselves on the vineyard, its Lord, its nature and its destiny. The fact that the guilty must pass judgment and be condemned by their own mouth and conscience is a psychological principle that is found again and again in Scripture. Undoubtedly the same will be true of all the lost. They, too, will agree that their sentence is just and justified. The Lord Himself appears before these judges to repeat His complaint. It is graphically depicted here that all the care of the Lord was intended to call forth *fruit* in their lives.

The Destruction of the Vineyard

> 5. And now go to; I will tell you what I will do to my vineyard: I will take away the hedge thereof, and it shall be eaten up; and break down the wall thereof, and it shall be trodden down:
> 6. And I will lay it waste: it shall not be pruned, nor digged; but there shall come up briers and thorns: I will also command the clouds that they rain no rain upon it.
> 7. For the vineyard of the LORD of hosts is the house of Israel, and the men of Judah his pleasant plant: and he looked for

judgment, but behold oppression; for righteousness, but behold a cry.

Evidently the judges kept silent after the sharp appeal to their conscience by the Vinedresser. If they chose silence, then He will speak and remove the *hedge,* i.e., the wall, the fence of the vineyard.

Actually, this is a prediction of the breaking down when Christ died on the cross. Then the *law* was not abolished, for according to the Word of the Lord it is eternal, but the *administration* of the law was abolished since it was a wall of partition and a schoolmaster to lead to Christ. After the breaking down of that fence, Israel was dispersed among all the nations and the animals of the world have devoured its vineyard. This devouring is still going on today, but as soon as the times of the Gentiles will have sped past, this will come to an end. The exact fulfillment of verse six up to this very day is striking, for Jerusalem and Canaan have been totally destroyed. For many ages they were not cultivated, pruned or weeded; thorns and thistles grew in abundance, but there were no crops to keep even a handful of people alive. All of this was the result of the Lord's destruction of and His curse upon this vineyard. He, who sits enthroned above, rules the clouds making them His chariots and the footstool of His feet and commanding them to withhold their rain.

Verse seven gives us the unmistakable explanation of the vineyard, its turning away and its actual sin. The last clause contains a remarkable play on words which is hard to convey. The Lord looked for *mishpat,* judgment, justice, but instead found *mispach,* scabs, leprosy, which refer to the most repulsive immorality. He waited for *tsedakah,* justice, but instead His ear caught everywhere *tseakah,* the cry of the wretched who were oppressed by the judges whose calling it was to maintain and carry out justice and righteousness. The Jewish translator Isaac Leeser, to some extent, retains the play on words when he translates: *"justice,* but behold *injustice; equity,* but behold *iniquity."* De Wette has: *"Gutthat... Blutbad."*. and others: *"Beglückung ... Bedrückung";* while Ridderbos, following others, has the most beautiful translation: *"goed regiment ... bloed-regiment;*

rechtsbetrachting . . . rechtsverkrachting." In any case, the Vinedresser's disappointment is expressed in an ironic way.

Finally, the observation should be made that the Saviour in His teaching and parables frequently alluded to this beautiful parable (cf. Matt. 20:1-15; 21:28; Mark 12:1; Luke 20:9-18). This parable, presented in the form of a stirring song of gripping earnestness, contains a treasure of historic, dogmatic, psychologic and literary ideas. Hence, it is no wonder that throughout the ages entire books have been written on this song of the vineyard.

The First Woe: Unto the Greedy Rich

8. Woe unto them that join house to house, that lay field to field, till there be no place, that they may be placed alone in the midst of the earth!

9. In mine ears said the LORD of hosts, Of a truth many houses shall be desolate, even great and fair, without inhabitant.

10. Yea, ten acres of vineyard shall yield one bath, and the seed of an homer shall yield an ephah.

The prophets repeatedly cast their lightning condemnations against the insatiable greed of the rich oppressors who succeeded in acquiring the little houses and fields of the poor until in the end there was no place left for the poor. It looked as though these rich people were the only inhabitants of the country. Even if the rich bought these possessions honestly, which was not always the case, then this was still against the will of the Lord. In His law He had commanded that the land should be equally divided and remain so (Num. 33:54); houses could be taken from the owners only until the Year of Jubilee (Lev. 25). The economic laws were based on the principle that it was not Israel but Jehovah who was the ultimate Owner of all possessions. Thus, beside the sins of greed and pride, there was also the sin of disobedience and violation of the law, causing the anger of the Lord to cease not.

The Lord again presents Himself through the mouth of the prophet as the Lord of hosts; and this does not spell anything good for the people. For this is His battle name, indicating that He will march against those who hate Him with great armies. His warriors are so powerful that every single one of them can fell an army of 185,000 in one moment. The Lord will turn their houses into ruins and leave their palaces uninhabited because of the depopulation of the country while their acquired lands will yield practically no harvest. Calvin interprets the meaning of the latter very well, when he says, "It will hardly be possible to press one vat of wine from a huge vineyard and instead of a tenfold yield of the seed sown, exactly the opposite will take place: the harvest will hardly yield one-tenth of the seed sown." Stolen goods do not prosper. Avarice is the root of all evil!

The Second Woe: Against Revelry and Drunkenness

11. Woe unto them that rise up early in the morning, that they may follow strong drink; that continue until night, till wine inflame them!

12. And the harp, and the viol, the tabret, and pipe, and wine, are in their feasts: but they regard not the work of the LORD, neither consider the operations of his hands.

13. Therefore my people are gone into captivity, because they have no knowledge: and their honourable men are famished, and their multitude dried up with thirst.

14. Therefore hell hath enlarged herself, and opened her mouth without measure: and their glory, and their multitude, and their pomp, and he that rejoiceth, shall descend into it.

15. And the mean man shall be brought down, and the mighty man shall be humbled, and the eyes of the lofty shall be hunbled:

16. But the LORD of hosts shall be exalted in judgment, and God that is holy shall be sanctified in righteousness.

17. Then shall the lambs feed after their manner, and the waste places of the fat ones shall strangers eat.

It is a divine ordinance that man shall eat bread in the sweat of his brow and go out to work from sunrise to sunset (Ps. 104:23). When he does this, then he may also drink a glass of wine in moderation (Ps. 104:15), but both ordinances of God were violated by Judah and Jerusalem. They did not get up to work in the morning but to consume wine and strong drink. This was something unheard of (cf. Acts 2:15). Hand in hand with this indulgence went the greatest luxury. And luxury led to refined wantonness and sensuality. These people loved culture like the people of the northern kingdom in Amos's day (Amos 6:6, 7), and like the apostate of today are carried away with an oft-times Christ-hating culture. Harps, viols, tabrets and pipes are good, not evil, but they are generally used in the service of sin. If even Jerusalem, the city of God, did so, what then can be expected of the children of the world?

In and of itself it was not wrong to make use of music at festive occasions, but sin entered when they were wholly taken up with those things so that they forgot *the work of the Lord*. It dulled their senses and blinded them to the great works of God and the needs of His people and inheritance. They did not see the signs of their times. Is that not also the case today?

Punishment simply had to follow. Verses thirteen thru seventeen speak of this. It will consist in four judgments. First, there will be a carrying away into captivity because His people have *no knowledge* (cf. Hos. 9:17). The initial fulfillment of this threat occurred about a century later when Judah was carried away into captivity. The full materialization came with the destruction of Jerusalem in A.D. 70.

Secondly, the swilling rich, described before as wallowing in immorality, will suffer hunger and thirst. What is meant here is hungering after natural food, as this was experienced at both destructions of Jerusalem. But we need not exclude here a thirst after the Word (cf. Amos 8:11). The grave (hell, Heb. *sheol)*, will open wide its mouth like a hungry monster to receive its victims. The word *sheol* here does not only mean grave, but also the realm of the dead, which for the wicked includes the aspect of hell. Job. 10:21, 22 gives us a poetic image of *sheol*. This place is frequently portrayed as a devouring monster, which cracks its jaws wide open to devour its prey. Even the name *sheol* is derived from the verb *to ask*, which indicates that this monster is never satisfied but constantly demands more victims. Here it is particularly gluttonous for the luxury just portrayed. Just as Korah and his people were once swallowed up alive, so the nether world will open up to devour Jerusalem and all its luxury and culture — a terrifying prospect indeed! And history tells us that this was not merely a poetic picture. When this takes place, no one will escape, but all will be humbled (v. 15), the common man as well as the wanton rich man.

In a beautiful contrast to the shameful humiliation of the proud, the exaltation of the Lord is now presented (v. 16a). By means of justice, *i.e.,* the judgment by which justice is maintained, the Lord in His majesty will be acknowledged. On the basis of 26:9 we know that the people remaining from the judgment of the nations will seek and glorify the Lord. *And God that is holy* (v. 16b) obviously refers to Christ.

Finally, the complete destruction is dramatically depicted when it is said that the lambs will feed in the destroyed areas and that strangers — by whom are meant the uncivilized tribes of herdsmen, the Bedouin — will feed the depopulated land of the fattened and wanton nations, a representation found frequently in Isaiah. To portray depopulated and completely destroyed areas the prophet uses few words. In his own original way he lets cattle roam in them, or he depicts these regions as dangerous with wild animals so that they cannot be visited or traveled except with bow and arrow. Whoever wishes to study nature poetry, let him study Isaiah. He surpasses all others.

The Third Woe: Unto the Brazen Scoffers

18. Woe unto them that draw iniquity with cords of vanity, and sin as it were with a cart rope:

19. That say, Let him make speed, and hasten his work, that we may see it: and let the counsel of the Holy One of Israel draw nigh and come, that we may know it!

Just as a beast of burden plods on in its harness, so the debauched scoffers plod on as slaves of sin. The load of sin, which they pull, will one day descend as a crushing load on their guilty heads. This section points to hardened sinners, who have their consciences seared. Not until man has sunk so low as these people does he dare to mock and scoff at the word of the Lord. These are the kind of Old Testament scoffers mentioned in II Peter 3:4. Since God's judgments did not come immediately but tarried on account of God's longsuffering, they thought they would not come at all. Thus, the sinner is adept at misusing God's patience. In irritated impatience, they scoffingly cry out for God to make haste to carry out His threatenings so that they themselves may see it. Since the name *Holy One of Israel* is a regular Messianic term with Isaiah, the second part of verse nineteen tells us that they scoffed not only at the threatened judgments but at Israel's Messianic expectation as well.

The Fourth Woe: Against the Falsifiers of Concepts

> 20. Woe unto them that call evil good, and good evil; that put darkness for light, and light for darkness; that put bitter for sweet, and sweet for bitter!

The concepts evil and good, etc., are basic moral concepts, which depraved human ingenuity can never change. *Evil* is everything that is at variance with God's will, and *good* is everything that is according to His holy will. These two basic moral concepts, on which all Christian morality is founded, are as opposed to each other in the moral world order as light and darkness are in the natural world, and as bitter and sweet in the realm of taste. Whoever in the latter realm calls bitter sweet and sweet bitter is devoid of all taste, or worse, has a perverse taste. Whoever calls light darkness and darkness light is worse than blind. This now was the condition of the morally corrupt people of Isaiah's day. They were the Nietzschians of that day with their *Unwertung aller Werten,* their devaluation of all values, the overturning of all values and basic concepts. As Mrs. Roland Holst, a socialist, expressed it once they had reshuffled morality. When such a morality has become general, a land and a nation are close to ruin!

The Fifth Woe: Against the Conceited

> 21. Woe unto them that are wise in their own eyes, and prudent in their own sight!

Now, those who are wise in their own eyes have to hear

the thunder of God's judgments. The prophet does not dwell long on these people, because they are not really a class by themselves but undoubtedly belong to the same class of people who are addressed in the fourth woe. Imagined wisdom is always a despicable characteristic in man. He who is afflicted with it is incapable of learning any more, is satisfied with himself and is disdainful of others. Paul fulminates against it when he says to the conceited, "If any man among you seemeth to be wise in the world, let him become a fool, that he may be wise." Whoever is wise in his own eyes does not have the wisdom that is from above but that which is earthly and satanic. All the treasures of wisdom are hid in Christ Jesus, the ultimate Wisdom.

The Sixth Woe: Against the Cowardly Leaders

22. Woe unto them that are mighty to drink wine, and men of strength to mingle strong drink:
23. Which justify the wicked for reward, and take away the righteousness of the righteous from him!
24. Therefore as the fire devoureth the stubble, and the flame consumeth the chaff, so their root shall be as rottenness, and their blossom shall go up as dust: because they have cast away the law of the LORD of hosts, and despised the word of the Holy One of Israel.
25. Therefore is the anger of the LORD kindled against his people, and he hath stretched forth his hand against them, and hath smitten them: and the hills did tremble, and their carcases were torn in the midst of the streets. For all this his anger is not turned away, but his hand is stretched out still.

This woe does not announce the punishment of two classes of people, but of the one class of cowardly leaders, so that this ominous and somber group of woes forms a climax. It is not the prophet's intent to once again point out the sin of revelry as in verse eleven, but he is railing with holy ridicule against the mighty men. These judges are indeed "heroes," but only with regard to drinking wine; they are brave men, men of valor, but only in the mingling of strong drinks. It was a custom to mix herbs and spices in wine to make it hotter and stronger; these foolish leaders excelled in this noble art. And these same cowardly leaders did not dare to convict the affluent, but let themselves be bribed with gifts to declare the guilty absolved and convict the innocent. Hence, with their very way of life they illustrated the truth of Solomon's proverb that a bribe destroys the heart. The condition of a nation is very sad indeed, when its leaders do not have the moral courage to fight for justice and righteousness without respect of persons. Thus equity falls not only in the street but also in the courtrooms and councils of the land and even on the lecterns and pulpits. And this, alas, is exactly the condition of our nation today!

All those reprehensible sinners are called rejecters of the law of the Lord and despisers of the Word of God. The forms of their unrighteousness might vary widely; but in rejecting the Word of God they were the same. For that reason the fire of judgment will descend on them like a prairie fire that consumes dead grass, and they will burn like chaff. The wicked who perish in this judgment are always presented as totally worthless, whether as straw or stubble, hay or chaff, dross or dregs. This affords us the comforting thought that, viewed from God's side, nothing of real value is lost. In the second part of verse twenty-four the imaginative prophet compares the wicked with a tree whose root is rotting, and whose *blossom* is torn off by the wind and flies away like dust.

The anger of the Lord is kindled against His people on account of their brazen rejection of His Word. He lifts His hand threateningly to strike, indeed, with heavy blows it has already come down, so that the mountains trembled on account of it. We must not merely think of the earthquake in the days of Uzziah, for we are dealing with prophetic style; the prophet points to what will take place in the great day of judgment of the nations. His hand will be stretched out as never before; all the mountains will shake before the face of the God of Israel, and the whole world will be full of dead bodies, as verse twenty-five predicts. It is wrong to understand this prophecy or any of the prophets by thinking that the prophets only looked at their own day and what would follow immediately. Nearly all their utterances have a certain historical background, but at the same time they looked across the rolling ages to the great judgment of the nations of which all the local judgments in their day were aspects and symbols. Half of the book of Isaiah has yet to be fulfilled.

The Advance of the Army of the Enemy

26. And he will lift up an ensign to the nations from far, and will hiss unto them from the end of the earth: and, behold, they shall come with speed swiftly:

27. None shall be weary nor stumble among them; none shall slumber nor sleep; neither shall the girdle of the loins be loosed, nor the latchet of their shoes be broken:

28. Whose arrows are sharp, and all their bows bent, their horses' hoofs shall be counted like flint, and their wheels like a whirlwind:

29. Their roaring shall be like a lion, they shall roar like young lions: yea, they shall roar, and lay hold of the prey, and shall carry it away safe, and none shall deliver it.

30. And in that day they shall roar against them like the roaring of the sea: and if one look unto the land, behold darkness and sorrow, and the light is darkened in the heavens thereof.

Two subjects are described here: the king and the terror of his enormous advancing army. There is no doubt that the prophet sees the army of the Assyrians, then that of the Babylonians, and even that of the Romans in A.D. 70. But the final fulfillment of these words does not dawn until the advance of the terrible armies of Gog and Magog at the time of Israel's initial restoration after the Rapture of the Church. The Lord of hosts Himself is presented as the great Commander who plants His ensign on the top of a high mountain, according to the military tactics in the ancient world, in order to summon His dispersed warriors to come together. In the same verse the prophet seizes another simile, that of a beekeeper or landowner who whistles softly to call his bees together. In 7:18 the soldiers of Assyria are also compared to swarms of bees. There too, Jehovah is symbolically portrayed as a beekeeper who whistles to his alert bees.

The hostile armies are described as being magnificent and mighty and advancing swiftly. No one among them is weary or stumbling. Every single soldier is an unconquerable hero whom nothing can stop. They need no sleep for they can march not only during the day but even during the night. If they rest occasionally, they do not undress but simply throw themselves down to the ground without loosening their girdles or latchets. It is obvious that the prophet's purpose is to call attention to the contrast between them and the drinking heroes in verse twenty-two. The weak and enervated people shall have to flee before the vigorous and heroic peoples from the ends of the earth.

Verse twenty-eight describes their equipment. Their arrows are sharp and deadly. Their bows are drawn taut as they march toward the enemy on the battlefield. Their cavalry ride horses whose hoofs are hard as rocks. Some ride in chariots whose wheels are like a whirlwind. The earth roars when they approach from the distance. Their wild battle cries sound like a roaring lion. They are as bloodthirsty as young lions who leap at their prey. There will be no one to snatch their prey from their claws. They roar like the angry waves of the sea. When that terrible day shall dawn when Gog and Magog's hordes shall be on the march, there will be darkness and consternation in the whole world.

The second part of verse thirty points to a black night of thunderstorms, when it will be totally dark, while the violent fire of lightning, which otherwise might provide some light, is even extinguished by the black storm clouds. This agrees with Zephaniah's description of the day of the Lord: "That day is a day of wrath, a day of trouble and distress, a day of wasteness and desolation, a day of darkness and gloominess, a day of clouds and thick darkness" (Zeph. 1:15).

ISAIAH 6

The Vision of Isaiah's Calling

1. In the year that king Uzziah died I saw also the Lord sitting upon a throne, high and lifted up, and his train filled the temple.

2. Above it stood the seraphims: each one had six wings; with twain he covered his face, and with twain he covered his feet, and with twain he did fly.

3. And one cried unto another, and said, Holy, holy, holy, is the LORD of hosts: the whole earth is full of his glory.

4. And the posts of the door moved at the voice of him that cried, and the house was filled with smoke.

5. Then said I, Woe is me! for I am undone; because I am a man of unclean lips, and I dwell in the midst of a people of unclean lips: for mine eyes have seen the King, the Lord of hosts.

6. Then flew one of the seraphims unto me, having a live coal in his hand, which he had taken with the tongs from off the altar:

7. And he laid it upon my mouth, and said, Lo, this hath touched thy lips; and thine iniquity is taken away, and thy sin purged.

In this vision the youthful Isaiah received a fivefold view of the transitoriness of all earthly glory. The first verse does not merely contain a time reference but also the reason for this vision. After Solomon, Uzziah had been the most powerful king of Judah. Many tribes had subjected themselves to him; he had a large standing army, built many fortifications and obtained great prosperity through peaceful activities. He had been king longer than any other, with the exception of Mannaseh although the latter had been imprisoned in Babylon for some time. However, the eminent King Uzziah died ignominiously as a leper. Having become intoxicated by his unheard of prosperity, he had desired the office of priest for himself. This was such a great evil that the priests collectively cast their sovereign king, struck by leprosy, out of the temple. Now this erstwhile honored and very powerful king had gone the way of all flesh as proof of the truth that all flesh is like grass and all glory of man (culture) is like a flower of the field.

Was it not entirely logical that, besides the deep impression of the uncertainness of worldly grandeur, all manner of questions vexed the heart of the youthful prophet as he entered the house of the Lord? As in the temple where long ago the light dawned in the heart of Asaph in his deep turmoil of spirit, the light also dawned in the darkness of the prophet's heart. In contrast to the empty throne of Judah, God showed him the King on His throne. In contrast to the leprous and decayed flesh of the erstwhile powerful Uzziah, He showed him the real King of Jerusalem whose throne is established and who fills the whole earth with His glory. Compared to the king who attempted to be a priestly king, but was not allowed to be such, the Lord showed him the only Priestly King, who not only had a high and elevated throne, but also an altar that could remove guilt and forgive sin. Hence, it seems that the first clause of this vision is not merely a pinpointing of time but definitely indicates a psychological reason for this vision.

After his initial look at vanished human glory, he next saw the true and glorious King. Isaiah received this vision in the temple at Jerusalem. We are not told in what manner this grand vista came to him, so we need not guess at it either. To assume that it took place in a sort of trance or dream is not only not stated but is highly questionable. Every aspect of it was intended to make an indelible impression on the young man. The throne is said to be *high* and *lifted up* meaning highly elevated or exalted. It was not vacant as was Uzziah's for the Lord was sitting on it in quiet majesty. Fortunately, we need not guess who is meant here, since the Lord Jesus Himself told us so in John 12:41. The prophet beheld no one else but Christ Himself, not the Christ in His humiliation but in His glory which He one day will manifest in the sight of all nations in the day of His return. At His first coming, there was neither beauty nor comeliness in Him but here the whole earth is full of His glory. In His humiliation, He was not sitting on a throne but was hung on a cross. Even after His ascension, He did not sit down on His own throne but on His Father's throne. Hence, there is no doubt that Isaiah saw Him in His future glory, when as Priest and King He will sit on His own mediatorial throne to fill the earth with His glory. Today, the nations still labor unto destruction and fire; men weary themselves in vain. Someday the earth will be filled with the knowledge of the glory of the Lord as the waters cover the sea (Hab. 2:14). Not only His throne and position were magnificent and majestic but the same can be said of His royal attire. The train of it alone filled the temple. Isaiah did not see the whole glistening robe of light of this great king but only parts of it like Moses.

Glorious *names* are attributed here to the Lord of glory. In verse one He is called *Adonai,* the plural of *Adon* — lord, master, usually the master of the house who legally possesses all power and authority over his family, his wife, children and slaves. In Genesis twenty-four Abraham is called *Adon.* In I Kings 1:16-18 Bathsheba calls David her *Adon* twice. Here however, He who is more than David is called *Adonai* in the plural on account of the greatness of His glory and the abundance of His dominion. In verse three He is exalted as *Jehovah Sabaoth,* the Lord of hosts. Isaiah himself also calls Him by that name (v. 5). Generally speaking, this is God's battle name denoting Him as warring against His enemies or for His friends. The usage of this name in Scripture is very instructive. It does not appear in the books of Moses, Joshua, Judges, Job, Proverbs and Ecclesiastes. In the books of Samuel, Kings, Chronicles and the Psalms it occurs very infrequently. The prophets, however, used this name very often: Jeremiah, almost eighty times, Haggai, in his two chapters, fourteen times, Zechariah, fifty times; in the short prophecy of Malachi it appears no less than twenty-five times. Hannah, the mother of Samuel, was the first to use this battle name of God in her triumphant battle song. From the way it was used it is clear that it was not used in the beginning of Israel's history, but mainly toward the end. By then Israel had kindled the anger of the Lord with her apostasy and deserved that the Lord, as a Warrior with His army of angels came to do battle against her. So it can be proven here that the Lord of hosts was none other than

Christ Himself. Finally, He is called by the name Jehovah in verse twelve His rich covenant name.

Seeing that the exalted King bears three names, it is more than fitting that He is lauded by a triple *holy, holy, holy.* This chapter contains a threefold proof for the Holy Trinity. Three different names of God, a triple use of the word holy and, in verse eight, the single "Whom shall *I* send" is used with the plural "who will go for *us."*

A third view in this vision is that of the retinue, the brilliant train of the king's faithful servants. Are cherubim the same beings as seraphims? Obviously not, for the *names* are different. Cherubs means the *seizers* and seraphims the *burners,* those who burn away sin. The *position* of both groups also indicates a difference. According to verse two the seraphim stood *above* the throne, while the cherubim, according to Ezekiel 1:5 are the *bearers* of God's throne. Their *activities* are also different; the cherubim always carry out justice and judgment (Gen. 3; Ps. 18; Ezek. 10) while the seraphim sing praises to the holiness and glory of God. They also remove sin by the fire of the altar and engage in works of peace. In Revelation four these beings are united together. Through the cross of Christ righteousness and peace kiss each other (Ps. 85:10).

Each of the seraphim had six wings, three pairs. With the first pair, they covered their faces. These were the wings of reverence, manifesting the deepest reverence for the glorious King. By this act, the seraphim testified that they were not worthy to behold the King in His glory. The second pair of wings expressed their deep humility. By covering their feet with them, they testified that they were not worthy to be seen by the King nor to serve Him. The third pair of wings were used for flying. They were the wings of obedience and readiness to serve. At the command of their King, they flew, and with lightning speed, carried out His holy will. All this was shown to the youthful prophet so that in his prophetic service he would always follow the exemplary readiness of those glorious servants of the King. It is striking therefore that with Isaiah, we always find these three traits: a deep reverence for the most holy being of God, a deep humility and an unlimited obedience. His constant pointing to the

Holy One of Israel is nothing else but an echo of the triple *gadosh, gadosh, gadosh* of the flaming seraphim; his glorious prophecies of salvation are but variations on the song of glory by the seraphim that *the whole earth is full of his glory.* This was sung with such tremendous power and force by these celestial beings that the door posts shook.

At the same time, this is an example for us to speak with a powerful voice and sing with jubilation about the glory of the Lord. But alas, the lips of many of us are dumb with regard to the coming glory of the Lord. Every child of God should cause the house of the Lord to resound, since the celestial ones are in ecstasy about it. While the thresholds and posts shook from the sound of the singing, the house was filled with smoke. This smoke was not that of incense, nor merely a sign of praising of the Lord, but as in Revelation 15:8 and Psalm 18:8, it was a sign of His majesty and anger with His enemies. In the day of His coming, fire and pillars of smoke will go before His countenance and devour His enemies. Understood this way, we can much better understand how Isaiah cried out, "Woe is me! for I am undone." He did not say this because he was stupefied by the incense, but because he received a glimpse of the consuming holiness and majesty of the Lord.

This constitutes the fourth view of Isaiah — a view of himself. He had just pronounced six woes unto others; here he pronounces the seventh unto himself. He does so in the presence of the Lord, the only place where man can do it and must do it. It is an old question whether these verses refer to Isaiah's conversion. There is no basis for this idea. What is described here is an important turning point in his life. His spiritual life is deepened, his insight broadened; he received impressions that stayed with him all his life. This passage is similar to that of the miraculous catch of fish when Peter in deep emotion cried out, "Lord, depart from me, for I am a sinful man!" Yet Peter had become a follower of the Savior, prior to this occasion. That is why Isaiah does not say, "Woe is me! because I am a man of unclean *heart,"* but of unclean *lips.* The contrast is not between an insignificant man and a great ruler, but between an unholy man and an immaculately holy King. The fact that Isaiah pronounces a woe unto himself and utters a self-accusation concerning the uncleanness of his lips after having pronounced six woes unto others, leads one to think that his omniscient Sender gave him a preventative means against all self-exaltation above his contemporaries. For is not the Lord an expert in supplying such preventative means? Consider the painful thorn of Paul. Isaiah lived in the midst of a people of unclean lips whom he would have to admonish continuously. How necessary it was for him always to remember that he in both his private life and in his public ministry was a man of unclean lips; a man far removed from all unrighteousness and self-righteousness who, before pronouncing a woe unto others, had first pronounced a condemning woe unto himself. Whoever judges himself will no longer be judged.

Although this is not explicitly said, it nevertheless appears from the last part of verse seven that God had found some particular sin in Isaiah's life which needed blotting out. Adding to this the complaint about unclean lips, it is evident that in Isaiah's prior prophecies there had been some uncleanness of lips. It is not necessary to ask of what kind, for this question is futile as it is not revealed. It is entirely possible that he pronounced the sixfold woe with some hatred in his heart or with some self-righteousness. His message was divine and perfect, and remained the same in spite of the situation in his own heart. It is possible that a divine message is sometimes given in a less than holy frame of mind. Whatever the case may have been, it was quite fitting that a young man such as Isaiah, when pronouncing all those woes unto others, should pronounce one unto himself as well. For in the presence of the Lord, we are all unclean and even the fiery seraphim are not clean before Him or worthy to behold Him. How fortunate, however, that Christ as the Priestly King has not only an exalted *throne,* but also an *altar,* where sins can be burned away, as happened with this seer.

Isaiah's Calling

8. Also I heard the voice of the Lord, saying, Whom shall I send, and who will go for us? Then said I, Here am I; send me.

After the remarkable four views in the one vision of his calling, the prophet receives a fifth view concerning his call. The resounding song to God's holiness and glory had hardly died out when he heard the voice of Him who sits upon His throne, *Adonai*. Just as Abraham, as the lord of his household, once sent his servant to bring a bride for his son, so the Lord Jesus sends out His servants. For that reason He asks, not as someone who is perplexed but as the mighty Sender, "Whom shall *I* send?"

Will the prophet with his sense of self-abhorrence and his fear of perishing dare to offer himself as servant of the mighty *Adonai* and triune God? Will his fear or sense of unworthiness prevent him from doing so? Indeed, no; he voluntarily offers himself with the right attitude of heart. If there be one frame of mind and heart in His servants that is pleasing to the Lord, it is that they condemn themselves before God's countenance. When Gideon thinks he has no strength, then he can go forward in the strength and power of God. Only when we are weak, we are mighty; only when we are an empty vessel can the full flood of His grace and of His Spirit flow through us. Only when we are nothing, can He be all and in all. Oh, that all servants of the Lord might understand this!

Isaiah's Mandate

9. And he said, Go, and tell this people, Hear ye indeed, but understand not; and see ye indeed, but perceive not.

10. Make the heart of this people fat, and make their ears heavy, and shut their eyes; lest they see with their eyes, and hear with their ears, and understand with their heart, and convert, and be healed.

The Lord accepted the self-condemning young man, and said, *Go.* But before He let him go, He gave him a carefully circumscribed mandate. This mandate was, in a word, terrible. First of all, it was this way because the Lord does not say, Go to *My* people, but to *this* people. Already, the Lord considers His people as *Lo-Ammi — Not-My-People.* Secondly, Isaiah must show the apostate people its total blindness, deafness and hardness, which was the reason she would not convert and God would not heal her. From the wording it appears that Isaiah himself had to make the heart of the people *fat, i.e.,* hard and senseless. Physically, a fat heart is very dangerous and can result in death at any moment; spiritually, it is infinitely more dangerous. Isaiah indeed made the heart of the people fat, not purposely but accidentally, since all his preaching had only the result that the people ridiculed, rejected, and hardened themselves against his message. Because of the people's unbelief, his prophecy did not become a savor of life unto life, but of death unto death. The triune God — recall the little word *us* in the second question of verse eight — nevertheless told him this at the outset of his calling sparing him from disappointment. When people call others to a certain task or office, they usually try to charm the senses with all kinds of rosy pictures, but not so the Lord. In John 12:39-40, Christ quotes this word and in Acts 28:25 the Holy Spirit does; this is proof that the Lord who is speaking here, along with Christ and the Holy Spirit, are fully one in Being.

An Important Question by Isaiah Answered

11. Then said I, Lord, how long? And he answered, Until the cities be wasted without inhabitant, and the houses without man, and the land be utterly desolate,

12. And the LORD have removed men far away, and there be a great forsaking in the midst of the land.

13. But yet in it shall be a tenth, and it shall return, and shall be eaten: as a teil tree, and as an oak, whose substance is in them, when they cast their leaves: so the holy seed shall be the substance thereof.

When the prophet hears the heavy task that awaits him, he suddenly cries, "Lord, how long?" As a rule this question is not understood correctly. From the answer it is clear that it was not Isaiah's intent, at least not in the first place, to hear how long the hardening of Israel would last, but to know how long he himself would have to be the proponent of this terrible judgment. His Sender answers him and it must not escape our attention that as yet He does not introduce him to the whole mystery of Israel's hardening. This mystery is revealed to the Church, which for that reason should not be ignorant of it (Rom. 11:25). The hardening of Israel is *partial* and *temporal.* God during the time of Israel's hardening will nevertheless have a people unto His name on earth and one day will save all Israel (Rom. 11:25). In the year 722 B.C., Isaiah experienced the destruction of Samaria and the carrying away of the northern tribes. Verse eleven obviously refers to this, but we must not exclude the calamities of war inflicted upon Judah by Syria, Israel, Edom and Moab in the days of Ahaz. Hence, the prophet was going to see horrible scenes and experience terrible calamities in his days. For at least a half-century, he would have to speak to a very stiffnecked people. When at last the prophet went the way of all flesh, there certainly must have been no more left than a tenth of the population. It cannot be said of the remnant after the second destruction of Jerusalem that a tenth of the inhabitants was left in the holy land. But this tenth part will also be carried away once more, for this is the meaning of the words *it shall return.* Even that tenth part will not remain in the land but be destroyed, just as when a terebinth (or an oak tree) is hewn down. How terrible all this must have sounded to the young prophet! It appeared that nothing would be left of his people, of the Lord's covenant people. It looked as though the destruction had been unalterably decided upon and that nothing would remain of the Lord's land, people, city and temple, indeed of the promised Messiah.

When the thunderclouds of judgment are at their blackest, God lets the sun of His gracious promises penetrate the clouds. This is what the Lord is doing here as well. He does not forsake the works of His own hands! His unconditional and faithful covenant never fails, no matter how dark everything may appear. He promises to the comfort of the youthful prophet, that there will be a remnant after all the terrible judgments. The image of a cut-down oak clarifies this beautifully. For this kind of tree has, as it were, an indestructible life. They may be cut down, but they always propagate themselves. The Lord promises to leave some *substance,* i.e., a piece of the trunk, a stump. In the same manner there will be left a *holy seed* after all the judgments that shall descend upon this hardened people. Here again is the rich and comforting idea of the remnant, by which He perpetuates His covenant.

We have to settle one more question before leaving the subject of Isaiah's calling, contained in this chapter. Why has this chapter been placed here, and not at the beginning! The question is very old indeed and always returns again and again. It seems that not only the year of the death of Uzziah was psychologically the most suitable time to receive such a vision, but also that the prophet could hardly have preached about the hardening of Israel before it actually manifested itself. Only when the people rejected more of his preaching, was it useful to let them know that God had revealed the fruitlessness of his preaching long before. At the same time of his calling, Isaiah makes known his mandate to preach the woes of judgment.

ISAIAH 7

The Allied Armies Advance Against Jerusalem

> 1. And it came to pass in the days of Ahaz the son of Jotham, the son of Uzziah, king of Judah, that Rezin the king of Syria, and Pekah the son of Remaliah, king of Israel, went up toward Jerusalem to war against it, but could not prevail against it.

In order to understand the history contained in this chapter, it is necessary to consider II Kings 16 and II Chronicles 28 carefully. There something is discovered concerning Ahaz's reign and wickednesses. He was a cowardly, superstitious and hypocritical ruler, one of the worst kings Judah ever had. His superstition caused him to pass his son through fire. He sacrificed in the high places and under every green tree. The results of his abominable wickedness were bound to catch up with him. Whoever does evil is bound to meet evil. God must punish it. Let us never forget that. God deals with sin in only two ways; He either washes it away by the blood of His Son, or He punishes it with His fierce anger. He did the latter with regard to Ahaz. Pekah, the king of Israel, and Rezin, the king of Syria, formed an alliance against him. In one day, Pekah killed 120,000 of his soldiers in battle while Rezin carried a great multitude of prisoners away. Pekah also carried 200,000 away captive although these were later released at the urging of the prophet Oded. Zichri, a giant from Ephraim, killed a son of the king and a couple of ranking men. The country's treasures were robbed. In spite of all this, Ahaz did not humble himself but robbed the temple of its treasures and sent them as an enticement to Tiglath-pileser, king of Assyria, requesting him to hasten to his aid against Syria and Israel. From the last clause of verse one it is clear that the allied armies were not able to invade Jerusalem. They succeeded to some extent against Ahaz, against his country and against his people, but not against the holy city.

A Message of Calamity

> 2. And it was told the house of David, saying, Syria is confederate with Ephraim. And his heart was moved, and the heart of his people, as the trees of the wood are moved with the wind.

It is deeply stirring and serious when it is said that this was told to *the house of David.* According to the promise of the Davidic covenant, the family of David would continue to reign if it continued to walk in obedience. Only in the way of disobedience would it be chastised with the rod. This was the condition that the covenant people were now in. Mighty armies marched up to do battle against an exhausted little nation. The representative of the house of David was a superstitious weakling. When he received the message of the alliance and the advance of the armies, his heart fainted from fear. But what courage could the apostate have? His confidence in the king of Assyria was not strong enough to put him at ease in this hour of anxiety. Since he did not trust in God, he could not say:

> *Though flesh and heart should faint and fail,*
> *The Lord will ever be*
> *The strength and portion of my heart,*
> *My God eternally.*

Only the quiet confidence of faith gives courage; unbelief and superstition make one cowardly and afraid. Not only Ahaz, but also his apostate people were very fearful. In a beautiful simile it is said that their hearts were moved like the trees of the woods when shaken by a windstorm.

A Message of Deliverance

> 3. Then said the LORD unto Isaiah, Go forth now to meet Ahaz, thou, and Shearjashub thy son, at the end of the conduit of the upper pool in the highway of the fuller's field;

4. And say unto him, Take heed, and be quiet; fear not, neither be fainthearted for the two tails of these smoking firebrands, for the fierce anger of Rezin with Syria, and of the son of Remaliah.

5. Because Syria, Ephraim, and the son of Remaliah, have taken evil counsel against thee, saying,

Against the news of calamity is the quiet, peaceful message of deliverance by the prophet. What a contrast not only between the message the king had just received and the one he will hear from Isaiah, but also between the fearful and trembling king and the quiet, courageous Isaiah. In the one, we see the fearful fruit of unbelief; in the other, the precious fruit of a steadfast faith in the Word of the Lord. Isaiah's very appearance should have had a soothing influence on the king, but wicked people like Ahaz flee even when there is no pursuer. There is no telling what they would do when there is a pursuer as was the case here!

Isaiah was commanded to take his little son Shear-jashub along. This son had to come along for the instruction and reassurance of the king. His name contained a prophecy, for it means *The remnant shall return.* Ahaz would learn from it that there would indeed be a judgment upon Judah, but that his house and people would not be totally destroyed and that a remnant would return from exile. Isaiah with his children were often used as signs and wonders in Israel (8:18); his two other sons also had symbolic names. The place where Isaiah would meet him is carefully indicated. It was not in the palace but where Ahaz must have been working, fortifying the city. Ahaz wanted to send for help to Assyria; thus, the prophet had to proceed tactfully to keep him from taking this futile step. This is why we have here the remarkable language which is addressed to the wicked king: *be quiet, fear not, neither be fainthearted.* He does have to be on the alert as the words *take heed* indicate; he may take defensive measures, but not such evil ones as he obviously was already contemplating. The description Isaiah gave of the two allied kings was also encouraging. He called them *tails of smoking firebrands,* i.e., the blackened ends of almost consumed firebrands. Like the firebrands, Pekah and Rezin would soon be spent. If only the king had believed these comforting words of the Lord. Unbelief is destructive to the soul and dishonoring to God.

The Satanic Object of the Allied Kings

> 6. Let us go up against Judah, and vex it, and let us make a breach therein for us, and set a king in the midst of it, even the son of Tabeal:

It is remarkable that Pekah is always called *the son of Remaliah.* This is a scornful reference that expresses the name of this man of blood, a murderer of kings and usurper of thrones. His history is described in II Kings 15:25-32; it is simply not worth mentioning, though his father's name is. Judging by verse five, pagan Syria had made the plans to invade Judah, and then sought the support of the northern kingdom to materialize them.

Verse six tells of their satanic plan. This plan was to make a joint invasion in Judah to *vex* this small nation, squeeze it into a corner and worry it to death. Then, they would divide the land between them. So they were motivated by a desire for annexation and extension of power. They intended to exterminate the Davidic family and make a certain *son of Tabeal* their vassal king. The northern tribes must have sunk very deep indeed for them to support such satanic plans. It is obvious that these plans were forged in hell, since it was promised that one day the Messiah would be born from the Davidic royal family. Satan has always made his attacks on this family, because he wanted to make the coming of David's great Son and Lord impossible. But God was thoroughly aware of their demonic intent. Even the discovery of their plans by the Omniscient God should have caused Ahaz to reconsider. However, there has seldom been a ruling king who was more depraved and foolish than Ahaz.

The Fall of Edom Foretold

> 7. Thus saith the Lord God, It shall not stand, neither shall it come to pass.
> 8. For the head of Syria is Damascus, and the head of

Damascus is Rezin; and within threescore and five years shall Ephraim be broken, that it not be a people.
9. And the head of Ephraim is Samaria, and the head of Samaria is Remaliah's son. If ye will not believe, surely ye shall not be established.

The demonic plan will not succeed; the allied kings will be bitterly disappointed because they do not know the counsel of the Lord. Within sixty-five years Ephraim would cease to be an independent nation. Exegetes have always had trouble with the time reference here, since Samaria was actually destroyed after only about twenty years. Like Vitringa, many assume a copyist's error and think it should be sixteen and five, so that the time indication would be correct. The critics usually follow Gesenius, who has expressed himself in favor of accepting a gloss. But everything agrees quite well with the time reference if we apply it not to the time of the destruction of Samaria but to the time when Esarhaddon carried off the last inhabitants of Ephraim and replaced them with new populations. At that time, the kingdom was terminated and the people could no longer be called a nation. For the time being, however, Damascus would remain the capital of Syria and Samaria that of Ephraim. These kings would also continue for some time to be the head of their nation.

This was truly a comforting message in days of panic on the part of both king and people. However, what good does even the most comforting message do if it is not believed? Herod *loved* to hear John the Baptist, but the serious words of this preacher of penitence were not accepted by the heart of the ruler. It was the same way with Ahaz. The prophet warned him; yet if there was no trust or faith in him, he would not be *established.* The matter at issue was faith. On it depended Ahaz's crown, his life and the continuance of his kingdom. When the deadly frightened jailer in Philippi cried out, "What must I do to be saved?" the only answer given him was: *"Believe on the Lord Jesus Christ!"*

Ahaz May Ask for a Sign

10. Moreover the LORD spake again unto Ahaz, saying,

11. Ask thee a sign of the LORD thy God; ask it either in the depth, or in the height above.

Believing without seeing? That is too easy and simple in the eyes of a sinner, for he loves to have something tangible and visible. That is the way Ahaz felt. So God, in His condescending mercy, takes this into account and gives him the right to ask for a sign. Was not the Lord somewhat too indulgent here with this scoundrel? Apparently, He was. But in His mercy God was remembering His people and His house: He wanted to keep Ahaz from an alliance with Assyria, which would result in a world of misery. For this reason, He made it very easy for Ahaz. He was allowed to ask for a spectacular sign from Jehovah, whether in the depth or in the height. Hence, he was allowed to ask for an earthquake, or a similar miracle as befell Korah and his gang, or he could ask for lightning and thunder or hail from above, or even for a sign as that which had taken place in Joshua's day. We observe here that the Lord's miraculous power is as limitless as His goodness is unsurpassed. He gives the choice wholly to Ahaz; whatever he demands will take place. Christ refused to perform a miracle to please the Evil One, but God is willing to do it here for the benefit of wicked Ahaz. How great must have been the faith of Isaiah, however, under these circumstances. We admire him both for his unwavering faith and his undaunted courage and holy self-control. The king and the prophet, here confronting each other, are a perfect contrast in more than one respect. The one has no faith and wants a sign; the other, with his faith, was a sign for Israel.

Ahaz Refuses to Ask for a Sign

12. But Ahaz said, I will not ask, neither will I tempt the LORD.

Ahaz had no faith in God's promise and no desire for the Lord's help. Obviously, he had already put his secret trust in Assyria's king. For that reason, a spectacular sign did not suit him at all. For once a miraculous sign was given him, then he would be compelled, and maybe even forced by the people, to trust in Jehovah, and to abandon his own little plans to make an alliance with the king of Assyria. Ahaz was too much of a coward to tell this honestly and forthrightly to the prophet. It has been demonstrated through all ages that wicked people love to cover their evil works with a Biblical text. And Ahaz was no exception. How many wicked deeds have been rationalized and excused with an appeal to the Bible! He had read in Deuteronomy 6:16, *"Ye shall not tempt the Lord your God."* The injunction was grist for his mill. I will not tempt the Lord, he says apparently very piously to the prophet.

God Himself Offers a Sign

13. And he said, Hear ye now, O house of David; Is it a small thing for you to weary men, but will ye weary my God also?
14. Therefore the Lord himself shall give you a sign; Behold, a virgin shall conceive, and bear a son, and shall call his name Immanuel.
15. Butter and honey shall he eat, that he may know to refuse the evil, and choose the good.
16. For before the child shall know to refuse the evil, and choose the good, the land that thou abhorrest shall be forsaken of both her kings.

It is not only Ahaz, but the entire house of David who is addressed here. This was the issue at stake. This was what Satan, Syria and Ephraim were after. This was also what God had in mind. Verse thirteen shows the controlled anger of the prophet. It is evident that he is not at all thinking of himself when he says that Ahaz is wearying *men*. To weary men, to bother them, is a great sin but how much greater a sin it is to weary God, like Ahaz was doing right then. This is a remarkable expression containing a tremendous truth and reality. Almighty God, who always works and never becomes tired or weary, *can* become *weary* on account of the sins of men. It is obvious that this is an anthropomorphism, but words like these are not mere hollow sounds in the infallible Word of God.

The sign is that of *Immanuel.* The fact that this is a Messianic prophecy is indisputable on the basis of Matthew

1:22, 23. However, if some prefer to think of this as an indirect, rather than a direct, Messianic prophecy, that would be acceptable also. Anyone who is familiar with New Testament quotations from the Old Testament will readily admit that Matthew 1:22 does not compel us to the direct Messianic interpretation. Nevertheless, after taking everything into account, we are inclined to prefer and accept the direct Messianic interpretation, since the word *Almah,* translated as virgin, as a rule refers not to a married but an unmarried woman, or a virgin. It is true however, that Leeser, a Jew, translates this as *young woman,* to prevent any Jew from thinking of Mary. It is also argued that this sign could not be actually a sign to Ahaz, since it would not take place until after some seven centuries. To this it can be answered, however, 1) That Ahaz, by his stubborn unbelief, had fully forfeited an immediate sign, 2) That an immediate sign would not have benefited Ahaz anyway. For he, notwithstanding all warnings to the contrary, wanted to ally himself to the king of Assyria, 3) That the sign of Immanuel being born of a virgin was proof for him that his house and Judah would not totally perish, and 4) That it sufficiently proved to him the Lord's omnipotence to protect and deliver his house and people.

Immanuel shall eat *butter and honey,* i.e., He will be reared in the simplest rural manner until He has come to the years of discretion. *Butter* simply means thick, sour milk or possibly cream, which is a favorite drink with the Bedouins. *The child* in verse 16 does not refer to Immanuel, but to the little son of Isaiah. We can imagine the prophet pointing with his finger at Shear-jashub, the little fellow he held by the hand. Before the lad would come to the years of discretion, the lands of Syria and Ephraim, before whose kings Ahaz trembles will be destroyed. The subsequent history has proven the literal fulfillment of this prophecy. Tiglath-pileser, whose aid Ahaz bought with the temple treasures, conquered Syria, killed Rezin and carried the nations' inhabitants as captives to Assyria (II Kings 16:9). This same king also took possession of the northern part of Israel and carried a great multitude of the people of the land captive to Assyria. See II Kings 15:29 and I Chronicles 5:26.

The Judgment of Judah's Exile

17. The LORD shall bring upon thee, and upon thy people, and upon thy father's house, days that have not come, from the day that Ephraim departed from Judah; even the king of Assyria.

18. And it shall come to pass in that day, that the LORD shall hiss for the fly that is in the uttermost part of the rivers of Egypt, and for the bee that is in the land of Assyria.

19. And they shall come, and shall rest all of them in the desolate valleys, and in the holes of the rocks, and upon all thorns, and upon all bushes.

20. In the same day shall the Lord shave with a razor that is hired, namely, by them beyond the river, by the king of Assyria, the head, and the hair of the feet: and it shall also consume the beard.

21. And it shall come to pass in that day, that a man shall nourish a young cow, and two sheep;

22. And it shall come to pass, for the abundance of milk that they shall give he shall eat butter: for butter and honey shall every one eat that is left in the land.

23. And it shall come to pass in that day, that every place shall be, where there were a thousand vines at a thousand silverlings, it shall even be for briers and thorns.

24. With arrows and with bows shall men come thither; because all the land shall become briers and thorns.

25. And on all hills that shall be digged with the mattock, there shall not come thither the fear of briers and thorns: but it shall be for the sending forth of oxen, and for the treading of lesser cattle.

With subdued anger the prophet further addresses Ahaz. Not only Syria and Ephraim will be destroyed, but also Judah since it committed the accursed sin of making the Assyrian flesh his arm. The Lord will cause the tsetse flies from Egypt and the bees from Assyria, *i.e.* the soldiers of Egypt and Assyria, to advance on Judah. Like swarms of grasshoppers, they will cover and destroy the entire country and all the pleasant gardens of the land. Presently, Ahaz is hiring at a great price the king of Assyria as his helper. Later, God Himself will use him as a borrowed razor to denude the entire country and its inhabitants. All the jewelry and beautiful things of the people will be taken away; there will be a great mourning and a complete removal into slavery. To shave off the beard of an Oriental was an unbearable shame to him and was a sign of great sadness and mourning as well as of despicable slavery. All these things would come upon Judah! As a result of the depopulation of the country, the land would no longer be tilled. Nowhere would there be the rustle of waving fields of grain nor the sound of harvest songs; only here and there a cow would graze, for there would be plenty of grass and, as a result, plenty of milk for the few inhabitants. Where once there were beautiful vineyards, thorns and thistles would spring up. The whole land would be a wilderness full of wild animals, so that it would be unsafe to travel through it unarmed.

ISAIAH 8

A Significant Public Document

1. Moreover the LORD said unto me, Take thee a great roll, and write in it with a man's pen concerning Maher-shalal-hash-baz.

2. And I took unto me faithful witnesses to record, Uriah the priest, and Zechariah the son of Jeberechiah.

3. And I went unto the prophetess; and she conceived, and bare a son. Then said the LORD to me, Call his name Maher-shalal-hash-baz.

4. For before the child shall have knowledge to cry, My father, and my mother, the riches of Damascus and the spoil of Samaria shall be taken away before the king of Assyria.

These four verses actually belong to the previous chapter. The prophets not only used many symbolic words but also engaged in symbolic acts in order to drive the truth home more effectively. To compliment the sign of Immanuel, which referred to the faraway future, Isaiah was commanded to offer a sign to Ahaz and his people that would in the near present become full reality. He had to take a big roll and write on it with a letter type the people could read: *Hasten the spoil, rush on the prey!* These are the same words as the name of the baby in verse three. The prophet did so in the presence of two credible witnesses, Uriah the high priest and a certain Zechariah. What was the purpose of having these two witnesses? As a public document which undoubtedly was displayed, it needed to have the ratification of trustworthy men. Therefore, these men either signed their names on it or attached their seal to it (see also Hab. 2:2). Uriah was the high priest during Ahaz's reign and at the same time his spiritual kin and fellow idolater. II Kings 16:10-16 contains a very ugly story about him. Such a witness can never be suspected of deceit. As a witness he was all the more reliable.

Who Zechariah was cannot be ascertained. Most likely he was the Levite mentioned in II Chronicles 29:13.

The little son born to Isaiah received the same name. And before this little fellow could say Father or Mother, the two allied powers which still threatened Judah would become the prey of the king of Assyria. For the fulfillment of this prophecy, see II Kings 16:9, 17:1-6.

Despising the Waters of Shiloah

> 5. The LORD spake also unto me again, saying,
> 6. Forasmuch as this people refuseth the waters of Shiloah that go softly, and rejoice in Rezin and Remaliah's son;

The little stream of Shiloah sprung from Mount Zion on the southwesterly side of Jerusalem. It flowed as softly as oil without any murmur. Jerusalem's existence and continuation depended on it for a city cannot live without water. Thus, this little stream became a symbol of the house of David, on which Jerusalem's spiritual well-being depended. By now, this house was despised by Pekah and Rezin and many people in Judah. When the two foreigners advanced on Judah, with their satanic plan to replace the theocratic government of David's house by putting a foreigner on Judah's throne, many in Judah and Jerusalem rejoiced in it, revealing their unbelief, gross ingratitude and pride. Most of all, their pride. For the softly running brook, or without using the metaphor, the small and despised kingdom of Judah, was much too insignificant to suit them. They hankered for worldly greatness. By way of punishment, worldly greatness would inundate them.

The Torrent in Assyria

> 7. Now therefore, behold, the Lord bringeth up upon them the waters of the river, strong and many, even the king of Assyria, and all his glory: and he shall come up over all his channels, and go over all his banks:
> 8. And he shall pass through Judah; he shall overflow and go over, he shall reach even to the neck; and the stretching out of his wings shall fill the breadth of thy land, O Immanuel.

Beautifully contrasted here are the mighty waters of the River Euphrates, symbol of the Assyrian world power, and the humble brook of Shiloah. The destructive invasions of the Assyrians are handsomely depicted as an enormous flooding of the Euphrates. The strong and mighty waters would first cascade as a torrent over Judah's two enemies. But the ever swelling and irresistible waters would rage on until they also covered Judah to the neck. When it is remembered that the Euphrates flooded its banks twice a year and changed the bordering lands to marshes and mud pools, all can see that this comparison is not only very beautiful, but also very well chosen and fitting. Of course, its flood waters never reached Judah, but figuratively speaking this is quite possible. The branches of the Euphrates are called *wings*. All this would happen to Immanuel's land, the country of the just promised Messiah. This must have made the hearts of the God-fearing people in Judah even sadder. He, who had just been designated as a sign of Judah's continued existence, would, according to this word not prevent Judah from being inundated up to the neck.

The Breaking in Pieces of All Nations

9. Associate yourselves, O ye people, and ye shall be broken in pieces; and give ear, all ye of far countries: gird yourselves, and ye shall be broken in pieces; gird yourselves, and ye shall be broken in pieces.
10. Take counsel together, and it shall come to nought; speak the word, and it shall not stand: for God is with us.

The prophet suddenly points to the fall of all world powers. The sight of the river of Assyria flooding its banks affords him the occasion. The world powers will not always have dominion over the Lord's people and Immanuel's nation. The *times of the Gentiles,* the times of brutal violence, will speed past and then all Israel will be saved. But before that age of bliss dawns, a terrible association of nations with hostile intentions will first advance on Jerusalem. This massing of nations against Israel in the last days is again and again described in the prophets and is seen frequently in Isaiah. Inspired by the Spirit of God, the prophet sees from the distance their plans, battle arrangements and deliberations. In the most defiant language, he cries to them that they may freely advance with all their craftiness and force because their doom is sealed. No weapon formed against Israel will prosper (54:17). The worm Jacob will one day be like unto a new sharp threshing instrument, having teeth, and will thresh those proud nations and kingdoms. The daughter of Zion will *beat in pieces many people* (Mic. 4:13). The most important reason why no power in the world can destroy Israel, nor exterminate the Davidic royal house, is that *Immanuel* is with them. There is jubilation in Isaiah's heart when he looks at that. There are those who wrongly interpret this to mean only the death of the 185,000 Assyrians.

No Confederacy and No Fear

> 11. For the LORD spake thus to me with a strong hand, and instructed me that I should not walk in the way of this people, saying,
> 12. Say ye not, A confederacy, to all them to whom this people shall say, A confederacy; neither fear ye their fear, nor be afraid.
> 13. Sanctify the LORD of hosts himself; and let him be your fear, and let him be your dread.
> 14. And he shall be for a sanctuary; but for a stone of stumbling and for a rock of offence to both the houses of Israel, for a gin and for a snare to the inhabitants of Jerusalem.
> 15. And many among them shall stumble, and fall, and be broken, and be snared, and be taken.

Strictly speaking, the prophet is defending his conduct and viewpoint here against his fellow inhabitants of Jerusalem. They must have often taken him to be evil for many times he did not go along with the great majority of the people. He had no enthusiasm for the politics of Ahaz and his court; on the contrary, he publicly opposed it. Undoubtedly, they must have accused him of lacking patriotism. This is why he says that Jehovah instructed him with a *strong hand*. What he means is that the Lord treated him like a strict teacher who may forcefully grab an unruly pupil. It is true, that Isaiah's heart, by nature, was just as much inclined to evil practices and capable of trusting in man as did most of the people in his day. It was only by grace that he courageously dared to take and defend a position that was diametrically opposed to that of the king and the people. The fact that he spoke the way he did and walked separately on the narrow road of self-denial was only due to the fact that God Himself with His irresistible grace had conquered him and had clearly shown him the other and better way.

All that men talked about in those days was federation and alliance. Some time later there was also an influential party which had great expectations of an alliance with Egypt which Isaiah in the Lord's name resisted. Does not Isaiah in verse twelve speak the language of our own day? There are many today who expect everything from a united nations in the realm of politics and from a federation of churches in the realm of religion. But also, in our day, the Lord through His Word and Spirit says to his faithful servants: *Say not, A confederacy!* God does not want a union of light and darkness, Christ and Belial, but He does want a union and oneness in His beloved Son. The world's goal in unity is supremacy; God's goal in oneness is holiness!

Notwithstanding all their talk about it and their trust in the federation with the Assyrian world power, the heart of Ahaz and his people was full of anxious fear. This fear was also the fruit of unbelief. The righteous is as courageous as a young lion. Whoever has the fear of God is not afraid of men as Ahaz and his people were. They were stricken by panic at the approach of the united armies of Israel and Syria. The Lord had also warned Isaiah and his family and their followers against this fear, saying, *Neither fear ye their fear.* Even in this respect they were not allowed to be like their contemporaries. Today, the heart of man almost melts again for fear of the things that will happen on earth. But now, too, God's people do not have to be like unto them with regard to this fear.

After having said that they don't have to fear the mob of Judah's oppressors, he continues to say that they do have to fear Jehovah Sabaoth. They must sanctify themselves unto the Lord, for He is indeed a terrible God for His enemies. A glorious promise is added for all who put their trust in the

Lord. In the day of calamity He wants to be a sanctuary, *i.e.,* a holy hiding place for them. Michaelis, Van Hamelsveld and others translate this as *holy stone,* thinking of an Eben-Ezer, a stone of help, like the one Samuel erected. Contrasting this to the *stone of stumbling* makes a very striking argument. On behalf of God's people, God would then be a stone of help and for the wicked a stone of stumbling. Whatever the case may be, we have to think of a hiding place in the hour of danger, which is *holy, i.e.,* inviolable, completely safe for those who remained faithful to God. In the Orient temples and altars were usually an asylum, a safe place of refuge for the persecuted.

Thus, the Lord Sabaoth Himself would be such a holy place of refuge. He would not merely *afford* a hiding place, but *be* one Himself for them. On the other hand, He would be a *stone of stumbling and a rock of offence* to both houses of Israel. The second word explains the first here. Imagine a narrow footpath in a dark mountain area on which a hunk of rock has tumbled down from the top of the mountain, so that a traveler might easily stumble over it. And as if this one simile were not sufficient, another one is added, that of a *gin* (trap) and a *snare.* Like wild animals, the wicked will be captured and carried off to Babylon. From a comparison with Psalm 118:22, Isaiah 28:16, Luke 2:34, Romans 9:33 and I Peter 2:7-8, it is clear that this *stone of stumbling* refers to none but our Lord Jesus Christ, who is a safe hiding place from the raging flood of judgments for all those who believe on Him, but is a cause of eternal lamentation for the unbelievers.

Verse fifteen describes in a succession of terrible terms the fall and destruction of the wicked by His hand. What Simeon expressed when he held the newborn child in his arms is but an echo of this terrible word of the Lord through Isaiah. Christ is set either unto a fall or unto a rising again, unto death or unto life. And whoever runs along with the great multitudes on the broad way of sin, as the people in Isaiah's day did, is a lost person. In those days the public opinion had been poisoned by the leaders with their futile politics. Today, politics are still totally influenced by a Christ-rejecting majority. It is the same now as it was then. It is not the Holy

Spirit who determines the spirit of the times, but the evil spirit of Satan. May God give the grace to take a firm position against the unholy majority, as did Isaiah, for in the end they will plunge us into eternal death!

The Sealing of the Testimony

16. Bind up the testimony, seal the law among my disciples.
17. And I will wait upon the LORD, that hideth his face from the house of Jacob, and I will look for him.
18. Behold, I and the children whom the LORD hath given me are for signs and for wonders in Israel from the LORD of hosts, which dwelleth in mount Zion.

In close connection with the preceding, Isaiah is commanded to bind up and seal in the middle the very significant testimony just received in the presence of the Lord's pupils. This shows that Isaiah was not alone but, like Jeremiah later, had gathered a small circle of kindred minds around him. The word *law, tora* does not refer to the entire Mosaic law, but to the testimony that had been given a moment ago. The prophet and his friends had to observe it as strictly as the unchangeable law of the Lord. There are some who take this word to mean the Mosaic law, so that it no longer is a rule or guide and can now be safely put away. But such a command the Lawgiver would never give. For does He not even say on the last page of the Old Testament: *"Remember ye the law of Moses my servant"* (cf. v. 20)? No, for the word *tora* can also be translated *instruction, indication,* and that is obviously what is meant here. The wealth of instructions and indications God had just given Isaiah had to be scrupulously kept and adhered to in the small circle of the holy remnant. As has been already observed, these words are still a guide for the believers of today.

Since the apostasy would continue to increase, and during that time of apostasy it would become increasingly difficult for the true believers to remain faithful, Isaiah suddenly expresses his holy intent to wait for the promised Redeemer. Judah's king Ahaz could not bring about salvation for the Lord's people. For He himself, with his people, were beyond "rationality, beyond reasoning and beyond rescue." Assyria could not provide deliverance and no federation or alliance with whatever world power could usher in the dawn of Judah's weal. Therefore the prophet responds to the Lord's admonitions by saying that he will wait upon the Lord who presently in anger hides His face from the house of Jacob. And not only he himself, but also the children God had given him would share in this expectation and would walk with him the way of separation. Thus they would be used more and more for *signs* and for *wonders* in Israel. Already with their long and strange names they were a sign in Israel, but by means of the godly instruction of the prophet they would be increasingly so.

This contains the greatest lesson for believers of our own day. Today, there are a great number of sincere believers who run from one conference to another to find "food for their souls," as they call it. But at the same time they show little interest in a godly upbringing of their children in the home, in school and in church. In the natural realm they would not think of taking care only of their own food. Yet Spiritually, they are doing this, for many have no qualms about entrusting their little ones for five days to *this present evil world,* while placing them for one or two hours at the feet of Jesus in Sunday School or Catechism class. Oh, that they would follow the example of Isaiah! The prophet was herein a beautiful type of the Savior and His Church. Hebrews 2:13 quotes these words by him and applies them to the Lord and His Church in that day.

The Spiritism of Isaiah's Day

> 19. And when they shall say unto you, Seek unto them that have familiar spirits, and unto wizards that peep, and that mutter: should not a people seek unto their God? for the living to the dead?
>
> 20. To the law and to the testimony: if they speak not according to this word, it is because there is no light in them.

Times of desperation, such as after the world wars, are times in which spiritism, *i.e.,* consulting the dead for the living, flourishes. King Saul had consulted the dead when the living could no longer help him. After the big wars, spiritism increased enormously as many parents desired to speak once more with their fallen sons. It was that way already in Isaiah's day. Then, there was fear and desperation also. Apparently there were many who sought counsel from the *wizards and familiar spirits.* The law did not even allow the existence of such people. The Lord ridicules the foolish generation of soothsayers. The text imitates their muttering and mumbling, and reminds us of ventriloquism. In their pride, these people pretended that they could replace religion and the gods of all nations. Is it not noteworthy that this is still the proud pretension of spiritism? Today, it offers itself as the only true religion worthy of the world, which must and will replace all other religions.

The question, *Should a people ask the dead for the living?* is holy irony to expose the foolishness of their actions. At the same time, it can be safely concluded from this question that the dead know nothing of or about the living, or at least have no communication with them. When we are most solemnly assured today that at their seances, the assemblies of the spiritists, they can really speak with the dead, we must not take this as humbug, but as reality, inasmuch as they are not speaking with the dead but with demons who falsely pretend to be the dead. Against the spiritism of his day Isaiah had no other defense than the Word of the Lord. And he himself must have sought his strength not only in isolation but in the infallible Word of the Lord. The only means to check apostasy is God's Word, which gives counsel in desperation and light in darkness. But all those who do not speak and act according to this Word shall have no light of happiness and prosperity either in this time or in eternity. This is further stated in the following two verses, which are a fitting conclusion to this chapter.

The Results of Departing from God's Word

21. And they shall pass through it, hardly bestead and hungry: and it shall come to pass, that when they shall be hungry, they shall fret themselves, and curse their king and their God, and look upward.

22. And they shall look unto the earth; and behold trouble

and darkness, dimness of anguish; and they shall be driven to darkness.

These verses give a gripping description of the apostates who have departed from the Word of God. They will wander about in misery and hunger from one place to another. Yet in their oppression and hunger they will not turn to God; rather, full of rancor, they will curse God and their king. In this remarkable chapter, we have met *federation, spiritism* and *bolshevism.* The basic traits of all these terrible movements were depicted by the prophet some hundred years before Christ. And is it not remarkable also that in each of these three movements the apostate Jews take the lead? Together, however, they are *driven to darkness.* But this cannot be the fearful end of Israel as a nation. That is why in the next verse the glorious light of salvation in Christ again shines through the clouds.

ISAIAH 9

The Great Light of Salvation

> 1. Nevertheless the dimness shall not be such as was in her vexation, when at the first he lightly afflicted the land of Zebulun and the land of Naphtali, and afterward did more grievously afflict her by the way of the sea, beyond Jordan, in Galilee of the nations.
>
> 2. The people that walked in darkness have seen a great light: they that dwell in the land of the shadow of death, upon them hath the light shined.

In verse one the prophet is referring to the ravaged areas whose inhabitants were the first to be carried off into captivity by Assyria. They were *at the first lightly afflicted, i.e.,* first depopulated. That is why it pleases the Lord to let the light of the Messiah shine there first. In Matthew 4:14-16 we see that this was literally fulfilled with the first coming of the Savior. Nevertheless, this may not be the final fulfillment. According to the following context there will come a final fulfillment at a later time. Although we readily admit that the Savior was a great light for Galilee at His first Coming (He lived for a time at Capernaum near the sea and thus exalted that city to heaven, dwelled for the most part in Galilee where He chose His disciples and performed most of His miracles there), we, nevertheless, believe that the Lord, according to the unchangeable law of compensation, will one day gloriously reward despised Galilee at the time of His return to Israel. The next three verses speak of the unique joy Israel will experience in that glorious day.

The Great Joy of Restored Israel

> 3. Thou hast multiplied the nation, and not increased the joy: they joy before thee according to the joy in harvest, and as men

rejoice when they divide the spoil.

4. For thou hast broken the yoke of his burden and the staff of his shoulder, the rod of his oppressor, as in the day of Midian.

5. For every battle of the warrior is with confused noise, and garments rolled in blood; but this shall be with burning and fuel of fire.

The translations and interpretations of verse three vary widely. Today, however, commentators are unanimously of the opinion that the word *not* does not belong in the text, since it causes some contradiction and is not found in many manuscripts. If it is retained, then it must be interpreted in this way, "Thou hast in former times made this nation great in number, but not in joy." Then, in the second part of the sentence it is prophesied that this will be altogether different in the future. In contrast with the former sorrow, the coming joy will be the greater. This approach is very striking and agrees not only with the main thought of the context, but can be defended linguistically as well. At any rate, it is certain that Scripture elsewhere teaches sufficiently that Israel will not only have great joy in its restoration, but also that it will be greatly multiplied thereafter. The great joy Israel will experience is expressed here in two comparisons. Their joy will be as great as the joy of harvest and victory in battle when the soldiers are given the spoil. The second comparison is with an ox, whose oppressive yoke has been lifted from its shoulder after having toiled all day long, while the stick with which the tired animal had been beaten on the shoulder is broken. Indeed, Israel's deliverance will be so great that only the glorious deliverance by Gideon from the hand of Midian can to some extent be compared with it (Judg. 7:22). The second part of verse five does not refer to the past but to the future, for it contains a glorious prophecy that all armaments will be burned with fire. All soldiers' shoes and cloaks, still damp and dripping with blood, will be consumed in the fire of the judgment of the nations (cf. 2:4, Micah 4:3).

The Birth and Dominion of Christ

6. For unto us a child is born, unto us a son is given: and the

government shall be upon his shoulder: and his name shall be called Wonderful, Counselor, The mighty God, The everlasting Father, The Prince of Peace.

7. Of the increase of his government and peace there shall be no end, upon the throne of David, and upon his kingdom, to order it, and to establish it with judgment and with justice from henceforth even for ever. The zeal of the LORD of hosts will perform this.

It is regrettable that many people see in these words only a beautiful reference to the Advent and birth of the Babe in Bethlehem. This superficial interpretation does not do justice at all to the coordinative conjunction *for* — which is of such great significance here — nor to the context. The question why this despised people would obtain such great joy, victory and peace has not been answered yet. These words give the answer. It is because unto this people a Child is born and a Son is given. The two names *Child* and *Son* indicate the humanity and divinity of the Savior. When we look at these words in their natural context, we automatically realize that it was not the intent of the Spirit at all to emphasize the birth and work of the Savior in His humiliation. Rather, He presents Him here as a great Conqueror who has defeated all His enemies in the battlefield and delivered His people from the yoke of those who hated them.

The government shall be upon his shoulder. It is equally common today to speak of a king as being clad with authority, a figure of speech derived from the ceremonial robe worn by a king as a symbol of his authority and rule. But there is another reason why this is expressed in these terms; a reason already pointed out with keen insight by Calvin. We have here a striking contrast between the *staff* of the driver on the shoulder of Israel in verse three and the *government* which Christ bears on his shoulder. Israel was bowed down under the dominion of the anti-christian world powers, while Christ on the contrary executes all dominion Himself. The Christ does not have five names, but a fivefold *name.* With Him there is one office and a glorious manifestation of His qualifications and attributes. He was, and is, and will be Wonderful in His being and works. He is a *Counsellor,* One who gives advice and counsel. If only Ahaz and his people in their perplexity and desperation had turned to Him! With Him there is a solution in the greatest calamity and even in the face of death. *The mighty God* – this is a beautiful proof of His divinity and His almighty power. He is the mighty One on whom God has laid help against death, the grave, Satan, sin and hell. The *everlasting Father* – we do not consider it likely that this is meant as another proof of His divinity. In our opinion, the Vulgate has translated this expression correctly by rendering *pater futuri saeculi,* i.e., *Father of the coming age.* In connection with His last name as *Prince of Peace,* this is obviously a reference to the glorious fact that Christ alone will be great in the coming age of salvation when He shall reign. This is not to be taken as a reference to the Father as the first Person of the holy trinity, but to Christ's authority and power in that age of felicity which will be equal to the right and authority of a father in his family. Verse seven favors this idea greatly. It speaks of the greatness of His government and peace. It also suggests that He, while sitting on the throne of David as the Prince of Peace, like Solomon before Him, will not receive this kingdom in all its future glory. Rather, upon receiving it, He will strengthen it by His righteousness and justice; and there will be growth in His Kingdom. The fire of the zeal of Jehovah Sabaoth guarantees this ultimate glory.

The Speech of the Outstretched Hand

8. The Lord sent a word into Jacob, and it hath lighted upon Israel.

9. And all the people shall know, even Ephraim and the inhabitant of Samaria, that say in the pride and stoutness of heart,

10. The bricks are fallen down, but we will build with hewn stones: the sycamores are cut down, but we will change them into cedars.

11. Therefore the LORD shall set up the adversaries of Rezin against him, and join his enemies together.

12. The Syrians before, and the Philistines behind; and they shall devour Israel with open mouth. For all this his anger is not turned away, but his hand is stretched out still.

Here the second part of this chapter begins and continues

to verse four of the following chapter. In regular sequence, it is said again and again: *His hand is stretched out still.* That is why this section is called "The Speech of the Outstretched Hand." It is addressed to the northern kingdom. Although Isaiah labored especially in Judah and Jerusalem, he nevertheless frequently had a message for the north. Apparently, the tribes of the north expected golden returns from their alliance with Rezin of Syria. These verses severely condemn this foolishness. And not only their foolishness but also the pride of heart it revealed. Instead of humbling themselves before the face of God on account of the many calamities that had already descended on them, they still entertained a lighthearted optimism regarding the future. This optimism manifested itself in the slogans that were current in that day and apparently were on everybody's lips. Just as a few years ago in our own country such slogans had their enchanting influence upon thousands: "making the world safe for democracy," "banishing wars by one big war," etc.

Evidently many houses had been broken down and many trees cut. Frivolously they cried, *"Brick —* houses built from ordinary bricks — *are fallen down; but we will build with hewn stone!"* Had the enemy cut down wild fig trees, they would replace them with a much better kind of tree, cedars. Hence, they wanted to replace the poor little houses with grand palaces; they wanted to make the hewn-down woods far more beautiful than they had been. What a brief but deeply psychological picture this is of an unfaithful generation that keeps on dreaming of better times to come and lightheartedly ignores the severe judgments of God. A generation that has the face of a whore and refuses to blush with shame! When God's judgments do not bring men to humiliation, God visits them with more and more severe punishments. According to verse eleven, He will send Rezin's enemies, the Assyrians, against Ephraim. By this alliance with Rezin, Israel only gained more enemies. It is the greatest foolishness for a nation to trust in its allies; for every ally it gets it gains a few more enemies. Assyria was an enemy of Syria and through this federation it was also an enemy of Israel.

He *shall join his enemies together.* Here, the nature of

anti-Semitism comes to the surface again. Actually, Israel's enemies were also enemies of each other, but in His anger God joined them. That means He made them one and they pitched in battle against Israel. The Assyrians, Syrians and Philistines would surround Israel, so that it could neither advance nor retreat, and they would *devour Israel with open mouth.* The image is that of a savage animal which throws itself with a wide-open mouth upon its prey to devour it completely. Thus would Israel be totally devoured by the nations which vexed her, so that she could no longer exist as a nation in her own country.

The Head and the Tail

13. For the people turneth not unto him that smiteth them, neither do they seek the LORD of hosts.
14. Therefore the LORD will cut off from Israel head and tail, branch and rush, in one day.
15. The ancient and honourable, he is the head; and the prophet that teacheth lies, he is the tail.
16. For the leaders of this people cause them to err; and they that are led of them are destroyed.
17. Therefore the Lord shall have no joy in their young men, neither shall have mercy on their fatherless and widows: for every one is an hypocrite and an evildoer, and every mouth speaketh folly. For all this his anger is not turned away, but his hand is stretched out still.

The second part of this speech contains a description of the destruction the enemies of Ephraim would soon bring about. The leaders who led the people astray would be exterminated. Again this section ends with the somber refrain, *For all this his anger is not turned away, but his hand is stretched out still.* We came across this expression already in 5:25. Scripture mentions three kinds of God's stretching out His hand; it is either a sign of protection, of invitation or of judgment. In Isaiah it constantly appears in the last of the three meanings.

The *head* and the *tail,* which will be cut off from Israel, are fortunately explained by God Himself, so that error is excluded here. The head and the tail are the two extremities of an animal, the most noble and most ignoble parts. The head is the old and venerable ruling person, while the tail means the false prophets. With inner joy this true prophet must have placed this divine explanation concerning the false prophets between parentheses. In Isaiah's day we do not hear as much about false prophets as in the days of Jeremiah and Ezekiel. What we do hear about them is worth a volume of description. Compare with this expression what is said in 28:5ff. Isaiah had pointed out earlier that the leaders of the people were leading the nation astray (3:12) and devouring the people like a savage animal. The foolish throngs were allowing themselves voluntarily to be led to destruction. "My people like it that way," Jehovah complained at one time through Jeremiah. The world as well as an unfaithful covenant people wants to be deceived. The expression *branch and rush* indicates the same thing as *head and tail*. A branch grows upward and hence refers to the high and important people of the population; the rush grows in muddy marshes and refers to the lowest element of the population, the scum.

The Lord is very angry with Ephraim. He will have no pleasure in their young men, who are usually the hope, the flower, the pride of the nation and the strength of the army. Even more, He will have no mercy on their orphans and widows, for they have all together become *hypocrites* and *evildoers,* and *every mouth speaks folly,* or rather, *abominations* or *filth.* These three expressions tell us how complete the moral corruption must have been in the northern kingdom. It was one corrupt, loathsome mass which was beyond healing, a God-forsaking people. They were not *heathen,* but *covenant people,* who had received the light of the Lord's law and to whom frequently faithful messengers had been sent. Was it a wonder that the Lord's fierce anger had been kindled and that He could no longer show mercy? With Van der Palm we can also say that "the disasters of the Assyrian war must have been terrible if we are to judge them by these and similar predictions." The Assyrian kings were fearfully cruel; Tiglath-pileser certainly must not have shown any mercy to the young men, the widows and the orphans in Ephraim.

A Terrible Civil War

> 18. For wickedness burneth as the fire: it shall devour the briers and thorns, and shall kindle in the thickets of the forest, and they shall mount up like the lifting up of smoke.
> 19. Through the wrath of the LORD of hosts is the land darkened, and the people shall be as the fuel of the fire: no man shall spare his brother.
> 20. And he shall snatch on the right hand, and be hungry; and he shall eat on the left hand, and they shall not be satisfied: they shall eat every man the flesh of his own arm:
> 21. Manasseh, Ephraim; and Ephraim, Manasseh: and they together shall be against Judah. For all this his anger is not turned away, but his hand is stretched out still.

These verses describe a bloody civil war using the image of a consuming forest fire which fills the entire country with pillars of fire and smoke. The experience in verse twenty, *"they shall eat every man the flesh of his own arm"* is not a description of a great famine, but of civil war and fratricide. Even the two tribes that were closest to each other would fly at each other's throat in hot fury. Only in their hatred of Judah will they be one. When one asks about the fulfillment of these predictions, one can easily point to the anarchist days under the last kings of Israel (see II Kings 15). Israel's abominations were the full cause of war of which would consume all of them like chaff. The prophet saw the hand of the Lord stretched out; that hand that doeth all things both in judgment as well as in mercy.

ISAIAH 10

His Hand is Stretched Out Still

> 1. Woe unto them that decree unrighteous decrees, and that write grievousness which they have prescribed;
> 2. To turn aside the needy from judgment, and to take away the right from the poor of my people, that widows may be their prey, and that they may rob the fatherless!
> 3. And what will ye do in the day of visitation, and in the desolation which shall come from far? to whom will ye flee for help? and where will ye leave your glory?
> 4. Without me they shall bow down under the prisoners, and they shall fall under the slain. For all this his anger is not turned away, but his hand is stretched out still.

Once more, the chapter division is unfortunate here. As anyone can see, these verses still belong to the preceding chapter. The picture of the moral corruption in Ephraim is completed here by pointing out that the judges of the country were guilty of all kinds of extortion and oppression of the poor, the defenseless widows and the orphans. The faithful prophets were always at loggerheads with the unrighteous judges and other influential officers of justice. The false prophets flattered the rich extortioners, but the true prophets always had great sympathy with the underdogs (cf. 1:17, 23; 3:14; 5:7, 23). In the first verse a woe is pronounced against those who made unjust laws, which weighed heavily on the poor, such as very high taxes. With those *that write grievousness* is not meant a second class of people, but the same unrighteous lawmakers whose prescriptions were meant only to oppress the lower classes. Those people with their evil practices went diametrically against the laws of Moses, which were designed to always hold a protecting hand above the heads of the weak and wretched. But this tyranny will not go unavenged. For the

Lord is an observer of men's ways. With the contrary He will show Himself to be contrary. Suddenly, the Lord turns to these wicked oppressors and asks what they would do if the oppression came upon themselves; to whom would they flee for help and where would they hide their illegally obtained treasures? Oppression and calamity would come upon them too, for already the thunder of His anger rumbles in the distance. But the storm is coming closer and closer, until it breaks loose upon their guilty heads; and then they will be taken prisoner to be carried away to Assyria or fall in battle.

Woe Unto the Assyrian, the Rod of God's Anger

> 5. O Assyrian, the rod of mine anger, and the staff in their hand is mine indignation.
> 6. I will send him against an hypocritical nation, and against the people of my wrath will I give him a charge, to take the spoil, and to take the prey, and to tread them down like the mire of the streets.
> 7. Howbeit he meaneth not so, neither doth his heart think so; but it is in his heart to destroy and cut off nations not a few.

A new prophecy begins here which runs on to the end of the chapter. To appreciate this beautiful prophecy against the Assyrian situation fully, two things must be kept in mind. First, it should be remembered that wicked Ahaz had sold himself as a vassal to the king of Assyria at the expense of the Lord's favor, the Lord's servant and the Lord's house. By remembering this, this beautiful description can become a courageous act on the part of Isaiah in our estimation. For this prophecy is directed against the powerful ally of the king and the nation. During World War I American citizens were not allowed to speak one word against France or England since these nations were our allies. What a courage of faith it must have taken therefore to pronounce a prophecy like this one against Judah's partner!

Second, this prophecy was pronounced after Samaria and the northern kingdom had already fallen into the hands of Assyria, as is very clear from verses nine to eleven. These historical facts are significant here for the hearts of many in Jerusalem must have trembled, and many must have wondered in silence whether after Samaria it would be Jerusalem's turn. Since, then, Damascus and Samaria and many other cities had fallen to the mighty conqueror, was it again not a message of special courage on the part of Isaiah and a wonderful tiding of comfort for the believers in Jerusalem and Judah? They could learn that this mighty Assyrian was nothing but the *rod* of God's anger, which He Himself had *ordered* and *sent* (v. 6).

Howbeit he meaneth not so, neither doth his heart think so. Indeed, by no means did he consider himself as a rod in Jehovah's hand. Rather, he considered himself a god who was much mightier than all the gods of other nations. Neither was it his intention to chastise Israel with the rod for its unspeakable abominations and to give it a sound thrashing with a stick. It was definitely in his heart to destroy it and to do away with a large number of nations. His plan and intention were therefore entirely different from Jehovah's. Nevertheless, God wanted to use him as a rod and a staff, an axe and a saw. In this chapter, the most beautiful contrast between the Sovereign God and the greatest sovereign of that time is seen. The latter, however, was but an insignificant instrument with which the former did what He pleased. And after He had used the instrument, He broke it in pieces and threw it away. At the same time we have a picture here of the greatest contrast between the Kingdom of God and the kingdom of the world. Indeed, we may go a step further and say that we do not understand this prophecy correctly if we do not see something in it of the Christ and the Antichrist. The king of Assyria is the type, if not of Antichrist himself, then of the wicked king from the north in the end time.

The Proud Boasting of the King of Assyria

8. For he saith, Are not my princes altogether kings?
9. Is not Calno as Carchemish? is not Hamath as Arpad? is not Samaria as Damascus?
10. As my hand hath found the kingdoms of the idols, and whose graven images did excel them of Jerusalem and of Samaria;
11. Shall I not, as I have done unto Samaria and her idols, so do to Jerusalem and her idols?
12. Wherefore it shall come to pass, that when the Lord hath

performed his whole work upon mount Zion and on Jerusalem, I will punish the fruit of the stout heart of the king of Assyria, and the glory of his high looks.

13. For he saith, By the strength of my hand I have done it, and by my wisdom; for I am prudent: and I have removed the bounds of the people, and have robbed their treasures, and I have put down the inhabitants like a valiant man:

14. And my hand hath found as a nest the riches of the people: and as one gathereth eggs that are left, have I gathered all the earth; and there was none that moved the wing, or opened the mouth, or peeped.

In times past it was often thought that the prophet was merely giving a poetic description of the absurd self-glorification of the Assyrian king. But scientific Assyriology has made abundantly clear that this passage also gives us a very real picture of the proud imagination of the Assyrian kings. On the stones that for centuries lay hidden in the ground and later were unearthed still can be read today the boastful enumerations of their own grandeur and famous acts. In verse eight, he boasts about the greatness of his *princes* or high-ranking officers. They were comparable to the *kings* of other nations. Now if his government servants were that majestic, how grand and exalted must be their lord and emperor! The braggart continues to boast about his conquests. He depicts himself as the invincible and unconquerable one before whom all cities and nations must bow down. *Calno* is the same as Calneh in the land of Shinar in Genesis 10:10. *Carchemish* lay on the west bank of the River Euphrates where the River Chabor joins it. *Hamath* was a city and kingdom on the Orontes. *Arpad* is little known, but it is thought that it was a city situated between the Euphrates and the Orontes, north of present-day Aleppo which we often heard of during World War I in connection with the quarrels about the oil fields of Turkey. Finally, *Samaria* and *Damascus* are mentioned as having fallen by his power.

In verse ten, the vain and unbridled bragging turns to blasphemy against the service of the Lord. Yet, this blasphemy contained an element of truth. Jerusalem and Samaria were indeed full of *graven images*. As far as the art and outward appearance of them are concerned, they may have been far less beautiful than those of other nations. Israel was not a nation of culture and aesthetics. It should be remembered, however, that the ancient heathen always had a certain respect for the gods of other nations. To Israel this respect became all too often a snare unto its own shame and detriment. But this crowned braggart had no such respect at all. He reminds us of the description Paul gives of the man of sin "who opposeth and exalteth himself above all that is called God" (II Thes. 2:4). On the basis of all his conquests, he in his arrogance is of the opinion that Jerusalem, too, will have to surrender to him. The Lord makes it very clear that this proud Assyrian imagination made no distinction between Israel and the Gentiles. To him Jehovah was merely another god like all the others. The advanced critics of today have still the same view as this pagan braggart. Verse twelve is an interjection which makes us sense that God had little patience with his flagrant manner and pride. After having used him as a rod for Judah and Jerusalem, He will cast him down according to the rule that "pride goeth before a fall." Verse thirteen elaborates on this pride. Verse fourteen uses the imagery of a boy taking the eggs from a bird's nest. The king had done with the nations what a mischievous boy does with a little bird's nest. He had gathered the eggs, the treasures of the nations, and none had dared to lift a wing against him, nor opened their beaks or peeped. Hence, the subjugation of the nations and the robbing of their treasures and the carrying away of the inhabitants were to him mere child's play.

The Light of Israel is a Flame to Assyria

15. Shall the axe boast itself against him that heweth therewith? or shall the saw magnify itself against him that shaketh it? as if the rod should shake itself against them that lift it up, or as if the staff should lift up itself, as if it were no wood.

16. Therefore shall the Lord, the Lord of hosts, send among his fat ones leanness; and under his glory he shall kindle a burning like the burning of a fire.

17. And the light of Israel shall be for a fire, and his Holy One for a flame: and it shall burn and devour his thorns and his briers in one day;

18. And shall consume the glory of his forest, and of his fruitful field, both soul and body: and they shall be as when a standardbearer fainteth.

In verse fifteen the ridiculousness of the king's bragging is presented in the imagery of a carpenter's tools. Imagine an ax boasting against the one who swings it, a saw boasting against the sawyer or a staff and stick boasting against the one who lift them and you have, to some degree, a picture of the vaunted tyrant. He acted as though he ruled Jehovah, while it was He who made use of him as an axe and saw against His house and as a rod and stick against the sheep of His pasture.

Verse sixteen again uses two metaphors, this time to depict the punishment upon his haughtiness and pride. With an allusion to the *princes* in verse eight, of whom the king boasted, God says that he will send leanness among his *fat ones.* Scripture frequently refers to rich and brutal rulers as fattened oxen (cf. Ezek. 34). The second metaphor is that of a great fire that will consume all the power, the riches, the luxury and the grandeur of the braggart. Whereas Assyria was first as a rod to Israel, now the roles are reversed and Israel becomes the means in God's hand to punish Assyria.

II Kings 19:35 and Isaiah 37:36 are to be taken as the fulfillment of this prophecy. As is so often the case, the prophet suddenly transposes himself from history or the near future to the faraway future of the day of the Lord. At the same time, he turns away from the historic example, Assyria, to the prophetic counterpart of Assyria, the wicked king of the north in the last days.

The *light of Israel* is meant the *Holy One of Israel* in verse twenty, *i.e.,* the Lord Jesus Christ. Already in 4:5 we saw that Israel will then have the light of His presence. When it is said here that the Light and the Holy One of Israel will devour the thorns and briers *in one day,* we have to think of the appearance of the lightning of His future coming (cf. Ezek. 37, 38; Hos. 14 and Rev. 19). It is also a striking metaphor when all the glory of Assyria, of which its king vaunted himself so outrageously, is compared with *thorns and briers,* the image of the curse, of worthlessness and of desolation.

Verse eighteen still retains the idea of an all-consuming fire which devours both soul and body. Calvin warned against inferring from this that the soul is not immortal. What is meant, according to this keen expositor, is that the soul of this tyrant will have to pay for his wicked deeds on earth after the destruction of his body. The last part of verse eighteen is translated and explained in a great variety of ways. The Septuagint has: "And he will flee as one who flees before a consuming fire." The Vulgate has: *"et erit terrore profundus,"* i.e., "he will flee in terror." And Luther: *"Und wird vergehen und verschwinden,"* i.e., "And will perish and vanish." Michaelis: "That will be melting and boiling!" Van der Palm: "Indeed, it will be totally consumed, it will melt away like dry twigs." Ridderbos: "So that it will be as when a languishing one pines away." Isaac Leeser: "And he shall be as a tree eaten to powder by the worms." Sachs: "As the fading away of a sick man." In our opinion, it is again Calvin who hit the mark best when he makes this comment: "The third metaphor sounds very peculiar, but that is due especially to the unfortunate verb *melt away,* which has been translated too literally. The Hebrew here has an untranslatable play on words, which, combined with the idea of a flame, causes wax dolls to melt, justifies this expression in the original. But in matter-of-fact prose, this *melting away* means nothing but to fall in battle and lose one's standard in the process. The ancient Greek and Roman historians often speak of losing the standard as a disaster, which was almost equal to losing the battle in which this ensign was lost. Hence, this imagery indicates that the situation of the Assyrian will be no less hopeless than if his army had been robbed of its standard-bearer and standard."

A Twofold Remnant

19. And the rest of the trees of his forest shall be few, that a child may write them.
20. And it shall come to pass in that day, that the remnant of Israel, and such as are escaped of the house of Jacob, shall no more again stay upon him that smote them; but shall stay upon the LORD, the Holy One of Israel, in truth.
21. The remnant shall return, even the remnant of Jacob, unto the mighty God.

> 22. For though thy people Israel be as the sand of the sea, yet a remnant of them shall return: the consumption decreed shall overflow with righteousness.
> 23. For the Lord GOD of hosts shall make a consumption, even determined, in the midst of all the land.

Here we have a striking contrast between two different remnants. The first verse speaks metaphorically of the remnant of Assyria as the few trees that have survived a consuming forest fire mentioned earlier. This metaphor, too, appears often in Isaiah. The trees of the erstwhile proud woods will be so few that a little child can count and write them down. The remnant of this proud world power will have no future.

How entirely different it will be with the remnant of Israel. Three marvelous things are said of this remnant: (a) In the future they will no longer trust in him who conquered them as they did in Isaiah's day. Ahaz put his trust in Assyria, but it was this same world power that oppressed Judah so fearfully afterward. (b) The remnant will return from exile. It is almost childish to insist that this is a reference to the return from the seventy year exile. For then Israel was not as the *sand of the sea* nor did Israel trust wholeheartedly in the Lord. What is meant here is the great and final return in the last days as can be safely concluded from the *determined consumption* of verse twenty-three by which is meant *the time of Jacob's trouble* (Jer. 30:7), the time and the judgment of the Great Tribulation. *The consumption will overflow with righteousness* means that Zion will be redeemed with judgment, *i.e.*, by the terrible upholding of His inviolable justice which spells judgment for the wicked and deliverance for the believer. Israel's deliverance and complete restoration will not come about as by magic, but by justice, righteousness and by destroying of its oppressors at that time. The fall of the world power and Israel's deliverance are always juxtaposed. Babylon and a restored, holy Israel cannot exist side by side. Not until *the times of the Gentiles* have sped by can all Israel be saved.

Finally, the observation is by no means amiss that in these verses there is a beautiful explanation of the prophetic name of one of Isaiah's children, Shear-jashub (7:3).

Fear Not: Yet a Little While

> 24. Therefore thus saith the Lord GOD of hosts, O my people that dwellest in Zion, be not afraid of the Assyrian: he shall smite thee with a rod, and shall lift up his staff against thee, after the manner of Egypt.
> 25. For yet a very little while, and the indignation shall cease, and mine anger in their destruction.
> 26. And the LORD of hosts shall stir up a scourge for him according to the slaughter of Midian at the rock of Oreb: and as his rod was upon the sea, so shall he lift it up after the manner of Egypt.
> 27. And it shall come to pass in that day, that his burden shall be taken away from off thy shoulder, and his yoke from off thy neck, and the yoke shall be destroyed because of the anointing.

When Hezekiah, the son and successor of Ahaz, refused to pay the tribute, and the mighty Sennacherib invaded Judah with a mighty army and laid siege around Jerusalem and was at the point of taking the city, God suddenly gave deliverance by His avenging angel. His whole army was slain, and Sennacherib himself fled to his country where he indulged in debaucheries and was killed by his own sons. That, in short, was the main event to which Isaiah's prophecies allude again and again. It can be considered beyond all doubt that this is also the case in these words. We may also safely assume that these words contained the greatest comfort and encouragement for the people of God in Isaiah's day, confronted as they were by the Tiglath-pilesers and the Sennacheribs, but yet not losing sight of the end time. Furthermore, two main topics are noteworthy in these verses.

First, that the history of the exodus from Egypt will repeat itself on a much grander scale. This one historical comparison speaks volumes of Israel's misery and deliverance. Isaiah's historical metaphors are no less rich than his natural ones. It must also have been of great comfort to the God-fearing people that it would be *for yet a very little while*. This reminds us of the *little wrath* in 54:8. This is God's view of things. Calvin says correctly: "That all earthly time indications have but a relative value is true especially in the prophets." We might call this a basic rule of prophecy, and a rule that is ignored all too often. Verse twenty-six refers back to the judgment of Midian in the days of Gideon, when a miraculous delivery was wrought for Israel. Just as Oreb and Zeeb one day fell into the hands of Gideon, so the Antichrist and the false prophet will fall before the face of the Lord Jesus Christ.

The second main topic of these verses is found in the last part of verse twenty-seven. There it is said by whom this great deliverance of Israel will be brought about, the *Anointed One.* This text actually does not mention the Anointed One, the *Messiah,* but *oil.* For that reason many wild translations and explanations have resulted. We believe, however, that the expression *because of the anointing* synecdochically stands for the *Anointed One,* our Lord Jesus Christ, since the preceding context mentions Him three times and later, in verse thirty-four, He is once again referred to as the *mighty one.* Moreover, it was entirely fitting that after the description of the downfall of the great enemy mention would be made of Him who brought about this downfall. Even if God's anointed Son were not meant in this difficult expression, nevertheless it can be known with absolute certainty that the Lord Jesus Christ will one day inflict a crushing defeat on all the antichristian powers in the end time. Every oppressive and shameful yoke will be removed from the necks of His beloved people. The entire earth will enjoy rest and peace during His blessed reign.

The Advance of the Enemy

28. He is come to Aiath, he is passed to Migron: at Michmash he hath laid up his carriages:

29. They are gone over the passage: they have taken up their lodging at Geba; Ramah is afraid; Gibeah of Saul is fled.

30. Lift up thy voice, O daughter of Gallim: cause it to be heard unto Laish, O poor Anathoth.

31. Madmenah is removed; the inhabitants of Begim gather themselves to flee.

32. As yet shall he remain at Nob that day: he shall shake his hand against the mount of the daughter of Zion, the hill of Jerusalem.

33. Behold, the Lord, the LORD of hosts, shall lop the bough with terror: and the high ones of stature shall be hewn down, and the haughty shall be humbled.

34. And he shall cut down the thickets of the forest with iron, and Lebanon shall fall by a mighty one.

This is a highly poetical description of Assyria's advance on Jerusalem. Again, it is evident the king of the north is in view from the fact that the places named are all north of Jerusalem. Later on chapters thirty-six and thirty-seven tell us that Sennacherib marched past Lachish and Libnah, cities that lay southwest of the holy city.

The description here is very lively. An enormous army is moving from city to city causing nervous excitement, terror and dread everywhere. From the distance the prophet hears their cries of fear and lamentation. At *Michmash* he saw the enemy *laying up his carriages* apparently to camp for the night. According to others, he first left his vehicles behind there because the army had to descend a very steep slope and on the other side ascend a similar height. It cannot be determined where all these little towns were situated and it is meaningless to guess at it. The prophet also sees the villagers fleeing in deadly fear before the face of the tyrant. He calls out to the *daughter of Gallim* to lift up her voice in lamentation. We must not think of a young daughter here, but of the entire town, represented as a daughter. It is quite common in Scripture to call cities *daughters*. We need only to recall the expression *daughter of Zion,* so often used for Jerusalem (v. 32). When he approaches Jerusalem, he stays a night at Nob, undoubtedly for reconnaissance of the area and to plan the most effective strategy, and to allow the army some rest before the deadly blow will be executed. From there he marches on again toward the holy city. The mighty conqueror lifts up his hand to administer the deadly blow. Yet a little while, and the entire city will be crushed underneath his iron fist.

But *behold!* Man proposes, and God disposes. While he is ready to smash Israel, God is ready to crush him. Standing there with uplifted hand, he looked like a proud tree. But the Lord will lop off all his branches with a strong hand. Previously, this enemy was represented as a forest whose trees are tall and high. It was exactly this characteristic that the proud king of Assyria had in common with the stately trees. His flagrant manner and pride has been pointed out before. When it is said that *Lebanon* shall fall, this means, of course, the mountain forest of its tall cedars. In like manner Psalm 72:16 speaks of the *shaking of Lebanon,* by which is meant its trees. Whoever will cut down this proud forest must have great strength. The last verse says the *mighty one* shall do it! This is no one less than the *rod* of chapter eleven, who will stand as the ensign and oracle of all nations.

ISAIAH 11

Prince of Peace

> 1. And there shall come forth a rod out of the stem of Jesse, and a Branch shall grow out of his roots:
>
> 2. And the spirit of the LORD shall rest upon him, the spirit of wisdom and understanding, the spirit of counsel and might, the spirit of knowledge and of the fear of the LORD;
>
> 3. And shall make him of quick understanding in the fear of the LORD: and he shall not judge after the sight of his eyes, neither reprove after the hearing of his ears:

Indicated here are the origin, the sevenfold Spirit and the fear of the Lord of the Prince of Peace. It has not always caught the attention of Bible students that we are dealing here with a beautiful contrast between the proud mountain forest of Assyria and the humble shoot of the cut-off trunk of Jesse. That forest was tall of stature but had been leveled; this *Rod* is of humble stature but will be exalted to such an extent that all nations will ask for Him. His rest will be glorious for the entire world. The world power has fallen, the Kingdom of God has come. This chapter is one more proof that the enemy of the previous chapter is not exclusively Sennacherib, but has his counterpart in the end time in the king of the north.

The origin of King Messiah was very humble. We see a bare, withered tree stump, robbed of its trunk and top, and it looks as though the stump will never bear any fruit any more. But, a small shoot sprouts from the root of this dry stump which is the Davidic dynasty. Because of its unsightliness and misery, it is not named after David but after his father. When Christ was born, there was nothing royal about that dynasty. But a new shoot sprang from this old stem. Christ was born in Bethlehem, and a heavenly messenger said of Him that He would sit on the throne of His father David and reign over

the house of Jacob forever (Luke 1:33). This image of the
Shoot does not point to His divinity but to His human nature
and origin.

He is depicted as equipped with the sevenfold Spirit of the
Lord. According to the keen observation of the learned
Delitzsch, the elements of verse two remind us of the golden
candlestick with its seven branches filled with oil and giving
light. This candlestick had one stem in the center from which
protruded three branches to the right and three to the left.
Similarly in this text, three pairs of names of the Spirit are
grouped around the central stem formed by the words: "And
the spirit of the Lord shall rest upon him." Taken as a whole,
these words express that the Spirit rests on Him, fills Him
and permeates Him in unlimited plenitude with all His gifts,
powers and operations. He is *anointed above His fellows.* All
the gifts that had been scattered among the prophets, priests,
kings and sages throughout the ages were combined in His
most glorious person. Someone has correctly observed that
the three Spirits on the right are concerned with *thinking,*
theory, and the three on the left with *action,* the practice of
the service of the Lord.

The Work of the Prince of Peace

> 4. But with righteousness shall he judge the poor, and reprove
> with equity for the meek of the earth: and he shall smite the
> earth with the rod of his mouth, and with the breath of his lips
> shall he slay the wicked.
> 5. And righteousness shall be the girdle of his loins, and
> faithfulness the girdle of his reins.

After first describing His Person, the text now describes
the *work* of the Prince of Peace. Remarkably enough, this
too, is described in the form of a septet.

1. His *breath* shall be in the fear of the Lord. A great
variety of explanations have been given of this word, but
since another six organs of the Savior are mentioned, it will
be best here to think of the organs of smell. The sense of
smell is the finest man has. With it we can detect the slightest
smells, whether pleasant or unpleasant. The Prince of Peace
will have a keen sense of smell to detect everything. He did

this at His First Coming, He will do so at His Second.

2. He will not judge after the *sight of His eyes.* This is what the judges in Judah did in the time of Isaiah. They were influenced by the prominence of the rich and trampled on the poor of the land. This Judge will be entirely different. He will judge, but as the omniscient One who knows the heart and tries the reins; who will judge not only external actions but even the thoughts and contemplations of the heart.

3. He will not reprove after the *hearing of His ears.* Earthly judges and prominent men are always dependent on what their fallible senses and the ears and eyes of witnesses point out, but that will not be the case with this illustrious Prince. When in the day of His coming, He will punish great nations, He will not do this on the basis of the testimony of others, or on external evidence. He will judge according to the divine rule of holy and inviolable justice and without the respect of persons. Even the God-fearing remnant, called the *meek of the earth,* will be punished with equity.

4. He will smite the earth with the *rod of His mouth.* From Revelation nineteen it is known that out of His mouth goes a sharp sword. This verse speaks of the *rod of His mouth,* which also means the mighty Word of the Lord.

> The voice of the LORD is upon the waters: the God of glory thundereth: the LORD is upon many waters. The voice of the LORD is powerful; the voice of the LORD is full of majesty. The voice of the LORD breaketh the cedars; yea, the LORD breaketh the cedars of Lebanon. He maketh them also to skip like a calf; Lebanon and Sirion like a young unicorn. The voice of the LORD divideth the flames of fire. The voice of the LORD shaketh the wilderness; the LORD shaketh the wilderness of Kadesh. The voice of the LORD maketh the hinds to calve, and discovereth the forests: and in his temple doth every one speak of his glory   (Psalm 29:3-9).

This is the grand description of the powerful voice of Jehovah. It is this voice the Lord Jesus will use in the day of His coming.

5. With the *breath of His lips* He will slay the wicked. Dr. V. Hepp, in his book on the Antichrist, says about this text:

From of old, the Rabbis have adhered to the first interpretation and seen in this wicked (one) Armillus, the Jewish Antichrist. And what strikes us even more is that Paul in his second letter to the Thessalonians quotes these words and applies them to the lawless one, the man of sin. Now, according to the well-known rule that whatever is hidden in the Old Testament is revealed in the New, this prediction of the wicked (one) by Isaiah may be unhesitatingly applied to the Antichrist.

We are in total agreement with this explanation.

6. Righteousness will be the girdle of His *loins.* Scripture often compares virtues with the clothes and girdle a person wears (cf. Job 29:14; Ps. 109:18, 19; Eph. 6:13-17, and Rev. 19:8). In the Orient, girdles were worn by the rich and prominent as adornment and for comfort to tie up their dragging clothing. While working or traveling they used them to increase quickness of movement, safety and proficiency.

7. Also truth will be the girdle of His *loins.* This does not say the same thing as the preceding expression, for two different words are used. The fact that His girdle is mentioned twice serves to indicate His royal pomp, riches and beauty, because the rich had many girdles. Thus, the glorious virtues of righteousness and truth (faithfulness) will cleave unto Him as a girdle cleaves to the loins of a man. Both will be put into the service of His glorious Kingdom. At last there will be a world Ruler possessing righteousness and faithfulness.

The Reign of the Prince of Peace

6. The wolf also shall dwell with the lamb, and the leopard shall lie down with the kid; and the calf and the young lion and the fatling together; and a little child shall lead them.

7. And the cow and the bear shall feed; their young ones shall lie down together: and the lion shall eat straw like the ox.

8. And the sucking child shall play on the hole of the asp, and the weaned child shall put his hand on the cockatrice' den.

9. They shall not hurt nor destroy in all my holy mountain: for the earth shall be full of the knowledge of the Lord, as the waters cover the sea.

10. And in that day there shall be a root of Jesse, which shall stand for an ensign of the people; to it shall the Gentiles seek: and his rest shall be glorious.

His dominion is described once again in the number of completeness, seven. In 4:1, we saw that seven, as such, is not the number of holy perfection but the number of completeness, whether unto evil or unto good. There it was used in a bad sense; here in a good sense:

1. *The wolf also shall dwell with the lamb.* This is the main thought around which all the rest is grouped. It is impossible to conceive of a greater contrast than what exists between these two animals. For that reason this contrast is used again and again to represent the bloodthirsty wicked and the defenseless followers of Christ (Matt. 7:15; Luke 10:3; John 10:12; Acts 20:29).

2. The *leopard* shall lie down with the *kid.* The leopard is one of the sliest, furtive animals ever lying in wait for prey, while the kid is one of the dullest little animals, always playful and frisky. Experts tell us that kids are especially enticing to a leopard or panther; but here they lie alongside of each other in perfect peace. The leopard is no longer bloodthirsty and the kid is no longer afraid of its former sworn enemy.

3. Next the prophet sees a curious flock consisting of a calf, a young lion and fatlings, and a boy of tender age is their shepherd. Such a flock had not existed on earth since the state of rectitude under the dominion of the first Adam. But now, after a long and oppressive history of sin and grace, the second Adam has come and He has restored everything the first Adam had destroyed and subjected to vanity. A little boy, symbol of weakness and innocence, will be able to lead a young lion, the most bloodthirsty of all animals and always hungry. A young lion prefers to pounce upon calves and fattened young oxen, but under the dominion of King Jesus he will no longer have a bloodthirsty nature.

4. The *cow* and the *she-bear* will feed together. A she-bear cannot run very fast and so a milk cow is an easier prey for her than the fast young oxen. So here, too, is the reconciliation and unification of former enemies. The she-bear no longer has a desire for blood and for tearing her prey to pieces; there is no longer any danger for the cow. Their friendship and peace include also their young; the little calf rests peacefully beside the young bear.

5. *The lion shall eat straw like the ox.* From the statement that the she-bear would feed together with the cow it could not only be inferred that the wild animals have abandoned their savage nature, but also that they must have undergone a great organic, physical change under the reign of the Prince of Peace. Presently, a she-bear does not graze; a she-bear lives on flesh, berries and honey. When she gets very hungry, she does not eat grass, but tree roots. What is said indirectly of the she-bear is here specifically said of the lion. He will not eat flesh any more, but grass, hay and straw like the ox.

6. A *sucking child* will entertain itself with the hole of an asp. Under the reign of King Jesus sucking children will be born in Israel and the nations. The sucking children will play according to the nature of sucking children. The seer sees a very young child of about one year of age playing near the hole of an adder. The marvelous thing is not that the little child is playing near the hole of an adder and curiously looking into the hole, but that the asp or adder, a very poisonous snake, has lost its venom and meanness. All this is meant as a blessing of King Messiah.

7. A *weaned child* will stick its hand into the den of a *cockatrice*. A weaned child is a child that has just been taken from its mother's breast so is about two years old. Just as the child is older than the first one, so the cockatrice is more venomous than an asp. The reference is a snake with little tentacles such as the Cerastes or Horned Viper. The little toddler is beautifully depicted as putting its little hand into the den of this very dangerous reptile to stroke it. But even if it should put its finger into the open mouth, it will not experience any evil effects for the Lord Jesus reigns.

Dr. Ridderbos in his commentary on this chapter says correctly,

Calvin certainly does not do justice to these verses when he, following in the footsteps of the Church Fathers, sees only metaphorical language here, pointing out that men who were formerly wicked and unruly have now become pious and gentle. Scripture teaches that when the meek shall inherit the earth, the realm of nature shall also be delivered from the bondage of corruption (Rom. 8:19); in this renewed creation, the removal of the Paradise curse, which also fell on the earth and the animals and caused them to degenerate and turn wild is shown in a lovely scene. Meanwhile the features of it are derived from life on this earth, hence, from these verses it cannot be concluded that in the kingdom of glory there will also be animals that will eat straw . . .

With the first part we agree, but not with the last sentence. It negates the first statement to a large extent. The animals are subject to the curse, as he stated before. Will they now be freed from that curse by being annihilated? Is restoration from the curse annihilation, or deliverance and glorification? Undoubtedly, the latter. He says that in the realm of glory there will be no animals. If one is of the opinion that the realm of glory consists only of a new heaven, then this might be granted. But we, according to His promise, look for new heavens and *a new earth* (II Pet. 3:13). Hence, the realm of glory will also include the earth, according to this explicit apostolic statement. Why then should there not be in the realm of glory on earth a new kingdom as well as a restored world of animals? Was there not a glorious world of animals on earth before the fall? If God could create a glorious world of animals, why should He not be able to recreate it as well? If the fall could degenerate the animal world so fearfully, why could not grace lift it up again out of this fallen state? If the animals were dragged along in the fall of the first Adam, why could not the much mightier second Adam lift them out of that fall and place them on the height of the glory of God? On this basis, we reject with full conviction all the allegorical and so-called spiritual explanations of these words. We adhere to the simple, unforced and discerning literal interpretation according to which all these things will one day become a glorious reality under the reign of peace of our Lord Jesus Christ.

That we are to think mainly of the restored land of Israel is evident from verse nine. *All my holy mountain* means all of Canaan. Nevertheless, the second part of this verse prevents us from thinking that this peace and glory is restricted to

Canaan only. In a significant metaphor of the waters covering the sea, we are told that the whole earth with all its inhabitants will be full of the knowledge of Jehovah. No hurt or destruction will be caused any more; there will be no more war, revolution, murder, pillaging or plundering. The sword is beaten into a sickle, the spear into a spade and the gun is made into nails. In the same millennial day all nations will gather under the banner of King Jesus (v. 10). Whereas the first verse portrayed Him in His humanity as a shepherd the humble shoot from the cut-down trunk of Jesse; here He is portrayed as the *root of Jesse,* as God, from whom Jesse and the whole Davidic royal family originated. He is, as this chapter teaches us, both Lord and Son of David. Even the last page of God's Word points out this truth (Revelation 22:16). All nations will acknowledge Him, who once hung on the cross as the King of the Jews, as their sovereign King and Commander. The *root* of Jesse will then be an ensign, a banner, a tall *tree* which can be seen by all nations and around which all nations will gather. They will seek Him! This banner will be at the same time their oracle. In the Kingdom of Peace all problems will either have been solved by Christ or willingly presented to Him for solution.

And his rest shall be glorious. During His first presence He said, "I will give thee rest," but that promise was not fulfilled then. This rest is the rest of Shiloh, the Provider of peace, of whom Jacob had prophesied on his deathbed (Gen. 49:10). It will be enjoyed by the entire earth, when all nations shall be obedient unto him (cf. 14:3, 7).

The Restoration and Reunification of Israel, the People of the Messiah

11. And it shall come to pass in that day, that the Lord shall set his hand again the second time to recover the remnant of his people, which shall be left, from Assyria, and from Egypt, and from Pathros, and from Cush, and from Elam, and from Shinar, and from Hamath, and from the islands of the sea.
12. And he shall set up an ensign for the nations, and shall assemble the outcasts of Israel, and gather together the dispersed of Judah from the four corners of the earth.
13. The envy also of Ephraim shall depart, and the adversaries

of Judah shall be cut off: Ephraim shall not envy Judah, and Judah shall not vex Ephraim.

14. But they shall fly upon the shoulders of the Philistines toward the west; they shall spoil them of the east together: they shall lay their hand upon Edom and Moab; and the children of Ammon shall obey them.

15. And the LORD shall utterly destroy the tongue of the Egyptian sea; and with his mighty wind shall he shake his hand over the river, and shall smite it in the seven streams, and make men go over dryshod.

16. And there shall be an highway for the remnant of his people, which shall be left, from Assyria; like as it was to Israel in the day that he came up out of the land of Egypt.

These verses clearly prove Israel's complete restoration to the land of its fathers (at least if any power of proof may be ascribed to the words of Holy Scripture). For: (a) This restoration coincides with the reign of the Prince of Peace over all nations. (b) It cannot refer to the first return from exile, for it emphatically says that the Lord shall gather His people *the second time.* (c) Never before has there been such a gathering together of Israel from among all nations as is described here. (d) The uniting of Ephraim and Judah can never be explained as referring to the Church. (e) The Church never flew on the shoulder, *i.e.,* the mountain ridge, of the Philistines. Nor, has it ever taken spoil of the nations of the east other than in unfair trade and the stealing of land before the mouth of the cannon by so-called Christian nations. Finally, the most discerning expositors have not succeeded in giving an undistorted exegesis when excluding Israel's restoration. Dr. Ridderbos wants no literal fulfillment of this prediction, but allows for a partial fulfillment in the return from the Babylonian exile. He admits, however, that the past has never brought the full materialization of this prophecy. He finally says that it refers to the glorified Church, but this does not explain these texts. The final three verses point to the miracles and judgments which will accompany Israel's exaltation above the nations.

ISAIAH 12

Israel's Future Deliverance

1. And in that day thou shalt say, O LORD, I will praise thee: though thou wast angry with me, thine anger is turned away, and thou comfortedst me.
2. Behold, God is my salvation; I will trust, and not be afraid: for the LORD JEHOVAH is my strength and my song; he also is become my salvation.
3. Therefore with joy shall ye draw water out of the wells of salvation.
4. And in that day shall ye say, Praise the LORD, call upon his name, declare his doings among the people, make mention that his name is exalted.
5. Sing unto the LORD; for he hath done excellent things: this is known in all the earth.
6. Cry out and shout, thou inhabitant of Zion: for great is the Holy One of Israel in the midst of thee.

This chapter is the continuation and conclusion of the preceding prophecy. The glory of the Messiah, His Person, His work, His Kingdom and His people were so phenomenally great that the oracle had to transform into a song of praise and thanksgiving; it was placed on the lips of the delivered and exalted Jews in the Kingdom of Peace. But even in this glorious prophecy of salvation, the historical connection is undeniable. In the last verses of the preceding chapter, allusion was made to the great signs and wonders of God accompanying the deliverance from Egypt. These will repeat themselves on a much grander scale at Israel's ultimate restoration. Indeed, it will be very appropriate that a similar song of thanksgiving be repeated as it was at the exodus from Egypt and after the passage through the Red Sea, as is described in Exodus 15 (cf. Hos. 2:14).

This beautiful song consists of two parts. In the first part restored Israel gives thanks for the great deliverance and in the second it calls on the whole earth to sing praises to the Lord. In the first verse God is not thanked for His *anger,* but that the anger *is past,* and is now turned away and has given place to rich comfort. The nation that once was so very sinful now glorifies God's free grace. *Behold, God is my salvation!* She cries out. In the Hebrew word for the name *Jesus* is hidden. Today, the Jews still call Him *Yesu* which is formed from the first letters of the terrible expression: "His name and remembrance be expurgated from the earth!" But then, the triune God will be unto Israel *salvation, strength* and a *psalm.* Then Israel will draw water from the wells of salvation. In the past Israel always used this expression at their. Feast of Tabernacles. Here it is a word of prophecy which this enthusiastic man of God cries out to them while gazing at their future bliss. We also believe that this prophecy will one day be literally fulfilled for restored Israel; for we know that the Scriptures frequently represent Christ Himself as the Fountain of life (55:1). Once He Himself cried out, "If any man thirst, let him come unto me, and drink" (John 7:37; 6:35,54; cf. Rev. 22:17). So here we obviously have a reference to Him as the Fountain of Salvation; His blessings in the natural and spiritual realms are called the *wells of salvation.*

The second part of this song is found in the last three verses. Restored Israel is enjoined there to urge all nations to give thanks unto Jehovah; not only to *give thanks,* however, but also to *call upon His name,* to *preach,* to *sing psalms* and to *cry out and shout.* And the ground for all these glorious activities will be that the *Holy One of Israel,* the Lord Jesus Christ as the great Prince of Peace, will be *great in the midst* of Israel. Then Israel will, like Thomas once did, see and believe the Resurrected Savior and, like Thomas and the other apostles, hasten to the utmost ends of the earth and to the faraway islands which as yet have not heard the news that Christ has returned and which as yet have not seen His glory. They will declare Christ's glory among the Gentiles (66:19). Then will be fulfilled the glorious promise given Abraham that one day all nations would be blessed in him.

ISAIAH 13

The Prophecies Against the Nations

With chapter thirteen a new series of prophecies against the heathen nations begins. The series runs through chapter twenty-three. The main idea of all of them is the same: God will bring down all that is haughty and order things so that He, His Anointed One and His people alone, will be high and exalted in the day of His coming. Hence we must view these heathen nations as prototypes of every world power that opposes God. This is why the downfall of these world powers usually results in the restoration and exaltation of Israel. When the times of the Gentiles have passed, all Israel will be saved.

The typical character of these prophecies, must not be misunderstood. Their symbolical and prophetic reference to the antichristian world power of the last days by no means excludes the literal and historical fulfillment of these divine pronouncements. For instance, historical Babylon was once literally invaded and captured by the Medo-Persians under the command of Cyrus the Great.

All these prophecies against the nations are listed under the heading, *The burden* (of Babylon, etc.). For the sake of brevity it is not necessary to elaborate on this remarkable expression every time it occurs; thus we offer an explanation now. The Hebrew word *massa* is derived from the verb *nasa,* which means *to lift, to lift up.* And so the word *massa* means a burden, a heavy load. The divine pronouncements often weighed heavily as a great burden on the wicked cities and proud nations. The Lord's prophecy is a *burden (massa)* unto us, the people who are derisively spoken of in Jeremiah's predictions. There is, however, another thought which we may safely connect with the preceding, i.e., that every ominous prophecy also weighed like a burden on the usually very sensitive seers. We need but recall the expressions of grief such as are recorded of the prophet himself in 15:5, 16:9-11, 21:4. It is vexingly grievous to one's feelings when one has to announce eternal damnation to his fellow men. Hence, when the word *burden (massa)* was used to designate the message from above in its crushing descent on the wicked, it frequently weighed heavily on the impressionable and flammable heart and mind of the prophet.

Finally, it is beyond doubt that these predictions come from Isaiah. This is generally doubted and denied by the critics, but without any ground. The Leyden Translation with Annotations, which represents the most radical and progressive high criticism, writes about Isaiah thirteen, *"This prophecy did not originate with Isaiah."* According to its translators this would have been imcomprehensible. It is no wonder that these men do not want to consider this prediction as coming from Isaiah. For then they would also have to accept the divine wonder of literal prediction, since Isaiah predicted this conquest in the minutest details some two centuries before the downfall of Babylon. According to these unbelieving gentlemen miracles and predictions are impossible. To them, it is a basic unassailable dogma. According to the Leyden Translation and others, these predictions about Babylon originate with an unknown author who after the destruction of Jerusalem lived in Babylon and boiled with hatred against Babylon. Hence, the critics demand us to believe their dreams rather than the Word of God in verse one, which says that *Isaiah* saw the burden.

God, as Commander, Summons His Army Against Babylon

1. The burden of Babylon, which Isaiah the son of Amoz did see.
2. Lift ye up a banner upon the high mountain, exalt the voice unto them, shake the hand, that they may go into the gates of the nobles.
3. I have commanded my sanctified ones, I have also called my mighty ones for mine anger, even them that rejoice in my highness.
4. The noise of a multitude in the mountains, like as of a great

people; a tumultuous noise of the kingdoms of nations gathered together: the LORD of hosts mustereth the host of the battle.

5. They come from a far country, from the end of heaven, even the LORD, and the weapons of his indignation, to destroy the whole land.

In these verses, there is divine mobilization against Babylon. In true Isaiahic fashion God is presented as the Commander of the army who gives His snappy, authoritative commands. In days of old, the sign for war was given by the erection of banners during the day and the burning of signal fires on top of a high, bare mountain during the night. Actually the Hebrew has *on a bare mountain, i.e.,* a deforested mountain, so that the sign for war could be seen from afar and no trees or woods would be burned. The heralds of the king were sent out. They lifted their voices and hands to call the soldiers to battle indicating that they must first assemble in the gates of the officers to be inspected. Others think that the expression *that they may go into the gates of the nobles* refers to the gates of Babylon. Still others read with Michaelis: *So that my volunteers assemble at my gates,* for the purpose of being inspected by the Commander Himself in the gates of His palace. There is no reason, however, to depart from our translation.

The *sanctified ones* in verse three are the selected and dedicated soldiers of the army of the Medes and Persians who will advance on Babylon. God in His anger has summoned His warriors from the mountains of Media and Persia. These warriors are His because He will use them as a rod of correction against Babylon. They will serve Him by subjugating other proud nations. Who are those who *rejoice in my highness?* They are the same warriors and soldiers who will rejoice in the greatness and glory of their Commander. This, at least, is the generally held opinion, but it does not satisfy us completely. Although we fully agree that here, on the basis of verse seventeen, it is primarily the mighty armies of the Medes and Persians in view. However, it is possible to think of another and much grander army of angels and saints who will accompany Christ unto judgment. We prefer to think of the *mighty ones* as the angels of His power and of them that *rejoice in my greatness* as the saints who one day with Christ will execute judgment on all ungodly world powers. Is it not known from I Thessalonians 4:16 that the Lord Jesus with the *shout* of a commander will gather His Church from the graves and from the four corners of the earth to judge shortly with them the antichristian world powers? In Revelation 19:14, there are the rejoicing ones who descend with Him from on high to the battle of Armageddon. Our reasons for this explanation are: (a) The language used here is far too strong for the advance of the Medo-Persian army of Cyrus. Consider the expressions *a tumultuous noise of the kingdom of nations, the host of the battle,* and *from the end of heaven,* etc. (b) Again and again reference is made to *the day of the Lord,* the day of Great Tribulation. (c) It is said that God will not only destroy Babylon, but will also visit *the whole land, i.e.,* the *world,* and will lay low the haughtiness of the terrible. (d) Verse ten speaks of the kind of mighty signs that elsewhere are said to accompany the day of the Lord's coming (Ezek. 32:7; Joel 2:31, 3:15; Matt. 24:29). (e) According to verse thirteen both heaven and earth will be moved *out of their places.* Most certainly all this did not take place at the conquest of Babylon. Hence, it is our opinion that this is not merely the mobilization of the Medo-Persian army against Babylon, but also the coming of the Lord with His angels and saints to judge all the ungodly world powers.

The Terrors of the Day of the Lord

6. Howl ye; for the day of the LORD is at hand; it shall come as a destruction from the Almighty.

7. Therefore shall all hands be faint, and every man's heart shall melt:

8. And they shall be afraid: pangs and sorrows shall take hold of them; they shall be in pain as a woman that travaileth: they shall be amazed one at another; their faces shall be as flames.

9. Behold, the day of the LORD cometh, cruel both with wrath and fierce anger, to lay the land desolate: and he shall destroy the sinners thereof out of it.

10. For the stars of heaven and the constellations thereof shall not give their light: the sun shall be darkened in his going forth, and the moon shall not cause her light to shine.

11. And I will punish the world for their evil, and the wicked for their iniquity; and I will cause the arrogancy of the proud to

cease, and will lay low the haughtiness of the terrible.

12. I will make a man more precious than fine gold; even a man than the golden wedge of Ophir.

13. Therefore I will shake the heavens, and the earth shall remove out of her place, in the wrath of the LORD of hosts, and in the day of his fierce anger.

14. And it shall be as the chased roe, and as a sheep that no man taketh up: they shall every man turn to his own people, and flee every one into his own land.

Generally most commentators see here a picture of the feat that will grip the inhabitants of Babylon at the approach of the Medo-Persian army. But for several reasons this explanation is inadequate. Besides the considerations given above, it is evident that Babylon had no fear whatsoever of the army of Cyrus. According to 21:5, they were still eating and drinking at their festive banquets when the hostile army was already at the gates. But in the days of the Great Tribulation all that is said here will be literally fulfilled. When the fourth avenging angel will pour out his vial of wrath upon the sun in that day, the people will be scorched with fire and blaspheme the name of the Lord because of it (Rev. 16:8, 9). Then verse eight will also be literally fulfilled: *their faces shall be as flames.* Whoever understands the great terrors of the day of the Lord — and everyone who believes the Scripture ought to understand or seek to understand them — must agree that these verses give us a picture of it. The *evil of the world* will be punished in that day as well as the *haughtiness of the terrible* tyrants. As a result of this visitation, the population will be diminished to such a degree that a man will be *more precious* i.e., *scarcer,* than fine gold (v. 12) cf. 6:8. Then we shall understand the imagery of verse fourteen where the remnant is compared to a chased, scared roe or gazelle, or to a defenseless sheep which, separated from its shepherd, wanders about searching and bleating, and at any moment may fall prey to wild animals. One flees in one direction, the other in another. They are looking for their kinsmen and country without being able to find them.

The Cruelty of the Medes

15. Every one that is found shall be thrust through; and every

one that is joined unto them shall fall by the sword.

16. Their children also shall be dashed to pieces before their eyes; their houses shall be spoiled, and their wives ravished.

17. Behold, I will stir up the Medes against them, which shall not regard silver; and as for gold, they shall not delight in it.

18. Their bows also shall dash the young men to pieces; and they shall have no pity on the fruit of the womb; their eye shall not spare children.

Cyrus himself was not cruel, but it seems that this cannot be said of his army. Especially the Medes were known to be very cruel and heartless. Whomever they found they stabbed. They snatched the babies from the arms of the Babylonian mothers and smashed them before their eyes. What the psalmist sang in Psalm 137:9 will take place. They went into houses and plundered them and raped their women. Such abominations always accompanied wars in those days; nevertheless verse seventeen says that the Medes were not after treasures. The Medes were wild and uncivilized mountain tribes who hardly knew the value of the noble metal. They were more thirsty for blood and bestial activities than for the countless treasures of Babylon. According to verse eighteen, they had no mercy on *young men, pregnant women* or *children,* but struck down all who crossed their path. Verse nineteen indicates the total collapse of all the beauty, luxury and pride of Babylon. What was once the *glory of the kingdoms* is overthrown like Sodom and Gomorrah.

Babylon Irreparably Destroyed

19. And Babylon, the glory of kingdoms, the beauty of the Chaldees' excellency, shall be as when God overthrew Sodom and Gomorrah.

20. It shall never be inhabited, neither shall it be dwelt in from generation to generation: neither shall the Arabian pitch tent there; neither shall the shepherds make their fold there.

21. But wild beasts of the desert shall lie there; and their houses shall be full of doleful creatures; and owls shall dwell there, and satyrs shall dance there.

22. And the wild beasts of the islands shall cry in their desolate houses, and dragons in their pleasant palaces: and her time is near to come, and her days shall not be prolonged.

Not much can be said with certainty of the animals mentioned here. At this juncture two thoughts can be offered: one on the strange nature of these predictions, and one on the question whether this prophecy may be considered as already having been completely fulfilled.

There is no stronger proof for the divinity of Holy Scripture than the predictions already fulfilled. It is greatly to be deplored that people in believing circles have not made use of them as crushing weapons against unbelief. Maybe this must be explained from the fact that Christendom itself was often very slow to believe all that the prophets had spoken. When modernism advanced its bold denial not only of the miracles but also of prophecy, then the former evoked rather strong protest, but seldom were the latter defended. Yet the prophecies already fulfilled should have been the strongest weapons against bold unbelief. The Christians would not only have pitched philosophical reflections against philosophical reflections but would have advanced divine and crushing facts. The predictions concerning Babylon afford a mighty weapon.

According to Scripture, Babylon was the glory of kingdoms (13:19), the golden city (14:4), abundant in treasures (Jer. 51:13) and the praise of the whole earth (Jer. 51:41). In Daniel two, Nebuchadnezzar and his kingdom are called the golden head. The city of Babylon had one hundred massive gates of shining brass, and walls that were thirty-five feet high and so wide that six chariots could ride abreast on them. When this city was at the height of its glory and was still the queen of the nations, the prophets predicted not only its total overthrow but at the same time gave the minutest details of its fall. The specific *nations* that would seize and destroy it were mentioned more than a century beforehand (21:2; Jer. 51:11). The *time* when this would take place was mentioned (Jer. 25:11, 12). The name of the *commander* is even mentioned (44:28, 45:1). The expert *manner in which* the city would be seized is repeatedly described (44:27; Jer. 50:34, 38; 51:30, 36). The *exact hour of the nightly drinking party during* the capture is specifically described by Isaiah. When it is realized that at the time of Isaiah's prophesy, the Persians were a poor and insignificant people and did not count at all in the gallery of nations, then we see clearly the finger of God. What is said of Babylon holds partially true for Egypt, Nineveh, and other nations as well.

To the question whether this prophecy has been completely fulfilled, we answer in the negative. At Babylon's overthrow the entire land was not destroyed (13:5). Nor did the day of the Lord come (v. 6). At that time, the heavenly lights were not darkened (v. 10). Babylon has never been overthrown like Sodom and Gomorrah (v. 19). The Lord did not give rest to Jacob and the whole earth (14:1-7). There has never been a king of Babylon as described in 14:4-14. On the basis of these, and other considerations, it is to be considered probable that in the end time Babylon will be restored once again, as many Bible students today believe it will be. Revelation eighteen appears to point in that direction as well. Questions do remain, but the omnipotence of the Lord can in due time solve these problems.

Finally, we will quote here what the rationalist Michaelis notes in connection with this prophecy:

> This, too, is a very remarkable illustration of prediction, and its fulfillment was at the time it was made nothing short of impossible. If Babylon were to be conquered, then we should rather think, considering the situation of Asia at that time, of the Assyrians and, next, the Egyptians who, during the reign of Pharaoh Necho, indeed advanced to the River Euphrates, or of the Ethiopians who could invade from Arabia. At that time, the Medes were not very well known on the scene of Asia; during the final year of Hezekiah they elected their first king, Deioces, since they had had no king before. This was the first and most distant preparation for the fulfillment of this prophecy, of which, on account of the scarce mutual relationships in the old world, people in Isaiah's day had no knowledge at all. Even if such communication existed, what human mind could have conceived of a united nation under Deioces that would one day destroy a powerful Babylonian monarchy that did not even yet exist?

Now if the initial fulfillment was so remarkable that it even amazed men such as Michaelis, why then should not the ultimate fulfillment be even more remarkable?

ISAIAH 14

Babylon's Downfall is Israel's Raising Up

1. For the LORD will have mercy on Jacob, and will yet choose Israel, and set them in their own land: and the strangers shall be joined with them, and they shall cleave to the house of Jacob.

2. And the people shall take them, and bring them to their place: and the house of Israel shall possess them in the land of the LORD for servants and handmaids: and they shall take them captives, whose captives they were; and they shall rule over their oppressors.

The first little word *"For"* is very significant here. It speaks of Babylon's anti-Semitism, its hatred of Jews, which is the main reason for its downfall. On the other hand, this word speaks of Jehovah's love for Israel. Let us briefly point out a few things, for we shall have frequent opportunity to refer to Israel's restoration: (a) God will go out with His mighty warriors to do battle against Babylon and destroy it utterly, *for* as the faithful Covenant Jehovah He will have mercy on Jacob, the sly and deceitful nation. (b) He will yet *choose* Israel. Scripture often calls the reacceptance of Israel a *choosing* (see Zech. 1:17; 2:12). (c) He will set them *in their own land.* All the prophets in one way or another end with this promise of territorial restoration. Jonah alone symbolizes it in his own life and so does not speak of it. We only have to take the trouble to read attentively the last parts of the so-called Minor Prophets and it would be very evident whether the Jews will be taken to their own land again. (d) *Strangers* will join Jacob. This too is continuously taught by Scripture (2:3; 11:14; 44:5; 49:23; 60:2-12; 66:12). These are but a few references in this book which teach it clearly and incontestably. (e) *Anti-Semitism,* with which all nations in ages past were affected, will one day disappear. The day will come when Israel will no longer be despised and oppressed, but will be *accepted* and helped so that this miraculous people will be brought back to Canaan. God-fearing expositors have been for a long time of the opinion that Isaiah eighteen points to some great navigational power that will take Israel back to its own land. (f) Then Israel shall begin to rule over the nations of the world. The roles will be reversed. The former rulers will become servants and the former servants, once despised and rejected, will then be the rulers of the whole world. Oh, if people would only believe this! How much better would they understand the Word and the significant signs of our times!

The Satirical Song on the King of Babylon

> 3. And it shall come to pass in the day that the LORD shall give thee rest from thy sorrow, and from thy fear, and from the hard bondage wherein thou wast made to serve,
> 4. That thou shalt take up this proverb against the king of Babylon, and say, How hath the oppressor ceased! the golden city ceased!
> 5. The LORD hath broken the staff of the wicked, and the sceptre of the rulers.

Who is this king of Babylon? To this it can be answered that no matter to what extent Nebuchadnezzar is included in this concept, it must not be limited to him as most expositors do. For the powerful terms used here can in no way be applied to the fall of Nebuchadnezzar. For at that time the *staff of the wicked* and the *sceptre of the rulers* were not broken; No *rest, peace* and *joy* were poured out over the whole earth (v. 7). This will take place, however, literally and exactly, at the return of our Savior. For that reason, the downfall of the final, great and abominable king of Babylon, the first beast described in Revelation thirteen the head of the restored Roman Empire is in view here (cf. the little horn of Daniel seven). In order to depict their emotions, whether it be a matter of sadness or of joy, the prophets often present a song of lamentation or of triumph which frequently ridicules the enemy. The latter is the case here. Van der Palm calls it one of the most beautiful vestiges of Hebrew poetry.

Verses five and six sing of the fall of the oppressor as an object of amazement. It sounds to us as though we can hear the sighs of those under his reign change into sighs of relief because of his fall.

The Peace and Joy of the Kingdom of Peace

6. He who smote the people in wrath with a continual stroke, he that ruled the nations in anger, is persecuted, and none hindereth.
7. The whole earth is at rest, and is quiet: they break forth into singing.
8. Yea, the fir trees rejoice at thee, and the cedars of Lebanon, saying, Since thou art laid down, no feller is come up against us.

All expositors are full of praise for the beauty of the song in this chapter, of which the first verses form a fitting introduction and conjunction. Calvin calls it a fruit of Isaiah's Oriental poetic genius. Umbreit calls it a satire that is so striking, so bold, so terribly exalted that he cannot name another like it. He calls it cutting and at the same time as quiet as a peaceful evening after a fierce blizzard has raged all day through the world. Van Hamelsveld calls it a song that exceeds in beauty and art all other poems of Isaiah. Lowth says:

What a song! I believe that we may state with certainty that in no other language of whatever name exists a poem of this nature and in which the subject is so eminently organized; and, in such a brief form, is so well worked out with such a wealth of turns, with such a variety of images, persons and changing action, with such an enviable ease in its transitions, thoroughly worked out, as in this majestic ode. With regard to exactness of lines, vitality of color, clearness and truth and power of expression, it has no rival among all the writings of antiquity!

And Ten Kate calls it "a masterpiece of imagination, composition and execution."

All this has been beautifully stated, and we can also learn from this that from the standpoint of *aesthetics* the Bible soars above all the books of the world. Whoever wishes to practice the art of poetry ought to go first of all to the prince among Israel's prophets. But do we have only beautiful and exalted poetry that merely sings of a proud monarch of early antiquity and therefore has little more than poetic and historic value? We think not! On the contrary, we believe that in this strikingly beautiful and exalted poetry we have at the same time divine *truth* that one day will become fully divine *reality, i.e.,* the whole earth, which presently is still vexed with unrest and rebellion, will be at *rest.* The present clatter of weapons and the roaring of the nations will make a place for holy quietude. The nations, which now bleed from a thousand wounds and cause rivers of blood and tears to flow, will one day truly *break forth into singing.* It is known from Revelation nineteen that the heavens will resound with joy over the fall of the last Babylon. Also, the earth will have no less reason to rejoice. Thus, it is infallibly predicted here that after the fall of Babylon's king has hardly been announced, the world will be caught up in the ecstasy of joy which is even shared by the trees of Lebanon. Says Umbriet,

> It sounds great and overwhelming when cypresses and cedars rustle in the storm of joy, but greater still is the meaning of this forest song from on high falling on the prophet's ear: *Since thou art laid down,* no one comes up to us any more to hew us down.

On the eastern slope of Lebanon pine trees grew, on the western slope cedars. Both kinds of trees are presented as rejoicing in the downfall of their destroyer. In war, trees are usually destroyed whether for the purpose of hurting the enemy or out of necessity for use as fuel. (But, cf. God's command to Israel in Deut. 20:19, 20.) From history it is known that Nebuchadnezzar, as king of Babylon, utilized the trees of Lebanon as building material. All of creation is still groaning because of man's sin, but after the fall of the world powers it will be completely set free.

The Arrival of the King in the Realm of the Dead

9. Hell from beneath is moved for thee to meet thee at thy coming: it stirreth up the dead for thee, even all the chief ones of

the earth; it hath raised up from their thrones all the kings of the nations.

10. All they shall speak and say unto thee, Art thou also become weak as we? art thou become like unto us?

11. Thy pomp is brought down to the grave, and the noise of thy viols: the worm is spread under thee, and the worms cover thee.

The fall of the tyrant was first a subject of general astonishment, then of joy and here of commotion and ridicule in the realm of the dead. The word here for *hell* is *sheol.* It appears very often in the Old Testament, but its meaning is by no means clear and obvious to everyone. Some think it refers to the place of the damned, hell with its eternal fire; but the old translators have wisely translated it with *grave* or *pit* in the following places: Genesis 37:35; 42:38; I Kings 2:6, 9; Job. 7:9; 14:13; 17:13; 21:13; 24:19; Psalm 6:5; 30:3; 31:17; 49:14, 15; 88:3; 89:48; 141:7, Proverbs 1:12; 30:16; Ecclesiastes 9:10; Song of Solomon 8:6; Isaiah 38:10, 18. In most of these instances, the translation *hell* as the place of the damned would not be possible since some passages refer to believers going down to *sheol.* Jacob most certainly did not expect to descend into hell. Job most certainly did not pray to be allowed to hide in hell (Job. 14:13), nor did the prayerful *Heman* and *Ethan* entertain the expectation of going to the place of the damned (Ps. 88:3, 89:48). Others insist that this word *always* means *grave,* but when one checks all the instances where the word is used, it is soon evident that this simply won't do. Korah and his mutinous gang are told that they will *descend into hell (sheol) alive* (Num. 16:30), which certainly does not mean that they would be lying in the grave alive. Moses sang that God's anger would burn unto the lowest hell *(sheol).* This certainly does not mean the grave. The same is true of such references as Job 10:21; 21:13; Psalm 9:17, 18; Proverbs 5:5; 9:18; 23:14. And also such texts as Numbers 16:30, 33; Deuteronomy 32:22; I Kings 2:6, 9; Psalm 49:14, 15, and Isaiah 5:14, even though they also include the grave, cannot have reference to it only, since the idea of punishment and pain are most closely connected with it.

Taking all aspects into consideration, it can be said that

sheol is a very broad and flexible idea which stands for the following concepts: the subterranean realm of the dead, the spirit underworld, the realm of the spirits, the gathering place of the deceased, the grave and the place of the lost who are locked up there to endure dreadful misery. Job calls *sheol* the land of darkness and the shadow of death (Job. 10:21). From Amos 9:2 it is evident that *sheol* was considered an underworld beneath or deep in the earth. According to Psalm 16:10 David had been there, too, and it was not only the sorrows of *sheol* that struck him there (Ps. 116:3). Also from Psalm 139:8 and Proverbs 5:5 and 15:24 it is evident that *sheol* was thought to be below in contrast with heaven which is always thought to be on high. Similarly here in verse nine the prophet speaks of *sheol from beneath.* He does not mean the lowest part of *sheol* but *sheol that is under the earth.* From our preceding remarks, it is more than evident that *sheol* as such indicates no more than a neutral underworld into which the godly as well as the wicked descend at death. *It is the intermediate state of all bodiless persons, but where the wicked experience pain and sorrow and the righteous, on the other hand, peace and bliss, awaiting the day of resurrection.* So both the above-mentioned ideas are wrong and do not do justice to the broad concept of *sheol.*

It need not be argued that *sheol* in verse nine means the place of initial punishment, which one day, at the resurrection of the wicked when they will rise to shame and everlasting contempt, will be greatly increased. *Sheol,* which is frequently represented as the realm of fearful silence, becomes extremely excited at the arrival of the king of Babylon. *All the he-goats of the earth* (Dutch) are *all the chief ones of the earth* (KVJ). Usually, in the Orient, a he-goat or bellwether led the flocks. This is why mighty commanders, princes or other leaders are often compared to such he-goats or rams in Scripture (see also 60:7; Ezek. 34:17; Micah 2:12, 13; Zech. 10:3). Thus, the erstwhile powerful leaders and kings of the nations are stirred by the arrival of the tyrant to get up from their seats to greet him with astonishment, ridicule and scorn. Whereas they had flattered him as a mighty lord before, now they mock him, for he is no longer their lord but has become like them. They emphasize this equality to hurt him; they ridicule him with his haughtiness, his music and song — culture! — which have descended with him into *sheol.* Your bed has been made for you, they cry to him, a bed of *maggots* and a cover of worms. Gone is his golden chariot; gone also is his royal robe of embroidered sheets.

From this picture it is evident that the concept *sheol* in the sense of a place of punishment and *sheol* in the sense of the grave are not strictly separated. One can hardly think of worms or maggots being anywhere else but in the grave of decomposition. But we also see in this horrible representation what it will mean one day to have to be in the company of the lost. The wicked often slavishly and cringingly flatter each other here on earth, even though they hate each other; but below in the place of punishment they will reveal themselves in their true hatefulness. All masks and semblances will be discarded there and there will be no longer similated love and subservience.

Satan Fallen from Heaven

12. How art thou fallen from heaven, O Lucifer, son of the morning! how art thou cut down to the ground, which didst weaken the nations!

13. For thou hast said in thine heart, I will ascend into heaven, I will exalt my throne above the stars of God: I will sit also upon the mount of the congregation, in the sides of the north:

14. I will ascend above the heights of the clouds; I will be like the most High.

15. Yet thou shalt be brought down to hell, to the sides of the pit.

Together with a long list of respected students of Scripture such as Scofield, Gray, Gaebelein, Jennings, Blackstone, Wertheimer and others, we believe that we are dealing here with no one less than Satan, of whom the king of Babylon was and will be, but an instrument. Just as the king of Tyrus in Ezekiel 28:12-16 is represented as a type of Satan, so is the king of Babylon here. Just as in the former text his greatness and fall are described, so it is here. Once he shone in heaven as a light-bearer, the *son of the morning, i.e.,* one who had the substance of light of the beautiful dawn. But alas, as a brilliant star he has been slung from heaven to earth, there to become a deceiver and oppressor of the nations (cf. Luke 10:18; Rev. 12:9; 20:1-10). Verse thirteen points to his pride as the cause of his fall, as do Ezekiel twenty-eight and other texts. He did not merely want to become like unto God but even surpass God in glory.

The final clause of verse thirteen is very difficult.

What is the *mount of the congregation in the sides of the north?* Certainly not, as some have thought, the temple mount of Moriah. Calvin translates *mount of the covenant,* and says, "Meant is, at any rate, Mt. Zion, which in Psalm 48:2 is called the mountain of God's glory and which is said to be situated on the sides of the north." But it is obvious that the language used here transports us to much higher regions. Others explain this clause from mythology, the teaching of the ancients concerning the gods. They say that just as the Greeks pictured their gods congregating on Mt. Olympus, so the ancient Orientals pictured the place of the assembly of the gods on a very high mountain in the north. And perhaps inspired by the northern lights, they pictured these mountains as mountains of light, just as we still imagine the celestial beings and everything connected with heaven to be in the form of light. It is true that there have existed such ideas in the myths and fables of the ancient Oriental nations, but the question is whether Scripture utilizes this idea in this expression. We are of the opinion that this question must decidedly be answered in the negative. Thus, Calvin's explanation is to be preferred. Finally, there are exegetes today who claim that this is actually a local indication of the heaven of glory, the dwelling place of the celestial beings. Although the arguments for this position are not convincing, one dares not reject the idea since the immediate context forces one to think of some place of glory. Maybe the mysterious and grand phenomenon of the northern lights, which can fill the heart with wonderment, is a pale reflection of the immaculate light of heaven.

The general idea of these verses is very clear, however, Satan, who wanted to be like God, indeed wanted to surpass God, was cast to the earth. Verse fifteen tells us, however, that he will not remain on earth but be thrust down into *sheol, to the sides of the pit.* If pit is taken to mean *grave,* we have another indication that *sheol* must be taken to mean the place of the punishment of hell. When everything that Scripture says about Satan is compared, it becomes evident that he will reach his final destination in a fourfold fall. First, he was cast out from the third heaven — where manifestly, before the countenance of God, he sinned — into the spacial heavens; here he still is and remains until the Rapture of the Church. Then, his second fall will take place from the heavens to the earth, where he will manifest his great wrath for a short time (cf. Rev. 12:12). Then, the man of sin will come after the working of Satan (II Thess. 2:9). Christ comes to earth, Antichrist comes to earth and Satan comes to earth. Oh, that the inhabitants of earth might take this to heart! From earth, Satan will be locked up in the abyss for a thousand years. Finally, he will be cast into the lake of fire, which is the ultimate hell. Scripture teaches these things clearly, and who knows how near at hand these terrible things already are. We ought to be found daily praying and watching, lest this day come upon us unawares!

Babylon's King is Deprived of the Honor of a Burial

16. They that see thee shall narrowly look upon thee, and consider thee, saying, Is this the man that made the earth to tremble, that did shake kingdoms;

17. That made the world as a wilderness, and destroyed the cities thereof; that opened not the house of his prisoners?

18. All the kings of the nations, even all of them, lie in glory, every one in his own house.

19. But thou art cast out of thy grave like an abominable branch, and as the raiment of those that are slain, thrust through with a sword, that go down to the stones of the pit; as a carcase trodden under feet.

20. Thou shalt not be joined with them in burial, because thou hast destroyed thy land, and slain thy people: the seed of evildoers shall never be renowned.

21. Prepare slaughter for his children for the iniquity of their fathers; that they do not rise, nor possess the land, nor fill the face of the world with cities.

22. For I will rise up against them, saith the LORD of hosts, and cut off from Babylon the name, and remnant, and son, and nephew, saith the LORD.

23. I will also make it a possession for the bittern, and pools of water: and I will sweep it with the besom of destruction, saith the LORD of hosts.

These words contain a further explanation of the expression *to the sides of the pit,* which prevented us from thinking that *sheol* in this instance was the same as the grave. Babylon's ruler was in *sheol* but not in a grave. We must imagine the corpse of the king — and this time apparently Belshazzar is meant — as lying among other corpses, contemptuously thrown away. Afterward it is discovered, however, that it is the corpse of the king. In the surprise attack on Babylon and Belshazzar, in that memorable night so incomparably described by Daniel, it was quite possible that he, together with the corpses of others slain in battle, was contemptuously thrown away on a heap and that no one recognized him as the king.

Later, the victors make this discovery and are seized by astonishment and cry out in amazement: *Is this the man that made the earth to tremble, that did shake kingdoms; that made the world as a wilderness, and destroyed the cities thereof; that opened not the house of his prisoners?* This, of course, refers to captured Judah. Nebuchadnezzar, too, had shown no mercy to the wretched of the Lord (Dan. 4:27). Both Nebuchadnezzar and Belshazzar were anti-Semites. From of old it was a terrible dishonor not to be buried. This is why the people, staring at the remains of the king, lying there before them as a prey to decomposition, say *All the kings of the nations, even all of them, lie in glory, every one in his own (memorial) house.* But he has been cast far away from his tomb as an *abominable branch, i.e.,* as someone who indeed is a royal offspring, but a shoot, a sprout, a branch that is broken off and disdainfully thrown away.

Here we have the perfect contrast with the *shoot* from Jesse's root (11:1). He lies there covered by the other slain surrounding him from every side; they are not thought worthy of burial either but are thrown into a deep stone pit. This is described in such disdainful words that it is as though people are walking on his corpse and trampling it flat. The latter comparison puts the crown on all the preceding ones, says Calvin, for a corpse cannot be treated more disdainfully than by trampling it into the ground. We are reminded of the words spoken by Jeremiah regarding King Jehoiakim: "He shall be buried with the burial of an ass, drawn and cast forth beyond the gates of Jerusalem (Jer. 22:19)." He will not be buried with the kings of the nations, since he has destroyed the land and slain his people. His descendants are exterminated, for God commands his children to be slaughtered because of the iniquity of their fathers. From this, we can infer that these children were in agreement with their father. This slaughter is not only the execution of judgment but at the same time a gracious preventative act. For God prevents this wicked generation from filling the world with *cities* or their *ruins.* The prophet introduces God speaking solemnly and predicting Babylon's complete overthrow. As with a broom, He will sweep away all the glory of Babylon. Only night owls and pools will remain.

The Breaking of Assyria on the Mountains of Israel

24. The LORD of hosts hath sworn, saying, Surely as I have thought, so shall it come to pass; and as I have purposed, so it shall stand:
25. That I will break the Assyrian in my land, and upon my mountains tread him under foot: then shall his yoke depart from off them, and his burden depart from off their shoulders.
26. This is the purpose that is purposed upon the whole earth: and this is the hand that is stretched out upon all the nations.
27. For the LORD of hosts hath purposed, and who shall disannul it? and his hand is stretched out, and who shall turn it back?

The scenes keep changing constantly and sometimes very abruptly with the prophets. This chapter, in particular, is an example of that. For after having depicted Belshazzar's downfall, Jehovah is not, as some think, confirming with an oath, what was said concerning Babylon, but that which was said earlier concerning Assyria (cf. 10:33). This text is fully explained in the extensive description of Ezekiel thirty-eight and thirty-nine. Those chapters speak for themselves. In the end time there will be an alliance of northeastern nations, which after Israel's initial restoration, will advance on this nation in the holy land to extract great booty from her prosperity. Then Jerusalem will be attacked and oppressed for the last time. When the calamity has reached its zenith, the Lord Himself will descend with His angels and saints to execute judgment on Gog's hordes. There, too, shall take place the last great battle, near the mountains of Megiddo. God is the Warrior who has decided in His counsel. Who can frustrate this counsel? His hand is stretched out in anger upon the nations that hate the Jews; who then can turn His hand back and say: what doest Thou? The downfall of Assyria will be the deliverance of Judah (v. 25).

Prophecy Against the Philistines

28. In the year that king Ahaz died was this burden.
29. Rejoice not thou, whole Palestine, because the rod of him that smote thee is broken: for out of the serpent's root shall come forth a cockatrice, and his fruit shall be a fiery flying serpent.
30. And the firstborn of the poor shall feed, and the needy shall lie down in safety: and I will kill thy root with famine, and he shall slay thy remnant.
31. Howl, O gate; cry, O city; thou whole Palestina, art dissolved: for there shall come from the north a smoke, and none shall be alone in his appointed times.
32. What shall one then answer the messengers of the nation? That the LORD hath founded Zion, and the poor of his people shall trust in it.

The judgment against the world power of that time, Babylon, heads the cycle of predictions against the foreign nations. Now it is the turn of the nations closest to Judah. The name *Palestina* is derived from the country of the Philistines. This is what is meant here and not the entire land of Canaan. First, the *time* of this prophecy is given as the year when King Ahaz died. This *burden,* like the preceding ones, is connected with events in Isaiah's own day. The main thought is this: The Philistines must not rejoice in the downfall of David's house, for one day they will be destroyed by it. The purpose is to warn against an alliance with the Philistines to protect themselves against Assyria. A common explanation of this difficult *burden* is that the *rod* is identified with Ahaz, the *serpent's root, i.e.,* its body, with the house of David on account of its deterioration due to the misgovernment by Ahaz; the *cockatrice* with King Hezekiah who subjugated the Philistines, and finally, the *flying serpent* with the Messiah. Hitzig, Ewald, Knobel, Umbreit and Ridderbos think that with this brood of vipers Assyria is meant as the enemy that will bite the Philistines. After much hesitation, it seems to us that this is the most acceptable interpretation. The broken rod is not Ahaz, but the deep decline of David's house. The mighty Uzziah had beaten the Philistines severely (II Chr. 26:6). His death must have occasioned great joy to these uncircumcised heathen. And now that Ahaz had died, and His successor was still a mere boy, this must have increased their joy. But from the root of the serpent, that deeply degenerated house, a cockatrice would come forth. This refers to Hezekiah who smote them even more than his grandfather Uzziah (II Kings 18:8). The *(fiery) flying serpent* refers to Christ, who will be an even more dangerous enemy to them. In the desert, Christ had been represented as a serpent (Num. 21:9; John 3:14). The serpent is the symbol of the curse. It is represented here as the punitive justice to all nations that hate Israel. The fruit of Christ's coming and reign will be that the *firstborn of the poor, i.e.,* the poorest of Judah's poor, will have peace and prosperity and lie down like a flock of sheep. This is undoubtedly an allusion to the poor Jewish shepherds who lived near the border of the Philistines and who had to suffer most from the invasions of the uncircumcised hordes.

Verse thirty contains a glorious contrast. Against the superabundance of the very poor in Judah is placed the prediction of death by famine for the arrogant Philistines. Even their *remnant* will be slain by the enemy of verse thirty-one. At the same time, there is the contrast between the *root* of the Davidic house which one day will gloriously revive and obtain great power causing the *root* of the Philistines to wither completely.

Hence, not just a single calamity will befall the Philistines but a double one. This proud nation will be visited not only by Judah but also by the final great enemy from the north, Assyria. Initially this may have already been fulfilled by

Tiglath-pileser who penetrated as far as Gaza. But we are of the opinion that this prediction will also be fully fulfilled in the end time. Instead of having malicious pleasure at the misfortune of Judah, the Philistine people will howl on account of the enemy that will crush them. They will melt before this enemy like snow before the sun. The prophet already sees the clouds of smoke arising against the horizon. The expression *none shall be alone in his appointed times* means that when the army camps, there will not be a single soldier who deserts. It will not be a disorderly troop that advances upon them, but a well-trained army of disciplined soldiers. Jennings correctly translates this expression, "No straggler is there, 'tis a well-ordered band.' "

In mount Zion and in Jerusalem shall be deliverance (Joel 2:32; Obad. 17). What a pity that by spiritualizing this statement it has been made so meaningless! For how few believers today can tell what this really means, since this statement clearly points to a definite delivery at a definite time and place. When in the day of Christ's coming Assyria will rage and the Antichrist will play havoc, there will be deliverance from their raging on Mt. Zion and in Jerusalem. We are also reminded of the 144,000 on Mt. Zion of Revelation 14:1, the escapees of the rampage of the two beasts. This glorious fact also fully explains verse thirty-two, which usually is reduced to a beautifully sounding phrase.

It is quite possible and even very likely that also in Isaiah's day messengers from the Philistines came to Jerusalem to urge Judah to participate in an anti-Assyrian coalition, as Dr. Ridderbos thinks. It is also certain that this prophet of God must have resisted such a league of nations, for we already saw in chapter eight that Jehovah emphatically warned him against the federation movements which were prominent in his time. It is most certain, however, that the oppressed of His people will one day have a safe place of refuge in Zion.

ISAIAH 15

The Burden of Moab

1. The burden of Moab. Because in the night Ar of Moab is laid waste and brought to silence; because in the night Kir of Moab is laid waste, and brought to silence;

2. He is gone up to Bajith, and to Dibon, the high places, to weep: Moab shall howl over Nebo, and over Medeba: on all their heads shall be baldness, and every beard cut off.

3. In their streets they shall gird themselves with sackcloth: on the tops of their houses, and in their streets, every one shall howl, weeping abundantly.

4. And Heshbon shall cry, and Elealeh: their voice shall be heard even unto Jahaz: therefore the armed soldiers of Moab shall cry out; his life shall be grievous unto him.

5. My heart shall cry out for Moab; his fugitives shall flee unto Zoar, an heifer of three years old: for by the mounting up of Luhith with weeping shall they go it up; for in the way of Horonaim they shall raise up a cry of destruction.

6. For the waters of Nimrim shall be desolate: for the hay is withered away, the grass faileth, there is no green thing.

7. Therefore the abundance they have gotten, and that which they have laid up, shall they carry away to the brook of the willows.

8. For the cry is gone round about the borders of Moab; the howling thereof unto Eglaim, and the howling thereof unto Beer-elim.

9. For the waters of Dimon shall be full of blood: for I will bring more upon Dimon, lions upon him that escapeth of Moab, and upon the remnant of the land.

The burden of Moab, in this and the next chapter, is described in the most pitiful and melancholy language. The Moabites descended from Lot and so were related to Israel, but they were always filled with animosity against Israel. According to 16:13 this prophecy had been pronounced against Moab long ago, but here it is brought closer; it will be fulfilled within three years (16:14). Moab will be destroyed in the night, unexpectedly and suddenly. This will happen so surely that the prophet in his lively style speaks as though it has already become an accomplished fact.

He paints a very sad picture of the Moabites. *Ar of Moab* is the capital, which elsewhere is also called *Rabbah of the Moabites,* the front wall of the country. For the rest of the places mentioned here Calvin says: "We shall not dwell on the location of the places mentioned in these verses; of some of them it is unknown." *Bajith* means temple and *Dibon, the high places.* Isaiah presents the inhabitants of Moab as fleeing in their distress to their sanctuaries. When people are in great distress, they often flee to their places of prayer. Only in the general sense is it true that dire circumstances teach people to pray.

The Moabites were in such great distress that they caused the entire country to resound with their howling. As a sign of their mourning and grief, the women cut off their braids, while the men in their bitterness of soul plucked out their beards. In all the streets and on all the roads, people were running about in sackcloth. Everyone was howling — men, women and children, throughout the entire country. Even the *armed soldiers* of Moab, *i.e.,* the well-equipped army, could offer no help and cried themselves with vexation of spirit. The warriors had lost heart completely. Together with the others, they were suddenly overrun and could not turn back this assault on their homeland. We see that militarism easily disappoints. "There is no king saved by the multitude of an host: a mighty man is not delivered by much strength. Behold, the eye of the Lord is upon them that fear him, upon them that hope in his mercy."

My heart shall cry out for Moab. This short, full sentence affords us a look into the depths of Isaiah's soul. It tells us that this royal spirit was at the same time a man of deep feelings and sympathy. Moab was not his people. In fact, it had often plagued his land and people. But now that he observes the wretched condition of that nation his soul is deeply grieved and he laments as if he were one of them. Moab's *fugitives* flee to *Zoar,* the little town that was once a place of refuge for Lot, the ancestor of the Moabites. This town is called *an heifer of three years old,* apparently to indicate that it had never been under the yoke of strangers.

Because of the tradition regarding its ancestor, this town apparently had a good name. Maybe it was always considered as an asylum, a safe place of refuge. The people were so perplexed because the enemy had destroyed the water conduits and springs, filling them with sand which was usually done in wars. The result of this dastardly deed was that all the grass, herbs and green vegetables perished and withered from drought (v. 6). The accumulated treasures and that which the enemy had left them are hidden near the brook of the willows, so that the enemy would not rob these precious possessions. The Brook Dimon, which flowed through Moab, was colored red from all the blood that was spilled in that memorable night. However, still another calamity would strike Moab. Even its *remnant of the land* would not be spared but torn to pieces by lions. The text actually speaks only of one *lion,* so that we obviously must think of some mighty enemy, whether *Nebuchadnezzar,* or Hezekiah or maybe even the great Son of David, the Lion from the tribe of Judah.

ISAIAH 16

Good Advice Given to the Desperate Moabites

> 1. Send ye the lamb to the ruler of the land from Sela to the wilderness, unto the mount of the daughter of Zion.
> 2. For it shall be, that, as a wandering bird cast out of the nest, so the daughters of Moab shall be at the fords of Arnon.

On the basis of an incorrect translation by the Vulgate, some Catholic exegetes consider verse one a Messianic prophecy. The Vulgate has this translation: "Send the Lamb, O Lord, the Ruler of the earth, from Petra in the desert to the mount of the daughter of Zion." Also the Lutheran theologian Joseph Seiss in his famous *Exposition of Revelation* has defended this view. Calvin takes it as irony in the sense of: "Send as many lambs as you wish as sacrifices to Jehovah, to Zion's sanctuary, but it will not avail you; it is too late; your repentance is but hypocrisy!" But there is practically no basis for this interpretation either. On the contrary, we have just seen that the prophet was extremely moved with pity on Moab and cried out with them. So it would be strange indeed if he now were to mock Moab, even if in holy mockery. It is better to take it to mean that the Moabites had not paid their tribute of lambs to Judah and that this had resulted in some alienation between the two nations. Whereas they are now in the greatest misery, Isaiah advises them to send up their lambs to Judah as a proof of their renewed tributary obligations. He clearly indicates that with this advice he has their own well-being at heart. For if they refuse, they will soon experience the bitter results. Struck with severe punishment, the daughters of Moab will wander about at the fords of Arnon like young birds cast out of their downy nest. There was a similar image in chapter ten.

In case the Moabites might fear that Judah was adamant and would refuse to send help in their misery, the prophet shows that he is wholly inclined and ready to be an intercessor for Moab with his own people, as will be seen in verse three. The man of God indeed interceded powerfully on behalf of the poor refugees from Moab who in their perplexity did not know where to turn.

Isaiah Pleads for Moab with His People

3. Take counsel, execute judgment; make thy shadow as the night in the midst of the noonday; bewray not him that wandereth.

It is strange indeed that Calvin still thinks of mockery in this verse, for it is just the opposite. The prophet tried with all his might to move Moab to seek the friendship of Judah. Now he is doing his utmost to move his own people to give counsel to the desperate refugees from Moab. *Take counsel* means: decide in a judicial manner what must be done with them. He further admonishes the elders of his people to *make thy shadow as the night in the midst of the noonday,* which means that they must give shelter and protection in the heat of the oppression that now engulfs Moab. He also warns them not to deliver these poor wanderers treacherously into the hands of their enemies.

The Only Hope for Moab

4. Let mine outcasts dwell with thee, Moab; be thou a covert to them from the face of the spoiler: for the extortioner is at an end, the spoiler ceaseth, the oppressors are consumed out of the land.
5. And in mercy shall the throne be established: and he shall sit upon it in truth in the tabernacle of David, judging, and seeking judgment, and hasting righteousness.

It is difficult to decide who is the speaker and who are the ones addressed in these verses. According to Lowth, Eichhorn, Gesenius, Noyes, Dachsel, Ridderbos and others, the Moabites in verse four are beseeching Judah to afford them refuge, as they did in the preceding verse. But apparently we have here one of those sudden changes of subject which is often found in Isaiah and the prophets. Whereas he has just pleaded for Moab with Judah, now at the beginning of this verse he addresses Moab again and requests of her — he constantly portrays Moab as a woman — a place of refuge for Israel's outcasts. According to the nature of divine predictions, we are of the opinion that with the *spoiler* he is thinking of the final great enemy of Israel, the man of sin. We may take the *oppressor* to mean the last king from the north, usually indicated as Assyria; the *spoiling,* the Great Tribulation of Israel, and the *oppressors,* the armies of Gog and Armageddon. There are only a few expositors, and they are all of more recent date, who think of the last days of the Great Tribulation in connection with these and similar predictions. But this is totally in accordance with the nature of prophecy. Already there have been many examples and there will be more to come proving that the prophets never stayed within the circumstances of their own day or of the immediate future. But they always looked ahead to the great day of the Lord and its implications. Thus other places in Scripture teach us that in the end time Moab will again play an important role (11:14, 25:10-12, Dan. 11:41).

The reason why the *oppressors* will be consumed out of the land is indicated in verse five. Calvin says that this verse is one of the most significant in the whole Old Testament, as it contains a striking reflection of the kingdom of the Savior. He calls it an absurdity to apply this verse to Hezekiah. This is correct, for both the immediate context and the words themselves point to no one less than the Messiah. Ridderbos in his *The Messiah King in Isaiah's Prophecy* quite correctly observes that the well-known Messianic attributes, righteousness and justice, are ascribed here to the expected King, and he refers thereby to 9:6; 11:4; (cf. 32:1-4; Dan. 2:44; Luke 1:33). At times Hezekiah's throne shook before the Sennacheribs, and was not firm and established, nor did this righteous ruler consume the *oppressors* out of the earth. On the contrary, Hezekiah by his sin of pride became the reason why Judah was carried off to Babylon when the *times of the Gentiles* began under Nebuchadnezzar. So with the fullest justification one may think here of the future Messianic King.

Moab's Pride Goes Before Its Fall

6. We have heard of the pride of Moab; he is very proud: even of his haughtiness, and his pride, and his wrath: but his lies shall not be so.

7. Therefore shall Moab howl for Moab, every one shall howl: for the foundations of Kir-hareseth shall ye mourn; surely they are stricken.

8. For the fields of Heshbon languish, and the vine of Sibmah: the lords of the heathen have broken down the principal plants thereof, they are come even unto Jazer, they wandered through the wilderness: her branches are stretched out, they are gone over the sea.

Even though Moab had been advised to seek help from Zion's King, the seer foresaw at the same time the futility of this advice on account of Moab's pride. Whenever pride is not broken by humility, it will have to be broken by justice. For that reason the prophet continues to give a vivid picture of the judgment threatened earlier. Moab's pride is depicted in six words and is indicated as the true reason for its downfall. The words *his lies shall not be so* are translated and explained in a great variety of ways. Luther: "Pride and anger — the greater its power"; Van Ess: "His speech is not true"; De Wette: "the vanity of his boastings"; Calvin: "But his vain lying language will turn out badly"; the Vulgate, followed by the Catholic expositors: "His pride and hatred surpass his strength;" The Septuagint: "Not so is thy prediction, not so;" Michaelis: "His prophets spoke against the truth, against the truth;" Umbreit: "The indefensibility of his lies;" Van der Palm: "The falsehood of his lying prophets;" Van Hamelsveld: "His flattery is deceit and not meant uprightly;" Delitzsch: "The falsehood of his speech;" Barnes: "Vain are his self-confident boastings;" Jennings: "Yet how vain are his pratings." In the same vein are all the newer translations, and it seems to us that these renditions and explanations are the only tenable ones. Where there is great pride, there is always great boasting on the part of the false prophets. Undoubtedly they encouraged Moab in its flagrant pride. But when judgment suddenly struck with destruction as a whirlwind, all the soothing words of the leaders proved to be vanity and lies. Verses seven and eight point again at the total destruction of Moab. Moab had luxuriant vineyards. They are picturesquely presented as spreading their vines in a twisting manner through the desert and even across the sea. But the *lords of the heathen,* the kings of the nations, have uprooted these precious vineyards. So everything Moab prided itself on was destroyed.

The Prophet Bewails Moab's Downfall

9. Therefore I will bewail with the weeping of Jazer the vine of Sibmah: I will water thee with my tears, O Heshbon, and Elealeh: for the shouting for thy summer fruits and for thy harvest is fallen.

10. And gladness is taken away, and joy out of the plentiful field; and in the vineyards there shall be no singing, neither shall there be shouting: the treaders shall tread out no wine in their presses; I have made their vintage shouting to cease.

11. Wherefore my bowels shall sound like an harp for Moab, and mine inward parts for Kir-haresh.

12. And it shall come to pass, when it is seen that Moab is weary on the high place, that he shall come to his sanctuary to pray; but he shall not prevail.

13. This is the word that the LORD hath spoken concerning Moab since that time.

14. But now the LORD hath spoken, saying, Within three years, as the years of an hireling, and the glory of Moab shall be condemned, with all that great multitude; and the remnant shall be very small and feeble.

When the man of God beheld all the destruction of Moab, his heart fainted, just as it did in 15:5, causing him to break forth into a very sensitive lamentation. He no longer hears the happy harvest song of the grape pickers and treaders as before. Everything was destroyed; all joy had left and the festive song of all had died. The prophet pictures it as though his tears have sprinkled on all their past glory. His bowels rumble with pity for Moab and sound like an aeolian harp. When reading these songs of Lamentations, it must be remembered that Orientals were much more passionate than the phlegmatic Westerners. Meanwhile, Isaiah had all the more reason to lament because the people rejected Zion's

King. In their grief, they turned to Moab's idols which could not offer any help (v. 12).

Within Three Years Moab Will Fall

Verse thirteen contains the divine confirmation of this prophecy of which the main content had already been predicted by Balaam, Numbers 24:17. This remarkable prophecy reads: "I shall see him, but not now: I shall behold him, but not nigh: there shall come a Star out of Jacob, and a Sceptre shall rise out of Israel, and shall smite the corners of Moab, and destroy all the children of Sheth" — the children of rebellion (Num. 24:17). In order to understand these two chapters and all the threatenings against Moab correctly, one has to return again and again to this remarkable Messianic prophecy. For what was indicated there is further developed in verse five in this chapter. One day the Moabites will have to meet and face the great King of the Jews, seated on David's throne in Jerusalem. Verse fourteen drives the threatening prediction made earlier closer to home. Within three years, as the years of a hireling were counted, Moab's glory will have turned to contemptuousness, no matter how great its populous *multitude.* Still, there would be a small remnant, but very *small,* very *few,* and very *feeble.* Since we do not know for sure when this threat was pronounced, we cannot indicate the exact time of the destruction. We can be certain, however, that this prediction was promptly fulfilled within three years for His Word is ever faithfully fulfilled.

ISAIAH 17

The Burden of Damascus and Ephraim

> 1. The burden of Damascus. Behold, Damascus is taken away from being a city, and it shall be a ruinous heap.
> 2. The cities of Aroer are forsaken: they shall be for flocks, which shall lie down, and none shall make them afraid.
> 3. The fortress also shall cease from Ephraim, and the kingdom from Damascus, and the remnant of Syria: they shall be as the glory of the children of Israel, saith the LORD of hosts.

Since Damascus and Ephraim had been allied for some time against Judah, they are, although not mentioned together in the heading, combined in the judgments that will come upon them. This chapter is a further explanation of the seventh, where these nations advanced with evil intentions on Judah and Jerusalem. The judgment that will strike Damascus is that it will be no longer a city but a *ruinous heap*. This prediction has yet to be completely fulfilled, for in Jeremiah's day it was a flourishing city, and even today is said to be the oldest city in the world (cf. Genesis 15:2 where Damascus is already mentioned). According to II Kings 16:9 Tiglath-pileser captured it and killed its king Rezin; but he did not make it a *heap*. This chapter also, however, points to the terrible end time of the Great Tribulation when all the cities of the Gentiles will fall including Damascus (Rev. 16:19).

There were at least three cities by the name of Aroer, but those in Jordan are meant in verse two. These cities will be depopulated and abandoned to such an extent that sheep will peacefully graze there and be able to choose the vacated houses as shelters. The *fortress* of *Ephraim* will cease as well. *Fortress* is a collective name for all fortified cities and towns. Equally, these allied nations will fare poorly. Ephraim had lowered itself to an appendage of pagan Syria; therefore it will be treated the same way as Syria. Syria had been the object of confidence to Ephraim, thus its people will be revealed before the eyes of the Ephraimites as a broken reed that pierces the hand. II Kings 15:29 and 16:9 register the initial and partial fulfillment of these words.

The Ten Tribes in the Great Tribulation

4. And in that day it shall come to pass, that the glory of Jacob shall be made thin, and the fatness of his flesh shall wax lean.

5. And it shall be as when the harvestman gathereth the corn, and reapeth the ears with his arm; and it shall be as he that gathereth ears in the valley of Rephaim.

6. Yet gleaning grapes shall be left in it, as the shaking of an olive tree, two or three berries in the top of the uppermost bough, four or five in the outmost fruitful branches thereof, saith the Lord God of Israel.

The complete description of this chapter forbids us to limit its fulfillment to the fall of Samaria. Rather, we are forced to think of the day of Jacob's trouble. Verse four again contains the favorite image of a fat person getting thin or wasting away indicating the faded glory and destruction of luxuriant fields and luxurious palaces. They will be mowed down like standing corn in a field. Still, there will be a remnant; but it will be as small as the few ears left in the field by the mowers, which afterwards are gleaned by children. Isaiah had seen this often in the valley of Rephaim, southwest of Jerusalem, a valley that was very fertile and where the poor from Jerusalem eagerly gleaned the fat ears of corn. In another picturesque image derived from the gathering of olives the prophet says that after the shaking of the tree there will be only a few berries left on the fruitful branches, near the top of the tree. Compare this with what has been said earlier concerning the remnant in 4:3,4; 6:13; 10:21; 65:8,9. Glorious promises for the remnant of Israel are evident from what follows.

Idolatry Abolished Because of Christ's Presence

> 7. At that day shall a man look to his Maker, and his eyes shall have respect to the Holy One of Israel.
>
> 8. And he shall not look to the altars, the work of his hands, neither shall respect that which his fingers have made, either the groves, or the images.

Christ will suddenly come to Jacob in his great calamity. This is very vividly described in Zechariah 14:1-5. The prophet Isaiah, however, seldom describes the return of Christ as a future event. But frequently, as he does here, he presents Him as having already returned, cf. chapters four, seven, eleven and sixteen. The Holy One of Israel is no one else but Christ Himself, specifically in the day of His coming. The greatly vexed little nation of Israel will behold Him (Zech. 12, Matt. 23:39). It will be a fearful meeting, only vaguely reflected by the surprise meeting between Joseph and his brothers. Not only Israel, but all nations will see Him; thus, the text speaks of a *man* in the most general sense of the word. This glorious Messiah will take such a great place in the heart of all men that they will no longer look at the work of their own hands, but they will forget them, despise them and cast them away. "And the LORD shall be king over all the earth: in that day shall there be one LORD, and his name one (Zech. 14:9). In 2:20 we saw that at the coming of the Lord Jesus Christ all idolatry will be abolished and all false religions put away to make place for the one religion of King Jesus. Very few expositors of this prophet have an eye for these glorious vistas. This is due to the fact that they do not know the counsel of the Lord concerning Israel. As a rule this nation is considered as finished and replaced by the Church of the New Testament. All the promises for Israel's remnant which are still unfulfilled are taken to be spiritual blessings of the Church. This view has caused a world of misery and is without any basis whatsoever.

Ephraim's Sin and Fall

> 9. In that day shall his strong cities be as a forsaken bough, and an uppermost branch, which they left because of the children of Israel: and there shall be desolation.

10. Because thou hast forgotten the God of thy salvation, and hast not been mindful of the rock of thy strength, therefore shalt thou plant pleasant plants, and shalt set it with strange slips:

11. In the day shalt thou make thy plant to grow, and in the morning shalt thou make thy seed to flourish: but the harvest shall be a heap in the day of grief and of desperate sorrow.

Here the prophet is obviously referring back to Ephraim's history. Israel had put her trust in her *strong cities,* but they would become like the abandoned ruins that remained in the woods and on the mountains as remnants of the Amorite fortresses razed by the armies of the Israelites at the conquest of Canaan. This seems to be the historical allusion of verse nine. The next verse points to Israel's sin: they have *forgotten the God of their salvation* and while building their fortresses had not been mindful of the *Rock of their strength.* Israel is then compared to a man who made a pleasant garden and planted it with *strange slips.* Every morning he arose early to take care of them in hope of harvesting rich fruits. But when the harvest time came, all the fruits of his garden became nothing but *a heap,* a further reference to what was said in verse five. The prophet gives an incisive description of the sin of the northern kingdom: (a) From the moment of separation from Judah it had *forgotten the God of its salvation* and turned to the worship of calves. (b) By building fortresses, it clearly demonstrated refusal to acknowledge God as the Rock of its strength. (c) By building a luxurious pleasure house, by admitting foreign abominations and by developing a sensual life of sin, Samaria had filled the cup of God's wrath. The great nations came and carried it away to foreign lands where it is wandering about to this very day.

The Assembly of the Great Nations in the Last Days

12. Woe to the multitude of many people, which make a noise like the noise of the seas; and to the rushing of nations, that make a rushing like the rushing of mighty waters!

13. The nations shall rush like the rushing of many waters: but God shall rebuke them, and they shall flee far off, and shall be chased as the chaff of the mountains before the wind, and like a rolling thing before the whirlwind.

14. And behold at eveningtide trouble; and before the morning he is not. This is the portion of them that spoil us, and the lot of them that rob us.

The description of Gog's invasion into Canaan in the last days contains a remarkable statement, which has given expositors much difficulty. It is this: "Art thou he of whom I have spoken in old time by my servants the prophets of Israel, which prophesied in those days many years that I would bring thee against them (Ezek. 38:17)?" This verse tells us that Israel's prophets spoke often about Gog's invasion. For it is stated in such general terms that the pinpointing of a single place is impossible. Prior to this reference, nowhere is the name and indication of Gog found in detail. But this statement by Ezekiel gives us the significant hint that we must expect to find the same assembly of nations often in the prophets. Isaiah's verses refer to this terrible invasion into Canaan and not to the defeat of Sennacherib's army before Jerusalem. This contemporary sudden destruction by a miracle of God is to be considered a type, or prelude, of what will take place on a much more gigantic scale in the end time. So, the mighty Sennacherib can be thought of when reading the words *him* and *he* in verse fourteen, since he indeed fled like chaff before the wind to his own country. But in the final analysis, none other than Gog, the king of the north is in view.

> See how the mighty nations advance in battle array!
> This is how the seas roar, this is how they come storming in!
> Let the nations roar like mighty rivers,
> God wrinkles His eyebrows, and they are destroyed!
> Like drifting sand from the mountains they are scattered,
> Like chaff in the wind their threatening numbers dwindle!
> Deadly fear prevailed at night, and weeping and wailing —
> In the morning there is joy and the shouting of victory!

ISAIAH 18

Israel's Restoration

1. Woe to the land shadowing with wings, which is beyond the rivers of Ethiopia:

2. That sendeth ambassadors by the sea, even in vessels of bulrushes upon the waters, saying, Go, ye swift messengers, to a nation scattered and peeled, to a people terrible from their beginning hitherto; a nation meted out and trodden down, whose land the rivers have spoiled!

3. All ye inhabitants of the world, and dwellers on the earth, see ye, when he lifteth up an ensign on the mountains; and when he bloweth a trumpet, hear ye.

4. For so the LORD said unto me, I will take my rest, and I will consider in my dwelling place like a clear heat upon herbs, and like a cloud of dew in the heat of harvest.

5. For afore the harvest, when the bud is perfect, and the sour grape is ripening in the flower, he shall both cut off the sprigs with pruning hooks, and take away and cut down the branches.

6. They shall be left together unto the fowls of the mountains, and to the beasts of the earth: and the fowls shall summer upon them, and all the beasts of the earth shall winter upon them.

7. In that time shall the present be brought unto the LORD of hosts of a people scattered and peeled, and from a people terrible from their beginning hitherto; a nation meted out and trodden under foot, whose land the rivers have spoiled, to the place of the name of the LORD of hosts, the mount Zion.

To us, this brief chapter is the most difficult one of all the sixty-six chapters of Isaiah. For many years this chapter has been again and again an object of our study and contemplation; but we still dare not claim that we understand it well. It has been thought that the first two verses refer to such countries as Ethiopia, Egypt, Palestine, Assyria, America and England. Da Costa and the older premillennialists in England thought that these verses predict that one day England will lend its aid to the restoration of the Jews. They identified the *vessels of bulrushes* with the great steamships and *a nation scattered and peeled* with Israel. The indications are very mysterious and we do not know for what reasons.

After much reflection it appears to us that the main thought of this difficult chapter is that Egypt and Ethiopia, who were practically one nation at that time, are now sending ambassadors and presents to Judah to draw her deceitfully into world politics. This angers the prophet and he calls out in irony to those strange ambassadors to go to the people who, being scattered and peeled themselves, cannot offer help. But one day — after the judgment of the nations — the nations will in truth bring presents to Jehovah in Zion.

Six matters are briefly and mysteriously indicated here. First of all, the *political entanglements of Isaiah's day* is in view, specifically the attempt by Tirhakah, the mighty king of Egypt and Ethiopia, to make an alliance with Judah against the imminent attack by Sennacherib and in general against the growing power of Assyria. Isaiah sees his ambassadors coming in little ships made of papyrus reeds covered with pitch — little boats that could easily be carried overland in case they encountered strong currents — down the *sea*, as the River Nile is called here and elsewhere. They are *swift messengers*, for the king is in a hurry, and the enemy is not sitting still. Oh that the gospel messengers might be welcomed as *swift messengers!*

Secondly, *Israel* is mentioned here twice in very remarkable terms. Regardless of how strongly many expositors insist that reference is made here to the Egyptians or the Ethiopians or the Assyrians, after long deliberation we are convinced that this is a description of *Israel,* an opinion shared by the Rabbis and the expositors of more recent date such as Horsley, Kay, Kelly, Da Costa, Gaebelein, Tucker and others. Calvin with his usual keen insight already saw that this chapter contains a description of Israel. The annotators to the old Dutch Authorized Version[1] think the chapter is

[1] The version requested by the Synod of Dort in 1618-1619 and authorized by the States General of Holland shortly thereafter. In this respect it is like the King James Version of 1611—authorized by both an ecclesiastical and civil authority.

speaking of the Assyrians, but they add in the margin: "Others think it describes the Jewish people, who had suffered much and who had received from God *precept upon precept* (Isa. 28:10), and that was *terrible,* although many enemies (like rivers strong and many, Isa. 8:7) spoiled their land." Most translators and commentators have become the victims of preconceived notions. In our opinion Calvin explained *meted out* correctly as the tearing apart of Israel into two kingdoms. *Peeled* literally means *the hair plucked or shaved from the skin.* This word also appears in Ezekiel 29:18 and there refers to the spoiling and looting by Nebuchadnezzar's soldiers at the siege of Tyrus. In 50:6 it is used of the Messiah and translated *plucking off the hair.* Here it depicts Israel as being very oppressed and cruelly treated, not the least by the people that now came to beg for her favor. The Jewish scribe Aben-Ezra says of the first two words: "The Israelites are meant who have been dragged from their houses like sheep, and who were dragged so long until they were skinned." The word certainly means *skinned.*

Israel is further called *terrible.* This word is continually applied to Israel, since her origin, deliverance, history, future and especially her God are terrible, i.e., feared (cf. Exod. 23:27; 34:10; Deut. 28:58; Josh. 2:9; Ps. 139:14). In the past, Egypt experienced it, as will the nations in the future (Ex. 15:11; Num. 23:24; Zech. 12:3). *Meted out* might refer to the many laws, but it is better to take it in this context as referring to the (measuring) line of destruction. The plummet was used at the destruction of buildings (28:17, II Kings 21:13, Lam. 2:8) and therefore in Scripture it is the common symbol of destruction. Jerusalem has been destroyed more often than any other city in the world. Horsley follows the Septuagint and the Vulgate and translates it as *expecting,* interpreting it as Israel's constant Messianic expectation. On the *trodden down* the Great Prophet Himself comments in Luke 21:24. The *rivers* are a symbolic representation of the hostile nations and armies as in 8:5-8; 18:2.

Next, Isaiah informs the messengers as well as all the inhabitants of the world that God has revealed to him that He will first take His heavenly *rest* for a while and consider. But suddenly, this rest will be broken. War will be declared to all the nations by the erecting of the war banner on the mountains, and the call to war will be issued by the blowing of the trumpet. During the *times of the Gentiles,* God keeps silent and seems to be a disinterested beholder of evil, while the nations outside of Israel rage like wild beasts and Israel is oppressed and plucked as described in verse two, and sorely afflicted (Ps. 83:2; Isa. 42:14; 57:11; 63:15-19; 64:12).

Fourth, at the return of Christ, God will terminate His silence and annihilate His and Israel's enemies. He will arise and do battle against all those who hate Him. The *ensign* (banner) is no one but Christ Himself. According to 11:10, He will stand for an ensign of the people (cf. 49:22 where Israel's return is connected with it). Regarding the blowing of a *trumpet,* compare 27:13, Zechariah 9:14 and Matthew 24:31, where this sound is connected with the gathering and return of Israel. Until that time God will quietly consider all the vain activity of the nations. "He that sitteth in the heavens shall laugh: the Lord shall have them in derision (Ps. 2:4)."

The judging of the nations is the next item on God's program. This, too, is cryptically described, but it will obviously be very surprising to the wicked who interpreted God's silence as approval (cf. Psalm 50:21; II Peter 3:3-10; Isaiah 34:1-8; 57:11). We interpret *clear heat* as a bolt of lightning that suddenly shoots from a dark raincloud. Christ will come to the world, consuming, fast as the lightning (Matt. 24:27), and as a *snare* (Luke 21:35). Christ's judgment will be twofold. This is expressed by the two similes of verse four: He will be as lightning to the wicked and as a soft cloud of dew at harvest time to His people. Although nowhere is mention made of the Church here, we nevertheless know that it also will receive comfort and relief, while the others will receive retribution. Israel will experience the heat of harvest time, but to the elect remnant the Lord Jesus will be a cooling cloud of dew. Then the *times of relief* will dawn for Israel and the nations. Expanding on the suddenness of these happenings verse five depicts a wine harvest that begins even before the grapes have ripened. The Lord Jesus will beat down all the unripe grapes, the fruitless shoots and the dry branches, assigning them to the fire. This reminds us of the terrible judgment of purging that shall come upon Israel (Zech. 13:9) and, by extension, on all the nations (Rev. 6 - 19). The imagery changes again in verse six. Birds of prey and beasts of prey will feast on the corpses of men and beasts after the bloody battle of Armageddon. (The meaning of this verse is conclusively explained in Ezekiel 39:4 and Revelation 19:17-21.

Finally, *in that time, i.e.,* after Armageddon, a present will be brought to Jehovah Sabaoth in Jerusalem. Already in Isaiah's day an attempt was made to honor Judah with presents in order to draw it into the corrupt politics of the world. The ambassadors from far off undoubtedly carried these presents with them. No! the seer cries out, not until *that time,* and no sooner than after the judgment, will Jehovah receive a present. The bringing of gifts, of which we read in II Chronicles 32:23, was but a faint example and prelude. It is almost childish to consider that instance as a complete fulfillment of this reference. The verb for the bringing of a present is used elsewhere in connection with Israel's restoration (Ps. 45:15; 68:29; 86:9). The word *and* inserted here should be omitted, for Israel itself will be the rich gift which the nations will bring to Jehovah in Jerusalem. The reason for the repetition of the words of verse two in verse seven is to point out that not all the people but a remnant will be returned.

ISAIAH 19

The Burden of Egypt

1. The burden of Egypt. Behold, the LORD rideth upon a swift cloud, and shall come into Egypt: and the idols of Egypt shall be moved at his presence, and the heart of Egypt shall melt in the midst of it.

This chapter contains an oracle against Egypt. Beside Canaan there is no country that appears so often in Scripture as Egypt. This is because Israel lived there for over four hundred years and at last was brought out of it with a strong hand. Also, it is because in Scripture Egypt is the symbol of world power in general and of the house of bondage from which God's people must be delivered in particular. The first verse contains the key to this burden of Egypt. The man of God sees Jehovah approaching in an exalted manner in judgment upon Egypt. He rides on an airy chariot of cloud. Clouds in Scripture are frequently a symbol of judgment. Especially riding on a cloud points in this direction, for Jehovah Jesus ascended to heaven on a cloud and will also return on the clouds of heaven. The coming of the Lord will have an immediate twofold result for Egypt: (a) Its idols will be *moved*. In Isaiah's day there was no other nation on earth that was so much in the grip of superstition and filthy idolatry as Egypt. Apes, cats, frogs, crocodiles, lizards — everything was venerated by them. When these idols see Jehovah approaching for judgment, they scatter in fear from before His countenance. (b) The prophets and Revelation give many descriptions of the dreadful fear which the coming of the Lord will bring to the wicked who despised Him. The Egyptians will be no exception.

Civil War in Egypt

> 2. And I will set the Egyptians against the Egyptians: and they shall fight every one against his brother, and every one against his neighbour; city against city, and kingdom against kingdom.

This verse speaks of civil war as a further result of the Lord's judgment. When God wishes to destroy a nation, He has several means at His disposal. One means is the self-destroying civil war, which is evident today in Ireland and other nations of the world. It is a terrible situation indeed when brother is arrayed in battle against brother, friend against friend, city against city and kingdom against kingdom, until they perish together. That is the way it would come to pass in Egypt. All things exist together in Him and outside of Him there is no true unity.

The Wisdom of the Counselors Will Perish

> 3. And the spirit of Egypt shall fail in the midst thereof; and I will destroy the counsel thereof: and they shall seek to the idols, and to the charmers, and to them that have familiar spirits, and to the wizards.

The Egyptians were known as a very intellectual people. When the world powers feel threatened they turn to men wise in worldly matters. The prophecy of Daniel contains some of the most striking examples of this. Today the nations in their desperation also go to their learned inventors, mechanics and scientists to see if they may succeed in inventing the ultimate weapon or a poison gas to crush the enemy with a single blow. That is the way in which the Egyptians must have gone to their experts, but in vain. Their wisdom and counsel was exhausted. If science does not help, they then turn to their religion and idols.

Domination by Hard Masters

> 4. And the Egyptians will I give over into the hand of a cruel

lord; and a fierce king shall rule over them, saith the Lord, the
LORD of hosts.

According to Dr. Urquhart and other experts this
prophecy has been literally fulfilled during the coming and
going of the centuries. Egypt must always have had hard
rulers. The second part of this verse cannot be said to have
been exactly fulfilled throughout the ages. Many names of
Egyptian and other kings have been suggested for this cruel
lord, but considering the beginning and conclusion of this
chapter, it may be safest to think of the king of the restored
Roman Empire, the little horn of Daniel seven *or* of Gog, the
king of the north.

The Cessation of All Industry

5. And the waters shall fail from the sea, and the river shall be
wasted and dried up.
6. And they shall turn the rivers far away; and the brooks of
defence shall be emptied and dried up: the reeds and flags shall
wither.
7. The paper reeds by the brooks, by the mouth of the
brooks, and every thing sown by the brooks, shall wither, be
driven away, and be no more.
8. The fishers also shall mourn, and all they that cast angle
into the brooks shall lament, and they that spread nets upon the
waters shall languish.
9. Moreover they that work in fine flax, and they that weave
networks, shall be confounded.
10. And they shall be broken in the purposes thereof, all that
make sluices and ponds for fish.

All expositors agree that the *sea* mentioned here is the
Nile. As is well known, the prosperity of Egypt depends on
the Nile. By the annual flooding of this river, Egypt's arable
land is covered with a layer of silt, so that the Nile supplies
the necessary moisture and fertilizer to the land. Even if the
flooding skipped only one year the result was scarcity and
famine. These verses predict the drying up of Egypt's rivers
causing the farmers and fishermen to mourn. But there would
be another result. The little remaining water of the Nile, the
only water Egypt has, would stand still in pools and marshes

and cause stench sickness, and would be totally unfit as drinking water. The papyrus that grew on the banks of the river and supplied a branch of industry and livelihood would slowly die. As a result of this drying up of the river, all industry and crafts would be hit: trade and agriculture, cattle raising and fishing, weaving and brewing. This prophet with his rich imagery depicts the representatives of these crafts as mourning and lamenting. Even the members of the highest castes and classes would be crushed, and all the wage earning slaves would be grievously sad. It seems that this is what verse ten means: all the great, rich and mighty, as well as the poorer slaves, would be cast into suffering and mourning. It is difficult to pinpoint the fulfillment of these verses, but we may safely assume as a rule of interpreting prophecy, that even though we cannot always point to the verbal realization of a prediction, it can nevertheless already have been or yet be literally fulfilled. Either one will always be true; for not a single jot or tittle of the Lord's Word will ever fall unto the earth. His word will always be faithfully executed, whether it be in the past, the present or the future.

"Where is the Wise?"

11. Surely the princes of Zoan are fools, the counsel of the wise counsellors of Pharaoh is become brutish: how say ye unto Pharaoh, I am the son of the wise, the son of ancient kings?

12. Where are they? where are thy wise men; and let them tell thee now, and let them know what the LORD of hosts hath purposed upon Egypt.

13. The princes of Zoan are become fools, the princes of Noph are deceived; they have also seduced Egypt, even they that are the stay of the tribes thereof.

14. The LORD hath mingled a perverse spirit in the midst thereof: and they have caused Egypt to err in every work thereof, as a drunken man staggereth in his vomit.

15. Neither shall there be any work for Egypt, which the head or tail, branch or rush, may do.

It almost seems as though the Apostle Paul was thinking of these severe words concerning the worldly wise when asking the question used as the heading of this section. The wisdom of the Egyptians was proverbial in those days. Now the world actually has only two things, power and wisdom. Both would perish from Egypt, as they will one day from the whole world forever. There is a wisdom which is from above and another which is from below, which is earthly and devilish, and Egypt had only the latter. This wisdom is foolishness with God and can at any time turn men into fools. Egypt as well as Babylon had a separate class of sages, but this class gave foolish and unwise counsel. Usually the worldly wise manifest much arrogance and pride. This is clearly seen in the last part of verse eleven. According to verse thirteen, it was exactly these wise men with all their wisdom, and we may say *by* all their wisdom, who caused Egypt to err, to be seduced and become filthy fools, who *as a drunken man staggereth in his vomit.* The latter comparison says much about the spirit of Egypt. Its condition was hopeless. The curse of the Lord rested on everything they did. Regardless of whether the head of the state, the false prophet, or the common man might undertake something, nothing would succeed. As we may remember, the Lord Himself gave an explanation of these last expressions. Everything depends on the Lord's blessing. If He takes this blessing away, nothing will succeed. When He puts the cup of His fury and of trembling to the lips of a nation, its hour of doom has struck. When we think of the peace conferences of our day, which accomplish next to nothing, we can't escape the fearful thought that God has caused the wisdom of the civilized wise to pass away and given Europe the cup of confusion to drink. Already the wise are staggering. And soon the world will stagger like a drunken man.

Fear All Around

16. In that day shall Egypt be like unto women: and it shall be afraid and fear because of the shaking of the hand of the LORD of hosts, which he shaketh over it.

17. And the land of Judah shall be a terror unto Egypt, every one that maketh mention thereof shall be afraid in himself, because of the counsel of the LORD of hosts, which he hath determined against it.

We saw above that the Egyptians would no longer have any power, prosperity, or wisdom. Here we see that they will have no courage in that great and terrible day of the Lord, for these verses are again referring to that day. In that day, they will tremble and shake before the hand of the Lord that is stretched out over them in anger. And no wonder, for it is the mighty hand of Jehovah Sabaoth that is stretched out against them (cf. 5:25; 9:12, 17, 21; 10:4; 11:15; 30:32). Verse seventeen causes some uncertainty. Michaelis, Van Hamelsveld and Van der Palm translate the word for *terror* with *refuge* and see in it a prediction of the conversion of Egypt. Nevertheless the older and most common translation is to be preferred both linguistically and conceptually, for in that day Christ will reside in Zion and cause the restored Jews to be a terror unto the nations (cf. Zech. 10 and 11). Even on the last page of the Old Testament we read: "And ye shall tread down the wicked; for they shall be ashes under the soles of your feet" (Mal. 4:3). This, then, is the *counsel of the Lord,* that will cause Egypt to tremble.

The Conversion of Egypt

18. In that day shall five cities in the land of Egypt speak the language of Canaan, and swear to the LORD of hosts; one shall be called, The city of destruction.
19. In that day shall there be an altar to the LORD in the midst of the land of Egypt, and a pillar at the border thereof to the LORD.
20. And it shall be for a sign and for a witness unto the LORD of hosts in the land of Egypt: for they shall cry unto the LORD because of the oppressors, and he shall send them a saviour, and a great one, and he shall deliver them.
21. And the LORD shall be known to Egypt, and the Egyptians shall know the LORD in that day, and shall do sacrifice and oblation; yea, they shall vow a vow unto the LORD, and perform it.
22. And the LORD shall smite Egypt: he shall smite and heal it: and they shall return even to the LORD, and he shall be intreated of them, and shall heal them.

"When thy judgments are in the earth, the inhabitants of the world will learn righteousness," (26:9). This does not refer to the general judgments that occur throughout all ages, but to the judgments of the end time, the judgments of the Great Tribulation. At first, people will resist and harden themselves against these. But when the Lord Himself as a terrible Warrior will reveal His power and majesty, the nations remaining after the judgment will seek the Lord as Acts 15:17 quoting Amos 9:12 clearly teaches. For the *residue of men* (Acts 15:17) are those who are left after the judgment has destroyed most of the inhabitants of the world. And the *seeking* mentioned there will take place after the return of the Lord and after the house of David has been restored from its deep decline.

It is in the light of the conversion of the nations after the return of Christ for the restoration of Israel that these verses are to be understood. Throughout all ages expositors have been struggling with them because they lost sight of this fact. There is no reason to depart from the literal meaning of these words even when taking the figurative language into consideration. Five cities, whether big or small, right after the Great Tribulation and at the beginning of the reign of Christ will be converted unto Jehovah. This is poetically described in the sense that they will speak the language of restored Israel and swear by the God of Israel. The name *city of destruction* has caused great difficulty. Following the Vulgate, Catholic and other expositors read *Is-Cheres,* city of the sun, and think of Heliopolis, which also means city of the sun. Apparently this city was a place of sun worship. The Leyden Translation, together with many critics and following the Septuagint, renders it *Righteous City.* Whatever the case, the name has caused much difficulty since in the context one would expect something quite different than *destruction.* It may be best to retain the present translation and apply it to the disruption and destruction of the formerly flourishing idolatry.

The *altar* and the *pillar* in verse nineteen also create some difficulty. The most acceptable explanation is that Egypt will be a grateful nation serving Jehovah. The patriarchs and Noah built altars to show their gratitude to the Lord. The altar here is perhaps a sign of gratitude and communication with God. If one does not want to view this as figurative language, but as a literal altar in Egypt, a conclusive argument or objection cannot be presented against it. For just as restored Israel will bring blood sacrifices unto the Lord to keep in remembrance of the all-sufficient blood sacrifice of Christ, so this may also

take place in Egypt in that memorable day. Indeed, verse
twenty-one states this as a certainty. Regarding the *pillar,*
Joseph Seiss and many others think that this refers to the
Spinx or some pyramid. In Israel they used to have
commemorative stones and pillars on which they engraved as
it were their constant gratitude. We think of the stone of
Jacob in Genesis 28:18 and the twelve memorial stones
which were to be constant reminders to Israel of the crossing
of Jordan (Josh. 4). Similarly, in that great day Egypt will
not want to forget the great works of the Lord and for that
purpose will erect a pillar as a sign of its conversion. For did
they not call upon God in their great affliction and did He
not send them a *Saviour,* and a *Great One,* Christ?

Whereas the preceding verses tell us that the Egyptians in
that day will seek the Lord, now verse twenty-one indicates
why. The text says literally, "Jehovah will be a well-known
One unto Egypt," which presupposes that He has revealed
Himself in favor unto them, no longer as a terrible Enemy,
but as a Friend. As a result of this manifestation, Egypt will
know Him as their *Saviour, Great One* and *Deliverer.* The
blood of the Lamb will have become precious unto them;
they will symbolize it by shedding the blood of goats and
bullocks. Just as this blood could point forward, it can also
point backward to the one perfect sacrifice. This viewpoint
contains nothing dishonorable to the precious blood of
Christ. When the Epistle to the Hebrews is understood
correctly, it does not contain a single word that contradicts
this idea. Rather, the opposite is true. It is impossible for the
blood of goats and bullocks to *take away* sin, but it is not
impossible for sacrifice to symbolize it. It is true, He did not
desire sacrifice and offering as the actual ransom for sin; but
He did want it to symbolize sin and the sin offering as the
only ransom. It is most certainly true that by one offering He
has perfected forever them that are sanctified, and in that
one offering no blood of rams and bullocks was involved. As
a substitute for that one offering God was not pleased with
thousands of rams, or with ten thousand rivers of oil, nor yet
with our firstborn (Micah 6:7). But that does not change the
fact that all the sacrificial blood that flowed for almost two
thousand years pointed to that one sacrifice. Would it not be

altogether fitting that exactly the *uniqueness*, the *greatness* and the *preciousness* of this offering be symbolized to the nations that never knew this sacrifice? At any rate, Egypt will most certainly do so. This nation will *speak, swear, sacrifice* and *pay vows* in a holy manner to the glory of its Savior.

It is truly understandable that this nation will offer great gratitude to Jehovah Jesus, for He will first *smite* and afterward heal them. When they flee to Him in their great devastation and beseech Him for deliverance, He will be *entreated* by them and *heal* them, *i.e.,* completely restore them.

The Three Great Powers in the Kingdom of Peace

> 23. In that day shall there be a highway out of Egypt to Assyria, and the Assyrian shall come into Egypt, and the Egyptian into Assyria, and the Egyptians shall serve with the Assyrians.
> 24. In that day shall Israel be the third with Egypt and with Assyria, even a blessing in the midst of the land:
> 25. Whom the LORD of hosts shall bless, saying, Blessed be Egypt my people, and Assyria the work of my hands, and Israel mine inheritance.

These verses contain a key phrase, i.e., *in that day,* which appears no less than six times in these last verses dealing with Egypt's conversion. Hence, there is a time reference here that appears six times, as is the case in Revelation six. In both instances the beginning time is given, but not the duration of time. It is evident that this expression may not be identified with the last year (week) of Daniel, *i.e.,* the time of the Great Tribulation, but, also comprises the time of Christ's millennial reign. These verses speak briefly of the conversion of Assyria, Israel and Egypt. These nations, which were always at war with each other, will live in peace together and together will be a blessing in the midst of the earth. The word *land* must be substituted here by *earth* or *world.* In the Kingdom of Peace there will no longer be three world powers. For then Christ's Kingdom will embrace the whole world and all the nations. These verses tell us that the center of gravity in world history will then no longer lie in Europe or America but in Asia and Africa. No longer will the

Japhethites rule the world, but the Semites (the Israelites and Assyrians were Semites) and the Hamites (the Egyptians). Shem will then be the greatest.

ISAIAH 20

King Sargon

> 1. In the year that Tartan came unto Ashdod, (when Sargon the king of Assyria sent him,) and fought against Ashdod, and took it;

As late as 1779 J. D. Michaelis wrote concerning the Assyrian King Sargon, "Our great ignorance, due to no fault of ours, regarding Assyrian history is the cause that we do not know this king." At that time some identified him with Shalmaneser, others with Sennacherib, while many higher critics denied that there ever had been a Sargon. But by letting the stones speak, God has put this unbelief to shame and removed our ignorance. Today we know that he was one of the most powerful and martial Assyrian kings from 722 B.C., the year Samaria fell, to 705 B.C. He was the throne usurper and successor of Shalmaneser V and the father of the mighty Sennacherib, whose army perished so lamentably before the gates of Jerusalem. *Sargon* means *appointed by God, the rightful king,* a name that obviously was chosen to justify and cover up his usurpation of the throne. Extensive inscriptions of Sargon II have been found, translated and published.

It was not so much Ashdod that Tartan and Sargon were after but to crush the powerful Egyptian-Ethiopian King *Sua*[1] who reigned at that time. Ashdod, a border town of the

[1]i.e., "So king of Egypt" of II Kings 17:4; since So is not a name of a known Pharoah, recent studies identify So as an abbreviated form of Sibe, possibly a commander of a delta contingent, (Wilson, IDB) or (more recently) with Sais, a town in the western delta, serving as the residence of Pharoah Tefnakhte. Clearer knowledge of Egypt's history now requires a more modest estimate of her position at the time of Sargon. – ED.

Philistines, was the key to the conquest of Egypt. In those days there was a strong party in Jerusalem which favored a close alliance with Egypt for the purpose of ridding Judah of the tributary obligations to Assyria which it had been subjected to during the reign of Ahaz. It is this foolish trust which Isaiah so often depicts in a peculiar symbolical act for the purpose of driving his message home.

Isaiah Walking Naked and Barefoot

2. At the same time spake the LORD by Isaiah the son of Amoz, saying, Go and loose the sackcloth from off thy loins, and put off thy shoe from thy foot. And he did so, walking naked and barefoot.

3. And the LORD said, Like as my servant Isaiah hath walked naked and barefoot three years for a sign and wonder upon Egypt and upon Ethiopia;

4. So shall the king of Assyria lead away the Egyptian prisoners, and the Ethiopians captives, young and old, naked and barefoot, even with their buttocks uncovered, to the shame of Egypt,

5. And they shall be afraid and ashamed of Ethiopia their expectation, and of Egypt their glory.

6. And the inhabitant of this isle shall say in that day, Behold, such is our expectation, whither we flee for help to be delivered from the king of Assyria: and how shall we escape?

In the days of Isaiah the two great powers Assyria and Egypt sought each other's downfall. At about this time, Assyria had reached the zenith of its power and greatness. It had conquered the nations of Syria and Ephraim and this presented the right moment to give Egypt the death blow. Hence the king of Assyria sent Tartan into the field, the same general whom Sennacherib employed in the siege of Jerusalem.[2] Since quite some time prior to this Hezekiah had renounced his allegiance to Assyria, this was understandably a terrifying expedition for Judah. The northern kingdom had already been crushed by Assyria's army, the formerly powerful Syria subjugated, Ashdod of the Philistines already

[2]Now generally recognized to be an office or title, not a personal name; it means "commander." (Assyrian turtanu) —ED.

besieged; so there was every reason to fear an invasion by this powerful enemy. What else to do but lean on Jehovah who never leaves nor forsakes His people? But a sinner does not do so readily, not even a converted sinner. There is always the evil tendency to put one's trust in the flesh. Thus, there were in that perilous day many in Judah who put their trust in the flesh of Egypt's cavalry. The same people who had trusted earlier in Assyria's power now put their trust in Egypt's military strength. But this, too, would prove to be a broken reed that would pierce the hand. God demands that His people always lean on the golden staff of His promises; for all others pierce the hand.

In order to impress this indelibly on the mind and soul of Judah, Isaiah was told to carry out a symbolic act of walking naked and barefoot. According to the context and the style of Scripture, *naked* means without the outer garment. He also had to remove the sandals from his feet.

Was this not a peculiar command? Yet the prophet did not murmur against God but obeyed his Sender immediately. To him, the Lord was his Potter, and he was the clay; the Lord the Woodcutter, and he the ax. But what is the meaning of this strange act of the prophet? The Lord Himself tells us in verses three and four. In doing so Isaiah was a sign and prediction. Just as he walked about naked and barefoot, *i.e.,* in slave's clothing, so the Egyptians and Ethiopians in whose strength Judah trusted would soon be carried away as slaves by the Assyrians. Hence, the prophet in his own person had to portray the vicissitudes of these nations. For three long years he had to be such a sign. Some expositors take it to mean that three years after this symbolic and predictive act the fulfillment would come about, or that the fulfillment itself would take three years. But the simplest explanation is that the prophet appeared for three years in this slave's attire before the people. When the Judean party who favored an alliance with Egypt, saw the prophet walking in the streets of Jerusalem, they could take him as an object lesson of how the gods in whom they now trusted would fare. Assyria's mighty king would soon carry the Egyptians and the Ethiopians (their relief troops?) as slaves to the country of the conqueror. The real *purpose* of this symbolic act is indicated in verses five and six. Specifically Judah, which put its trust in the armor of Egypt, is admonished by it not to trust this powerful nation but only Jehovah. O that Judah would give heed, lest the day soon come when seeing the captive Egyptians, it will be forced to exclaim with an accusing conscience: *Behold, such is our expectation, whither we flee for help to be delivered from the king of Assyria: and how shall we escape?* We more often hear people *sing,* "Blest is the man who knows he must in God alone put all his trust," than we see *do* it!

ISAIAH 21

The Grievous Vision of Babylon's Fall

> 1. The burden of the desert of the sea. As whirlwinds in the south pass through; so it cometh from the desert, from a terrible land.
>
> 2. A grievous vision is declared unto me; the treacherous dealer dealeth treacherously, and the spoiler spoileth. Go up, O Elam: besiege, O Media; all the sighing thereof have I made to cease.

This chapter contains three different burdens: the first against Babylon, the second against Edom and the third against Arabia. All three have in common that they are indicated with symbolic names. The oracle of the following chapter, directed against Jerusalem, is also symbolically and mysteriously indicated as *the valley of vision,* so that with Jennings we may call these chapters *"The Burdens of the Emblemed Countries."* To understand this burden correctly, one must also read Jeremiah fifty and fifty-one, and Revelation seventeen and eighteen.

Why does the prophet refer to Babylon with such a strange name: *Burden of the desert of the sea?* Why a desert? Was not the city the *golden city?* Indeed, but spiritually it was extremely barren and the place where the demons skipped and danced, the dwelling and working place of Satan. It was situated on the Euphrates, a sea of water. But the phrase *of the sea* is more a metaphorical reference to the sea of nations than to a place or area (cf. Rev. 13:1; 17:15). To view the symbolical Babylon of the last days, John had to be taken to the desert where he saw it sitting upon many waters or nations. The hot whirlwinds coming from the Arabian desert scorched Babylon. Verse one depicts the approach of Cyrus' army in the image of such a terrible sandstorm. In his prophetic imagination, Isaiah saw in his *grievous* or terrible, vision the faithless and ravaging king of Babylon bring about destruction everywhere. Meanwhile he does not realize that the whirlwind will soon roar against him and snatch him away. *Go up, O Elam!* he cries as the spokesman of the Lord; *besiege them, O Media!* Cyrus was the servant of the Lord who must carry out the judgment on Babylon. The last part of verse two points to the deliverance of groaning Israel. Babylon's fall would be the freedom of Israel. Ezra one shows that Cyrus' first act was to set Israel free.

The Influence of the Grievous Vision on Isaiah

3. Therefore are my loins filled with pain: pangs have taken hold upon me, as the pangs of a woman that travaileth: I was bowed down at the hearing of it; I was dismayed at the seeing of it.
4. My heart panted, fearfulness affrighted me: the night of my pleasure hath he turned into fear unto me.

The *grievous* vision was grievous for Babylon, but also for the sensitive prophet. We have seen before how this man of God was not a cold and insensitive person, but much rather a man with a finely tuned conscience and a sympathetic heart. The thought of all the abominable things that would be committed in the night of Babylon's capture terrifies and vexes him. It is not wise to think exclusively of the personal feelings of the prophet, however, but also see his personal identification with the Babylonians and how he, in a bold poetic manner, depicts the feelings of the inhabitants of the doomed city in the night of the conquest. My heart *panted* means it *pounded* irregularly, as the Leyden Translation correctly renders it.

The words: *the night of my pleasure hath he turned into fear unto me* may mean that Isaiah received this horrifying vision in the evening or at night. But it is better to suppose that he depicts how longingly the Babylonians had looked forward to the festive night, while it was exactly that longed-for night of festivities that was turned into *fear,* misery and terror. Van der Palm says of it: "The greatest of all poets could not have given a stronger picture of Babylon's destruction." Verse five continues the description of the *grievous* vision.

The Description of Belshazzar's Carousal

> 5. Prepare the table, watch in the watchtower, eat, drink: arise, ye princes, and anoint the shield.

Van der Palm's translation is somewhat clearer:

> The table is prepared,
> The watchmen have been posted,
> They eat, they drink . . .
> Up, up, O princes, anoint the shields!

Here the prophet sees in a vision Babylon's king and his great men feasting. He sees them carousing and reveling, conscious of no danger. For were not Babylon's walls strong and impenetrable, and had the guards not been posted? Thus, they continued drinking and toasting, honoring the gods of Babylon while ridiculing the God of Israel. But what was that? A hand appeared and wrote mysterious words on the white wall before their confused eyes. It seems that at the same time the voices of the watchmen resounded and penetrated to the drinking rulers: Get ready and *anoint the shields, i.e.,* prepare for battle! Daniel five and Jeremiah fifty-one are infallible commentaries on this prophecy.

Isaiah a Watchman on the Lookout

> 6. For thus hath the Lord said unto me, Go, set a watchman, let him declare what he seeth.
> 7. And he saw a chariot with a couple of horsemen, a chariot of asses, and a chariot of camels; and he hearkened diligently with much heed:
> 8. And he cried, A lion: My lord, I stand continually upon the watchtower in the daytime, and I am set in my ward whole nights:
> 9. And, behold, here cometh a chariot of men, with a couple of horsemen. And he answered and said, Babylon is fallen, is fallen; and all the graven images of her gods he hath broken unto the ground.

In his true poetic fashion, Isaiah tells what he saw on his prophetic watchtower. In Scripture, the prophets are often compared to watchmen who had to guard the city at night near the watchtower on the city wall. In Ezekiel we find this metaphor again and again, and everyone will have to agree that it is a very fitting comparison for a seer (cf. Hab. 2:1). From verse ten it is clear that this watchman is none other than the prophet Isaiah himself. All day long he stood attentively at his post, and continued all night long. He watched *diligently,* constantly being on the alert. He had his eyes wide open and his ears pricked up to see whether he might find out something, as Babylon's fall was of the greatest importance to Israel. Did the watchman see anything? Yes, he saw an army of chariots and hordes of horsemen, one army division after another.

Dr. Ridderbos omits the words *a lion* on the scanty grounds that it does not make sense. That is why he, together with many others, suspects that the text has been handed down incorrectly, but in our opinion, it definitely belongs here. The intent of the watchman is not only as a lookout with his ears and eyes wide open, staring in the distance, but also for the sake of the Lord to roar like a *lion, i.e.,* very loud. "Will a lion roar in the forest, when he hath no prey?" Amos asks. What Amos means is that a prophet has to talk loudly when he has received a message from God. Hence it does not mean, as Delitzsch and others think, that the prophet is roaring with impatience. That would hardly befit the dignity of a prophet, let alone one of Isaiah's caliber and faithfulness, whom these commentators nevertheless portray as being that impatient. As far as the judgments are concerned, they were always proclaimed loudly, and that is the idea here (cf. Rev. 10). The prophet calls out twice, to express his great excitement and emotion (cf. Jer. 51:8; Rev. 14:8; 18:2). As a special reason for rejoicing it is stated that the judgment of the Lord has also fallen on the gods of Babylon and that all the graven images and the idols have been dashed to pieces on the ground.

Isaiah's Exclamation

10. O my threshing, and the corn of my floor: that which I

have heard of the LORD of hosts, the God of Israel, have I declared unto you.

This verse tells us that it is the Lord Himself who has revealed all these things. Many expositors today wish to explain everything on the basis of the rich inner life of the prophets. But the prophets themselves explain nothing on that basis; they rather constantly point to the objective and actual revelation the God of Israel gave them. The prophet says three things in this verse. First he explains the metaphorical posting of a watchman. He himself was the watchman who stood on his post, stared, listened, roared. He was, on the one hand, deeply touched with burning grief concerning Babylon's tragic and horrible fall; on the other hand, however, he was extremely happy about the fall of Israel's enemy and its idols. Did not the Lord contrast gloriously with the crushed idols of Babylon? Then, the prophet addresses the exiles in Babylon, i.e., Israel, which is literally called *son of the threshing floor.* Babylon had, as it were, threshed and fanned Israel. Grieved and sad, he identifies himself with his suffering people when he cries out: *my threshing!* Finally he says that it is Jehovah Sabaoth who does battle for His people and against His enemies, who has revealed all these terrible and glorious things. It is not by his own authority but by God's that he has loudly raised his voice.

Prophecy Against Edom

11. The burden of Dumah. He calleth to me out of Seir, Watchman, what of the night? Watchman, what of the night?
12. The watchman said, The morning cometh, and also the night: if ye will enquire, enquire ye: return, come.

These two verses constitute a separate prophecy against Edom. This brief burden has always been a great burden to expositors!

According to some, Dumah is only a change of name for Edom, an abbreviation of Idumea. Others refer to Genesis 25:14 in which *Duma* is mentioned as one of the sons of Ishmael. Still others translate this word by *silence,* the horrifying silence of the grave, as in Psalm 94:17 where we read: "Unless the LORD had been my help, my soul had almost dwelt in silence" *(dumah).* According to this view-point, this word gives a prophetic indication that the land of the Edomites will be the land of a horrible and deathly silence after the destructive judgments have passed over it, exactly like it has been described by later travelers. It seems appropriate to combine the three opinions because it is beyond dispute that this is a prophecy against Edom. *Seir,* which means *hairy, rough,* apparently derived its name from the rough, hairy Esau. Scripture continuously depicts Edom as a symbol of the enemies of the Lord and His people.

Typically, this was already depicted by the contrast and enmity between Jacob and Esau. Edom once refused to let Israel pass through its country. When Israel was carried away captive, Edom did not mourn about its sister nation but instead rejoiced exceedingly in Israel's misery. That kindled God's anger and He withdrew His light more and more from Edom until Edom ended in a black night of misery. It is in this night that we meet Edom here. The night was long, fearful, cold and icy; no star of hope illumined it. But as so often is the case in the world, when adversity strikes, it seeks help from the believers. The same was true here. The all-devouring kingdom of Assyria, which consumed and trampled nations under foot, apparently had put its foot on Edom's neck. And when the night of suffering weighed heavily on Edom, a voice from Seir came to Israel's prophet Isaiah, saying, "Watchman, what of the night?"

So we must picture the entire nation of the Edomites as cast into deep misery and mourning, and crying out to Isaiah with a scream to see if he has any good message for them. When the deeply mysterious and symbolic aspect of this prophecy is kept in mind, it is unnecessary to think that a legation of Edomites actually came to Isaiah's house in Jerusalem, or that the prophet made a journey to the Edomites.

The answer of the watchman does not sound favorable to Edom. The *morning* — symbol of deliverance, just as the night is the symbol of misery — has initially come to Israel with the fall of Babylon and the consequent decree of freedom. But for Edom, it is still night, fearful night. Further suffering is even predicted for Edom. God's anger will continue to burn against it. The night will continue and not make a place for the joyful morning of liberation. The fulfillment of this and other prophecies concerning Edom is striking. The unbeliever Volney notes that in all of Idumea there is not one suitable place for living. Signs of past glory are still to be found there, but the land that was once heavily populated has become one awful, howling wilderness.

Nevertheless a light ray of the grace of God is revealed to Edom. Edom may *ask, enquire, pray;* it may *return, i.e.,* convert and *come* to the salvation that is available in Israel's Messiah. These last words are not as a rebuttal or a holy ridicule, but rather an urgent plea for conversion. For that possibility is not totally excluded even for Edom. Daniel 11:41 suggests that Edom will escape the oppressive hand of the Antichrist.

Prophecy Against the Arabian Tribes

13. The burden upon Arabia. In the forest in Arabia shall ye lodge, O ye travelling companies of Dedanim.
14. The inhabitants of the land of Tema brought water to him that was thirsty, they prevented with their bread him that fled.
15. For they fled from the swords, from the drawn sword, and from the bent bow, and from the grievousness of war.
16. For thus hath the Lord said unto me, Within a year, according to the years of an hireling, and all the glory of Kedar shall fail:
17. And the residue of the number of archers, the mighty men of the children of Kedar, shall be diminished: for the LORD God of Israel hath spoken it.

The original text does not have *Arabia,* but *Ereb,* or evening. The contents indicate, however, that this burden is meant for the wild Arabic tribesmen. So this burden also is metaphorically presented, a fact that no one as yet has correctly explained. It is evident that this burden announces that Arabia's day is far spent and that the night, with its darkness of misery and woe, is at hand. The wandering, trading Dedanites occupied a territory near Edom. They are presented as having been beaten in a war and are now, not walking as usual on a caravan road, but hiding themselves in a forest. There they suffer from hunger and thirst. The inhabitants of Tema are called upon to supply these wretched people with bread and water (cf. Deut. 23:3, 4). Verse fifteen points out the cause of their wretched condition. The Kedarenes were a mighty Arabian tribe (Gen. 25:13). Within a year, carefully delineated as the year of a hireling, their fame and power will perish, according to God's Word.

ISAIAH 22

The Prophecy Against Jerusalem

> 1. The burden of the valley of vision. What aileth thee now, that thou art wholly gone up to the housetops?
> 2. Thou that art full of stirs, a tumultuous city, a joyous city: thy slain men are not slain with the sword, nor dead in battle.
> 3. All thy rulers are fled together, they are bound by the archers: all that are found in thee are bound together, which have fled from far.

This chapter consists of two very unequal parts. The first part reveals God's anger over the conduct of the inhabitants of Jerusalem who at the time of the siege of the holy city conducted themselves in such an unholy and undignified manner. There has been much speculation concerning the symbolical name given to Jerusalem. The Jewish scholars considered it a very suitable name since they were of the opinion that Jerusalem was the place where the Lord gave visions to His servants. In that case, however, there is still the problem with the word *valley;* for Jerusalem was not situated in a valley but on mountains. There were, however, high mountains all around Jerusalem, as is found in Psalm 125:2, so that in relation to these mountains Jerusalem could be called a valley. Or, it is possible that the word *vision* is an allusion to Mt. Moriah, a name which is also derived from prophetic *seeing* and *appearing.* At any rate, it is certain that this is a prophecy against Jerusalem. On that point all expositors agree. Possibly it is called a valley because of its deep fall.

Another question is this: to which siege does the text refer? Is it the one by Sennacherib, or that by Esarhaddon during Manasseh's reign, or that by Nebuchadnezzar or that by Titus? Also, it could refer to the one mentioned in Zechariah 14:1-7. We favor the one by Sennacherib since the description is so vivid that it impresses one as the description of an eye witness. That does not alter the fact, however, that this is at the same time a generic, general prediction concerning future sieges of Jerusalem, particularly the one in the far future which will be the last and most terrible one during the reign of terror of the man of sin (cf. II Kings 18-19, II Chronicles 32, and Isaiah 36-37).

Jerusalem is presented as in total turmoil. The people have gone to the flat roofs of their houses to see what was happening outside the city. In days of turmoil they climbed up to the rooftops since the houses had few windows on the street side and from the rooftops they could see further in the distance. The first part of verse two speaks of the frivolity of the city. It was *skipping happily* towards destruction, just as today "the cities of the Gentiles" are doing. And for that reason they will fall one day as surely as Jerusalem did. Verses two b and three do not become clear until, with Van der Palm, we assume that Jerusalem had an army in the field, which even before it made contact with the enemy had fled cowardly and was therefore struck down from a distance by the archers and some of them were taken prisoner. The latter were most disgracefully chained together like dumb cattle. *They have fled from far, i.e.,* these heroes, with their officers leading them, had already taken flight when they saw the enemy approaching in the distance; they were no Gideon's band of heroes! There was a casual connection between the *happy skipping* and the *fleeing from far* of these city dwellers. A frivolous group never has the courage of a hero, and no heroic courage can avail anything, for whether they can read it or not, before their eyes is the divine writing: You have been weighed and have been found wanting!

Isaiah's Grief

4. Therefore said I, Look away from me: I will weep bitterly, labour not to comfort me, because of the spoiling of the daughter of my people.

This is a little jeremiad by Isaiah! Sometimes people speak

of the prophets Isaiah and Jeremiah as though these two had nothing in common whatsoever. But whoever does so knows neither one. Jeremiah could be as forceful as Isaiah, and the latter could be as sensitive as his colleague. Many in Jerusalem in this critical time continued to skip and dance happily and went on eating and drinking. The prophet, however, had separated from the crowd and walked a different way. The sad singer would sooner squirm in the dust than live like his contemporaries. He can hardly stand the sight of those unholy crowds; he cries vehemently: *Look away from me!,* an exclamation which was no more literally meant than Peter's exclamation to his Master: *Lord, depart from me!* The prophet does not wish to go to the rooftops with the rest but rather to be alone with his grief. For that reason he cries out to them to not comfort him because of the calamity that had befallen his fellow citizens. The *daughter of my people* means Judah which is here, as so often elsewhere, called a virgin. O that all preachers were as this prophet, who never hesitated to preach the judgments of God, but who always did so with a bleeding heart.

The Army of the Enemy Surrounding the City

5. For it is a day of trouble, and of treading down, and of perplexity by the Lord GOD of hosts in the valley of vision, breaking down the walls, and of crying to the mountains.
6. And Elam bare the quiver with chariots of men and horsemen, and Kir uncovered the shield.
7. And it shall come to pass, that thy choicest valleys shall be full of chariots, and the horsemen shall set themselves in array at the gate.
8. And he discovered the covering of Judah, . . .

In these verses the prophet motivates his grief even more. We can imagine the fleeing crowds surging into the city. To justify their cowardice, they give terrible descriptions of the army of the enemy to the citizens. The city is now totally in an uproar, striken with terror and despair. The people are milling about without knowing what they want to do or where to go. It is a day of Jehovah Sabaoth, which vividly points to the great and terrible day of the Lord in the future.

Someone cries, "Strengthen the wall!" Another cries, "To the mountains!", as Van Hamelsveld describes the last part of verse five. Next the various nations with their armor, who served in the Assyrian army as supplementary troops, are sketched. What a contrast we find here between the quiet valley of the vision of God's holiness and the wild and savage tumult of the foreign nations! The valley of vision is mentioned again in verse five probably to drive this contrast home. The place where the heavens were inclined to meet the earth now looks like a place of unbridled demons. The fruitful valleys around the city are covered with the chariots of the wild hordes. The enemy's horsemen are already approaching the gates. Those who are watching on Jerusalem's rooftops can be sure that the enemy is ready to attack.

He discovered the covering of Judah. Covering refers to the veil of a woman. Judah is again depicted as a virgin, whose veil is roughly torn from her face. It was a great shame and deep humiliation for an Oriental virgin when her veil, which covered her face, was snatched off. The meaning of this figure of speech is that Judah's outer wall is rendered defenseless.

Preparations for the Defense of the City

> 8b. ... and thou didst look in that day to the armour of the house of the forest.
> 9. Ye have seen also the breaches of the city of David, that they are many: and ye gathered together the waters of the lower pool.
> 10. And ye have numbered the houses of Jerusalem, and the houses have ye broken down to fortify the wall.
> 11. Ye made also a ditch between the two walls for the water of the old pool: but ye have not looked unto the maker thereof, neither had respect unto him that fashioned it long ago.

After having recovered somewhat from the first shock, Jerusalem's inhabitants seem to have collected their senses to some extent. The prophet sees them make some hurried preparations to defend the city. They are not thinking of surrendering at all. They are rushing to the *house of the forest.* This house was an armory built almost entirely of wood by Solomon (I Kings 7:2), who kept in it his precious armor of golden bucklers and shields. These had later been stolen by Shishak, king of Egypt, but Rehoboam had replaced them with brass ones. At this time it must have contained plenty of weapons. Everything shows that these foolish people commit the sin of making flesh their arm and not putting their trust in the mighty God of Israel.

They are also closing the breaches and cracks of Zion's wall. When it is said that these are *many,* it means that the people had lived as those that are *at ease in Zion* and had not cared for the walls. Allow one little crack in your spiritual life and the enemy will take advantage of it. He most certainly will succeed in crawling through it to get inside! To repair the walls, they needed bricks and stones and so they broke down the houses they could best do without. They also changed the course of the water conduits in such a way that the besiegers would, and the besieged would not, suffer a shortage of water. This was undoubtedly one of the wisest precautionary measures (cf. II Chr. 32:3, 4; Isaiah 7:3).

Precautionary measures as such are not bad. Isaiah will not berate them for that. But it grieves him to the depths of his righteous soul that with all these precautions they are not looking unto Israel's Keeper who never sleeps nor slumbers and who brought all this upon Judah according to His determined counsel. For according to Amos there is no evil in the city unless the Lord sends it. God had determined this upon Judah *long ago.* He had sent the Assyrians as His executioners to chastise Judah. It was He alone who could deliver Judah from them, though Judah did not acknowledge this.

"Let Us Eat and Drink; for Tomorrow We Shall Die"

12. And in that day did the Lord GOD of hosts call to weeping, and to mourning, and to baldness, and to girding with sackcloth:

13. And behold joy and gladness, slaying oxen, and killing sheep, eating flesh, and drinking wine: let us eat and drink; for to morrow we shall die.

14. And it was revealed in mine ears by the LORD of hosts, Surely this iniquity shall not be purged from you till ye die, saith the Lord GOD of hosts.

All precautionary measures avail nothing if there is no humbling before the face of God. Instead of repenting of their sins, the people of Jerusalem put their trust in flesh and walked in the flesh. The words *and behold* point out a touching contrast. God calls them to brokenness of heart on account of their sin and misery. But the frivolous people, especially the wanton rich, made their belly their god and pursued frivolous pleasures in the midst of the inexpressible misery of the people. The only thing they thought of was killing oxen, slaying sheep, eating meat, and drinking wine. This was all the more irresponsible in view of the possibility of long siege, since there would be scarcity and shortage of food. But they did not care! They no longer cared about God, about the people or even about themselves. Finally, Isaiah points out the inescapable judgment of God.

The Denouncement of Shebna

15. Thus saith the Lord GOD of hosts. Go, get thee unto this treasurer, even unto Shebna, which is over the house, and say,

16. What hast thou here? and whom hast thou here, that thou hast hewed thee out a sepulchre here, as he that heweth him out a sepulchre on high, and that graveth an habitation for himself in a rock?

17. Behold, the LORD will carry thee away with a mighty captivity, and will surely cover thee.

18. He will surely violently turn and toss thee like a ball into a large country: there shalt thou die, and there the chariots of thy glory shall be the shame of thy lord's house.

19. And I will drive thee from thy station, and from thy state shall he pull thee down.

Many people think, with Calvin, that the denouncement of Shebna has no connection with the preceding verses. But we are of the opinion that they are mistaken; for this courtier is presented here as an example of the guilty, indeed, as the guiltiest among the corrupt in Jerusalem. Judging by the first two brief questions in verse sixteen, Shebna must have been a foreigner living in Jerusalem. He was *unbelieving,* for he must have heard from Isaiah that the people would be carried away into exile. But by hewing out a sepulchre for himself in the city, he showed that he refused to believe it. He is further depicted as a very proud man. Even during his care-filled days he only thought of his own greatness and of his fame after death. What kind of office he held cannot be ascertained. Some think that of treasurer, others that of councilor, or chamberlain, or minister of the palace or perhaps governor of the fortress. In any case, it is obvious that he was a prominent officer of the palace, a grand vizier or first government official — a premier, as we would say. His high office brought with it a great responsibility, but he had a loftier idea of himself than of his responsibility.

Go, get thee unto this treasurer. This manner of speaking expresses a deep disdain for this worthless man. The sin of this courtier was not the building of a mausoleum but his unbelief, his ridiculous pride and the disregard for the interests of the people. The building of the mausoleum was but a symptom of the malady, not the malady itself. The rich had their graves hewn out in the rocks. He did this too, high up in the rocks as if this were symbolic of his high position and pride. In today's world, there is the same haughtiness and arrogance. For even though the whole world is shaking on its foundations, yet millions are chasing after gold and pleasure, games and sports, dancing and drinking, while far removed from their minds they keep the thought of death and the grave.

His punishment is unavoidable. Whoever does evil will meet with evil. He will soon experience this. Jehovah will cast him away with a mighty hand as when we cast away something loathsome. He will seize him, cover him with His strong hand, press him as it were into a ball and then throw him away like a ball. He will never occupy the grave which he had hewn out high up in the rocks in the midst of the graves of the Davidic kings. Nor will he any longer ride the *chariots of his glory.* For God will not let him ride on a chariot to a far and foreign country, but throw him at it as a ball. The fact that he rode *glorious chariots* is one more indication of his haughtiness and ridiculous ostentation. The phrase *the shame of thy lord's house* indicates that he did not serve his king faithfully. It cannot be determined with certainty what this terrible expression implies, but it can be safely assumed that he shamefully misused the confidence of his master. In a word, he was a scoundrel who neither feared God nor regarded any man. In II Kings 18:37 Shebna is called a scribe. Some are of the opinion that he merely had been demoted, but the words are much too strong to justify this opinion. The words are indeed so strong, that they point to the Antichrist who at the last siege of Jerusalem will play the roll of this Shebna.

Eliakim Replaces Shebna

20. And it shall come to pass in that day, that I will call my servant Eliakim the son of Hilkiah:

21. And I will clothe him with thy robe, and strengthen him with thy girdle, and I will commit thy government into his hand: and he shall be a father to the inhabitants of Jerusalem, and to the house of Judah.

22. And the key of the house of David will I lay upon his shoulder; so he shall open, and none shall shut; and he shall shut, and none shall open.

23. And I will fasten him as a nail in a sure place; and he shall be for a glorious throne to his father's house.

24. And they shall hang upon him all the glory of his father's house, the offspring and the issue, all vessels of small quantity, from the vessels of cups, even to all the vessels of flagons.

25. In that day, saith the LORD of hosts, shall the nail that is fastened in the sure place be removed, and be cut down, and fall; and the burden that was upon it shall be cut off: for the LORD hath spoken it.

Gaebelein says, "It is Christ displacing Antichrist, which is seen in verses fifteen to twenty-five." We must agree, if we first of all keep in mind the two persons living in the time of Hezekiah. For the Holy Spirit, who moved and infallibly inspired the holy men, manifestly was thinking of the great end time, the time of which Christendom seldom thinks and Scripture thinks so often. Eliakim will be appointed in the place of the scoundrel Shebna. In 37:2 Eliakim is mentioned as the *master of the palace,* and Shebna as the *scribe.* Those who place these verses chronologically after chapter thirty-seven are of the opinion that Shebna usurped Eliakim's post. And now Jehovah has removed the scoundrel from his office and calls the good man Eliakim back to the office he once held. That is the opinion of Calvin and others, but without any basis.

It must have been shocking to the proud Shebna that his successor is mentioned by name. Eliakim will be clothed with Shebna's stately robe, strengthened with his girdle. He will carry out his office as a *father* to the inhabitants. The Lord calls him *my servant,* from which it may conclude that, in contrast to Shebna, he would be a God-fearing and theocratic servant of the palace. Revelation 1:18 and 3:7 apply verse twenty-two to Christ. The verse does not refer to the key of the church's discipline but to the fact that no one comes to the God and Father of our Lord Jesus Christ but by Him: "No man cometh unto the Father, but by me." At the coming of His reign no one will obtain "the sure mercies of David" but by Him. He is both the *door* and the *door-keeper.* He has the key to the treasure house of the Father.

The Lord Jesus would be *as a nail in a sure place.* This is a rich metaphor and, if considered well, says everything. To appreciate this rich metaphor we must keep in mind that Oriental houses had no separate kitchens and cupboards and only very few pieces of furniture. Almost everything in the houses of the poor was hung on *nails, i.e.,* wooden pegs in the wall. So when it is said here that Eliakim will be *as a nail in a sure place,* it means that his reign will be *lasting.* On this nail will be hung everything that is in *the house of his father.* Many expositors interpret verse twenty-four as sinful nepotism, *i.e.,* favoritism toward members of one's own family. But we see it as expressing the joyful thought *that everything in the house of the Father, and everything in the Church, is dependent on Christ.* He Himself has said, "Without me ye can do nothing." All bottles, basins and jars, both large and small, in a household hang on Christ, who is truly a nail in a sure place. We are reminded that his great honor is indicated by carrying the key on his shoulder and sitting on his *glorious throne.* In Isaiah's day people carried large wooden keys on their shoulders. Not only kings, but also the nation's high dignitaries sat on a throne of glory. The entire description here is of such a nature that we are forced to think of Christ.

He has the true key of David. Eliakim never had all that glory and long-lasting rule. Christ is the true Eliakim, *the one established by God.* Verse twenty-five is interpreted in many ways. Those who consider verse twenty-four to be a description of Eliakim's nepotism, view this verse as a prediction of his downfall. Some view it as a reference to Christ's suffering. It is, however, as Umbreit observes: "Logic dictates that it refers back to Sebna." Gesenius, Ewald, Knobel, Van Hamelsveld, Van der Palm, Jonckbloet, Jennings and others are of the same opinion.

ISAIAH 23

"The Burden of Tyre"

> 1. The burden of Tyre. Howl, ye ships of Tarshish; for it is laid waste, so that there is no house, no entering in: from the land of Chittim it is revealed to them.
> 2. Be still, ye inhabitants of the isle; thou whom the merchants of Zidon, that pass over the sea, have replenished.
> 3. And by great waters the seed of Sihor, the harvest of the river, is her revenue; and she is a mart of nations.

This chapter contains a prophecy concerning the downfall and restoration of the famous merchant city Tyre. Everything is written in a lofty and poetic style. W. B. Flaming has written a book on the history of Tyre. His work clarifies many texts in the numerous descriptions of Tyre by the prophets. Men such as Keith and Urquhart have pointed out many striking and literal fulfillments of prophecies concerning this city. Tyre is the Greek word for *tsor,* meaning rock, apparently because the city is built on a rock in the sea, near the coast. It had its zenith in the tenth and ninth centuries B.C. It was besieged more than once, so it is impossible to determine which siege the seer is referring to here. The first siege we know of is the one by Shalmaneser, king of Assyria who, according to Menander and quoted by Josephus, blockaded the city for five years without being able to take it. The second was by Nebuchadnezzar who besieged the city for thirteen years, but in vain, according to some writers who think they can deduce this from Ezekiel 29:18. A third well-known siege of Tyre was that by Alexander the Great, who conquered it after seven months in the year 332 B.C. and destroyed it. Later it was besieged by the Syrian King Antigonus and during the Middle Ages more than once by the crusaders. Hence, this prediction must be taken more generically than specifically; every siege must be included. When we compare everything Scripture tells us of Tyre's trade, navigation, pride, wealth, luxury, ruler, fall, recovery and conversion, it is beyond question that we may not limit our view to the ancient past of a single heathen city or settlement. But we have to view Tyre as an example and type of *world trade* and its wickedness, wealth, pride and humiliation as it is all subjected to the god of this age. The remarkable words of Ezekiel 28:11-19 point this out. In our day we have seen Tyre in its full strength with its satanic ruler. Prophetically it was Tyre which was responsible for the great World War I[1] whose evil consequences are still felt so painfully in Europe and which, taken as a whole, dragged nearly forty million people to their graves.

As usual, the text contains more of a description of the results of the devastation than of the devastation itself. The merchant ships returning from Tarshish, and apparently still ignorant of the fall of their city, are enjoined by the prophet to begin howling on account of the fall of the city that sent them out. The destruction originated from Chittim and from there the message of the fall of Tyre reached them. *Chittim* does not mean only Cyrpus but the entire European coast of the Mediterranean Sea and in even a broader sense all of Europe. Those who are of the opinion that this chapter refers to the capture of the city of Tyre by Alexander the Great see here a reference to his Macedonian armies from the land of *Chittim.* If one were to think of one single siege, then he would prefer this viewpoint. In verse two all cities in and around the Mediterranean are called upon to become speechless with astonishment and grief over the fall of the city whose merchant ships they filled with merchandise. To Tyre the sea was what fruitful farmland was to other nations. *Sihor* means *trouble,* and refers to the River Nile. The revenue of Tyre was the *seed,* the *harvest* of the Nile. We must keep in mind that Tyre itself, built as it was on a rocky

[1] This may be an allusion to Germany's attempt to establish a railway from Berlin to Baghdad before World War I in order to greatly increase its trade with the Middle East. —ED.

island, did not, indeed could not have a harvest. But her merchant ships carried to her the harvest of the Nile, and thus she became the *mart* of the nations.

Zidon Called to Mourn Its Daughter Tyre

> 4. Be thou ashamed, O Zidon: for the sea hath spoken, even the strength of the sea, saying, I travail not, nor bring forth children, neither do I nourish up young men, nor bring up virgins.

Zidon was the mother city of Tyre but was later surpassed by her more prosperous daughter. It was mainly Tyre which founded flourishing colonies in Africa and Europe. Now Zidon, as the mother, is urged to mourn over her daughter who has been struck with such a great calamity. Tyre is called *the sea* and *the strength of the sea,* meaning a fortress or fortification of the sea, on account of its enormous power of resistance during its sieges. But the erstwhile powerful and proud queen of the sea is compared with an old spinster who never had a husband or children; who was an utterly lonely woman, something which was a gruesome idea to an Oriental. Her *children* means her colonies. When calamity struck, it was as though Tyre had never possessed flourishing settlements. As we saw during World War I, when a nation is conquered, it also loses its colonies in other parts of the world. This is what happened to Tyre.

The Report of Tyre's Fall

> 5. As at the report concerning Egypt, so shall they be sorely pained at the report of Tyre.
> 6. Pass ye over to Tarshish; howl, ye inhabitants of the isle.
> 7. Is this your joyous city, whose antiquity is of ancient days? her own feet shall carry her afar off to sojourn.

The prophet returns once again to the idea expressed in verse two, i.e., the great fear that would seize the nations upon hearing of Tyre's fall. Amost all known countries at that time carried on trade with Tyre. So, its welfare was very much their concern; the tiding of its fall had to strike them with great grief.

There are, however, three different explanations of verse five. Some take it as a historical comparison with the fear that gripped the nations after the Exodus of the children of Israel from Egypt (cf. Exodus 15:14-20). This was the position of the translators of the Authorized Dutch version of the Bible. Others take it as a reference to the fear that seized the small nations when Egypt was conquered by Assyria (cf. Isaiah 20). Another opinion is that the report of Tyre's fall will terrify the Egyptians because Egypt's abundance of corn would find no market in Tyre any more (v. 3), and that they were in danger of being invaded by the conqueror of Tyre (v. 3). Ezekiel 29:17-20 indicates that Nebuchadnezzar indeed did so.

Tarshish or according to the Greek spelling, *Tartessos* is an old city in Spain. According to Genesis 10:4, it received its name from one of the descendants of Japheth. This city was one of the most flourishing and populous colonies of Tyre. The prophet now tells the inhabitants remaining after the destruction of Tyre to turn with howling to Tarshish. This is in contrast to verse two, where he pictured the inhabitants of Tyre as being struck dumb with fear and woe; now they must howl. They have somewhat recovered from the initial shock and began to consider what they can do under the circumstances. There is no doubt that many sought refuge in the colonies of the mother land. The formerly frivolous city, which had skipped and danced toward its destruction and was so proud of its great age, is now forced to wander about as a wretched exile. Calvin says correctly, "The tone here is that of devastating mockery." This misery was all the more unbearable since its luxury, wealth and pride had provoked heaven greatly.

A Significant Question and Answer

8. Who hath taken this counsel against Tyre, the crowning city, whose merchants are princes, whose traffickers are the honourable of the earth?

9. The LORD of hosts hath purposed it, to stain the pride of all glory, and to bring into contempt all the honourable of the earth.

10. Pass through thy land as a river, O daughter of Tarshish: there is no more strength.

11. He stretched out his hand over the sea, he shook the kingdoms: the LORD hath given a commandment against the merchant city, to destroy the strong holds thereof.

12. And he said, Thou shalt no more rejoice, O thou oppressed virgin, daughter of Zidon: arise, pass over to Chittim; there also shalt thou have no rest.

13. Behold the land of the Chaldeans; this people was not, till the Assyrian founded it for them that dwell in the wilderness: they set up the towers thereof, they raised up the palaces thereof; and he brought it to ruin.

14. Howl, ye ships of Tarshish: for your strength is laid waste.

There is no book in the world that can ask questions more psychologically than the Bible. In verse eight one of those psychological and at the same time deeply theological questions is asked. To arouse interest and to urge man to seek an answer, the question is asked who has thought out and brought about this terrible fate on Tyre, the city that was not only crowned with glory and fame like a queen, but which also passed out crowns in its colonies, whose merchants were *princes* in riches, luxury, honor and pride and whose tradesmen were the greatest of the whole world. The expression *honourable of the earth* means that the merchants of Tyre were the great men of the world. Some three centuries ago this was the case with the merchants of the Dutch nation.

The question is put not in order to become wise but to become wise by the answer God Himself gives. No one else has done it but Jehovah Sabaoth, the Lord of hosts. He has brought about this fate on Tyre in order to desecrate and cast into the mire its proud recklessness, its luxury and beauty and to bring down all its proud worldly dignitaries. With respect to Tyre, one sees pride going before a fall.

Very different explanations are given of the short tenth verse. After serious consideration the following seems to us to be its meaning. Tyre is still in the context. This city was the mother of Tarshish. But by her destruction and flight to Tarshish she became as it were a daughter of Tarshish. Now Tyre is ironically compared to a fleeing woman who, robbed of everything, wades through a stream without even having a girdle to bind up her loose garments. In Scripture girdles are frequently a symbol of prosperity. Undoubtedly this verse suggests that she did not have a girdle in which to hide even a single jewel. Girdles served the rich as pockets and satchels in which they put small jewelry. This explanation not only makes sense but also agrees best with the preceding and following context.

In verse eleven there is the image of the hand stretched out in anger. This hand causes the kingdoms to shudder. As the Commander of the hostile armies He has commanded that *Canaan's* strongholds be destroyed. Canaan is the Hebrew name for Phoenicia. She who used to skip and dance happily is now compared to a violated virgin. She is further told that at her crossing over to *Chittim,* Cyprus, and the coasts of Spain, Italy and Greece, she will find no rest and peace. After the capture of Tyre 15,000 inhabitants escaped and 30,000 were sold as slaves. After the Author and the results of Tyre's destruction have been indicated, the *instruments* that will destroy Tyre are mentioned − the wild, uncivilized desert dwellers of Chaldea who descended from Arphaxad, the third son of Shem (Gen. 10:22). This name is actually Arpha-*chesed*. In Genesis 22:22 there is a son of Nahor, the brother of Abraham, named *Chesed*. The Hebrew word for Chaldeans is *Chesdim,* descendants of *Chesed*. In Job 1:17 they are described as wild desert dwellers. Assyria made them into a nation, but in the days of Nebuchadnezzar they outstripped and destroyed both Assyria and proud Tyre (cf. Ezek. 26 to 28). Nebuchadnezzar did not destroy Tyre completely. This did not happen until two and a half centuries later at the hands of Alexander the Great. Verse fourteen contains the conclusion and climax of the burden of Tyre.

Tyre's Initial Restoration

15. And it shall come to pass in that day, that Tyre shall be forgotten seventy years, according to the days of one king: after the end of seventy years shall Tyre sing as an harlot.

16. Take an harp, go about the city, thou harlot that hast been forgotten; make sweet melody, sing many songs, that thou mayest be remembered.

17. And it shall come to pass after the end of seventy years, that the LORD will visit Tyre, and she shall turn to her hire, and shall commit fornication with all the kingdoms of the world upon the face of the earth.

In these verses, the oracle against Tyre takes a favorable turn. After having been forgotten for seventy years, Tyre will again flourish and begin trading anew. The expression *according to the days of one king* must be understood in the light of Jeremiah 25:11. In Scripture the word *king* often stands for a kingdom or a royal house. This is the way to understand this expression of the Babylonian domination. From Nebuchadnezzar's first year until Cyrus is exactly seventy years. During that time the nations and kings would serve the king in Babylon, including Tyre. Careful study of this chapter leads to the conclusion that it refers, though not exclusively to Nebuchadnezzar's long-lasting siege of Tyre. Consequently, it must be assumed that this mighty conqueror besieged the city for no less than thirteen years and finally captured it.

In order to understand verse sixteen correctly, it must be kept in mind that ancient Oriental cities had public women whose crafty intention was to attract men by their beguiling songs and music. Verse fifteen alludes to this custom. Van Hamelsveld is even of the opinion that seductive Tyre actually quotes part of one of the well-known harlot songs. According to verse seventeen, its seductive tricks will succeed. It will once more obtain the favor of its former devotees and receive its *hire* as a whore; the city will once more carry on trade with all the kingdoms of the world. Today we see that this is literally fulfilled. Historical Tyre has long since ceased to exist and for the most part is resting on the bottom of the sea. As Ezekiel predicted, fishermen now spread their nets where Tyre once lay. But Tyre in a prophetic sense and as a symbol of the mercantile powers of the world is still living and still seduces today all the nations of the earth.

Tyre's Future Conversion

> 18. And her merchandise and her hire shall be holiness to the LORD: it shall not be treasured nor laid up; for her merchandise shall be for them that dwell before the LORD, to eat sufficiently, and for durable clothing.

We must not think, Van der Palm says, that merchandise is presented here as something dishonorable or criminal, because it is called *whoredom* and the profit *harlot's hire;* fellowship with foreign nations, according to him, is called by that name in the style of Holy Scripture. Although it is true that Scripture uses this and other terms in a much broader sense than we are used to do today, the idea is nevertheless conveyed here that the world trade of Tyre was an unlawful, dirty, profit-hungry occupation just as it is perpetrated today. It is generally conceded today that the great World War I, which raged on so terrifyingly for a number of years, was begun and continued for the purpose of taking possession of world trade and to cause the treasures of this trade to flow into the participating nations' own coffers. Today there is no one who believes that this war was fought to terminate the oppression of the small nations. The most horrendous lies which the father of lies can conceive are eagerly believed today. Not only by the blind world but also by the churches that think they have such clear vision. Today the devil poisons with his poisonous breath the commerce of the world. But this text assures us that this will not always continue. All trade and profit will one day be consecrated to Jehovah. In that day people will no longer gather and accumulate treasures on earth, but will spend them for Jehovah, His house and His servants. Three centuries after Christ, Eusebius wrote that this prophecy was fulfilled in his day, since there was a church in Tyre whose members gave from their profit unto the Lord. Many expositors are still of this opinion, but this word will not be fulfilled until the Millennium.

ISAIAH 24

Without a heading or any transition, the series of predictions concerning some seven nations contained in chapters thirteen to twenty-three is followed by another series, which continues to chapter thirty-five, but chapters twenty-four to twenty-seven are one continuous unit that describe the same terrible but yet glorious events. All attempts to divide these chapters into distinct parts must be considered a failure, as J. A. Alexander writes: "The attempts which have been made to subdivide this portion of the book are for the most part arbitrary."

The *connection* between these chapters and the preceding ones appear to be as follows: the judgments pronounced upon the various countries and nations in those chapters are drawn together here into a focal point. The specific divine judgments described there become here the general judgment upon the nations, which will take place when the Lord Jesus Christ with His Church will return to this earth. That which happened to a specific city such as Tyre will happen to all the cities of the nations — they will be utterly destroyed. Whereas the previous judgments were often only local and limited, in this one the entire sinful and groaning creation, land and sea, city and desert, heaven, earth and hell will be moved. Whereas the glory after the judgment there appeared as but a shining star in the night, here we are constantly reminded of the great contrast between the great judgment and the great glory following it.

With these observations, we have indicated the *subject* of these prophecies. Some expositors are thinking here of the invasion by Sennacherib during Hezekiah's reign, others of the destruction of Jerusalem by Nebuchadnezzar and the exile into Babylon and still others of the period during the Maccabean rulers. There are also some who think of the destruction of Jerusalem by Titus, while others think these predictions concern the end of the world or the last day. These views, however, do not take into account the character of divine prediction, which one way or another always carries us along not into the ocean of eternity but to the great day of the Lord, the awesome end time and what it involves. Calvin writes concerning these prophecies, "I cannot believe that here we are to think of a scene of the end of the world or the last day." No wonder, for these predictions speak of all kinds of glorious scenes on this earth which cannot exist after its end and after the last day. We shall have plenty of opportunity to show that the main theme of these chapters is the destruction of all wicked world powers with all their knowledge and culture, and that the kingdom of our Lord Jesus Christ will rise up with power and majesty on the ruins of the destroyed world powers. Even the Catholic expositors do not limit themselves to the judgments of the past but think of the judgment of the world. It is certainly not redundant to add that even with a futuristic view on these chapters we concede that the prophet at times presents features which already in the past obtained initial or partial fulfillment.

Total Destruction of the Earth

1. Behold, the LORD maketh the earth empty, and maketh it waste, and turneth it upside down, and scattereth abroad the inhabitants thereof.
2. And it shall be, as with the people, so with the priest; as with the servant, so with his master; as with the maid, so with her mistress; as with the buyer, so with the seller; as with the lender, so with the borrower; as with the taker of usury, so with the giver of usury to him.
3. The land shall be utterly emptied, and utterly spoiled: for the LORD hath spoken this word.
4. The earth mourneth and fadeth away, the world languisheth and fadeth away, the haughty people of the earth do languish.

In the first verse, there is the metaphor of a vessel or bottle. Just as its contents are poured out by turning it over, so the earth will one day be robbed of its inhabitants. The word *behold* introduces something very significant and terrible (cf. chap. 2, Zeph. 1 and Zech. 12-14). From verses six and thirteen it is evident, however, that in that day there will be a remnant of the nations *among the people.* Verse two teaches that in that great day all classes and ranks among the people will be wiped out. Christ will judge righteously and without respect to persons. This was already pointed out in 11:3-5.

The LORD hath spoken this word. This guarantees the certainty and sure fulfillment of the prophecy. Truly, the primary continuous main theme of the prophets is the judgment of the nations and their ensuing salvation. The language is very decisive: all classes and the whole earth will be destroyed, the horror will be unspeakably great. It is impressive to simply count the verbs in verse four which are used to describe the great desolation: *mourneth, fadeth away, languisheth, fadeth away* and *languish.* These words are not merely poetically strung together, but represent a fivefold woe.

Connection Between Sin and Punishment

> 5. The earth also is defiled under the inhabitants thereof; because they have transgressed the laws, changed the ordinance, broken the everlasting covenant.
> 6. Therefore hath the curse devoured the earth, and they that dwell therein are desolate: therefore the inhabitants of the earth are burned, and few men left.

The inhabitants of the earth have defiled the Lord's beautiful creation. For that reason the Lord will come to destroy them who destroyed the earth (Rev. 11:18). The earth is polluted with the blood and tears of the innocent. The people have transgressed God's laws, changed His ordinances and broken the everlasting covenant. These three together describe how the inhabitants of the earth have rejected the Word of the Lord and violated all institutes based on His Word. This description very aptly depicts our own day of apostasy.

Therefore the curse devours the earth — *therefore* the inhabitants of the earth are burned. The repetition of the word *therefore* points out the connection between disobedience to God's Word and punishment. Disobedience turns everything upside down and evokes God's curse. The prosperity of a nation declines as soon as its inhabitants start turning their backs upon God. The wicked inhabitants of the first world caused a flood of water to come upon them. The wicked inhabitants of the second world will bring a flood of fire upon themselves. They will be burned by the consuming heat of God's anger.

Great Bitterness of Soul

7. The new wine mourneth, the vine languisheth, all the merryhearted do sigh.
8. The mirth of tabrets ceaseth, the noise of them that rejoice endeth, the joy of the harp ceaseth.
9. They shall not drink wine with a song; strong drink shall be bitter to them that drink it.
10. The city of confusion is broken down: every house is shut up, that no man may come in.
11. There is a crying for wine in the streets; all joy is darkened, the mirth of the land is gone.
12. In the city is left desolation, and the gate is smitten with destruction.

These verses tell us that even during the wine harvest, which was usually a time of great mirth, there will be no joy. The *city of confusion* does not refer to Jerusalem, but the whole world represented here as a large city. It is obvious, however, that it also contains an allusion to the depopulation of the city by Nebuchadnezzar.

The Converted Remnant of the Nations

13. When thus it shall be in the midst of the land among the people, there shall be as the shaking of an olive tree, and as the gleaning grapes when the vintage is done.
14. They shall lift up their voice, they shall sing for the majesty of the LORD, they shall cry aloud from the sea.
15. Wherefore glorify ye the LORD in the fires, even the name of the LORD God of Israel in the isles of the sea.
16. From the uttermost part of the earth have we heard songs, even glory to the righteous . . .

Van Hamelsveld catches the idea of verse thirteen well when he translated: "That is how the situation is domestically (in Judah); but among foreign nations it will be like . . . ," etc. The prophet returns to the scene of the harvest, but differently than before. There it was said that there would be no more harvest joy, here, it is said, there will be but a small remnant that will be converted to God. A comparison of the remnant to *gleaning grapes* was made in 17:6. Scripture teaches that there will be past, a present and two future remnants — one from Israel and one from the nations. It is well to keep both of these future remnants in mind here. Just as a bunch of grapes or a single olive can escape the searching eye of the gatherers at harvest time, so there will be some people remaining on earth after the terrible judgments of God. When we read the descriptions of the Great Tribulation with all its judgments — of the seven seals, trumpets and vials — we might easily assume that not a mortal will be left alive on earth. But Scripture teaches us often that there will indeed be a remnant both from Israel and from the nations. It is of the utmost importance to realize this in order to understand the prophetic Word correctly. For it is from this remnant that the converted nations of the kingdom of peace will originate. Hence these verses clearly teach not only that there will be a remnant, but also, very definitely, that it will be a converted remnant. Then a happy song to the glory of the Lord will resound from the uttermost coasts of the sea. For then the Lord Jesus will have returned to display His majesty on earth.

The fires means the East, and *the isles of the sea* means the West. What is the ultimate object of their song? They sing a doxology to the *glory* of the Righeous, *i.e.,* Christ. Because of the judgments He sent to earth, this remnant of the world has at long last learned righteousness.

The Great Tribulation

16. . . . But I said, My leanness, my leanness, woe unto me! the treacherous dealers have dealt treacherously; yea, the treacherous dealers have dealt very treacherously.
17. Fear, and the pit, and the snare, are upon thee, O inhabitant of the earth.

18. And it shall come to pass, that he who fleeth from the noise of the fear shall fall into the pit; and he that cometh up out of the midst of the pit shall be taken in the snare: for the windows from on high are open, and the foundations of the earth do shake.

19. The earth is utterly broken down, the earth is clean dissolved, the earth is moved exceedingly.

20. The earth shall reel to and fro like a drunkard, and shall be removed like a cottage; and the transgression thereof shall be heavy upon it; and it shall fall, and not rise again.

With this description the prophet returns to the terrors of God's anger on earth (cf. II Thess. 1:7-10). The prophet places the most glorious doxologies alongside the most heart-rending lamentations, for at the coming of the Lord both will go hand in hand. In the original language this stands out more beautifully than in the translations. For there we find all kinds of plays on words and onomatopoeias. Those of verse seventeen are derived from the hunt of wild animals. We hear the wild animals howling as it were and we see them lying down with wide-open mouths in pits or snares. One judgment will follow the next with crushing speed. Who is not reminded here of the seals, trumpets and vials of God's anger? For this is what the Holy Spirit points out when He says that the *windows from on high* are opened. In that day the powers of heaven, earth and hell turn against sinful mankind. The earth will then be *broken down, dissolved* and *moved*. The most terrible natural disasters will take place. The two metaphors of a *drunkard* and a *cottage,* or rather, a night shanty, indicate a tremendous earthquake. Sin, like a heavy load, will crush the world, so that it will perish.

The Judgment of the Wicked Angels by Christ and His Saints

21. And it shall come to pass in that day, that the LORD shall punish the host of the high ones that are on high, and the kings of the earth upon the earth.

22. And they shall be gathered together, as prisoners are gathered in the pit, and shall be shut up in the prison, and after many days shall they be visited.

23. Then the moon shall be confounded, and the sun ashamed, when the LORD of hosts shall reign in mount Zion, and in Jerusalem, and before his ancients gloriously.

To understand these verses correctly we must consult I Corinthians 6:1-8, Ephesians 6:10-19 and Revelation 20:1-10. There is *spiritual wickedness* in high places, and this is what is meant by *the host of the high ones that are on high,* and not the heavenly bodies as objects of idolatry as some think. Nor are the great men on earth meant here since they are mentioned separately. They are gathered together and shut up in a pit, an abyss, which serves as a prison. Here especially we must realize that no prophecy of Scripture is of any private interpretation (II Pet. 1:20); for Revelation 12:9; 19:19, 20; and 20:1-3 provide an infallible commentary on these verses.

These wicked angels will be visited *after many days.* This wholly agrees with Revelation twenty. The duration of these *many days* are not indicated here, nevertheless it will be a period of one thousand years. Then the devil will be removed from the scene and Christ with His ancients will *reign in Mount Zion.* As King of the Jews He will reveal His glory first of all and most of all in Jerusalem. Then the light of the sun and moon will fade in the glistening light of His glory, for He is the real Sun, the Sun of righteousness. He will reign as the *Jehovah Sabaoth,* for that comprises His divinity, His omnipotence and His army of ancients. It is not quite clear who these *ancients* are. It may be considered a title of honor for all His saints, or one might appropriately think of His apostles who, according to His promise, in that day will be sitting on twelve thrones, judging the twelve tribes of Israel.

ISAIAH 25

A Doxology by Restored Israel

1. O LORD, thou art my God; I will exalt thee, I will praise thy name; for thou hast done wonderful things, thy counsels of old are faithfulness and truth.

2. For thou hast made of a city an heap; of a defenced city a ruin: a palace of strangers to be no city; it shall never be built.

3. Therefore shall the strong people glorify thee, the city of the terrible nations shall fear thee.

4. For thou hast been a strength to the poor. a strength to the needy in his distress, a refuge from the storm, a shadow from the heat, when the blast of the terrible ones is as a storm against the wall.

5. Thou shalt bring down the noise of strangers, as the heat in a dry place; even the heat with the shadow of a cloud: the branch of the terrible ones shall be brought low.

This chapter contains three parts: a song of praise by the God-fearing remnant for His marvelous delivery, the glory of all nations in the kingdom of peace and the annihilation of the Moabites. Both the psalmists and the prophets composed many songs of praise that will be sung by converted Israel in the end time (Ps. 46, 67, 96 - 100, Isa. 12). In the next chapter, there is another song of praise, and we shall come across them again and again in Isaiah, for this prophet is also a psalmist.

In verse one, God is praised for His marvelous deeds and the fulfillment of His Word. In the next verse, the fall of Babylon is celebrated in song. The fall of future Babylon is to be emphasized here more than its fall in the distant past, for the future Babylon will nevermore be rebuilt. At Babylon's destruction by Cyrus the city was not made into a heap and a ruin. But as a result of the fall of antichristian Babylon, the conversion of the Gentiles will take place — a comforting truth that is pointed out again and again. *The strong people* represents any and all strong nations, and the *city of the terrible nations* represents the capital of all great and tyrannical nations. Whom will these nations fear? Who else but Christ who then will have displayed His glory before the eyes of all nations! Verse four praises His preciousness.

There is notice of the glorious names restored Israel gives Him. He is called a *strength* for the poor and needy. Israel had always been weakest and downtrodden among all nations, but He will become a Strength, a Fortress and Fortification to His people. He was a *Refuge* from the raging flood of Antichrist, which almost wiped out Israel, and a *Shadow* from the heat. In Scripture *shadow* is the constant symbol of protection. In the Great Tribulation, the heat of God's wrath and the heat of hell will burn against Israel. He at last comes as Israel's protector when her wretchedness reaches its zenith. He laughs at the *blast, i.e.,* the raging and wrath of the arch tyrants, for to Him it is no more than a rainstorm against a wall. The raging of the mighty oppressors is further compared to the burning of summer heat on a dry and withered field. If the sun burns down on such a field, then everything is scorched. Thus, Christ will consume those wicked ones by His burning wrath against them. In still another metaphor it is finally stated that like the shadow of a thick thunder cloud removes the heat, so He will beat down the victory song of the tyrants.

The Glory of All Nations in the Kingdom of Christ

6. And in this mountain shall the LORD of hosts make unto all people a feast of fat things, a feast of wines on the lees, of fat things full of marrow, of wines on the lees well refined.

7. And he will destroy in this mountain the face of the covering cast over all people, and the veil that is spread over all nations.

8. He will swallow up death in victory; the Lord GOD will wipe away tears from off all faces; and the rebuke of his people shall he take away from off all the earth: for the LORD hath spoken it.

9. And it shall be said in that day, Lo, this is our God; we have waited for him, and he will save us: this is the LORD; we have waited for him, we will be glad and rejoice in his salvation.

In these verses we are told what the Lord Jesus in the day of His coming will do unto all nations, what He will take away from them and, finally, what Israel will confess in that day. The salvation of the nations is presented as a *feast of fat things.* To Israel, the main meal of the day, which in the case of the well-to-do was more or less like a festive meal, conveyed the idea of friendship, peace, freedom, joy, fellowship and satisfaction. It is these glorious aspects which the Savior put into the Lord's Supper; they are present here as well. Many expositors think that these verses are a reference to the Lord's Supper, but that is not the case either here or anywhere else in the Old Testament. That supper is not for all nations; it does not swallow up death in victory and wipe away tears from all faces. On the contrary, at the Lord's table we still feel that as believers we lie in the midst of death, and there we frequently wipe a sorrowful tear from our eyes because of our sins.

We find here a remarkable Host – the Lord of hosts; a wonderful restaurant – in this mountain, *i.e.,* Zion; a great multitude of guests – all nations; and a very rich meal. There is no convincing objection to a simple literal explanation. For on the basis of Luke 22:18 and related texts, it is known that the Lord and His people will drink of the *fruit of the vine.* If in the days of the Old Covenant, angels who have no bodies, could eat of Abraham's fatted calf, then believers with their new bodies *can* certainly partake of a meal. One does not even have to think of resurrected believers but only of glorified people of the earth – Israel and the nations of the kingdom of peace. Nevertheless it seems best to interpret it as meaning, besides the above-mentioned blessings, the marrow of the strengthening of life and the wine of the vivification of life. The psalmist sings of the wine that gladdens the heart of man. *Wines well refined* indicate the soundness of the drink. There will be no more strong and intoxicating elements in them.

And what does the Lord take away from the nations? (1) The face of the *covering.* The nations are presented here as being blindfolded. And indeed they are, no matter how they boast of their enlightenment. The god of this world has blinded their minds. Christ removes this blindness. (2) He will swallow up *death* in victory. Paul quotes this phrase in 1 Corinthians 15:54 and then breaks out into a song of victory over death and *hades.* We too can be saved by hope here and now. Yet we know that during the kingdom of peace there will still be death for the nations — not for the Church and God-fearing Israel — although it will not have the power and dominion it now has. Thus, not only the earthly aspect of the kingdom of peace is pointed out but also to some extent the heavenly aspect. (3) The same can be said of the *tears.* The inhabitants of heaven and the righteous people on earth will not weep any more. For the rest there will still be occasion to shed tears on earth because there will still be sin. Still, by that time tears will already have been wiped off the faces of all those who fear God. (4) He will take away the *rebuke* of His people from off all the earth. This will take place because *the Lord hath spoken it.* Finally the last verse points to the glorious confession converted Israel will make at that time, and not as lip service but as the deeply felt expression of the heart. How wonderful and glorious this is!

Israel's Song of Victory at the Fall of Moab

> 10. For in this mountain shall the hand of the LORD rest, and Moab shall be trodden down under him, even as straw is trodden down for the dunghill.
> 11. And he shall spread forth his hands in the midst of them, as he that swimmeth spreadeth forth his hands to swim: and he shall bring down their pride together with the spoils of their hands.
> 12. And the fortress of the high fort of thy walls shall he bring down, lay low, and bring to the ground, even to the dust.

It is still converted Israel who is singing here. Israel sings of Moab's destruction, contrasting it with the glory of Zion's King. The Moabites were always considered the most dangerous enemies of Israel. Hence when singing of Moab's humiliation and fall, she is singing of the fall of all her enemies. Moab is said to be threshed under His feet *even as straw is trodden down for the dunghill.* This is a peculiar expression, since wheat is indeed threshed to straw, but not straw to manure. Van Hamelsveld sheds the necessary light on this expression when he says, "the East straw," threshed out and minced by the threshing sled, is trodden into clay and loam to make bricks, which are dried in the sun. There are a great variety of opinions on the metaphor of the *swimmer*. Who is meant by *he* in this verse? The annotators to the Dutch Authorized Version think it is God or Christ, and many commentators agree. Calvin too is of the opinion that the Lord is compared to a swimmer who swings his arms left and right in order not to drown. It is better, however, to refer this pronoun to Moab, as many competent expositors do. The prophet still has in mind the image he applied to Moab before, i.e., the treading down of Moab into the water of a manure pit. Now the trodden-down straw suddenly becomes a person, who is thrashing about in the mud pool and trying in vain to get out of it. This severe punishment of Moab is due to its pride, which casts its high walls to the dust.

ISAIAH 26

The Song of the Two Cities

1. In that day shall this song be sung in the land of Judah; We have a strong city; salvation will God appoint for walls and bulwarks.
2. Open ye the gates, that the righteous nation which keepeth the truth may enter in.
3. Thou wilt keep him in perfect peace, whose mind is stayed on thee: because he trusteth in thee.
4. Trust ye in the LORD for ever: for in the LORD JEHOVAH is everlasting strength:
5. For he bringeth down them that dwell on high; the lofty city, he layeth it low; he layeth it low, even to the ground; he bringeth it even to the dust.
6. The foot shall tread it down, even the feet of the poor, and the steps of the needy.
7. The way of the just is uprightness: thou, most upright, dost weigh the path of the just.

This chapter continues the preceding one and points to the day when Moab, representative of all the enemies of Judah, will be destroyed. This song of thanksgiving will be taken up by the saved people immediately after the Great Tribulation with its judgment of the nations and Armageddon. When explaining this section we must keep in mind that it is an Oriental song. A. Maclaren writes, "This song is to be interpreted as a song, not with cold-blooded accuracy proper to a scientific treatise. The logic of emotion is as sound as that of cool intellect, but it has its own laws and links of connection." The first four verses sing of Jerusalem, the city of God, of its strength, its walls, gates, righteous inhabitants and the peace and trust that reign in its dwellings.

Verse five contrasts with this glorious city of God, the *lofty* city, the proud city. This city is presented as having been laid low and crumbled to dust. The pedestrians will walk on its debris. The opinions concerning this city vary widely, but it undoubtedly means future Babylon. In chapter thirteen, it was called *the lofty city*. The *time* when this song will be sung points in this direction too. In verse seven the way of the just is called completely *smooth* (Dutch Version) in contrast to the ruins of the wicked. The way of the just may be dark at times, but it leads to eternal light.

Israel's Expectation

8. Yea, in the way of thy judgments, O LORD, have we waited for thee; the desire of our soul is to thy name, and to the remembrance of thee.

9. With my soul have I desired thee in the night; yea, with my spirit within me will I seek thee early: for when thy judgments are in the earth, the inhabitants of the world will learn righteousness.

10. Let favour be shewed to the wicked, yet will he not learn righteousness; in the land of uprightness will he deal unjustly, and will not behold the majesty of the LORD.

Israel had a different expectation than the Church has now. We expect that before the actual judgments of the world break loose the Lord will draw us up in the clouds to meet Him in the air, but Israel expected Him in the way of judgments. This agrees with the other Scriptures which teach that Christ will come to Israel in its greatest distress.

In this glorious hymn there is the richest variety of songs, alternate songs, and solos. Verse nine is a solo in which the lyrical soul of the prophet unburdens itself. He expresses in it his great longing for the Messiah. He even contemplated and longed for His coming at night upon his bed, and when he arose in the morning his innermost thoughts were still with Him. The wickedness of his day had been a burning grief to him and had made him look forward all the more eagerly to the promised salvation. He could sing with David: "My zeal hath consumed me, because mine enemies have forgotten thy words. Thy word is very pure: therefore thy servant loveth it" (Ps. 119:139, 140).

The *judgments* in verse nine are not a reference to the general judgments which come down on the nations today.

The inhabitants of the world are not yet learning righteousness but are becoming increasingly more careless under the chastising hand of the Lord. In fact, they will even become more so in the days of the Great Tribulation. Revelation sixteen tells us three times that the people who are struck by the vials of God's wrath *blasphemed* God. Nevertheless we know from Revelation 15:4 that all the nations remaining after the judgment will come and worship the Lord *because* His judgments have been made manifest. The wicked did not give in to God's *mercy,* but one day they will bow before the terrible judgments of the Lord. Hence the first part of verse ten contains a justification for the judgments of God. The latter part of that verse says that even in the sanctified and partially glorified earth there will be some who deal unjustly and pay no heed to the majesty of our Lord Jesus Christ. The heart of man is only evil *continually* — even in the days of the kingdom of peace.

Peace for Israel, Fire for His Enemies

11. LORD, when thy hand is lifted up, they will not see: but they shall see, and be ashamed for their envy at the people; yea, the fire of thine enemies shall devour them.

12. LORD, thou wilt ordain peace for us: for thou also hast wrought all our works in us.

13. O LORD our God, other lords beside thee have had dominion over us: but by thee only will we make mention of thy name.

14. They are dead, they shall not live; they are deceased, they shall not rise: therefore hast thou visited and destroyed them, and made all their memory to perish.

15. Thou hast increased the nation, O LORD, thou hast increased the nation: thou art glorified: thou hadst removed it far unto all the ends of the earth.

16. LORD, in trouble have they visited thee, they poured out a prayer when thy chastening was upon them.

17. Like as a woman with child, that draweth near the time of her delivery, is in pain, and crieth out in her pangs; so have we been in thy sight, O LORD.

18. We have been with child, we have been in pain, we have as it were brought forth wind; we have not wrought any deliverance in the earth; neither have the inhabitants of the world fallen.

The Lord's hand had often been lifted up in anger, though the wicked did not notice it; but in that day they will see it and be ashamed. The fire of the wrath of Jehovah Jesus will consume His and Israel's enemies. But He will *ordain abundant peace* for Israel, for He is the Prince of Peace Other lords beside its sovereign King Jesus have had dominion over Israel for ages on end. But they have been consumed in the fire of the Great Tribulation and their memory has perished, while even their bodies remain in the grave until after the millennial kingdom (cf. Rev. 20). How solemn is the repeated use of the word *Jehovah!* Verse fifteen means that Israel's people will increase and its borders will be extended. The well-known image of the child-bearing woman suggests that all of Israel's previous troubles and efforts were in vain.

The Resurrection from the Dead

19. Thy dead men shall live, together with my dead body shall they arise. Awake and sing, ye that dwell in dust: for thy dew is as the dew of herbs, and the earth shall cast out the dead.

Opinions on this verse can be reduced to five. Many consider it a reference to the general resurrection of the dead. Others see it as a prayer that the deceased Jews might rise again to populate the depopulated land. Again others see in it the restoration of Israel which is comparable to a resurrection. Still others, the First Resurrection of deceased saints, while Calvin even sees in it the resurrection of the believers from their moral death. It seems to us that the third and fourth explanation must be combined, since these two facts happen almost simultaneously and have much in common. Because this subject is so solemn, we repeat here what we wrote on this and the fourteenth verse in *Maranatha:* "They are dead, they shall not live; they are deceased, they shall not rise . . . . " This does not mean at all, as some think, that there will be no resurrection of the wicked. Isaiah teaches such a resurrection clearly enough (cf. Daniel 12:2; John 5:29; Acts 24:15). What is meant here is that the wicked will not rise with the righteous and rule with them in the kingdom of peace.

What we have in verse fourteen is a song of victory by the people of the Lord who have been delivered from their former oppressors. They themselves are already completely delivered. For them death has been swallowed up in victory (25:8); the rebuke of His people has been taken away from off the earth and all tears have been wiped off their faces. They are no longer cross-bearers but crown-bearers with Christ, for He has returned (25:9) and has destroyed the face of the covering cast over all people (25:7). Hence, although the word may not be mentioned, it is emphatically stated that the First Resurrection had taken place. For the people mentioned in this song have not been resurrected yet. They are still lying dead in their graves. Nor will they rise until the end of the kingdom of peace. They are the wicked, and "blessed and holy is he that hath part in the first Resurrection." Hence the meaning of these words is clear enough. These wicked dead will not have dominion on earth again as they did before. They remain in their graves until the hour of their judgment has struck (Rev. 20:10-15). So there is no ground in verse fourteen for the evil doctrine of the annihilation of the wicked.

We now return to verse nineteen. Van der Palm expresses the meaning better than the Dutch Authorized Version. It is the chorus, the resounding closing song, of the redeemed.

> Now, now your dead live again,
> Now their dead bodies arise;
> Shouting with joy they awake
> Who dwelt in the dust!
> Your dew is as the dew
> That softly descends on the herbs,
> And for the second time the earth
> Brings forth those long since deceased!

The emphasis here is on *your dead.* It is true that the unbelieving dead in general are God's, but by no means in the glorious sense meant here. The believers die in Jesus. "Blessed are the dead who die in the Lord." Nothing can separate them from the love of God in Christ, not even death, for that mystical union is inseparable. These dead do not belong to death but to the Lord in life and in death. It is a totally different situation with the unbelieving dead. They belong to death in all the fearful sense of the word. As servants of God's severe justice, Satan and death have received a certain right to them.

The dead in verse nineteen are the Lord's and they shall have a glorious resurrection in contrast with the wicked of whom it was said in verse fourteen that they will not rise again. The Lord's dead will wake up shouting for joy. We need not marvel at this when we recall that Paul already shouts for joy at the mere prospect of the blessed resurrection.

"Your dew is as the dew that softly descends on the herbs." The thought of water always meant much to Israel. But dew meant even more. There were times when no rain fell and everything would burn up if no copious and refreshing dew descended on the thirsty earth. And what dew did for the realm of nature, the Holy Spirit does in the realm of grace. Here He is compared to the dew, as elsewhere to wind, fire and oil. Softly but irresistibly He quickeningly settles down on the barren field of death and causes it to sprout and bud forth unto life. The Holy Spirit is eminently the Author of all life, as will become manifest again in the day of resurrection. For He will make the vast cemetery of this world into a garden of delight for believers. When the Lord sends His Spirit, they are created; He renews the face of the earth when the wicked will be removed from it.

> And for the second time the earth
> Brings forth those long since deceased.

It is all quite clear that these words are referring to something different than the blessed Second Resurrection. The first part of this verse states that the dead are the property of the Lord. The emphasis here as well as in verse fourteen is on the state of death and on punishment. Here the dead are presented as something loathsome. They are cast away as carrion and the earth vomits them up. They arise to abhorring and judgment, of which the following verse and the first verses of the next chapter speak.

That we are dealing here with the resurrection of the wicked is evident from the very words and their construction.

The word used for the dead is *rephaim,* which actually means *giants* or mighty men, and is so translated in Deuteronomy 3:11; II Samuel 21:16, 18. But it is also often used in the sense of phantoms in the realm of the dead, which were imagined as being without flesh and blood, but not entirely without vitality. But apart from a few exceptions the word is mostly used to indicate the wicked dead. Also the verb translated *cast out* is definitely not a word we would expect in connection with the blessed resurrection of the believers. It refers to the disdainful casting out of a dead body or a miscarriage. Of them, it is not said that they will live or rise from the dead like the others, but cast out, slung away. They are worthless to creation and so it throws them out as a worthless mass. Nothing of real value in God's creation is wasted. All the images and metaphors of Scripture point this out. They will blow away as chaff before the wind, be removed from the earth as dross, be burned like stubble or be cast out like carrion. Chaff, foam, stubble and carrion have absolutely no value. That which is thrown away is not in a *standing* position, but Scripture generally depicts the righteous as *standing* before the Son of man in judgment (Ps. 1:5, Dan. 12:13, Luke 21:36) with confidence and boldness (I John 2:28, 4:17).

The wicked, on the other hand, are *cast away, cast down* at His feet, and slain. They will not stand before the countenance of the Lord but be cast out into outer darkness. Standing is hardly ever mentioned in Scripture in connection with the wicked. For the people of God the resurrection is a standing up in the full sense of the word. But for the wicked, it is in fact a deep falling, a total rejection, a sinking away under the wrath of the Almighty.

Of course we must not expect of a prophecy like this that it clearly delineates the long interval between the two resurrections. All commentators are agreed however that this last phrase contains some kind of time reference. The Dutch annotators write in the margin: *"After* thou hast cast the giants down to the ground." The conjunction *waw* frequently means: hereafter, after that, on the other hand, for the second time (cf. Judg. 2:19).

Finally, it is needless to say that the Jews who died

without Christ will not be saved in that day. Neither this text nor any other in Scripture can serve as a proof text for this error.

The Safety of God's People During the Great Tribulation

> 20. Come, my people, enter thou into thy chambers, and shut thy doors about thee: hide thyself as it were for a little moment, until the indignation be overpast.
> 21. For, behold, the LORD cometh out of his place to punish the inhabitants of the earth for their iniquity: the earth also shall disclose her blood, and shall no more cover her slain.

In these verses the *indignation* of the Great Tribulation of which the prophets speak so often is pointed out to Israel. Before the sun of salvation shall rise for Israel, she must pass through this tribulation. The strains of praise have died out; instead the prophet tells his people of the indignation with holy seriousness. But the Lord will not only cast Israel, but the entire world into inexpressible misery. He will visit the unrighteousness of the world and avenge the blood of the innocent; all innocent blood will be *disclosed,* which for centuries has cried to God for vengeance from the earth; that cry for vengeance will be answered. The Tribulation lasts only *a little moment* of seven years. During that time the Church is with her Bridegroom in the inner chambers. Here, too, protection is promised to the God-fearing remnant.

ISAIAH 27

The Doom of the Satanic Powers

> 1. In that day the LORD with his sore and great and strong sword shall punish leviathan the piercing serpent, even leviathan the crooked serpent; and he shall slay the dragon that is in the sea.

This verse should have been added to the preceding chapter, for with the next verse a new song begins. This verse is a further elaboration of the preceding one, i.e., that God wishes to visit the unrighteousness of the entire world. Expositors generally agree that this verse speaks of the doom of great hostile powers, but as to which enemies are meant the opinions vary widely.

The Song of the Vineyard

> 2. In that day sing ye unto her, A vineyard of red wine.
> 3. I the LORD do keep it; I will water it every moment: lest any hurt it, I will keep it night and day.
> 4. Fury is not in me: who would set the briers and thorns against me in battle? I would go through them, I would burn them together.
> 5. Or let him take hold of my strength, that he may make peace with me; and he shall make peace with me.
> 6. He shall cause them that come of Jacob to take root: Israel shall blossom and bud, and fill the face of the world with fruit.

In this touching song the Lord Himself is the Vinedresser who in restored Israel has a vineyard which will no longer bring forth *wild grapes* (5:1-7), but *red wine* and delicious fruit. It is a vineyard that is worthy of being exalted by alternate singing. God Himself is not only the Owner, but also the Keeper of the vineyard. He sends the dew of heaven's blessings on it and pulls out the thorns and thistles, Israel's enemies. There is no longer *fury* in him regarding His vineyard. After all, who would dare to set the thorns and briers against the Lord, *i.e.,* make Him into an enemy? Would not such a person be consumed by the burning of His glory? No, in that illustrious day no one will provoke Him to anger any more and make Him into an enemy, but take hold of Him and make peace with Him.

> Yea, all the kings shall bow to Him,
> His rule all nations hail;
> He will regard the poor man's cry
> When other helpers fail.

The vineyard of the Lord will be so fruitful in that day that it will send out its roots to the ends of the earth and will blossom and grow, indeed, it will fill the world with its fruit. Catholic and Protestant expositors usually speak of the glory of the Church in connection with this text, but the Church is never called *Jacob.* The very words and their context, as well as the continuous teaching of Scripture, tell us that the restored nation of the Jews will be a blessing to the whole world (see Ps. 67; 68; 102:15; Acts 15:17; Rom. 11:15).

Contrast Between the Chastisement of Israel and the Punishment of Its Enemies

7. Hath he smitten him, as he smote those that smote him? or is he slain according to the slaughter of them that are slain by him?

8. In measure, when it shooteth forth, thou wilt debate with it: he stayeth his rough wind in the day of the east wind.

9. By this therefore shall the iniquity of Jacob be purged; and this is all the fruit to take away his sin; when he maketh all the stones of the altar as chalkstones that are beaten in sunder, the groves and images shall not stand up.

10. Yet the defenced city shall be desolate, and the habitation forsaken, and left like a wilderness: there shall the calf feed, and there shall he lie down, and consume the branches thereof.

11. When the boughs thereof are withered, they shall be broken off: the women come, and set them on fire: for it is a people of no understanding: therefore he that made them will not have mercy on them, and he that formed them will shew them no favour.

This chapter began with a song of the Lord's great, tender care of His vineyard. The objection could quite readily have been made that God had punished His people long and severely. In verse seven God answers that He had never punished Israel as severely as its enemies. It is true, He had cast Israel from its city and country, but even that brought forth glorious fruit, for in doing so He purged Israel in the crucible of misery and cured it forever from every form of idolatry (v. 9). Jerusalem, which in times past had been a strong, fortified, populous city, may have been depopulated and destroyed, and for centuries been like a desert, where the calves lay down and ripped branches from the trees. The women may have picked the dead branches and the dry grass to make a fire on which to bake bread. Be that as it may, the Lord has two answers: In the first place, Israel had more than deserved all this misery, since it was a nation without knowledge; in the second place, all this misery was neither the beginning nor the end of Israel's history. At last the glorious day will dawn when Israel will be gathered together from all the nations to worship Jehovah on His holy mountain in Jerusalem.

Judgment and Mercy

> 12. And it shall come to pass in that day, that the LORD shall beat off from the channel of the river unto the stream of Egypt, and ye shall be gathered one by one, O ye children of Israel.
> 13. And it shall come to pass in that day, that the great trumpet shall be blown, and they shall come which were ready to perish in the land of Assyria and the outcasts in the land of Egypt, and shall worship the LORD in the holy mount at Jerusalem.

The word *beating* must be taken in the sense of Christ's judgments upon Israel and all the nations at His coming. According to the greatness of His promise He will strike the holy land from the Euphrates to the Nile with the rod of judgment. There are still indescribable judgments awaiting Israel and all the nations of the world, particularly the so-called Christian nations. When things are at their blackest, Israel's delivery will dawn, as the prophecy of Zechariah

14:1-4 describes it. The image of *beating,* in the sense of beating the fruit off a tree, provided the prophet with another image, i.e., gleaning or gathering fruit. Delitzsch, Nagelsbach and others take this as a reference to the First Resurrection when the believing Jews of the old dispensation who have not been raised with the *many saints* who arose with Christ, will arise from their graves. Not one single good fruit will be left behind. Verse thirteen refers to the gathering in of the living and elect Jews, as Matthew 24:31 says, "And he shall send his angels with a great sound of a trumpet, and they shall gather together his elect from the four winds, from one end of heaven to the other." There the Savior is also speaking of Israel's future restoration. This trumpet and the one mentioned in Isaiah 18:3 is not the same as that of I Corinthians 15:52 and I Thessalonians 4:16. "Those ready to *perish* in the land of Assyria" seems to refer to the lost ten tribes. They may seem lost to us, but God knows where they are and in the illustrious day of the Lord He will call them together and bring them to Zion. It is childish to take this as a reference to the edict of Cyrus or "the trumpet of the gospel."

ISAIAH 28

With this chapter a new subdivision of the first main section begins; it runs on through chapter thirty-seven, Chapters thirteen to twenty-seven describe the total overthrow of every power in heaven and on earth and under the earth which rises up against Jehovah. Now the prophet returns to the present and takes us with him in the midst of the inhabitants of Jerusalem.

Following the example of eminent expositors, we can readily subdivide this subdivision into three parts:

I. Chapters twenty-eight to thirty-three contain a sixfold *woe* to various wicked people in Ephraim and Judah, particularly since they despise God and His Word and seek aid from strange nations.

II. Chapters thirty-four and thirty-five give a description respectively of the doom of the kingdom of the world and the rise of the kingdom of peace in which everything will flourish and sing.

III. Chapters thirty-six and thirty-seven give a historical description of the siege and wonderful deliverance of Jerusalem, which gloriously justifies and confirms Isaiah's message. All these predictions were made after the fall of Samaria and during the reign of King Hezekiah.

An Old Prophecy Against Samaria Repeated for the Instruction of Judah

1. Woe to the crown of pride, to the drunkards of Ephraim, whose glorious beauty is a fading flower, which are on the head of the fat valleys of them that are overcome with wine!
2. Behold, the LORD hath a mighty and strong one, which as a tempest of hail and a destroying storm, as a flood of mighty waters overflowing, shall cast down to the earth with the hand.
3. The crown of pride, the drunkards of Ephraim, shall be trodden under feet:

4. And the glorious beauty, which is on the head of the fat valley, shall be a fading flower, and as the hasty fruit before the summer; which when he that looketh upon it seeth, while it is yet in his hand he eateth it up.

5. In that day shall the LORD of hosts be for a crown of glory, and for a diadem of beauty, unto the residue of his people,

6. And for a spirit of judgment to him that sitteth in judgment, and for strength to them that turn the battle to the gate.

A proverb says, "Example is better than precept," but there are many exceptions to this rule. In the year 722 B.C. Samaria had been conquered and the northern ten tribes carried away captive. This was Judah's sister nation and if the inhabitants of Judah and Jerusalem had climbed to their rooftops they could have seen the sky becoming red with the avenging fire of God's wrath, which had been set in the ivory palaces of Samaria. But Judah did not take this warning to heart; she walked in the same sins as her sister Samaria; indeed, she sinned even worse. The parable of the two sisters Aholah and Aholibah in Ezekiel twenty-three describes this in detail. These verses predict Samaria's sin, fall and restoration, and the first two had already been fulfilled some twenty years previously.

Samaria was built on a hill bordered by a very fat valley. This is what verse one is referring to; it also suggests that the rich at their festive meals wore a crown of flowers on their heads as an adornment. The city would be trodden under foot and the floral wreaths, which the proud and drunken people had worn at their orgies destroyed as well. When the *hail* and the *flood of mighty waters,* i.e., Israel's strong enemy in the time of the Great Tribulation, enters Canaan, then Israel as a nation will still be punished for all those abominations, of which the invasions of the Sargons and Sennacheribs in the past were only weak preludes (II Kings 17:3-18). Verses seventeen to twenty-two also mention this *mighty and strong one. Eateth it up* in verse four is a reference to eager eating of prematurely ripe fruit. Ephraim's *crown, i.e.,* Samaria, will have fallen from the heads of these proud people, but *in that day,* the day of the Lord, Jehovah Sabaoth will be a glorious *crown* and *diadem* to the elect remnant. We must not take this to mean Judah, as many expositors do, but the remnant of the end time. Christ as Zion's glorious Ruler will reveal Himself to this remnant, while He will be a Judge to all the enemies of Israel; He will give His Spirit to Israel's judges and His strength to Israel's army.

A Picture of Judah's Moral Collapse

7. But they also have erred through wine, and through strong drink are out of the way; the priest and the prophet have erred through strong drink, they are swallowed up of wine, they are out of the way through strong drink; they err in vision, they stumble in judgment.
8. For all tables are full of vomit and filthiness, so that there is no place clean.

These two verses give a powerful picture of the moral degeneration of Judah. Now that the prophet has painted before our eyes the drunken debauchery of the spiritual leaders, we need no longer ask how the situation of the average people must have been in the days of this man of God. The words *they also* indicate that the prophet used the first verses only as an introduction to strike Judah with the Lord's *woe!* Now he has come to his actual theme — the sin and punishment of Judah. Even the leaders made themselves guilty of the most shameful dissipations. They are presented to us as being constantly intoxicated by strong drink. They reel and totter through the streets and often fall down and lie there as though out of their mind and completely insane. The priests, whose calling it was to pronounce judgment in difficult judicial matters, prostituted their holy office before the people because even in their judging they were under the influence of strong drink; their heads reeled when they gave verdict. The word prophet here does not mean the ordinary teachers of morals nor the true prophets but the false prophets who from their own heart always predicted peace and prosperity to the people. We do not read often about false prophets in Isaiah, but it seems that in his day they began to multiply rapidly. That had something to do with the advance of the apostasy and heathen influences. As long as

Israel was a holy nation the false prophets could not flourish in the midst of the people. But when the nation began to put its trust more and more in the heathen world powers, first in Assyria and then in Egypt, it prepared the field on which these weeds could flourish. Thus, we find them here in league with the apostate priests and the wanton aristocrats. They head the party that advocated alliance with Egypt, against which the faithful servant of the Lord for the sake of his Master fulminates so vehemently.

Verse eight gives a most realistic picture of a carousel of the prophets and priests in order to show the disgusting and dissolute nature of it. These "venerable" leaders sometimes tumbled, totally intoxicated, from their seats and wallowed in their own vomit and excrements until there was not a clean spot left in the entire hall. The prophet's words contain bitter irony for in the original he imitates the stammering of the drinkers. The next two verses make this clear.

Judah's Leaders Ridicule Isaiah

> 9. Whom shall he teach knowledge? and whom shall he make to understand doctrine? them that are weaned from the milk, and drawn from the breasts.
> 10. For precept must be upon precept, precept upon precept; line upon line, line upon line; here a little, and there a little.

The drunken priests are introduced as speaking. They ask Isaiah indirectly whom he wants to teach indicating that they are not the least interested in his admonitions. They did not care to be instructed by him. Were they not the enlightened ones and the men of knowledge in Israel themselves? And whom, so cries another one — this time a prophet, would he make to understand *doctrine?* Let Isaiah go to the little ones who have just been weaned from the milk, but let him not prophesy to them, for are they not grown-up men, men of culture, of art, of knowledge and of prominence? How does this man Isaiah dare to bother them with an accumulation of precept upon precept and line upon line? There is no doubt that by onomatopoeia they intend to ridicule his prophetic teaching. They not only mock the prophet's manner of teaching, but also the message as such. Hitzig is of the opinion that the expression *here a little, and there a little* is a reference to little children learning to walk, who at one time are pulled first to the right, and then to the left.

The Punishment of the Mockers

11. For with stammering lips and another tongue will he speak to this people.
12. To whom he said, This is the rest wherewith ye may cause the weary to rest; and this is the refreshing: yet they would not hear.
13. But the word of the LORD was unto them precept upon precept, precept upon precept; line upon line, line upon line; here a little, and there a little; that they might go, and fall backward, and be broken, and snared, and taken.

Referring to the mocking drunkard's prattle of the preceding verses, the prophet tells these mockers with his person and his message that God, too, will mock *them.* God will send upon them enemies whose foreign language will sound like stammering in their ears. And since they considered Jehovah's message fit for sucklings, He will treat them like little children. They can't blame this to anybody but themselves, for the Lord had given them the most comforting promises. If they had listened to His well-meant word and given rest to the weary, Israel would have found rest from without and peace and freedom in the midst of the nations (cf. Ps. 81:13-16). The way of obedience would have been the way of happiness. "But my people would not hearken to my voice" is the sad complaint heard again and again in the Psalms and Prophets. This stiffnecked disobedience and mockery of the Lord's word would not remain unavenged. Since they had rejected and ridiculed the word of the Lord, they would have to groan under the commands and rules of foreign nations. They are represented here as stones Israel would run into and be crushed by, and snares and nets in which the foolish people would be caught.

Throughout the many ages since this word was spoken it has been and still is being most literally fulfilled. Israel has fallen (Hos. 14:1, Rom. 11:12) and has been broken into pieces like dry branches (Rom. 11:17-20) and scattered among all the nations of the world (Deut. 28:64, Zech. 7:14, Luke 13:34); but all the nations among which Israel was scattered have treated her as a stranger and made her subject to all kinds of laws, regulations and restrictions. In the Middle Ages this went so far that a Jew could have only a certain kind of house, had to have his hair cut a certain way, and had to wear a certain kind of clothing; so that everyone would immediately recognize him as a Jew.

Two Kinds of Refuge

14. Wherefore hear the word of the LORD ye scornful men, that rule this people which is in Jerusalem.

15. Because ye have said, We have made a covenant with death, and with hell are we at agreement; when the overflowing scourge shall pass through, it shall not come unto us: for we have made lies our refuge, and under falsehood have we hid ourselves:

16. Therefore thus saith the Lord God, Behold, I lay in Zion for a foundation a stone, a tried stone, a precious corner stone, a sure foundation: he that believeth shall not make haste.

The wicked leaders and deceivers of the people have still to hear more, however. In their coarse ridicule they have apparently intimated that they did not fear *death* and *hell (sheol,* the realm of the dead). These were the same people who on an earlier occasion had quoted the insane slogan, "Let us eat and drink, for to morrow we die!" They were like the many thousands today who with contempt of death can face all dangers, but who, some day soon, after having tired not of sin but of sinning, seek refuge in death by committing suicide. This contempt of death is expressed in a peculiar way; it is stated that they have made a covenant with death and an agreement with *sheol,* i.e., they have made a pact with them. Enemies make no covenant with each other; only friends do. These people have an unshakable optimism; they claim that the passing enemy will not come near them. They call this enemy *the overflowing scourge.* In a primary sense this was Sennacherib, but in the final analysis we agree with Gaebelein, Scofield, Gray and others that Antichrist is meant, with whom Israel in the end time will make an alliance according to Daniel 9:27. That will literally be a covenant with death and hell, but Jehovah-Jesus will destroy this covenant. We must not think that these leaders spoke the last words of verse fifteen themselves; rather the Lord, who knew their hearts and lives, declared this through Isaiah.

God then contrasts the false refuge with the true one which is in Christ Jesus for everyone who believes on Him. Quite abruptly, but solemnly, Christ as the true Son of David, the King of Israel, is contrasted with Judah's lying politicians, who trusted in deceitful Egypt. Politics has never made one single nation happy, and never will.

In times past it was generally agreed, even by Catholic and Rabbinic expositors, that the *foundation stone in Zion* meant the Messiah. The modern expositors see nowhere a reference to Christ, and in this phrase anything but Christ. The believing heart, however, does not doubt for a second that Christ and no one else is meant. For has not God laid Him as a foundation stone? And no one can lay another than that is laid. The following references point to Messianic explanation: Psalm 118:22, Matthew 21:42, Acts 4:11, Romans 9:33, Ephesians 2:20, I Peter 2:6-8. As a foundation stone He is *tried, precious* and *sure* — words that express His riches, significance, preciousness, glory, trustworthiness and indispensability. Whoever lets himself down — for that is what the word *believe* can appropriately be said to mean here — on this foundation stone, shall not make *haste,* or take flight when the predicted calamity comes. When the apostle Paul quotes this word in his Greek translation, he does not say something different in the phrase "shall not be ashamed," but only gives a broader application of it, which is already included here.

The Building Erected on the Foundation Stone in Zion

17. Judgment also will I lay to the line, and righteousness to the plummet: and the hail shall sweep away the refuge of lies, and the waters shall overflow the hiding place.

Actually this verse should have been incorporated in the preceding section, but in order to better bring out its meaning, we shall discuss it separately. By inserting this beautiful Messianic prophecy the prophet has by no means lost sight of his original thought. His double thought is judgment upon the wicked and glory upon the faithful. The former will be scourged by Antichrist, the latter will be glorified by Christ. The refuge of lies of the former will be swept away, the latter will have a safe hiding place in the Savior. The prophet especially retains the idea of a foundation in this verse, for with a foundation or foundation stone belongs a building and a builder. The Lord will build a glorious building on this stone, but He will do so in the way of judgments, for Zion will be saved by justice. The word building refers to Christ's glorious Kingdom which will be built in the way of the most terrible judgments. Just as a builder uses a line and plummet to erect everything in straight lines and to hack away and saw off all that is crooked, so Christ in the day of His coming will, according to His inviolable justice, destroy that crooked and perverse generation from the earth and establish His Kingdom with equity and justice. Righteousness and justice are presented elsewhere as the foundation pillars of the future Messianic state (cf. 11:4 and 32:1-8). The *hail* and the *overflowing waters* as scourges will sweep away their refuge of lies. Perhaps the Lord Jesus in His parable of the two builders was thinking of this text. Concerning the *hail,* Revelation 16:21 indicates that in the days of Antichrist there actually will fall hailstones on the wicked of about fifty pounds each.

No Safety for the Wicked

18. And your covenant with death shall be disannulled, and your agreement with hell shall not stand; when the overflowing scourge shall pass through, then ye shall be trodden down by it.

19. From the time that it goeth forth it shall take you: for morning by morning shall it pass over, by day and by night: and it shall be a vexation only to understand the report.

20. For the bed is shorter than that a man can stretch himself on it: and the covering narrower than that he can wrap himself in it.

21. For the LORD shall rise up as in mount Perazim, he shall be wroth as in the valley of Gibeon, that he may do his work, his strange work; and bring to pass his act, his strange act.

22. Now therefore be ye not mockers, lest your bands be made strong: for I have heard from the Lord God of hosts a consumption, even determined upon the whole earth.

The general train of thought in these verses is easy to follow. The wicked generation of mockers will find no hiding place, but destruction. Verse seventeen refers back to their arrogance already expressed in verse fifteen. Both this verse and the next make abundantly clear that we are not dealing here merely with a hostile army such as that of Sennacherib, but with a terrible enemy which will trample down the wicked in Israel like chaff and a report of which will already strike terror. Whoever hears about him and his acts of terror will be seized with dread. In a proverbial expression verse twenty indicates the great consternation in which the people will find themselves; they will not know where to hide and the world will seem too small. The bed will be too short for a person to stretch out on and the covering too narrow to cover the body. The person who has discovered how dangerous this can be to one's health will understand the power of this proverb. Whoever has to put up with such a situation may toss and turn in an effort to find rest, but it will be to no avail. So it will be in that dreadful day. In Revelation 9:6 we read of people in the Great Tribulation who will seek death as a way of escape but will not find it, as death will flee from them. None of the God-forsaking people will be safeguarded against perdition. No mountains or hills will cover them and no death or grave will afford any relief from the face of that fierceful scourge who is more than Sennacherib in evil and power. There will be no covering whatsoever with which to cover body or soul.

The coming of the Lord Jesus is further referred to in the expression *the Lord shall rise up*. The coming of the Lord for judgment is frequently called a *rising up* and an *arising*. During the times of the Gentiles the Lord is still *sitting* at the right hand of God, but He *arises* as soon as He returns to earth. Isaiah was not only a great prophet but also well acquainted with Israel's history, as is evident from the many historical examples he incorporates in his prophetic instructions. *Perazim* means *cleaving* and reminds us of the cleaving of the Mount of Olives (cf. Zech. 14:4). Even so these place names primarily refer back to the past, to the places where David in the power of the Lord defeated the Philistines (II Sam. 5:17-25, I Chron. 14:11-16). So it may be said indeed that the Lord's work will be *strange,* unheard of, unparalleled, in that terrible day.

Finally, a serious warning is given to the mockers to no longer ridicule God, His word and His servant, lest their damnation in the bands of eternal death be the heavier. Judgment upon them and the entire nation is determined and is inescapable. Their terrible portion will not be hiding in the lies of abrupt politics, but perdition; but they could aggravate their judgment by continued mockery. The prophet also makes it very clear that he has not spoken these things of himself but that he has heard them of the Lord Jehovah Sabaoth. He has thereby let it be known to these mockers that they had not merely offended a man and the word of a man, but the Lord Himself and His infallible Word. The day would come when they would experience what it means to mock the Lord Sabaoth whose servants are the flaming angels of His power. *He* will *mock* when their fear comes.

"His God Doth Instruct Him"

23. Give ye ear, and hear my voice; hearken, and hear my speech.

24. Doth the plowman plow all day to sow? doth he open and break the clods of his ground?

25. When he hath made plain the face thereof, doth he not cast abroad the fitches, and scatter the cummin, and cast in the principal wheat and the appointed barley and the rie in their place?

26. For his God doth instruct him to discretion, and doth teach him.

27. For the fitches are not threshed with a threshing instrument, neither is a cart wheel turned about upon the cummin; but the fitches are beaten out with a staff, and the cummin with a rod.

28. Bread corn is bruised; because he will not ever be threshing it, nor break it with the wheel of his cart, nor bruise it with his horsemen.

29. This also cometh forth from the LORD of hosts, which is wonderful in counsel, and excellent in working.

These verses are generally well known and have supplied many topics for preaching. Spurgeon used the heading of this section as the title for one of his most beautiful books. This section is a parable demonstrating the wisdom of God in His judgments. The Lord in his judging is like a capable farmer who does not keep on plowing and harrowing to break up the soil and to make it soft and level; for as soon as he has prepared the field with plow and drag — a symbol of judgment here — be begins to sow. He plowed and harrowed in order to sow. The judgment of the Lord also has a goal. It is to sow the world with meek people who will inherit the earth. In the choice of seed this wise farmer also shows his great expertise, even though he never took a course in agriculture by not simply sowing *fitches* and *cummin,* i.e., small garden produce, but also the best kind of *wheat, barley* and *rye.* His God instructs him as to the manner in which he must sow and cultivate these grains. Uniquely beautiful is the expression *his God.* It is as though the Lord thereby gives a hint that farmers usually live closer not only to nature but also to God than city dwellers. The greatest percentage of people who forsake God must be sought in the cities rather than in the country.

If the farmer displayed wisdom in working and sowing his field, this is no less the case in his threshing the various kinds of grain. Here, too, the farmer's discretion is a faint reflection of the much greater acts of God. In the Orient threshing was done in different ways, depending on the kinds of grain. The farmers had threshing carts and sleds with sharp pegs which they rode across the sheaves. They also used oxen that ran across the grain. According to some expositors they tied pieces of brass to their hoofs so that the animals could do better work. Revelation 1:15 may allude to this custom. To thresh the finer seeds they used a flail or simply a stick. These seeds demanded a lighter treatment than the usual kinds of grain such as wheat, barley and rye. The fitches (fennel) were beaten with a staff and the cummin with a rod. Bread, corn (wheat) and barley to some extent, had to be *bruised,* so the threshing cart had to be rolled over it to loosen the grain from the chaff. But even the harder grains are not constantly and continually bruised and crushed by the threshing cart. This, too, comes to an end. Now the application of this parable is clear. The wisdom of the farmer displayed in his plowing, harrowing, sowing, cultivating and threshing is a reflection of God's judgments. In His wrath He always remembers mercy and He will not contend forever. The object of all His judgments is not to obtain the weeds and the chaff but the nourishing grain. In other words, He sends His most fearful judgments for His own glory and the salvation of His children.

ISAIAH 29

"Woe to Ariel, to Ariel!"

> 1. Woe to Ariel, to Ariel, the city where David dwelt! add ye year to year; let them kill sacrifices.
> 2. Yet I will distress Ariel, and there shall be heaviness and sorrow: and it shall be unto me as Ariel.

The second woe concerns Ariel, the city that long ago served David as a capital. Five woes in this portion (chapters 28-33) are directed at Jerusalem on account of a false hope, a false religion, false politics, a false covenant and a false trust, while a sixth woe is directed at Israel's *spoiler* (33:1). The name *Ariel* means *lion of God* or *hearth of fire* in the sense of *place of sacrifice.* Ezekiel 43:15, 16 indicates that this name refers to the altar hearth. This hearth of fire had undoubtedly received the name *lion of God* because like a lion it devoured many sacrificial animals. Some are of the opinion that this hearth of fire or hearth of God had the form of a lion. In any case, it is clear that here this name is symbolically applied to Jerusalem since a great slaughter will take place there.

We must further keep in mind that in order to understand this prophecy correctly one must recognize again the characteristic confluence and combination of that which lies close at hand and that which lies far in the future, which has been observed so often in this study. Not without irony the city is told that it will kill sacrifices for one year and then be struck by a terrible disaster. There will be great fear, sorrow and sadness. The city will indeed serve Jehovah as a hearth of fire and a place of burning. Umbreit, Jonckbloet and others interpret the last phrase of verse two as a limitation and promise: *yet it is an Ariel, i.e.,* yet the city will not be destroyed and its temple will remain the place of My worship; but we are obviously dealing here with a serious threat. We have no doubt that the initial and partial fulfillment can be found in the siege of Jerusalem by Sennacherib, when the Assyrian army was destroyed by God's direct intervention (37:33-36). The time reference also points in this direction. But we are equally convinced that this prophecy did not have its complete fulfillment in that event and that Dr. Ridderbos simply cannot prove his statement when he says, "This prophecy was fulfilled when Jerusalem was surrounded by the Assyrians." This statement does not take into account the eschatological character of the prophecy, because the final fulfillment of all unfulfilled prophecy will not take place until the end time. That is the *terminus ad quem,* the grand finale, the great objective and final stage. Neither Sennacherib, Nebuchadnezzar or Titus is ultimately meant here, but the final great Assyria, the king of the north whom we met earlier as the rod of God against Israel and of whom Sennacherib is a clear type (cf. Isaiah 10; 28; Daniel 8:11, 12, 23-25; 9:27; 11:40; Micah 4:11; 5:4-15; Zechariah 12 to 14). A separate study, describing this clearly and succinctly on the basis of Scripture, would be very desirable. We must not identify this last king from the north with Antichrist, for the former descends as a judgment of the Lord on the blasphemous idolatry of the latter in Jerusalem and thereby terminates the *worldly* power of Antichrist. Those who are interested in making a further study of this important subject should read the book by Klein Haneveld, *De Toekomst van de Volken der Aarde* (The Future of the Nations of the World).

Afflicted, but Suddenly Delivered

3. And I will camp against thee round about, and will lay siege against thee with a mount, and I will raise forts against thee.

4. And thou shalt be brought down, and shalt speak out of the ground, and thy speech shall be low out of the dust, and thy voice shall be, as of one that hath a familiar spirit, out of the ground, and thy speech shall whisper out of the dust.

5. Moreover the multitude of thy strangers shall be like small dust, and the multitude of the terrible ones shall be as chaff that passeth away: yea, it shall be at an instant suddenly.

6. Thou shalt be visited of the LORD of hosts with thunder, and with earthquake, and great noise, with storm and tempest, and the flame of devouring fire.

7. And the multitude of all the nations that fight against Ariel, even all that fight against her and her munition, and that distress her, shall be as a dream of a night vision.

8. It shall even be as when an hungry man dreameth, and, behold, he eateth; but he awaketh, and his soul is empty: or as when a thirsty man dreameth, and, behold, he drinketh; but he awaketh, and, behold, he is faint, and his soul hath appetite: so shall the multitude of all the nations be, that fight against mount Zion.

The fourth verse poetically points to the great distress of the inhabitants of the city. To symbolize their fear and sadness they will sit in the dust and speak softly. Wherever there is great grief, such as at a funeral, people do not speak loudly but whisper in hushed tones. In their soft mumbling they are compared to a medium or enchanter who by his demonic tricks is able to evoke all manner of strange sounds from the demons. It seems to us that we find here a rather clear reference to the general practice of spiritism in the last days. Although spiritism is an ancient craft, it nevertheless has made more inroads recently than ever before. We could quite appropriately call it one of the most ominous phenomena of our time. Verse five indicates the enormous size of the army in which almost all nations will be represented (cf. Ezek. 38:1-8).

Suddenly, however, deliverance dawns for the distressed city! The wrath of God bursts loose against the innumerable enemies in a storm of thunder and lightning, accompanied by earthquakes, hurricanes and all-devouring flames. This is a grand description that points to the Lord's coming unto judgment (cf. 28:21, 30:30, Zech. 14:1-6, and II Thess. 1:6-8).

The enemy will suddenly disappear like a dream in the night, which upon awakening is not only not there but can hardly be recalled. The enemy will not only have vanished but will never be able to rear its head again. In still another change of metaphor, verse eight says that the disillusionment of the enemies will be as great as that of a hungry person who dreamed he was eating and of a thirsty person who dreamed he was drinking but who upon awakening will be just as empty and miserable as before. This is followed by a clear, divine application.

Foolishness, Blindness, and False Religion

> 9. Stay yourselves, and wonder; cry ye out, and cry: they are drunken, but not with wine; they stagger, but not with strong drink.
>
> 10. For the LORD hath poured out upon you the spirit of deep sleep, and hath closed your eyes: the prophets and your rulers, the seers hath he covered.
>
> 11. And the vision of all is become unto you as the words of a book that is sealed, which men deliver to one that is learned, saying, Read this, I pray thee: and he saith, I cannot; for it is sealed:
>
> 12. And the book is delivered to him that is not learned, saying, Read this, I pray thee: and he saith, I am not learned.
>
> 13. Wherefore the Lord said, Forasmuch as this people draw near me with their mouth, and with their lips do honour me, but have removed their heart far from me, and their fear toward me is taught by the precept of men:
>
> 14. Therefore, behold, I will proceed to do a marvellous work among this people, even a marvellous work and a wonder: for the wisdom of their wise men shall perish, and the understanding of their prudent men shall be hid.

With these words the prophet returns to the circumstances around him in the wanton city.

Some expositors are of the opinion that the causes of the announced disaster are described, and that is most certainly the case; but we must not overlook the fact that these words themselves are describing the terrible divine judgment of delusion and spiritual blindness. As the Lord's spokesman the man of God enjoins his audience to be astonished at the frivolity of the city in this great calamity. It can be described only as a moral drunkenness. In contrast with the literal drunkenness of the previous chapter we are dealing with spiritual stupor.

Jeremiah and Ezekiel often use the image of moral, religious stupefaction and confusion. They present it as the result of drinking from the cup of trembling which God in His anger put to their lips. Delusion is a righteous judgment of God upon the foolishness of sin. This delusion and blindness is still further detailed by Isaiah. The prophets were to be an *eye* to the people to discern God's will, the spiritual dangers and signs of the times. But by means of a *deep sleep*

God had closed the eyes of the people. This suggests the deceiving nature of the false prophets who ultimately became the greatest scourge of Judah and Jerusalem. The *seers* are called *rulers* here, which does not mean a separate class of prophets but the prophets in general as the spiritual leaders of the nation. The characteristics of a sleeping person are that they are without sensation, without consciousness, without wakefulness, inactive and without prayer. This will be the moral and religious condition of Israel's leaders. It is emphatically stated that the Lord has poured on them a *spirit* of deep sleep. He sends an evil spirit on them to effect this. There is absolutely no reason to take this expression figuratively rather than literally. It is the consistent teaching of Scripture that there are evil spirits who, under the supreme authority of the Lord, can even be sent to a man such as Paul to keep him from pride.

The result of this delusion is described in two examples. The prophets can no more understand the divine visions than that they can read a sealed book. Regardless how well they can read otherwise and how educated they may be, they must acknowledge their inability and say: *I cannot.* Unwillingness is always followed in an aggravated measure by inability. The book of God's visions is given to one who cannot read with the request to read it. But he, too, must acknowledge his inability by saying: *I cannot.* That is how powerless Israel's many prophets would be in the future to read God's visions.

Finally, the prophet delivers a scourging lecture to the hypocritical formalists of Hezekiah's day, who comprised a great multitude. For when Hezekiah began his reformation and energetically carried it through, there were many who outwardly turned from idolatry and converted to Jehovah, but did not do so from the heart. They drew near to Jehovah with their mouths and their lips, but their hearts were far removed from Him. They observed human traditions and rules more than the one rule of God's Word. This one verse contains a volume of biblical psychology. In religious matters God is concerned with the heart, and it was exactly the heart that remained far from Him. They had the form of godliness but denied the power thereof, while it is exactly a manifestation of power the Lord is looking for — power of the Spirit, of faith, of hope and of love. They were blind with respect to God's visions, but they scrupulously adhered to the *precepts of men* (cf. Matt. 15:8). Because of all these abominations God will continue to deal marvelously with these people. In His righteous judgment He will cause the *wisdom* and *understanding* of Israel to perish completely. This marvelous work means punishment of their foolishness and blindness.

The Woe Upon the Secret Politics

15. Woe unto them that seek deep to hide their counsel from the LORD, and their works are in the dark, and they say, Who seeth us? and who knoweth us?
16. Surely your turning of things upside down shall be esteemed as the potter's clay: for shall the work say of him that made it, He made me not? or shall the thing framed say of him that framed it, He had no understanding?

The third woe is directed against Egyptian politics. The words *seek, hide* and *work in the dark* point out the secrecy of intrigue with Egypt. From 30:1 it is evident that initially Judah sought a secret alliance with Egypt. Apparently they wanted to keep hidden from the people their wicked plans to put their trust not in Jehovah but in flesh. For that reason they resorted to secret intrigues. Secret societies! Works of darkness! And all the while they were imagining that they were also hidden from the all-seeing eyes of the Lord, so that it looked as though they were saying defiantly, *Who seeth us?* and *Who knoweth us?* This proves that secret meetings for the purpose of forging evil designs are of a very early date. When man hides like a night owl, he usually has something in mind that is not very good. The Savior said that men loved the darkness more than the light, *because their works were evil.* This was also the case with these people in Jerusalem: they sought the darkness because their deliberations could not stand the light.

Their *turning* the ordinances of the Lord *upside down,* and their meeting in secret are exposed as the height of folly in this short parable of a potter and his clay. If the clay were to say to the potter and the thing made to its maker *you made me not,* or if a fired vessel were to speak disdainfully of its maker and say *he has no understanding* (of his trade), that would be no more foolish than what these leaders of Judah perpetrated with their secret politics; they acted as though God knew nothing about their scheming.

God's Public Plan of Salvation Contrasted with the Secret Plans of Judah's Rulers

17. Is it not yet a very little while, and Lebanon shall be turned into a fruitful field, and the fruitful field shall be esteemed as a forest?

18. And in that day shall the deaf hear the words of the book, and the eyes of the blind shall see out of obscurity, and out of darkness.

19. The meek also shall increase their joy in the LORD, and the poor among men shall rejoice in the Holy One of Israel.

20. For the terrible one is brought to nought, and the scorner is consumed, and all that watch for iniquity are cut off:

21. That make a man an offender for a word, and lay a snare for him that reproveth in the gate, and turn aside the just for a thing of nought.

22. Therefore thus saith the LORD, who redeemed Abraham, concerning the house of Jacob, Jacob shall not now be ashamed, neither shall his face now wax pale.

23. But when he seeth his children, the work of mine hands, in the midst of him, they shall sanctify my name, and sanctify the Holy One of Jacob, and shall fear the God of Israel.

24. They also that erred in spirit shall come to understanding, and they that murmured shall learn doctrine.

The Lord will put man's unbelief to shame. After only a short while the Lord will put the foolish generation to shame and perform wonders of grace and glory. He will change the face of the Holy Land by recreating it into a garden of pleasure and giving His people *joy upon joy.*

Joy upon joy — that is exactly what every man ultimately desires. The playing child, the lighthearted youth, the serious businessman — everyone seeks happiness, joy upon joy in one form or another. But no matter how much the sinner desires and chases after happiness, he will never find it under the sun. Even the whole world cannot satisfy the heart of a mortal. After all his efforts to obtain happiness, all that remains is the unutterable hunger of the soul, often aggravated by a polluted conscience and an unnerved body.

To *whom* does the Lord promise joy upon joy? To the meek, the people whose stony hearts have been removed. These are the people with a heart of flesh. They are no longer cold, hard, lifeless and senseless like a stone, but soft, tender, warm and receptive to the Lord and His blessed service, His Word and His people. Here it is Israel converted and restored.

When will this joy upon joy be given? The expositors say that this section contains no time delineation, but in the context there are no less than seven indications, which point to a certain time: (1) When inhospitable and rugged Lebanon will have been turned into a fruitful field. (2) When the *deaf,* the disobedient, listen to the Book. (3) When the *blind* will see. (4) When the *terrible one,* Satan, will be brought to nought. (5) When the *scorner* is consumed. (6) When all unrighteousness is cut off. (7) When *Jacob,* Israel, will no longer be ashamed. Whoever seriously contemplates these things must agree that this glorious time has not dawned as yet. We are still living in the days of disobedience, blindness and satanic seduction; unrighteousness is still not cut off and Israel is still wandering about. But as soon as all this has come to an end, at the coming of the Lord, this joy upon joy will truly be known upon earth by the meek who will inherit the earth.

What does this entail? A Christ who will be present, clothed with majesty and glory. In this verse He is called the *Holy One of Israel.* Satan, that arch tyrant, will then be bound. And for God's people sin, sickness and solicitude will vanish. Sin galls everything here and misery weighs us down. The evil world vexes us and the brooks of Belial terrify us; we are burdened and sigh because of Magor-Missabib, fear on every side.

Who will give this joy? Who else but He who loved us to the utmost. Outside of Him God is a consuming fire with whom no one can dwell. In Him are hid all the treasures of salvation. Outside of Him there is no light, no life, no love. What an encouragement this is for you, weary pilgrim, in the strife of life! What a comfort when you are overwhelmed by oppression and adversity! Wait upon the Lord, ye who fear the Lord, and keep courage! But what will then befall the sinner? He will be destroyed as described above. Jacob will no longer be ashamed or turn pale from fear. Those who suffered from spiritual delusion and those who *murmured* against God's ordinances will, after all those wonders of God's grace through Christ, wisely accept God's doctrine.

ISAIAH 30

The Woe Upon the Promoters of Egyptian Policy

1. Woe to the rebellious children, saith the LORD, that take counsel, but not of me; and that cover with a covering, but not of my spirit, that they may add sin to sin:

2. That walk to go down into Egypt, and have not asked at my mouth; to strengthen themselves in the strength of Pharaoh, and to trust in the shadow of Egypt!

3. Therefore shall the strength of Pharaoh be your shame, and the trust in the shadow of Egypt your confusion.

4. For his princes were at Zoan, and his ambassadors came to Hanes.

5. They were all ashamed of a people that could not profit them, nor be an help nor profit, but a shame, and also a reproach.

This chapter is a continuation of the preceding one and links up with verse fifteen. Some expositors are of the opinion that these words are directed at Ephraim, since II Kings 17:4 notices a covenant between Hoshea, the last king of the northern kingdom, and So, the king of Egypt, rather than a covenant between Judah and Egypt. But the entire context shows that this section speaks of Judah and Jerusalem. As far as the fact that it does not specifically mention a covenant is concerned, the expression *cover with a covering* could have been better translated by *making an alliance,* as many indeed do. Literally, the word means *pour out water,* but this refers to the pouring out of an oblation by which solemn agreements were confirmed. The Lord was Israel's Father, and He considered the people as His *children.* by refusing Him and putting their trust instead in the flesh of Egypt, they became disobedient, degenerate, rebellious and unfaithful; thus He calls them *rebellious children.* They had forsaken their Father to waste themselves on pagan Egypt. This was not according to the Spirit of the Lord, who through the mouth of the prophets had warned against such heaping of sin upon sin. It was a sin of unbelief, of disobedience, of pride and of foolishness. It was even a great sin of negligence, for they had neglected to ask of the Lord's mouth when they sought refuge in the *shadow* of Egypt, *i.e.*, the safety of Egypt. They refused to listen to the Lord's servant Isaiah, and it was exactly he whom they should have asked concerning a matter of such great importance.

To expose the folly of their policy, the prophet depicts the arrival of Judah's princes in Egypt. They have completed their long, difficult and dangerous journey in the hope of getting help and protection, but it is all in vain and to no avail. Even worse, it is unto shame and confusion to Judah. An alliance with Egypt will anger the Assyrians and provoke them to revenge. The question has been asked how it was possible that the God-fearing Hezekiah could assent to such a foolish act, since he was a reformative and theocratic king. It is certain that the initiative to this alliance was not his. We get the impression that among the rulers there was a strong party that favored close contact with Egypt. By secret maneuvering and intrigue it succeeded in bringing about this Egyptian alliance without the knowledge of their sovereign. Hezekiah was not a very powerful figure and was not the man to stand up courageously to the rebellious group of insolent princes. Hezekiah's reformational activity, like Josiah's later, affected the outward fringes of religious life. The leaders, the prophets, priests and rulers, only outwardly accommodated their "pious" king, who was influenced by that troublesome Isaiah.

The Burden of Behemoth of the South

6. The burden of the beasts of the south: into the land of trouble and anguish, from whence come the young and old lion, the viper and fiery flying serpent, they will carry their riches upon the shoulders of young asses, and their treasures upon the bunches of camels, to a people that shall not profit them.
7. For the Egyptians shall help in vain, and to no purpose: therefore have I cried concerning this, Their strength is to sit still.

The prophet inserts a brief oracle concerning the *behemoth* of the south in his lecture. The Hebrew word means hippopotamus, which at that time still lived in the Nile and the River Jordan. If we wish to translate it, then we have to think of a caravan of beasts of burden by means of which the Jews traveled to Egypt. The *south* means specifically the desert south of Judah, which they had to traverse to get to Egypt. This area is described here as very dangerous, a land of trouble and anguish, where lions in great numbers lurk for prey, where the most poisonous snakes and adders slither about and where the *fiery flying serpent* lives. Scripture frequently presents the desert as the habitat and scene of activity of the devil. It is wise to take this as a reference to the devil rather than "an image from the world of fantasy," as many do. Elsewhere Satan is represented as a *great red dragon* (cf. Rev. 12:3). When the men of Judah left the way of the Lord and their holy land of inheritance, they set foot on the land of the evil one. The prophet pictures these fools as they travel along with difficulty and surrounded by dangers, having their treasures loaded on the backs of asses and the humps of camels. What an activity, and all for nothing! For verse seven tells us, *Rahab shall sit still,* as the expression, *Their strength is to sit still,* means in the original. Elsewhere the poetic name for Egypt is *Rahab* (see Ps. 87:4, 89:10, Isa. 51:9). The word means, *great one, proud one, vaunted one, boaster.* Egypt will take on proud airs as though it is willing to help, and will deceive these men by making beautiful promises. But when worse comes to worse, it will do nothing and just sit still watching Judah being carried away captive to Babylon. What did proud Rahab care about despised Jewry! The Jews were just as much an abomination to them then as they were in the days of Jacob (Gen. 43:32; 46:34). And how blind and foolish the Jews were for seeking help from proud Rahab!

Isaiah is Charged to Write Down His Message

8. Now go, write it before them in a table, and note it in a book, that it may be for the time to come for ever and ever:

The accursed sin of making flesh their arm must be etched deeply into the memory of the people. The prophet is commanded to write especially the words *Rahab shall sit still* on a large tablet, so that everyone can see it. Oral preaching was soon forgotten, but this word had to be kept for posterity to serve as instruction, admonition and warning.

Isaiah's writing was considerable. He was not only a preacher and a poet, but also a writer. According to II Chronicles 26:22 and 32:32 he wrote a biography of King Uzziah and King Hezekiah. Back in 8:1-3 he was commanded to write a certain truth on a big roll so that everyone might read it. Thus Judah would be taught what the poet expresses so beautifully in these words:

> Trust not in man who soon must die,
> But on the living God rely;
> Most blest the man whose help is He
> That made the heav'n and earth and sea.

Judah's Register of Guilt

9. That this is a rebellious people, lying children, children that will not hear the law of the LORD:
10. Which say to the seers, See not, and to the prophets, Prophesy not unto us right things, speak unto us smooth things, prophesy deceits:
11. Get you out of the way, turn aside out of the path, cause the Holy One of Israel to cease from before us.

Isaiah must not only publicly expose Judah's folly, but he also had to write the preceding text in a book. The latter, of course, he did not do publicly but in his home. There he heaves a sigh of grief over Judah's sins. His heart groans under this burden and therefore he describes them in the strongest terms. They are degenerated children who deny their own Father. He alludes once again to the tragic and mysterious unsuccessful rearing of the Lord's children as in 1:2.

These rebellious children do not want to listen to the Father, to His law or to His servants the prophets. We must not imagine that the people of Judah expressed themselves in the same words as he uses in verse ten. As a rule people are not that honest and forthright regarding their disobedience, especially not religious people. The prophet rather depicts in brief and powerful strokes what it amounted to, the essential bent of their entire life regarding the Lord and His servant. The text is not referring to two classes of prophets when mentioning *seers* and *prophets.* Some Bible students see an essential difference between these words and think that they were two classes of prophets, but this is without any basis. When comparing references such as I Samuel 9:11; II Samuel 24:11; II Kings 17:13; I Chronicles 9:22; 26:28, II Chronicles 9:29; 12:15; 19:2; 33:18; Amos 7:12-14; Micah 3:7, it is obvious that Scripture wants us to view these words as wholly synonymous.

The way of the Lord was far too narrow for them. It was always and ever the same. It all seemed so monotonous, so narrow-minded, so insignificant to them. And Isaiah was forever talking about the Holy One of Israel. That seemed to be his hobbyhorse, his stopgap, the speech that betrayed him. For that reason they fervently wished that he would depart from the way of separation and cease talking about the *Holy One of Israel.* This crowd no longer wanted the truth. They had an aversion to it and could no longer stomach it as it condemned everything they did. But that was not all. They not only refused to hear the truth, but they decidedly wanted to hear the lie, *smooth things, deceits.* "Because they received not the love of the truth, that they might be saved. And for this cause, God shall send them strong delusion, that they should believe a lie" (II Thes. 2:10, 11). In our apostate days, we too see the rejection of the truth going hand in hand with the eager acceptance of the lie. The historic Church has no reason whatsoever to reproach Israel. They both have corrupted their way before the Lord. Judah's sin was in direct conflict with the basic law of the theocratic kingdom as laid down in Deuteronomy seventeen, for there Israel is emphatically told that she may not return to Egypt to multiply horses. Now, however, Judah wants to go exactly that way and says concerning the Lord's way of putting her trust in God: *Get you out of the way!*

The Bitter Fruit of Trusting in Egypt

> 12. Wherefore thus saith the Holy One of Israel, Because ye despise this word, and trust in oppression and perverseness, and stay thereon:
> 13. Therefore this iniquity shall be to you as a breach ready to fall, swelling out in a high wall, whose breaking cometh suddenly at an instant.
> 14. And he shall break it as the breaking of the potters' vessel that is broken in pieces; he shall not spare: so that there shall not be found in the bursting of it a sherd to take fire from the hearth, or to take water withal out of the pit.

Isaiah does not give in to the evil wishes of the people. He is not the kind of man to cut the truth in half or to twist it. Whereas his fellow citizens had said, "Cause the *Holy One of Israel* to cease from before us!" the prophet tells them, "Thus saith the *Holy One of Israel!*" In verse fifteen he uses this name again. This is most courageous and gives all timid preachers an example to follow. Verse twelve once more mentions the two main sins: the rejection of the Word of the Lord and trusting in *oppression and perverseness,* as he calls the fraudulent politics of Egypt. As a result of their sin they will be like a high wall in which there is a severe break. On account of this break the wall bulges and is ready to fall. Even with this break the wall may stand for some time, but it may also suddenly crash at any moment. How strikingly is this metaphor chosen! It is indeed Egyptian politics that caused the break in the life of both Israel and Judah. After the break had been effected, the wall *swelled out* for some time, signifying that Judah was a vassal state to this or that ruler, but at last the entire wall collapsed.

This wall will completely collapse, as another beautiful metaphor tells us. The wall will be totally crushed, just as when someone crashes an earthen vessel to the ground. Such a jar breaks into countless pieces and not one piece is big enough to scoop fire from the hearth or water from a pit. Thus the Lord will soon send Nebuchadnezzar to destroy Judah completely, which as a rebellious nation is again and again in league with Egypt. With his battering rams he will cause the high walls of Jerusalem to crash down into ruins.

"And Ye Would Not"

> 15. For thus saith the Lord GOD, the Holy One of Israel; In returning and rest shall ye be saved; in quietness and confidence shall be your strength: and ye would not.
>
> 16. But ye said, No; for we will flee upon horses; therefore shall ye flee: and We will ride upon the swift; therefore shall they that pursue you be swift.
>
> 17. One thousand shall flee at the rebuke of one; at the rebuke of five shall ye flee: till ye be left as a beacon upon the top of a mountain, and as an ensign on an hill.

The prominent people in Christ's time gloried in Abraham and in the law; but *they would not.* The contemporaries of Isaiah gloried in Egypt; but *they would not.* In both instances it was the corrupt state of their proud heart that made them reject the Word of the Lord. They refused to *return* from their proud schemes, to rest in the saving promise, to be quiet like a weaned child at its mother's breast, and to surrender trustingly to their Father. To be quiet! Indolent people have often misused this word. They did not realize that there are different kinds of quietness. There is the quietness of laziness and sleepiness, of death and the grave and of mute grief. None of these are meant here, of course. What is meant is the quietness of childlike faith. Judah was constantly in fear, today of one enemy, tomorrow of another. The wicked man has no peace but, rather, many griefs. They flee when there is no pursuer. Judah did not have that love of God that casts out fear. Judah's eyes were not constantly on the Lord but on Egypt's chariots and horses. That is where help would come from, they thought. But meanwhile they were very nervous and ran to and fro without accomplishing anything. The strong horses of Egypt were their weakness. Whereas they were strong indeed, they were alas very weak. When calamity struck, they could always flee on the fast horses. So, the Lord says, you will indeed use them to flee, but your enemies will pursue and overtake you on even faster horses.

> Not human strength or mighty hosts,
> Not charging steeds or warlike boasts
> Can save from overthrow . . .

King Zedekiah experienced the truth of these words when he fled on one of the fastest horses of the royal stables. But he was overtaken by the even faster enemy horsemen afterward to endure the most horrible tortures.

Nor will Judah's courage in the hour of affliction amount to anything. At the rebuke of one single enemy soldier a thousand of Judah's men will cowardly throw away their weapons and take flight, while only five of the army of the enemy will cause the whole army of Judah to flee. But, again, there will be a remnant of Judah, though it will be very small. It is compared with a mast on a mountain, a pine tree, which is used as a banner, an ensign. Just as such a tree is alone and forsaken, so it will be with depopulated and captive Judah, which at the same time is a warning sign to us.

A Waiting God and a Waiting People

> 18. And therefore will the LORD wait, that he may be gracious unto you, and therefore will he be exalted, that he may have mercy upon you: for the LORD is a God of judgment: blessed are all they that wait for him.

In the preceding verses we heard of Judah's sin, punishment and remnant. This promise is for the remnant. Nevertheless, it is said that the Lord will *wait* with His grace. In this context this expression is very significant. It reminds us of the father who continues to wait for the prodigal son. In Jeremiah 31:20 we read these touching words: "Is Ephraim my dear son? is he a pleasant child? for since I spake against him, I do earnestly remember him still: therefore my bowels are troubled for him; I will surely have mercy upon him, saith the LORD." Presently, the Lord still hides Himself from His beloved people (45:15). During the times of the Gentiles this word is fulfilled: "I will take my rest, and I will consider in my dwelling place" (18:4). For ages He has adopted a waiting attitude. But waiting implies His intention to visit Israel again with His salvation. He has thoughts of peace concerning Israel and is waiting to be gracious unto her. This is His determined intent, His promise, His longing. And this long waiting of God is a terrible chastisement to

Israel. After this waiting the Lord will be *exalted* in Christ's coming for Israel's deliverance. At this exaltation two things will take place: He will manifest Himself as the *God of judgment,* and He will have mercy upon Israel. These two concepts contain almost the entire eschatology of the future.

Blessed are all they that wait for him! the man of God cries. It is already blessed that His punishment of the wicked is not immediately carried out, but *blessed* indeed are they who wait for Him. In our day the God-fearing people who wait for Him are considered fanatics and fools, but not by Isaiah. Nor is this waiting for God a passive thing, as many seem to think, but rather the highest spiritual activity. Isaiah was suggesting that waiting for God implied staying away from Egypt; the psalmist sang:

> My soul, in silence wait for God;
> He is my help approved,
> He only is my rock and tower,
> And I shall not be moved.

Whoever waits for God today refuses to be taken in by all kinds of worldly designs and movements, and abstains from seeking all paths of carnal trust.

Israel Restored and Very Blessed

19. For the people shall dwell in Zion at Jerusalem: thou shalt weep no more: he will be very gracious unto thee at the voice of thy cry; when he shall hear it, he will answer thee.

20. And though the Lord give you the bread of adversity, and the water of affliction, yet shall not thy teachers be removed into a corner any more, but thine eyes shall see thy teachers:

21. And thine ears shall hear a word behind thee, saying, This is the way, walk ye in it, when ye turn to the right hand, and when ye turn to the left.

2. Ye shall defile also the covering of thy graven images of silver, and the ornament of thy molten images of gold: thou shalt cast them away as a menstruous cloth; thou shalt say unto it, Get thee hence.

23. Then shall he give the rain of thy seed, that thou shalt sow the ground withal; and bread of the increase of the earth, and it shall be fat and plenteous: in that day shall thy cattle feed in large pastures.

24. The oxen likewise and the young asses that ear the ground shall eat clean provender, which hath been winnowed with the shovel and with the fan.

25. And there shall be upon every high mountain, and upon every high hill, rivers and streams of waters in the day of the great slaughter, when the towers fall.

26. Moreover the light of the moon shall be as the light of the sun, and the light of the sun shall be sevenfold, as the light of seven days, in the day that the LORD bindeth up the breach of his people, and healeth the stroke of their wound.

Those who wait for Jehovah will not be put to shame. Suddenly the prophet again lifts himself out of the present miseries and transports himself and his audience into the glorious future which Christ will prepare for Israel and the nations at His return. We have seen more than once that such transports often appear in the prophets. Isaiah forgets the present miseries of his people and rejoices in the glorious future. In order not to dwell too extensively on these glorious promises we shall only touch upon their main aspects: (a) The people of Israel will dwell in *Zion*. This does not refer to the heavenly Zion, but to Zion on earth, as is indicated in the preceding and following contexts. (b) The restored people will *weep no more*. Among the other nations there will still be some sin, suffering, tears and dying, but no longer among the restored people. Now Israel's tears still flow every morning, but then they will flow no more. (c) There will be an immediate answer to prayer. As soon as the people make their desires known to God, He hears and answers them from His fullness. In a later description of the kingdom of peace this statement is intensified: *"Before* they call, I will answer"* (65:24). Israel has been calling for deliverance from its misery for ages, but her prayer has remained unanswered all these centuries. (d) Before Israel's deliverance dawns she will have much affliction: she will have to pass through the waters of the Great Tribulation. Michaelis translates this beautifully: "Upon your siege and affliction He will cause an abundance of food and drink to follow." Compare the expression *water of affliction* with the expression *overflowing scourge,* which we came across earlier. (e) The restored nation will behold her *Teacher* and *Leader, Christ.* Many take the word *teachers* to mean preachers; others think it means prophets who sometimes are hidden like those one hundred by Obadiah (I Kings 18:4) or who fled like Uriah (Jer. 26:21). The Greek translation has *false teachers, seducers,* but the Vulgate, Luther, Ewald, Kay, Wellhausen, Robert Smith, Jonckbloet, Ridderbos, Van Ravesteyn and others take this word in the singular. That is undoubtedly the way we must take it here, for not only the verb, which is in the singular, but also the whole context point in this direction.

Dr. Ridderbos has again given the correct translation when he renders these words: "But then your teacher will no longer hide himself, but your eyes will see your teacher." The only qualification is that *teacher* must be capitalized, as no one else is meant but our Great Teacher, Christ. In the Messianic prophecy of Joel 2:23 He is given the same name.[1] Israel will see its Messiah! (f) Israel will hear and obey the *word* of her returned Messiah who now, as the people's Teacher, will remain close to them and give them continual spiritual guidance. As a result of this constant guidance and instruction Israel will no longer turn to the right hand or to the left.

(g) Still another blessed result is vividly portrayed in verse twenty-two which says that Israel will despise and cast away its former idols *as a menstruous cloth.* They are abhorred even though they were idols of precious gold and of silver. (h) The restored nation will have the greatest fertility of her land. The cattle will find lush pasture. Even the beasts of burden such as oxen and asses will eat the finest fodder, grain that has been purified with the shovel and fan. A *shovel* was simply a tool that was used to throw the grain into a strong wind on the top of a hill, which was the usual method of winnowing. (i) The land will be so fruitful that even the high mountains and hills will have sufficient water. Before there was often a great lack of water, especially in the mountainous regions, now there will be springs and waterbrooks everywhere. The promise of abundant water is often found in Isaiah and this is always a promise of rich natural and spiritual blessings. Israel never thought of a sharp separation

---

[1]The reference is to the Dutch Authorized Version; in the KJV the words of Joel 2:23 are translated "the former rain." The Hebrew moreh has both meanings. —Trans.

between the natural and the spiritual as we do. (j) The sun and moon will have seven times their usual strength. Many people explain this, as well as all the preceding promises, symbolically as the blessings of the Church. Especially Vitringa with his great influence has caused many to err by spiritualizing these promises. But God's Word is spiritual enough and does not need to be more spiritual than it is. The Church Father Jerome took these words literally of the glorification of creation as it is also promised in the New Testament (cf. Rom. 8:21 and II Pet. 3:13). In that day of great wonders this will not be too wonderful for the Lord.

Finally, these glorious promises will not obtain their fulfillment in this dispensation nor in heaven, but, as is emphatically stated, *in the day of the great slaughter, when the towers fall.* The *towers* here stand for all that is high, proud, strong and exalted in the Christless culture of men. When the Lord comes to establish His kingdom of peace, He will first of all bring low all that is high with men and is an abomination with God. This He will do at the onset of His long day of a thousand years. But, beside this time reference another is given; it will be in the day when Jehovah-Jesus as the great Physician of His people will bind up their breach and will heal the wound which He Himself inflicted. For the Son of righteousness will have healing in His wings. Hence the great judgment and the great deliverance are once more beautifully juxtaposed.

A Description of Christ's Coming in Judgment

27. Behold, the name of the LORD cometh from far, burning with his anger, and the burden thereof is heavy: his lips are full of indignation, and his tongue as a devouring fire:

28. And his breath, as an overflowing stream, shall reach to the midst of the neck, to sift the nations with the sieve of vanity: and there shall be a bridle in the jaws of the people, causing them to err.

29. Ye shall have a song, as in the night when a holy solemnity is kept; and gladness of heart, as when one goeth with a pipe to come into the mountain of the LORD, to the mighty One of Israel.

30. And the LORD shall cause his glorious voice to be heard, and shall shew the lighting down of his arm, with the indignation of his anger, and with the flame of a devouring fire, with scattering, and tempest, and hailstones.

31. For through the voice of the LORD shall the Assyrian be beaten down, which smote with a rod.

32. And in every place where the grounded staff shall pass, which the LORD shall lay upon him, it shall be with tabrets and harps: and in battles of shaking will he fight with it.

33. For Tophet is ordained of old; yea, for the king it is prepared; he hath made it deep and large: the pile thereof is fire and much wood; the breath of the LORD, like a stream of brimstone, doth kindle it.

Most expositors are of the opinion that this is a grand description of the miraculous destruction of Sennacherib's army; although many agree that Assyria is presented here as the type of all world powers that are at enmity with God. There is no doubt about it, however, that here the Lord's return unto judgment is depicted. This coming is the main theme, of which the ruin of the Assyrian army was but a pale image. For verse twenty-seven emphatically states that the *name of the Lord,* Christ, *cometh from far.* He went to a faraway country and now He is coming back from there. His anger blazes and scorches everything that opposes Him; the *burden* of His hot anger is heavy. Woe unto these people, cities and nations on which this burden will rest! His *lips, tongue* and *breath* blaze and devour. Of His breath it is said that it will be *as an overflowing stream* that reaches *to the midst of the neck* (cf. 11:4). With it He will kill the *wicked* (one), Satan or Antichrist. II Thessalonians 2:8 suggests that His breath means the Holy Spirit who in 4:4 is called the *Spirit of judgment* and the *Spirit of burning.* He *sifts* the nations to such an extent that they perish, then come to naught, and are no longer. He puts a bridle in the jaws of the nations with which He will lead them to destruction. With this word *sift* the prophet harks back to the metaphor of verse twenty-four. On the metaphor of *bit* or *bridle,* see 37:29 and Ezekiel 29:4, 38:4. By it the Lord means that He keeps the nations in check like a wild animal. When it is said that this is an *erring* bridle it means that with it He leads the nations unto destruction.

In sharp contrast with the destruction of the nations, verse twenty-nine indicates that in Israel there will be a festive song of praise as in the paschal night (see Exod. 12:27; Matt.

26:30). When Egypt was severely afflicted, Israel had great joy. Thus, the same will be true but in a much greater measure in that *day of great slaughter.* Israel will have joy as one who *goeth with a pipe,* as one who goes up to the temple mountain accompanied by the happy music of flutes to meet the Rock of Israel.

Verse thirty is an incomparable description of the Lord's judgment. His glorious voice resounds through the world like the sound of many waters. His arm comes down in furious anger with devouring flames, tempest, cloudburst and hail (cf. 29:6; Rev. 11:19; 16:21). Assyria is beaten down by this powerful voice of the Lord — first Sennacherib, but especially the last king of the north. When we read Psalm twenty-nine, which speaks of the voice of the Lord in connection with this description, it is evident that this beautiful psalm is not merely poetry but prophecy concerning the coming of the Lord in judgment. The exact translation of verse thirty-two is very difficult, but the main idea is clear enough: Assyria will be destroyed and restored Israel will rejoice with the battle music of victory. Tophet was located in the valley of Hinnom where the people passed their children through the fire (II Kings 23:10; cf. Jer. 7:31; 19:6). The word is derived from *tephet,* altar, but the spelling *tophet* is ironically intended to give it the despicable meaning of *vomit.* This horrible place became a symbol of hell, the lake of fire and brimstone. It was prepared long ago for the king of the north who, like Antichrist, will apparently be cast into hell alive. The arch-criminal will be placed on the great pyre. There will be plenty of fuel. Christ is his executioner who by His Spirit (v. 28) will kindle him in a burning stream of fire and brimstone.

ISAIAH 31

The Folly of Egyptian Help

1. Woe to them that go down to Egypt for help; and stay on horses, and trust in chariots, because they are many; and in horsemen, because they are very strong; but they look not unto the Holy One of Israel, neither seek the LORD!

2. Yet he also is wise, and will bring evil, and will not call back his words: but will arise against the house of the evildoers, and against the help of them that work iniquity.

3. Now the Egyptians are men, and not God; and their horses flesh, and not spirit. When the LORD shall stretch out his hand, both he that helpeth shall fall, and he that is holpen shall fall down, and they all shall fail together.

This chapter is of the same period and of the same context as the preceding. It is only natural to assume that an important subject such as the wicked Egyptian politics is treated more than once and from different angles by Isaiah. Now the fifth woe is pronounced in connection with that hapless policy. Judah's rulers thought themselves to be very wise, since they trusted in the many and strong horses of Egypt and not in the *Holy One of Israel.* But Isaiah tells them with holy irony: *Yet he also is wise.* He will manifest His wisdom by bringing upon it the evil of a curse and by not calling back His words spoken through Isaiah, but promptly fulfilling them. He will arise in judgment against the *house of the evildoers* as Jerusalem is called here. At the same time He will visit their *help* or helpers, the wicked Egyptians, with His wrath. In His anger He will stretch out His hand against them and cast both the helper and the helped into an abyss of misery. The first part of verse three points out the reason why trust in Egypt is vain and foolish. The Egyptians were only weak, insignificant mortals and totally powerless to offer help against the enemy. Their horses were mere *flesh and not spirit.* With these brief, powerful strokes, the prophet depicts the basic thought of his message: God is everything and man is nothing; God is worthy of all trust and adoration and man is flesh, transient and powerless. At the time Egypt was renowned for its herds of horses and the Egyptian army for its cavalry, but all this was mere *flesh.* Is not all flesh grass and all the goodness thereof as the flower of the field (40:6)?

Jerusalem is Delivered Not by Egypt but by God Himself

4. For thus hath the LORD spoken unto me, Like as the lion and the young lion roaring on his prey, when a multitude of shepherds is called forth against him, he will not be afraid of their voice, nor abase himself for the noise of them: so shall the LORD of hosts come down to fight for mount Zion, and for the hill thereof.

5. As birds flying, so will the LORD of hosts defend Jerusalem; defending also he will deliver it; and passing over he will preserve it.

6. Turn ye unto him from whom the children of Israel have deeply revolted.

7. For in that day every man shall cast away his idols of silver, and his idols of gold, which your own hands have made unto you for a sin.

8. Then shall the Assyrian fall with the sword, not of a mighty man; and the sword, not of a mean man, shall devour him: but he shall flee from the sword, and his young men shall be discomfited.

9. And he shall pass over to his strong hold for fear, and his princes shall be afraid of the ensign, saith the LORD, whose fire is in Zion, and his furnace in Jerusalem.

These verses depict in a beautiful Isaiahic metaphor how it is not Egypt but God Himself who protects His city from its besiegers. A young and bloodthirsty lion has stolen a sheep from the flock. Roaring, it has caught its victim and, roaring, it hangs on to it. Shepherds came from every side in order to save the prey. According to the law, shepherds had to show proof when a sheep was missing that it had been taken by a wild animal. So, they tried to retrieve a leg or a piece of an ear (cf. Amos 3:12). The shepherds dare not approach the roaring lion so they stop at a distance and with loud cries and screams try to chase off the monster. But with its paw on the prey, it remains where it is and rends the air with its roaring. It is not scared off by their united efforts. The application is not hard to make. Just as that lion catches and protects its prey from a drove of screaming shepherds, so Jehovah-Jesus will descend to protect the holy city. The *birds flying* is no reference to aviators in air ships.[1] The Lion from the tribe of Judah can manage quite well without them in that day. It is rather the beautiful image of a mother bird which swoops down and protectively spreads its wings over its brood. In that day Israel will convert to Him. Verse six is not a command but a prophecy — they will cast away their idols (cf. 30:22). Assyria will fall before Him; not before Egypt, but before Him who at Jerusalem has the *fire* of grace and judgment!

---

[1] This was a popular interpretation advocated by some millennialists in the post-World War I period. —ED.

ISAIAH 32

The Blessed Reign of Christ

1. Behold, a king shall reign in righteousness, and princes shall rule in judgment.
2. And a man shall be as an hiding place from the wind, and a covert from the tempest; as rivers of water in a dry place, as the shadow of a great rock in a weary land.
3. And the eyes of them that see shall not be dim, and the ears of them that hear shall hearken.
4. The heart also of the rash shall understand knowledge, and the tongue of the stammerers shall be ready to speak plainly.
5. The vile person shall no more be called liberal, nor the churl said to be bountiful.
6. For the vile person will speak villany, and his heart will work iniquity, to practice hypocrisy, and to utter error against the LORD, to make empty the soul of the hungry, and he will cause the drink of the thirsty to fail.
7. The instruments also of the churl are evil: he deviseth wicked devices to destroy the poor with lying words, even when the needy speaketh right.
8. But the liberal deviseth liberal things; and by liberal things shall he stand.

This chapter is divided into three parts. The first eight verses depict the blessed reign of Christ that will dawn after Assyria's fall. The second part is directed against the frivolous women, while the final six verses return once more to the time of bliss under the direct reign of Christ. There are many Bible students who think that Hezekiah is meant by this king, but during his reign there was hardly a shadow of all the glory promised here. According to verse three, the curse, once announced in the occasion of Isaiah's calling, is removed, and the tongue of the stammering mockers of chapter twenty-eight will, during the reign of this King, be *ready* to speak *plainly,* clearly and distinctly. It is evident that this curse did not rest with all its weight on the people of Hezekiah's day, although they were extremely blind, foolish and hypocritical.

Israel as a nation, her land, her city, her temple, her priesthood and her kingship will be re-established in unheard-of glory. The renewed kingship will be the culmination of this restoration. These verses speak of a fulfillment similar to the remarkable annunciation of the angel in Luke 1:32, 33. We must not picture the Lord Jesus as an earthly king on an earthly throne who will day in and day out be in one and the same place here below. He will indeed be revealed, seen, acknowledged, admired and honored here on earth. But, references such as Jeremiah 30:9; Ezekiel 34:24; 37:24-25; 44:3; 45:16-17; 46:2, 16-18 seem to teach that He will commit the practical government to a resurrected David or one of his descendants. The Lord Jesus reigns, but He will leave the mundane aspect of this reign to a viceroy who in His name will reign as sole ruler. Some Bible students think that with this king a viceroy is meant, but in view of what is said of this *king* in verse two we would much rather think of Christ Himself. He Himself is the King of kings and the Lord of lords and under Him the ideal rulers reign according to His holy will. He will rule as a *man*, as a Man of God.

Verse two depicts His reign in powerful images. This King will be a *hiding place from the wind.* To a traveler in the desert it was precious to find a hiding place from the choking siroccos. A *covert from the tempest* is another metaphor expressing the idea of safety. The Lord Jesus is a safe hiding place from death, damnation and from the storms of judgment to all who believe in Him from the heart. The last two images of *rivers of water* and the *shadow of a great rock* express the refreshing, relief and comfort which Christ *in the times of refreshing* will bring to the inhabitants of the world. These images are very striking to anyone who can at all imagine the conditions in the Near East. The word *shadow* must be taken in the broad meaning of protection and relief. The results of Christ's reign are depicted in verses three to eight. The main idea is that the former judicial blindness, stupefaction and foolishness will be gone. In this connection one might notice once more 6:9-10; 29:18; 30:21. Under the reign of King Jesus, Israel's sin, punishment and wretchedness will have come to an end. Nor will there be any more bluffing and flattering during His reign; people and things will be called by their actual names.

Denunciation of the Careless Women

9. Rise up, ye women that are at ease; hear my voice, ye careless daughters; give ear unto my speech.
10. Many days and years shall ye be troubled, ye careless women: for the vintage shall fail, the gathering shall not come.
11. Tremble, ye women that are at ease; be troubled, ye careless ones: strip you, and make you bare, and gird sackcloth upon your loins.
12. They shall lament for the teats, for the pleasant fields, for the fruitful vine.
13. Upon the land of my people shall come up thorns and briers; yea, upon all the houses of joy in the joyous city:
14. Because the palaces shall be forsaken; the multitude of the city shall be left; the forts and towers shall be for dens for ever, a joy of wild asses, a pasture of flocks;

Again the prophet returns to the matters of everyday life. Whoever has no eye for the sudden changes in Isaiah's addresses does not understand this prophet. Hence, it is not necessary to seek for a different time of origin for these words, as some expositors do. Psychologically they fit perfectly in the framework of this particular time and train of thought.

Isaiah understood the seriousness of the times; his people did not. The leaders were muddled by strong drink, staggered on their feet, spouted forth gibberish and scornfully flouted all his warnings. The ladies, frivolous and fashion-crazed as they were, apparently had no favorable influence on the moral condition of the people. Meanwhile, it does not surprise us that those who assume that the first eight verses describe the wise and noble reign of Hezekiah think that this section is speaking of the women of Samaria; they compare this preaching of Isaiah with that of Amos four. These are foolish exegetical antics, however, for clearly the preceding verses cannot refer to Hezekiah but must be applied to Christ. The description of Jerusalem's women in chapter three tells us sufficiently that the prominent women of Jerusalem were not a hair better than those of Samaria. They

continued their wanton and vain behavior despite the serious
condition of the times, and that they were not in the least
concerned about the breach of their people. We would not
want to exclude the women outside of Jerusalem in the other
cities of Judah, either.

The prophet addresses them in a very dignified albeit
vehement manner to awaken them from their false
complacency and slumber. Both mothers and daughters were
very sure and self-confident, and thought of no danger which
would overtake them as a snare. With holy earnestness, Isaiah
admonishes them to accept his preaching. From the sequence
of his speech, we get the impression that he is addressing a
multitude of women who on the occasion of the wine-harvest
festivities, were dressed up gaily and were in a happy mood.
If so, this is another manifestation of his fearlessness and
courage. As a preacher of penitence, he was again and again
the spoilsport of the drinking and dancing crowd. The word
many has been inserted incorrectly. He means that after a
little over a year the terror and misery of a siege will descend
on them. There will be no harvest feast as the enemy will
have eaten the harvest. They will tremble and be troubled
and no longer be able to deck themselves in festive array, but
will drape themselves in clothes of mourning. They will smite
their breast for the destroyed fields and vineyards. Where the
harvest waved before, now thorns and briers will shoot up.
They will even grow in the very palaces and cities where the
people used to make merry. Instead of bustle and noise there
will be dead silence; in a word, prosperity will give way to
adversity, and joy to sadness and loneliness. *Ophel* means
knoll, hill, or fortress. It was the southern end of the temple
mount where the rich lived (cf. II Chron. 27:3; Neh. 3:26,
27; Song 4:4; Mic. 4:8). From now on robbers and wild asses
will take up their abode there. For how long? Isaiah will give
the answer:

The Outpouring of the Spirit from on High

15. Until the spirit be poured upon us from on high, and the
wilderness be a fruitful field, and the fruitful field be counted for
a forest.

> 16. Then judgment shall dwell in the wilderness, and righteousness remain in the fruitful field.
> 17. And the work of righteousness shall be peace; and the effect of righteousness quietness and assurance for ever.
> 18. And my people shall dwell in a peaceable habitation, and in sure dwellings, and in quiet resting places;
> 19. When it shall hail, coming down on the forest; and the city shall be low in a low place.
> 20. Blessed are ye that sow beside all waters, that send forth thither the feet of the ox and the ass.

Most expositors apply the pouring out of the Spirit to His outpouring on Pentecost, but this event lies entirely outside of the prophet's vision. Explanations of this kind have caused much confusion and are the result of misunderstanding the future work of the Holy Spirit. According to Joel 2:28 the Holy Spirit will be poured out upon *all flesh,* on all nations, classes and animals. For when the nature of lions will be changed so that they will no longer devour other animals but be as tame as domestic animals, eat straw like an ox and can be led by a little boy together with other wild animals, then this is the fruit of the glorious outpouring of the Spirit. "Thou sendeth forth thy spirit, they are created (also re-created!): and thou renewest the face of the earth" (Ps. 104:30). This the Lord will do in the great day of His coming. In the future the Spirit will have many things to do and He Himself longs for the future and prays for the return of Christ (Rev. 22:17). In the future He also will have work to do with regard to *Christ* (11:2), with regard to *Antichrist* (II Thes. 2:8), with regard to *Satan* (11:4), with regard to Israel (Ezek. 36:27; 37:6, 10, 14; 39:29; Zech. 12:10), with regard to the *judgment* (4:4, 30:28), with regard to *all flesh* (Joel 2:28) and with regard to the entire *creation.* It is this last-mentioned work of Christ that our text is referring to. Again and again Scripture refers to the Spirit as a fluid that can be poured out (cf. 44:3, Ezek. 39:29, Joel 2:28, Zech. 12:10). This can be explained from the fact that He is often likened to rain and oil. Here He is presented as a copious fruitful rain that changes the wilderness into a *fruitful field.* What in Isaiah's day was considered a fruitful field will in that joyful day be considered as an untillable forest. Hence, the prophecy of Psalm 104:30 will be literally fulfilled in the day when the wicked will be annihilated from the earth. In Old Testament times, the right of the strongest obtained among the wandering nomadic tribes of the desert. This, too, will be entirely different. In the desert justice will have a safe and lasting dwelling place, while righteousness will have a seat in the fruitful fields. On the basis of justice and righteousness there will be an abundance of peace and quietness. Right now the nations cannot obtain justice, since they are trying to establish peace on the basis of injustice and oppression. But then, this will never succeed, for righteousness, truth and peace are the unchangeable order of God. Surrounded by the bliss of this peace every man in Israel will sit under his vine and under his fig tree; and none shall make them afraid by wars, sieges or captivity (cf. Mic. 4:4). Verse nineteen means that in the Great Tribulation hail will fall on the proud forest, Assyria will come crashing down, and the city, the proud world power (25:2; 26:5), will be utterly debased. The prophets always take pains to make perfectly clear that the kingdom of peace will never come into being gradually but only after the most terrible judgments. The last verse pronounces a benediction upon those who will share in this promised bliss and who will inherit the new earth and who, after the curse has been removed, may tend and till it. Whoever enjoys this kingdom will be able to sow anywhere. Then, there will be living waters everywhere. He will be able to let his ox and ass graze freely since there will no longer be any thief or animal of prey to endanger them.

ISAIAH 33

The Sixth Woe

> 1. Woe to thee that spoilest, and thou wast not spoiled; and dealest treacherously, and they dealt not treacherously with thee! when thou shalt cease to spoil, thou shalt be spoiled; and when thou shalt make an end to deal treacherously, they shall deal treacherously with thee.

By way of climax, and in contrast to the *blessed* of the last verse of the preceding chapter, a *woe* is pronounced upon Assyria, which is mentioned for the last time here—except in the historical chapters—which describe its siege and downfall. Once again it must be said that the initial, partial and typical fulfillment of this oracle is found in Sennacherib and his pathetic defeat. But the real and final fulfillment is to be found with the terrible king from the north of the end time. Here he is reproached for his violence and unfaithfulness. Also, verse eight speaks of the breaking of the covenant by Sennacherib, which is described in II Kings 18:14-17. He will be dealt with, however, according to the stern law of retribution: the destroyer is destroyed, the treacherous one dealt with treacherously. But he must first have accomplished his destructive activities. The Lord must first use him as the rod of His anger. The day of final reckoning is coming to all the wicked.

A Prayer in Extremity by the Faithful Remnant

> 2. O LORD, be gracious unto us; we have waited for thee: be thou their arm every morning, our salvation also in the time of trouble.
> 3. At the noise of the tumult the people fled; at the lifting up of thyself the nations were scattered.

4. And your spoil shall be gathered like the gathering of the caterpillar: as the running to and fro of locusts shall he run upon them.

5. The LORD is exalted; for he dwelleth on high: he hath filled Zion with judgment and righteousness.

6. And wisdom and knowledge shall be the stability of thy times, and strength of salvation: the fear of the LORD is his treasure.

A prayer of this kind was most likely already uttered when Sennacherib stood before the walls with his armies, but in the day of Jacob's great fear the God-fearing remnant will pray this again against her cruel enemies. Perhaps Isaiah uttered this prayer as the representative and mouthpiece of the pious remnant. It is a touching supplication for grace, for help and rescue *in the time of trouble,* with a declaration that they have waited for the Lord. The actual prayer is wholly contained in verse two; in the remaining verses the supplicant again turns to the happy state of bliss resulting from the coming of the Lord. At His *lifting up,* at His exaltation as the King of kings and Lord of lords the nations will scatter abroad like chaff. The *noise of the tumult* refers to His glorious voice of thunder, which will cause the nations to tremble. Verse four may already have had an initial fulfillment after the death of the Assyrian soldiers, for undoubtedly the inhabitants of Jerusalem congregated like caterpillars around the corpses and the implements of war. We know, however, that immediately after the Great Tribulation Israel will plunder its former oppressors and take the treasures of the nations, as it once did from the Egyptians. The image of caterpillers and locusts tells us that they will take away everything from the nations. According to verse five, the returning Christ is the highly exalted and all powerful King whose throne is in the highest heavens and who has filled Zion with judgment and righteousness. Finally, verse six points out the secret of Israel's salvation and glorious state. Spiritual wisdom and knowledge are her strength, her treasure and her stability. The fear of the Lord is no slavish fear, but one based on love; it will be their treasure and lasting happiness.

The Country's Condition at the Invasion by the Enemy

> 7. Behold, their valiant ones shall cry without: the ambassadors of peace shall weep bitterly.
> ` 8. The highways lie waste, the wayfaring man ceaseth: he hath broken the covenant, he hath despised the cities, he regardeth no man.
> 9. The earth mourneth and languisheth: Lebanon is ashamed and hewn down: Sharon is like a wilderness; and Bashan and Carmel shake off their fruits.

The crying of the *valiant* is a reference to the provocative boasting of the Rabshakehs and the *ambassadors of peace* does not refer to angels or prophets, but the messengers who were sent to try to obtain peace. We must picture these messengers as returning with loud lamentations and uttering out the short impassioned sentences of verse eight. After their sad report no one dares to travel any more for fear of falling into the hands of the cruel enemy who does not spare a single city and has no regard for any man. In visual personifications the prophet presents the entire country as mourning and dolefully weeping. In Israel people were ashamed of things that were barren and unfruitful: Lebanon too is ashamed. Sharon, Bashan and Carmel, normally the most fruitful and delightful places, are withered and have become like a desert.

Jehovah Himself Announces His Coming to Judge Assyria

> 10. Now will I rise, saith the LORD; now will I be exalted; now will I lift up my self.
> 11. Ye shall conceive chaff, ye shall bring forth stubble: your breath, as fire, shall devour you.
> 12. And the people shall be as the burnings of lime: as thorns cut up shall they be burned in the fire.
> 13. Hear, ye that are far off, what I have done; and, ye that are near, acknowledge my might.
> 14. The sinners in Zion are afraid; fearfulness hath surprised the hypocrites . . .

There are several different voices speaking in this grand piece of poetry. First, the Lord Himself speaks and announces His *rising* unto battle. His coming again is often presented in Scripture as a rising unto battle. We have but to think of the well-known paraphrase of Psalm 68:1,

> God shall arise and by His might
> Put all His enemies to flight . . . ,

which also refers to His coming in judgment against the wicked. When He returns He will be exalted to His highest glorification. With different words it is further stated that He will manifest His highness. Secondly, Jehovah-Jesus addresses the enemy. With crushing irony He compares the enemies, who were full of plans against Jerusalem, to people who conceived chaff or straw and hay and who brought forth stubble. The metaphor of pregnancy and birth appears again and again in the prophetic announcements of judgment. Isaiah 26:18 speaks of bringing forth *wind.* Straw, hay, stubble and chaff in Scripture stand for that which is worthless. Their spirit, their own breath or breathing with anger and wrath will kindle the stubble. This expresses the striking thought that the wicked effect their own destruction and with their own sins ignite the fire of hell. The nations will be burned as *lime* and as *thorns.* The latter metaphor is also frequently used by the psalmists and prophets (cf. 5:24; 9:18). In verse thirteen Jehovah admonishes the faraway nations to give heed to his mighty acts and to acknowledge His might.

> Say ye to God, How terrible
> In all Thy works art Thou!
> To Thee Thy foes by Thy great power
> Shall be constrained to bow.

When Christ rises in judgment the wicked in Zion will also be seized by terror. We are not dealing here with a beneficial fear that some suppose fell upon the wicked in Jerusalem after Sennacherib's downfall, but with the fearfulness that will befall the unfaithful when beholding the person of Christ. This sight will be so unbearable to all the wicked that they will pray to the mountains to hide them from *His* sight.

A Significant Question Answered

> 14b. Who among us shall dwell with the devouring fire? who among us shall dwell with everlasting burnings?
> 15. He that walketh righteously, and speaketh uprightly; he that despiseth the gain of oppressions, that shaketh his hands from holding of bribes, that stoppeth his ears from hearing of blood, and shutteth his eyes from seeing evil;
> 16. He shall dwell on high: his place of defence shall be the munitions of rocks: bread shall be given him; his waters shall be sure.

We believe that this question will be asked in the day when Christ reveals His overwhelming majesty in Jerusalem (cf. 2:9, Hosea 10:8; Mal. 3:2; 4:1; Rev. 6:16-17; 9:6). The prophet does not fail to give the correct answer to this question. It *is* possible *to stand before the Son of man* (Luke 21:36). In his answer the prophet enumerates a series of virtues that remind us of the righteous man of Psalm fifteen. That person can face with boldness the Judge of the future who (a) walketh righteously, (b) speaketh uprightly, (c) despiseth the gain of oppressions, (d) disdainfully shaketh his hands from receiving bribes, (e) stoppeth his ears from listening to bloody plans and (f) shutteth his eyes from seeing evil. The person with these qualities is said to be righteous.

Such a righteous person will not only be standing before the Judge but will be exalted with Him, and protected and cared for by Him in the day of Jacob's calamity. When Antichrist wants to starve the faithful remnant to death (Rev. 13), Christ will miraculously take care of them (Rev. 12). In the final analysis that is what this prophecy is referring to.

Seeing the King in His Beauty

> 17. Thine eyes shall see the king in his beauty: they shall behold the land that is very far off.
> 18. Thine heart shall meditate terror. Where is the scribe? where is the receiver? where is he that counted the towers?
> 19. Thou shalt not see a fierce people, a people of a deeper speech than thou canst perceive; of a stammering tongue, that thou canst not understand.
> 20. Look unto Zion, the city of your solemnities: thine eyes shall see Jerusalem a quiet habitation, a tabernacle that shall not

be taken down; not one of the stakes thereof shall ever be removed, neither shall any of the cords thereof be broken.

21. But there the glorious LORD will be unto us a place of broad rivers and streams; wherein shall go no galley with oars, neither shall gallant ships pass thereby.

22. For the LORD is our judge, the LORD is our lawgiver, the LORD is our king; he will save us.

23. Thy tacklings are loosed; they could not well strengthen their mast, they could not spread the sail: then is the prey of a great spoil divided; the lame take the prey.

24. And the inhabitant shall not say, I am sick: the people that dwell therein shall be forgiven their iniquity.

Many expositors think that *the king in his beauty* is a reference to King Hezekiah and that by *his beauty* is meant his joy on account of the destruction of Sennacherib's army; the *land that is far off* is mentioned in contrast to the construction of the siege. Now it can safely be considered a rule that Scripture would never describe the glory and majesty of earthly rulers in such terms. If an earthly king had been meant, his name would have been mentioned or it would have said *thy* king. Moreover the context irrefutably points to Christ who in verse ten announced His coming and exaltation above all nations. Subsequently in verse fourteen, it is said of the wicked that they cannot stand to be in His presence. He was to them a *devouring fire* and eternal burnings. Now, however, in glorious contrast to those wicked it is said that the righteous will see the King in His beauty. Many Psalms describe the same contrast (cf. Ps. 68:1-6; 96-98). See for instance the first two verses of Psalm 68 and compare them with the following four. The same is true in Psalms 96, 97 and 98. Here follows an example:

> Consuming flames deploy
> Before Him, to destroy
> His foemen round about Him,
> Who vainly seek to flout Him.

Contrasted with this is:

> Jehovah's kindly face
> Gives happiness and grace
> To all that are pure-hearted;
> To them in life imparted.

In that day King Jesus will not only be *beautiful,*
illustrious, and majestic but he will reign over a *land that is
far off.* Whether this means the land of Canaan, which
according to the promise will extend from the Nile to the
Euphrates, or the entire world over which His sceptre will
sway, both make good sense and both will one day be full
reality.

Then His people Israel will be eternally beyond the reach
of all *terror* and know it only as belonging to their past
history. Their contemplation is graphically described by the
questions: Where is the scribe? Where is the receiver? Where
is the counter of towers? When contemplating all the terrors
they endured in the past, they ask where all those enemies
who came to tax them have gone. To the delivered people the
present glory is all the greater since it contrasts so brilliantly
with the oppression of the past. All three words of verse
eighteen refer to the officers of the enemy, and the counting
of towers was a preparation for levying war taxes. The
receiver, actually the weigher, had to examine the weight of
the collected gold and silver, while the scribe was the
bookkeeper. The enemy did these things tauntingly and with
malicious pleasure. Harsh officers filled the hearts of the
people with terror and dismay. They are called *fierce* and *of a
stammering tongue.* In spite of their misery the Jews still had
to smile when hearing the halting Hebrew of their enemies. It
is noted in II Kings 18:28 that Rabshakeh spoke Hebrew.

Now the text turns from the past to the future again. The
King was beautiful and illustrious, His land of great size, His
people happy and His city, Jerusalem, will be a *quiet
habitation,* a safe city, surrounded on all sides by rivers and
broad streams, unapproachable and unconquerable. A *tent*
was but a slender, temporary dwelling, but the city of God
will be like a tent the stakes of which will never be pulled up
and the ropes of which will never be broken. Jehovah-Jesus
Himself is present there with Israel. Verses fourteen and
seventeen implied this but here it is emphatically confirmed.
Verse twenty-one must be seen as a metaphor to express the
glorious reality. The city of the great King is compared to a
inpregnable fortress that is surrounded by water. No ship of
the enemy, large or small, can penetrate it. *Gallant* ship in

our language would be warship. The reason for the invincibility of restored Jerusalem lies in Christ of whom the restored people shout with joy that He is their Judge, Lawgiver and King. We must not overlook the fact that it is restored Israel who cries this. Christ will still be a Lawgiver to Israel. The Sermon on the Mount of Matthew 5-7 will be the nation's law and constitution. No inhabitant of the holy city will any longer report sick, for Israel's sins are forgiven and there are no wounds any more. It is true that no sickness is found in heaven. This text, however, is not speaking of heaven but of restored Jerusalem on earth during the kingdom of peace. It is not true that no sickness will be found on earth any longer, since it will still be found among the nations outside of Israel. Verse twenty-three presents no difficulties if we only keep in mind that it contains the beautiful image of an enemy ship attempting to approach the fortress with hostile intentions — remember Assyria! — and is wrecked in full view of the city. Everything is destroyed — the ropes, the mast and the sails. Judah sees this and jeers, and the *lame* take the prey. Again how brilliant and original this picture is!

ISAIAH 34

The End of the World

1. Come near, ye nations, to hear; and hearken, ye people: let the earth hear, and all that is therein; the world, and all things that come forth of it.

2. For the indignation of the LORD is upon all nations, and his fury upon all their armies: he hath utterly destroyed them, he hath delivered them to the slaughter.

3. Their slain also shall be cast out, and their stink shall come up out of their carcases, and the mountains shall be melted with their blood.

4. And all the host of heaven shall be dissolved, and the heavens shall be rolled together as a scroll: and all their host shall fall down, as the leaf falleth off from the vine, and as a falling fig from the fig tree.

In these verses all nations are summoned to give heed to the great judgment acts of the Lord. The Lord will perform dreadful things among the nations, so that it will be of the utmost importance to pay heed to them and to behold the superior majesty of God above all nations. Even the inanimate creation is summoned to watch the Lord execute judgment. Let the world see, hear and be silent, for God will speak and act! The reason for this solemn summons is given: the Lord's indignation is poured out upon all the nations and His flaming fury upon all their armies, on all their culture; He has utterly destroyed them: He has assigned them to the curse of hell and to the slaughter. The number of the slain will be so great that they are not buried but cast out in great heaps; the stench of their carcases will contaminate the air and the mountains will be soaked, indeed be melting and dripping, with their blood (cf. Rev. 14:20). This old, sinful earth has seen countless calamities for ever so long, but it will have to endure the greatest of agonies in the future. The description in verse four must be taken literally and not be evaporated in meaningless generalities. But when taking it literally, we must at the same time have an eye for the rich imagery which we meet time and again. For instance, will the heavens be literally rolled together? But the phrase *as a scroll* is a metaphor, of course, or rather, a simile. The description of the removal of the heavenly bodies agrees fully with that in the New Testament (Matt. 24:29; Rev. 6:12-14). Finally, this judgment will be complete and all-encompassing. In these four verses the little word *all* appears no less than five times. The *host of heaven* means the spiritual wickedness in high places (cf. 24:21; Eph. 6:12; Rev. 12:7-9; 20:1-8).

The Judgment Upon Edom as a Type of the Anti-Semitic World Power

5. For my sword shall be bathed in heaven: behold, it shall come down upon Idumea, and upon the people of my curse, to judgment.
6. The sword of the LORD is filled with blood, it is made fat with fatness, and with the blood of lambs and goats, with the fat of the kidneys of rams: for the LORD hath a sacrifice in Bozrah, and a great slaughter in the land of Idumea.
7. And the unicorns shall come down with them, and the bullocks with the bulls; and their land shall be soaked with blood, and their dust made fat with fatness.
8. For it is the day of the LORD'S vengeance, and the year of recompences for the controversy of Zion.

Edom was a sister nation to Israel, but it hated Israel more than any other nation. Throughout all of history we see a burning hatred of Edom against Israel. It is for this reason that Edom is frequently presented as a representative of all the nations that hated the Jews. Verse eight clearly indicates that this is the reason why judgment descends on Edom. My sword has *become drunk in heaven,* says the Lord. This means that it is full of God's anger and will strike without respect of persons the enemies of exiled Israel. Then this sword of the Lord is presented as a priest's butchering knife and the Edomites as the defenseless cattle that must be sacrificed. His sword drips with blood and gleams with the fat of the sacrificial animals. At that time *Bozrah* was the capital of Edom. There used to be quite a difference of opinion regarding the word *unicorns,* but today the general opinion is that it does not mean rhinoceros but aurochs, or wild bison. According to Deuteronomy 33:17 this animal did not have one but two horns (cf. Num. 23:22; Job. 39:9-10; Ps. 22:21). It is now extinct. These powerful *oxen* together with the *bullocks* and *bulls* stand for the mighty ones. Edom's land will be totally covered with blood and fat in that day of vengeance. The Lord will do all these things for the sake of His Zion, His beloved people, who were forever hated by Edom.

The Total Destruction of the Land of the Edomites

9. And the streams thereof shall be turned into pitch, and the dust thereof into brimstone, and the land thereof shall become burning pitch.

10. It shall not be quenched night nor day; the smoke thereof shall go up for ever: from generation to generation it shall lie waste; none shall pass through it for ever and ever.

11. But the cormorant and the bittern shall possess it; the owl also and the raven shall dwell in it: and he shall stretch out upon it the line of confusion, and the stones of emptiness.

12. They shall call the nobles thereof to the kingdom, but none shall be there, and all her princes shall be nothing.

13. And thorns shall come up in her palaces, nettles and brambles in the fortress thereof: and it shall be an habitation of dragons, and a court for owls.

14. The wild beasts of the desert shall also meet with the wild beasts of the island, and the satyr shall cry to his fellow; the screech owl also shall rest there, and find for herself a place of rest.

15. There shall the great owl make her nest, and lay, and hatch, and gather under her shadow: there shall the vultures also be gathered, every one with her mate.

These verses contain two representations of the destruction of Edom. The first one in verses nine and ten, alluding to the total annihilation of Sodom and Gomorrah, depicts a land that is burning forever and ever. It seems that during the millennium there will be on earth places that will always tangibly remind the inhabitants of the earth of the abominations of mankind and the judgments of God (cf. 66:24; Ezek. 47:11; Rev. 14:11; 19:3). This first representation is the more prophetic of the two, which will obtain its literal fulfillment in the future.

The second representation is that of a howling wilderness, as the land of Edom has been for centuries, according to Keith and Urquehart. The experts are still very uncertain about which animals are referred to; there are variances in translation and each one doubts his own translation. The *cormorant* is a bird that belongs to the heron family and lives in marshy areas. Instead of *bittern,* read *hedgehog.* Just as an architect uses a *measuring line* and *plumb line* when erecting a building, so the Lord will use them to turn the structure of the state of Edom into a desolate chaos like the earth was before its formation — without form and void. There will be no nobles or princely rulers. In the erstwhile luxurious palaces *thorns, nettles* and *thistles* will come up and be a habitation of *dragons* and *owls.*

The *wild beasts of the desert* (lynxes?) and the *wild beasts of the island* (jackals?) will meet each other in the destroyed land of the Edomites. It will be full of all kinds of predatory animals. The *satyr* will cry to his fellow. The Hebrew word used here is *sair,* which as an adjective means *hairy* (Gen. 27:11) and as a noun *he-goat* (Gen. 37:31, Lev. 4:23). For this reason Izak Leeser translates "one goat shall call to his fellow." The same word is translated by either *devils* or *satyrs* in the King James Version. *Seirim* reminds many expositors of the Egyptian deities which had the form of goats, and which the Jews allegedly took over from the Egyptians. The Egyptians worshipped goats as gods and had a beautiful temple near the Nile where this worship was perpetrated in the form of such abominations as are described in Leviticus 18:23. This idea is very debatable, however, on the basis of the fact that the references to Egyptian deities, such as in Joshua 24:14 and Ezekiel 23:3, 8; 20:7, makes no mention of the *seirim.* Baudissen and others are of the opinion that the *seirim* stand for all idols, but a text such as II Chronicles 11:15, 16 contradicts this idea. Dr. J. H. de Visser says in his book *Daemonologie van het Oude Testament:* "The *seirim* are nothing but hideous, unclean spirits, which inhabit desolate places and of which the superstitious are afraid, for which reason they sometimes sacrifice unto them." This idea is acceptable. Because of their uncleanness and hideousness, people imagined them as being hairy. On the basis of this idea the best translation of *seirim* is satyrs, demons, or field devils. The last of these three names fits best in this context.

The creatures of the night will also settle there. Which creatures are they? The word *lilith* is the feminine form of *lil* = night and hence means literally *the nocturnal*. Once again we quote what Dr. J. H. de Visser says about this in his dissertation mentioned before: *"Lilith* derives its origin from that which was extremely gruesome, and which was a common phenomenon during the night in such regions. When everything that ran around and frolicked during the day was at rest, *lilith* arose to be awake. Later Jewish superstition made it into a goddess of the night, who restlessly wandered about, killed children, defiled men, and was pictured as having wings and long, loose, flying hair." According to him, she dwelt in ghastly and spooky places. We can add to this that the Jews pictured this night ghost as a beautiful woman who seduced men and pursued and killed children. We must not think, however, that the prophet agrees and adopts this popular superstition here. Rather the opposite is true and Jewish superstition seized this text for its own purpose. The Holy Spirit obviously is referring to an evil spirit, which was especially active during the night and did as it liked in the darkness.

On the authority of Bochart most expositors think that with the *great owl* the very poisonous viper is meant, a small serpent that lives in some parts of Africa and Arabia. Dr. Ridderbos translates here: "There the viper nests and lays and gathers and hatches her eggs." The fact is however, that neither the viper, nor any other snake, hatches her own eggs. Like the turtles, they let the sun hatch them. The things that are said further on of this animal remind us more of a bird than of a serpent. The viper was dreaded because it could strike lightning fast at people and afflict a mortal bite. The *vultures* are predatory birds that spread a terrible stench; they are not the ordinary lammergeiers. Van der Palm says correctly that this last section is inimitably painted with the most daring poetic colors.

"Seek Ye out of the Book of the Lord"

> 16. Seek ye out of the book of the LORD, and read: no one of these shall fail, none shall want her mate: for my mouth it hath commanded, and his spirit it hath gathered them.
>
> 17. And he hath cast the lot for them, and his hand hath divided it unto them by line: they shall possess it forever, from generation to generation shall they dwell therein.

Scripture frequently speaks of a book of the Lord, which sometimes means the book of life, and other times the book of retribution (Exod. 32:32; Ps. 56:8; 69:28; Dan. 7:10; Mal. 3:16; Rev. 3:5; 20:12; 21:27). Neither of these books is meant here, however, but simply the black register of horrors that is predicted for Edom. This shows that the Lord Himself has written this book and wants it to be considered as such. It also shows that the Lord wants His people to read and examine this prophecy. We do not find many commands in Isaiah's prophecies, but here is a clear and stern command to search the divine predictions. It is said that none of these terrifying animals will fail. His mouth has infallibly predicted all these things through Isaiah and therefore everything that may not have been literally fulfilled as yet will be literally fulfilled in the day of the Lord's coming. The Spirit of the Lord Himself, who infallibly foretold these things, will also gather these wild animals in Edom's land. After the destruction of Jerusalem by Nebuchadnezzar, this prophecy was partially fulfilled. Umbreit correctly comments on the last clause of verse sixteen: "In this manner the man of God indicates that his words must not be taken in a poetic but a prophetic sense." In the last verse these animals of prey are compared to a colony of people who have been gathered by the hand of the Lord and led by Him, as the Head of the colony, to that place. Just as Israel received the land of Canaan as an inheritance out of His hand by lot, so the Lord will do the same in Edom with respect to these revolting animals. Hence it was Jehovah Himself who not only foretold all these things but also fulfilled them, or will fulfill them; the battle of Armageddon as described in Revelation 19:11-21 will bring about the complete fulfillment of this remarkable prophecy (cf. 49:7-22; Ezekiel 25:12-14; 35;

Amos 1:11-12) to illustrate the distinction between historical and prophetic Edom.

An interesting question, however, is whether in the *times of restitution of all things* there will also be a restoration for Edom. Both opinions are held. Rev. J. Fles, an eminent student of prophecy, wrote concerning this in his Bible lectures of 1879:

> There will also come a time of life and peace for the world. When the Lord Jesus will destroy the kingdom of Satan, every knee will bow before Him, and every tongue will confess Him. Israel's sealed ones will preach happiness and salvation to the world. Nations and lands that are still sitting in darkness and anxiously look for deliverance will hear of the salvation of our God. Esau left the home of his father (Gen. 36) and his descendants lost the knowledge of God and became bitter enemies of God's people. But Esau's people has a future that is glorious. This people must, like Ammon and Moab, and also like the ten tribes of Israel, appear as a nation, and that before Antichrist sits on the throne, for they will escape from his hand and his destructive sword (Dan. 11:41). And when the Lord Himself will decide the great battle in the land of Israel, His threshing floor (cf. Isa. 21:10), when he will save His people as wheat on the threshing floor, a voice of Seir will cry out: Watchman what of the night? The Watchman shall answer: The morning cometh, and also the night, unto you, O Edom! That night may no longer continue. If you will only humbly and earnestly ask, our King is merciful; hence ask, and pray, and thus return, O people of Edom! and come with us to the Lord and His mercy, for there is healing under the shadow of His wings. And Edom will hear and come and be saved. Saviors and liberators will come upon Seir, Esau's mountains, who will reform, restore, and judge the people in truth, and the Kingdom will be the Lord's (Obad. 21).

With respect to this exposition it can be argued, however, that the Lord, through Jeremiah, has expressly said of Moab and Elam that in the last days He will bring again their captivity, but *not* so of Edom (Jer. 48:47, 49:39).

ISAIAH 35

The Kingdom of Peace Following Armageddon

> 1. The wilderness and the solitary place shall be glad for them; and the desert shall rejoice, and blossom as the rose.
> 2. It shall blossom abundantly, and rejoice even with joy and singing: the glory of Lebanon shall be given unto it, the excellency of Carmel and Sharon, they shall see the glory of the LORD, and the excellency of our God.

In contrast to and as the result of the punishment of all the wicked, the sun of Israel's salvation will rise and all of creation will blossom as a rose. Those expositors who view this chapter independently from the preceding one do not see the glorious connection between the judgment upon the nations and the kingdom of peace. There, a blooming area was changed into a dismal desert; here, the arid land is changed into a blossoming garden of delight, so that we have a perfect contrast. Marginal notes in the Dutch and English Bibles as well as most Protestant expositors take these verses as a reference to the glorious state of the Church. Even Catholic expositors have been more logical in this respect than Protestant commentators. All too often the latter have given to the Church what belonged to Christ and Israel. Calvin identified the Kingdom of God with the Church. Keeping this in mind we quote his view on this chapter:

> I am convinced that the often vague image the prophet received was that of the Kingdom of God on earth, which one day will come about by the spreading of the gospel. I say 'will come about,' for today it is still far off. After the many kinds of horrors that fill the preceding chapters, it is a relief now to behold his vision of such a happiness as is found, we regretfully admit, only sporadically as yet on earth. Many trials, indeed, many severe chastisements, are

undoubtedly in store for us before we are ready for a state of bliss as is depicted here. That will not take place until men everywhere will have gratefully and humbly seized the hand of the Saviour, and only then the ideal conditions such as this chapter describes — after we eliminate the fantastic images of the prophetic style — can to a large extent be materialized.

These words rather accurately reflect Calvin's view concerning the prophecies of salvation that have not been fulfilled as yet. This shows that he had just about the same view as the present-day postmillennialists, the men of federation of churches, who also do not take similar prophecies literally, but only those that as beautiful ideals can be materialized by the united and courageous effort of men.

Many expositors think that this chapter is referring to Israel's return from Babylon, but this thought is too absurd to take the time to refute it. For we may search all we want in the books of Ezra and Nehemiah and of the post-Babylonian prophets, but we shall not find a trace of all the glory predicted here, but rather the opposite. Dr. J. van Oosterzee writes correctly:

Indeed, we would have to rob this prophecy completely of its venerable character in order to reduce it to mere poetry, albeit inimitable and beautiful poetry, but meaningless and exaggerated poetry nevertheless, if we were to claim that this exalted presentation was already completely fulfilled at Israel's return from its Babylonian exile.

Still others think this prophecy is a reference to the life and miracles of the Messiah, but with the renowned Van der Palm we say also of this explanation:

We cannot agree with this, but find in this chapter an oracle that is still awaiting fulfillment and that will obtain it in those final, glorious days when Jehovah will have gathered His people once more from the diaspora and made them confess their and our Saviour. Contents, language and style agree with this best of all, and that the prophet could have such exalted vistas we know, among other things, from chapters eleven and twelve.

Keep Courage, for the Lord Is Coming!

> 3. Strengthen ye the weak hands, and confirm the feeble knees.
> 4. Say to them that are of a fearful heart, Be strong, fear not: behold, your God will come with vengeance, even God with a recompence; he will come and save you.

Israel will *see* — not merely as we believe without seeing — the *glory* of Jehovah, the *beauty* of our God, Christ; but it will be a long time hence and many afflictions will come upon His people. For this reason the prophet cries to them to keep courage, to be strong and not to fear His coming. The long-awaited and strongly desired Messiah, Israel's God, will come with vengeance: He will recompense Israel's enemies and deliver Israel with an everlasting deliverance. All commentators who apply these words to Hezekiah's day, or to the return from Babylon, or to Christ's first coming, or to the Church's prosperity are not taking these verses, which point out the second coming of the Lord, seriously. For, viewed correctly, this is the key word of this glorious prophecy; this key gives us the significant hint that all this glory comes only *after* and *through* the return of our Lord Jesus Christ.

The Results of Sin Removed by the Lord's Return

> 5. Then the eyes of the blind shall be opened, and the ears of the deaf shall be unstopped.
> 6. Then shall the lame man leap as an hart, and the tongue of the dumb sing: for in the wilderness shall waters break out, and streams in the desert.

Those who apply this prophecy to the First Coming of the Lord do so on the basis of this text, since it was partially quoted by the Lord Jesus in His answer to the messengers sent by John the Baptist. We can wholeheartedly agree that Christ by the miracles performed during His humiliation already manifested an initial and partial fulfillment of these words. It seems to us, however, that here, in connection with the commission given Isaiah at the occasion of the vision at his calling, and further in connection with 28:11-13; 30:21;

32:3-5, we are to think of the moral and religious restoration of Israel. Blindness, deafness, lameness and dumbness will cease. The spiritual is always represented by the natural. We believe wholeheartedly, however, that as Christ at His First Coming commenced these miracles of physical healing, He will do the same a thousand times more for the naturally blind, deaf, lame and dumb. In the millennium there will be no institutions for the deaf and dumb, nor will any lame person hobble about on crutches. For is it not an incontestable rule that the second Adam will restore on earth what the first Adam spoiled there? The Christ will do no half work, but a complete work; hence in His Second Coming, He will remove all the results of sin. We take this word in the broadest sense possible.

The Renewal of the Earth

> 7. And the parched ground shall become a pool, and the thirsty land springs of water: in the habitation of dragons, where each lay, shall be grass with reeds and rushes.
>
> 8. And an highway shall be there, and a way, and it shall be called The way of holiness; the unclean shall not pass over it; but it shall be for those: the wayfaring men, though fools, shall not err therein.

Already the last part of verse six pointed out the closest correlation between the moral and religious change and the renewal of the earth. These verses tell us more about it. In this delightful picture of the recreation of nature we are struck again by what we saw several times, that many streams will rise in places that were barren and arid before. Of course, this image does not have the same appeal to us as it must have had to Israel at that time, for our climate is not as hot and scorching and we have enough rain, lakes and rivers everywhere. The situation, however, was entirely different in the holy land. Scarcity of water was a constant threat and many a traveler in the desert died from thirst. We must keep this in mind when reading the beautiful description of an abundance of water. See, besides the texts already commented on, 41:17-20; 43:18-20; 44:3-4; and Ezekiel 47:1-12. The abnormal condition of a lack of water for man and beast, this heavy curse, will be removed. In that day of Christ's peace there will no longer be deserts and wildernesses as such, for verse one already said that the wilderness and the solitary place will be glad and blossom as the rose. Gone will be the desert of Sin, gone the wilderness of Paran, gone also the barren steppes of Russia, the heath and moors of the Netherlands, the infertile prairies of North America and Sahara of Africa — all will be gone! For He, our Lord Jesus Christ, reigns.

The word translated *parched ground* actually means *mirage,* air reflection, an atmospheric phenomenon frequently seen in Eastern deserts which is caused by the reflection of the hot rays of the sun. From a distance it looks as though the surface of a lake lies on top of the sands. The thirsty traveler, who is inexperienced, stumbles toward it, soon to be bitterly disappointed and perhaps even lured from the right way and lost. Now the prophet brings the glad tiding that what used to be a mere semblance and an illusion will one day become glorious reality.

Much has been written and said in sermons about the *highway,* but it is still to come and has not been built to this very day. We can look forward to a literal materialization of it in the great day of miracles. This way will be *holy,* as restored Israel, will then be holy. No unclean person will walk on it and even fools will not err therein. All this may very well be *applied* to Christ or the way of salvation, but this does not *explain* it. For in that day there will be in and to the holy land a highway so that people from all parts of the world can without difficulty reach the temple for it will be the house of prayer of all nations. In the past there hardly were any good roads to get to Jerusalem quickly to seek God's face, but at the coming of the Lord this will be entirely different.

No Ravenous Beasts Anymore

9. No lion shall be there, nor any ravenous beast shall go up thereon, it shall not be found there; but the redeemed shall walk there.

We can safely assume that it was not always a smooth and safe road which pilgrims in the ages gone by had to walk when at festive days they were called to hurry to the temple. During Israel's early centuries as a nation there were many lions and other wild animals and snakes, or dragons; but they too, will be there no more in that day. This is a frequent feature in the descriptions of Christ's Kingdom (cf. chap. 11 and 65).

Israel's Complete Restoration

10. And the ransomed of the LORD shall return, and come to Zion with songs and everlasting joy upon their heads: they shall obtain joy and gladness, and sorrow and sighing shall flee away.

This very holy way will first of all be used by Israel which, ransomed from the fetters of sin and from the claws of the nations, will return and come to Zion with joy. All the people of the nation are anointed with the oil of gladness on their heads to indicate that she is a nation of priests, prophets and kings. According to this verse, we apparently must picture them also as having their heads crowned with the crown of victory.

> There will the ransomed of the Lord,
> Forever safe, rejoice in Him,
> And, freed from bondage and the sword,
> Return to Zion's holy hill.
>
> There, joy and gladness, like a crown,
> Adorn their heads forevermore;
> Peace fills their bosom to the full
> And grief and sorrow are no more!

"And grief and sorrow are no more!" This applies to the entire restored nation, after two of the three parts have been exterminated in the Great Tribulation. This, more than anything, is what Scripture teaches continuously. It was already embryonically included in the promises given to the fathers (Gen. 18:18-19; 26:4; 28:14; Zech. 8:23). The Jews will not only be restored but also be abundantly blessed by the Lord (Ps. 67; Isa. 28:6; Jer. 31; Micah 4:8; Zeph. 3:17; Zech. 12-14; Mal. 3:12; Rom. 11; Rev. 7:4). Israel will become a great nation (Lev. 26:44-46; Deut. 28:12-13; Isa. 45:14; 50:5-12), a holy nation (Isa. 4; 60:21; 61:3; Zech. 13:1, 8, 9), after it will first have been purged by the fire of the Great Tribulation. Finally, it will be a nation which through her Messiah will be a blessing to all the nations of the world (Ps. 67:1, 2; Isa. 27:6; 61:6, 9; 66:19; John 4:22; Acts 15:13-17; Rom. 11:15). There is no erudition, wisdom or eloquence in the world which can break the power of these words of God, which could readily be multiplied. Especially in our days, when the fig tree is budding, we cannot but call it a sign of stubborn unbelief or great ignorance and blindness that those who claim to believe the entire Scripture dare to doubt this. To him who does not believe these words of God no proof can be given here below for Israel's restoration. He will have to wait until God himself does it.

ISAIAH 36

With chapter thirty-five we have actually come to the end of the first part of Isaiah. The next four chapters form a separate unit and may properly be considered a conclusion of the preceding chapters and an introduction to the following chapters. For what was depicted prophetically in the preceding chapters is being told historically here. Almost the same material was already recorded in II Kings 18:13-20, 19 and II Chronicles 32. Bible students have never been able to agree where the original story is given or whether both stories are based on the same common source. But this entire question is of no practical value and can moreover not possibly be settled. As far as we are concerned, we are fully convinced that both stories were directly inspired by the Holy Spirit, albeit by means of different men of God. On the basis of II Chronicles 32:32 some expositors are of the opinion that these historical chapters contain part of the biography of Hezekiah by Isaiah. This idea sounds plausible but, again, cannot be proven.

Sennacherib Invades Judah

> 1. Now it came to pass in the fourteenth year of king Hezekiah, that Sennacherib king of Assyria came up against all the defenced cities of Judah, and took them.

In order to understand this entire story correctly we need to have a clear picture in our minds of the history of Hezekiah and especially of the invasion by Sennacherib which is partially described in II Chronicles 32:32 and in II Kings 18:14-16. These accounts show that Hezekiah first courageously did all he could, with the assistance of his people to defend the nation, but that afterwards he gave up his courage.

Rabshakeh

2. And the king of Assyria sent Rahshakeh from Lachish to Jerusalem unto king Hezekiah with a great army. And he stood by the conduit of the upper pool in the highway of the fuller's field.

3. Then came forth unto him Eliakim, Hilkiah's son, which was over the house, and Shebna the scribe, and Joah, Asaph's son, the recorder.

From II Kings 18:17 we know that Sennacherib had sent two officers with Rabshakeh by the name of *Tartan* (Isa. 20:1) and *Rabsaris.* Hence there was a commission of three persons, but since Rabshakeh alone did the talking, Isaiah mentions him only. Rabshakeh is really not a name, but a title and means *chief cupbearer,* a prominent post at a Mid-Eastern court. Originally these high dignitaries were in charge of the royal wine cellar and had to taste the wine before the king drank to prevent the danger of poisoning. Later on such a chief cupbearer took on other functions as well. At the least, this title covered much more than merely pouring the king's wine. It is noteworthy that this delegation of Sennacherib appeared by the mouth of Rabshakeh to mock the Lord, on the same spot where Ahaz had earlier mocked Jehovah (Isa. 7). Concerning the persons of *Eliakim* and *Shebna,* see the comments on chapter twenty.

Rabshakeh Taunts Hezekiah and Jehovah

4. And Rebshakeh said unto them, Say ye now to Hezekiah, Thus saith the great king, the king of Assyria, What confidence is this wherein thou trustest?

5. I say, sayest thou, (but they are but vain words) I have counsel and strength for war: now on whom dost thou trust, that thou rebellest against me?

6. Lo, thou trustest in the staff of this broken reed, on Egypt; whereon if a man lean, it will go into his hand, and pierce it: so is Pharaoh king of Egypt to all that trust in him.

7. But if thou say to me, We trust in the LORD our God: is it not he, whose high places and whose altars Hezekiah hath taken away, and said to Judah and to Jerusalem, Ye shall worship before this altar?

8. Now therefore give pledges, I pray thee, to my master the king of Assyria, and I will give thee two thousand horses, if thou be able on thy part to set riders upon them.

9. How then wilt thou turn away the face of one captain of
the least of my master's servants and put thy trust on Egypt for
chariots and for horsemen?

10. And am I now come up without the LORD against this
land to destroy it? the LORD said unto me, Go up against this
land, and destroy it.

For *I say* we had better substitute as II Kings 18:20 does
Thou sayest, since this makes better sense in the mouth of
the proud boaster. He calls his king *the great king, the king of
Assyria* while at the same time not deeming Hezekiah worthy
of the title *king.* The proud statements by this courtier and
general of Sennacherib fully agree with the boastful royal
inscriptions which Assyriologists have deciphered. He speaks
of Hezekiah as though he were a mere beardless lad, calls his
words vain prattle and ridicules his trust in Jehovah. He
mocks not only Hezekiah's trust in God but also Judah's
trust in Egypt. Since reeds grew in abundance in Egypt and
were used for several purposes, he appropriately compares
this trust in Egypt with leaning on a reed stalk, and a broken
stalk at that, which pierces the hand of him who leans on it.
This beautiful and meaningful comparison contained more
truth than Rabshakeh himself realized. He expressed a truth
which Jehovah Himself had already expressed by the mouth
of Isaiah (cf. chap. 20; 30:3). The vaunter may not think
much of Hezekiah, but he does not think any more of
Pharaoh. He expresses a mixture of truth and lies. We get the
impression from Rabshakeh's whole demeanor that he was a
smart and sly person. He first wounds Hezekiah in regard to
his politics and then with respect to his religion, his trust in
God. He obviously knows more about the Jewish religion and
about Hezekiah's character than most heathen in his day. He
considers Hezekiah's trust in God of such importance that he
returns to this subject four times. This was indeed the main
issue at stake and he seems to have sensed that instinctively.
But he reveals his gross ignorance regarding Israel's religion,
in thinking that Hezekiah had broken down Jehovah's altars.
Obviously the smart fellow wishes to stir up the people
against Hezekiah, unless, as others think, he wants to
illustrate Jehovah's impotence.

In verse eight, he ridicules Hezekiah's army on account of

its lack of cavalry. Mocking, he says he wants to make a bet with Hezekiah, and will give him two thousand horses if Hezekiah can supply as many riders able to do battle on horseback. Besides, what would Hezekiah do with cavalry, since he is counting on help from Egypt's excellent horsemen and horses? Rabshakeh's words could not have been prouder, more defiant, more aggravating and more taunting! At last the proud braggert returns to the help of the Lord. If Hezekiah thinks that Jehovah will help him, then he is completely mistaken, for He is also an Ally of Rabshakeh! He claims that Jehovah told him to advance on Judah and to destroy the land. Undoubtedly, he was making an appeal to the nation's conscience. The foolish and superstitious people could easily be induced to believe this lie, the more so since it had not accepted the truth of Isaiah's preaching. Some expositors are of the opinion that he knew of the prophecy of 10:5, and although this may have been possible, it is not certain and so it is better to suspect this sly character of trying to deceive the people by lying.

The Request for Rabshakeh to Speak in Syriac

11. Then said Eliakim and Shebna and Joah unto Rabshakeh, Speak, I pray thee, unto thy servants in the Syrian language; for we understand it: and speak not to us in the Jews' language, in the ears of the people that are on the wall.

This request was made politely by Hezekiah's three men, as they wanted to prevent the people from being influenced by the smooth tongue of this cunning person. Rabshakeh spoke in Hebrew and so could be understood by all the ignorant people on the wall. This could have had severe consequences, indeed, even civil war. It is no wonder that they want to prevent such a consequence. Even though this request was polite and was made for a good purpose, it was nevertheless not very wise to make it to a person such as Rabshakeh. They should have known beforehand that such an arrogant character would not be willing to do any favor for them. Hence we see how with true satanic glee and according to the satanic principle of *divide and rule,* he commences to scream even louder in his gibberish Hebrew in the hearing of the people. Hezekiah's men should have realized that this was exactly what he was after, and for the very reason that he could speak Hebrew, he had been sent by Sennacherib. Even though Syriac or Aramaic was the diplomatic language of that time, he had spoken Hebrew from the start. If these men felt that they had to make this request, they should have omitted the final clause: "in the ears of the people that are on the wall." For the latter now heard this request and it must have been somewhat painful to them — the populace may be ignorant but it always feels deeply! — while on the other hand it must have inclined them favorably towards Rabshekeh since he wanted them to understand him. For now they could remain on the wall and thus satisfy their curiosity. Thus this request, no matter how well intended, now had the exact opposite result, as desired. The diplomats of Jerusalem were no match for those of Assyria!

Rabshakeh Addresses the People

12. But Rabshakeh said, Hath my master sent me to thy master and to thee to speak these words? hath he not sent me to the men that sit upon the wall, that they may eat their own dung, and drink their own piss with you?

13. Then Rabshakeh stood, and cried with a loud voice in the Jews' language, and said Hear ye the words of the great king, the king of Assyria.

14. Thus saith the king, Let not Hezekiah deceive you: for he shall not be able to deliver you.

15. Neither let Hezekiah make you trust in the LORD, saying, The LORD will surely deliver us: this city shall not be delivered into the hand of the king of Assyria.

16. Hearken not to Hezekiah: for thus saith the king of Assyria, Make an agreement with me by a present, and come out to me: and eat ye every one of his vine, and every one of his fig tree, and drink ye every one the waters of his own cistern;

17. Until I come and take you away to a land like your own land, a land of corn and wine, a land of bread and vineyards.

18. Beware lest Hezekiah persuade you, saying, The LORD will deliver us. Hath any of the gods of the nations delivered his land out of the hand of the king of Assyria?

19. Where are the gods of Hamath and Arphad? where are the gods of Sepharvaim? and have they delivered Samaria out of my hand?

20. Who are they among all the gods of these lands, that have delivered their land out of my hand, that the LORD should deliver Jerusalem out of my hand?

Here the proud man goes a step further and now disdainfully ignores Hezekiah's diplomats by speaking only to the people. And he delivers one of the most horrible and blasphemous speeches that have ever been delivered to these people. Yet, objectively considered, there is never anything new under the sun, for between the two World Wars France followed the same Rabshakeh methods with regard to the German people. Long before Rabshakeh, the seed of the serpent applied the same wiles of the devil. He calls their attention to the fact that Sennacherib sent him to the people and not to the government of Judah. For these people — and here he flatters them again — will have to bear the burden of a siege. When hunger and thirst will soon grip them, they will, together with the government "eat their own dung and drink their own piss." No statement could have struck home more forcefully than this reprehensible picture. Everything he says is for the purpose of exciting the people to rebellion against their lawful government and to prod them to revolt and run over to the enemy. He was, however, unaware of Hezekiah's wise provision for water; the attackers would suffer a shortage of water before the beseiged (cf. II Chron. 32:3-4). To contrast the strangling lack of provisions during a seige, he points out the abundance the people will enjoy in Assyria if they voluntarily surrender: everyone will eat his own fruits of the field and drink his own well water and will have plenty in a land of plenty just as in their own country of Canaan. The main theme of his despicable speech, however, is that *Hezekiah is a deceiver. Let him go and come over to us.* The words are shocking: "Let not Hezekiah deceive you. Let not Hezekiah make you trust in the Lord. Hearken not to Hezekiah but to King Sennacherib. Beware lest Hezekiah persuade you with his trust in God!" One can just feel that the fear the delegation showed makes him bolder and that he has good reason to hope that the people will revolt against their sovereign and defect with all they have to Sennacherib. Whatever Rabshakeh can effect with his words, he is not going to do with battering rams. A victory of the former kind is easier, cheaper and safer. The blasphemous character of his speech is evident from the fact that he returns again and again to Hezekiah's trust in the Lord in order to ridicule it and to present it as criminal and as deceiving the people. He refers to the gods of the foreign nations and even to those of *Samaria* and asks: *Where are they? Have they saved the nations out of my hand?* Taking advantage of the people's lack of faith and superstition he boldly demands of them how they could be so foolish as to believe that the Lord would save Jerusalem from the hand of Sennacherib. In truth Hezekiah might say with the psalmist:

> I will say to God, my fortress:
> Why hast Thou forsaken me?
> Why go I about in sadness
> For my foes' dread tyranny?

> Their rebukes and scoffing words
> Pierce my bones as pointed swords,
> As they say with proud defiance:
> Where is God, thy soul's reliance?

Rabshakeh's Stratagem Foiled

21. But they held their peace, and answered him not a word: for the king's commandment was, saying, Answer him not.
22. Then came Eliakim, the son of Hilkiah, that was over the household, and Shebna the scribe, and Joah, the son of Asaph, the recorder, to Hezekiah with their clothes rent, and told him the words of Rabshakeh.

It was the treacherous object of Rabshakeh to win the people over to his side. His whole speech was geared to that end. But he did not succeed, for Hezekiah's subjects on the wall did not answer him a word. The word *they* does not refer to the three delegates but, according to II Kings 18:36, to the people on the wall: "But the people held their peace, and answered him not a word." It is precious indeed that the speech intended to stir up the people to disobedience is immediately followed by the statement that they kept silent in obedience to Hezekiah's command not to answer Rabshakeh. The house of David always had enemies and in

Jerusalem there were many who despised the softly flowing waters of Siloam. But in this hour of danger the people apparently gathered as one around the throne of Hezekiah.

Meanwhile the speech of Rabshakeh was not wholly without effect. This is indicated in the last verse of the chapter, where it is said that the three courtiers of Hezekiah rent their clothes as a sign of sadness and consternation and because they were offended by the blasphemous speech, and so went to the king. When they appeared before the king there must have been in their hearts a mixture of anger, sorrow, and fear on account of Rabshakeh's words. Their task had not been an easy one.

ISAIAH 37

Hezekiah Mourns, Prays and Sends a Delegation to Isaiah

> 1. And it came to pass, when king Hezekiah heard it, that he rent his clothes, and covered himself with sackcloth, and went into the house of the LORD.
> 2. And he sent Eliakim, who was over the household, and Shebna the scribe, and the elders of the priests covered with sackcloth, unto Isaiah the prophet the son of Amoz.

The king shared in the feelings of his officers and upon hearing of the blasphemies uttered by Rabshakeh he rent his royal robe and put on mourning clothes as an indication not only of his grief but also of his humiliation before the face of God (cf. 3:24; 22:12; 32:11). In this condition he set out for the temple to unburden his soul before God's countenance. His touching prayer is found in verses fourteen to twenty. The pious king could not have done better than to humble himself and pray. But he also felt the need of the intercessory prayer and advice the prophet of the Lord could offer him in his perplexity. For that reason he sent an honorable delegation, consisting of Eliakim, Shebna and the chief priests, all robed in sackcloth, to Isaiah with the request: "Lift up thy prayer for the remnant that is left."

What must have gone on in the heart of the man of God? He was now an old man in the service of his God. For years on end the people had ignored him in order to lean on the flesh of Egypt. When for three years he had walked barefoot and in his underclothes as a captive prisoner robbed of everything, these same proud princes ridiculed him. But now that everything seems to have turned upside down, the king sends a delegation to him. Now that the Egyptian armies did not come to their rescue, perhaps a prayer by Isaiah might bring deliverance.

The Delegation Submits His Request to Isaiah

3. And they said unto him, Thus saith Hezekiah, This day is a day of trouble, and of rebuke, and of blasphemy: for the children are come to the birth, and there is not strength to bring forth.

4. It may be the LORD thy God will hear the words of Rabshakeh, whom the king of Assyria his master hath sent to reproach the living God, and will reprove the words which the LORD thy God hath heard: wherefore lift up thy prayer for the remnant that is left.

5. So the servants of king Hezekiah came to Isaiah.

The sad procession of prominent men has finally arrived at the house of Isaiah. Hezekiah is completely crushed, as is evident from his message to Isaiah; nor does it contain any indication of his wishing to appear strong and courageous or to minimize the danger. It is a sign of his true humility that he presents himself exactly the way he is in this hour of dire need. His politics had not always been equally irreproachable. Evidently he, too, had had Egypt more in mind than Jehovah and His servant. He had at times toadied to his audacious princes more than was proper. It seems that he did not seek the Lord through the prophet in any of the political experiences of his nation. His giving away the temple treasures to Sennacherib a short time prior to this (II Kings 18:14-16) cannot possibly have met with Isaiah's approval. At that time he should not have confessed to Sennacherib, "I have sinned," but to Jehovah, for he indeed had sinned, not by refusing to pay Sennacherib the taxes but by his temporary lack of faith and its courage. Nevertheless, one should not come down too hard on this otherwise very pious king, for there is question whether we would have done better or even as well as he in similar grievous and dangerous circumstances. The comparison in the second half of verse three is very striking. One expositor makes the following observation concerning it: "We cannot picture a moment of greater dread and mortal danger than when a woman to be delivered has carried her baby with endless pain and care to the moment of birth but who then, totally exhausted, has no strength left and hence cannot deliver." Hezekiah compares his and the nation's situation with that kind of a terrible situation. Not only was Hezekiah's situation desperate, but a temporary cloud had covered his faith as he repeatedly speaks of "the Lord *thy* God." We would have preferred to hear the words "our God" coming from his lips. The timorous beginning of his message, "It may be," also points in this direction as well. He is not all that sure that Isaiah's prayer will be answered. What he is sure of, however, is that Jehovah has heard Rabshakeh's derisive and blasphemous speech. He does not want to repeat those blasphemies in the ears of the prophet, but he assures him that Jehovah had heard them.

Finally, Hezekiah's request of Isaiah to raise up intercessory prayer for the *remnant* is worthy of attention. It indicates not only that many towns and villages of Judah had fallen to the enemy, but also that Hezekiah accepted in faith Isaiah's prophetic view which, at the Lord's command, he had preached for many years, i.e., that the nation as such was doomed to extinction and that only a remnant would be saved. Already as a young man Isaiah had in days of similar extremity, while holding the hand of his little son *A-Remnant-Returns,* preached by words and signs the truth that only a remnant of the people would be saved in the time of judgment. Only a handful! Judah was not very big, only about the size of a province of the Netherlands or a county of our United States, and there were some two million inhabitants. But even of this small nation only a small remnant would be saved. Such preaching was intended to beat down all pride and worldly greatness. And it is this kind of humiliating preaching Hezekiah accepts and on which he bases his request. Isaiah's answer follows:

Isaiah's Answer to Hezekiah

6. And Isaiah said unto them, Thus shall ye say unto your master, Thus saith the LORD, Be not afraid of the words that thou hast heard, wherewith the servants of the king of Assyria have blasphemed me.

7. Behold, I will send a blast upon him, and he shall hear a rumour, and return to his own land; and I will cause him to fall by the sword in his own land.

Isaiah did not at first get ready to make a long, moving intercessory prayer. He must have poured out his heart in prayer and supplication before the arrival of the delegation, and not only had *he* spoken to God, but God had already spoken to him. Once again his answer is calm and soothing as it was years ago during the Syro-Ephraimitic war, when Ahaz and his people were shaking like the trees of the woods. *Be not afraid!* Only those who forsake God have reason to fear grief upon grief – not those who seek Him like Hezekiah does. *Be not afraid,* for Jehovah is greater than Assyria's armies; *be not afraid,* for Rabshakeh's words are untrue, but the Lord's word is true. Truth is simple, as we observe here, for how soberly does this true word of the prophet contrast with the boastful and flaunting bragging of Rabshakeh! Isaiah is a unique master of irony (holy mockery) and he does not hide his art. He calls Rabshakeh and the other officers of the army the *slaves* or *servant boys* – we could say the *errand boys* – of the king of Assyria. This noble heart does not know fear but only holy disdain of the attackers of Judah.

The *blast* of verse seven must be taken in the sense of the operation of an evil spirit or demon in Sennacherib's heart. Scripture frequently uses the word spirit in a broad sense and often means man's soul, or life's energy, or even all of man's inner life. But Scripture also teaches abundantly that there is a realm of evil spirits which though subject to God's sovereignty, does battle continually against mankind. Thus it seems that an unclean spirit of whoredoms tempted Hosea's contemporaries in the northern kingdom to commit unspeakable abominations, although this did not diminish the guilt of the people themselves (Hos. 4:12; 5:4; Isa. 19:14; 29:10; Judg. 9:23; I Sam. 16:14; 18:10; 19:9; II Kings 19:7; Zech. 13:2). If we place these references alongside each other and compare them, we cannot escape the idea that in these cases we are dealing with a demonic influence on the spirit of man. Just as the good Spirit can influence our lives in a good sense, so an evil spirit can influence a sinner in a bad sense. Scripture teaches that there are all kinds of evil spirits. God, according to His righteous judgment, sent a terrifying spirit upon the proud but courageous Sennacherib so that he became afraid of King Tirhakah. Finally the prophet summarizes briefly the entire judgment upon Sennacherib. For its fulfillment see verse thirty-eight.

Rabshakeh Returns Empty-Handed

> 8. So Rabshakeh returned, and found the king of Assyria warring against Libnah: for he had heard that he was departed from Lachish.
>
> 9. And he heard say concerning Tirhakah king of Ethiopia, He is come forth to make war with thee. And when he heard it, he sent messengers to Hezekiah, saying:

One can imagine the anger of "the great king" when Rabshakeh brought him the message at *Libnah* that he would flee to his country and there would be killed by the sword. The army apparently stayed behind under the command of Rabsaris and Tartan, while Rabshakeh hastened to Libnah near Lachish. Undoubtedly, Rabshakeh now expected that he officially had to start the assault on Jerusalem, but suddenly something took place that made such an assault impossible. The mighty conqueror Tirhakah of Egypt advanced with his army to do battle with his archenemy Assyria. Sennacherib heard about this just when Rabshakeh came with his report.

A Second Attempt to Persuade Jerusalem to Surrender

> 10. Thus shall ye speak to Hezekiah king of Judah, saying, Let not thy God, in whom thou trustest, deceive thee, saying, Jerusalem shall not be given into the hand of the king of Assyria.
>
> 11. Behold, thou hast heard what the kings of Assyria have done to all lands by destroying them utterly; and shalt thou be delivered?
>
> 12. Have the gods of the nations delivered them which my fathers have destroyed, as Gozan, and Haran, and Rezeph, and the children of Eden which were in Telassar?
>
> 13. Where is the king of Hamath, and the king of Arphad, and the king of the city of Sepharvaim, Hena, and Ivah?

The question has been asked why the courageous and mighty Sennacherib, who certainly did not lack bravery, made such hurried attempts at departure. We must keep in mind, however, not only that he was surrounded by hostile nations but also that Tirhakah was known as a very powerful king. Moreover, the king of Egypt was not advancing to do battle with Sennacherib but to invade Assyria to cut off his return march. For if he had advanced on Sennacherib, he could better have stayed where he was. Some commentators are of the opinion that it was only a false rumor, but this cannot be proven and the account itself does not give that impression. Upon hearing this report, Sennacherib understood only too well that in order to do battle with Tirhakah successfully without being endangered by an enemy at his rear, he had to settle accounts with Jerusalem first if at all possible. For that reason he made one more attempt to take the city without bloodshed. This time he wisely did not send the arrogant Rabshakeh, but other messengers to Hezekiah who were commissioned to give a written message to Hezekiah. Although the content of this missive is just as blasphemous as the previous one, it is not quite as insulting to Hezekiah as the first. The king's excessive boldness must have been tempered somewhat by the circumstances. Ridderbos observes correctly: "We may consider this an example that also in those days the servant acted higher and mightier than his lord." Briefly put, his message was: "I conquered all nations and their gods; how then will your God deliver you from my hand?" As is evident, Israel's God was once again derided and His honor defamed. Sennacherib put Him on the same level with the non-gods of the nations. This God would be able to do nothing against Sennacherib. Hence it was no longer a matter between Sennacherib and Hezekiah but between Jehovah and the gods of the nations. So the decisive moment had arrived when the issue at stake was the power or the powerlessness of Jehovah. Aware of this, the pious king Hezekiah went to the temple to inform Him in prayer of Sennacherib's challenge.

Hezekiah's Prayer

14. And Hezekiah received the letter from the hand of the messengers, and read it: and Hezekiah went up unto the house of the LORD, and spread it before the LORD.
15. And Hezekiah prayed unto the LORD, saying,

16. O LORD of hosts, God of Israel, that dwellest between the cherubims, thou art the God, even thou alone, of all the kingdoms of the earth: thou hast made heaven and earth.

17. Incline thine ear, O LORD, and hear; open thine eyes, O LORD, and see: and hear all the words of Sennacherib, which hath sent to reproach the living God.

18. Of a truth, LORD, the kings of Assyria have laid waste all the nations, and their countries,

19. And have cast their gods into the fire: for they were no gods, but the work of men's hands, wood and stone: therefore they have destroyed them.

20. Now therefore, O LORD our God, save us from his hand, that all the kingdoms of the earth may know that thou art the LORD, even thou only.

Hezekiah was a man of prayer. On five occasions we read of him that he sought his strength in prayer. Isaiah's reassuring prediction had already put him somewhat at ease; yet threatening danger was still great, and he felt the need to call the Lord's attention to Sennacherib's attack on His honor. He received the letter of the messengers, read it and took it to the temple. There he spread it open before the Lord's countenance so that the Lord Himself could read the blasphemous contents. Solemn are the opening words of his prayer. He calls Him Lord Sabaoth, the God of Israel, who dwells between the cherubims — a name that often appears in Scripture (I Sam. 4:4; II Sam. 6:2; II Kings 19:15; I Chron. 13:6; Ps. 80:1; 99:1). This expression is derived from the spreading wings of the cherubs, which were also represented on the lid of the ark. According to some expositors, the *Shekinah* always stood above it as a sign of God's presence.

Hezekiah now praises the Lord as the King of all the nations and Creator of all things. He magnifies God thus at the beginning of his prayer to emphasize the contrast between "the great king," Sennacherib, and Jehovah. Then he beseeches God to take notice of Sennacherib's horribly scornful language. We like to picture it as though he, with his finger, pointed out the words of the letter to God. Then he continues to remind the Lord of the element of truth the words contained. *Of a truth,* Jehovah, he cries, the kings of Assyria have destroyed all nations and their people. *It is true,* he says. We may learn from this that we may never and under no circumstances call the truth a lie, wherever we meet it and regardless of how much untruth is mixed in with it. Sennacherib had indeed conquered the gods of his subject nations, but the king hastens to add that these gods were only the work of men's hands and that the king therefore had only destroyed some wood and stone. It is obvious that Hezekiah here contradicts the false conclusion Sennacherib had drawn from it.

The end of this prayer is very beautiful as well. It contains two precious motives for urging God to hear his plea. First of all, he urges that He who is *the God of all the kingdoms of the earth* is nevertheless in a special sense the God of Israel. He had already called Him *God of Israel* in the beautiful opening words. Here again, he calls Him *Jehovah our God,* as though he wants to remind God of His glorious covenant and close relationship with Israel. Actually this relation is already contained in the name Jehovah, which indicates the wholly unique relationship of love by which God united Israel to Himself as His beloved wife. The second motivation to deliverance Hezekiah derives from the expansion of the name of the Lord over all the earth. God's honor was involved; the pious king had understood it very well. He had also understood that by appealing to this fact he touched a string of God's heart, which is God's deepest ground for hearing our prayers. Truly, a ruler who can pray like this deserves to be honorably mentioned among the most pious kings of Judah.

The Answer to This Prayer

21. Then Isaiah the son of Amoz sent unto Hezekiah, saying, Thus saith the LORD God of Israel, whereas thou hast prayed to me against Sennacherib king of Assyria:

22. This is the word which the LORD hath spoken concerning him; The virgin, the daughter of Zion, hath despised thee, and laughed thee to scorn; the daughter of Jerusalem hath shaken her head at thee.

23. Whom hast thou reproached and blasphemed? and against whom hast thou exalted thy voice, and lifted up thine eyes on high? even against the Holy One of Israel.

24. By thy servants hast thou reproached the Lord, and hast said, By the multitude of my chariots am I come up to the height

of the mountains, to the sides of Lebanon; and I will cut down the tall cedars thereof, and the choice fir trees thereof: and I will enter into the height of his border, and the forest of his Carmel.

25. I have digged, and drunk water; and with the sole of my feet have I dried up all the rivers of the besieged places.

On this occasion Isaiah reached the pinnacle of his prophetic labor. When De Buck in his book on the prophets comes to this event in the life of Isaiah, he exclaims: "What a triumph for the old man! This is the moment for which he had waited for years and years!" This is true, as long as we do not mean a triumph for *the old man,* but for Jehovah. First he assures Hezekiah that his prayer has been answered and that he can rest in peace. Verse twenty-two is again an example of true Isaiahic irony. Judah will no longer tremble before but mock at Sennacherib with all his power and proud boasting. He presents Sennacherib as boastfully speaking. He could reach the top of Lebanon and cut down its tallest cedars. Success followed at his heels. He could stamp water out of the ground and dry up the streams of water-rich Egypt. Nothing was too miraculous for him!

The Lord Speaking to Sennacherib

26. Hast thou not heard long ago, how I have done it; and of ancient times, that I have formed it? now have I brought it to pass that thou shouldest be to lay waste defenced cities into ruinous heaps.

27. Therefore their inhabitants were of small power, they were dismayed and confounded: they were as the grass of the field, and as the green herb, as the grass on the house tops, and as corn blasted before it be grown up.

28. But I know thy abode, and thy going out, and thy coming in, and thy rage against me.

29. Because thy rage against me, and thy tumult, is come up into mine ears, therefore will I put my hook in thy nose, and my bridle in thy lips, and I will turn thee back by the way by which thou camest.

Now the prophet introduces God Himself as speaking. He presents Him as calling Sennacherib to order. The Lord contrasts sharply His power and wisdom with Sennacherib's outrageous arrogance. He calls attention to His counsel according to which all that had been done, also what Sennacherib had done had taken place, according to the counsel of the Lord. The Lord had since long determined everything in his life and that he would be His rod who would vehemently descend like a destructive hurricane upon nations and cities. To this, and this only, Sennacherib owed all his military success. Why could Nebuchadnezzar too be so successful in his campaigns? It was because he was a servant of the Lord. Why could Cyrus the Great cast down nations and loosen the loins of kings as none other? It was because the Lord had anointed him and holden his right hand. How can we explain that a young man such as Alexander the Great with a small army of mercenaries conquers the known world of his day in twelve years? Was it not because he, too, was an instrument of the Lord to do the Lord's work and to hasten the coming of His Son? And − to name one of the later date − what made Napoleon such a unique general and mighty ruler so that he distributed kingdoms like toys? Again, the reason is none other than that God wished to use this little Corsican as a scourge of the nations of Europe. God's counsel and world dominion was the secret of the power of all world conquerors. Verse twenty-seven shows marvelously how God also used Sennacherib as a scourge of the God-forsaking nations. This explains why the nations were before him as without hands, without any courage or power of resistance. They were like a field covered with tender blades of grass beneath the feet of the victors. To Sennacherib they were like the grass on the Mid-Eastern rooftops which quickly withered as it had neither depth of earth nor shadow. To the two metaphors of a meadow full of tender blades of grass and that of grass on the rooftop that suddenly turns to hay a third one is added, i.e., that of blasted grain that has lost its moisture and strength before its ears are formed. It bends before the slightest wind that stirs about. All these things being as they were, what reason did Sennacherib have to boast?

Verse twenty-eight says that Jehovah knew Sennacherib through and through. He knew him when he was yet sitting still in Assyria, when he departed from Assyria and when he entered the holy land. The Lord lets him know that He knows him inwardly as well as outwardly, when He says that in everything he does he is *raging* against the Lord. He is what Antichrist later will be, anti-God and anti-Christ in all that he does and does not do. But since Sennacherib rages against Jehovah like a wild animal, God will also treat him as a wild animal. Hence, his sentence: God will hook a ring in his nose and put a bridle between his teeth. All this was language Sennacherib could understand very well. With this nose ring and bridle, God will lead this mad and uncontrollable beast wherever He wants him to go. Again this prophecy is expressed in very imaginative and picturesque language and every reader of Scripture can easily understand what is meant by these striking metaphors.

God Gives Hezekiah a Sign of the Remnant

> 30. And this shall be a sign unto thee, Ye shall eat this year such as groweth of itself; and the second year that which springeth of the same: and in the third year sow ye, and reap, and plant vineyards, and eat the fruit thereof.
> 31. And the remnant that is escaped of the house of Judah shall again take root downward, and bear fruit upward:
> 32. For out of Jerusalem shall go forth a remnant, and they that escape out of mount Zion: the zeal of the LORD of hosts shall do this.

Here the Lord is speaking to Hezekiah and promises him a glorious sign. His intent is to remove all concern and uneasiness regarding the frightful results of Sennacherib's invasion. During the year there had been no sowing or harvesting because of the enemy. This could easily lead to famine or at least great scarcity of food. The red horse of war is always followed by the black horse of hunger as the people of that day frequently experienced in a painful manner. Now, however, they will not have to suffer famine, for this year they will have enough of what has grown by itself without sowing. Even the following year the destroyed fields will not yield a normal harvest; in that year, too, they will have to make do with what the Lord causes to grow of itself. But in the third year after the invasion everything will be done as usual. From the context, it is clear that the Lord wishes to teach the people an important lesson by this natural remnant by which he will keep them alive. The natural remnant of the fields serves the imaginative prophet as an example and mirror of the spiritual remnant of Judah in the future. The expression "take root downward and bear fruit upward" is often used in the so-called "language of Canaan," especially in the prayers of God's people. But how little is this expression understood according to the intent and meaning of the Spirit as it is indicated here. It does not speak of the individual child of God but of the future remnant of the Jews. The promise concerning the remnant as indicated in verses thirty-one and thirty-two indicates: (a) Israel will never be exterminated, for even if the world expires in its present form, a remnant from Israel will *escape* this judgment. (b) This remnant will again be planted in its country and in *Jerusalem* (v. 32). (c) The remnant will take root so deeply that it can never be uprooted. (d) The remnant will shoot upward and bear fruit unto God. (e) The remnant will spread out from Jerusalem over the entire earth and fill the world with its fruit. (f) The burning fire of Jehovah's love *will do this*. Precious also is the thought that this glorious promise is given to Hezekiah, since he had just clung in faith to the remnant, as we saw in verse four. Here the Lord crowns his steadfast faith and living hope.

The Assurance That Sennacherib Will Not Enter Jerusalem

33. Therefore thus saith the LORD concerning the king of Assyria, He shall not come into this city, nor shoot an arrow there, nor come before it with shields, nor cast a bank against it.
34. By the way that he came, by the same shall he return, and shall not come into this city, saith the LORD.
35. For I will defend this city to save it for mine own sake, and for my servant David's sake.

How lovingly the Lord wishes to remove with the tenderest of care all anxious fear from Hezekiah's heart! How beautiful is the life of faith and trust in the Lord! Those who believe have indeed nothing to fear; on the other hand, those who forsake Him can expect grief upon grief. Sennacherib will not come into the city or even shoot an arrow at it from a distance. He will not storm the walls. Soldiers did this while covering themselves with their shields lifted above their heads. No *bank, i.e.,* no dam on which a battering ram was advanced towards the city, will be put up against the wall. He will return to Assyria – a prophecy shortly afterwards literally fulfilled – while leaving his army behind – dead. The cause of all this lay not in Judah or in Hezekiah's stirring prayer, but in God Himself, His name, and his covenant with His beloved servant David.

The End of Sennacherib and His Army

> 36. Then the angel of the LORD went forth, and smote in the camp of the Assyrians a hundred and fourscore and five thousand: and when they arose early in the morning, behold, they were all dead corpses.
> 37. So Sennacherib king of Assyria departed, and went and returned, and dwelt at Nineveh.
> 38. And it came to pass, as he was worshipping in the house of Nisroch his god, that Adrammelech and Sharezer his sons smote him with the sword; and they escaped into the land of Armenia: and Esarhaddon his son reigned in his stead.

In this brief, sober passage we have a description of the downfall of this proud enemy of God. How believing expositors can talk about some severe pestilence or other immediate causes is beyond us, for the Lord describes it as a miracle performed by the angel of the Lord. We would much prefer that the word angel were capitalized, for undoubtedly no one else is meant but the Lord Jesus before His incarnation. One day He will also with His own hand do away with him who is more than Sennacherib in the last days and defeat and destroy his armies in His wrath. According to II Kings 19:35 this miracle took place *in that night,* i.e., the night that followed upon this prophecy of Isaiah.

There must have been songs of rejoicing in the tents of the righteous. This was the finger of God! Here pride and blasphemy were visibly and manifestly punished. Judah had suffered much by his hand. In one of the inscriptions that were found some years ago in the ruins of Nineveh, Sennacherib tells the following:

I attacked Hezekiah of Judah who had not subjected himself to me, and took forty-six fortresses, forts and small cities. I carried away captive 200,150 people, big and small, both male and female, a multitude of horses, young bulls, asses, camels and oxen. Hezekiah himself I locked up in Jerusalem like a bird in its cage. I put up banks against his city. I separated his cities whose inhabitants I had taken prisoners from his realm and gave them to Mitinti, king of Ashdod, Padi, king of Ekron, and Zilbel, king of Gaza and thus diminished his country. And I added another tax to the one imposed on him earlier.

The braggert pretends that his campaign against Hezekiah ended in triumph, but on the basis of God's Word we know better. We may safely assume that as a rule the monuments never related the kings' defeats but always their victories.

And (he) *dwelt at Nineveh.* This does not mean that he never left his capital — the inscriptions give an account of another twenty years of his reign and several campaigns — but that he never undertook another campaign against Judah and Jerusalem.

His end was lamentable. In the place which heathen consider safest on earth — in the temple of one of his gods — he was killed by his own sons. In verse seven, it was already foretold that he would die by the *sword* in his own country. The later Jewish scribes have embellished this sober description. According to them Sennacherib had consulted an oracle concerning the question of why he could not conquer the Jews, to which he received the following answer: "The reason is that Abraham in his day had wanted to sacrifice his son to his God, that is why Jehovah is always intent on showing His gratitude for that great liberality to his descendants." When the tyrant had learned this, he decided to improve on Abraham's act and to sacrifice *two* sons to his patron god — then Nisroch would certainly confound the attempts of his Jewish colleague. But his plans leaked out, and driven on by bitterness and the desire of self-preservation, his sons prevented their own murder by murdering their father. It is obvious that this legend originates with the Jews. May we learn from Sennacherib that *pride goeth before a fall!*

ISAIAH 38

"Set Thine House in Order: For Thou Shalt Die"

1. In those days was Hezekiah sick unto death. And Isaiah the prophet the son of Amoz came unto him, and said unto him, Thus saith the LORD, Set thine house in order: for thou shalt die, and not live.

Bible students have often argued as to when the pious king became sick, but from verses one and six it is evident that his sickness must be placed at the time of Sennacherib's invasion. He became very sick, even unto death. We are not told what the nature of his sickness was. Many think of the plague as a result of the siege. Others explain his sickness as the result of a nervous breakdown in body and spirit, since it is certain that the king was subject to great anxiety in those days. But these are only guesses and verse twenty-one rather points to a sickness accompanied by a dangerous boil. According to some, a plague *botch* is meant. The prophet Isaiah was sent to the king with the sad message: *Set thine house in order: for thou shalt die.* This was a shocking announcement, for the king was at that time still a young man of thirty-nine years of age. At that age, a person usually manifests no tiredness of life but rather a zest for living. Moreover, his afflicted people could hardly do without him. He was sick *unto death.* People around him must have fluctuated between hope and fear, but the man of God removed all hope with his sad tiding. *Set thine house in order* means that he had to make out his last will and testament.

Effect of the Death Announcement on Hezekiah

2. Then Hezekiah turned his face toward the wall, and prayed unto the LORD,

3. And said, Remember now, O LORD, I beseech thee, how I have walked before thee in truth and with a perfect heart, and have done that which is good in thy sight. And Hezekiah wept sore.

The king was completely crushed and burst into loud wails when he heard the death announcement.

Hezekiah has been compared with Paul who desired to depart and be with Christ, but this comparison is unfair, for Hezekiah still lived under the shadow of the Old Dispensation. Israel knew of an immortal life but did not quite have the glorious hope the Church now has. This is the reason why the fear of death in Israel was much greater than that of believers of the New Dispensation. Israel's spirit of bondage to fear manifested itself especially in its view of death. *Sheol* was thought of as a horrible realm of phantoms, while the Conqueror of death and the grave, of Satan, sin and hell was seen only from a gray, nebulous distance.

Yet this does not explain everything in Hezekiah's case, for there may have been many God-fearing people in that day who would not have uttered such lamentations. There were special reasons for his great sadness and we would do him a great injustice if we were to think only of a fear of death on his part. Nor is his unusual sadness to be ascribed to his rather young age or to the sad conditions of his kingdom, no matter how much we must agree that a long and happy life on earth was one of the most coveted things to a Jew.

The main reason for his sadness was undoubtedly the fact that he as yet had no successor to the throne. Manasseh had not been born yet (II Kings 21:1). If he were to die now, what would become of the promise once given to David, i.e., that his seed would be established and that there would always be one of his house to sit on the throne? Thus, he was to some extent confronted with the same difficulty as Abraham when seemingly contrary to the covenant promise, he was commanded to sacrifice his own son. Moreover the pious king seems to have entertained the constant desire to see the promised Messiah during his lifetime. For he literally cries out in verse 11: *"I shall no more see Yahweh, Yahweh in the land of the living; I shall behold Adam no more with the inhabitants of rest."* The Greek translators took these words in a Messianic sense, for they translate: "I said, I shall no more see the salvation of God in the land of the living: I shall no more see the man from my generation." Hence we do not doubt that we are dealing with a Messianic idea expressed in these words by the sick king. Obviously he had lived in the expectation that during his lifetime on earth he would see Yahweh, who was the second Adam, the central man, the real man, the representative of all of mankind. Many kings and prophets have desired to see what later the Apostles were privileged to see; among those many was Hezekiah. As is the case with every fervent wish, he had expected the coming of the Lord in the near future, not very far off. If this interpretation is correct, then it is understandable that the announcement of death was so shocking to him. Hope deferred marketh the heart sick, according to the wise proverb of Solomon.

Nevertheless, the noble king in his crushing grief was neither without hope nor desperate, but turned his face to the wall to wrestle with God without interference. He prayed! He was a man of prayer. Whenever there was a crisis in his life he poured out his heart before the face of the Lord. He was not only an active ruler but also a praying king. He prayed and besought and interceded. He could plead and wrestle with God as few others. The ground for his plea, which he presents to God in verse three, is not self-righteousness but a frank reminder to God that He is dealing with one of His true children. We come across similar pleas again and again in the prayers of God's children of old. The Psalms abound with them. But we do not find them in the New Testament. The Church bases its pleas on Christ's righteousness.

Hezekiah's Prayer Answered

4. Then came the word of the LORD to Isaiah, saying,

5. Go, and say to Hezekiah, Thus saith the LORD, the God of David thy father, I have heard thy prayer, I have seen thy tears: behold, I will add unto thy days fifteen years.

6. And I will deliver thee and this city out of the hand of the king of Assyria: and I will defend this city.

The answer to Hezekiah's prayer came very quickly. According to II Kings 20:4, Isaiah was still in the palace where he most likely remained with the courtiers to give spiritual advice regarding the dying king and the soon to be unoccupied throne. The text does not say how the word of God came to him. It seems that the Lord spoke to him the way he did to Moses, i.e., mouth to mouth. Isaiah was always absolutely certain of his message. The expression *the God of David thy father* is significant and indicates, among other things, that Hezekiah had been very concerned about the house of David. God heard his *prayer* and saw his *tears.* Good health would soon come to him so that after three days he would be able to go up to God's house according to the desire of his heart, while his life would be lengthened by fifteen years; and the holy city will not fall into the hands of Sennacherib (see 37:33-35). The latter indeed meant good health to Hezekiah.

The Sign of Ahaz's Sun Dial

7. And this shall be a sign unto thee from the LORD, that the LORD will do this thing that he hath spoken;
8. Behold, I will bring again the shadow of the degrees, which is gone down in the sun dial of Ahaz, ten degrees backward. So the sun returned ten degrees, by which degrees it was gone down.

According to verse twenty-two Hezekiah had asked for a sign. His wicked father had been offered a sign but out of so-called piety he did not want to ask for one. The pious son is not offered a sign and yet he asks for it. This was not evidence of unbelief but it did show that his faith was weak. However, the Lord accommodated him in it.

The miracle itself is considered a great wonder by the Holy Spirit and is described three times, while it is indicated by the words *oth* (sign), and *mopheth* (a striking and spectacular miracle-sign, which amazes everybody and which also indeed aroused the amazement of the Chaldean astrologists). The Hebrew word does not actually mean sun dial, but *stairs, ascent, going up.* It is used for the stairs of a throne (II Chron. 9:18-19), the stairs of the altar (Exod. 20:26; Ezek. 43:17) the stairs of a house (II Kings 9:13; Amos 9:6), the stairs of the court of the temple (Ezek. 40:6, 22-37), the stairs of a ring wall of a city (Neh. 3:15; 12:37), and finally it is the same word we meet in the songs *hamaaloth* (of ascends) (Psalms 120 - 134). Hence, the Septuagint translates: *shadow of the stairs.* The importance of the miracle is further evidenced by the fact that it took place upon the prayer of Isaiah (II Kings 20:11). Talk about this sign spread far and wide and even reached Babylon (II Chron. 32:31).

If we ask, however, what this miracle entailed and how it must be explained, we have to confess humbly that it is beyond our comprehension, as is the case with the two other great natural wonders, the standing still of the sun upon Joshua's prayer and the darkening of the sun at the Savior's death, indeed with all miracles. A miracle as such is inexplicable, unfathomable, divine; it is a rock that is too high for our comprehension. It is a sudden interference by God's hand in the usual order of things whereby the connection between causes and results simply eludes us. All the expositors have written about it is but wild speculation. Even the special booklet written on it by Professor Dilloo, *Das Wunder an den Stufen Achaz* explains nothing about this miracle as such. As a further elucidation on this verse, read II Kings 20:8-11 where the matter is discussed in greater detail.

The Title of Hezekiah's Memoir

> 9. The writing of Hezekiah king of Judah, when he had been sick, and was recovered of his sickness.

Hezekiah was a worker and teacher and one who prayed. Evidently he loved God's Word and desired to acquaint others with it. From Proverbs 25:1 we learn that he had his men collect and publish a great number of Solomon's Proverbs. At the celebration of the great Paschal feast, he again had in mind the instruction of the ignorant people. But besides all that, he was also a poet. Hezekiah's prayer is actually a song, which he composed when he was sick and facing death and in which he poured out his heart in distressed and heart-rending laments. Finally, we observe that in this, as well as in publishing the Proverbs of Solomon, he wanted to be spiritually helpful to others of his nation. Thus, he even made his sickness profitable to his people.

Hezekiah's Song of Lamentation

10. I said in the cutting off of my days, I shall go to the gates of the grave: I am deprived of the residue of my years.
11. I said, I shall not see the LORD, even the LORD, in the land of the living: I shall behold man no more, with the inhabitants of the world.
12. Mine age is departed, and is removed from me as a shepherd's tent: I have cut off like a weaver my life: he will cut me off with pining sickness: from day even to night wilt thou make an end of me.
13. I reckoned till morning, that, as a lion, so will he break all my bones: from day even to night wilt thou make an end of me.
14. Like a crane or a swallow, so did I chatter: I did mourn as a dove: mine eyes fail with looking upward: O LORD, I am oppressed; undertake for me.
15. What shall I say, he hath both spoken unto me, and himself hath done it: I shall go softly all my years in the bitterness of my soul.
16. O Lord, by these things men live, and in all these things is the life of my spirit: so wilt thou recover me, and make me to live.
17. Behold, for peace I had great bitterness: but thou hast in love to my soul delivered it from the pit of corruption: for thou hast cast all my sins behind thy back.
18. For the grave cannot praise thee, death can not celebrate thee: they that go down into the pit cannot hope for thy truth.
19. The living, the living, he shall praise thee, as I do this day: the father to the children shall make known thy truth.
20. The LORD was ready to save me: therefore we will sing my songs to the stringed instruments all the days of our life in the house of the LORD.

These verses contain the song of lamentation which he imploringly poured out before God's countenance in the dreadful hour of danger. It is divided into two parts. Verses ten to fourteen describe in four metaphors his great perplexity, when he thought he would live only a few more hours. Verses fifteen to twenty describe his great gratitude as well as his earnest intentions and solemn promises he made to the Lord after the assurance that his life would be lengthened. We must not overlook the fact that the image of *sheol* appears again and again. Compare this with comments on this subject in Chapter fourteen. Although he was a sincere believer, he nevertheless imagined that he was going to a dreadful place, at least a place that to his mind was ominous. Verse ten expresses his grief that he would be deprived of the rest of his days. We have already discussed the Messianic meaning of the next verse. In verses twelve to fourteen he uses the most striking images to express his death and sorrow.

Suddenly his life is broken up like a shepherd's little tent, which was constructed very poorly and of which the pegs had already been pulled up. Paul, too, uses the metaphor of tent or tabernacle for the human body (II Cor. 5:1), as does Peter also (II Peter 1:14). The second image is that of a weaver who cuts his woven cloth loose from the loom. We likewise speak of the severing of the thread of life. Hezekiah believed that this would happen to him that very night. The metaphor of weaving is also beautifully expressed in Job 7:6. The third metaphor is that of a lion that breaks all the bones of its victim, while in the fourth place he compares his utterings with the doleful sound of some birds. Apparently, his voice had already weakened considerably due to his illness and his eyes grew dim, but imploringly he lifted them up and prayed: *Undertake for me!* The idea of surety is found throughout Scripture. Judah said to Jacob: "I will be *surety* for him," i.e., guarantee his life with mine. Usually, however, the word means a monetary surety (Prov. 11:15, 20:16, 27:13). Here the word means a prayer to God to prevent him from dying.

Between verses fourteen and fifteen we must insert in our minds the promise that his life would be lengthened. It is remarkable that as soon as Hezekiah pleaded upon a Surety, he was saved. Prophetically this is a striking reference to the only Surety, Christ. As soon as we flee to Him in our distress we are saved from death and doom.

The second part of verse fifteen is translated and interpreted in widely different ways. Luther, Michaelis and the Lutheran theologians translate: "All my life I shall be remembering this bitter hour with trembling." The Vulgate, Jerome, Lowth and others translate: "For the rest of my life I shall think about and contemplate this bitter thing."

Vitringa, Schmidius, Holreisel, Dathe, Rosenmuller, Leeser and Jonckbloet translate: "I shall stately tread toward the temple." But Calvin, Sibersma, Henderson, Delitzsch, Ewald, Umbriet, Orelli, Martin, A. Clarke, Alexander, Cowles, De Wette, Darby, Whedon, Kay, Dachsel, Cheyne, Kelly, Wade, Ellicott, and Klinkenberg translate it the same as the Dutch Authorized Version. The Greek translators even omitted the entire verse. The Hebrew word *daddah* points to a soft tripping and pattering as that of a toddler at his mother's hand and thus also to the solemn climb to the temple. So the Dutch Authorized version is preferred. Ridderbos translates with a recent German expositor: "Restlessly I toss about during the time of sleep on account of the bitterness of my soul," but this is unfounded.

We explain these words as a solemn intention of the God-fearing king. He was answered in his totally lost condition after he poured out his heart in prayer. Now he may look to the future again. God grants him another fifteen years. All these things, he makes a solemn decision to spend his remaining years in ever increasing seriousness and with complete dedication to the Lord. He no longer wants, as perhaps in the past, to rush through life; on the contrary, he now wants to walk softly, sweetly, demurely and humbly through life, which to him is like a journey. If he once condoned his princes' trust in Egypt's chariots and horsemen, he now determines solemnly that this will be different from now on. As the shepherd of his people he wants to subject himself carefully, humbly and totally to God's will. It is a solemn resolve of a broken and truly grateful heart. He wants to remain faithful to this resolution all the days of his remaining life. And he wants to do so *because of,* or better, *after* the bitterness of his soul, which at the same time was the immediate cause of his holy resolution. What this resolution was worth is told in the next chapter. Good intentions, even by the greatest of God's children, mean absolutely nothing if they are not carried out prayerfully and watchfully. For every time a pious soul makes a good resolution, hell breaks loose and Satan at once resolves to make it impossible to carry it out. With Hezekiah, Satan succeeded only too well.

"O Lord, by these things men live, and in all these things is the life of my spirit!" This statement is often applied to the experiences of God's people, but that is not what Hezekiah had in mind. Nor was he thinking of his own marvelous experiences. He rather was thinking of the promise of God, or, even more broadly, of the *words* and *miraculous acts* of God which he had received and experienced. We live indeed by the words and works of God. His creative Word quickened us and it is also His Word that maintains our spiritual life. When he says: *But thou hast in love to my soul delivered it,* he is speaking of his sweet experience. The end of verse seventeen shows the close connection between his sickness and sin. The king not only rejoiced in his physical healing but also in the forgiveness of his sins (cf. 33:24). The last two verses of this section enlarge on his good intentions; as a living person he wishes to praise Jehovah; as a father he wishes to make known the truth to his children; as a blessed person he wishes to sing his songs to the stringed instruments in the temple.

The Means of His Cure

21. For Isaiah had said, Let them take a lump of figs, and lay it for a plaister upon the boil, and he shall recover.
22. Hezekiah also had said, What is the sign that I shall go up to the house of the LORD.

Recently, the words of verse twenty-one have evoked intensified interest. Due to the increased attention for faith healing, the question has been asked if we really must accept a means of healing here. We are convinced that the text is definitely dealing with such a means. This does not detract from the divine miracle of healing, for it remains just that. But fig plasters are still useful and are frequently used in the Near East to cure swellings. They soften and ripen boils. According to some faith healers, Hezekiah needed a remedy since he had asked for a sign.

ISAIAH 39

Ambassadors of Babylon Visit Hezekiah

1. At that time Merodach-baladan, the son of Baladan, king of Babylon, sent letters and a present to Hezekiah: for he had heard that he had been sick, and was recovered.

2. And Hezekiah was glad of them, and shewed them the house of his precious things, the silver, and the gold, and the spices, and the precious ointment, and all the house of his armour, and all that was found in his treasures: there was nothing in his house, nor in all his dominion, that Hezekiah shewed them not.

This brief chapter is actually an introduction to the second half of Isaiah, but, according to tradition, we shall discuss it here. It contains the lamentable attitude of the otherwise very pious king. As a divine elucidation on this chapter we quote here II Chronicles 32:24-31:

24. In those days Hezekiah was sick to the death, and prayed unto the LORD: and he spake unto him, and he gave him a sign.

25. But Hezekiah rendered not again according to the benefit done unto him; for his heart was lifted up: therefore there was wrath upon him, and upon Judah and Jerusalem.

26. Notwithstanding Hezekiah humbled himself for the pride of his heart, both he and the inhabitants of Jerusalem, so that the wrath of the LORD came not upon them in the days of Hezekiah.

27. And Hezekiah had exceeding much riches and honour: and he made himself treasuries for silver, and for gold, and for precious stones, and for spices, and for shields, and for all manner of pleasant jewels;

28. Storehouses also for the increase of corn, and wine, and oil; and stalls for all manner of beasts, and cotes for flocks.

29. Moreover he provided him cities, and possessions of flocks and herds in abundance: for God had given him substance very much.

30. This same Hezekiah also stopped the upper watercourse of Gihon, and brought it straight down to the west side of the city of David. And Hezekiah prospered in all his works.

31. Howbeit in the business of the ambassadors of the princes of Babylon, who sent unto him to enquire of the wonder that was done in

the land, God left him, to try him, that he might know all that was in his heart.

Regarding Hezekiah's fall we must keep in mind three facts: (a) God left him, that is to say, left him alone for a moment to try him, and see all that was in his heart. (b) Satan, although he is not mentioned here, has throughout the ages, as here again, made the fiercest attacks on the house of David. (c) The *heart* of Hezekiah was *lifted up* and he *rendered not again* for the blessing of healing bestowed on him. God not only considered his sin of commission but also his sin of omission. Hezekiah knew what Babylon was from Isaiah's descriptions. He should have told the Babylonians of the glory of Israel's God and praise the grace bestowed upon him to them. He should have witnessed in love to them about their abominable idolatry. He should not have displayed his treasures to them but the treasures of the grace of God. The well-known expositor Kohlbrugge correctly says in his forceful style: "Just as Samson revealed his strength to the whore, so Hezekiah revealed God's glory to the devils as though he were their companion and had received favors from Babylon." The question is asked again and again why it was such a great sin that he showed his treasures; if showing one's treasures as such is already sin, all museums and all displays of merchandise are sin also. No, having and showing treasures per se is not sin, but showing treasures is usually accompanied by the sin of pride, and this was the case here. With a vainglorious selfish pleasure, the greatly blessed king showed his treasures to the uncircumcised heathen — and he did not think of his solemn intentions!

The name *Merodach* is the same as that of the Assyrian and Babylonian Deity Marduk, which is similar to Jupiter of the Romans (Jer. 50:2). His name often appears in proper names of persons, as do the names of Bel and Nebo. Merodach-baladan in 721 B.C. usurped the throne of Babylon, was conquered and driven off by Sargon in 710, but returned in 703 and held out for nine months against the mighty King Sennacherib. Now it was only natural that he rejoiced in the calamity that had struck Sennacherib's army before the walls of Jerusalem. Therefore, the general opinion today is that his delegation's object was not merely to congratulate Hezekiah with his victory and healing, or to examine the miraculous sign of Ahaz's sun dial, but to gain diplomatic ground, i.e., to turn Hezekiah against the dominion of Assyria and induce him to become a friend and ally of Babylon — an idea which has little that is objectionable and much that is plausible. Seen in this light, Hezekiah's sin becomes all the more irresponsible. The Lord had just shown him the vanity of all worldly power. Egypt on the one hand had not offered any help and Sennacherib on the other hand had not been able to resist God's power. How can he now behave so cordially and affectionately to the ambassadors of Babylon. He was finished with Egypt and Assyria but Satan easily caught him in the snares of Babylon. Are we not often subject to the same temptations as Hezekiah?

Isaiah Visits Hezekiah and Questions Him

3. Then came Isaiah the prophet unto king Hezekiah, and said unto him, What said these men? and from whence came they unto thee? And Hezekiah said, They are come from a far country unto me, even from Babylon.
4. Then said he, What have they seen in thine house? And Hezekiah answered, All that is in mine house have they seen: there is nothing among my treasures that I have not shewed them.

Those legs are strong indeed that can bear up under luxury, as became all too evident to Hezekiah. He conducted himself much better in adversity and oppression than in prosperity. Prosperity has always proved to be extremely dangerous to Israel, the Church and every individual believer. The Lord was very angry with Hezekiah's sin, which consisted of carelessness, unbelief, ingratitude, inattentiveness and pride. He sent His servant Isaiah to the king. The prophets were the correctors of the kings and when the latter sinned, the former came storming at them like birds. Here Isaiah comes as such a bird to announce judgment. His face must have looked ominous when he demanded an account of his king in short, clipped questions. He puts three questions to the king. First, *What said these men?* Actually, this was the most important question, and exactly the one Hezekiah left unanswered. He apparently did not dare tell the man of God what insipid flattery he had allowed them to subject him to. Hence the king's answer is not as forthright and courageous as is sometimes thought. The fact, however, that Hezekiah does not become furious at Isaiah so that he snaps at him, "What business is that of yours!" shows on the other hand that in his conscience he was already aware of what was going on, agreed with the prophet and inwardly regretted his misdeed. Many monarchs in a case like this would have exploded in anger. And even God-fearing kings such as Asa could not always humbly accept the stern admonitions of the prophets. The fact that Hezekiah does not resist Isaiah is a good sign.

The Babylonian Exile Foretold

5. Then said Isaiah to Hezekiah, Hear the word of the LORD of hosts:
6. Behold, the days come, that all that is in thine house, and that which thy fathers have laid up in store until this day, shall be carried to Babylon: nothing shall be left, saith the LORD.
7. And of thy sons that shall issue of thee, which thou shalt beget, shall they take away; and they shall be eunuchs in the palace of the king of Babylon.

After a solemn opening Isaiah now announces the Babylonian captivity. The expression *that which thy fathers have laid up* indicates that the royal palaces at that time were at the same time the museums in which all kinds of documents and war trophies were preserved for future generations. Hezekiah must have shown with pride what David had captured from his enemies long ago and what others of his renowned ancestors had been able to take from their enemies. These treasures were carefully preserved, the descendants were proud of them and they would have hated to lose such historical monuments. Hence it must have cut Hezekiah's soul that all these highly valued treasures would be carried off to Babylon. Babylon had now, by his own doing, cast a covetous eye at all those treasures and after about a century it would covetously reach out for them. Finally, in the days of Belshazzar, it would use them to mock the God of Israel. The cultured heathen had been much too smart for the pious covenant king! We may observe here the law of commensurate retribution — Hezekiah had sinned with Babylon, now he would be punished with Babylon.

Even more severe punishment would descend upon Hezekiah's house. Not only his treasures, but also his *sons* — his descendants from the line of David — would be carried away captive to Babylon and there as castrated chamberlains serve in the palace of the king of Babylon. Daniel one describes the literal fulfillment of this prophecy.

The question has been asked why such severe punishment was pronounced on such a minor offense. We must answer that here we are not dealing with a minor transgression but rather with a very serious one. The sin of pride has a true Satanic nature. Moreover we must not forget that Judah went into the Babylonian exile not only because of Hezekiah's sin, but also because of Manasseh's sins and the sins mentioned in II Chronicles thirty-six and other places.

Hezekiah Humbles Himself Under the Continuous Punishment

8. Then said Hezekiah to Isaiah, Good is the word of the LORD which thou hast spoken. He said moreover, For there shall be peace and truth in my days.

It cannot be denied that this verse contains some difficulty. For here we find Hezekiah, who otherwise is very impassioned of nature, extremely calm and controlled. When his own end was announced, he filled the air with lamentations. When the end of his nation is announced, he remains so calm that many have accused him of selfishness. Some expositors, in an effort to save his character and piety, have assumed mute grief, as this grief is deeper than that which made him weep uncontrollably. On the basis of II Chronicles 32:25, 26, however, we may speak of humiliation on his part. Here, too, he says in effect to Isaiah, "The word of the Lord which thou hast spoken is *good.*" There was quiet submission to and acceptance of God's ways. We cannot disguise the fact, however, that the last clause points to some egotism. We must observe that obviously not everything is told here. It even makes a great difference *how* these words were said. Intonation, attitude and look can indeed say much. Such things escape us in a brief account like this. Finally, one thing is certain — we clearly see the law of history, the law of apostasy in the life of this noble ruler.

INTRODUCTION

ISAIAH 40-66

INTRODUCTION

ISAIAH 40-66

The critical science of today does not recognize the second part of Isaiah as the work of Isaiah the prophet but assumes the author to be some great unknown person from the time of the exile whom it calls Deutero-Isaiah or Second Isaiah. Hence Isaiah's book experienced the same fate as (according to tradition) his person — it was sawn asunder. It was the rationalistic theologians from Germany who in the second half of the eighteenth century were so bold as to undertake this venture. It took another century, however, before the denial of these chapters became general, as is now the case in the scientific world. In the year 1880 the renowned Hebrew scholar, Professor Franz Delitzsch, in other regards a believing Lutheran theologian, hesitantly at first, abandoned his belief that Isaiah was the author of the second part. From that time on a flood of books have appeared which deny Isaiah's authorship of this part. Even many theologians who still confess Christ as their Savior accept it as an established fact that these chapters are not nor cannot be by Isaiah. Dr. J. J. P. Valeton, Jr. of Utrecht reflects the viewpoint of the moderate critics when he says, "Isaiah 40 to 66 are just as much the book of comfort par excellence, the gospel of the old dispensation, whether they are to be dated back to the sixth century or whether they are the work by a prophet from the eighth century."

This viewpoint must be rejected as foolish and dangerous. For that reason we wish to indicate briefly our basis for accepting the genuineness and the Isaiahic authorship of the second part. Of all the theologians in Europe and America who have written on this subject none has, in our opinion, produced such a thorough book as the Dutch theologian,

Prof. Dr. A. Rutgers, the father of the well-known Amsterdam professor. Under point (9) in our list of arguments below, we have included some information derived from his book which have never been refuted.

(1) In the first place it is very strange that this second Isaiah was discovered at such a late date, and then by the rationalistic theologians who became renowned by anything but their deep insight in the Scriptures. The old Rabbis, the Church Fathers, and the Reformers never even dreamed of his existence. But how could such a great prophet remain hidden for such a long time? Regarding the greatness of this prophet the thoughts are unanimous. He is admired by everyone as a stylist, poet, thinker and orator who with unequaled courage makes his message known in a manner that is commanding, admonishing, comforting, lamenting and jubilating. It is impossible from a psychological standpoint that a genius of this caliber would be unknown to both contemporaries and later generations. The greatly beloved man Daniel was already in his day generally known and renowned.

(2) Josephus presents external proof for the genuineness of this part. In Book XI (i.2) of his *Antiquities* he says that the Lord's will to rebuild the temple "was known to Cyrus by reading the book Isaiah had written. When Cyrus read this he was seized and moved by the great desire to fulfill what had been written concerning this matter." So it is obvious that Josephus in his day knew only of one Isaiah. His testimony is confirmed moreover by what we read in Ezra 1:2, 3 and 6:2, 3. There we read that King Cyrus in his edict acknowledged Jehovah the God of heaven and earth as the source of his authority and that He commanded him to build a house in Jerusalem. This proclamation was preserved as an important document of state in the royal library. The only source of Cyrus's knowledge is undoubtedly these words by Isaiah,

That saith of Cyprus, He is my shepherd, and shall perform all my pleasure: even saying to Jerusalem, Thou shalt be built; and to the temple, Thy foundation shall be laid . . . Thus saith the LORD to his anointed, To Cyrus, whose right hand I have holden, to subdue nations before him; and I will loose the loins of kings, to open before him the two leaved gates; and the gates shall not be shut (44:28; 45:1).

Let us suppose Isaiah had not written this but an unknown great man in Cyrus' days. Then two things follow from this: 1) that this unknown writer was an impostor and Cyrus a fool for believing this deceit, and 2) Josephus' story which is recognized as genuine proves to be worthless.

(3) It is impossible that an impostor could have such exalted views of God and His Kingdom and possess such high moral standards as he did. The critics usually smile benignly at the word *impostor* in this connection and try to justify this as "pious deceit" and as something quite common, innocent, naive and natural. But this only proves that these gentlemen are in a state of moral decay and degeneration. For so-called pious deceit is deceit — not pious, but reprehensively untrue and deeply sinful. A Jew who lived during the exile knew that Isaiah had been dead for more than a century. If an impostor wanted to see his book find acceptance by attaching the authority of Isaiah's name to it, this would be simply branded as what psychology calls Jesuitism, which has always been condemned by all right-minded Protestants as immoral. Again, psychologically it is inexplicable how such an impostor could have such exalted religious views, for is not a man's style identical with the man? And it is also baffling that a man such as Valeton could continue to call such deceit comforting gospel.

(4) It is argued that this author assumes the exile and presents the country as already having been destroyed, the cities depopulated, the people as mourning and in need of comfort. Since Isaiah lived about a century and a half before the exile, he should have presented these things as taking place in the future. But a refutation such as this, if sincerely meant, shows great ignorance regarding the style of the prophets in Holy Scripture. Ever since Enoch prophesied, "Behold, the Lord *came* with ten thousands of his saints," the prophets used this manner of writing. Dr. Aalders says of the custom of the prophets to describe future events in the

present or even in the past tense, "They identify themselves with the future events that are revealed to them to such an extent that they speak of them in the past tense, the so-called *prophetic perfectum,* which often alternates with the future tense." We can add to this that this indicates the divine certainty of the fulfillment. In the first part of Isaiah we can point out examples of this manner of writing in almost every chapter. For example, 9:1-5 speaks of the people that walked in darkness and *have seen* a great light and of the Child that already *is born.* In the New Testament we find the same phenomenon. In his commentary on James in *Text en Uitleg* Dr. H. M. van Nes writes on James 5:1-6, "This Messianic judgment is actually presented as having already come, since the treasures are described as already having been corrupted and motheaten and cankered." It must be admitted that we find this peculiar presentation here more than elsewhere, but for a stylistic artist like Isaiah this was nothing too strange and under the circumstances indeed necessary.

(5) Another reason for the rejection of the authorship of Isaiah lies in the style. It is alleged that it is entirely different from the prophet who is recognized as the genuine Isaiah, much more beautiful and exalted and making much more use of the figure of speech known as personification. To begin with the last item, it must be conceded that the second part contains the richest and most beautiful personifications. So the little worm can as a man who is threshing with a new sharp threshing instrument thresh and pulverize the mountains (41:14, 15); a sevenfold song resounds through all of creation (42:10, 11); the beasts of the field, the dragons and the young owls will exalt God (43:20); heaven and earth, mountains and woods shout with joy about Israel's restoration (44:23); the heavens and clouds are commanded to drop down righteousness on earth (45:8); the idols of Babylon are powerless beings that weary the beasts of burden to death (46:1); Babylon is a lusting, frivolous young woman (47:1-10); Israel is a barren and forsaken woman who to her own amazement receives many righteous children, so that her tent will become too small (49:20, 21; 54:1-6); God is viewed a man who in His own house is treated disdainfully (50:2); heaven goes in mourning and clothes itself in

sackcloth (50:3); Jerusalem is a slave woman who is set free (52:1, 2), and therefore totally the opposite of Babylon (cf. 47:1-10); the mountains and trees break forth into singing and clap their hands on account of Israel's restoration (55:12); the Messiah is a warrior in complete armor (59:17), and a treader of the winepress (63:3); Lebanon comes to beautify Israel with its rich variety of trees (60:13), and restored Jewry is a bride over whom God as the bridegroom rejoices (62:5).

But it is exactly this argument regarding style that can be turned crushingly against this criticism. As Prof. Rutgers says,

> It is unthinkable that an unknown man living in Babylon, when toward the end of the captivity, the Hebrew language had deteriorated, would have equaled the first master in writing, and would have succeeded in putting the stamp of Isaiah's perfection on his deceptive composition. Rather, the language points out the age of the author, and the style his further development.

Besides, why should not a brilliant intellect as that of Isaiah be able to use a different style? And, to quote an example from our day, Dr. P. D. Chantepie de la Saussaye writes the following about Dr. Abraham Kuyper, Sr., in his book *Eene Halve Eeuw* (A Half Century), "Together with a few others (among whom the writer who calls himself R. van Deyssel and also A.J.) he permits himself the abnormal luxury of more than one style: the sweet style of 'honey from the rock,' the scathing style of the 'triasterics' and the majestic broad style of the great speeches." How much more, then, may not a man like Isaiah, who moreover was inspired by God's Spirit, have spoken and written in two different styles?

Moreover, this whole argument regarding language and style is extremely exaggerated. In the year 1871 J. J. P. Valeton took his doctor's degree in theology at the University of Utrecht on the thesis "Isaiah According to His Writings Generally Accepted as Authentic," in which he, when speaking about Isaiah's incomparable mastery of language, said this among other things about the exalted style of the known Isaiah:

By no means bound to the decidedly didactic form of a continuous speech, the lyric and elegiac element suddenly appears with him and he succeeds in the most fortunate manner to express his thoughts in the form of stories and proverbs. He frequently uses antitheses and paronomasia but always in a perfectly natural way. His metaphors are simple and derived from ordinary and generally known matters, but always well chosen, fresh and sublime. His oratory, without being in the least overburdened, gives evidence of his fiery imagination and his poetic spirit and is thereby free from all dryness and excessive soberness.

All this can with equal justification be said of the style of the second part. Finally, it is of interest to note that most likely Isaiah wrote these final chapters at a very old age, when his deep, broad mind had fully developed and matured. This would naturally influence his style in connection with the difference in theme.

(6) Dr. F. Hosse in his book on Isaiah called the argument based on style "pure illusion," but this can be said with even more justification of the argument based on the contents of the so-called Deutero-Isaiah. Nearly ten decades ago much was made particularly about the "universalism" of the second Isaiah. The totally modernistic W. Haverkamp based his thesis on this aspect. The first Isaiah was allegedly more narrow-minded and particularly Jewish while the second's view encompassed far more of all the nations. At times one is amazed at the childish nonsense of the critical gentlemen. They want to be known as erudite, profound, strictly scientific and fair, but as a rule they are neither as they come up with "the merest rot and rubbish" like little children. This is a case in point. Are they not acquainted with the "universalism" of 2:2-4 which speaks of the conversion and happiness of all nations? Have they never read and understood the glorious meaning of 11:4-10, where the glory of the Lord is even so universal that it includes the most ravenous beasts of prey and the most poisonous snakes? Is the glory of 12:4-6 hidden to them? Is it not an example of glorious universalism when in 25:6, 7 it is said that the Lord will make a feast of fat things *unto all people* and will

destroy the face of their covering? Dr. J. H. Gunning once spoke of the "bad faith of the Modernists." With equal justification we may speak of the bad faith of the critics, for these men deliberately close their eyes upon the clearest light and then complain about the darkness.

(7) The second Isaiah does not show us his credentials as a prophet. The prophets almost always mention their person, time and calling, and Isaiah, Jeremiah and Ezekiel even make extensive mention of the vision of their calling. This prophet, however, has no title above his bundle of prophecies. He does not list his name, nor the time, nor the place where he lived. With his "Comfort ye, comfort ye my people, saith your God" he places his readers in the heart of the matter and thereby indicates the subject of his preaching. To us, who are fully convinced of the unity of the two parts of this prophet, all this is natural and exactly as we would expect it, since Isaiah recounted his calling in chapter six. Whereas he had spoken earlier of sin and judgment, we would expect nothing less than that he would also point at God's mercy and complete deliverance. Those who want to speak of a different prophet, however, must consider it an almost inexplicable phenomenon that this evangelist of the old covenant, as they lovingly call him, does not show his credentials at all.

(8) The writer of the last twenty-seven chapters identifies himself fully with the author of the first thirty-nine chapters. Hence it runs diametrically counter to the truth when P. de Buck in his book on the prophets writes, "Not a single word in all these twenty-seven chapters indicates or suggest that they want to be taken for the work of Isaiah. On the contrary, they most clearly indicate and say in almost every sentence that they cannot possibly be by him." For the sake of brevity we mention here only a few facts: (a) the basic idea of the holy remnant runs like a golden thread through both parts. (b) The idea of judgment, expressed in the name *Maher-shalal-hash-baz* is also found in both parts. (c) Isaiah prophesied during the reign of the pious King Hezekiah, whose name means *Yahweh is (my) strength.* In different ways he alludes in both parts time and again to this beautiful name (1:24; 4:1; 22:21; 27:5; 28:22; 33:22; 35:3); in

the second part we find in the original this play on words in 41:6, 7, 9, 13; 45:1; 51:18; 54:2; 56:2, 6; 64:7. (d) The poetic name Rahab for Egypt appears in 30:7 and also in 51:9. This poetic name, which also appears in Psalm 87:4 and 89:10, presents Egypt as the proud and arrogant one. (f) As we pointed out earlier, the name Holy One of Israel appears about the same number of times in both parts. (g) The image of the erection of a banner in connection with Israel's restoration is also used in both parts (11:12; 18:3; 49:22; 62:10; 66:19). (h) The idea of idolatry in gardens appears in 1:29 and also in 65:3 and 66:17. (i) Also the expression "The mouth of the LORD hath spoken it" appears in both parts (1:20; 21:17; 22:25; 24:3; 25:8; 40:5; 58:14). (j) The two main parts of Isaiah contain the same eschatological presentations. Both country and nation will be restored and will receive growth and glory from the hand of the Lord. In 1910 T. L. W. van Ravesteyn wrote a voluminous dissertation on "The Unity of the Eschatological Presentations of the Book of Isaiah," in which he, although he was a radical critic belonging to the Leyden School, nevertheless pointed out the unity of these presentations. If we realize that "the last things" receive the lion's share of attention both from Isaiah and the other prophets, we can say that this destructive critic proved the unity of Isaiah in spite of himself. (k) Finally, the author of both parts comes through as one who knows the history of his people thoroughly.

(9) The author of the last twenty-seven chapters shows clearly that he is not living in Babylon but in the holy land. In the past it was quite generally accepted that he lived among the exiles in Babylon, but great linguists such as Duhm, Ewald, and Holscher saw clearly that this was not true. Duhm placed him in Phoenicia and the others in Egypt. Nevertheless most expositors assume that he lived in Babylon, even though this idea is quite untenable in light of the facts.

(a) The *geography* of these chapters points to a writer in Canaan. In Babylonia there were several large heavily populated cities beside Babylon, of which more than one lay close to Babylon; yet not one of these cities is mentioned in these chapters. Nor do we find any proper name of a Babylonian province, district, area, fortress or village; indeed, the name Babylon itself appears no more than three times. This may be considered extremely strange when we remember that this name appears often in the books of all writers that lived during the time of the exile. In Jeremiah the name appears more than 160 times! Against this significant fact is the peculiar fact that of Canaan not only the most well-known names appear frequently, but also the least known such as Achor in the north and Sharon in the south.

(b) The author's *knowledge of the nations* points in the same direction. Of the nations surrounding Babylonia not a single one is mentioned in all these chapters, while Israel's neighbor nations appear again and again. The so-called Second Isaiah speaks very often of mountains and hills, rocks and caves, mountain roads and clefts, valleys, brooks, and pits. All these things refer to Canaan and not to Babylonia, since this country was a monotonous plain, interrupted only by dug canals.

(c) The *mineralogy* is that of Canaan. This author speaks very frequently of all kinds of *stones,* such as the sand of the sea and its gravel (48:19), the smooth stones of the brooks (57:6), the stones on the road (62:10), the rock (51:1), the hardened clay or flint (50:7). In Babylonia, however, no such stones are found on or in the ground.

(d) The *flora* mentioned by the author points to Canaan. Babylonia had very few trees, but cultivated several fruit trees such as peaches, apricots, mulberries, cherries, and apples, while in the wild only palms, poplars and willows were found. Of all these different trees only the willow is mentioned in 44:4, but with the addition *by the water courses,* which proves that he is referring to those in Canaan. Trees native to Canaan are mentioned again and again, such as cedar, myrtle, olive, pine, beech, cypress, fir, elm and grapevine.

(e) *Architecture,* particularly the use of wood as it appears in these chapters, points to an author in Canaan. The

Babylonians used palm-tree wood for building and fuel, while on the other hand the so-called Second Isaiah speaks of a carpenter cutting down and working the wood of a cedar or cypress, an oak or a pine tree, in order to make an idol from part of the wood and to warm himself and bake his bread and fry his meat by burning the other part (44:13-16); these trees grew in Canaan but not in Babylonia.

(f) *Field crops* appearing in this part of Isaiah point the same way. He does not mention a single plant peculiar to Babylonia, but he does mention spices, reeds, flax and others, which grew in Canaan. When describing the future prosperity, we might reasonably have expected that he would have spoken of fruitful grains, such as wheat and barley which grew in Babylonia.

(g) The situation is no different with respect to the *fauna.* Although he mentions no less than twenty-five kinds of animals, there is not a single one among them that was particularly peculiar to Babylonia. He does mention the scarce animals of Canaan, but, living in Babylon, he certainly would have mentioned the animals that live there in abundance, such as beaver, otter, porcupine and alligator, and such birds as pheasants, flamingos and pelicans, and such fish as carps and bluegill. Again, he is totally silent on these animals, birds, and fish.

(h) *Idolatry,* as depicted by the author, points us again from Babylon to Jerusalem. Babylonians perpetrated their idolatry in the most beautiful temples, but he describes it in these chapters as carried out under oaks or terebinths, underneath all green trees (1:29, 57:5-7), alongside brooks, at the caves of the rocks, and on mountains and hills, but neither these trees and brooks, nor such mountains and clefts were found in Babylonia. The *slaughtering of children* points in the same direction, for the sacrifice of children was an abominable form of Caananite idolatry. It did not exist in Babylon; there they sacrificed lambs to the deities Bel and Nebo, but not children. Hence in cruel and idolatrous Babylon the people were never as inhuman as in Judah. This author knows of only two main kinds of idols, i.e., cast images of base metal which were merely covered with gold, and wooden ones which were made by a carpenter. In Babylon the people would have answered the holy mockery of the prophet with their own striking mockery by saying, "Ridicule those who pay homage to such images! We do not venerate such gods, but only those who glitter with blinding beauty and are made of solid gold!"

(i) In Babylon there were four very remarkable masterpieces of architecture, i.e., the high and wide wall of Babylon, the temple of Bel, the royal palace of Neriglissar[1] and the hanging gardens. Now since this writer is a man who notices and observes everything and derives his metaphors from everything he sees, is it not strange that he does not even mention these wonders of the world? Of a man like he, living in Babylon, this is simply unthinkable.

(10) Finally we must point to the witness of Christ and His Apostles which to the true believer is absolutely conclusive. Ultimately at the base of the rejection of Isaiah's authorship by the modern destructive criticism lies the hatred of God and His beloved Son, of the miracles and predictions of God and of the land and the people of the Lord. Many who want to adhere to Christ to be saved by Him apparently allow themselves in the pride of their hearts and out of a foolish fear of the wrath of the vaunted critical science to be overpowered. Thus they come not only to a denial of the genuineness of this part of Isaiah, but also violate the honor of the Savior and of His Apostles by carelessly brushing aside their testimony. If they say that the Savior did not know better, then they injure His omniscience; if they claim that He knew better but adapted Himself to the opinion of the people, then they make Him a participant in this kind of deceit and a menpleaser either out of fear or out of ambition, something that borders on blasphemy.

It is remarkable that exactly from this contested part of Isaiah the New Testament quotes more often than from any

[1] King of Babylon, 559-556 B.C. —ED.

other book, stating that it was written by Isaiah. Quotations from 40:3; 42:1; 61:1, 2; 40:3; 53:1; 53:7, 8; 65:1, 2 are successively found in the following places: Matthew 3:3; 12:17; Luke 4:17-19; John 1:23; 12:38; Acts 8:28-33; Romans 10:20. Hence there need not be any doubt whether Christ and His Apostles believed in Isaiah's authorship of these chapters.

A word of caution with regard to these quotations must be added, however. Many people think on the basis of such quotations that the entire prophecy of Isaiah has been fulfilled in the New Testament, and that of course is not the case at all. The Hebrew word for fulfillment, *mala* has two meanings: *to complete* in the sense of bringing to an end as in I Kings 1:14, where Nathan says to Bathsheba that he will *confirm* her words (cf. I Kings 2:27), and *to fulfill* in the usual sense of the word. The same can be said of the Greek word for *to fulfill, pleroo,* which in places like Matthew 5:17 appears in its first meaning, but in Luke 22:37 in its second meaning. We must keep this always in mind with regard to the quotations from Isaiah and the rest of the Old Testament in the New Testament. For Isaiah is only partially fulfilled and will not be completely fulfilled until the blessed coming of the Lord, which will frequently become clear to us from the explanation itself.

Having briefly indicated some bases for the genuineness of Isaiah, we shall not come back to it at all in the exposition.

ISAIAH 40

The Main Theme of the Second Part

1. Comfort ye, comfort ye my people, saith your God.
2. Speak ye comfortably to Jerusalem, and cry unto her, that her warfare is accomplished, that her iniquity is pardoned: for she hath received of the LORD's hand double for all her sins.

The Leyden translators have this to say here: "How forty to sixty-six have become part of Isaiah we do not know. Maybe by accident, maybe by guesswork. Whatever the case, they have no connection with the prophet Isaiah and his time." By this, they thereby show that they accepted the view now so popular. As is evident, they are strong in their denial, which at best is no more than doubt and uncertainty. To us it is irrefutable that these words follow quite naturally after the preceding chapter. For Isaiah's word must have caused great consternation in the hearts and minds of the king and the God-fearing people. And the seer, enlightened by God's Spirit, saw how long Israel would be in exile and what a history of suffering his poor people would have to endure. His eagle's eye scanned the ages as far as the coming of the Lord. Was it not altogether understandable and fitting that after having struck them with the words of judgment he would speak words of comfort to the people who languished in exile?

The word *comfort* composes the main idea of this entire part. Its repetition indicates not only the intense feeling with which the thought is expressed, but also the double measure of comfort the suffering people will need during their anxious exile which still continues. They will receive their comfort after the exile at their reacceptance and complete restoration. Israel will for many centuries be *Lo-ammi,* i.e., *not-My-people,* but in connection with the future reacceptance it is called here *My people*. *"Saith your God,"* is richer in meaning than when Isaiah had merely said that God had commanded him to comfort Israel. As written here, it means that not only is Isaiah the prophet of comfort, but all the prophets are summoned to comfort Israel, indeed all of Israel and the entire Church. Whoever acknowledges Jehovah as his God has the solemn responsibility to comfort His people Israel. As far as the prophets who appeared after Isaiah are concerned we can see that after the announcement of the thunder of judgments they concluded with the most tender comforting words.

The Dutch word for comfort, *troost,* is related to the English *true. To comfort* means literally *to cause to see the truth.* Here it is further explained as a speaking *to the heart of Jerusalem,* an expression that often appears in Scripture (Gen. 34:3; 50:21; Judg. 19:3). And what would be more to the *heart of Jerusalem* — which stands for the entire nation — than that her *warfare* is accomplished, her *iniquity* is pardoned and that she has received *double* for all her sins from the chastening hand of the Lord which has lain so long and so heavily on the people? Because of the absolute divine certainty of these facts they are put in the prophetic past perfect tense. This means that the suffering people must look to the joyful end. At the end of the long road of suffering there is light; there a reconciled God is waiting mercifully to accept them again as His people. The word *double* has caused many expositors to stumble since they have thought that a righteous God would not punish more severely than usual, i.e., according to works. But that is precisely what He is doing, for it must be remembered that Israel did sin doubly; her first sin is found in the prophets and her second in the gospels. Thus, there is double punishment for double sin.

The Preparation of the Lord's Way

3. The voice of him that crieth in the wilderness, Prepare ye the way of the LORD, make straight in the desert a highway for our God.
4. Every valley shall be exalted, and every mountain and hill shall be made low; and the crooked shall be made straight, and the rough places plain:

5. And the glory of the LORD shall be revealed, and all flesh shall see it together: for the mouth of the LORD hath spoken it.

After the end of Israel's sin and warfare have been mentioned, the King of glory who will bring all this about is identified. He is an illustrious Monarch and He has a personal forerunner to prepare the way. From the New Testament we know that John the Baptist applied these words to himself. It would have been perfectly in order, however, not to mention John's name here, for the attention ought not to be called to the herald but to the coming King.

In order to understand the work of a Mid-Eastern herald correctly, we have to keep in mind that the roads in that part of the world were often in a desolate condition. This has been the case up to our own day, and only the great war and the automobile have brought about some change for the better. If some dignitary came to visit Palestine, the Turkish government suddenly showed great diligence in making the roads passable. Then the *valleys,* the deep holes, must be smoothed, and the *mountains,* the humps, be leveled, so that soon the monarch and his retinue could pass through without hindrance. Thus the Messiah is presented here as an arriving King who will travel through the entire country. Hence, the herald who ran ahead of his sovereign cried that everything should be made ready for his arrival.

The herald himself did not prepare the roads; how could he do this all by himself? We must make a distinction between the herald and the people who prepared the roads. The entire nation is summoned to level the roads and remove the stumblingblocks so as to receive its King festively. For that reason we did not use the term *preparer* but *preparation* of the Lord's way above this section. The emphasis is not on John but on all of Israel who is summoned to receive her King. Thus, this text must not be interpreted "spiritually," whereby the mountains and hills that must be made low means the pride of men, and the valleys that must be exalted means the humility of the believers. In practical application this truth may be inferred, for the Lord also desires that there be passable ways in our hearts and that morally we hate crooked and perverse ways; but this is not the primary explanation of the text. The awful splendor and majesty, the beauty of the holiness of King Jesus, will be revealed before the eyes of Israel and of all the nations, and *all flesh.* All of mankind besides Israel shall *see,* and not merely believe, but *see* that the Lord fulfills His Word. When He comes He will first by means of the most terrible earthquakes change the face of Palestine and make this mountainous land into a level plain. This is why the prophet cries that all valleys will be *exalted* and all hills be made *low.* Christ Himself will in a physical sense make low that which is elevated and exalt that which is low. Nevertheless we must not interpret this phrase in a merely physical and geographical sense but also in a moral-religious one. He will make straight all that is morally and religiously crooked.

Almost everyone agrees that many things are presently crooked, and very crooked indeed. Actually no one is satisfied with the conditions of today. Only a few *Post-tribulationist* preachers stubbornly maintain the figments of their imagination, but no wonder, for they are as deaf and blind, indeed as dead, as a pot. Today the moral, social, political, ecclesiastical and international relations are extremely crooked.

All men agree that this crookedness is abnormal and should be different, better and rectified. Almost everyone is very busy rectifying what is crooked, the one in one way, the other in another way. Even the Bolsheviks think after their fashion that they are ridding the world of its crookedness. According to them, religion is what is crooked and must be exterminated root and branch if the much desired utopian state is to dawn. Their antichristian nature becomes more evident by the day. But meanwhile no one will succeed in ridding the world of all that is crooked. Crookedness actually resides in the heart of man in Satan. There is only One who has dominion over it — Christ. When the glory of the Lord Jesus will be revealed, then, and only then will all that is crooked be made straight. It is He who will do it. He will do it well and He will do it in His own time and in His own way (40:1). A "crooked and perverse generation" cannot straighten the crooked; darkness will not drive away darkness.

The Contrast Between Flesh and the Word of God

> 6. The voice said, Cry. And he said, What shall I cry? All flesh is grass, and all the goodliness thereof is as the flower of the field:
>
> 7. The grass withereth, the flower fadeth: because the spirit of the LORD bloweth upon it: surely the people is grass.
>
> 8. The grass withereth, the flower fadeth: but the word of our God shall stand for ever.

Those who think that a great unknown prophet wrote these chapters are generally of the opinion that these verses contain the calling to his prophetic office. We view these matters that are contained in very dramatic and oratorical images as so: the prophet Isaiah upon hearing of the herald of salvation and upon beholding the coming and the glory of the King, is so overwhelmed that he is silent with amazement. The same had happened to him earlier, when he had seen the King seated on the throne of His glory. At that time he was struck by the distance between himself and the glorious King; here he is overwhelmed by the contrast between the wretched state of his people and the King of glory. And it is then that the Lord gives him a new commission which, again is in contrast to his earlier one. Then, he was charged with preaching judgment; but now with the preaching of comfort to Israel. *Cry!* the Lord's voice commands him, that is to say, *Prophesy!* When he humbly asks what he must prophesy to the people, whom he envisions as being in exile, he is answered in connection with his original vision that he must preach the antithesis between all flesh and the Word of the Lord. It is this immense contrast that lies at the root of the entire book of Isaiah, of the first part as well as the second. When this contrast is worked out and rightly viewed, it contains the richest comfort for the people in her suffering and oppression. For her oppressors are mere flesh and will wither like the grass and all her proud culture will fade like a flower, while on the other hand God's Word, which contains innumerable promises for her, will survive all her oppressors; indeed, it will stand forever. The touching repetition, *The grass withereth, the flower fadeth,* has a unique effect on man's soul, a pathos that cannot be described in words. Actually, these words sound like a dirge at the grave. Isaiah is a master of such pathetic repetitions. Recall "Watchman, what of the night? Watchman, what of the night?"

"Because the spirit of the Lord bloweth upon it. The Spirit is the Author of life (Ps. 104:30). He even prepared the natural body of the Savior in the womb of the virgin Mary. When He blows upon life, however, it perishes. He who gave life can also take it away again. We take the word Spirit in the same eschatological sense as in 4:4, where He is presented as the Spirit of judgment unto Israel in the days of the Great Tribulation. In that context we also have an eschatological presentation. Both *glory* and *reveal* are concepts that refer to the appearance of Christ. And *all flesh seeing it* points in the same direction. Not until the days of the Great Tribulation will the truth of these words be fully seen. Only then will the Spirit of judgment fully blow upon all flesh and all the glory of human civilization. When all pride of men has been put to shame, the Word of God as the absolute truth will gloriously shine forth.

Zion will Bring the Tidings of the Lord's Coming

9. O Zion, that bringest good tidings, get thee up into the high mountain; O Jerusalem that bringest good tidings, lift up thy voice with strength; lift it up, be not afraid; say unto the cities of Judah, Behold your God!

10. Behold, the Lord GOD will come with strong hand, and his arm shall rule for him: behold, his reward is with him, and his work before him.

11. He shall feed his flock like a shepherd: he shall gather the lambs with his arm, and carry them in his bosom, and shall gently lead those that are with young.

12. Who hath measured the waters in the hollow of his hand, and meted out heaven with the span, and comprehended the dust of the earth in a measure, and weighed the mountains in scales, and the hills in a balance?

13. Who hath directed the Spirit of the LORD, or being his counsellor hath taught him?

14. With whom took he counsel, and who instructed him, and taught him in the path of judgment, and taught him knowledge, and shewed to him the way of understanding?

The Shepherd King with His tender mercy on the flock is at the same time the Creator of all things. Seven times the holy number indicating the divine-human — His creative power and wisdom are pointed out. By His omnipotence and omniscience He measured all the *waters* of the oceans in His closed hand, so that there is not one drop too many or one drop lacking. He has taken the *measure* of the limitless *heavens* with the span of His fingers; all the *dust of the earth* He has measured with a measure. Some think that this *measure* refers to three fingers, but we prefer to think of a small measure with three legs the size of about one-third of a bushel or ephah.

The poetic power of this comparison is clear to anyone. The earth's globe is so small to the Messiah that He could scoop and carry away its dust in a small measure. The *mountains* He has weighed in scales. When one rides for a whole day on a train through the rocky mountains of America, he is often overwhelmed by the sight of high and well-nigh unreachable mountaintops with their permanent snow. How glorious then is the thought of knowing that our Lord Jesus Christ has as it were weighed in a balance all those proud mountains which seem to soar to the heavens. Even the hills have been weighed by Him in a *balance*. The countless rolling hills have been carefully weighed and measured by Him, so that not one of them is too high or too low.

Not only creation as such but also the marvelous order of the universe is ascribed to the wisdom of the Messiah. He has measured, apportioned and weighed everything in heaven and on earth, so that the space of the heavens is neither too great nor too small. The oceans have not a drop of water too much nor are they short of one drop. The earth has exactly enough grains of sand, and no mountain or hill is too high or too low.

This, astronomers and wise inventors, is mathematics and mechanical ability! Bow before King Messiah and render Him your homage, for all of your highly acclaimed achievements are insignificant and vain in comparison with His great works. Waters, heavens, dust, mountains, hills — these are the five elements in verse twelve while verse thirteen mentions two more which are enlarged upon in the following verse. Calvin thinks that *spirit of the Lord* does not mean the Holy Spirit, but God's omniscience. The Septuagint translates, "Who has known the mind of the Lord?" and remarkably enough, it is this translation which the Apostle quotes in Romans 11:34. This is a frequently occurring fact in the New Testament,[1] and is well known, but it has never been solved satisfactorily. Finally, the wisdom of the Messiah is summarized in the question about who has taught Him as a counselor. The answer to this question is, of course, no one. In Romans 11:34 Paul also quotes this question; he does not apply it to the creation of all things but to Israel's rejection and reacceptance. With regard to the latter, no one has been His adviser either. He is sovereign and knows and does things only according to His omnipotent good pleasure. No one can give Him counsel or knowledge, verse fourteen goes on to say. No one can teach Him in the realm of morals and no one can instruct Him in knowledge and understanding. No one can be His guide in any matter, for all the plans of His counsel are made in wisdom and are carried out with irresistible power throughout the rolling ages. At the end of the ages everything will be found in the holy number of seven — the number of divine completeness and perfection.

A Further Description of the Greatness of the Messiah

15. Behold, the nations are as a drop of a bucket, and are counted as the small dust of the balance: behold, he taketh up the isles as a very little thing.

16. And Lebanon is not sufficient to burn, nor the beasts thereof sufficient for a burnt offering.

17. All nations before him are as nothing; and they are counted to him less than nothing, and vanity.

The insignificance of all nations contrasts strongly with the overwhelming greatness of the Lord. The nations, which in their unspeakable foolishness ever want to rule the world, are to His greatness no more than a drop hanging from a bucket, or remaining in it after its contents have been poured out,

---

[1] Bultema is referring to the frequent New Testament use of the Septuagint, not this particular text from Isaiah forty. Some progress has been made in explaining particularly aspects of this phenomenon.—ED

and as a little particle of dust on a balance. Not much may stick to the tongue of a balance, for that would influence the balance, but who would bother with one small particle of dust? According to the biblical representation, Europe and America are counted among the islands. Just as easily as a seaman scatters a handful of dust on the waves of the sea, so the Lord scattered the islands across the boundless sea. Just as humiliating as this grand representation is to the proud and vaunted nations, so it is just as comforting to the believing heart, for viewed in this way it is a very easy task for our Savior to judge the nations righteously, to purge them by His judgments and to convert and exalt them in His day. Verse seventeen increases even more the contrast between the Messiah and the nations. There it is said that the nations are *as nothing* and *less than nothing* before Him. The prophet could not have used any stronger expressions. In his poetic fervor he proceeds from *a drop,* a particle of *dust* and a *very little thing,* to *nothing* and *less than nothing.* Meanwhile the last representation gives us some justification for usually quoting verse fifteen as "the nations are counted as less than a drop," etc., although that is not yet said there.

The representation of verse sixteen is also powerful and grandiose. The main thought is that no sacrificial fire or sacrifice is great enough to honor the God who is coming to the cities of Judah. At that time the mountains of Lebanon were covered with thick woods of proud oaks and cedars in which many wild animals frolicked, while in the valleys great herds of cattle roamed. But if one would want to burn a sacrifice to the Savior who is coming to Zion, what would be equal to His greatness, majesty and holiness? All the wood of Lebanon would not be sufficient for the fire and all the animals roaming about would not suffice as a sacrifice. Lebanon itself would be a worthless altar for Him and the beauty of nature displayed there an unholy temple.

Expositors vie with each other in praising the poetic talent of the prophet. How could it be otherwise! The representations here are inimitable and majestic. There are also sharp contrasts. First he used the everyday images of a drop, a bucket, a particle of dust and scales, and now he suddenly points to a sacrifice which has never been burnt and which would still be too small in spite of all its grandeur. In the literature of the nations one would search in vain for similar profound ideas and exalted representations. The poets of today are simply poetasters compared to Isaiah.

Not One Idol Can Be Compared to Messiah

18. To whom then will ye liken God? or what likeness will ye compare unto him?

19. The workman melteth a graven image, and the goldsmith spreadeth it over with gold, and casteth silver chains.

20. He that is so impoverished that he hath no oblation chooseth a tree that will not rot; he seeketh unto him a cunning workman to prepare a graven image, that shall not be moved.

After the prophet has depicted the imcomparable greatness of the Messiah, he suddenly makes a transition to the ludicrousness of all idolatry in verse eighteen. Whenever Isaiah speaks about idolatry, he cannot keep from using the most cutting mockery. He cannot limit himself to a single word but goes into the minutest details with the holy object of exposing the absurdity of all idolatry. Next, he leads us as it were by the hand through the workshop where idols are made and lets us see and hear the artisans. In verse nineteen he shows us the foolish wastefulness of the rich person who squanders his gold and silver to obtain a metal idol. With *silver chains* he expresses humor and irony of the finest kind. The object of this fine hint, which reveals his vocabulary and art of description, is to ridicule the expensive idol of the rich. For what kind of a god is it that must be tied with chains lest it topple over or be stolen by thieves who covet its gold and silver?

The prophet then presents an idolator who has become impoverished by oppression — for that is what the original word implies — and has nothing to sacrifice to his god. He pictures this poor man as being serious about making himself a god, for although he cannot afford a metal image, he nevertheless wants a durable god. Hence he wanders about in the woods or in the lumber yard and carefully selects a piece of wood that does not easily rot, for a god that would rot would be something terrible! After he has finally found and selected the wood he desires, he goes searching once more, this time for a capable workman. For who would want to put an incompetent workman to work on a god! Moreover, the god must be made so well that it will *not move.* This subtle hint expresses much more than what the words do, of course. It implies that this god, although made by the finest craftsman of the finest wood, has no legs to stand on and no strength to keep himself upright. The unexpressed conclusion can be made by everyone: how can a god who cannot keep himself standing upright keep and protect his worshipers! May Israel then not succumb to the foolishness of idolatry while dwelling amongst the idolatrous nations! May they continue to serve Israel's God who can keep her feet from falling! For we must not forget that this is the point of the prophet's mockery and ridicule of idols. He continues to point at the creation and says that even a glance at the heavens and the earth should cause the idolaters to blush on account of their idolatry.

Another Description of the Greatness of the Messiah

21. Have ye not known? have ye not heard? hath it not been told to you from the beginning? have ye not understood from the foundations of the earth?
22. It is he that sitteth upon the circle of the earth, and the inhabitants thereof are as grasshoppers; that stretcheth out the heavens as a curtain, and spreadeth them out as a tent to dwell in:
23. That bringeth the princes to nothing; he maketh the judges of the earth as vanity.
24. Yea, they shall not be planted; yea they shall not be sown: yea, their stock shall not take root in the earth: and he shall also blow upon them, and they shall wither, and the whirlwind shall take them away as stubble.
25. To whom then will ye liken me, or shall I be equal? saith the Holy One.
26. Lift up your eyes on high, and behold who hath created these things, that bringeth out their host by number: he calleth them all by names by the greatness of his might, for that he is strong in power; not one faileth.

Once again the prophet continues his grand poetic description of King Messiah, for the entire context and the character of comfort point to Him and no one else. What is ascribed here to the Messiah He is already now doing or will most certainly do in the day of His coming. From the context and verse twenty-one we conclude that these words are addressed first of all to the sottish idolaters. Even the book of nature or that of history could cure them from their foolishness.

Again it is in seven forceful strokes that this picture is presented. In the preceding verses the prophet used seven fine images to ridicule idolatry. There he depicted the completeness of folly; here the completeness of power and wisdom (1) The Messiah is first of all described as He who *sitteth upon the circle of the earth.* Believing astronomers have marveled that long before astronomy discovered that the world was round Isaiah penned this. Seven hundred years before Christ, he wrote as though this were common knowledge. There the Son of God is *sitting* before His incarnation, rejoicing in the bosom of His Father, and after His exaltation He sits at the right hand of the Father. (2) All the inhabitants of the earth are *as grasshoppers* to Him. This reminds again of the drop and the particle of dust. (3) He stretches out the *heavens* as a tent cloth. The metaphor of a tent often appears in Scripture and always recalls the nomadic life of the patriarchs and Israel's dwelling in tents during her passage through the desert. But even after Israel lived in houses in Canaan the word tent continued to be used in the daily language of the people and served there metaphorically in all sorts of circumstances. Even in David's time the people still cried, "To your tents, O Israel!" (4) He brings the *princes* to nothing. In days of old He broke down the proud Nimrods and Nebuchadnezzars and Alexanders and in our days the Napoleons and the emperors of Russia, Austria and Germany. (5) He makes the *judges* of the earth as vanity, or desolation, as the original has it. The Greek translation alludes to the desolation of the earth at the beginning of creation. This destruction and annihilation of the great ones of the earth is described in rich imagery as sudden and complete. These great men are compared to plants and tender sprouts and a little tree trunk. After hardly having been planted, sown and rooted, they are blown upon by His Spirit. According to verse seven, they wither, and a whirlwind blows them away like stubble. In verse twenty-five, there is another soul-searching question similar to that of verse eighteen, the intent of which is to point out the everlastingness of God's holy being. (6) The idolaters are commanded to lift up their eyes, to look at the starry heavens and ask themselves who made and numbered and called into being all those stars. From the New Testament we know that Christ made all things, both those that are in heaven and those that are on earth. The astronomers are still busily engaged in counting and classifying the stars, but Christ has described, counted and ordered them already. (7) The stars are presented here as a great army of which every one is a soldier. The Messiah, great in power and strength, is their Field Commander who knows all of them by name, and calls and commands them so that none dare to disobey Him. After centuries of study the astronomers have still not found a name for every star; yet Christ has.

Jacob Comforted with the Greatness of His Messiah

27. Why sayest thou, O Jacob, and speakest, O Israel, My way is hid from the LORD, and my judgment is passed over from my God?

28. Hast thou not known? hast thou not heard, that the everlasting God, the LORD, the Creator of the ends of the earth, fainteth not, neither is weary? there is no searching of his understanding.

29. He giveth power to the faint; and to them that have no might he increaseth strength.

30. Even the youths shall faint and be weary, and the young men shall utterly fall:

31. But they that wait upon the LORD shall renew their strength; they shall mount up with wings as eagles; they shall run, and not be weary; and they shall walk, and not faint.

Now the prophet has reached the application of his glorious argument.

These words are of stirring beauty and of fathomless depth, and their purpose is to make Israel see the unreasonableness of her distrust of God's omniscient and omnipotent dominion. The orthodox Jews of our day would do well to heed verse twenty-seven, for they generally are of the opinion that the God of their fathers is unconcerned about the upholding of their rights. They say, "Our bones are dried, and our hope is lost: we are cut off for our parts" (Ezek. 37:11). In two questions Israel's attention is called to four attributes of God (v. 28). He is the Eternal One, the Creator, the Almighty, who never faints or becomes weary, and the Omniscient One whose wisdom cannot be fathomed by any creature. Every one of these shining attributes is a ground for comfort to the enslaved people. God's everlastingness should teach Israel that Jehovah is eternally the same Covenant God in His love and faithfulness to Israel. At the same time He has the time to save Israel so that there should not be any nervous impatience on the part of His people. As the Creator He can also recreate His people. Whereas He is never faint nor weary, He is able to bear His people for many future centuries. Finally, as the Omniscient One He can deliver His people in the most unexpected manner.

Higher and higher soars the song of this poet-prophet. Jehovah Himself never tires, but on the other hand He does give strength to the weary. Man, whose constitution has been weakened by sin, tires quickly; even believers easily tire of waiting for the Lord and working for Him. The Lord, however, who is the life of their life, is also the strength of their strength; blessed is he who expects *all* his strength and help only from Him! In the physical realm we cannot multiply with zero, but in the spiritual realm God does do this for His people (v. 29). The glory of young men is their strength, the wise king says, but Isaiah says that they will not only be faint and weary, but that they will utterly fall. This strong expression is confirmed daily in mankind's history. When the Spanish influenza raged, it was usually the strongest young men who were snatched away by it first.

Israel must wait upon the Lord for many centuries. In order to excite the people to do so, the final verse contains a special promise. They will renew their strength which, according to the biblical presentation, means enjoy eternal youth. According to the conception of those days the eagle renewed its youth. This bird grows very old as ornithologists assure us. *They shall mount up* on high as eagles powerfully and rapidly. In this beautiful metaphor we may readily see a faint reflection of the taking up of believers when the Lord comes. Then they will also be made conformable to Jehovah-Jesus and in their new bodies which are like His, they will no longer be faint or weary.

ISAIAH 41

God Summons the Idolators to Judgment

1. Keep silence before me, O islands; and let the people renew their strength: let them come near; then let them speak: let us come near together to judgment.
2. Who raised up the righteous man from the east, called him to his foot, gave the nations before him, and made him rule over kings? he gave them as the dust to his sword, and as driven stubble to his bow.
3. He pursued them, and passed safely; even by the way that he had not gone with his feet.
4. Who hath wrought and done it, calling the generations from the beginning? I the LORD, the first, and with the last, I am he.

Once again the presentation is grand and magnificent. We have seen that the preceding chapter pointed out the greatness of Israel's God and His Messiah, this chapter has the same basic thought. There, everything in heaven and on earth pointed to the greatness of God: the earth, in verses twelve to fourteen; the nations, in verses fifteen to seventeen; the idols, verses eighteen to twenty; the heavens, verses twenty-one, twenty-two, twenty-six; the powerful men of the world, verses twenty-three to twenty-six and finally Israel, verses twenty-seven to thirty-one. Let now the controversy between Jehovah and the idolatrous nations be settled in a public debate, a controversy like one once settled by Elijah on Mt. Carmel! Jehovah is presented as Himself summoning the *islands,* a poetic name for the idolatrous distant nations – to judgment. This grand presentation is nevertheless simple. The Lord will present His case first then the nations theirs (v. 21). He is not asking much of the nations, only that they predict the future events (vv. 22, 23). In verse thirty-one it was said that the people of the Lord who wait upon Him will renew their strength. Now the Lord challenges the nations to renew their strength as well. But, hearken! the lawsuit has commenced and the Judge is speaking. He asks a question, as He had done several times in chapter one and will keep on doing in the following chapters (see 40:12, 21, 25, 28; 41:26). In the New Testament it is Paul who constantly asks such heart-searching questions. The question is "Who raised up *the righteous man from the east,* from the rising of the sun, who as a mighty conqueror subdued the nations and made kings bow before him?" all of which is described in a poetic manner. There are three schools of thought concerning this: (1) The Rabbis usually take it to mean Abraham; Calvin also says that this *righteous man* can be no one else but Abraham. The same idea is expressed in the marginal notes of the D.A.V. and by H. Grotius. Van der Palm observes, "If we explain it as a reference to Abraham, then everything is at once light, power and life!" Of the same opinion are Sikkel, Hausschein, Piscator, Lowth, Bengel, Birks and A. Clarke. (2) Many Church Fathers, such as Jerome, Cyril, Eusebius, Theodoret and Procopius were of the opinion that it referred to the Messiah, as also Sibersma and many Premillennialists of today. (3) Most of the recent commentators think it refers to Cyrus. The entire critical school is of this opinion. They present it this way: the great unknown prophet already saw the great conqueror of the nations, Cyrus, appear on the scene to destroy Babylon and its many vassal nations.

We cannot totally agree with any of these three views and are fully convinced that we must certainly think first of all of *Cyrus* and that his conquests are described here in the ordinary prophetic perfectum. Both secular and sacred documents present him as righteous and good, and he can be called *righteous* or, as the text actually has it, *justice,* especially since he carried out the righteousness of vengeance on Babylon and that of the deliverance of Israel. Later in Isaiah, his conquests are mentioned in the same vein as here. On the other hand, however, we are equally convinced that in the final analysis and in the deepest sense of the word, the *righteous man* refers to Christ. We must view Cyrus here as well as elsewhere *as a type of Christ in His coming for the deliverance of Israel from its centuries-long exile.*[1] *Called to his foot* is a Hebrew idiom for following and serving in battle. Verse two(b) describes poetically how Cyrus chased the nations ahead of him like dust and stubble. He pursued them in places where his foot had never trod. We know that when Christ sits in judgment, He too will chase away the wicked like chaff before the wind. In verse four God Himself gives the answer to His own question.

The Terror of the Idolatrous Nations Because of their Summons

5. The isles saw it, and feared; the ends of the earth were afraid, drew near, and came.
6. They helped every one his neighbour; and every one said to his brother, Be of good courage.
7. So the carpenter encouraged the goldsmith, and he that smootheth with the hammer him that smote the anvil, saying, It is ready for the sodering: and he fastened it with nails, that it should not be moved.

It may not escape our attention that with this summons to all nations for judgment God's ultimate objective is His own glorification, and that He is doing everything Himself. It is He who summons and calls all the nations. It is He who as a sheriff's officer calls for silence in the great hall of judgment: *Keep silence before me!* It is imperative that in a courtroom there be a solemn silence, since there holy justice will be pronounced. He Himself is also the Advocate, who pleads and defends His own cause, and finally He is the great Judge, who decides everything. As the Judge, He asks the questions, and since no one can answer Him, He Himself answers the questions that have been asked.

How do the nations react to God's summons? The Lord had said: *let them come near* and *let us come near together to judgment.* Verse five now adds that as a result of this summons they drew near and came together; but they *feared*

---

[1] Messianic titles and functions are ascribed to Cyrus both here and in Isaiah 44:24-45, and to Israel's own post-captivity leaders in Haggai 2 and Zechariah 3-4. —ED.

and *trembled* (Dutch Version). These two words describe the tremendous effect which the summons of the Lord had on them. They panicked as it were; and not without holy irony and divine glee the prophet describes that they put their heads together supporting and encouraging each other. We mention divine glee, for one day God, too, will laugh at the destruction of the wicked, and mock when their fear comes (cf. Isa. 2:3-4). We find something similar here. With unconcealed joy, the prophet describes how the one encourages the other and says: *Be of good courage!* Indeed, one had better be strong on his way to meeting God in judgment.

The prophet describes further how they became feverishly busy making new idols of whose support they want to assure themselves. He depicts the goldsmith and the forger of iron who hastily help each other and who rejoice that there is good *solder* to work with. *Solder* refers to the thin golden plates with which the various parts of the idol were joined. With barbed scorn Isaiah describes that they are happy and consider themselves fortunate that their products will not easily come apart. But in order to support their gods even better they fasten them with *nails* to the ground. The *nails* mentioned here are as eloquent as the expression *that shall not be moved* in 40:20. The prophet wants to indicate mockingly that they are gods who have no power to keep themselves upright. For the rest anyone can draw his own conclusion from this fact. If these gods were so unstable themselves that iron pegs had to keep them in position, how then could they ever keep the foolish nations who worshiped them from topling and falling? If the nations were mute and could not answer Jehovah, their gods, too, were unable to answer Him; worse still, they were seized with terror. Will Israel, too, fear in the midst of this general despair? No, for when Cyrus overpowers Babylon, he delivers Israel. When Christ tramples the nations in His fury He will restore Israel and use the worm Jacob to thresh mountains.

Glorious Comfort for Israel

8. But thou, Israel, art my servant, Jacob whom I have chosen, the seed of Abraham my friend.

9. Thou whom I have taken from the ends of the earth, and called thee from the chief men thereof, and said unto thee, Thou art my servant; I have chosen thee, and not cast thee away.

10. Fear thou not; for I am with thee: be not dismayed; for I am thy God: I will strengthen thee; yea, I will help thee; yea, I will uphold thee with the right hand of my righteousness.

Israel is designated here with three names, and for that reason it is simply inexcusable for commentators and preachers to assign these glorious promises to the Church from all the nations. These words of comfort appear in groups of the holy number Three: three names for Israel in connection with its past; three *acts* with regard to Israel's future: *taken called, chosen* (v. 9); and three wonderful deeds of God for Israel's present: I will *strengthen* thee, I will *help* thee, I will *uphold* thee.

The great significance of Abraham is evident from his name *my friend.* "And he was called the Friend of God" (Jas. 2:23). The New Testament indicates that this name was very special, and rich in content and significance; but in John 15:15 all the disciples of the Savior are honored with this name. This proves that the glory of the New Dispensation exceeds that of the Old Covenant. Then there was only one who was the friend of God; now all those who truly love and obey the Lord Jesus Christ are called His friends. Even among the Mohammedans the Koran calls Abraham the friend of Allah. Verse nine again contains a prophetic perfectum, because the election mentioned there does not refer to the election of the past, as in verse eight, but to the second election of the nation in the future, as is frequently mentioned in the prophecies of Zechariah (1:17; 2:12; 3:2). That verse nine is not referring to the past but to the future election as a nation is evident from the words "and not cast thee away." This statement would make no sense at all in connection with the first calling of Abraham. But, it has the greatest significance in the light of Israel's lamentation during her exile: "My way is hid from the LORD, and my judgment is passed over from my God" (40:27). Also in 49:14 we hear Zion lament, "The LORD hath forsaken me, and my LORD hath forgotten me!" Over against this dejectedness of the nation sighing in exile, God repeatedly assures them that He has not rejected His people but will yet elect them. Nor was Abraham called from *the ends of the earth. From the chief men thereof* means from the noblest of the nations. The Lord will fetch His people from among the noblest nations, from the most powerful, the greatest, the most civilized and the most religious; in short, He will choose His noble people from among the noblest so that the Jews should glorify Him.

Fear not! He cries out to the sighing people. All nations have reason to fear, but not Israel. The reason why Israel has nothing to fear lies in the close relationship between Jehovah and His nation. Jehovah is *with thee.* That is the meaning of Immanuel. Jehovah is Israel's God. If Israel is as weak as a worm, then He *strengthens* the worm so that she can thresh mountains. If Israel is in need of help, He will not withhold His help, but His strong right hand will uphold her. The *right hand* of the Lord is manifestly contrasted with the *nails* which propped up the idols in verse seven.

The End of Anti-Semitism

11. Behold, all they that were incensed against thee shall be ashamed and confounded: they shall be as nothing; and they that strive with thee shall perish.

12. Thou shalt seek them, and shalt not find them, even them that contended with thee: they that war against thee shall be as nothing, and as a thing of nought.

Over against the sense of safety and confidence that must inspire His people God now indicates that the consternation of the nations is fully warranted. Their new idols, which had to be fastened with bolts and nails, will not be able to save them in the great day of reckoning. The nations are described here as fierce anti-Semites who are *incensed* against Israel and strive, contend and war against her. These four words, which as it were designated the nations of the four winds of heaven, indicate both the universality and depth of their hatred of Israel. Indeed, where is there a nation that has not hated Israel? Where is there a nation that has not in some way or another vexed Israel? Nearly all of them have plowed upon her back and made long their furrows.

There are four kinds of anti-Semitism: (1) Political anti-Semitism. We find it already with Pharaoh who commenced oppressing Israel more than two thousand years before Christ. The drowning of the Jewish baby boys in the Nile was a political measure. (2) Ecclesiastical anti-Semitism. Throughout the ages this has inspired both the Roman and Greek Church. Protestantism too has systematically ignored and secretly despised the Jews, stolen their promises and applied these to itself, denying them a future. (3) Social anti-Semitism is found throughout history in all nations and not too long ago also in our country, where many a hotel refused to lodge Jews. (4) Philosophical anti-Semitism was brought into the world by the Germans not too long ago. Higher criticism can properly be included in this kind, for it is based on the philosophical principle of development. Higher criticism under the command of the evil one wages war against Israel and her Messiah and promises, so that we are dealing here with what is by no means the least dangerous form of anti-Semitism. All four kinds of enmity against Israel are in essence one. They will also in the great and fast approaching end time, when everything comes to a head in one evil principle and one evil person, the antichrist, reveal themselves as one and unite themselves in the antichrist, Gog and Armageddon against Israel and her Messiah.

In these two verses the end of all anti-Semitism is presented in the strongest terms. They will be ashamed, confounded, be as nothing, perish, not found and as a thing of nought. Remarkably enough, the total destruction of all those who hate the Jews is expressed in the number of completeness.

The Worm Jacob Shall Thresh Mountains

13. For I the LORD thy God will hold thy right hand, saying unto thee, Fear not; I will help thee.

14. Fear not, thou worm Jacob, and ye men of Israel; I will help thee, saith the LORD, and thy redeemer, the Holy One of Israel.

15. Behold, I will make thee a new sharp threshing instrument

having teeth: thou shalt thresh the mountains, and beat them small, and shalt make the hills as chaff.

16. Thou shalt fan them, and the wind shall carry them away, and the whirlwind shall scatter them: and thou shalt rejoice in the LORD, and shalt glory in the Holy One of Israel.

In the verses ten to fourteen, it is said to Jacob three times, *Fear not!* That was indeed necessary because the poor exiles feared so many things. But Jehovah, the faithful covenant God, uses all kinds of motives and inducements, to put His people at ease and remove her fears. In verse thirteen, He again points out that as Jehovah He is Israel's possession, *I the Lord thy God.* When God sent Moses to deliver Israel from the slavery of Egypt, He emphatically called Himself *Jehovah* (Ex. 3:14; 15; 6:2). At that point in Israel's history His adoption of that name was beautiful and comforting. With it, God said that He unswervingly kept His promise to Abraham (Gen. 15:14) and fulfilled it. The description of the name *I am that I am* contained the assurance to Israel that in the future He would always remain the same. Whatever else might change, He would always remain the same in His love and promises and faithfulness. Often He connects this richest of all His names to other ones. The best known of these compound names are: (1) *Jehovah-jireh* (Gen. 22:14), *Jehovah will provide,* which, in the context means, to provide a sacrifice. Alluding to this the poet may sing, "The Lord is my shepherd; *I shall not want* (Ps. 23:1). (2) *Jehovah-shalom* (Judg. 6:24), i.e., Jehovah is peace; Jehovah-Jesus is our peace (Eph. 2:14). (3) *Jehovah-ropheka* (Ex. 15:26), the Lord thy Healer; He wants to heal the sickness of both soul and body. (4) *Jehovah-zidkenu* (Jer. 23:6), the Lord our righteousness; He is made unto us righteousness, so that now we are *righteousness in Him* (I Cor. 1:30). (5) *Jehovah-nissi,* Ex. 17:15, the Lord is my banner; His banner goes before the warring armies. (6) *Jehovah-yah* (Isa. 12:2), *I am that I am.* (7) *Jehovah-shammah* (Ezek. 48:35), *The Lord is there.* This will be one of the names of restored Jerusalem during the millennium.

But we should almost lose sight of the *worm Jacob* when dwelling on God's glorious names. It is an eminently fitting name for the people in exile. A (little) worm wriggles in the mud and has neither strength nor beauty and glory. A pedestrian steps on it without paying any attention to its painful twisting. Our Savior was a worm and no man, especially when He was in agony in Gethsemane. Israel, too, is called a worm, for this people has nearly all the characteristics of it in common. Pharaoh stepped on this worm; Pharaoh is dead but the worm still alive. Sennacherib and Nebuchadnezzar trod on it, but these world conquerors are also dead but the worm still very much alive. The Roman emperors and the popes of Rome as well as Russia, Rumania, Spain, Portugal — indeed, all nations — stepped on this worm, but they never succeeded in killing it for this worm refuses to die. But God can take the worm and thresh mountains with it, He not only can but He will do this one day. He will take this still despised and trodden-down people of the Jews and make it *a new sharp threshing instrument having teeth,* to thresh, strike, punish and crush the mountains and hills, the great and small kingdoms of the world, so that they blow away as chaff before the wind. On the very last page of the Old Testament we still read these words regarding Israel: "Ye shall tread down the wicked; for they shall be ashes under the soles of your feet in the day that I shall do this, saith the LORD of hosts." A strange people is this people of Israel, and now misunderstood!

Israel Athirst in Exile

17. When the poor and needy seek water, and there is none, and their tongue faileth for thirst, I the LORD will hear them, I the God of Israel will not forsake them.
18. I will open rivers in high places, and fountains in the midst of the valleys: I will make the wilderness a pool of water, and the dry land springs of water.
19. I will plant in the wilderness the cedar, the shittah tree, and the myrtle, and the oil tree; I will set in the desert the fir tree, and the pine, and the box tree together:
20. That they may see, and know, and consider, and understand together, that the hand of the LORD hath done this, and the Holy One of Israel hath created it.

In the arid Near East people knew what it meant to suffer thirst. Zion's exiles are presented here as those who languish with thirst and are consequently utterly miserable and destitute. They wander about looking for water in the brooks and streams, but find none. Their tongues are parched and stick to the roofs of their mouths, while their hope for water is constantly frustrated. Of them Solomon's saying is doubly true, that hope deferred maketh the heart sick. In their misery they call on God, however, as we may infer from the words, *I the Lord will hear them.* Although it is not stated in so many words, it is nevertheless clear that we are to think of the dreadful days of the Great Tribulation, for as a nation Israel does not begin to call on God before those days. Only then, Israel's prayer for the coming of the Messiah will be answered. "Upon their cries and supplications the Lord will one day free all Israel from their deprivations." The answer to this prayer is poetically described in the following two verses. The Lord will give so much water that it will change the face of Palestine. To those perishing with thirst, much water was the most fitting metaphor to give an impression of great bliss and abundance. Moreover, in Scripture much water is the greatest of metaphors for rich blessings. This abundance is described as the breaking forth of streams, fountains and ponds in all places. On the high plateaus, which otherwise could not produce grass because of their elevation; in the valleys, in the deserts and other arid regions there will be water in abundance.

As a result of this abundance of water the lush trees will come up in former deserts, the poet mentions no less than seven kinds of trees which will grow in the desert and wilderness. This holy number is intended to point out the fullness of God's material blessings in the kingdom of peace. Verse twenty points out the glorious purpose of all these blessings; with a truly Isaiahic fullness of words he ascribes them to God.

When the Lord Jesus Christ, who was born, who suffered and was crucified and rose again as the King of the Jews, will come again to His people Israel, His footsteps will drop fatness for Canaan and for the entire world. Around the area occupied by Israel there were many deserts. Because of the curse resting upon the land for many centuries, it was itself changed into a desert. In these dry regions hardly a scrubby bush grew to serve as good for the camel, the ship of the desert. But, according to this promise, that will change completely. At His coming He will change all these arid, dead steppes into blossoming pleasure gardens in which an abundance of stately, fragrant, lush, shade and fruit-bearing trees will grow. Once again, seven kinds of trees point to the fullness and perfection of glory; according to 42:10, 11 a seven-fold song will be sung in the desert.

Jehovah Challenges the Nations to Prophesy

21. Produce your cause, saith the LORD; bring forth your strong reasons, saith the King of Jacob.
22. Let them bring them forth, and shew us what shall happen: let them shew the former things, what they be, that we may consider them, and know the latter end of them; or declare us things for to come.
23. Shew the things that are to come hereafter, that we may know that ye are gods: yea, do good, or do evil, that we may be dismayed, and behold it together.

While Jehovah was pointing out His great and marvelous deeds both in nature and in grace with respect to the past, the present and the future, the idolatrous and anti-Semitic nations had remained mute throughout. Therefore the Lord challenges them once more to plead their cause and produce their strong argument. He says this as the *King of Jacob*. Scripture nowhere calls Christ the King of the Church, but dozens of times it calls Him the King of Israel. The name of *Jacob,* as applied to Israel here, always points back to Israel's lowly and deceitful past, so that it is by no means an honor to the Church to call itself by the name of Jacob. In the epistles of Paul the Lord Jesus is constantly presented as the Head of the Church and of all things. *King* is a juridical concept of power, while *Head* is an organic concept indicating unity of life. These two entirely different concepts already indicate the great difference between Israel and the Church. The actual test in this passage is the literal fulfillment of prophecy. God invites the nations to point out to Him the things that will take place in the future and the things that are now taking place which were predicted by them in the past. "One of the cherished basic ideas of the prophet is that idols have no true prophecy, no true proclamation of the divine counsel about the present and future, while Israel can point to countless prophetic predictions that have been fulfilled, and hence can confidently await also the new and as yet unfulfilled prophecies regarding Cyrus" (Gunning). The main reason why many refuse to accept that Isaiah wrote these chapters is that they do not believe in the miracle of prophetic prediction, which one day will be literally fulfilled. For if we accept Isaiah's authorship of these last chapters, we are also forced to accept his prediction of the appearance, the name and the character and activities of Cyrus the Great more than two centuries before his time. Here we see that the Lord Himself claims to have made these predictions, which will be accurately fulfilled, in contrast to the nations and their dumb idols. He constantly points this out to the glory of His great name. This should also be the boast of all His children. Here is apologetic material with which we can silence the mouths of all Bible-undermining critics and with which we can strengthen faith in the Bible among all the fainthearted. It is truly sad when a man such as Dr. G. C. Aalders in his otherwise excellent book on the prophets weakens the accurate fulfillment of the prophecies by all manner of half-believing arguments and drivel about a *symbolic* fulfillment, in order to undermine the dreams of the Chiliasts. If such people would be honest they would also have to call Isaiah a dreamer.

Jehovah Wins the Argument

24. Behold, ye are of nothing, and your work for nought: an abomination is he that chooseth you.

25. I have raised up one from the north, and he shall come: from the rising of the sun shall he call upon my name: and he shall come upon princes as upon morter, and as the potter treadeth clay.

26. Who hath declared from the beginning, that we may know? and beforetime, that we may say, He is righteous? yea, there is none that sheweth yea, there is none that declareth, yea there is none that heareth your words.

27. The first shall say to Zion, Behold, behold them: and I will give to Jerusalem one that bringeth good tidings.

28. For I beheld, and there was no man; even among them, and there was no counsellor, that, when I asked of them, could answer a word.

29. Behold, they are all vanity; their works are nothing: their molten images are wind and confusion.

It is instructive to find in these verses that the Lord identifies His words with His works. His words, whether they be promises or threatenings, are so sure of fulfillment that they are completely identical to His works. In verse twenty-four the great Judge pronounces the verdict upon the summoned nations and especially upon their idols. The verdict is three-fold and applies to their *being,* their *works,* and their *worshippers.* They are less than nothing, their work is worse than a poisonous adder D.A.V. or, as the English and most other translations have it, of nought, and they that choose them are themselves an abomination. Now these fools know what they are! So let Israel not be tempted by these worthless idols, which are vainer than vanity itself. Let Israel remain faithful to its God who will do great and glorious things for His people! He will raise up Cyrus from the north (Media), and from the east (Persia).

The works of God are mentioned after the works of the nations have been declared to be as nought and abominable. Cyrus had the greatest respect for Jehovah, as we can read in his proclamation concerning the freeing of Israel in Ezra one. In it he states correctly that Jehovah had given him all the kingdoms of the earth. Nevertheless we know from both Scripture and history as well as from recent excavations that he did not hesitate to honor other gods as well.[2] He seems to have been filled with respect for any religion, but most of all for Jehovah, the God of Israel. When it is said, "He shall call upon my name," we must not take this in a saving sense on Cyrus' part. With regard to the Savior, we must take it in the

---

[2]The reference is to the "Cyrus Cylinder," a decree of Cyrus the Great inscribed on a cylindrical clay barrel about 9 inches long in c. 536 B.C. It bears a remarkable resemblance to Ezra 1. For text see D. W. Thomas, "Documents from Old Testament Times" (N.Y. Harper, 1961) pp. 92-94.

most absolute sense of the word, for He will realize this prophecy fully in the day of His coming. He will tread upon the great ones of the earth as does a potter on lime and clay. The metaphor of a potter often appears in Scripture with respect to Christ as Judge of the nations; the image is usually derived from the smashing of the potter's vessels. Here, however, the treading of the potter's clay is the image which indicates the total subjugation of the nations to the One who is greater than Cyrus. Once more Jehovah points out the fact that no one can equal Him in similar predictions. Only of Him, and of no one else, can it be said, *He is righteous,* or better, *It happens exactly as He predicted. In everything He is the First,* and no one in heaven or earth can be compared with Him. He will gladden Jerusalem by returning its children and by giving it *one that bringeth good tidings* of salvation and peace. The first verse of the next chapter identifies this *bringer of good tidings.* Among the nations, however, there is no one who can give advice in their calamity. Together with their idols they are altogether vanity and nothingness, wind and a vain thing. The prophet has a message for our confused times too. Even today the nations with all their wisdom and idols are at their wit's end. But He is near who will tread them as lime, but will bring to Jerusalem glad tidings of complete restoration.

ISAIAH 42

The Elect Servant of the Lord

> 1. Behold my servant, whom I uphold; mine elect in whom my soul delighteth; I have put my spirit upon him: he shall bring forth judgment to the Gentiles.
> 2. He shall not cry, nor lift up, nor cause his voice to be heard in the street.
> 3. A bruised reed shall he not break, and the smoking flax shall he not quench: he shall bring forth judgment unto truth.
> 4. He shall not fail nor be discouraged, till he have set judgment in the earth: and the isles shall wait for his law.

The Greek translation explains this of Israel, the Rationalists with Grotius at the head, of Isaiah; the recent critics all think it refers to Cyrus. It is nothing short of mutilating the Scriptures if these words are applied to anyone else but Christ. Matthew 12:17-21 definitely settles the matter here. This entire beautiful passage concerning Him is governed by the holy numbers three and seven. He is called by three names: *my servant, whom I uphold,* and *mine elect,* while in seven features His character and work are pointed out. For the sake of brevity we only mention: (1) The word *elect* does not refer to a selection of one from among many but to the great love the Father has for the Messiah. This love is further delineated by the words: *in whom my soul delighteth.* All of the Lord's delight is in Him. Already from eternity He was rejoicing in the inhabitable part of His earth. During His incarnation the Father three times gave Him the assurance of His love, and after His resurrection God gave Him the highest place of honor. (2) *I have put my spirit upon him.* This was fulfilled at His baptism in Jordan. Yet these words do not refer to this event only, but also to what is mentioned in 11:2 concerning the Spirit of the Lord with regard to the Messiah. Christ obtained His body by the Spirit,

He performed His miracles by the Spirit, He sacrificed Himself by the Spirit, He arose by the Spirit, and one day He will judge by the Spirit. He received the Spirit without measure, but was anointed with the oil of gladness above His fellows. (3) *He shall bring forth judgment to the Gentiles.* The word *mishpat,* here translated *judgment,* has several different meanings and is not always easily translated. It seems to us that the basic meaning is usually that by punishment unrighteousness is removed and justice triumphs. This is most likely the meaning here. The Lord Jesus will judge the nations, and from that judgment good will result for them. He will crush their oppressors and then govern them as the King of kings in peace and wisdom. (4) *He shall not cry,* etc. This verse indicates that with Him there will not be found any effort nor any hollow slogans. This statement refers rather to His quiet and unobtrusive behavior as a Teacher at His First Coming. This statement does not condemn any public preaching in the street or any loud speaking from the pulpit so that all may hear the good tidings; rather it does condemn all spectacular publicity and advertisement, as is the practice today of certain churches to get the attention of a fickle public. The Lord Jesus avoided the sensational and spectacular. Let us, as His faithful followers, do the same. (5) *A bruised reed shall he not break,* etc. This text obtained great familiarity by Smytegelt's volume of sermons under this title; it seems to us that this old divine has penetrated deeper into this text than many who despise him. It indeed refers to the Savior's condescending goodness toward that which is weak and miserable; but — and this Smytegelt did not see! — not in the first place to the members of the church but to broken and decimated Israel in exile. Christ at His Second Coming will turn His hand to the despised and oppressed Jewish nation. (6) *He shall bring forth judgment unto truth.* His great mission is already indicated in verse three; He will restore justice among the nations. Now it is said that He will do so to *truth.* Together with righteousness He will also cause truth to dwell in the whole earth. That is a great comfort, for today truth does not find a place for the hollow of its feet. But He will banish all lying and falsehood from the earth and fill the earth with the knowledge of the Lord. (7) *The isles shall wait for his law.* Here *isles* stands for all of Europe, America and Australia. During His reign, these continents will look longingly for His teachings. His Word will be the law for all nations. The word *fail* is a prophetic reference to His death.

The Lord of the Elect Servant

5. Thus saith God the LORD, he that created the heavens, and stretched them out; he that spread forth the earth, and that which cometh out of it; he that giveth breath unto the people upon it, and spirit to them that walk therein:

6. I the LORD have called thee in righteousness, and will hold thine hand, and will keep thee, and give thee for a covenant of the people, for a light of the Gentiles;

7. To open the blind eyes, to bring out the prisoners from the prison, and them that sit in darkness out of the prison house.

8. I am the LORD: that is my name: and my glory will I not give to another, neither my praise to graven images.

9. Behold, the former things are come to pass, and new things do I declare: before they spring forth I tell you of them.

The Lord is referring here to the great works of creation and providence, to indicate that He is mighty to raise the Messiah. He says further that He will call the Messiah, of which Cyrus was a type, and will take His hand, will keep Him, and give Him for a *covenant of the people* and *a light of the Gentiles.* This expresses His relationship to Israel and the Gentiles. How some exegetes can take the first concept to mean the Gentile nations outside of Israel, we do not understand, as both the context as well as the idea of a covenant contradicts this interpretation. The question is, however, why Christ is called the *covenant* of the people of Israel. Michaelis reads this, with a slight change in vowel points *potash,* in the sense of purifier, as *potash* was used in the purification of silver, to separate the silver from the slag. But this rationalist always takes pleasure in reasoning away the most glorious thoughts of Scripture by making small changes in the vowel points. There is no reason at all to depart from the concept *covenant.* According to Romans 9:3, 4, the covenants pertain to Israel. Now some commentators prefer to take the word *covenant* in the sense of *angel of the covenant* and then compare this promise with the one in Malachi 3:1 where Christ is also called by that name. But we prefer to take it as a pregnant expression for Him in whom all the promises of the covenant will find their fulfillment. The Messiah will fulfill the covenant of grace with all its inherent promises. Already in His death everything is assured and sealed; at His Coming everything will be fully materialized. The name *light of the Gentiles* is explained in verse seven. At His blessed Coming, the Lord Jesus will open the blind eyes, and loosen and free the prisoners morally and physically. To be sure, in a spiritual sense He is already doing this all through the ages of this dispensation, but that is not what the prophet is thinking of here. As is evident from what follows, he has his eye on the Second Coming of the Lord. Hence we must not take it as a reference to the freeing of Israel from Babylon. In the last two verses, the Lord again points to His honor which He will not give to idols, and to the miracle of prophetic prediction and fulfillment. He is *Jehovah;* that is His name; it contains His omnipotence, omniscience and faithfulness.

The Sevenfold New Song of Creation

> 10. Sing unto the LORD a new song, and his praise from the end of the earth, ye that go down to the sea, and all that is therein; the isles, and the inhabitants thereof.
> 11. Let the wilderness and the cities thereof lift up their voice, the villages that Kedar doth inhabit: let the inhabitants of the rock sing, let them shout from the top of the mountains.
> 12. Let them give glory unto the LORD, and declare his praise in the islands.

The second part of Isaiah is a continuous description of the glory which the coming Christ will bring to this groaning creation. Here it is said that He will change the sighs of creation into songs. The number of completeness indicates how the entire creation, after His return and after His purifying judgments, will break forth into jubilation and joyful noise. It will be a *new* song that will be sung, a song that as yet, because of Satan, sin and misery, cannot be taken up. It will be an absolutely universal song as is indicated by the number seven and the terms of the description. All seafaring men and inhabitants of the sea, the inhabitants of the islands and the deserts, of the cities and the villages and of the caves — those who live in the high rocks of the mountains — will give vent to their joy over the deliverance brought about by the King of Israel. Verse twelve points out the object of the song. It will be sung in that day to the honor of our Lord Jesus Christ.

The Coming of the Lord to His Enemies and to His People

13. The LORD shall go forth as a mighty man, he shall stir up jealousy like a man of war: he shall cry, yea, roar; he shall prevail against his enemies.

14. I have long time holden my peace; I have been still, and refrained myself: now will I cry like a travailing woman; I will destroy and devour at once.

15. I will make waste mountains and hills, and dry up all their herbs; and I will make the rivers islands, and I will dry up the pools.

16. And I will bring the blind by a way that they knew not; I will lead them in paths that they have not known: I will make darkness light before them, and crooked things straight. These things will I do unto them, and not forsake them.

17. They shall be turned back, they shall be greatly ashamed, that trust in graven images, that say to the molten images, Ye are our gods.

Before the breaking of the dawn of salvation sung about in the preceding verses, the Lord Jesus will come as a terrible warrior and punish the nations with severe justice. Van Hamelsveld correctly notes on these verses: "I believe that here a future total change of the condition of the world is predicted." If anyone should think that the happy song of praise of the whole world will be the result of human civilization, this prophecy will remove this vain imagination. Such jubilation cannot be heard in this dispensation, for presently all of creation is travailing in pain together. The Lord must first have purified the entire creation by His judgment, and only then will the sevenfold new song be heard. When viewed correctly, the cause of this joy is described here. The Lord Jesus is compared to a warrior who utters His field cry and loudly exclaims his song of vengeance. We must not overlook the marked contrast with verse two. There it was said that in connection with His First Coming He would not *cry* nor *lift up his voice,* but here with regard to His Second Coming it is stated that He will *cry like a travailing woman* (v. 14). With a view to the long-lasting *times of the Gentiles* it is said that He has *long time holden* His *peace* and has been *still.* Isaiah often alludes to this long silence during which the Lord hides His face from Israel and allows the heathen to rage like wild animals against His people, whom He considers as Lo-Ammi, *not* His people (cf. 8:17; 30:20; 33:2; 45:15; 54:8; 63:15-19; 64:7-12). The duration and nature of these times are described at length in Daniel, while the end of these times is depicted in vivid colors in Revelation. The image of the war cries of an advancing warrior alternates with that of the wails of a travailing woman, which is a favorite metaphor with Near-Eastern writers. This image, which speaks to us Westerners less than to them, contains the prophecy concerning a new world. As a travailing woman brings forth something new into the world, so Christ at His Coming will bring forth a new world. In John 16:21 the Lord Jesus expanded on this image to comfort His disciples. The *mountains and hills* (v. 15) are to be understood as the nations, both greater and smaller; but the entire verse can also simply be taken literally. For we know that the revelation of Christ will influence all of nature; first, during the Great Tribulation unto evil; then, unto a blessing (2:12-14; 7:23-25; 24:1-4; 19, 23; 32:19; 33:9; 34:4; 42:15; 50:2, 3; 51:6).

For Israel, however, Jehovah-Jesus will provide salvation. On account of their spiritual blindness (Rom. 11:8), which was already pointed out in Isaiah's vision of his calling, the Jews are called here *the blind.* As their shepherd, Christ will lead them by a way unknown to them. He Himself is the Way, which Israel as a nation has never known. He will remove the darkness of error and of misery from Israel and make everything light for His people. This image of the removal of darkness and blindness and the giving of light also appears frequently in Isaiah (29:18; 32:3; 60:1). Christ is presented here as the Way and the Light of life to the restored nation. Idolatry and all its attending practices will be dealt a death blow. When beholding the Christus Trimphator all idolators will shrink with terror from Him and be covered with shame as a sign of their awakened consciences.

Address to the Blind People of Israel

18. Hear, ye deaf; and look, ye blind, that ye may see.
19. Who is blind, but my servant? or deaf, as my messenger that I sent? who is blind as he that is perfect, and blind as the LORD'S servant?
20. Seeing many things, but thou observest not; opening the ears, but he heareth not.
21. The LORD is well pleased for his righteousness' sake; he will magnify the law, and make it honourable.
22. But this is a people robbed and spoiled; they are all of them snared in holes, and they are hid in prison houses: they are for a prey, and none delivereth; for a spoil, and none saith, Restore.
23. Who among you will give ear to this? who will hearken and hear for the time to come?
24. Who gave Jacob for a spoil, and Israel to the robbers? did not the LORD, he against whom we have sinned? for they would not walk in his ways, neither were they obedient unto his law.
25. Therefore he hath poured upon him the fury of his anger, and the strength of battle: and it hath set him on fire round about, yet he knew not; and it burned him, yet he laid it not to heart.

The Jewish exegetes, for obvious reasons, do not want to take this section as applying to Israel and so they explain it as applying either to the heathen or to some individuals such as David, Isaiah or Cyrus. But both the context and the whole presentation point to none other than Israel in her incorrigible wickedness and blindness. Her blindness and deafness to the words and works of the Messiah is the standard description of Israel by Isaiah and all the prophets. The basis of this presentation is found in the words of 6:9 on which all other descriptions of this kind are based. It cannot be denied that Israel is frequently called the *servant* of the Lord. References such as 41:8; 44:1, 21; 45:4; 49:3 are unmistakable. Verse twenty says in different words the same thing as 6:9, while verse twenty-one points to God's sovereign grace in Israel's origin and past. The Lord delighted in Israel because of *His righteousness' sake.* At Horeb He made her a priestly kingdom by giving her the Law as a constitution. Hence He made her great by the law and *honourable* above all nations.

In this connection, the words *he that is perfect* has caused some difficulty. It was almost impossible to imagine how the blind and deaf nation could at the same time be called *perfect,* and consequently this word has occasioned great difference in translation and explanation. The word *meshullum* is the same as the Arab word *muslim* as the Mohammedans call themselves. Calvin, who finds more irony in Scripture than any other commentator known to us, takes it to mean *bitter mockery.* Others interpret it as having reference to Israel's pretense and profession. But it seems best to interpret this word the same as *messenger* and *servant* and as having reference to Israel's calling among the nations. It was Israel's original destiny to be a perfectly committed and dedicated people unto Jehovah among the nations.

So interpreted, we can freely agree with Calvin that the word used is not entirely without holy irony. The people whose destiny it was to be perfect, and in her self-righteousness thought she was, were far removed from being perfect. Indeed, she was blind and deaf. Worse still, she was a *robbed* and *spoiled* people, a *prey* to other nations and without anyone to save and restore her. The description in verse twenty-two of Israel in exile among the nations reminds one of the one in 18:2 and 7.

It must not escape our attention that this description is again sevenfold, with the purpose of indicating that Israel's misery is total and complete. Whoever knows anything of Israel's history at all, notices immediately that those seven brief but powerful strokes depict Israel's history of the last two thousand years. The final two verses point out the cause of Israel's wanderings and oppression among the nations. Israel transgressed His *law* and would not walk in His *ways.* Therefore He Himself in His anger, surrendered *Jacob* to the plundering robbers.

ISAIAH 43

The Indestructibility of Israel

1. But now thus saith the LORD that created thee, O Jacob, and he that formed thee, O Israel, Fear not: for I have redeemed thee, I have called thee by thy name; thou art mine.
2. When thou passest through the waters, I will be with thee; and through the rivers, they shall not overflow thee: when thou walkest through the fire, thou shalt not be burned; neither shall the flame kindle upon thee.

As a rule this glorious promise is explained as having reference to the safety of the Church, but that this promise is given to Israel is obvious and incontestable. The context, which is always the best exegete, indicates this irrefutably. The words *But now* indicate that this glorious promise is contrasted with the preceding sins, punishments and wanderings of Israel. Jehovah had said that He had abandoned His guilty people as a spoil to the rapacious nations and had visited Israel in His anger with the destructions of war and fire. Here, He gives the assurance that He will not utterly consume His people by the destructive elements of water and fire, and that, in spite of Israel's unrighteousnesses, He remains her faithful covenant Jehovah and the Immanuel. *Jacob* is a name which usually points to Israel's infamous origin, a name which the Church should prefer not to apply to herself. He is also Israel's *Creator* and *Former.* As a nation, Israel came into being in a unique way by a double wonder of God's omnipotence. This is why Israel is constantly reminded of her origin, cf. v. 21. Jehovah is not only Israel's Creator; He is also her Deliverer. He had prepared manifold deliverances from the hand of Israel's enemies, but the one great national deliverance, exceeding all others, is that from Egypt which is alluded to here. Created, delivered, married —

these are the three great works of God for Israel. The Hebrew word *gaal,* translated *redeemed* has reference to the payment of a ransom; it implies that the deliverance from Egypt took place by the ransom of the blood of the Lamb, or was in any case a type of it. To call a person *by* his *name* in Scripture often has the rich meaning of intimate acquaintance, as the love of two lovers. Thus the good shepherd knows His sheep by name. The text refers to the close covenantal relationship at Horeb, where the Lord by virtue of the covenant of grace said, "Thou art unto me a peculiar people."

And now Jehovah says that He has never broken this covenantal marriage; what is more, He will never leave nor forsake His people, but will protect them in the midst of the greatest dangers. He does not promise Israel that He will keep her from the fire and the water; on the contrary, He predicts that she will enter them. Indeed, this has taken place throughout the revolving ages up to our own day. In Egypt Israel lay between two rows of bricks near the fire of the kilns, under the fire of the Mid-Eastern sun and under the fire of the hotheaded slave drivers. She did not perish, and while burnt black by the fire of the oven, she retained the promise that one day she would glimmer and shine like the gold in the feathers of a dove. In Babylon, the little remnant, represented by the three God-fearing young men, went literally through the flames again, but the Lord sustained them with His protecting arm. The flames were there, but the young men were not consumed. The fire constantly purified Israel, but it never consumed her; the water cleansed her, but it could never swallow up the Jew. Israel is just as indestructible as God's Word and Covenant are. Whoever can annihilate Israel can do more than Satan and all the powers of hell have been able to do in ages past. What is true of Israel, however, is equally true of the Church. Against it, too, the flames have raged and the waters have boiled but, according to His promise, the Lord Jesus has always been with her.

Promise of Israel's Restoration

3. For I am the LORD thy God, the Holy One of Israel, thy Saviour: I gave Egypt for thy ransom, Ethiopia and Seba for thee.

4. Since thou wast precious in my sight, thou hast been honourable, and I have loved thee: therefore will I give men for thee, and people for thy life.

5. Fear not: for I am with thee: I will bring thy seed from the east, and gather thee from the west;

6. I will say to the north, Give up; and to the south, Keep not back: bring my sons from far, and my daughters from the ends of the earth;

7. Even every one that is called by my name: for I have created him for my glory, I have formed him; yea, I have made him.

8. Bring forth the blind people that have eyes, and the deaf that have ears.

This chapter could fittingly be called the *I-Chapter*, for it is full of the Self-glorification of God. The personal pronoun *I* appears no less than thirty-six times in this chapter of twenty-eight verses. Of the human *I* Bilderdijk said in his powerful style:

> *Go to the devil, boastful word,*
> *For there is where it should be stored.*

But here we are dealing with the divine I, the I above all other I's. What does Jehovah, the Unchangeable I, promise His Israel:

I have redeemed thee.

I have called thee by thy name.

I will be with thee (in the waters of oppression)

I am the Lord thy God, the Holy One of Israel, thy Saviour.

I gave Egypt for thy ransom, Ethiopia and Seba for thee.

I have loved thee.

I will give men for thee.

I am with thee.

I will bring thy seed from the east.

I will gather thee from the west.

I will say to the north, Give up!

I have created him for my glory.

I have made him.

I have formed him.

I have chosen my servant.

I am he: before me there was no God formed.

I, even I, am the Lord (the Unchangeable in promise, love
and faithfulness).

I have declared.

I have saved.

I have shewed.

I am God, ye are my witnesses.

I am he before the day was.

I will work, and who shall let it?

I have sent to Babylon.

I am the Lord, your Holy One, the creator of Israel, your
King.

I will do a new thing.

I will even make a way in the wilderness.

I give waters in the wilderness.

I have formed this people for myself.

I have not caused thee to serve with an offering.

I have not wearied thee with incense.

I, even I, am he that blotteth out thy transgressions for
mine own sake.

I will not remember thy sins.

I have profaned the princes of the Sanctuary.

As we can see, the entire history of Israel is dominated by
this divine I — its past, present and future. In chapter
forty-five this pronoun again appears thirty-one times. We
point this out because it proves clearly that the prophets did
not go to the people with their own wise opinions, as so
many people claim today, but with the words of the Lord. It
must also be said that this I is no one else but Christ.

The word *ransom* (v. 3) deserves some further attention. It
is a very instructive word since it highlights the glorious
subject of Christ's satisfaction. The word *kaphar* is similar in
sound and meaning to the English word *cover*. It means
covering; it can denote a little village that offers refuge or a
hiding place to the inhabitants; or as in Gen. 6:14, the pitch
which covered the ark. In Solomon's Song 4:13 it is used of
the cypress flower, which received this name because its
leaves were ground to a powder used to paint fingernails red,
i.e., to cover them with paint — something which women in
the East thought very beautiful. Finally, it is used in Exodus

21:30; 29:36 and 30:10, 16 to express the idea of objective satisfaction and reconciliation. The basic idea is that God does not see sin on account of the covering sacrificial blood; and that which God with His all-seeing eye does not see, no longer exists. The idea of *kaphar* when applied to the three countries mentioned as God's *ransom* for Israel is variously interpreted. Some take it to mean a past event, others a future one; the latter is undoubtedly correct, for it never happened in the past. God gave these three countries to Cyrus' son as a reward for freeing His people. At His Second Coming Christ will annihilate many nations to make place for His people.

God will gather His people from all corners of the earth. The word *north* refers especially to Russia, where about half of the Jews live. *Give up my people,* God will say to that country, and the voracious lumbering bear will let go of its prey. In verse eight, Israel is once again called the *blind* and *deaf* people.

Summons to a General Meeting of the Nations

9. Let all the nations be gathered together, and let the people be assembled: who among them can declare this, and shew us former things? let them bring forth their witnesses, that they may be justified: or let them hear, and say, It is truth.

10. Ye are my witnesses, saith the LORD, and my servant whom I have chosen: that ye may know and believe me, and understand that I am he: before me there was no God formed, neither shall there be after me.

11. I, even I, am the LORD; and beside me there is no saviour.

12. I have declared, and have saved, and I have shewed, when there was no strange god among you: therefore ye are my witnesses, saith the LORD, that I am God.

13. Yea, before the day was I am he; and there is none that can deliver out of my hand: I will work, and who shall let it?

Again Jehovah summons the people to decide who is God and again He puts the prediction and the fulfillment of His words to the test. He can, though the nations cannot, predict future things. The Lord challenges the nations to predict in the presence of their witnesses Israel's deliverance from the four corners of the earth, as He has just done, or to point to the fulfillment of their earlier predictions. We might call this Jehovah's *apologetics.* Today there is a tendency to make use of apologetics, for it is realized that unbelief manifests itself more boldly by the day. But it is already noticeable that those who are so inclined want to do this in a philosophical manner; but they do not practice the defense of the truth in the way of Isaiah and Jehovah Himself. Why do children of God not follow God's manner of defending the truth? Again and again God pointed all gods and idolaters to His prophetic Word as His miraculous and unique prerogative. If the nations were able to point out to Him the literal fulfillment of their own predictions so that their witnesses could hear it and say, *It is truth,* then they would thereby justify their idolatry over against God (v. 9); even Jehovah Himself would admit that they had truly gods who were almighty and omniscient. This proposition is bold and should incite all readers of Scripture to serious consideration and all true believers to be divinely fanatic with regard to the Word of Prophecy. It should incite them to challenge the gods of our age to do like Jehovah the God of Israel did — to predict the things of the future so that they will come about ages later. This divine method of apologetics, if we may call it that, also has in its favor that it is simple, even a small child can understand it.

In this trial the nations stood mute again with their idols; for this reason Jehovah points to *His* witnesses: "You are my witnesses," He says to the Jews. This saying was quoted by the Savior when He applied it to His disciples and by extension to all believers. God wants Israel as His chosen servant to *believe* and *understand* His Word and to know from it that He alone is the true God, Israel's Covenant God and Savior who alone delivers His people, and from whose Almighty hand no one can deliver.

Once more the Lord says, *You are my witnesses.* Note well that He says this to the restored people of Israel. When Christ, after His resurrection adopted this expression and spoke it to His disciples, it obtained only partial fulfillment. The most glorious fulfillment will take place in the future. Then the redeemed nation will believe and understand and no longer be blind and deaf like she is now. Only then will Israel be truly the *servant of the Lord* who will serve Him and proclaim His praise among all the nations (12:5, 6).

Finally, verse thirteen points to eternity and Jehovah's omnipotence. Grand and lofty is the statement: *I will work, and who shall let it?* Someone has called this God's "I. W. W." On such a glorious God His people can rely wholeheartedly.

Babylon Punished for Israel's Sake

> 14. Thus saith the LORD, your redeemer, the Holy One of Israel; For your sake I have sent to Babylon, and have brought down all their nobles, and the Chaldeans, whose cry is in the ships.
> 15. I am the LORD, your Holy One, the creator of Israel, your King.
> 16. Thus saith the LORD, which maketh a way in the sea, and a path in the mighty waters;
> 17. Which bringeth forth the chariot and horse, the army and the power; they shall lie down together, they shall not rise: they are extinct, they are quenched as tow.

Israel has repeatedly been called *blind.* Nevertheless in their blindness they could testify to the literal fulfillment of the Lord's Word. Thus after two centuries and still in a sinful and blind state, they will be able to witness to the literal fulfillment of the prediction concerning Babylon. This does not alter the fact that only after her complete restoration can Israel be the true witness to Jehovah among the nations.

The Lord will punish Babylon for the sake of Israel (v. 14). This is the main thought of this verse, which is translated in many different ways. Calvin calls the original text confusing, but the main idea is clear enough. To depict the complete certainty of the deliverance from Babylon God again speaks as though it is already an accomplished fact and belongs to the past. God as the Commander in Chief of the hostile armies has sent the Medes and Persians to Babylon. And there He has brought about such a terror that the inhabitants of the city have fled in great haste. Elsewhere the word *barichim* is translated *bolts,* and therefore the English translation is *nobles,* most likely because bolts in Scripture frequently denote nobles who protected the city. But this word is also used of Jonah's fleeing. The idea of fleeing fits very well here, so that again we prefer the D.A.V. translation. The picture is as follows: The city was suddenly overtaken by the hostile armies of the enemy. Terrified, the people fled in every direction. Many rich people fled to their ships that were moored on the Euphrates and the Tigris. The problem that Babylon was not a maritime power does not matter here for the simple reason that the text does not require large merchant ships at sea but only the pleasure boats of the rich. This can be inferred from the fact that they were *shouting* for joy on them. In times past the frivolous rich made merry on their private yachts. Now, they find no safe refuge in them from the enemy, and their happy activity ceases.

In verse fifteen, Jehovah is again called by three glorious names when Israel is assured that He is Israel's *Holy One, Creator* and *King.* Christ is never called the King of the Church, but very often Israel's King. Whoever does not see this is blind indeed. These names are used here because they express the real relationship between Jehovah and Israel and because they would be of great comfort to the imprisoned people. With the same object of comforting Israel, verse sixteen recalls her passage through the Red Sea and the annihilation of Pharaoh's power (v. 17). Jehovah has not only exterminated Israel's haters, but He has done so in such a way that they will never again arise against Israel. This is further elaborated in a simple metaphor of extinction as only Isaiah's genius could use it. In those days, lamp wicks were made of flax, called *tow.* The sudden and complete destruction of Pharaoh's power is compared to the quenching of a wick. In that day, Jehovah will deliver His people from the power of Babylon!

The Lord Will Do a New Thing

18. Remember ye not the former things, neither consider the things of old.

19. Behold, I will do a new thing; now it shall spring forth; shall ye not know it? I will even make a way in the wilderness, and rivers in the desert.

20. The beast of the field shall honour me, the dragons and the owls: because I give waters in the wilderness, and rivers in the desert, to give drink to my people, my chosen.

21. This people have I formed for myself; they shall show forth my praise.

Israel was shown great and glorious things of the past in the preceding verses according to the rule that the past can guarantee the future. But those former things will turn pale in comparison with the *new* things God is going to do in the future (a) to the inanimate creation, (b) to the animal creation, and (c) to His people Israel. It is more than childish to explain these glorious promises as referring to Israel's return from Babylon. For that return was not really a restoration of Israel, as the number of returning Jews, including men and women slaves, did not quite amount to fifty thousand people. It is safe to say that the people as a nation chose to remain in Babylon.

Whereas in the past the Lord had made a way in the sea, He promises to make a way in the sandy deserts for His people in the future. The steppes and arid wilderness will disappear on account of an abundance of living water. This future glory will be so new, so great and so surprising that God's wondrous deeds in Israel's past will seem very insignificant and be hardly remembered. Not only the inanimate but also the animate creation will change completely when God does that *new thing.* Wild animals, lions, bears, wolves, tigers and panthers will praise the God of Israel, and the dragons and owls as well. The Greek Translation has *sirens* for *dragons,* which were thought to be seductive sea monsters able to bewitch seamen and carry them to their death with enchanting songs. It is very difficult to determine what Scripture means with *tannim.* In times past it was actually thought that mysterious snakelike creatures existed, which were called *dragons,* but there really are no dragons. Hence what is referred to are either snakes or jackals. Present day commentators usually hold to the latter. The main thought is clear enough. Not only the wildest but also the most repulsive and hideous animals will honor Christ in the day of His Coming, for that is what is referred to here. Even the most timid animals, such as *owls* (Dutch has *young ostriches;* the Jerusalem Bible[1] also) will honor Him as their Master. In Mark 1:13 we see already a small prophetic example. Rivers of water will wind their way through wild plains and arid steppes to afford Israel drink. For this fact, according to verse twenty, all the beasts of the field honor Jehovah (cf. chs. 11, 65).

They shall show forth my praise, verse twenty-one says of Israel. In numerous sermons this statement has been lifted from its context and applied to the Church. The Lord speaks of no one else but Israel, particularly of her miraculous origin and final destination. The Lord formed Israel in a wholly unique way for His own sake. Israel's calling as His peculiar nation was to show forth His praise among the nations. But by her unbelief and unrighteousness Israel has not been faithful to this calling to this very day. However, part of the *new thing* God will do is that Israel as His people will reach her destination and will show forth the manifold praises of Jehovah-Jesus among the nations.

God Complains About His Ungrateful People

22. But thou hast not called upon me, O Jacob; but thou hast been weary of me, O Israel.
23. Thou hast not brought me the small cattle of thy burnt offerings; neither hast thou honoured me with thy sacrifices. I have not caused thee to serve with an offering, nor wearied thee with incense.
24. Thou hast bought me no sweet cane with money, neither hast thou filled me with the fat of thy sacrifices: but thou hast made me to serve with thy sins, thou hast wearied me with thine iniquities.
25. I, even I, am he that blotteth out thy transgressions for mine own sake, and will not remember thy sins.

Israel's present ingratitude is in sharp contrast with the brilliant light of its future and that of all creation. The

---

[1] This cannot refer, of course, to the French Catholic Jerusalem Bible of 1956 (ET, 1966); "The Cambridge History of the Bible" does not identify any earlier translation under this title; the reference remains obscure. —ED.

complaints the Lord pours out about His people are heartrending. The real meaning of these verses is found in verse twenty-five: *Israel's sins are forgiven out of mere grace.* In verse fourteen the Lord had still said, "For your sake I have sent to Babylon." This could easily create the self-righteous imagination on their part that they were virtuous and worthy before God. These words are said to dispel that imagination and point instead to the greatness of God's free grace which forgives, indeed, blots out, the sin of such a deeply sinful people. According to Dillman, this verse marks the pinnacle of God's grace in the Old Testament. And what it says is by no means the least reason why Isaiah is sometimes called the prophet of free grace.

Again in seven statements Israel's sins of omission are pointed out. (1) *Prayerlessness* was the first evil. They had not *called upon* the Lord. This is a great evil, for a prayerless person is like a city without a wall, which the enemy can invade unhindered. (2) *The small cattle of burnt offerings* have not been brought to Jehovah. The burnt offering is mentioned first because it was the outstanding sacrifice in Israel's worship service. It was brought every morning and every evening as the sacrifice of total commitment. The fire of the burnt offering was never allowed to die out. The offer consisted of the males of the small cattle. Poor people were allowed to bring doves. In distinction from other sacrifices, which were burned only partially, the burnt offering went up entirely in flames. This was to express the total surrender and dedication to the Lord. (3) *Thou hast not honoured me with thy sacrifices.* One must not think that these sacrifices were not brought at all in Israel. Isaiah 1:11 and Amos 5:25 teach us differently. But with all their sacrifices the people did not give Jehovah the *honor* due to Him. The *zebachim* (sacrifices) were those offerings of which a part was due to the priest, or which were eaten by those who brought them after the fat was kindled on the altar. This refers to the bloody sacrifices in general. (4) the food offering is mentioned. The word *mincha* means gift, a gift of gratitude. It was a bloodless offer of flour mixed with salt, oil and incense. These sacrifices always accompanied the burnt and thanksgiving offerings. A food offering must consist of something derived from the

vegetable kingdom: wheat, whether in the form of parched
corn or flour with the three ingredients just mentioned, or in
the form of unleavened bread cakes prepared in three
different ways with oil. God says that He had not made them
serve Him as slaves. This implies, however, that Israel had not
brought these sacrifices out of gratitude but in a slavish
manner. (5) *I have not wearied thee with incense.* The basic
thought is the same as that mentioned under (4). The word
incense is derived from the word *lebonah,* i.e., being white. It
consisted of white kernels which were obtained in Arabia and
Canaan from incisions in the bark of a certain tree. When the
kernels were burnt, they produced a holy smoke and scent,
hence the name *incense.* It symbolized the pleasant scent of
prayer and was used profusely in Israel's sacrificial service.
(6) *Thou hast bought me no sweet cane with money.* The
main idea is repeated: Israel could not spare a thing for the
service of the Lord. Whatever was sacrificed in Israel had to
be the possession of the people and must originate from the
holy soil of the land. Only that could be offered to Jehovah
which came from Israel's stables and fields, and from Israel's
animal and vegetable kingdoms. What had been obtained by
trade from foreign countries and nations lay beyond the holy
circle of the covenant and could not be a well-pleasing
sacrifice. Still, *cane* was a sweet and fragrant reed, which
according to Jeremiah 6:20 and Ezekiel 27:19 was imported
as an article of commerce from faraway countries. According
to Exodus 30:25, it was used as one of the components of
the holy oil of anointing and of the holy incense that was
offered daily on the altar. Hence the Lord had not absolutely
forbidden everything from foreign countries. We are also
reminded of Hiram's help with the building of the temple. In
the language of today we might say that an element of
common grace was incorporated in the holy service of the
Lord, undoubtedly as a prophecy of the future sanctification
of the entire earth. In a truly Isaiahic play of words the
original says that Israel has not bought *kaneh kanitha.* The
Lord loves its sweetness and requires it of His people. He
loves to see them buy something for Him. He wants to be
served in trade also. Israel had indeed engaged in trade, but
wholly without Him — just as commercialism today also

perpetrates this unholy art. All the gold of the earth belongs unto Him and hence He wants to be served by it. His will one day will be reality and will be done on the whole earth, for the kings of the earth will bring their glory into the new Jerusalem (Rev. 21:24-26). (7) *Thou hast not filled me with the fat of thy sacrifices.* The fat of the sacrifices was the very best offering one could bring to the Lord. The Lord is depicted here as drinking this fat with relish, or rather, as wishing to fill Himself with it, for He complains that His people have not filled Him with it. On the basis of this text we must not assume that Israel did not sacrifice at all, but that they did so in a slavish, stingy manner, as a burden rather than a joy. In general, it seemed that the idols were better supplied than the only true God.

By using the number of fullness, Isaiah indicates that Israel's religion of the heart was very imperfect. What the glorified Christ later said of Sardis, He is saying to Israel in different words: "I have not found thy works perfect before God." In the estimation of the Jews they were full indeed, but not *before God.* And yet this is what is important. The Lord enumerated mainly the sins of omission rather than those of commission. Usually only the latter is considered by men, but with God the former is equally serious.

Finally, with a single statement, God points out the sin of commission and says with holy irony, what the people *had* brought Him. In verse twenty-three He said that He had not made them toil like slaves in His service. Alluding to this and by way of contrast He now says that Israel had burdened and wearied Him with their unrighteousnesses. One cannot help but be reminded of the load of our sins which burdened the innocent Lamb of God at one time. In His suffering and death He was truly wearied with our unrighteousnesses. Now how gloriously and brilliantly does verse twenty-five contrast with those abominations of Israel! Here love is completely a one-sided affair. Here we have a striking example not only of unmerited but of totally forfeited grace, the love of God bestowed on utterly guilty people. Here indeed all boasting on their part is out of place.

God Justifies His Putting Jacob Under a Ban

> 26. Put me in remembrance: let us plead together: declare thou, that thou mayest be justified.
>
> 27. Thy first father hath sinned, and thy teachers have transgressed against me.
>
> 28. Therefore I have profaned the princes of the sanctuary, and have given Jacob to the curse, and Israel to reproaches.

God is righteous in all His ways and works, and He appreciates it when His people see and accept this. As in ordinary human justice in all courts of the world, it is a principle that not a single guilty person is condemned without a hearing. The same is the case here as well. God invites the guilty to advance something, no matter how insignificant, in their favor or to be declared innocent. Calvin detects "cutting mockery" in these verses and says:

> With cutting mockery, the possibility is left open here that God might have overlooked something that could prove the worthiness of Israel's descendants. For that reason these people are invited to advance all the evidence available to them to prove the Lord's forgetfulness.

We prefer not to call it mockery but a human presentation of God's condescending goodness and stern righteousness. God is willing to take all circumstances into consideration to avoid every semblance of injustice. But Israel does not heed His invitation, however, but remains mute as there is nothing to advance that may excuse or mitigate her guilt. There is nothing to advance in self-defense. So the righteous Judge speaks again, summarizes her guilt, and then pronounces the ban upon the guilty part, which, as all must agree, is wholly just.

Some question who is meant with the *first father;* the expression has occasioned much difference of opinion. It has been said that it is a reference to Adam, Terah, Abraham, Jacob, Moses, Jeroboam, Ahaz or Manasseh. Many have thought of Israel's ancestors and compared this expression with Ezekiel 16:3: "Thy father was an Amorite." Others follow the learned Vitringa and translate *chief father;* they take it as a reference to the high priest, Uriah, who in the days of Ahaz, and as his slave, led the people to idolatry (II Kings 16:10-16). Still others understand it to mean all kings and high priests collectively, or more generally still, all leaders. Each of these explanations has both support and difficulties. It seems to us that the oldest opinion, shared by many Church Fathers and the Rabbis — that Adam is meant — is the most acceptable. Although Adam was not just the first head of the Jews but the father of all of us, Israel had nevertheless inherited its corruption from the womb through him (48:8; Ps. 51:5; Rom. 5:12; 6:23; Eph. 2:2, 3). *And thy teachers have transgressed against me.* This would be a suitable motto for all the books in history that explain the Holy Scriptures. Actually, it is a reference to the priests who had to explain the Word of the Lord to the people. Even then it was the same as today. Most likely the people did not deny the Word point-blank, but they mixed it with human wisdom, the wisdom of the world. When spiritual leaders sin in this way, it is easy to understand what the situation of the people was. Punishment was bound to come and is pronounced as a short judicial verdict. The *curse* is pronounced upon the idolaters (Deut. 13:6-11; 27:15; Josh. 7:10-26; I Sam. 15:3). The ban was an abandoning to the curse and a severe revealing of those who forsook God and rejected His authority. Not only God but also the nations would turn away from Israel with disgust (cf. Psalm 79:4; Jeremiah 24:9; Daniel 9:16; Zechariah 8:13). Until this very day Israel is scoffed by the nations.

ISAIAH 44

The Outpouring of the Spirit Promised to Israel

1. Yet now hear, O Jacob my servant; and Israel, whom I have chosen:

2. Thus saith the LORD that made thee, and formed thee from the womb, which will help thee; Fear not, O Jacob, my servant; and thou, Jesurun, whom I have chosen.

3. For I will pour water upon him that is thirsty, and floods upon the dry ground: I will pour my spirit upon thy seed, and my blessing upon thine offspring:

4. And they shall spring up as among the grass, as willows by the water courses.

5. One shall say, I am the LORD'S; and another shall call himself by the name of Jacob; and another shall subscribe with his hand unto the LORD, and surname himself by the name of Israel.

The verdict that had been pronounced was terrible. Israel has experienced this during her centuries-long wanderings in all its terrible weight when she was hated and scoffed at among the nations. But this can never be the end of her history, for then all the promises the Lord made to her must fail. In glorious contrast, therefore, to the verdict of the curse, Israel is now addressed and given the comforting promise that one day the nations will consider it an honor to name themselves with the name of Jacob and to be allowed to be the possession of Jacob's God. Hence, as usual, the condemnatory address is followed by a glorious address of comfort. Already it must be a great comfort to Israel that the Lord heaps up many lovely names one upon another by way of an antidote against the nations' scoffings of Israel. With these many names He again shows His covenant relationship with His people. He, who once formed Israel so miraculously in the womb of the barren Sarah, will never leave not forsake His people. His calling and election are immovably sure in

Himself. Israel may be dispersed and the nations may scoff; but in spite of all her sin and misery, *Jesurun* remains His elect, His beloved. The name *Jesurun* appears only three more times in the Old Testament: Deuteronomy 32:15; 33:5, 26; and it in all cases is used of Israel. It is a diminutive of the word *Jashur,* which means *upright.* Hence this word bespeaks a wonder of grace, for He calls His deeply sinful people His beloved, His upright one. Davidson, in his lexicon, translates it *darling honest one.* In 63:8 the Lord calls His lying people *children* that will not lie. God can do so only when He looks upon His people in the Son of His love, in whom resides all His good pleasure. Only in Him can He address His people with such tender love.

This glorious promise is made to His beloved people. He promises to pour water upon him that is thirsty. It is not necessary to demonstrate again that Israel in exile is often presented as perishing with thirst and that in Isaiah the image of water is that of every conceivable blessing. Israel's land will completely dry up, while Israel itself will wander among the nations; but this too will one day change completely. He will pour out floods upon the land parched with thirst. The Lord will not only give water; He will give no One less than the Holy Spirit Himself to the entire nation of the future. That the Lord will not do so to the polluted nation of Isaiah's day is evident from the references to *seed* and *offspring.* The generation of Isaiah's day is morally and religiously sick from the crown of the head to the soles of the feet; it makes itself ripe for the curse and the exile. But the Lord will do so when the Savior comes to Zion. All the threats God has ever pronounced upon His people have always been literally fulfilled until this very day. One need only look at Leviticus 26:27-35, 44; Deuteronomy 29:23-28; Isaiah 6:9-12; Ezekiel 20:32 and Hosea 3:1-5. Why then should His promises fail? Why should Jehovah's faithfulness and Word fail?

Hence we must not think that the promise of the outpouring of the Spirit mentioned here has already been fulfilled at Pentecost, as is usually unhesitatingly assumed. According to Calvin, the description here is merely symbolic to depict the return from Babylon and the outpouring of the

Holy Spirit. This opinion is shared by almost all of the commentators. But regardless of how general this opinion is, it is definitely not Scriptural. The idea here is the still future, general outpouring of the Spirit upon Israel, on all flesh, and on the entire creation; this did not take place at Pentecost at all. It is also mentioned in 4:4 and 32:15-18 as well as Ezekiel 36:27-35; 37:6, 14; Joel 2:28 and Zechariah 12:10.

Not a single one of these promises was fulfilled at Pentecost, as is evident from the following considerations: (1) On Pentecost the Spirit was not poured out on the entire people but only on a few thousand. (2) As a nation Israel is still wandering about, thirsty, dry and unfruitful, among the nations. Israel has as yet not been made a pure and holy people by the purifying, refreshing and fructifying floods of the Spirit. The glorious fruits of this outpouring have as yet never been witnessed in Israel or the nations. Israel is still not growing as willows full of shadows and leaves by the water courses, but is still like a dormant tree in winter. Willows growing near water brooks never suffer from thirst and grow very rapidly above the lush grass, but that has never yet been the picture of Israel as a nation. On the contrary, far from greening and growing, the nation until this very day is spiritually still as barren and emaciated as she was in Isaiah's day. (3) After Pentecost the land of Israel has for many centuries been wild and arid, hardly being able to sustain several thousand people. Until our own day it has been like the desert which Israel traversed long ago, a land that is burning with heat and where nothing can find refreshing relief. Places such as Isaiah 32:15-18 and Ezekiel 36:27-35 clearly indicate that this outpouring of the Spirit will also change the appearance of the land and make of Canaan a pleasure garden like the garden of Eden. (4) Finally, the fruits of this outpouring of the Spirit have never been materialized among the heathen nations. For verse five clearly points to the conversion of the nations outside Israel.

The nations still do not consider it an honor to bear the name of Jacob and be called by the surname of Israel and to be the possession of Jehovah, the God of Israel. Due to the hapless influence of higher criticism, Jehovah in the estimation of the so-called Christian nations is a cruel and salacious old tribal god of the Jews. Not only Israel but also Israel's God is scoffed at in the most ignominious manner. But after the coming of our Savior all this will change completely. In the Near East it was a custom to have the name of the god or master one served branded in one's hand. God had forbidden His people to do this, but Scripture frequently derives proverbs from this custom (49:16; Rev. 7:3; 13:16; 14:11).

God Appeals to Israel and Prophecy for Confirmation of His Divinity

6. Thus saith the LORD the King of Israel, and his redeemer the LORD of hosts; I am the first, and I am the last; and beside me there is no God.

7. And who, as I, shall call, and shall declare it, and set it in order for me, since I appointed the ancient people? and the things that are coming, and shall come, let them shew unto them.

8. Fear ye not, neither be afraid: have not I told thee from that time, and have declared it? ye are even my witnesses. Is there a God beside me? yea, there is no God; I know not any.

There can be no doubt that it is Christ, the Savior, who is speaking here, for according to His own good confession before Pilate He is the *King of Israel.* He and no one else is the Savior. The well-known word *gaal,* used here, is frequently used in the Old Testament, and specifically by Isaiah, to refer to Him as the One who buys the freedom of His imprisoned people from the power of the enemy with a ransom. In the day of His Coming He will reveal Himself as the mighty supreme Commander of the heavenly hosts of angels and saints. And, in Revelation 1:8, 17 and 22:13 He has repeatedly said that He is the *First and the Last.*

In verse seven He glorifies Himself over against the idols with respect to two matters: 1) the calling and appointment of Israel as an *ancient people* and 2) the prediction of future things. Israel is called the *eternal* people (D.A.V.). Many translators weaken this word by substituting *ancient, very old.* Luther translated this term as follows: "Since I from (the beginning of) the world found(ed) the nations"; and De Wette: "the people founded from before the ages." But all those and similar translations are wrong, since this expression points not only to the past but also to the future. If one compares this with Jeremiah 31:35-37, Isaiah 65:17 and 66:22, we are clearly taught that Israel's seed and name will endure as long as the new heaven and the new earth endure. Van der Palm correctly comments:

> Indeed, when we consider how many ages Israel had already existed when Isaiah wrote this, and how many ages (already increased to thousands of years) it has existed after Isaiah lived, until this very day; and how it has remained the same unmixed people all those ages notwith-standing the most cruel vicissitudes and calamaties that befell it and still befall it — I say, whoever considers all this will not hesitate very long to call Israel an eternal people, destined to be present until the end of the existence of our globe!

The gods of the nations could not call such an *eternal people* into existence. Nor can they predict the *things that are coming,* as Jehovah has predicted them of His eternal people. Israel and prophecy are two great miraculous works of Almighty God. They are inseparably connected. Whoever does not know prophecy does not know Israel either, and whoever does not know Israel does not understand prophecy. Does anyone wish to combat increasing unbelief? Very well, but then he had better begin by being a follower of God and pointing the gods of our day to these two powerful apologetic facts. This does not call for close or cunning arguments; we can only point to firm, hard, irrefutable miracles which everyone can see. Let us give the doubting generations of our day facts and not merely hollow sounds! *Fear not!* Jehovah cries out once more to His *eternal* people. We hear this again and again (43:1, 5; 44:2). This word of comfort is also characteristic of our Savior. He constantly said to his fearful disciples, *Fear not!* even to John when on Patmos he fell as one dead at His feet (Rev. 1:17). He is the only true God, equal with the Father; He is also the only Rock. The Apostle in I Corinthians 10:4 says, *And that Rock was Christ.*

Idolatry Mocked

9. They that make a graven image are all of them vanity; and their delectable things shall not profit; and they are their own witnesses; they see not, nor know; that they may be ashamed.

10. Who hath formed a god, or molten a graven image that is profitable for nothing?

11. Behold, all his fellows shall be ashamed: and the workmen, they are of men: let them all be gathered together, let them stand up; yet they shall fear, and they shall be ashamed together.

12. The smith with the tongs both worketh in the coals, and fashioneth it with hammers, and worketh it with the strength of his arms: yea, he is hungry, and his strength faileth: he drinketh no water, and is faint.

13. The carpenter stretcheth out his rule; he marketh it out with a line; he fitteth it with planes, and he marketh it out with the compass, and maketh it after the figure of a man, according to the beauty of a man; that it may remain in the house.

14. He heweth him down cedars, and taketh the cypress and the oak, which he strengtheneth for himself among the trees of the forest: he planteth an ash, and the rain doth nourish it.

15. Then shall it be for a man to burn: for he will take thereof, and warm himself; yea, he kindleth it, and baketh bread; yea, he maketh a god, and worshippeth it; he maketh it a graven image, and falleth down thereto.

16. He burneth part thereof in the fire; with part thereof he eateth flesh; he roasteth roast, and is satisfied: yea, he warmeth himself, and saith, Aha, I am warm, I have seen the fire:

17. And the residue thereof he maketh a god, even his graven image: he falleth down unto it, and worshippeth it, and prayeth unto it, and saith, Deliver me; for thou art my god.

18. They have not known nor understood: for he hath shut their eyes, that they cannot see; and their hearts, that they cannot understand.

19. And none considereth in his heart, neither is there knowledge nor understanding to say, I have burned part of it in the fire; yea, also I have baked bread upon the coals thereof; I have roasted flesh, and eaten it: and shall I make the residue thereof an abomination? shall I fall down to the stock of a tree?

20. He feedeth on ashes: a deceived heart hath turned him aside, that he cannot deliver his soul, nor say, Is there not a lie in my right hand?

In a world in which many thousands of gods and goddesses were worshiped it was truly a bold question Jehovah asked in verse eight: *Is there a God beside me?* Many in Israel would have been inclined to answer, "Yes!" to this question. This is why idolatry is mocked once more with divine irony. This entire section is comic, and it surprises and tantalizes the reader without actually causing him to laugh. The prophet's words retain a form of holy seriousness. Although he goes into the minutest details, he never resorts to empty banter and hollow jests. Even in his most biting satire and most cutting mockery he continues his heroic style in which the Messiah is the great Conqueror.

Let us follow him into the idol factory and behold the making of idols. Our eyes see first of all the makers of idols, who are called *vanity,* hollow, meaningless, worthless. With this one word he knocks this whole group upside down, for if the makers of gods themselves are worthless how then can they produce gods of any value? This he expresses emphatically in the next clause: *their delectable things shall not profit. Delectable things* refers to the beautiful images which soon they will worship as their favorite gods. We believers have a God who *does profit* us, who casts our sins into the depths of the sea and takes us into the heaven of His glory; but the idols of the nations do not do this. Their dumbness and blindness and total powerlessness testify to their unprofitableness. The Lord said to Israel: "You are my witnesses;" of the idols He says: *They are their own witnesses.* It would be impossible for one worshiper to tell about the virtues of these idols. And what *witnesses* these idols are! Imagine the folly: they are witnesses who do not see and know nothing. They will become a disgrace as worthless pieces of wood or metal. Verse ten contains an ironic question.

Verse eleven indicates the complete ruin of all worshipers and makers of idols. No matter how much trust they have put in their artful objects, one day they will be put to shame together with their gods and be doomed to complete destruction. Jehovah challenges them to array themselves together in battle. They may freely measure their imagined and acclaimed power against His, but He will arise and cover them with shame and dash them to pieces. Verse eleven is a clear indication that Isaiah's *vis comica,* his comic ability, stands totally in the service of the truth and is not calculated to please or tantalize the reader.

With holy impatience, as it were, the prophet has already twice said that the idols and their makers and worshippers will be brought to nought with shame, but he still can not turn away from this subject. His holy passion and fiery imagination take pleasure in showing his readers the utter foolishness of idolatry. The sparks of his genius fly as the sparks of the smithy into which he has taken us. A *metal* god is in the making. The prophet simply calls this god *it*. To him it is merely a piece of metal and nothing more. It is his intention to give a description of the entire process of making an idol and so he even goes back as far as the making of the instruments. He depicts a smith as he is first making an ax. There he stands, with his shirt sleeves rolled up so that we can see his muscular arms. He stands near the glowing fire with his tongs, the lump of metal still without form or fashion beside him. But the smith will now fashion the arms and legs and mouth and nose and ears, and so he vigorously swings his hammers. Look how he swings the heavy sledge-hammer and how he pounds and taps and strikes. He is in a great hurry to make this god, so he allows himself no time for eating and drinking. Some are of the opinion that his pious zeal and superstition prevent him from interrupting this important work by taking some food and drink, but whatever the case, his idol cannot give him either strength or food. If the living God of Israel were not to uphold him, he would drop dead alongside his dead god. His strong arm becomes paralyzed from all that swinging and slamming and the prophet shows us how he almost *fails* and *faints* and collapses. This much as far as the making of a metal god is concerned!

Now the prophet tells us how a *wooden* idol is made; again he takes us on the wings of imagination to another workshop. In all his extended descriptions the prophet is never tedious. Even in his expansions he is brief, powerful, terse and he sets in motion neither the yawning nor the laughing reflex. In a word, he is always inspiring and enchanting. In a single verse he showed us sufficiently the smith; now he will show us that the smith in his frenzy is not alone. We see the carpenter stand in front of a hewn giant of the forest of a large log. He takes his measure to determine exactly the length and width of the god he intends to make. Next with a stylus he roughly outlines his god on it. Then he lustily works with chisel, plane and compass until at last he obtains the figure of a well-proportioned man. But it is not a man; only the *figure of a man*. What to do next with the finished god? It will remain *in the house*. Motionless it will stand stiff and silent year in and year out in some corner or niche of a house or temple. This addition contains bitter ridicule, as Calvin correctly says.

But the prophet is still not finished with his description. He goes more extensively into the origin of an idol and takes us along into a park or forest. His intention is to show that the wood that is used to make an idol owes its origin to the rain of the God of heaven. The idol maker wanders about in the forest where all kinds of trees grow and looks for the best and hardest of wood, for he must make a solid god. There he sees trees which he himself planted years ago and which have already grown tall because of the rain. The new trees are to take the place of the ones that were cut down and have been used for making idols. Not all the wood of a tree can be used for making a god, however. Many pieces remain and those the man uses to build a fire, when the weather is cold, in order to warm himself. He kindles them and bakes bread on the fire. He does not burn the whole tree, however, but retains a large block and of it makes the god before whom he will kneel in adoration.

Verses sixteen and seventeen need no further explanation, for that would be a weakening of their force. Isaiah presents the maker and worshiper of gods as turning his piece of meat on a roasting spit above a lustily burning fire and quickly eating it until he is full. He then rubs his hands with delight at such a nice fire and exclaiming with great self-satisfaction that he finds it very pleasant to warm and fill himself before such a cozy fire. The man is delighted with his fire and his meat. He also makes a god of his belly. But at the same time he is quite religious, for soon he will cry out, lying on his face before his little wooden god: *Deliver me; for thou art my god!*

The actual application is found in verses eighteen to twenty. The tone of the prophet changes to a lament. Sad and grieved, he cries out that their eyes are blinded and their hearts shut to the brightness of the truth. They are, as it were, snared in a net of lies and their minds are totally darkened so that even the thought about this foolishness does not enter their hearts. If they had only considered their ways with their hearts, then even a little child would have been able to see the folly of their doings! Their corrupted taste is complete: they feed on *ashes.* They no longer see, understand or taste. The deceitful and deceived heart allows itself to be led to the Evil One who is the master of all idolatry; they allow themselves to be led astray to the depths of hell where their souls are hopelessly lost. The prophet considers them as already hopelessly lost since in their blindness, ignorance and tastelessness they do not want to acknowledge that they carry a lie in their right hand. What a terrible situation the prophet has depicted! He showed to us people who almost worked themselves to death for their religion, who very piously knelt and prayed, who exerted themselves and sacrificed for their religion and who in spite of all this retained a lie in their right hand and therefore must helplessly and irretrievably perish. Is this not also a true picture of many thousands of people in our day?

Israel's Nature, Past, Present and Future

21. Remember these, O Jacob and Israel; for thou art my servant: I have formed thee; thou art my servant: O Israel, thou shalt not be forgotten of me.
22. I have blotted out, as a thick cloud, thy transgressions, and, as a cloud, thy sins: return unto me; for I have redeemed thee.
23. Sing, O ye heavens; for the LORD hath done it: shout, ye lower parts of the earth: break forth into singing, ye mountains, O forest, and every tree therein: for the LORD hath redeemed Jacob, and glorified himself in Israel.

It is not in vain that the prophet has given such a long description of the absurdity of idolatry. He did so to drive home the vanity of idolatry to his people. The blind idolaters had neither knowledge nor understanding and did not contemplate their foolishness; but by way of contrast he cries out: *Remember these, O Jacob and Israel!*

Again it is pointed out that Israel is the *servant* of Jehovah. When considered rightly, this is the essence of this wondrous people. Israel's origin and past is expressed in the words *I have formed thee.* In a general sense, of course, He has formed all things and all peoples, but we may not take it here in this general sense. When He presents Himself again and again as Israel's Maker, He always means to point out the special act of creation by which He called Israel into existence and by which He called forth this wondrous nation so totally different from other nations. Is it any wonder that Scripture again and again calls attention to this double miracle and reminds Israel of it? Israel was not allowed to forget from which rock she had been hewn, for if she did, she would forget the most important part of her origin and past history. God wanted her to see her marvelous origin as the guarantee of her equally marvelous future.

Israel's past is contained in the words, *Thou shalt not be forgotten of me,* or, better translated, *Thou remainest unforgettable to me.* This expresses the Lord's love for the people descended from Abraham. They are enemies with regard to the gospel, but beloved ones because of their fathers. God does not forget them; they remain unforgettable to Him, as the elder son remained unforgettable to his father according to the touching description of the parable. His bowels still sound with mercy concerning His firstborn. Is there anything that does not totter before the hellish powers of revolution? The foundations of the family, of the church, of society and of the nation totter; but Israel is growing faster now than ever before. How must this riddle of history be explained? Only on the basis of the fact that Jehovah does not forget His people. He is united to this people with the bond of the Covenant.

At last we see Israel's glorious future! Israel's unrighteousness makes a separation between her and her God, but these sins, which hung as a heavy poisonous mist before the kind countenance of her God, will be blotted out. The sun causes all mists and fogs to disappear completely. The Sun of righteousness will arise over Israel (Mal. 4:2), and will blot out that pestilent cloud of Israel's trespasses; and then Israel will turn to Jehovah-Jesus as a redeemed people. Then Jehovah-Jesus will manifest Himself gloriously in Israel as her King and as the King of kings and Lord of lords. As a result of Israel's redemption and readoption the entire creation will burst out in jubilation, as arisen from the dead, and sing a song of triumph over the powers of hell. Heaven and earth, mountains and woodlands — all will shout with joy to the honor of Israel's Redeemer.

The Lie Put to Shame and the Word of God Glorified

24. Thus saith the LORD, thy redeemer, and he that formed thee from the womb, I am the LORD that maketh all things; that stretcheth forth the heavens alone; that spreadeth abroad the earth by myself;

25. That frustrateth the tokens of the liars, and maketh diviners mad; that turneth wise men backward, and maketh their knowledge foolish;

26. That confirmeth the word of his servant, and performeth the counsel of his messengers; that saith to Jerusalem, Thou shalt be inhabited; and to the cities of Judah, Ye shall be built, and I will raise up the decayed places thereof:

With the striking image of a misty cloud, God has assured Israel that He will blot out her sins quickly, completely and without leaving a trace. He presents Himself again as the Creator of Israel as a nation, and as the Ruler and Supporter of all things. He spreads out the heavens as a shepherd's tent and the earth like a carpet. These striking predictions, too, we have come across before. The question arises automatically why Jehovah points so often to His greatness and unlimited power; the answer must be that He does so to instruct and comfort Israel. He thereby wishes to teach Israel not to trust in vain idols but only in Him, and to urge the exiles to rely wholly on His omnipotence for the future. He wants Israel to consider the past as a solid guarantee of the future and to view her creation as an adumbration of her recreation. Hence it is remarkable that present-day Christendom is so interested in Israel's past but not in the least in its wondrous future.[1]

---

[1] This situation has changed since 1948, though not much among the Dutch Reformed groups the author has in mind. —ED.

The diviners and soothsayers — the men of wisdom in those days — will be put to shame by Jehovah. These men were of old in the service of idolatry and world power. The book of Daniel repeatedly depicts in the most graphic manner how this worldly wisdom could not save in time of need but had to retreat in shame. Science as such is good and excellent, a gift from heaven; a soul without knowledge is not good. God is called the *God of sciences.* But we see that there is also a foolish knowledge. We readily admit that this applies first of all to the foolish knowledge of Babylon. Undoubtedly the wise men told Belteshazzar that he could safely trust in the walls and gates and watchmen of the city; but the enemy took them by surprise and their knowledge was turned into foolishness. This word is also rich in meaning for our scientific world. For the world has become very scientific, so scientific in fact that the Christ of God is excluded everywhere, even though He is the *Supreme Wisdom* and *Wisdom* personified. Indeed, the science of today has rejected His Word. "How then would they still have wisdom?" we might ask with Jeremiah. Let believing people never forget that the wisdom of this world is foolishness with God.

The *servant* of verse 26 is Isaiah and the *messengers* are the prophets. The beautiful contrast between the lying prophets and the true prophets should not be overlooked. The former will be put to shame; the latter will not, however, for God will fulfill their prophecy by causing Jerusalem to be inhabited, the cities of Judah to be rebuilt and the decayed places to be raised.

The Prophecy Concerning Cyrus

> 27. That saith to the deep, Be dry, and I will dry up thy rivers:
> 28. That saith of Cyrus, He is my shepherd, and shall perform all my pleasure: even saying to Jerusalem, Thou shalt be built; and to the temple, Thy foundation shall be laid.

There are many interpretations of verse twenty-seven. Some simply view it as a poetic description of God's omnipotence; others take it as a reference to the crossing of the Red Sea and Jordan; most commentators follow Vitringa who applies this verse to Cyrus' conquest of Babylon by his well-known stratagem of diverting the Euphrates from its bed, and of whom it may therefore be said that he dried up the river. In favor of this view it can be said: (a) that Cyrus' name is specifically mentioned in this context; (b) that this verse in a few words describes the exact manner of conquest. Yet we must not forget that both Babylon and Cyrus are but vague types of future events and persons.

Cyrus is mentioned here for the first time in Scripture, more than two centuries before he appears on the world's stage. Isaiah mentions him only once more, but he constantly alludes to him and his acts of war and the freeing of the Jews. Elsewhere in Scripture he is mentioned frequently as proof that this heathen played a considerable role in God's counsel. (cf. II Chronicles 36:22, 23; Ezra 1:1, 2, 7, 8; 3:7; 4:3; 5:13, 14, 17; Daniel 1:21; 6:28; 10:1. His name in Persian means *sun* and in Aramaic *shepherd,* according to Davidson.

The mention of Cyrus' name and the precise descriptions of his acts are the main reason why the critics decided that he already had appeared on the scene when the prophet wrote this, which by no means is true. These people cannot or will not accept the miracle of prophecy; hence they assume a second Isaiah, which is no more than a figment of the wind on the part of unbelieving and semi-believing critics. Josephus in his *Antiquities* relates that when Cyrus came across his name mentioned in this place in Isaiah 220 years before he lived, he was seized by a holy desire to fulfill what was written of him. Besides the miraculous mentioning of Cyrus' name, the form of this prophecy, is grand and lofty. We could properly write above these words: *He speaks and it is done; He commands, and it stands fast.* For He speaks to Jerusalem: *Thou shalt be inhabited;* to the cities of Judah: *Ye shall be built;* to the deep: *Be dry!;* to Cyrus: *He is my shepherd, and shall perform all my pleasure;* to Jerusalem: *Thou shalt be built!* and to the temple: *Thy foundation shall be laid.* When the prophets wish to express the certainty of a future saving fact, they often do so either by presenting it as an already accomplished fact, or as a command with the presupposition that God's command will be unconditionally obeyed. It is in this sense that we must take these commands here. Finally, compare these divine commands with Cyrus' proclamation as recorded in Ezra 1:2 and II Chronicles 36:23.

ISAIAH 45

The Lord's Address to Cyrus

1. Thus saith the LORD to his anointed, to Cyrus, whose right hand I have holden, to subdue nations before him; and I will loose the loins of kings, to open before him the two leaved gates; and the gates shall not be shut;

2. I will go before thee, and make the crooked places straight: I will break in pieces the gates of brass, and cut in sunder the bars of iron:

3. And I will give thee the treasures of darkness, and hidden riches of secret places, that thou mayest know that I, the LORD, which call thee by thy name, am the God of Israel.

4. For Jacob my servant's sake, and Israel mine elect, I have even called thee by thy name: I have surnamed thee, though thou hast not known me.

5. I am the LORD, and there is none else, there is no God beside me: I girded thee, though thou hast not known me:

6. That they may know from the rising of the sun, and from the west, that there is none beside me. I am the LORD, and there is none else.

These verses contain an address by Jehovah to Cyrus. It contains three main points: How Jehovah views Cyrus; what He will do for Cyrus; and with what objective He will do this. The entire address clearly indicates that the great *I* of Jehovah, which appears sixteen times in the first seven verses of this chapter, will be the secret of Cyrus' famous victories. The chapter is one continuous Self-glorification of Jehovah. In chapter forty-three His *I* appeared no less than thirty-six times, here it appears thirty-one times. Cyrus shall not have the honor of his victories, neither shall his generals or armies, but He who is greater than Cyrus, Christ, the Son of God.

It is totally a unique phenomenon in Scripture for Cyrus to be called Jehovah's *Anointed* or, as the original has it, *Messiah,* the Hebrew name for Christ. Cyrus was a "Christ" because he had been anointed with the Spirit of qualification. By this alone one can neither affirm nor deny that he had the Spirit in a saving sense. But the fact that in the following verses it is said twice that Cyrus does *not know* Jehovah does not hold out much hope. It used to be thought that he was at least a monotheist, a worshiper of one God, but recent excavations have disproved this idea, since he also honored other gods. It is certain, however, that Jehovah anointed him in a qualifying sense. This is the exact secret of his exceptional victories and prosperity. Jehovah had taken hold of his right hand for the purpose of striking down the nations before His countenance. This fact points out not only the Lord's favorable attitude toward Cyrus but also His support of him. God took the war hero by the hand as a father does his little boy who can hardly walk by himself.

Secondly, Jehovah says that he will loosen the loins, the girdles of kings. This proverb means the removal of the Kings' power, of which the girdle was the symbol.

Thirdly, Jehovah promises to go before him to open the shut doors and gates. All fortifications, strongholds and cities will be taken without much trouble by Cyrus. Jehovah will also straighten the crooked and bumpy roads before him, break down the brass doors and destroy the iron bars.

Fourthly, Jehovah will give Cyrus all the hidden treasures of Babylon and other kingdoms. Warfare is always very costly, but the Lord would see to it that His anointed servant would not lack. In Babylon the treasures were hid in dark secret places, where they could not be found easily, but God knew very well where they were and He gave them to Cyrus.

And what was God's object in doing this? That Cyrus would acknowledge Him in His greatness as Israel's God. His proclamation of freeing the Jews tells us that this objective was reached. The second and broader object lay in Jacob, His servant, His elect. Cyrus would let Israel go. And finally the main objective was that people everywhere, east and west, would glorify Jehovah's name and see the worthlessness of all idols.

Jehovah the Creator of Good and Evil

7. I form the light, and create darkness: I make peace, and create evil: I the LORD do all these things.

Verse seven actually belongs to the Lord's address to Cyrus. At least, when we hold to this, a surprising light is shed on it. For Cyrus was a Persian, and Persians had a dualistic concept of God and the world. Their good god they called Ahura-mazda and the evil god Angra-mainya. The former had created the light, the second the darkness. It is more than likely that Cyrus was not wholly free from this dualism, for he was by nature very religious. With this one statement, God removes all ground for this dualism when He says that He is the Creator of both light and darkness and of peace and evil. But we must not misinterpret this majestic statement by understanding it to mean that God is the cause of sin and moral evil. The word *ra,* used here, does not mean sin but the result and punishment of sin, i.e., sorrow, oppression and misery. In this sense Jeremiah says in Lamentations 3:38, "Out of the mouth of the most High proceedeth not evil and good?" And does not Cyrus ask in the same sense: "Shall there be evil in the city which the Lord worketh not?" Calvin seems to be thinking of moral evil, but adds, "Undoubtedly the Lord is no representative of evil as such, but He does make use of evil so that it may bring forth good."

Isaiah's Prayer

> 8. Drop down, ye heavens, from above, and let the skies pour down righteousness: let the earth open, and let them bring forth salvation, and let righteousness spring up together; I the LORD have created it.

Earlier Cyrus was called Jehovah's Anointed, since he was enabled by God's Spirit to cast down mighty nations; but there is another and more profound reason why he received this special name. His freeing the Jews from Babylon was a type and adumbration of another and far more glorious deliverance of Israel and the nations and the entire groaning creation from the bondage of Satan and sin. A deliverance that will be brought about by the Great Anointed One, our Lord Jesus Christ. This is what Isaiah has in mind and when he hears Jehovah say that He creates peace and evil, he suddenly turns from Cyrus to Christ and breaks out into a earnest prayer for the coming and reign of the latter. Again he speaks in a truly poetic manner using the metaphor of dew and rain which, in Scripture, is so often the image of great blessing. The Latin Vulgate, followed by all Catholic expositors, applies this verse to Christ the Righteous One with much better insight than those who apply it to the return of the Jews from exile or the beneficent reign of Cyrus. The idea here is rather the same as the one we come across elsewhere regarding the bliss of the Messianic reign (cf. Ps. 67:7; 85:11-13). Shortly before he died David sang of Messiah, "He shall come down like rain upon the mown grass: as showers that water the earth." And his swan song even began with the words,

"He that ruleth over men must be just, ruling in the fear of God. And he shall be as the light of the morning, when the sun riseth, even a morning without clouds; the tender grass springing out of the earth by clear shining after rain."

Isaiah's prayer and David's prophetic song are heard and answered. As though it had already taken place, God says, *"I the Lord have created it."*

God Justifies His Choice Regarding Cyrus

9. Woe unto him that striveth with his Maker! Let the potsherd strive with the potsherds of the earth. Shall the clay say to him that fashioneth it, What makest thou? or thy work, He hath no hands?

10. Woe unto him that saith unto his father, What begettest thou? or to the woman, What hast thou brought forth?

11. Thus saith the LORD, the Holy One of Israel, and his Maker, Ask me of things to come concerning my sons, and concerning the work of my hands command ye me.

12. I have made the earth, and created man upon it: I, even my hands, have stretched out the heavens, and all their host have I commanded.

13. I have raised him up in righteousness, and I will direct all his ways: he shall build my city, and he shall let go my captives not for price nor reward, saith the LORD of hosts.

The idea is quite commonly held that the Jews murmured about God's decree that a heathen would deliver them, and that these words are a rebuke. Although there is not much proof for this idea, the words do give some occasion to it and this reaction is quite natural when we take into consideration how proud Jewry was over against heathendom. If we accept the idea that this is a rebuke, the words can be explained quite naturally; it even sheds a surprising light on them.

A double woe is pronounced upon all who dare argue with their Maker and fume against the heathen Cyrus. Both Jews and Gentiles are, as far as their bodies are concerned, formed out of clay and are like potsherds, which, as is indicated here, are also made of earth. Notwithstanding all the holy seriousness emanating from this verse it nevertheless contains crushing ridicule of all grumbling and striving between men. When people quarrel with each other, then there is war between potsherds, broken water vessels that can no longer hold water and are useless. For man is fallen and broken and by nature good for nothing. More foolish still, however, is man's quarreling with God. God is the Potter and we the baked clay products. Will now the baked clay demand an account of the Potter's action or retort to Him, *He hath no hands,* "Thou hast made me in an awkward, foolish, crude manner"? Another example is adduced to reprimand the foolishness of man's murmuring against his Maker, but it needs no further explanation.

Verse eleven contains another repetition of the great and important truth that Jehovah is Israel's Maker. In addition, this verse must be understood as an enlargement of the idea expressed in the two preceding verses. The idea is simply that Israel wants to know from God what the future will be concerning her own destination; but Israel would, on the other hand, also tell Him how to fulfill these future events, a boldness Jehovah refuses. For is He not the Creator of heaven and earth and all that is in them (v. 12)? Again it is said of the heavens that they are spread out like the cloth of a tent, while the stars and the angels and evil spirits are presented as His army, of which He is in complete command.

Finally God terminates the murmuring of the people when He returns to Cyrus and emphatically repeats that He has raised him up *in righteousness*. This says not only that God has not made a mistake by raising up Cyrus as the liberator of Israel, but also that He wishes to use the Persian to do justice to His people and carry out vengeful justice upon Babylon. Once more Jehovah says that He will make all Cyrus' pathways straight, that he, and no one else, will build Jerusalem and will free His prisoners; and Cyrus would indeed receive a reward from Jehovah for it. He was not, however, to demand a ransom or tribute from delivered Israel. The latter has been fulfilled for the book of Ezra shows us that Cyrus selflessly returned the Jews their freedom.

"A God That Hideth Himself"

14. Thus saith the LORD, The labour of Egypt, and merchandise of Ethiopia and of the Sabeans, men of stature, shall come over unto thee, and they shall be thine: they shall come after thee; in chains they shall come over, and they shall fall down unto thee, they shall make supplication unto thee, saying, Surely God is in thee; and there is none else, there is no God.

15. Verily thou art a God that hidest thyself, O God of Israel, the Saviour.

Just as in the New Testament the destruction of Jerusalem and the coming again of the Lord flow constantly into each other, so this happens constantly with Cyrus and Christ in these chapters. Everything that is said of Cyrus' liberation of the Jews will be done completely by Christ in His coming again to Israel. Hence this text places us suddenly in the midst of Israel's complete restoration and the flowing of all nations to restored Israel and Israel's God. It is the misfortune of the older orthodox expositors and of present-day critics that they have no eye for this and that they do not see that the prediction never ends with the very insignificant deliverance from Babylon, but always and only culminates in the complete restoration of Israel and of the entire groaning creation. All prophecy stretches itself as it were toward that day, so that again and again one comes across this remarkable phenomenon, that without any apparent transition it transposes us from the past into the midst of Israel's future glory. This prophecy has never been fulfilled either in the past or the present, but after the coming of Christ it will be gloriously fulfilled to Israel. The Egyptians, Moors and Sabeans will be converted to God and bring their sanctified culture to Israel and Israel's God in Jerusalem. The Sabeans are depicted as giants who will humbly bow down before Israel, surrendering themselves as a possession to Israel, and wishing to serve as her servants. Their pride is completely crushed, and humbled, they cast themselves upon the earth, crying, *God is in thee; and there is none else, there is no God.* The same thought appears many times in Isaiah (cf. 2:1-3; 11:9; 12:4; 14:1; 25:3, 6, 7; 42:1, 4; 44:1-45:24; 51:4; 55:5; 60:2; 61:9; 62:2). The glorified people will one day take a place of honor among the nations (53:12); kings will pay their respectful homage (49:7, 23; 52:15). Israel will reign over all nations (54:3); enjoy their riches (61:6); and even the great men of foreign nations will serve the restored people (49:23; 60:16).

Interpreting verse fourteen thus opens the way to the correct understanding of verse fifteen. During the course of the centuries many pious speculations developed concerning this text. On the basis of it it was even thought that a poor sinner could cry out for grace for a long time, and for days and years receive no answer from God. This is but a single sample of the evil applications which result from misunderstanding God's Word. For it is Isaiah who, as the mouthpiece of the people, cries this when he on the one hand looks at the future glory and on the other at Israel's present miserable condition. When he sees how God for many centuries hides His face from Israel, he cries out these words, overcome by rapture and emotion. The Lord hides Himself from Israel during the *times of the Gentiles* (18:4; 40:27; 49:14; Hos. 3:3-5). For many days Israel will sit down as a woman forsaken. So it is clear that we may not apply these words to a seeking sinner. From such God does not hide Himself. That even holds true for Israel. But when in the last days Israel will seek Him, she will find Him (Hos. 3:5). The God who hides Himself from Israel is no One less than the Savior (cf. Matt. 24:39).

All Idolatry Put to Shame, Israel Saved Everlastingly

16. They shall be ashamed, and also confounded, all of them: they shall go to confusion together that are makers of idols.

17. But Israel shall be saved in the LORD with an everlasting salvation: ye shall not be ashamed nor confounded world without end.

18. For thus saith the LORD that created the heavens; God himself that formed the earth and made it; he hath established it, he created it not in vain, he formed it to be inhabited: I am the LORD; and there is none else.

19. I have not spoken in secret, in a dark place of the earth: I said not unto the seed of Jacob, Seek ye me in vain: I the LORD speak righteousness, I declare things that are right.

20. Assemble yourselves and come; draw near together, ye that are escaped of the nations: they have no knowledge that set up the wood of their graven image, and pray unto a god that cannot save.

21. Tell ye, and bring them near; yea, let them take counsel together: who hath declared this from ancient time? who hath told it from that time? have not I the LORD? and there is no God else beside me; a just God and a Saviour; there is none beside me.

Israel will be saved with an *everlasting salvation,* but in the way of judgments and of the utter confusion of idolatry. While this is the main thought of these verses, the prophet cannot mention idolatry without ridiculing it some more. The contrast here is again precious. The idols cannot save themselves; they go, covered with shame, to confusion, while Israel is completely saved and will never be put to shame.

Verse eighteen points to Jehovah once more as the Creator of all things; He does not lack the power and authority to bring about the everlasting salvation of His people. All the objections and counter arguments some Bible-believing people produce to contest Israel's eternal salvation and territorial restoration are refuted by this verse. He who created and upheld the heavens and the earth can also recreate them and make them a fitting dwelling place for His people. Meanwhile, that Israel is not as yet delivered as indicated here, anybody who has eyes to see can know. The Church already has its eternal salvation, but Israel still must, at the coming of the Lord and by His powerful judgment upon the nations, be delivered from the hand of all her oppressors.

The expression *he created it not in vain* demands our special attention. The word for *vain* (Dutch: *void)* is the same as in Genesis 1:2, "And the earth was without form, and *void.*" In the following verse this word *is* translated by *vain.* Some expositors think that *earth* refers to Canaan, but here it seems to clearly refer to the whole earth. The Jews infer from this text that the earth was inhabited after the resurrection. More recently many deduce from it that the earth in Genesis 1:2 was already the result of a fall and judgment and that the prophet is referring to this event when he says that God had never created it so. Genesis 1:2 is then translated: "The earth *was made* without form and void." It must be admitted that Isaiah frequently uses this word in connection with judgment, especially for the result of some kind of judgment (cf. 34:11; 44:9). This is not the place to talk about the restoration hypothesis of creation, but we only wish to state that this text alone is not sufficient proof for it. In any case it is clear that the ultimate purpose for the earth is not to be void but that it be inhabited by converted Israel and the converted nations. In verse nineteen God contrasts His prophetic revelations with heathen oracles which as a rule were pronounced in dark, hidden caves. The Lord always spoke openly, straightforwardly, unequivocally. In John 18:20 Christ said much the same thing to the high priest. This text, as well as Deuteronomy 30:11 condemns all secret societies. The Lord continued to speak kindly and invitingly to Israel of *righteousness* and *things that are right.* The witness of Jesus is the Spirit of prophecy. He is the faithful Witness. The term *ye that are escaped of the nations* does not refer to the leaders of the nations, nor to the Babylonians, nor to the proselytes, nor to those who escaped slaying by Cyrus, but to the remnant of the nations that will survive the judgment and enter the millennium (cf. chapter four regarding the four remnants). The word *palit* refers to someone who has been spared in a battle (cf. Gen. 4:12). The Lord shows those who escaped Armageddon and Gog's downfall the folly of idolatry.

A Kind Invitation to the Salvation in Christ

22. Look unto me, and be ye saved, all the ends of the earth: for I am God, and there is none else.

23. I have sworn by myself, the word is gone out of my mouth in righteousness, and shall not return, That unto me every knee shall bow, every tongue shall swear.

24. Surely, shall one say, in the Lord have I righteousness and strength: even to him shall men come; and all that are incensed against him shall be ashamed.

25. In the LORD shall all the seed of Israel be justified, and shall glory.

It is the Savior of sinners who is speaking here. It is of the utmost importance to realize this clearly. An ordinary mortal has no right to call the entire world to himself. There have been people indeed who wanted to see the whole world kneel at their feet, but none who dared to promise the whole world the salvation of their souls on the condition that they look up to him. That no one else is referred to here but Christ can safely be inferred from Romans 14:11 and Philippians 2:10, and furthermore from the context. However, it is not the Christ of the Old Testament who is speaking here but the one of the future dispensation. This we conclude from the undeniable fact that the actual idea of mission and commission was totally foreign to the Old Covenant and had to be foreign as long as the wall of separation remained intact between Jew and Gentile. The context points in the same direction. Christ invites to Himself the ends of the earth, the furthest nations after He no longer hides Himself, as is the case now, from Israel (v. 15), after the Near-Eastern nations bordering Canaan have already turned to Israel and Him (v. 14), after Israel has been saved with an everlasting salvation (v. 17), and after all idolatry has been abolished. Now in glorious contrast to the gods of the nations who could not save, Christ calls to the still unconverted nations who escaped the judgment (v. 20) to turn to Him. For at the beginning of His kingdom of peace there will still be people living in Europe who have not heard about His judgment and His fame (66:19); it is those faraway nations who are invited by Christ to come to Him and His salvation. Whereas the gods of wood and stone, of science and culture, could not deliver, Christ can, and His willingness is as wide and extensive as His power. He calls all nations, for with Him there is an abundance of grace. Blacks, Indians and whites — they are all equally welcome with Him. The Kaffirs in the kraals of South Africa, the Cossacks on the steppes of Russia, and the cannibals on the islands of the sea are all equally invited. The judgment of the nations will have been terrible in that day, especially among the civilized Christian nations. Millions upon millions will have been struck by the judgments of the seals, the trumpets and the vials of the wrath of the Lamb. Entire areas will have been made desolate and all their inhabitants murdered, but there will also be many millions, especially in heathen lands, who will never have heard of the Savior.

Thus far already three questions have been answered concerning this invitation, i.e., who does the inviting, who are invited and when this invitation is given. Briefly stated, Christ invites the remaining people after the Lord has returned to rebuild the tabernacle of David.

Now let us ask for *what purpose* the nations are invited. The answer is simply their salvation in Christ. This summons presupposes that the nations are living in a state of aversion to rejection and estrangement from God; indeed they live without God and without hope, as there is salvation in none other than Christ. The word translated by *turn ye* (Dutch) means in the first place *to see, to look for, to cast one's eye at,* as the English and other versions usually translate it. There is life in a look. According to some commentators there is an historical allusion here to the brass serpent. But this word also points to the coming of the desired object that was first only glimpsed. It is this kind of coming the Dutch translation has in mind; first we see the desirability and indispensability of the Savior and then we come to Him to be saved. This is why the Savior cries out *be ye saved.* It is a simple way: only a believing look at Him and a coming to Him. Salvation is absolutely free. The Lord does not pose difficult conditions which the nations first have to meet. Salvation is most surely given to anyone who only comes to Him. Finally, we can call this salvation perfect and eternal.

The Lord adds urgent incentives to His kind invitation.

Strictly speaking, *be ye saved* is motivated by self-love. He beseeches them, as it were, to think of the eternal welfare of their souls, for their souls are very precious. The second urgent reason He derives from the excellence of His Person when He says, *I am God, and there is none else.* He is their Maker; they are His possession. All gods had already proved to be worthless; only Christ can save them.

Will the faraway nations heed His call? Today there are thousands of missionaries who call the nations to salvation in Christ, but very few people respond to it. The heathen nations already think much more of Hegel, Darwin and Spencer than of Christ. The nations as a whole do not want Him. They have no place for Him in their schools, temples and council halls. But in that day Christ will not call in vain. He swears an indication of absolute certainty — that unto Him *every knee* shall bow and every tongue shall confess that He is the Lord. They will swear by His name, for they believe in Him as the true and faithful One. Verse twenty-four contains a further elaboration of their confession. The nations will praise His righteousness and power and will joyfully testify that He alone is God and that there is salvation in Him, and that all His enemies will perish. *All the seed of Israel* will be justified in Him (cf. 54:13; Jer. 31:34; 33:8). All the people of the Lord will glorify Him among the nations; hence Israel's destiny as a nation will have been reached. But if every knee in heaven, on earth, and in hell *one day* must bow before Christ, why then should the sinner not gladly do so *now?*

ISAIAH 46

The Gods Are Being Carried, Jehovah Carries Israel

1. Bel boweth down, Nebo stoopeth, their idols were upon the beasts, and upon the battle your carriages were heavy loaden; they are a burden to the weary beast.

2. They stoop, they bow down together; they could not deliver the burden, but themselves are gone into captivity.

3. Hearken unto me, O house of Jacob, and all the remnant of the house of Israel, which are borne by me from the belly, which are carried from the womb:

4. And even to your old age I am he; and even to hoar hairs will I carry you: I have made, and I will bear; even I will carry, and will deliver you.

The contrast in these verses is typically Isaiahic. He gloats over the powerlessness of Babylon's gods, which had been taken down and loaded on beasts of burden, causing them to labor and pant under their heavy load of trash. David Nelson in his valuable book, *Unbelief the Greatest Malady of Our Times,* tells of a man who, upon reading this, cried out, "What nonsense!"; but here we find the most precious truth expressed very forcefully. *Bel* is really the same as Baal and is the Babylonian word for *lord.* Many now identify him with the god Marduk, called Merodach in the Bible. He was one of the chief gods of Babylon, as is indicated by his name. He was represented as a great man, royally garbed with a crown on his head, and with the horns of a bull. Every night large quantities of food and drink were presented to him and it was believed that *Bel* himself consumed everything. But according to the apocryphal book, "Bel and the Dragon," which is added to the book of Daniel in the Septuagint, Daniel at one time had ashes thrown on the temple floor and the next morning they revealed the footsteps of the priests of Bel who during their nightly orgies ate and drank the delicious food and drink of Bel. It is no wonder that the expression "priest's deceit" has become so well known. Like the Egyptian bull, Bel was the symbol of strength, while Nebo, another Babylonian chief deity, was the symbol of wisdom. Since writing was considered the chief wisdom, he was venerated as the god of the art of writing. World power and worldly wisdom are the two greatest, but the only powers the world possesses. The book of Daniel constantly exposes their powerlessness.

Now the prophet beholds by spiritual sight the conquest of Babylon. The mighty *Bel* bows down and the wise god Nebo stoops from his pedestal. The gods, richly adorned with gold, have fallen into the hands of Cyrus' army and the soldiers load them on beasts of burden — asses and camels — and carry them off. But, the gods are so unwieldy and heavy that the animals that carry them toil and pant beneath their burden, and soon bow and stoop down and eventually expire. Hence, the mighty and wise gods were carried off as loot by the Persians. One senses the ridicule Isaiah has again put in this representation. The chief gods of Babylon were so powerless that they had to be carried by the dumbest of animals, such as asses and camels. The mighty Bel could not walk and the wise Nebo could not move. Not only could they not save their worshipers, but they themselves were ignominiously carried away as captives. Therefore let Israel — for that again is the unmentioned conclusion and divine moral lesson — beware never to put her trust in such gods!

The prophet does not only wish to urge the people away from idolatry but also to urge them to cast themselves completely on the Lord. He places the mighty God of Israel over against the powerless idols. They had to be carried by dumb beasts of burden; He bears His children with the tender love of a mother. The contrast could not be stronger. He has, as it were, carried Israel in His womb under His heart. It should not escape our attention that this comforting word is directed to the *remnant*. Frequently the Lord is presented as carrying His people, sometimes like a man, then again like a mother, and often like an eagle carrying its young (Num. 11:12; Deut. 1:31; 32:11, 12; Isa. 40:31). Here it is presented as motherly love that bears the infant. When the child grows up, however, its Mother can no longer carry it, as she is weak or dead, but the mother love of God is totally different. He not only carried His children in the past, but He also bears them today and He will carry them in the future, even in old age and hoary hairs.

This is a very comforting word for the God-fearing remnant. On the one hand it implies that Israel will always remain dependent upon its God like a little child, but on the other hand it implies that His love will never wax cold and His power never diminish. No matter how old and large Israel may become, He will always be able to carry her, for He is not powerless like the gods of Babylon. When Israel was freed from bondage and exile, she was already thirteen hundred years old. The Chaldean empire was not even two centuries old when it fell, and most world dominions lasted only a few centuries. At that time Israel was still in her childhood, for even since that time she has existed for twenty-five centuries. Today she is more numerous and influential than ever. She is also more hopeful with regard to the future than ever before, for while all nations are burdened and bowed down under the load of their mountain-high debts, the Jewish people are still the main money-lenders of the nations, and whereas all nations see their national existence threatened, Israel's chances to become an independent nation are increasing daily.[1] Where lies the secret of Israel's toughness and ineradicable condition? The mighty world dominions of Babylon, Persia, Macedonia, and Rome have come and gone; Israel not only remained standing but even increased in spite of all oppression. The answer is: that strength lies not in Israel. Israel is as weak as a baby; the secret of that strength lies in Jehovah who carries her and will never allow her to fall.

[1] A striking prognosis considering the events of 1948 and after. One must keep in mind that this commentary was written shortly after the end of World War I. —ED.

Idolatry Ridiculed Once More

> 5. To whom will ye liken me, and make me equal, and compare me, that we may be like?
>
> 6. They lavish gold out of the bag, and weigh silver in the balance, and hire a goldsmith; and he maketh it a god: they fall down, yea, they worship.
>
> 7. They bear him upon the shoulder, they carry him, and set him in his place, and he standeth; from his place shall he not remove: yea, one shall cry unto him, yet can he not answer, nor save him out of his trouble.

Some expositors are of the opinion that the prophet is addressing the Babylonians here, but there is no need to think so. He had seen the making of gods from close by in Israel or Judah. For the rest it may be safely assumed that he is speaking to Israel of the Babylonian manufacture of gods. In order to express the height of folly, he again describes the foolishness in seven images. After all the preceding descriptions of idolatry it is not necessary to go into all the details once more. The sparks of his sanctified and Holy Spirit-inspired genius again fly vigorously when he gets to the baseness and foolishness of the manufacture of gods. Once he mentions this subject he just cannot let go of it but feels constrained to depict the whole process of the making and veneration of idol gods in shrill colors. In the light of God's absolute sovereignty and spotless holiness he had to consider the service of idols as vain and base. The same thing is found in Ezekiel. Ezekiel exhausts himself in finding the most derisive names for the idols. No less than seventy times he mentions them with a derisive onomatopoeia of *Elohim – Gelolim,* i.e., dung gods. In essence the same holy anger toward idolatry with both these great prophets, but they differ only in the manner of their attack. Ezekiel concentrates more on the filthiness and detestableness of idolatry; Isaiah constantly depicts the folly, ludicrousness and utter absurdity of it. Ezekiel simply is not such an artist, such a master in descriptive ability and in the holy art of humor and satire. The inspiration of the prophets was not mechanical but organical. The Spirit of God did not violate the natural talents of the men of God but adapted Himself to them. He wished to make use of the satirical genius of Isaiah to exhibit idolatry in all its ludicrousness so that, if the Jews had retained a grain of self-respect, they would loathe every form of idolatry. Finally, his description must have sounded all the more ridiculous in their ears after he had first seen how the gold-covered idols had been carried off in caravans of camels from Babylon to Persia. Beside the ludicrousness he also depicts the useless waste of gold and silver as well as the disappointment that would result from idolatry.

God Calls Cyrus as a Predatory Bird from the East

8. Remember this, and shew yourselves men: bring it again to mind, O ye transgressors.

9. Remember the former things of old: for I am God, and there is none else; I am God, and there is none like me,

10. Declaring the end from the beginning, and from ancient times the things that are not yet done, saying, My counsel shall stand, and I will do all my pleasure:

11. Calling a ravenous bird from the east, the man that executeth my counsel from a far country: yea, I have spoken it, I will also bring it to pass; I have purposed it, I will also do it.

12. Hearken unto me, ye stouthearted, that are far from righteousness:

13. I bring near my righteousness; it shall not be far off, and my salvation shall not tarry: and I will place salvation in Zion for Israel my glory.

After having once more depicted the foolishness of idolatry, the prophet as the mouthpiece of the Lord makes the application. He wants His people to blush with shame at the thought that at times they, too, had practiced idolatry. He wants Israel to contemplate her way and to admit that there is no other God beside Jehovah. Israel must consider her ways with her heart and realize that idolatry and image worship were the main reasons for her exile in Babylon. To show again that God is unique and unchangeably great, He points out His prerogative of being able to infallibly predict future things. This has frequently been pointed out before so it needs no further explanation. In the second place, however, He points out the stedfastness of His *counsel,* His decree. The certainty and wisdom and all-inclusiveness of Jehovah's counsel should also convince Israel to worship and glorify Him as the only true God. The certainty and immutability of God's counsel is a very comforting doctrine to the believing heart. The idols of the nations could be carried away by the enemy at any time, but not so Jehovah. His wise decree concerns all things and nothing on earth or in hell can ever change it. Verse eleven contains a further development of the thought of verse ten. We can conclude from this that prophecy is nothing short of the revelation of His decree concerning the future. Therefore it is very strange, to say it mildly, that many people rave about God's counsel, especially in connection with the silence of eternity, of which we know next to nothing, while they know nothing of and want to have nothing to do with prophecy. God indicates here, however, that His counsel is the foundation of all prophecy and that He wishes us to connect His counsel with the future. Cyrus is called a *ravenous bird,* since he will descend forcefully and swiftly on Babylon to rob its gods and treasures. In the explanatory parallel expression he is called *the man that executeth my counsel.* Christ is *the* Man of God's counsel, Cyrus *a* man of His counsel. Cyrus was included in God's counsel and therefore his name could be accurately mentioned two centuries before his appearance. Those who place this second part of Isaiah after the exile cannot possibly save the honor of God and His prophet. For they assume that the prophets never predicted anything or could predict anything any intelligent statesman or genius could not know or predict equally well. If this were the case we would be forced to brand the prophets as deceivers, for they, and especially Isaiah, stated repeatedly that he predicted future things. By making known the unknown future God Himself lays His honor on the line, so to speak, over against the idols. How then does anyone dare to doubt the miracle of prediction? To the critics it may also be said, "Hearken unto me, ye stouthearted!"

ISAIAH 47

The Great Debasement of Babylon

> 1. Come down, and sit in the dust, O virgin daughter of Babylon, sit on the ground: there is no throne, O daughter of the Chaldeans: for thou shalt no more be called tender and delicate.
> 2. Take the millstones, and grind meal: uncover thy locks, make bare the leg, uncover the thigh, pass over the rivers.
> 3. Thy nakedness shall be uncovered, yea, thy shame shall be seen: I will take vengeance, and I will not meet thee as a man.

After describing Cyrus as predatory eagle, who has swooped down on Babylon and carried away its gods as loot, the prophet now gives a description of the humiliation of Babylon itself. It is presented in the bold image of a rich, frivolous and sensual young woman who, as a prisoner, is doomed to the despicable state of a slave and in every respect is treated like a Near-Eastern slave woman. In his usual plastic way of presentation he cries out to her to take millstones to grind meal. This was hard work; the mill consisted of two large basalt stones of which the lower one was fastened with a pin in the center that reached through a hole in the upper stone so that it could also turn. The grain was poured into the hole around the pin and then dropped on the lower stone and was ground by the turning of the top stone. Because this was heavy work, it was usually done by two women, as in Matthew 24:41. It does not surprise us that it took two women to operate this mill when we realize that millstones at the time of Christ were so heavy that they had to be driven by a donkey. This is why Christ in the Greek said of him who offended the little ones that it would be better for him if an *ass's millstone* were put around his neck and he were drowned in the depths of the sea. Grinding grain and fetching water was the work of women in the Middle East. Hence it was all the more dishonorable for the young men when they were carried off during the destruction of Jerusalem that they had to work the mills, as Jeremiah laments in Lamentations 5:13. The double mourning of Babylon is indicated by the repeated exclamation that it will be sitting in the dust (cf. Josh. 7:6; Job. 2:12; 10:9; Ps. 22:15; Lam. 3:29). That cities were compared to virgin daughters is known from other places as well (1:8; 37:22; cf. Jer. 31:21; 46:11; Lam. 1:15). The assumed reason for this standing metaphor varies, but the most likely one is that a city was usually seen as frivolous and beautiful, lovely and desirable, and thus is fittingly compared to a beautiful young woman. *Uncover thy locks* indicates that her face and loose braids will be unveiled, which was also a shame to a rich Near-Eastern young woman. Next she will gather up her skirts and wade through the rivers whereby her naked parts will be seen by the conquerors who are carrying her away, and who subject her without excuse or respect to the most shameful humiliations. All this would be the *vengeance* of the Lord upon Babylon. The phrase, *I will not meet thee as a man* is translated in many different ways, but the main thought remains the same in all translations — none will turn away the vengeance of the Lord upon Babylon. He will not meet it as a man, not even as Cyrus, but as God, with irresistible power and in holy vengeance without stopping for or sparing anyone. Babylon may be understood not merely in a historical sense but in its apocalyptic meaning. The following verses have great similarity to the description of future Babylon in Revelation seventeen and eighteen.

The Reason for Babylon's Debasement

4. As for our redeemer, the LORD of hosts is his name, the Holy One of Israel.

5. Sit thou silent, and get thee into darkness, O daughter of the Chaldeans: for thou shalt no more be called, the lady of kingdoms.

6. I was wroth with my people, I have polluted mine inheritance, and given them into thine hand: thou didst shew them no mercy; upon the ancient hast thou very heavily laid thy yoke.

The prophet, as the mouthpiece of the entire delivered nation, suddenly breaks into joyful jubilation over Israel's *Gaal,* her Deliverer. This glorious name is constantly applied to Christ, for the word is a reference to Him and not merely to Cyrus except in a foreshadowing, prophetic sense. In Israel a redeemer could free persons or inheritances. Christ will do this too when He frees the children of Israel and their country. A *gaal* had to be a close relative. Christ is this too, for according to His humanity He came forth from the Jews. A *gaal* had to be able to deliver. The Holy One of Israel does not lack this ability. Sometimes a *gaal* had to exercise bloody vengeance. Christ will work bloody vengeance upon Babylon for its oppression of His people. Frequently a *gaal* had to pay a ransom to free a prisoner. The Lord Jesus paid with his blood on Golgotha to ransom His people. On the basis of these considerations, to which could be added many more, it is evident that the name *Gaal* is very fitting for the Savior. According to 59:20 the *Gaal* will come to Zion in connection with the conversion of the remnant. In the form of a command verse five once more points out the mute grief, adversity and the sadness of Babylon. Its silence indicates grief and despair, and walking in *darkness* indicates its calamity. In Isaiah's day Babylon was still queen of the kingdoms, but it will no longer be so. The barbaric treatment of His people Israel is the first and main reason of Babylon's deep fall. God admits that He Himself was very *wroth with,* that He *polluted* His *inheritance,* and that He gave His people *into* the *hand* of Babylon. But that severe punishment did not give Babylon the right to treat His people with outrageous cruelty. Psalm 137 offers a good commentary on this text. The Babylonians did not excuse either sex or venerable old age. Even upon the *ancient* they *heavily* laid their yoke. The metaphor of the yoke is derived from the image of beasts of burden plodding beneath their yoke. According to this statement the Babylonians laid heavy burdens even on the elderly whose strength was already diminishing and who already bowed under the burden of old age. The Medes and Persians never treated the Jews with such inhuman cruelties.

Verse six affords a striking proof of Jehovah's love to

Israel even in His anger. Though He used Babylon as the rod of His anger with His guilty people, He nevertheless did not want her to be treated inhumanly. Jehovah was married to Israel; the relationship was that of a husband and wife. Even though a wife may behave so badly that her husband is very angry with her, he nevertheless does not wish others to mistreat her; his love reawakens, the fire of his anger is kindled, and he defends her against all attackers, striking them in his anger.

Babylon's Pride and Self-Confidence

7. And thou saidst, I shall be a lady for ever: so that thou didst not lay these things to thy heart, neither didst remember the latter end of it.

8. Therefore hear now this, thou that art given to pleasures, that dwellest carelessly, that sayest in thine heart, I am, and none else beside me; I shall not sit as a widow, neither shall I know the loss of children:

9. But these two things shall come to thee in a moment in one day, the loss of children, and widowhood: they shall come upon thee in their perfection for the multitude of thy sorceries, and for the great abundance of thine enchantments.

10. For thou hast trusted in thy wickedness: thou hast said, None seeth me. Thy wisdom and thy knowledge, it hath perverted thee; and thou hast said in thine heart, I am, and none else beside me.

11. Therefore shall evil come upon thee; thou shalt not know from whence it riseth: and mischief shall fall upon thee; thou shalt not be able to put it off: and desolation shall come upon thee suddenly, which thou shalt not know.

Babylon is charged here, as well as in Revelation 18:7, with frivolous pride and self-confidence. Sin has many forms, colors and gradations, but self-glorification is always presented in Scripture as the most dishonoring to God of all sins. Selfishness stays on earth, so to speak, to draw from there everything to itself, but pride storms heaven; it pulls God from His throne and seats itself on it. Pride is the fruit of the satanic whisper: *You will be as God.* Hence we must not seek the real manifestation of sin's wicked nature in man's bestiality, or in his self-dissipation, but in his self-glorification. Man does not want to debase himself but to elevate himself; therefore, God casts him down into the depths of hell. Only regeneration breaks the natural pride of the heart. This hateful pride of heart manifests itself even in the followers of the Lord. It can be seen in the Lord's disciples. For this reason the Savior constantly pointed out self-denial and self-humiliation to them. As though His words were not sufficient, at the end of His mission He gave His disciples an example in the washing of their feet, which they were to follow in a spiritual sense. With this, He gave them a lesson in the deepest self-humiliation.

But the historical Church has quite forgotten this lesson. As soon as the persecutions ceased, there was the greatest jealousy and controversy among the bishops over who was to be the greatest, just as it had existed earlier in the small circle of disciples. One after the other wished to be the greatest and none of them wished to bow before the other, until after a few centuries the pope in Rome set himself up as the visible head of the Church on earth and hence as the first and highest in the circle of disciples. Thereby the bride of Christ became a whore, unfaithful and filthy. She should have looked longingly for His return, but instead she endeavored to make things comfortable here on earth and to manage without Him. As a harlot she did not merely fall, but continued deliberately and frivolously, not with her Bridegroom but loving many strange men and hankering after all the kings of the earth. In her self-satisfaction and frivolous self-deception she says, *I shall be a lady.* She claims royal riches, power and honor for herself *for ever.* A queen feels she must reign, and that was also the Church's goal quite early. Soon it placed a cross on its steeple instead of on its shoulders. With all its veneration of the cross, it hated the cross in a spiritual sense and reached for the crown of the world. With precious sarcasm God says, *neither didst remember the latter end of it.*

It is always wise to keep the end of the road in mind, but it is folly to disregard the end and not to take the things of God to heart. It is a significant characterization when it is said of the lustful and self-confident Babylonian woman that she did not *lay* these divine things to *heart,* but on the other hand *said* in her *heart, I am, and none else beside me; I shall not sit as a widow, neither shall I know the loss of children.*

Her heart was turned aside and therefore she did wicked things. A *widow* has lost her support and in Scripture therefore is the standard image of defenselessness, poverty and loneliness. For that reason the Lord, who is especially concerned about the weak, considers it a crying sin to oppress widows. Neither historic nor future Babylon wants to be weak, poor and lonely. Both brag about their husband and children. In Scriptural language, a country is called a *widow* when it loses its kings, and *childless* when it loses its inhabitants.

In answer to her proud boasting the Lord says that both widowhood and childlessness will suddenly come upon her in one day. This has already been fulfilled initially as Daniel 5:30 indicates. Other sins as further causes of Babylon's fall are mentioned: (a) *enchantments* and *sorceries,* words that do not merely indicate superstition, but point to black art and remind us of today's spiritism; (b) trusting in *wickedness,* which most likely refers to the crafty politics and diplomacy of Babylon; (c) *None seeth me,* she said, which depicts her unscrupulousness — she thought that no one could check her hapless statesmanship or challenge it; (d) her *wisdom* and *knowledge* have perverted her, which reminds us of Paul's statement in I Corinthians 1:21 that the world did not know God by reason of its wisdom. Nebuchadnezzar and Belshazzar were alas not the only ones who trusted in it and put to shame. Today, too, we can safely write above most school entrances: *Thy wisdom and thy knowledge, it hath perverted thee.* These are undoubtedly two great powers, but outside of Christ they are terrible and corrupting forces; (e) finally the self-deification of Babylon is pointed out once more. The words *I am, and none else beside me* are the same words Jehovah uttered frequently about Himself.

Because of all these abominations Babylon's destruction is once again announced as totally unexpected, unforeseen, irrevocable and complete.

Babylon's Wise Men Mocked

12. Stand now with thine enchantments, and with the multitude of thy sorceries, wherein thou hast laboured from thy youth; if so be thou shalt be able to profit, if so be thou mayest prevail.

13. Thou art wearied in the multitude of thy counsels. Let now the astrologers, the stargazers, the monthly prognosticators, stand up, and save thee from these things that shall come upon thee.

14. Behold, they shall be as stubble; the fire shall burn them; they shall not deliver themselves from the power of the flame; there shall not be a coal to warm at, nor fire to sit before it.

15. Thus shall they be unto thee with whom thou hast laboured, even thy merchants, from thy youth: they shall wander every one to his quarter; none shall save thee.

No nation was more superstitious than Babylon. According to Daniel the country was filled with all kinds of diviners and interpreters of dreams. Now the prophet summons this horde of worldly wise men to appear with their arts of divination and magic. He challenges them to convoke all wise men and gather together all the arts of wisdom and do everything possible to save Babylon from its destruction. This description certainly refers back to the last part of verse three, where God already assured that no one could resist Him in His taking vengeance on Babylon. Now let those proud diviners attempt to do so! He challenges them to it. Mockingly the prophet cries out that possibly they might succeed. The foolishness of worldly wisdom deserves nothing but ridicule. These worldly wise men are exhausted from their counseling and predicting, and it is necessary for another group of wise men to undertake this task. God had foretold that the city would be suddenly overtaken and destroyed; now let them search the heavens and the stars, looking at new moons, till when this would take place; they might prevent the threatened destruction of the city by advising the necessary precautions in advance.

But far from supplying the city with a means of escape by their predictions, they will not even be able to save themselves from the power of the flames. They themselves will become as stubble or chaff when the fire of God's wrath kindles them. And in satire they are compared to a little fire that spreads absolutely no heat and is insufficient for warmth. Chaff and stubble make poor fuel and provide no heat. Even in the fire they are worthless as fuel. This is the way Calvin and others explain the last part of verse fourteen; but it seems preferable to us to understand it as part of the satirical style of Isaiah as a pointed and provocative figure of minimization and denial, and that in his crushing satire he means exactly the opposite of what he says. Hence, the meaning is that the burning of all those wise men of Babylon will not be a small sputtering fire in a hearth where one wants to warm himself, but a boundless sea of fire that consumes anyone who would dare to get near it. It is not only the wise men of Babylon who cannot save the city; neither can the merchants with whom it traded from its early days. They are presented in the last verse as those who are wandering about helplessly (cf. Revelation 18:11-23). This final verse is one more proof that we must not take the concept of Babylon merely in its historical sense but also at the same time in its apocalyptic meaning, something which very few expositors have done thus far.

ISAIAH 48

God Complains About the Jews' Despising Prophecy

1. Hear ye this, O house of Jacob, which are called by the name of Israel, and are come forth out of the waters of Judah, which swear by the name of the LORD, and make mention of the God of Israel, but not in truth, nor in righteousness.

2. For they call themselves of the holy city, and stay themselves upon the God of Israel; the LORD of hosts is his name.

3. I have declared the former things from the beginning; and they went forth out of my mouth, and I shewed them; I did them suddenly, and they came to pass.

4. Because I knew that thou art obstinate, and thy neck is an iron sinew, and thy brow brass;

5. I have even from the beginning declared it to thee; before it came to pass I shewed it thee: lest thou shouldest say, Mine idol hath done them, and my graven image, and my molten image, hath commanded them.

6. Thou hast heard, see all this; and will not ye declare it? I have shewed thee new things from this time, even hidden things, and thou didst not know them.

7. They are created now, and not from the beginning; even before the day when thou heardest them not; lest thou shouldest say, Behold, I knew them.

8. Yea, thou heardest not; yea, thou knewest not; yea, from that time that thine ear was not opened: for I knew that thou wouldest deal very treacherously, and wast called a transgressor from the womb.

We must visualize the people of Israel and Judah, who are addressed here by the prophet, as being in exile. In verse eighteen this is clearly presupposed and in verse twenty even more so. A series of sins is enumerated as the reason why Israel was carried away to Babylon and of these sins the rejection of the prophetic words was the most serious and most common. Israel is addressed in a solemn manner with three names, which are intended to remind Israel of her humble and yet very gracious origin. The name *Israel* means warrior, conqueror of God. The progenitor of a people is often compared to a fountainhead and his descendants with a brook that originated from this source; hence the remarkable expression *out of the waters of Judah,* as *Judah* was the progenitor of the kingdom of Judah (cf. Num. 24:6, 7; Deut. 33:28; Ps. 68:26). The people are described as religious, even rather orthodox, but at the same time as untrue and lacking in righteousness. The word *swear* sometimes stands for all of religion, as in Jeremiah 4:2. God simply did not care about all this religion if the heart was not upright and pure before Him — a principle that is equally true today. He still hates all lip-service when the heart is far from Him. With a hint of sarcasm the prophet says of the strict orthodox and hypocritical people that they call themselves the *holy* city and ostensibly trust in the strong Jehovah Sabaoth. When in danger, they soothed their fears by hollow phrases: "our strong God will surely take care of His poor people"; it all sounds very pious in the ears of one who sees no farther than the surface.

Further on the prophet gives an answer to the questions why God so frequently refers to deliverance from exile. It is because Israel is so *obstinate,* and has a neck as an *iron sinew* and a forehead of *brass.* He knew Israel's stiff-necked condition, and lest Israel should give the honor of her deliverance to idols, He foretold them of this deliverance long before hand. It is clear that here already Jehovah complains about Israel's hardness of heart toward the prophetic word. During the Savior's sojourn on earth this hardness was no better for He had to chide His followers with these harsh words, "O fools, and slow of heart to believe all that the prophets have spoken!" (Luke 24:25). We wish there were no occasion for a similar rebuke today! There would be every reason to expect that the Church, which has the entire Word, possesses the Spirit and has the many rich lessons of literally fulfilled prophecy before its eyes, would appreciate the prophetic word; but it ignores, despises and falsifies it. Even many upright pious people have not opened their ears to the voice of prophecy.

Israel Owes Her Deliverance Only to God

> 9. For my name's sake will I defer mine anger, and for my praise will I refrain for thee, that I cut thee not off.
>
> 10. Behold, I have refined thee, but not with silver; I have chosen thee in the furnace of affliction.
>
> 11. For mine own sake, even for mine own sake, will I do it: for how should my name be polluted? and I will not give my glory unto another.

These words are extremely serious and rich in instruction concerning the doctrine of free grace. The expressions *my name, my praise, for mine own sake, even for mine own sake* and *my glory* strongly express that God did not deliver Israel for something that was found in Israel, but only for the glory of His great name. He did not let go of Israel since His own honor was involved. For He Himself had called and chosen Israel to be His own people. He had united Himself forever to her with a covenant, while forecasting a glorious future with His rich promises. If God were to destroy Israel He would first have to negate His own acts, attributes and words; in short, cross out His own holy essence and being, something which is absolutely unthinkable. He cannot deny Himself. If the Lord were to deal with Israel only according to what she deserved, then He truly would not *refrain* Himself; He could not contain Himself from destroying Israel with one blow. For this reason Satan does not cease to point at her filthy clothing, but He who chooses Jerusalem rebukes Satan, not His people. He will not be wroth with them (54:9). He does not behold iniquity in Jacob, neither perverseness in Israel (Num. 23:21). He continues, notwithstanding the sins of His people, to call them His *Jeshurun, My little one, My upright darling,* and says, *Surely, they are my people, children that will not lie* (63:8). He *refines* His people, as the silversmith does his silver, for His people contain many ignoble elements. All the trials He sends His people are meant as purifications. The words *but not with silver* have been translated and explained in many different ways, but the meaning seems simply to be that when God refined and tested Israel in the crucible of misery, He found no silver but foam and dross. In the past Israel's trials never resulted in a lasting improvement.

It will never be well with Israel as a nation until the joyful sound of the King is ever present in her midst.

Once again Jehovah strongly indicates that His honor will never suffer Israel to perish. For He would, if He annihilated Israel, be polluted, desecrated and blasphemed. The nations and Satan and all of hell would derisively jeer, ha! ha!, and cry out and say, "He could not save His people!" To give His honor to others is something He will never do. He formed Israel to publish His praise and His honor among the nations; to cast away Israel would be to cast away His own honor. But how can those preachers save the honor of the Lord who teach that Israel as a nation has been rejected and has had her day? They will never succeed. If they were to be consistent in their hapless teaching nothing would remain of God's Word nor of His honor and faithfulness.

Christ Addressed

12. Hearken unto me, O Jacob and Israel, my called; I am he; I am the first, I also am the last.

13. Mine hand also hath laid the foundation of the earth, and my right hand hath spanned the heavens: when I call unto them, they stand up together.

14. All ye, assemble yourselves, and hear; which among them hath declared these things? The LORD hath loved him: he will do his pleasure on Babylon, and his arm shall be on the Chaldeans.

15. I, even I, have spoken; yea, I have called him: I have brought him, and he shall make his way prosperous.

16. Come ye near unto me, hear ye this; I have not spoken in secret from the beginning; from the time that it was, there am I: and now the Lord GOD, and his Spirit, hath sent me.

This chapter can be divided into three parts. Israel's journey to Babylon, her stay in Babylon and her exodus from Babylon are its three main topics; the prophet makes a solomn prediction of Israel's deliverance from Babylon with yet another appeal to the Lord's prophetic ability. We have come across verses twelve and thirteen more than once before; they point out God's incomparable greatness and close connection with Israel. Nor is the reference to His predictions strange to us. The question here, however, is who it is of whom the Lord says, *I have loved him*. Most commentators think of Cyrus exclusively; we, too, feel certain that this statement refers first of all to Cyrus. But it need not be inferred from this that Cyrus was an upright and sincere child of God; what must be inferred is that God loved this conqueror as the suitable instrument of His vengeance on Babylon and His mercy on Israel. The following verse also refers to Cyrus.

We feel equally certain, however, that Cyrus must be viewed as the example and type of Christ to whom the Father more than once declared His love. "The Father loveth the Son, and hath given all things into his hand," John the Baptist said to his disciples (John 3:35). One day He will carry out the Father's good pleasure against apocalyptic Babylon, the false church that became unfaithful to Him. He is *the* Anointed of the Father; Cyrus is only *an* anointed one.

The opinion that the speaker in verse sixteen is Isaiah is definitely wrong. According to many expositors Isaiah is referring to earlier predictions which he had made publicly, as well as to their prompt fulfillment, and to his divine commission and inspiration. But the presentation is far too majestic to apply to Isaiah; the words are too strongly reminiscent of Messiah's words elsewhere to exclude Him here. He speaks as Wisdom personified (cf. Prov. 8:23-32). The words *I have not spoken in secret* refer elsewhere to the Messiah (45:19; John 18:20) as do the words *the Lord God, and his Spirit, hath sent me* (61:1; John 3:34; 5:24; 6:44, 57; 7:16; 8:42; 17:18; 20:21). Many older expositors correctly saw here a proof for the holy Trinity. As far as the form is concerned, however, it is not clear whether the Holy Spirit is said to have also sent Christ or to have been sent together with the Messiah. Both are true and hence we may speak here, as the ancient expositors used to do in such cases, of a holy ambiguity.

Those expositors who apply these words to Isaiah himself as a type of Christ are not advocating an unreasonable explanation, for it can be said that Isaiah too is a type of Christ. But we must not think of Isaiah first, but of Christ, and secondly of the seer.

Israel's Happiness is Found in Her Obedience to God's Word

> 17. Thus saith the LORD, thy Redeemer, the Holy One of Israel; I am the LORD thy God which teacheth thee to profit, which leadeth thee by the way that thou shouldest go.
> 18. O that thou hadst hearkened to my commandments! then had thy peace been as a river, and thy righteousness as the waves of the sea:
> 19. Thy seed also had been as the sand, and the offspring of thy bowels like the gravel thereof; his name should not have been cut off nor destroyed from before me.

In the days of Isaiah there were more than enough teachers. But most of them taught Israel things that profited them nothing. In our day it is not any different. How many men and women teachers there are! Taking their great number in consideration, the earth should be full of the knowledge of the Lord; but the situation is quite otherwise — the earth is covered everywhere with the thickest darkness of ignorance. Dr. W. Pierson rightly complained in the *Christian Advocate* concerning the student community that they enter high school as Christians and leave it as atheists — a complaint that is no less applicable to theological schools.

The *Gaal* as the Supreme Wisdom teaches what is *profitable,* yet it is exactly this Teacher who is not wanted. So there is general ignorance and foolishness. He alone *leadeth in the way* Israel, and every person, must go. He Himself is the Way, the Truth and the Life. Israel, however, did not want Him and chose death instead of life; she was sent into an exile which has lasted not merely seventy years, but over twenty-five hundred years. For Israel has never been fully delivered from her exile. This long exile and wandering amidst the nations is presupposed in verse eighteen. The Messiah expresses here a heartrending lament about Israel's rejection of His teaching and guidance. What fearful results this disobedience to His commandments has had for Israel! How well it would have been with Israel if she had listened to the Lord's commandments! She would have had *peace as a river,* — a peace deep, wide and constant that would have permeated the whole nation. The people would also have had a *righteousness* like the waves of the sea; this metaphor refers to the deep, wide and lasting happiness of the people. We must not merely think of the righteousness of Christ merited by His blood but of the righteousness and peace He will establish on earth in the great day of His coming. *Righteousness* and *peace* are the stereotype characteristics of the Messianic Kingdom of Peace (11:1-6; 32:1, 17; Ps. 72; 85:10). It is the continuous teaching of Scripture that as soon as Israel is an absolutely obedient nation the Kingdom of Peace will be ushered in. The Lord's repeated complaints about Israel's disobedience again and again point out the great state of happiness Israel would have obtained in the way of faith and obedience (Deut. 32:19-31; I Sam. 12:20-25; Ps. 81:13-16; Luke 13:34, 35). The covenant promise that it would become a very numerous nation, like unto the sand and the gravel of the sea, would have been fulfilled. Israel would never have been cut off as an independent nation but would have stood before His face as a priestly kingdom and the pride of the nations (cf. I Kings 11:36; Jer. 33). *Walk before my face,* God said, when the covenant was made, but Israel never did so and consequently God destroyed the nation from before His countenance. This grieved His Father's heart, however, as we may conclude from this touching lament.

Prophecy Concerning the Deliverance from Babylon

20. Go ye forth of Babylon, flee ye from the Chaldeans, with a voice of singing declare ye, tell this, utter it even to the end of the earth; say ye, The LORD hath redeemed his servant Jacob.

21. And they thirsted not when he led them through the deserts: he caused the waters to flow out of the rock for them: he clave the rock also, and the waters gushed out.

22. There is no peace, saith the LORD, unto the wicked.

Here, as elsewhere, the command is at the same time a very certain prediction. Almost all commentators simply take this section as a reference to Israel's return from her seventy-year exile. But no matter how gladly we agree that this prophecy then received a partial fulfillment, the complete fulfillment is not found in that return, for at that time no more than a remnant returned. Israel did not become a free nation; according to the word of Nehemiah they remained *servants.* Nor was there a *shouting for joy* but *weeping* and *great distress* (Neh. 9:36, 37). This return of about forty thousand Jews under Zerubbabel was not published and heard *to the end of the earth*. No, His *servant Jacob* was not fully delivered then – not delivered from Satan, sin and sickness, nor from care, and not even from the ungodly world powers. Some take verse twenty-one as a reference to the exodus from Egypt, others as the one from Babylon; it refers to the great miracles of deliverance and the blessings of Israel's future when the past wonders will be magnified and multiplied.

There is no peace unto the wicked, this prophecy concludes. This verse refers back to verse eighteen, where peace is made absolutely dependent upon hearkening to God's Word. This disobedience does not cancel out God's faithfulness; He will not abandon Israel, but give her complete deliverance. But this does not alter the fact that the wicked, who have trodden His covenant under foot, will not enjoy His *peace*. The concept *shalom,* peace, means more in the original than in its translation. According to Jewish sentiment it contained the ideas of happiness, prosperity, well-being. All these concepts would one day be embodied in the Messiah. The angels sang of this peace in the fields of Ephratah, and the Apostle testified of Christ, "He is our peace." He came to this earth with thoughts, words and works of peace. He bore the chastisement that we might have peace. Shortly before His departure He blessed His disciples with peace, saying, "Peace I leave with you, my peace I give unto you: not as the world giveth, give I unto you." The Godless ones are those who according to the meaning of that word are *loose* from God and not united by the Mediator to Him. Hence, they cannot share in the Messianic peace obtained by the blood of the cross. Those who live in obedience but outside the Messiah may have a false peace such as the world gives, but they do not have the peace of a good conscience nor the peace of the Messianic Kingdom of Peace which will be peace in abundance. On the contrary, these Godless ones will be exterminated before the Kingdom of Peace is established by Christ. With this somber word, so ominous to the disobedient, ends the first subdivision of the second main part of Isaiah.

ISAIAH 49

Christ's Humiliation and Exaltation

1. Listen, O isles, unto me; and hearken, ye people, from far; The LORD hath called me from the womb; from the bowels of my mother hath he made mention of my name.

2. And he hath made my mouth like a sharp sword; in the shadow of his hand hath he hid me, and made me a polished shaft; in his quiver hath he hid me;

3. And said unto me, Thou art my servant, O Israel, in whom I will be glorified.

4. Then I said, I have laboured in vain, I have spent my strength for nought, and in vain: yet surely my judgment is with the LORD, and my work with my God.

5. And now, saith the LORD that formed me from the womb to be his servant, to bring Jacob again to him, Though Israel be not gathered, yet shall I be glorious in the eyes of the LORD, and my God shall be my strength.

6. And he said, It is a light thing that thou shouldest be my servant to raise up the tribes of Jacob, and to restore the preserved of Israel: I will also give thee for a light to the Gentiles, that thou mayest be my salvation unto the end of the earth.

7. Thus saith the LORD, the Redeemer of Israel, and His Holy One, to him whom man despiseth, to him whom the nation abhorreth, to a servant of rulers, Kings shall see and arise, princes also shall worship, because of the LORD that is faithful, and the Holy One of Israel, and he shall choose thee.

These verses are a further explanation of the statement of the Messiah in 48:16, *The Lord God, and his Spirit, hath sent me.* From here on the prophet will speak increasingly about Christ and His work. He no longer speaks of Cyrus, neither does he any longer mention the power of Jehovah to predict infallibly the future, nor does he from now on fulminate with cutting ridicule against the idols of nations. It seems that Christ and His humiliation and exaltation occupy his soul to such an extent that he loses sight of all else. It is true, that earlier he frequently pointed at Christ as the servant of the Lord (41:8-10; 42:1-9; 18-22; 43:10; 44:1-5, 21-28; 45:4; 48:16-22), but from now on he is going to deal with Him much more extensively and particularly as the Servant of the Lord that will be rejected by Israel and through humiliation and suffering obtain glorification.

From the foregoing it is already evident that we view this Servant as no one else but Christ Jesus. The only difficulty with this viewpoint lies in verse three, where it says, *Thou art my servant, O Israel.* The most widely accepted viewpoint today, that of nearly all the critics, is that Israel is that servant and for proof they appeal especially to this verse. But in verse five, the servant is clearly distinguished from Israel, and also in verses six and seven. Scofield in his annotated Bible has a footnote that solves the apparently insoluble difficulty. He says, "The Lord Jesus and the believing remnant of Israel are here joined. What is said is true of both." Christ alone is fully *Israel,* i.e., God's conqueror, the strong Warrior who conquers all the powers of Satan and Hell. So we find here something similar to the preceding chapters where Cyrus was *an* anointed of the Lord, while Christ is *the* Anointed. Hence, all that was said of the former could be taken in a much broader sense of Him, so that all that was said of either one applies to some extent to both. In the first verse, the calling *from the womb* applies equally to Sarah's as well as to Mary's miraculous conception. Also it applies to the *worm Jacob* whom God protected under the shadow of His hand. This is why throughout the rolling ages the nations have never been able to trample this worm to death. What is being said of the *mouth* of the servant, however, fits the mouth of the Lord far better (cf. Rev. 1:16; 2:16; 19:15, 21). The metaphor of the *polished shaft* (Dutch: *pure arrow),* a sharpened or split arrow must also be taken as a sign of His irresistible and effective power in the day of His battle against His enemies. We may call the prophets "arrows" because of their power with the words of God, but He is the *pure* (polished) arrow. Before His incarnation He was in the bosom of the Father, *hid in His quiver.*

God's Warrior, therefore, was well qualified for the battle.

Moreover He did not have to work aimlessly, since the Father desired to be *glorified* by Him (cf. John 17:1, 4).

The form of these verses is a dialog. After the Father has made known His objective to be glorified by His Servant, the latter answers that as far as His mission is concerned He was made to labor in vain and that He was made to waste and fritter away His strength. Viewed from the human standpoint and according to His human feelings, this was very much the case during the time of His humiliation. For did He not come to His own, and they did not receive Him? He wept and lamented loudly over the hardness of Jerusalem which refused to be gathered together underneath His protective wings. When He was taken prisoner as an evildoer all His disciples fled. Of one thing He was very sure, however: His *judgment* was with the Lord and His *strength* with His God. Judgment must be taken in the sense of a trial in which the Father will avenge the right of His Son over against His attackers and rejecters. Keeping this in mind, Christ, "when He was reviled, reviled not again and when He suffered He threatened not; but committed himself to him that judgeth *righteously."* The reward of His labor is the reward the Father gave Him upon the travail of His soul (Phil. 2:9).

In verse five the Father speaks again and says that in reality Christ's mission was not a failure, but on the contrary, God's set purpose will be fulfilled by Him. He glorified the Father, and The Father will glorify Him according to the desire of His heart (John 17:1). Christ was primarily sent to and in behalf of Israel. All His personal labor was only for the benefit of Israel. The Canaanite woman for example had difficulty when she asked Him to cure her daughter, who was not a Jewess. But if Israel refused to be brought back to God by Him and refused to be gathered underneath His wings, He would nevertheless be *glorified.* Whoever wishes to see the fulfillment of this prophecy, let him go to the Mount of Olives where He ascended forty days after His resurrection, leaving Israel behind in the slime of sin and as featherless chicks soon to be overtaken by the Roman eagles. Heaven *had* to receive Him, the same heaven which a few days earlier had hid its face from Him. In verse six, the Father gives Him the comforting assurance that He will not restore Israel alone

but that He will be a Light unto the Gentiles and will bring
salvation to the ends of the earth. Strikingly, the rejected
Messiah is called *him whom man despiseth, him whom the*
nation (Israel) *abhorreth.* The people of Israel still abhor the
name of Jesus. They despise Him in this dispensation; they
consider Him an infamous person, a slave, and a malefactor.
But one day the roles will be turned. Even kings will bow
before Him.

One Day Christ Will Restore Israel

8. Thus saith the LORD, In an acceptable time have I heard
thee, and in a day of salvation have I helped thee: and I will
preserve thee, and give thee for a covenant of the people, to
establish the earth, to cause to inherit the desolate heritages;
9. That thou mayest say to the prisoners, Go forth; to them
that are in darkness, Shew yourselves. They shall feed in the
ways, and their pastures shall be in all high places.
10. They shall not hunger nor thirst; neither shall the heat nor
sun smite them: for he that hath mercy on them shall lead them,
even by the springs of water shall he guide them.
11. And I will make all my mountains a way, and my
highways shall be exalted.
12. Behold, these shall come from far: and, lo, these from the
north and from the west; and these from the land of Sinim.
13. Sing, O heavens; and be joyful, O earth; and break forth
into singing, O mountains: for the LORD hath comforted his
people, and will have mercy upon his afflicted.

These verses contain a beautiful description of Israel's
complete restoration by our Lord Jesus Christ. In contrast
with the rejecters of the Servant, the Father says that He
hears, helps and *preserves* Him from the raging of hell. On the
expression *covenant of the people,* see 42:6. To establish
the earth is the same as the restitution of all things of which
all prophets have spoken according to Peter's statement in
Acts 3:21. The language here is derived from a country that
has been destroyed and trampled down by an enemy. The
earth is a country that has been trampled down and trodden
under foot by the devil and his henchmen. Until the present
day everything is still beaten down by sin and the prince of
this world. According to God's promise, however, Christ will
come to bind the devil for a thousand years, to destroy the

sinners that corrupt His world and to restore all that has been destroyed and make it into an inheritance. Christ has come, and will come, to destroy all the works of the devil. This *Gaal* will not rest until He will have established a new heaven and a new earth.

Closely related to this restitution of all things, indeed, as the first condition of it, He will free shackled Israel. In verse nine the Israelites are presented as prisoners held in deep, dark, subterranean holes. He breaks their shackles and makes them come forth into the light of His grace. In the middle of the verse the image suddenly changes; those who just before sighed in dark holes are compared to a flock of sheep whose Shepherd is the Messiah. As their Shepherd He goes before the flock and looks for the lushest pasture for them. Neither hunger nor thirst vexes them, nor unbearable heat or burning sun, because their Shepherd is so rich in mercy that He has the right to be called *He that hath mercy.* He remembers the nursing mother sheep as well as the tender lamb. He knows and chooses the way and clears a path by removing all obstacles. For the sake of the weak, the sick, and the nursing He leads His flock quietly to the still, pure stream of water. This Shepherd gathers His flock from all the corners of the earth, even from the land of *Sinim,* which as with many older and more recent expositors, may appropriately be taken to mean China; for even there Jews were found two centuries before Christ. Thus Christ will one day restore Israel!

When this glad event of salvation will take place, the entire creation will break forth into jubilation (v. 13). This presentation is more than mere poetic imagery. Creation will be given new glory; its centuries-long sighing and weeping will give way to festive singing. According to Paul's description in Romans 8:19-23 creation looks forward with great longing (cf. also on 42:10, 11; 44:23). When we believingly accept these comforting truths we can already shout for joy in the midst of the sorrows of life.

Zion's Lament of Unbelief

14. But Zion said, the LORD hath forsaken me, and my Lord hath forgotten me.

15. Can a woman forget her sucking child, that she should not have compassion on the son of her womb? yea, they may forget, yet will I not forget thee.

16. Behold, I have graven thee upon the palms of my hands; thy walls are continually before me.

17. Thy children shall make haste; thy destroyers and they that made thee waste shall go forth of thee.

In sharp contrast with the jubilation of the entire creation is this doleful lament of Zion. Zion must still be viewed as being in exile, for as every student of Scripture knows, Zion is the stereotype metaphor for Israel. When the glad tiding of deliverance is preached to the imprisoned people, they do not believe this message, but lament pitifully that Jehovah has forsaken and forgotten them. Already for many centuries this has been indeed the fearful complaint of many orthodox Jews. If this were so, it would be terrible indeed for Israel and for us, and for all nations, plus the entire creation as Israel's sins are worthy of God forsaking them a thousand times over, but, thanks be to God, Christ has been forsaken by God for Israel, so that Israel cannot be forsaken forever.

The Lord gives Zion a comforting answer in the form of a question derived from life with all its variations. *Can a woman forget her sucking child?* A mother does not do this easily. Even a she-bear and a tigress take tender care of their young. There are at times degenerated mothers who leave their children and even forget and murder them. We need only to think of the drowning of little girls in China, the feeding of little ones to crocodiles in India in former days, the throwing of little ones under the wheels of Juggernaut, the sacrificing of children to the fire god Moloch, the abandoning of newly born infants and the many divorces in our day, which all too often fulfills the Scriptural prediction that men will be *without natural love.* This becomes daily and increasingly a sign of the times. But regardless how much natural love may decline so that the possibility of mothers forsaking their children becomes more and more a fearful reality, Jehovah will not forsake Zion. His love does not wax cold as time moves on.

He cannot forget Israel, for, *behold,* He has *graven* them upon *both palms of His hands.* This metaphor is derived from the contemporary custom of tatooing, though forbidden in the law it serves here as a comparison; Paul also frequently derived his images from heathen games and customs. The image means that God keeps Israel in lasting remembrance, for whichever hand He lifts, He sees the name of His people. *Thy walls are continually before me* proves that we are to think of Israel and not of the Church, for only Israel has walls that lie in ruins. "His servants take pleasure in her stones, and favour the dust thereof" (Ps. 102:14); no less does God Himself. His eyes are continually upon Israel's land and cities. Zion's sons will hasten to Canaan once more, but her *destroyers* and *wasters* will be banished forever. The Lord has spoken clear words of comfort, but does Zion and the Church believe these words?

Israel's Great Future Happiness

18. Lift up thine eyes round about, and behold: all these gather themselves together, and come to thee. As I live, saith the LORD, thou shalt surely clothe thee with them all, as with an ornament, and bind them on thee, as a bride doeth.

19. For thy waste and thy desolate places, and the land of thy destruction, shall even now be too narrow by reason of the inhabitants, and they that swallowed thee up shall be far away.

20. The children which thou shalt have, after thou hast lost the other, shall say again in thine ears, The place is too strait for me: give place to me that I may dwell.

21. Then shalt thou say in thine heart, Who hath begotten me these, seeing I have lost my children, and am desolate, a captive, and removing to and fro? and who hath brought up these? Behold, I was left alone; these, where had they been?

22. Thus saith the Lord GOD, Behold, I will lift up mine hand to the Gentiles, and set up my standard to the people: and they shall bring thy sons in their arms, and thy daughters shall be carried upon their shoulders.

23. And kings shall be thy nursing fathers, and their queens thy nursing mothers: they shall bow down to thee with their face toward the earth, and lick up the dust of thy feet; and thou shalt know that I am the LORD: for they shall not be ashamed that wait for me.

Here Zion is addressed and urged to lift its eyes to the children who come streaming in. It was always very desirable for a Near-Eastern woman to have many children. Her children were her adornment and her jewels. Hence, it is quite in keeping with Near-Eastern custom when Zion is urged to clothe itself with the children who are approaching her as with an ornament, a bridal dress. The number of her sons will be so great that the land will become too small, while on the other hand the destroyers of Israel's land will depart far away. Zion's sons will say, *The place is too strait for me;* give me some elbow room. It certainly needs no argument that this has never happened in the past but will only happen in connection with the future coming of the Lord. It will be an amazing situation when this rapid increase of population takes place after such a long period of destruction and oppression. Zion is depicted as a lonesome and forsaken mother who is thought to be deprived of children and now suddenly sees a great multitude of children around her; for this reason she contemplates in her heart and wonders who brought forth and brought up all these children, whom she does not know. She thought she was left alone in prison and slavery; from where do all these children come?

In verse twenty-two God gives the answer to Zion's question. He says that He will *lift up His hand,* i.e., command, give orders, as a general in this connection, *and set up* the *standard* in the sight of all the nations. This *standard* is no one else but Christ, as we can deduce from 11:10; 12; 18:3. All nations will flow to Christ, first in hatred in the battle of Armageddon, but after that with the desire to be blessed by Him. As a result of the planted standard — the returned Christ — the nations will bring Zion's *sons and daughters* — the Jews — to Jerusalem. Whoever does not believe this needs to explain why in the past Egypt begged Israel, loaded down with presents, to leave the country. Surely, something similar and on a much greater scale could take place? For Israel is still alive, Israel's God is still living and the nations in whose midst Israel lives still exist. Not only will Israel be taken back to the land of promise, but she will obtain such great honor there that the kings of the earth will be her *nursing fathers,* her stepfathers, and queens will be her *nursing mothers.* Calvin and most expositors believe that the text teaches that one day the greatest in the nation will love and care for the children of the Church. This text has usually been made to serve as proof of the legitimacy of the church state (or state church); however, the prophet does not have the Church in mind here, but future Israel. The Church will find no glory, but only oppression, in the world. *Lick up the dust of thy feet* refers to the great honor which the great ones of the world will give Israel. It is mainly on the basis of this phrase that there is the practice of kissing the pope's feet.

The Downfall of Satan, Israel's Greatest Adversary

24. Shall the prey be taken from the mighty, or the lawful captive delivered?

25. But thus saith the LORD, Even the captives of the mighty shall be taken away, and the prey of the terrible shall be delivered: for I will contend with him that contendeth with thee, and I will save thy children.

26. And I will feed them that oppress thee with their own flesh; and they shall be drunken with their own blood, as with sweet wine: and all flesh shall know that I the LORD am thy Saviour and thy Redeemer, the mighty One of Jacob.

By comparing verse twenty-four with Matthew 12:29, Luke 11:21, Hebrews 2:14 and I Corinthians 15:57, it is clear that this section speaks of the victory over the terrible enemy of Israel, the devil, by the Righteous One, Christ. Israel is presented here as the *prey,* the captive, of Satan. Satan is the prince of this world who not only deceives and blinds all nations but also and particularly keeps Israel as his captive. Again nearly all expositors miss the point, as they do not see the close connection between Satan's downfall and Israel's restoration. Israel is depicted here as enjoying a prosperity she never had in the past as a result of the shutting up of Satan in the abyss. Only when the nations are no longer deceived and blinded by the prince of the world can the great ones of this earth be the nurses and nursing mothers and fathers of Israel. That is why this section on the downfall of the devil very naturally follows the preceding one which described Israel's great deliverance and glory. Satan is the strong one and here is called the mighty, the terrible, the vehement one, since he as the great head of his band of robbers has in fact all of Israel and the entire world, and even the corpses of believers in his power, for his is the power of death. Who is stronger than he who can penetrate the fortress of this head of a band of robbers and take away his *vessels,* his armor and prey? No one else is capable of doing this but our Lord Jesus Christ. He will come again to destroy the works of the devil and to capture Satan as the arch-criminal, to bind him and to lock him up in an impenetrable prison (Rev. 20:1-10). In that day the Lord Jesus will contend with the *contenders,* the anti-Semitic nations. This will take place in the battle of Armageddon and of Gog's hordes.

I will save thy children. The Lord Jesus and no one else will save Israel from the clutches of the devil and the shackles of sin and the nations. It is not the treasures of Jewish capitalists that will deliver Israel, nor the sham generosity of John Bull, but only our Lord Jesus Christ. He will *feed* the nations *with their own flesh* and make them *drunk with their own blood;* that is to say, He will set the nations warring against each other in such a way that they will consume each other. Is it not an undeniable fact that the nations of late are busily engaged in doing just that? Was there a nation that really won the first World War? There was not one, for they all lost more than they gained. Hence, they ate their own flesh and drank their own blood. And even this horrible process has not brought them to their senses but, as is indicated here, made them *drunken.* So we may safely conclude that Israel's deliverance must be close at hand.

Finally, the great goal of Israel's deliverance is indicated. It is that *all flesh,* and this includes even animal flesh, will acknowledge that Christ Jesus is Israel's *Saviour* and *Redeemer* and the *Mighty One of Jacob.*

ISAIAH 50

Israel Punished for Her Sin, Delivered by the Power of Christ

1. Thus saith the LORD, Where is the bill of your mother's divorcement, whom I have put away? or which of my creditors is it to whom I have sold you? Behold, for your iniquities have ye sold yourselves, and for your transgressions is your mother put away.

2. Wherefore, when I came, was there no man? when I called, was their none to answer? Is my hand shortened at all, that it cannot redeem? or have I no power to deliver? behold, at my rebuke I dry up the sea, I make the rivers a wilderness: their fish stinketh, because there is no water, and dieth for thirst.

3. I clothe the heavens with blackness, and I make sackcloth their covering.

This chapter follows the preceding one quite naturally. Christ is still the speaker. In the first two verses He justifies His rejection of Israel. To understand these words correctly it must be kept in mind that a Jew was allowed to give his wife a letter of divorcement and send her away or sell her as a slave to his creditors (Deut. 24:1-3). But now Jehovah who in His covenant of grace is married to Israel, demands that the letter of divorcement be shown to Him as proof that He out of fickleness allegedly cast out His lawful wife. No, He has not sent away His wife without a cause. Israel's conduct asked for it. He had found something shameful in her. With her abominable idolatry she had committed spiritual adultery and thus on her part had broken holy wedlock.

Wherefore, when I came, was there no man? etc. Here the Lord compares Himself to a man and father of a household who is treated shamefully by his own wife and children. When he came home, there was no one to welcome him and when he called, no one answered him. Hence, He who had the right to all their respect was treated as one without any rights. Because of this His anger was kindled righteously and He put His wife and children in the street; and the centuries-long wandering is the result of this.

The Jews could get the idea, however, that Jehovah could send them away but could not bring them back. It is actually this blasphemous thought which the churches in general entertain, and millions of Reform Jews as well. This is why He says in the form of a question that His hand is not shortened to deliver and that He lacks no power to save; to prove His divinity, He points at His mighty acts. By His threatening rebuke, His stern command, He dries up the ocean and makes the rivers into a desert so that the fish die and stink. Hence, He rules over the raging sea and the sea of the nations as well; the seething of great waters and the roaring of the waves do not terrify Him. By the word of His power He causes the heavens to mourn; they are clothed in black and girded with sackcloth as a person in mourning. Let no one ever doubt His power to save.

In a precious contrast which Israel knows how to use as no one else, He continues to describe His own obedience which contrasts beautifully with Israel's disobedience. The Almighty, who robs the mighty of his prey, and who can move heaven, earth and sea, obeys and allows Himself to be beaten and spit at and His beard to be plucked out. Is a greater contrast in attitude imaginable?

Christ's Obedience and Justification

4. The Lord GOD hath given me the tongue of the learned, that I should know how to speak a word in season to him that is weary: he wakeneth morning by morning, he wakeneth mine ear to hear as the learned.

5. The Lord GOD hath opened mine ear, and I was not rebellious, neither turned away back.

6. I gave my back to the smiters, and my cheeks to them that plucked off the hair: I hid not my face from shame and spitting.

7. For the Lord GOD will help me; therefore shall I not be confounded: therefore have I set my face like a flint, and I know that I shall not be ashamed.

8. He is near that justifieth me; who will contend with me? let us stand together: who is mine adversary? let him come near to me.

9. Behold, the Lord GOD will help me; who is he that shall condemn me? lo, they all shall wax old as a garment; the moth shall eat them up.

These words offer precious proof for the true humanity of the Savior whose divinity was described in the preceding section. For He has a back, hair, a face and cheeks. First, He describes Himself as the Teacher ordained by God, hence as the great Prophet. His Father gave *Him* the *tongue of the learned.* When some great intellect, as Einstein, for instance, makes a startling discovery, it arouses great interest on the part of those in the scientific world and excitement in the schools of the philosophers. There is a great desire to know the secrets of nature and to hear about the revolutions of the planets. We, as believers, should make known to the world that there is a man who has the tongue of the learned and not only knows the heavens but also is able to change them according to His will; he has the power to settle the arguments of the learned with one word. How this news would be welcomed by the wise men of the world! But their faces would change expression when told for what purpose this man was given *the tongue of the learned!* For this purpose is stated in these words: *that I should know how to speak a word in season to him that is weary.* Does this require a *tongue of the learned?* we hear the wise men of the world exclaim, with a look of disdain on their faces. Our answer must be: Yes, for with all your highly acclaimed wisdom you have not been able to do so. Those who are *weary* of the relentless pursuit of Satan and sin, of the struggle of life and of life itself, have never heard a word in due season from the wise men of the world. Only Christ can say, "Come unto me, all ye who are weary and heavy laden." He is the obedient apprentice of the Father, for that is the way verse four presents Him. Teachers awakened their pupils early since studying consisted mostly of memorizing, and one's memory works best in the early morning. Well, then, Christ is presented here as being awakened early and as being perfectly obedient. Just as a slave who in the year of jubilee had his ear pierced at the doorpost, so He served His Father in love and readiness. The zeal of His Father's house consumed Him. In all things He was obedient and persevering, for He turned not back. Verse six describes His terrible suffering and great humiliation as it is recounted by all four evangelists: (1) He absolutely gave Himself freely! *I gave my back.* (2) He gave Himself completely, for He gave His back, face, hair, and cheeks; He withheld nothing. (3) He suffered the deepest humiliation, for to pluck out the hair (of the beard) and to cover someone's face with spit was, according to Near-Eastern concepts, the most humiliating suffering that could be inflicted upon a man. (4) He suffered humbly and meekly like a lamb, for He does not use His great power to crush His enemies. (5) He suffered perseveringly, for He set His face like a flint, no mockery or humiliation could make Him swerve from the path of obedience. (6) He suffered in the full confidence that the Father would not put Him to shame. (7) He suffered as One inwardly righteous who shortly afterwards would be justified by the Father. His obedience was perfect.

Admonition Not to Be Disobedient to the Lord's Servant

> 10. Who is among you that feareth the LORD, that obeyeth the voice of his servant, that walketh in darkness, and hath no light? let him trust in the name of the LORD, and stay upon his God.
> 11. Behold, all ye that kindle a fire, that compass yourselves about with sparks: walk in the light of your fire, and in the sparks that ye have kindled. This shall ye have of mine hand; ye shall lie down in sorrow.

Only he who knows how to obey can call others to obedience. Today there is so much disobedience on the part of young people because the older people themselves have totally forgotten how to obey. Christ Jesus obeyed unequivocally and perfectly and therefore demands obedience of all. The *Servant* in this context is none else but the incomparable Sufferer just described.

Two entirely different classes of people are described in their relationships to Him. First there is the person — to indicate that there are but few who fear God and obey Christ — in contrast with *all* the wicked, who are numerous — who fears Jehovah with childlike fear and who obeys the Messiah.

What a fortunate man! we would be inclined to cry. Yet, his way at times is dark and thorny. Sometimes he must walk in a pitch-dark night of adversity and suffering, which is not penetrated by a single beam of light. The way of obedience, as is clearly taught here, is not always the easiest way. But when those sad circumstances of suffering and woe come upon him, he need not despair but must *trust* in the name of Jehovah and *stay* upon his God. He continues to hope and pray in the night of his suffering, for "God's goodness shall one day change his darkness into day." The sun of his salvation will soon arise.

It is entirely different, however, with those who love evil and disobey Christ. "He that believeth not the Son shall not see life; but the wrath of God abideth on him" (John 3:36). They are presented here as men of enlightenment who are not walking in complete darkness; but have the light of torches made of smoking pitch and sulfur. They do not lack light at all, but are girded as it were with a fire which they have kindled themselves. Happily they walk on. But, suddenly they are struck down in the greatest misery, not by any man but by the Servant of the Lord whom in their imagined enlightenment they rejected. Those who refuse to walk in Christ, the Light of the world, but choose to walk in their own imagined light will soon lie in the pangs of hell. But let believers too take this warning to heart! When their way is only somewhat dark they often break out in laments and are envious of the wicked who prosper. Let them lean on Christ rather than complain about the darkness of their way, for does not their way lead to the eternal mansions of light?

ISAIAH 51

Christ Addresses the Believers

1. Hearken to me, ye that follow after righteousness, ye that seek the LORD: look unto the rock whence ye are hewn, and to the hole of the pit whence ye are digged.

2. Look unto Abraham your father, and unto Sarah that bare you: for I called him alone, and blessed him, and increased him.

3. For the LORD shall comfort Zion: he will comfort all her waste places; and he will make her wilderness like Eden, and her desert like the garden of the LORD; joy and gladness shall be found therein, thanksgiving, and the voice of melody.

4. Hearken unto me, my people; and give ear unto me, O my nation: for a law shall proceed from me, and I will make my judgment to rest for a light of the people.

5. My righteousness is near; my salvation is gone forth, and mine arms shall judge the people; the isles shall wait upon me, and on mine arm shall they trust.

6. Lift up your eyes to the heavens, and look upon the earth beneath: for the heavens shall vanish away like smoke, and the earth shall wax old like a garment, and they that dwell therein shall die in like manner: but my salvation shall be for ever, and my righteousness shall not be abolished.

7. Hearken unto me, ye that know righteousness, the people in whose heart is my law; fear ye not the reproach of men, neither be ye afraid of their revilings.

8. For the moth shall eat them up like a garment, and the worm shall eat them like wool: but my righteousness shall be for ever, and my salvation from generation to generation.

In these verses Christ is described as the great Prophet who could and did obey perfectly, but who Himself in turn wants to be obeyed and therefore repeatedly calls for obedience (vv. 1, 4, 7). In flowery style He admonishes believing Israel to consider her ancestral father and mother, with the secondary intent that they would consider the covenant of grace. Both the *rock* and the *hole of the pit* are explained in

verse two as referring to Abraham and Sarah. God called
Abraham when he still had no children but He blessed him in
a most marvelous way with a numerous posterity. In verse
three, as elsewhere, this past blessing is taken as a sure
guarantee for even richer blessings in the future. He will have
mercy not only on the people but also on the land of Israel.
He will make her desert as the garden of Eden; Paradise will
return. The first Adam took Eden away from us; the second
Adam will restore it. It is terrible how some texts of
Scripture are twisted by those who deny Israel's future
restoration. Even the most unscrupulous lawyers would
hardly dare treat mere human laws in the way that many
Christian teachers and expositors do God's holy Word. How
can this text be taken as a reference to heaven? Does heaven
have waste places? The Church has never been destroyed.
Immediately after the exile in the days of Ezra and
Nehemiah, Palestine truly was no Eden! The only tenable
explanation of this and similar texts is that they speak of
Israel's territorial restoration. Both nation and country will
be fully restored; not by missions and not before the Coming
of the Lord but by it and after He returns. It is He who does
it and therefore it is done well, for He never does something
half way. Already with the marvelous origin of Israel He gave
the sure guarantee of His future Coming. He will give Israel a
cup of joy that will run over. His *law* will go forth from
Jerusalem to the nations (cf. 2:1-3; Micah 4:1-4) and by His
Word He will enlighten the nations with the knowledge of
truth, so that the earth will be covered with the knowledge of
His Name.

All these blessings for Israel and the nations do not come,
however, until after the most terrible judgments, as is evident
from the pregnant expression *mine arms shall judge the
people.* Verse six indicates that the entire present order and
form of the world must first be done away. *The heavens shall
vanish away like smoke* refers to the heavens of the clouds
and the air. He will cast away the earth like a worn-out
garment in order to clothe it with the garment of praise,
while the inhabitants of the world will *die in like manner,* or
perhaps better, *like insects.* His righteousness, however, will
surpass heaven and earth in durability, since it is eternal.

Taking into consideration then, this blessing of righteousness on the one hand and all that is perishable on the other, believing Israel is admonished not to fear, or succumb to, the attack of any enemy whatsoever.

A Prayer of Isaiah for Speeding Up the Promised Salvation

9. Awake, awake, put on strength, O arm of the LORD; awake, as in the ancient days, in the generations of old. Art thou not it that hath cut Rahab, and wounded the dragon?

10. Art thou not it which hath dried the sea, the waters of the great deep; that hath made the depths of the sea a way for the ransomed to pass over?

11. Therefore the redeemed of the LORD shall return, and come with singing unto Zion; and everlasting joy shall be upon their head: they shall obtain gladness and joy; and sorrow and mourning shall flee away.

For some time we have known Isaiah as a man of prayer. The great salvation of his people which the Messiah depicted has kindled his flammable emotions; as the mouthpiece of his people he passionately cries out, *Awake, awake, put on strength, O arm of the Lord!* In Scripture the idea that during the times of the Gentiles, when Israel is *Lo-Ammi,* Jehovah is sitting down or lying down as though doing nothing and forgetting about Israel, is not unusual. That is the way things seem to be and is the human side of the matter; on the part of God Psalm 121 is absolutely true. In this connection the coming of the Lord is depicted as a warrior's arise to battle. The *arm of the Lord* is the powerful revelation of His glory and is fully embodied in the Coming of Christ. Hence, the prophet actually is praying for the Coming of the Lord when He will move His now inactive arm against His haters and for Israel.

The prophet now prays that He manifest Himself mightily as in the days of old, when He defeated *Rahab,* the proud power of Egypt (30:7), and wounded the *sea dragon,* i.e., Pharaoh is the image of the old serpent (cf. 27:1; Ezek. 29:3). He reminds the Lord of His great acts for the benefit of Israel in drying up the Red Sea and making a pathway in the sea for His people to pass through (Exod. 14:21). At the beginning of this chapter the Lord Himself referred to His miracles in behalf of Israel's origin; now the prophet reminds the Lord of His great acts in connection with Israel's exodus. And the Lord loves such reminders from His children. Without waiting for the Lord's answer, the prophet expresses his well-founded hope and joy that the Lord once again will return His ransomed so that they will come to Zion with gladness. We must by no means apply this verse to the Church, for He has already come to Zion (Heb. 12:22), but as far as Israel is concerned that still lies in the future. Nor may these words be applied to Israel's return from Babylon for at that time there was no *everlasting joy* upon their heads. In 35:10, this image of joy upon the head is connected with the future restoration of Israel, for which see the commentary on that section. The returning exiles are presented as singing for joy upon their return as this was the ancient custom when caravans of festive pilgrims went up to the house of the Lord. *Sorrow and mourning,* presently still the daily portion of Israel as a nation, will then forever flee away from Israel as these will no longer be found with the restored nation. In the spirit the prophet sees the redeemed people marching with shouts of joy to the land of their fathers. We can somewhat imagine with what great longing the believing Jews looked forward to this promised future.

Jehovah's Answer to Isaiah's Prayer

12. I, even I, am he that comforteth you: who art thou, that thou shouldest be afraid of a man that shall die, and of the son of man which shall be made as grass;

13. And forgettest the LORD thy maker, that hath stretched forth the heavens, and laid the foundations of the earth; and hast feared continually every day because of the fury of the oppressor, as if he were ready to destroy? and where is the fury of the oppressor?

14. The captive exile hasteneth that he may be loosed, and that he should not die in the pit, nor that his bread should fail.

15. But I am the LORD thy God, that divided the sea, whose waves roared: The LORD of hosts is his name.

16. And I have put my words in thy mouth, and I have covered thee in the shadow of mine hand, that I may plant the heavens, and lay the foundations of the earth, and say unto Zion, Thou art my people.

It may safely be assumed that these words are the answer to Isaiah's prayer. The basic thought of these verses was expressed in verse seven. Since Jehovah does not forsake His people and will visit her again with His salvation, Israel need not fear the reproach of men. The address, here as there, is to the people *in whose heart is the law,* a precious name for the believers as in this respect they resemble their Savior (cf. Ps. 37:31, 40:8). As verse eight pointed out the insignificance of man, since a *moth* or *worm* can eat him up as wool, here the God-fearing people in exile are told that man is *as grass* and when the thread of life is cut off he becomes as *hay.* In contrast to the transience of man the incomparable greatness of the Almighty Creator is pointed out, whom the people are again and again inclined to forget because they fear the *fury of the oppressor.* Who is meant by this expression? Usually it is thought to refer to the fury of the king of Babylon, but we take it also to mean the great king of Babylon in the last days (cf. 14:4).

Jehovah's strong arm will make an end to the oppression of His people. The *captive exile* is the Jew bound in chains and compared to a prisoner in bowed-down position, locked up in a dismal dungeon. Jehovah takes care, however, that he does not perish and will feed him with bread in his terrible prison so that he does not die from hunger. The Lord's promises remain his portion, a thought expressed in the words *I have put my words in thy mouth.* Then, too, the Lord covers and protects him under the shadow of His hand. This is followed very significantly by the words *that I may plant the heavens, and lay the foundations of the earth.* This is a reference to the new heavens and the new earth in which righteousness will dwell. The word *plant* means, as Calvin noted, "to regulate, order, harmoniously." Because of sin everything became disordered and out of harmony, but God decided that in the dispensation of the fullness of times He will gather together in one head all things in Christ, both which are in heaven, and which are on earth (Eph. 1:10). The Lord gives us both the solution and the purpose of the riddle of the continued existence of the Jews. First, He preserves this strange and mysterious nation in order that some day He may enlarge the new heavens and establish this present restless earth on justice and righteousness. The object of the indestructible continued existence of the Jew lies in and points forward to the new heavens and the new earth. Secondly, the very existence of the nation is the object of divine protection. She has continued for many long and anxious centuries as *Lo-Ammi,* i.e., Not-My-People. And the Lord says that one day He will say to Zion, *Ammi.* In His grace He will drop the *Lo,* the *Not* in her name.

Address to Jerusalem

17. Awake, awake, stand up, O Jerusalem, which hath drunk at the hand of the LORD the cup of his fury; thou hast drunken the dregs of the cup of trembling, and wrung them out.
18. There is none to guide her among all the sons whom she hath brought forth; neither is there any that taketh her by the hand of all the sons that she hath brought up.
19. These two things are come unto thee; who shall be sorry for thee? desolation, and destruction, and the famine, and the sword: by whom shall I comfort thee?
20. Thy sons have fainted, they lie at the head of all the streets, as a wild bull in the net: they are full of the fury of the LORD, the rebuke of thy God.

As so often before, the prophet places himself once more in the midst of Israel's future glory. But what contrast looms up in his spirit between that joyful future and the sad present state of the nation. She is sunk away in the sleep of carelessness, indeed of death, lies on the earth as a miserable captive with no strength or courage to lift herself up. The chains of captivity lie heavily on her weakened limbs. This lamentable condition of Jerusalem is, however, the result of the unrighteousnesses of the people. On account of her abominations, the Lord has given Jerusalem the *cup of trembling.* Scripture frequently uses the metaphor of a cup. The handing out of a cup full of stupefying fluid was a symbol of a great visitation in anger and wrath, while the emptying of the cup typified blindly dancing toward destruction (cf. Jer. 8:14; 9:15; 23:15; 25:15; 49:12; Ezek. 23:31). Jeremiah, who had to preach the destruction of Jerusalem daily, returned again and again to this metaphor.

The image appears also, however, in a favorable sense in Scripture (Ps. 16:5; 23:5; 116:13). But usually it is used in connection with judgment (Ps. 11:6; 75:8; Lam. 4:21; Matt. 20:22-23; 26:39; John 18:11; Rev. 18:6). It is believed that this metaphor is derived from giving servants or guests at mealtimes a certain amount of strong drink. According to this idea, God is the father of the household who passes the cup to all the members of the family and table guests. According to other students of Hebrew antiquity it was drawn from the custom of handing criminals who were sentenced to death a cup of stupefying drink for the purpose of dulling their senses before the approaching punishment. Taken in this sense, the *cup of trembling* is a sign that the verdict has already been pronounced and the future of the unfortunate victim has been determined; the cup comes to him as a herald of execution. It seems to us that the metaphor of the cup must be taken in a good sense in connection with a meal and in a bad sense in connection with the preceding idea. Jerusalem had to empty the cup of wrath, which was filled to the rim, to the very last drop. She had to slurp it up, as the word really implies.

Then, the city is compared to a mother who is utterly despised by her own children. Had she not become a despicable, stone-drunk whore who lay on the ground completely intoxicated as a derision to all? According to Jeremiah she had committed two evils and hence the two evils of hunger and war had befallen her. The children did not merely feel ashamed about their mother. They themselves were also lying in a stupor and shame, like a *wild bull in the net.* The metaphor is clear. These animals were caught in large nets; when first ensnared they thrashed wildly but in the end they dropped from exhaustion. Thus the inhabitants of Zion sank down full of the wrath of God (cf. Lam. 2:10-12).

Zion's Oppressors Must Drink the Cup of Wrath

21. Therefore hear now this, thou afflicted, and drunken, but not with wine:

22. Thus saith thy Lord the LORD, and thy God that pleadeth the cause of his people, Behold, I have taken out of thine hand the cup of trembling, even the dregs of the cup of my fury; thou shalt no more drink it again:

23. But I will put it into the hand of them that afflict thee; which have said to thy soul, Bow down, that we may go over: and thou hast laid thy body as the ground and as the street, to them that went over.

At last the roles are turned around. For Israel, sin and punishment are never the final word. That is not to say that Israel deserved something else. Her sin and shame still speak clearly in the designation *drunken* with which Jerusalem is addressed. However, the Lord promises to plead the cause of His people against all His enemies. He takes the full cup of trembling out of their hand with the glorious promise that they will no longer have to drink it; He will give it into the hand of Israel's oppressors — something which He is manifestly doing in our own day.

The last part of verse twenty-three describes the humiliation which the nations afflicted on the Jewish people. It was once the custom in the Near East for conquerors to put their foot on the neck of the conquered. The victors shouted cruelly, *Bow down, that we may go over!* And Israel, in powerlessness albeit not in humility, bowed before all nations and became as a floor and a street on which the conquerors walked (cf. Josh. 10:24; Ps. 18:40).

Some expositors still see Israel as a stone-drunk woman in these verses, a woman who has been stupefied and who publicly and in the sight and to the amusement of the passers-by lies there in her intoxication, while some wanton ones do not shrink back from putting their foot on her back and pretending they are walking on a street. Whatever the case, Israel's misery is depicted here in all her reality; she has experienced the bitter reality of these words already for twenty-five hundred years. But at the judgment of the nations the Lord Jesus will visit the inhuman treatment of Israel; He will tread the nations in the winepress of His wrath.

Finally we may say that the next verses favor this idea, for there the prophet still has the image of the forsaken and despised woman in the back of his mind.

ISAIAH 52

Israel Restored, Adorned and Freed

> 1. Awake, awake; put on thy strength, O Zion; put on thy beautiful garments, O Jerusalem, the holy city: for henceforth there shall no more come into thee the uncircumcised and the unclean.
> 2. Shake thyself from the dust; arise, and sit down, O Jerusalem: loose thyself from the bands of thy neck, O captive daughter of Zion.

This chapter contains two very distinct parts. The first twelve verses continue and conclude the preceding chapter, while the last three verses actually belong with chapter 53. The prophet again places himself in Israel's future and gives commands to the nation as if he were confronting her future. We must remember that these commands have the power of prediction. He still presents Jerusalem as a mother in prison, long deprived of her children and prostrate in her fetters, dirt, shame and misery. Now he cries out to her to arise and to put on her beautiful festive garment to be ready to receive her children. From now on she will be a *holy city;* no circumcised and unclean heathen will invade her. *Shake off the dust* is a sign of mourning and sadness: *to loosen the bands of her neck* and seat herself as a free and beautifully adorned queen on her throne shows that she is now freed from her shackles.

"Redeemed Without Money"

> 3. For thus saith the LORD, Ye have sold yourselves for nought; and ye shall be redeemed without money.

The above title is that of an exegetical meditation in *De Heraut (The Herald)* of August 27, 1923, by Dr. A. Kuyper,

Jr., which by no means does justice to the Word. He refers, among other things, to the contrast between 43:3, where it says that God gives a *ransom* for His people, and 52:3, where God says that His people will be redeemed without money. The learned writer says of this: "We are indeed faced here with a great and mighty contrast." With respect to Babylon the Lord says, You will be redeemed without money. With regard to Persia He says, I have given men for thee, and people for thy life.

But the great and mighty contrast Dr. Kuyper sees here is not correct. Isaiah 43:3 does speak of the nations which God has subjected to the Persian throne as a ransom, a compensation, a reward, for the freedom Cyrus granted to Judah. But Isaiah 52 obviously is not talking of Israel's return from Babylon but of her final return from among all nations in the end time, and in connection with that Israel's complete restoration and great glory. This is evident from numerous facts as follows: a) From henceforth no uncircumcised nor unclean person will pass through Jerusalem (v. 1). b) Jerusalem will be freed from the bands around her neck (v. 2). c) The Lord Himself will speak to Israel on the day of her liberation and say, *Behold, it is I* (v. 6). d) Messengers will skip along on Israel's mountains and say to Zion (Jerusalem) *Thy God reigneth* (v. 7). e) Israel's watchmen will see with their own eyes that the Lord Himself and not Zerubbabel or Nehemiah will bring back Zion (v. 8). f) The Lord rebuilds the waste places of Jerusalem and on that occasion comforts His people (v. 9). g) The Lord has made bare His holy arm, *i.e.,* He has gone out to do battle against all nations (v. 10). h) All the ends of the earth will see the salvation which Jehovah Himself has brought to the Jews (v. 10). i) The returned Savior, who once was so humiliated, will at that time be exalted in the sight of all nations and rulers (vv. 13-15).

Not one of these events took place when Israel returned from Babylon. Hence the contrast of which Kuyper speaks of in *The Herald* is not the one between Babylon and Persia, but between Israel's first return from Babylon and the final return from among all the nations in the day of Christ's return. Nor, strictly speaking, was it the Babylonians who let

Israel go, for Israel returned after the fall of the first world power and through the mediation of the Persian King Cyrus. Certainly this king received a ransom for his noble deed consisting of many countries, but the nations of the future will receive nothing but the most terrible judgments because of their centuries-long oppression of the Jews.

God's Anger with Assyria Greater Than with Egypt

> 4. For thus saith the Lord GOD, My people went down aforetime into Egypt to sojourn there; and the Assyrians oppressed them without cause.
> 5. Now therefore, what have I here, saith the LORD, that my people is taken away for nought? they that rule over them make them to howl, saith the LORD; and my name continually every day is blasphemed.

The Returned Christ Present in Israel

> 6. Therefore my people shall know my name: therefore they shall know in that day that I am he that doth speak: behold, it is I.
> 7. How beautiful upon the mountains are the feet of him that bringeth good tidings, that publisheth peace; that bringeth good tidings of good, that publisheth salvation; that saith unto Zion, Thy God reigneth!
> 8. Thy watchmen shall lift up the voice; with the voice together shall they sing: for they shall see eye to eye, when the LORD shall bring again Zion.
> 9. Break forth into joy, sing together, ye waste places of Jerusalem: for the LORD hath comforted his people, he hath redeemed Jerusalem.
> 10. The LORD hath made bare his holy arm in the eyes of all the nations; and all the ends of the earth shall see the salvation of our God.
> 11. Depart ye, depart ye, go ye out from thence, touch no unclean things; go ye out of the midst of her; be ye clean, that bear the vessels of the LORD.
> 12. For ye shall not go out with haste nor go by flight: for the LORD will go before you; and the God of Israel will be your rereward.

The Lord will revenge His people and stop the mouth of those who blaspheme Him *in that day* — the standard expression for the great day of the future to which the seer often refers. The double *therefore* refers as before, to the cause of the judgment upon Assyria and its results for Israel. The result of the judgment upon the blasphemous anti-christian world powers will be twofold for Israel: she will know Jehovah-Jesus, and will have Him in her midst; she will see and hear Him. The presentation here is brief indeed, but very meaningful.

The salvation of the King of Israel who is present in her midst is so great that messengers are sent out everywhere; as the heralds of salvation they will publish it to all the cities of Judah. In verse seven one can sense the extreme haste in the prophet's presentation and a certain fullness and inflatedness of style on account of the presence of King Jesus. The whole salvation is comprehended, however, in this one expression *Thy God reigneth!* The heralds are fast racers and run very fast, and this is why their *feet* are so beautiful. They come running as with winged feet and that is why their feet as messengers of good tidings are so welcome. When they climb to the tops of the hills their voices resound far and near.

The watchmen are standing on the pinnacles of their towers and they see the messengers rapidly approaching; but at the same moment their eyes see that the Lord is returning to His Zion. At the sight of this memorable fact, they break forth into joyful noise at the rebuilding of the destroyed city and the gathering and comforting of His people as well as the mighty revelation of the majesty of Israel's King in the sight of all the nations. The expression *made bare his holy arm* is a Hebrew idiom derived from rolling up long, loose sleeves before starting to work. Then the arm was bared — the symbol of any mighty undertaking or initiative. The mighty works of Jehovah-Jesus are mentioned in verse nine. All nations, even the most distant, will see with their eyes, just as the messengers and watchmen do, the *salvation* of Israel as already envisioned by God. *Depart ye, depart ye, go ye out,* the seer, as the mouthpiece of the Lord, cries to the Jews who had stayed behind among the nations. They must separate themselves from the unclean people and never touch the unclean (cf. II Cor. 6:17). This still holds true for the Church. Those that *bear the vessels of the Lord* are the priests. The people will not return from the final exile in fear and haste as they once did at the exodus from Egypt, because Jehovah-Jesus will be their vanguard and *rereward*. At the exodus from Egypt He protected His people with the pillar of cloud and of fire, but then He will do so with His very person.

Here the Lord makes a distinction between Egypt and Assyria. Assyria refers first of all to the Assyrio-Babylonian world power, but not exclusively. The deepest meaning of Assyria is that of Israel's great enemy in the end time, as we constantly have noticed in the first part of Isaiah's prophecy (see commentary on 52:3). It could not be said however of Babylon in the past that it had oppressed Israel *without cause,* since Zedekiah had broken his solemn oath to remain faithful to Nebuchadnezzar and had, together with other small nations, revolted against the Babylonian kingdom. But this statement will be perfectly applicable to the arch-enemy of the future as well as to the blaspheming *continually every day* of the name of Jehovah-Jesus (cf. Rev. 13:5). The power of the contrast between Egypt and Assyria lies in an argument from the lesser to the greater as follows: If in former days Jehovah delivered His people from Egypt and punished Egypt to which His people had voluntarily gone, how much more would He beat Assyria which had dragged His people into exile without cause and made her to *howl* in distress. One translation has here *those who rule over it howl of vexation* or *roar for joy* but that is less desirable than the Dutch Authorized version. Dragging away Israel without reason, causing the exiles to howl, and constant blaspheming of Jehovah are three reasons why the Lord would punish Assyria more severely than He once did Egypt.

The Exaltation of the Servant of the Lord

13. Behold, my servant shall deal prudently, he shall be exalted and extolled, and be very high.

14. As many were astonied at thee; his visage was so marred more than any man, and his form more than the sons of men:

15. So shall he sprinkle many nations; the kings shall shut their mouths at him: for that which had not been told them shall they see; and that which they had not heard shall they consider.

Here we find a summons to look to Christ. When we have a beautiful portrait, we tell our friends, *Behold*. This is what the Father is saying here, for Christ is the image of the invisible God, and the Father thinks very much of Him. Again and again in His Word He points at His beloved Son with words such as, *Behold, your King is coming; behold, my servant; behold, the man whose name is the Branch; behold, Judah; behold your God*. It is by no means accidental that in the four Gospels we find this fourfold image of King, Servant, Man and God in this order.

We need not enlarge upon the concept servant after all that has been said before. This name points to Christ as the Mediator sent by God and the great Representative of the Father, who has the commission, the right and the qualification to take away sin and to subdue the rebellion in God's creation.

The first thing that is said of the *servant* is that He will *deal prudently*. Christ has always dealt prudently, since He is the supreme Wisdom. He always dealt wisely with Satan by using only the sword of the Spirit, the Word. His crafty interrogators always received a wise question or counter question. By His perfect sacrifice on the cross He satisfied God's justice, conquered Satan, saved creation and saved the sinner. The Hebrew word contains the secondary idea of *being prosperous*. Because He dealt prudently, He would prosper. This prosperity is expressed by three words referring to His exaltation: He was raised from the grave, He was *lifted up* into heaven and He was placed *on high* at the right hand of God and received a name above every name (Mark 16:19; Eph. 1:20-22; I Pet. 3:22). Just as in Philippians 2:5-11, the exaltation was proportional to His deep humiliation, as the word *as* indicates. His humiliation was of such a nature that many were *astonied* with revulsion. His face was so marred by the blows of fists, by the crown of thorns and by the saliva that was spit in His face that He hardly looked like a human being. This reminds us of His suffering shortly before He died. A whole night and a whole day He was dragged from one place to another, scourged, beaten and spit at so that the marble-white face due to lack of sleep, loss of blood and sorrow, with the red blood, the blue bruises and the grey saliva on it must have made Him look horrible. Before Constantine the Church taught that Christ was very ugly looking, but after Constantine that He was very beautiful. Both are true. Undoubtedly a spiritual beauty must have been present on His face, which could be discovered only by the spiritual eye. On the other hand, by abuse and suffering He must have showed a *marred* face and presented a repulsive sight. The Hebrew word *keen,* translated by *so,* once again points out the proportion that existed between His humiliation and exaltation. Few Christian exegetes have realized that chapter 53 is but a secondary description of the humiliated Christ, and that its real purpose is to point to His *exaltation.* The *servant* will *sprinkle* many nations with the *blood of sprinkling* (Lev. 14:51; 16:14; Ezek. 36:25; Heb. 9:13-14; I Pet. 1:2); out of respect for Him the kings of the earth will shut their mouths, and the blind heathen will fully understand His Word.

ISAIAH 53

An Important Question

> 1. Who hath believed our report? and to whom is the arm of the LORD revealed?

This chapter is so glorious and so dearly loved by God's people that we can't refrain from discussing it verse by verse, for regardless of how well known and simple it may be, it nevertheless contains depths which we shall continue to marvel at forever and ever. The chapter is extremely fascinating, a pathos inexpressibly tragic, and yet a sublimity that cannot be put into words.

In the preceding chapter the prophet spoke of the exaltation of Messiah, and of the proclamation of that exaltation. In verse fifteen he even depicted the glorious result of this preaching among the nations. This is not to be identified with our present-day missionary activity, for that does not produce such glorious fruits; it is rather a reference to the preaching of Christ after His return to Israel at the onset of the Kingdom of Peace, for not until then will all rulers and nations serve the Lord Jesus in full obedience.

In contrast with the general acceptance of Christ by the heathen, the question is asked here: *Who hath believed our report?* It is important to know who asks this question. Who is speaking here or, rather, who *are* speaking here, for it is more than evident from what follows, especially verse six that more than one person is speaking. Nor does the context allow us to think merely of Israel's prophets who found no response to their preaching among the people, though that was very much the case. From verse six, it is quite evident that all of Israel makes a public confession here. There is no reason to think that this question has any others in mind than all Israel. When we compare references such as 42:23 and 64:6, we discover that it may be considered a rule that whenever the pronoun *we* appears suddenly in a prophecy, it always refers to all of Israel. In addition, the following context actually allows for no other explanation. We may safely say that what is stated in the last parts of verses two, three and four applies uniquely to Israel. This explanation implies, of course, that Isaiah himself uttered these words at one time. But as we often find to be the case in prophecy, he does so as the mouthpiece of the people, as the interpreter of the multiplied thoughts that one day will live in the hearts of Israel after she has returned to God. For it needs no argument that unconverted Jewry could not speak thus of the Messiah. Initially this question was valid in the days of Christ and the apostles as is evident from the references to it in John 12:38 and Romans 10:16; but when the remnant of the end time will one day look at Israel's long-standing, stubborn unbelief, then this question will obtain increased significance. For stiff-necked Israel refused for many centuries to have anything to do with the humiliated and exalted Jesus, and hence the *arm,* the saving power of Jehovah-Jesus was not revealed to her. She did not believe and therefore she was not saved.

The Reason Why Israel Did Not Believe in Her Messiah

> 2. For he shall grow up before him as a tender plant, and as a root out of a dry ground: he hath no form nor comeliness; and when we shall see him, there is no beauty that we should desire him.

The principal thought of this verse is that the Messiah in His origin and appearance was very lowly and that for this reason Israel did not desire Him. The word *For* gives the causal connection with verse one. Here Israel supplies the answer to the question of verse one and indicates *why* she did not believe in her Messiah. It is because the Messiah, whose exaltation was depicted in the most glorious colors, did not at all correspond with the expectation and the ideal which had been formed of Him. On the contrary, He manifested

Himself in a lowly and unsightly form. Obviously, Israel had expected that He would manifest Himself in a royal manner and with majesty and pomp. In a metaphor derived from the realm of plants it is said that He appeared as a tender *plant* from the old trunk of Jesse. What is more insignificant than a small *branch,* a twig? Do they not appear silently and unheralded in spring by the millions? Who can become excited about a sprig! And who can believe in a sprig? Who can put his trust in it and place all his confidence in it?

Moreover the tender plant grew up *before him,* not before *Israel,* even though Israel, ever since the people had cried for gods to *go before them* at the foot of Mt. Horeb, forever hankered after spectacular signs and wonders. Israel did not want to believe but to live by seeing — seeing great and glorious wonders for her own glorification. The fact that this *tender plant* grew up *before Him* silently hints that as the Righteous and Holy One He completely fulfilled the requirement of the covenant. For God had said to Abraham, *Walk before me;* but Israel never did so. She walked everywhere, even as far as Egypt and Babylon; indeed, she now walks to the ends of the earth, but not *before him.* But what Israel has never done, the *tender plant* did. He is the true Israel.

Hence the tender plant represents Christ in His true and righteous humanity. The tender plant here is a sprout, a sprig, which as yet does not have life's saps within itself but derives them from the stump; it is dependent on something else, just as a baby receives food from its mother's breasts (The word *sprout* is sometimes used also in a zoological sense). Thus, the Messiah appeared among the people of Israel. Who is not reminded here of the tender babe at Bethlehem on that memorable day? This was so entirely different than Israel had expected. Israel's thought had not been guided by the truth but by a pleasant enough half-truth, an imagined carnal ideal to which the real Messiah did not correspond at all.

And as a root out of a dry ground. The word translated *root* actually refers to a shoot, a sprig from a root. This shoot came up from *a dry ground.* The words indicate that Christ came under the poorest of circumstances, poor and miserable from a poor and barren people. The sprouting of this sprig was not due to the moisture or richness of the soil, but to a miracle of the Lord. This is undoubtedly a reference to the lowly birth of the Messiah from the barren soil of the decrepit house of David, as pointed out in 11:1. No one could expect a shoot from this dry and sterile land or even from the cut-off stump. Messiah's whole appearance was incomprehensible and contrary to all expectations. But even this was not quite as unacceptable to Israel, since He, according to misconceived expectations would in any case restore the throne of David and make it famous once more; but that He came to such a place as humble Bethlehem and from such poor parents as Joseph and Mary and under such poor circumstances, and in that form would carry out His office — this Israel did not see with an eye of faith.

The prophet uses three words to describe the outward appearance of the Messiah. He had no *form,* that is to say, no beautiful physical appearance. Israel had imagined that He would be a tall, handsome Saul. The word *comeliness* also points to something beautiful. It means *beautiful specimen, ornament, jewel.* But, here it is stated that Christ had no adornment, beauty or splendor, and that His manifestation was totally devoid of the majesty or glory befitting a king. A third word is used to depict the appearance of the Savior. When we saw Him, converted Israel says, there was no *beauty* that we should have desired Him. Whereas the first word referred to the physical appearance as such, the second to the outward majesty of a king, throne, crown, scepter and courtiers, this word states that to an observer there was nothing attractive, nothing desirable about Him. They did not want to see Him like people want to see a king. He did not captivate, or appeal to, or excite others. On the contrary, He was unsightly and repulsive to the senses of unconverted Jewry. All they had to do was give Him one look to be turned off by Him and never to desire Him. Only the believing heart could say: "He is altogether lovely."

The contrast presented here is once more of such a nature as only Isaiah can do. On the one hand there is the grand expectation of the proud nation, which yearned, and hankered for glitter and glory, fame and splendor and enormous revelation of power; on the other hand there was only the humble, tender *plant,* which was averse from all splendor and worldly pomp. How wonderful this will seem one day to the converted nation!

The Deep Humiliation of Christ

> 3. He is despised and rejected of men; a man of sorrows, and acquainted with grief: and we hid as it were our faces from him; he was despised, and we esteemed him not.

The prophet, as the mouthpiece of the God-fearing people, continues here to further describe the humble state of the Christ. *He is despised,* he says, and by saying this without adding an accusative he emphasizes the generality of this contempt. The word translated by *despised* means first of all a mocking out of disdain and then despising as a worthless one. The Jews thought Christ ridiculous and despised Him as someone worthless because He was so quiet in His coming and so insignificant in His appearance. Now even stronger than before, we are told of Israel's relationship to the humble Savior. In verse two it was said that they did not desire Him; here it is positively stated that they despised him as being ridiculous.

History has all too clearly vindicated this statement. Christ was despised by Israel's learned men and by the Roman world in its representative Pontius Pilate, who scourged Him and delivered Him to the Jewish mob; its soldiers cast dice for His robe. And the Jews have despised Him to this very day; they have made fists against Him and gnashed their teeth against Him and spit to the ground upon hearing His name mentioned. In the Talmud He is called *Yesu,* which contain the first letters of the phrase "Let His Name and Remembrance Be Blotted Out!" They blaspheme His pure virgin mother, His words and His disciples.

And rejected of men. To us, who believe on Him, He is the most beautiful among men. This phrase really means that He was not counted in the circle of the great, but considered as the most worthless among men. Even the Josephs and Nicodemuses, who indeed believed in Him, did not dare to join Him publicly. And later on a Julian, then a Celsus, and much later a Nietzsche scornfully said that His followers were only slaves and that His religion was a religion of slaves. During His lifetime He was derided as a glutton and a winebibber, a friend of publicans and sinners. In the estimation of the leaders of Israel He was not a decent man with whom one could associate, and for that reason they turned their backs upon Him.

A man of sorrows means that sorrows were the characteristic aspect of His entire life. This is a reference to the popular belief in Israel that one who had to endure many sorrows was punished by higher powers, whether by God or evil spirits, for certain transgressions. And since the life of the Servant of the Lord was identical with suffering, Israel came to the common conclusion that He had made Himself especially worthy of the anger of the Lord for special sins. In an even deeper sense than Jeremiah the Lord Jesus could say, "Behold, and see if there be any sorrow like unto my sorrow." For He suffered at the hand of Satan, of sinners, of the disciples and of God.

And acquainted with grief. On the basis of this statement it has been assumed that Christ was often ill and had a sickly constitution, but for various reasons this idea seems unacceptable to us. The word *sickness* (Dutch version) also means weakness, sorrow, grief, misery, or adversity in general. It refers to suffering in the broadest sense and is best translated as in the King James version, *acquainted with grief,* i.e., familiar with and used to grief. Recall His statement, *And how am I straightened!* Already during His lifetime He was pressed by the wrath of God and by the unrighteousnesses of those who rejected Him.

And we hid as it were our faces from him. Literally, it says that there took place a hiding of the face from Him. There are some who translate, *He was as hiding His face,* and point out that mourners covered their faces (II Sam. 15:30, Ezek. 24:17). Others are of the opinion, on the basis of the verb *naga,* that the words mean Christ was struck with the affliction of leprosy and according to the injunction of Leviticus 13:45, covered His upper lip. But this explanation is wrong, since we read nowhere that Christ hid His face as an unclean one would have done because of a repulsive skin disease. The Lord Jesus indeed had a body like that of sinful flesh, and He bore not only sin, but also its results, so that He could be hungry, thirsty and tired; yet we never read in the Gospels that *He* was ever sick or afflicted with some terrible disease. On the basis of this text, and the next, the Talmudists have forged the legend that one of their famous teachers met the Messiah in Rome, lying there among the lepers. That shows that the Christ-rejecting Jews turn in revulsion and disgust from Him as from a leper. The word *we* does not include every Jew during His sojourn on earth, for many sought Him to supply them with bread, and the common people loved to listen to Him; it refers rather to the hardened Jews of this entire dispensation. They were so hostile to Him that they hid their faces from Him behind the wide folds of their cloaks. And the terrible result is that now God hides His face from them during this present dispensation.

He was despised, and we esteemed him not. With this repetition Israel gives a resumé of the reasons for such a disdainful attitude toward the Messiah. Israel declares here that after deliberation, evaluation and estimation He was found wanting. She measured Christ according to her own ideal. According to the carnal preference of Israel He had to be such and such and not otherwise; this is why she did not esteem Him at His coming into the world.

Christ Bore Our Griefs

4. Surely he hath borne our griefs, and carried our sorrows: yet we did esteem him stricken, smitten of God, and afflicted.

It is useful to say a few words about faith healing, of which so much is written and said nowadays, and which some see as the work of the Saviour and others as that of the devil. In this beautiful moving chapter converted Israel explains her rejection of the Messiah.

Surely, cries the now converted Israel, *he hath borne our griefs.* On the word *sicknesses* (Dutch version), see the observations on the phrase *acquainted with grief* in the preceding verse, where the same word is used regarding Christ; there it refers to all weakness and misery (cf. Rom.

8:3). From this it is clear that the word may not be limited to spiritual maladies, which are the same as sins. Neither does the evangelist limit the word when he says in Matthew 8:6-17 that the Lord Jesus healed *all those who were sick,* that it might be fulfilled which was spoken by Esaias the prophet, saying, Himself took our infirmities, and bare our sicknesses. Hence we are to think of physical suffering in its thousandfold manifestations and in the most general sense of the word.

People who believe in healing only upon prayer, appeal especially to this text. The school of Dr. A. B. Simpson, (The Christian Missionary Alliance) bases its agrument upon the fact that Christ has taken *our* sicknesses upon Himself and that as a result we no longer need to bear them. By way of analogy it is argued, "If Christ bore our guilt, then we are righteous before God as though we had never known or committed any sin or guilt; if Christ bore *our sicknesses,* then we are delivered from them just as well as believers we no longer need to bear any illnesses and therefore the sicknesses which believing people still bear are totally the result of unbelief, since they do not totally accept Christ's sacrifice."

This argument seems to be foolproof and even God-honoring; it is neither. First, the analogy is false. *Guilt* and *sickness* are totally different concepts that may not be identified. For *guilt* is a judicial concept and concerns the *state* of man, while *sickness* is a physical concept and concerns the *condition* of man. *Guilt* touches his relationship over against the law, while sickness concerns the natural body.

Secondly, if one were to argue consistently he would really have to say, "Christ bore our guilt, hence we *can* never be condemned as guilty ones any more; thus Christ bore our sicknesses, so that we *can* nevermore get sick." For the believer who hides in Christ is fully justified, even though he still finds many sins and miseries within himself. Hence if one wishes to view these two matters in the same way, he should advance a step farther and say: Christ bore our sicknesses, hence we *can* nevermore become ill." They do not dare go that far.

In the third place, we ask who is speaking here of *our*

griefs? The entire preceding and following context teaches us that it is converted Israel who says this, after she has returned to God. Here Israel has returned to her Shepherd and cries out, looking back upon her centuries-old wandering outside the Messiah, "All we like sheep have gone astray; we have turned every one to his own way." Israel laments her former blindness which prevented her from seeing the glory of the *sprout;* she did not appreciate the suffering and the death of Christ on the cross. Now this same converted Israel testifies that Christ took upon Himself *our,* that is, the Jews' sicknesses. Long ago the Lord had already declared through Moses that if Israel would be obedient, He would not lay the sicknesses of the nations upon Israel (Deut. 7:15), but Israel did not obey His voice and therefore already in the days of Elisha there were many lepers in Israel, without any one of them being cured. The only one to be healed was a heathen. And during Christ's sojourn on earth there were many who were grievously ill. But when Israel will one day be converted to God, Jehovah-Jesus will take all these illnesses from His people, for in the millennium there will no longer be heard any voice of weeping or crying from any sick or suffering person (65:19). This is what the God-fearing Israelites are thinking of in this confession.

Finally it must be noted that we do not wholly agree with Dr. Haldeman who recently wrote that the complete healing of all believers was not the fruit of Christ's satisfaction. We believe that the entire groaning creation was comprehended in Christ's satisfaction. He has tasted death for *everything,* as Hebrews 2:9 says, and not only for *every man* — even for a lion and leopard, a bear and a wolf. But what do we presently find as far as the world of these animals is concerned? All creation is still in travail; these wild animals are still predatory in nature. Only when Christ comes again will He deliver this ransomed creation and lift it up out of the corruption to which it is subjected; He will also change the nature of those wild animals (Isa. 11 and 65). The same is true of sickness. Christ has borne them for the entire creation, but presently He applies this glorious fruit of His crucifixion merits neither to Israel nor to the nations. As far as the Church is concerned, He already does so to the Church

Triumphant on high, but not here below. He will apply them to Israel as a nation in the next age of salvation, but to the nations that will be saved He will not do so until the everlasting eternity.

But, *we esteemed Him,* says redeemed Israel, that He was *stricken, smitten of God* and *afflicted.* For centuries this has been exactly the Jewish view of Christ's suffering. But when the scales will have been removed from the Jews' eyes, then they will truly begin to appreciate the suffering and death of our precious Savior, and in these words bewail and confess their blindness to their suffering Messiah.

The Mediatorial Suffering of Our Lord

> 5. But he was wounded for our transgressions, he was bruised for our iniquities: the chastisement of our peace was upon him; and with his stripes we are healed.

This verse contains a contrast with the last part of the preceding verse. It may be a continuation of the idea expressed in the first part of verse four. The first thing Israel says of Him is that He was *wounded,* literally *pierced through.* Just as many expressions in this remarkable chapter refer to particulars of the suffering of Christ, so here we apparently find a hint of the fact that Christ was *pierced* on the cross. The cause of it is said to be *for our transgressions.* This implies the sin of apostasy, forsaking, breech of covenant and marital unfaithfulness. Israel says that Christ received the thrust of death because of her rebellion and spiritual infidelity.

He was bruised for our iniquities. The substitutionary suffering of the Surety is further described. There is no other chapter in Scripture that emphasizes Christ's mediatorial suffering to the extent that this one does. In this verse alone the substitutionary character of the suffering is pointed out four times. Not only the substitutionary nature of Christ's suffering is revealed, but also the horrendous nature of sin. This is why another word for sin is used here, one that points out the wrong, the crooked and the perverse. The word indicates missing the goal, since man had veered away from the line of his intended destination. This word describes sin not merely as an act, but also as a *being wrong.* Man not only *does* what is wrong, but he *is* wrong, crooked, perverse and separated from God. Thus, Israel *is* wrong, crooked, perverse and separated from God. Thus, Israel says, this is why Christ was *buried, ground to dust.* He was struck into the dust of death for the sake of our crookedness.

The chastisement of our peace was upon him. To Israel the word *peace* had the wide meaning of temporal and eternal well-being. Whereas *we* wish someone much prosperity and blessing, the Jews say, "Peace to you!" There is no reason why the broad meaning of this word should not be maintained here, as may be concluded from the last clause of this verse that peace also implies *healing.* The punishment, meted out to Christ by God and men affords Israel peace, even a Kingdom of Peace. But also the believers from among the Gentiles may cry out with Paul, *"He is our peace!"*

With his stripes we are healed. Here we find again the glorious contrast between Him and us. The word translated *stripes* indicates the blueness of the skin as a result of scourging. Israel confesses that it beat the Surety's skin black and blue, so that we might have healing; what is more, it already healed the people of their sin and sickness. These words do refer to physical healing but not exclusively. Israel will be cured from all her hardness and blindness, from all the poisonous stabs, from the old serpent and not the least from the deadly sickness of her unbelieving heart.

The Confession of the Redeemed People

> 6. All we like sheep have gone astray; we have turned every one to his own way; and the LORD hath laid on him the iniquity of us all.

After God-fearing Israel in the preceding verses has repented of her great sin against the Messiah, she commences to speak in this verse about her misery as a result of that sin in a striking metaphor derived from pastoral life. There is here a great contrast between what Israel did and what the Lord had done.

All we like sheep have gone astray. What a touching, soul-stirring confession! The point of comparison is not the errant, stubborn and dumb nature of sheep, but the wretchedness of these animals once they have wandered away from the shepherd. Israel shows here that she knew not only her misery but also the cause of it. *They* had left the Shepherd, though the faithful Shepherd surely had not left them. The verb *gone astray* implies turning away, turning in another direction, and points to a moral turning away, apostasy and unfaithful forsaking. Indeed, the Lord is not like a hireling or the wicked shepherds of which Ezekiel speaks; they were more interested in the fat than in the feeding, in the wool than in grazing the sheep. Israel did not acknowledge the good and great Shepherd of the sheep as her Shepherd, and this was the real cause of all her misery, the wandering about outside of her country and the spiritual wandering outside of the Messiah and sovereign King. A faithful shepherd feeds and tends his sheep and since Israel wandered about in separation from her Shepherd, she has not had this privilege for many centuries. Already for many centuries Israel has been subjected to all kinds of misery. Wild animals, which love to stalk stray sheep, have devoured her, for she wandered about in all nations without a Shepherd.

We have turned every one to his own way. The flock, the entire nation, had forsaken the Shepherd, but afterwards the sheep did not stay together as one flock either. Hence, the general national wandering is individualized here. Almost casually we are taught that outside of Christ there is no unity. Both Scripture and experience teach this clearly enough, but since the tower builders of Babel man keeps on seeking unity outside of God and Christ. Notwithstanding all the cries of unity, equality, fraternity, federation, and similar hollow slogans and sounds, there is less unity in our day than ever before. Everyone seeks his own interest and chooses his own pathway and walks after his or her own god or goddess. Outside of Christ everyone walks according to the dictates of his own errant heart in ways of his own choosing, regardless of the lying trumpet sounds of unity. Roaming about, the seekers of happiness are going their own way and in their own manner toward death, the grave and hell.

And the Lord hath laid on him the iniquity of us all. The text speaks here in contrast with Israel's wandering. Because the Father caused the iniquity of us all to *rush against* Him (Dutch version), Israel once again obtained unity in the one Shepherd. Not only the substitutionary and sin-bearing, but also the judicial character of the suffering of the cross by Christ is beautifully demonstrated. He did not suffer like a martyr, for the latter was always comforted in his suffering; the Father caused the abomination of us all to crash into Him. Israel sobs while the tears of joy and gratitude on the one hand, and of the sorrow of forsaking and murdering that Shepherd on the other, flow freely. The word *run against* (Dutch version) is particularly rich in meaning. It means, Da Costa says, the converging of a large troop upon a certain point. Who is not reminded of the cattle and the dogs that encompassed Him, the strong bulls of Bashan that encircled Him and the congregation of evildoers that surrounded Him at the cross? An animals horde stormed at the immaculate and innocent Lamb of God.

The same word is used for the breaking of waves upon a rock. Just as the angry North Sea pounds the dikes of the Netherlands and the grey waves with their white crests come rolling on like huge serpents, so the waves and billows of God's fury over our sins came pounding upon the Rock of Ages. The taking of our sins upon Himself is beautifully stated here. The Lord took Israel's and our sins and placed them upon the innocent Lamb. The Lamb was of itself totally innocent, but God loaded Him down with our sins. He caused them to come down *upon* Him, not *into* Him. This important difference must ever be kept in mind. Just as in the olden days Israel's sin was symbolically placed on the head of the goat or ram, but never inside of it, so the Savior received them as it were on His innocent head; our sins have never been *in* Him. He was *made sin* for us, not a *sinner!*

If correctly understood, how comforting this statement should be to us, for when the Father has taken them away from us and put them upon His Son, then we no longer have them. Then He can no longer be wroth with us nor rebuke us. This is why we feel that redeemed Israel is sobbing for such a great blessing. O marvelous mystery of redemption! How high, deep, long and wide it is! Only when all the saints are together at last will they be able to measure it. He, the immaculate Holy One, became an accursed One who was banished outside the camp. The Father forsook Him and His own people rejected Him. The disciples fled from Him, and hell broke loose against Him; the devils swooped down on Him. All that because of *the iniquities of us all!*

The Manner in Which Christ Suffered

> 7. He was oppressed, and he was afflicted, yet he opened not his mouth: he is brought as a lamb to the slaughter, and as a sheep before her shearers is dumb, so he openeth not his mouth.

The first three verses of this chapter describe Christ's humble appearance; the next three His substitutionary suffering; now the manner of His suffering is described. In striking metaphors, the prophet indicates that His attitude during His suffering was that of quiet obedience and humble submission.

The opening words of the Dutch version, *When it was demanded,* is translated in various ways. The most common meaning of *demand* is the sense of demanding payment of debts or taxes. The Jewish expositors who do not take this chapter as a reference to Christ, take it to mean the extortion of heavy levies against the Jews. But it seems to us that the D.A.V. has the correct meaning. Payment for sin was demanded of Christ, hence He was summoned before the bar of God and was punished because our sins rested on Him.

He was oppressed. The wrath of God pressed down on Him, Satan pressed Him, and men tortured Him. He was oppressed by Satan, God and men. He did not destroy His attackers, but He allowed Himself to be tortured. Willingly and submissively He gave Himself as a sacrifice and endured the harshest treatment from the hand of His oppressors.

He openeth not his mouth. Is there anything more difficult than suffering innocently? And is there anything more natural than to open one's mouth in defense or in cursing? But Christ kept silent before Caiaphas, Pilate and Herod, and before His false accusers and murderers on Golgotha. What a meek submission!

He is brought as a lamb to the slaughter. Christ was and is a Lion in strength and courage. Yet He allowed Himself to be brought as a lamb to the slaughter. But He was not dull-witted as a lamb. He knew very well what was awaiting Him. The prophet in this touching metaphor is obviously thinking of the paschal Lamb. And he is manifestly still thinking of the wandering sheep of the preceding verse. The flock is led in the right way by a lamb. The Lord God always accomplishes great things by small means such as a branch, a twig, a lamb, a worm, or a small flock.

As a sheep before her shearers is dumb. Christ is compared to a full-grown sheep that is being shorn. It is a striking image, but as always with images, it is incomplete and does not fully reflect the reality. A sheep suffers without any self-consciousness; but it was entirely different with the Savior. A sheep suffers in powerlessness, because it is made to, and can't do anything about it. Christ suffered because He wanted to. Besides, the comparison is to be sought first of all in the meekness and dumbness of the sheep. It may groan under the hand of the shearers, but it does not roar. The shearing of sheep was a festive occasion in Israel. Christ was shorn on the feast of Passover.

Christ's Death

> 8. He was taken from prison and from judgment: and who shall declare his generation? for he was cut off out of the land of the living: for the transgression of my people was he stricken.

The story of the sufferings of the Servant of the Lord is continued here. It is said that He perished in His unfathomable suffering, and not, as some think, based on the sound of the words, that He was delivered from His suffering by His resurrection and ascension to heaven. Not until verse nine is there any mention of His burial. As far as the actual content of this verse is concerned, it may well be called a *crux,* for there are as many interpretations as there are possible translations. The preposition *mem* — *out or from* — is taken not only as an adjunct of time but also as *a means.* This indicates the unjust manner in which the Savior was put to death. Others translate it as a causal adjunct, *for,* in the sense of the *cause* of His death. Those who translate the preposition *mem* by *without,* point out that He was put to death without due imprisonment and a hearing, hence that He was judicially murdered. Finally there are those who translate it as *after,* meaning that the Savior was snatched away after the fear (Dutch version) and after judgment. Calvin's interpretation, followed by many, must be rejected. He comments: "When it is said of Christ that He 'is taken away from prison and judgment,' the meaning can only be that by His resurrection and ascension He advanced far beyond the reach of human justice, or rather injustice." There are serious difficulties with this. First, Christ never was in prison, nor does the word *hotzer* ever mean prison, but *fear, oppression.* Secondly, there is no reference to His ascension and resurrection, since His grave is not mentioned until the next verse. The Septuagint translates: "In His humiliation His judgment (i.e., His judicial judgment, His verdict) was taken away." It is remarkable that although this translation is not a correct rendition of the Greek, it is nevertheless stamped as being true by the Holy Spirit in Acts 8:33. It seems to us that in these two texts the two aspects of Christ's death are represented: the Hebrew gives the divine viewpoint; the Greek makes explicit the human viewpoint, as it is contained in the former.

As far as the translation is concerned, the D.A.V. is the most satisfactory. The verb form *taken* (away) has the accent here, so it means *snatched away* (cf. I Kings 19:4; Ps. 49:15; Isa. 49:25). Therefore we must not see it, as Calvin and others do, as the resurrection and ascension, but as a being snatched away from the dread of suffering and judicial murder by death in the sense that Christ's spirit went to the Father. We have here then on the one hand the climax of Christ's suffering but on the other hand also the turning point. Because when Christ died, He did not go to hell, as Roman Catholic, Greek Orthodox and Lutheran theology claim, but to the Father, while His body was laid in the grave. Although His death from the human point of view was the deepest humiliation of an accursed death on the cross, from

God's point of view it was an act of love, since He suddenly snatched His Son away from the hands of the tormentors, who had terrified, oppressed and tormented Him in the place of judgment. Hence, we take the unspecified subject of *lukach, snatched away,* to be God the Father. It was He who at the right time put a limit to the untold sufferings of the Son of His love by receiving His spirit. We are reminded here of the extraordinarily quick death of Christ, which surprised even Pilate when Joseph of Arimathea informed him that He had already died. It is said that crucified people at times lived for four or more days on the cross. Pilate apparently did not want to take only Joseph's word that Jesus had died, until the Roman centurion had emphatically confirmed it. For this reason, we also take the preposition *out* as a reference to locality, as this is its most obvious meaning. Once again, from the human point of view, Christ in His deep humiliation was murdered at the place of judgment, and this idea is found here in the Greek translation and in Acts 8:33. This is implied in the Hebrew text which mainly contains the divine aspect, according to which the Father snatched His dear Son away by a sudden death.

Who shall declare his generation? These words have caused the expositors as much trouble as the previous ones. The difficulty centers mainly around the word translated *age* (Dutch version) – *generation* (KJV) which has also been translated as generation, posterity, spiritual posterity, comtemporaries, life's course, manner of life, grave, place of residence, environment, age. Hence it is perplexing. Those who translate manner of life, the course of one's life, etc., had better with Kennicot and Lowth look for an explanation of this word in the Mishna and the Gemara of Babylon. For the Mishna speaks of a custom in olden days according to which a herald, forty days before the final judgment of a criminal, openly cried out, "Who knows anything of his life and innocence, let him testify!" The famous Jew, Maimonides, also speaks of this custom. According to Christian expositors, Jesus Himself alludes to the custom in John 18:20, 21, as did Paul in Acts 26:4, 5. According to this view, the prophet prophetically put this question in the mouth of Israel: "Who has expressed His innocence?" This is indeed a beautiful explanation on the part of Lowth and others, but it is doubtful whether it is the correct one. More recent translations, such as that of the English Revised Version (A.S.V.), by no means remove all difficulties. It has: "As for his generation, who among them considered that he was cut off out of the land of the living," etc. This is the translation of the German Rationalists Storr, Doederlein, Dath, Gesenius, Rosenmuller, De Wette, Van Ess, and Delitzsch, Van der Palm, and others. Hence this revised translation is not new. For years we ourselves considered this the correct translation, the more so since the poetic verb, translated here as *expressed,* can also mean consider, take to heart, contemplate. Then the idea is that converted Israel sadly states that almost no one in Israel considered and took to heart the meaning and significance of the Savior's suffering and death as far as its unique worth and merit is concerned. They did not know the significance and value of His life, but neither of His death. They saw His life as that of a worthless person and His death as that of a criminal. It cannot be denied that this idea as such is absolutely true and in harmony with the actual facts. This translation is far more acceptable than that of Lowth and others and the one which views it as a reference to His eternal generation or His miraculous incarnation.

But after repeated and serious examination we have returned to the oldest and most general translation and interpretation: *Who shall declare his generation?* This question refers to the far-reaching results of His death immediately after it has been mentioned. This same little word *dor,* generation, is used of Christ's Kingdom and rule in Daniel 4:3, 4. They will be from *dor* to *dor,* i.e., from generation to generation. It seems as though the Holy Spirit means to say: Christ has been murdered, but He has not been annihilated thereby, and His influence has not been permanently done away with, for He continued to live on in His generation, the generation of those that fear Him. The question of Isaiah is not answered here, and the omission is eloquent. The answer of course is: *no one can declare His generation.* The generation of the Messiah who died, in whom the Messiah continues to live on, is without number and without end. To a Jew it was a great honor to have a great and numerous posterity; likewise, the Messiah who was so ignominiously put to death has the same honor. This idea is about the same as that expressed by Calvin.

For he was cut off out of the land of the living. This is a standing expression for *murder.* Daniel 9:26 uses the same verb in connection with the Messiah. Actually it means to cut into two halves and in II Kings 6:4 it is used for the cutting down of a tree. Christ did not die a natural but a violent death.

The final clause once more indicates the cause why this Righteous One met with such an unnatural and horrible death. The word translated *transgression* indicates this sin to be *rebellion against lawful authority* (cf. I Kings 12:19; II Kings 8:20, 22; Isa. 1:2). This rebellion of Israel has been laid upon Him like a plague of leprosy, strongly emphasizes the substitutionary nature of His death.

Christ's Grave

> 9. And he made his grave with the wicked, and with the rich in his death; because he has done no violence, neither was any deceit in his mouth.

As in the preceding verse, we see here again that one and the same matter is viewed from two sides. On the one hand, the Savior's humiliation is further described, as the people went as far as assigning His final resting place with the wicked; on the other hand it is stated here that the Father took care of Him by sparing Him a most shameful humiliation by giving Him an honorable grave with the prominent. The English translation is quite unfortunate when it states, "He made his grave with the wicked," as it can neither linguistically nor factually be defended. In order to appreciate this expression it must be kept in mind that in Israel an honorable burial was considered of great importance, while on the other hand an "ass's burial" was considered shameful and reprehensible. The word *appointed* (Dutch version) *made* (KJV), actually means *given* and is used in the third person masculine singular to express the same idea as the impersonal personal pronoun *one* (as in "one would think . . . ,") when it refers to one or more persons in general. The Hebrew does not have a separate word for it, and the English actually does not either to the extent that the Dutch word *men* and the German word *man* does. The verb refers to the murderers of Christ. Christ had been *given* a grave, in the sense of *assigned,* appointed, relegated to, *with the wicked.* The word *grave* refers to a man-made cave in a rocky rise. The people of course thought that from then on Christ's dwelling place would be a grave, as Job expresses it. They saw this grave as being with and among the wicked. That was an assumed fact. They had killed Him as a wicked person; He would also be buried as a wicked person. Why should they deal differently with this criminal than with any other criminal? It would have been very strange indeed if He would have been given a better grave than that of the two malefactors crucified with Him.

And with the rich in his death. This reflects the divine viewpoint. Man deliberated, but God decided. The murderers had already made their plan: as a dishonorable person He would be dumped into a cave with other criminals. Because of a special intervention by God, however, His was not a shameful burial, but, on the contrary, He received a very honorable one. The literal fulfillment is extensively described in the beautiful history of the Savior's burial in the Gospels. *Because* he *had done no violence* states the reason for His honorable burial. He was fully deserving of this honor as He was innocent in both His words and deeds. Above it was said that He opened not His mouth because of His quiet resignation, obedience and meekness. Here it is stated that there was neither any deceit or cursing in His mouth. How different this is from a sinner whose throat is an open sepulchre, whose tongue uses deceit, whose lips hide asps' venom, and whose mouth is full of cursing and bitterness (Rom. 3:13-18). Christ not only *had* the truth, but He also *was* the Truth and Wisdom. Centuries before he appeared He was announced as the absolute sinless One. He was even without hidden aberrations.

Christ's Being Bruised by the Father

> 10. Yet it pleased the LORD to bruise him; he hath put him to grief: when thou shalt make his soul an offering for sin, he shall see his seed, he shall prolong his days, and the pleasure of the LORD shall prosper in his hand.

This verse stands in contrast with the last part of the preceding verse. If the Servant of the Lord was the absolute sinless One, the question might rightfully be asked why He had to suffer so grievously. This verse fully answers the question: He had to suffer because it pleased the Lord to bruise Him. That constituted the deepest ground, the reason for, and essence of, His suffering. It is the key to the whole mystery of His suffering. Without this explanation one might easily come to two wrong conclusions regarding His bitter suffering and death, i.e., that He either suffered so bitterly and died such an ignominious death because He was such a great sinner, or that He suffered so incomparably as an innocent martyr at the hand of evil people, as did other martyrs. But in order to remove this misconception, it is emphatically said here that it *pleased* the Lord to bruise Him. It is a strange Scripture, full of the divine mysteries of salvation! In view of the sentimentality and idolatry around the Babe of Bethlehem, it is good to be reminded of this word. In so-called passion sermons during the passion week this word is often kept in the background. It has specifically and emphatically been said of Christ that He was perfectly innocent and righteous. Even heathen seafarers were terribly afraid to pollute themselves with innocent blood and shrank back from casting an innocent person overboard (Jonah 1:14), so that these heathen were more merciful than the Father of our Lord Jesus Christ. If a true father's heart weeps when chastising a recalcitrant son, how then can the Father of the immaculate Holy One take pleasure in crushing the Son of His bosom and grinding Him to dust? Is He then a Father who punishes from a desire to afflict? Indeed, He is not. In fact, it is a wicked concept on the part of the Modern theologians when they view Jehovah as a vengeful and murderous god who insensitively keeps on demanding bloody sacrifices for His own satisfaction. All idolizing of the love of the Son at the expense of the love of the Father is sin. We need but to remember John 3:16 and II Corinthians 5:21. The Father brought just as much a sacrifice of love as did the Son. But for a correct understanding of this text we need to remind ourselves that the Son, although He was perfectly innocent as far as His nature and state were concerned, was nevertheless placed, for our sakes, under the law as a guilty one. As far as His state was concerned He was definitely guilty since *the Lord laid on Him the iniquity of us all.* We had deserved to be crushed by His feet, but now it pleased the Lord to crush Him as our Substitute. So whoever rejects Him can surely count on the fact that it will please God one day to slay such a one before His feet.

Furthermore, we must fully realize that God's bruising of His son was not the Father's object but His means. He wished thereby to establish something glorious and indeed He did. The objective must always determine the means. And since the objective was marvelously great, the means had to be great and awe-inspiring. The object was the deliverance of a creation that had deserved to be turned to rubble at His feet and of a people who had deserved to be crushed. In order to make such a deliverance possible, a Mediator and Substitute was needed, and now it pleased God to elect His Son to be that person so that He was now bruised in their place.

This text also intimates that we could not make any claim whatsoever to such a sacrifice. We owe the guilt-removing sacrifice of Christ only to the good pleasure of the Lord, to His great mercy. His good pleasure is the final cause of this sacrifice and the means of the bruising of His Son. The basic cause of both means and objective lay entirely in God. Hence it does not say: "It pleased the Lord that he was bruised," for this would not please Him at all. He hated and despised the work of the murderers. The Father *Himself* bruised Him; the people were but the instruments. All these things took place according to His determinate counsel and foreknowledge (Acts 2:23).

He hath put him to grief. What does this mean? For we read nowhere that He was *sick* (Dutch version). The word *sick* does not logically fit here. To have been made sick after

He had been crushed does not make sense. For an explanation, see the observations made on verse three, which also speaks of sickness. The word *sick* is derived from a verb meaning *to squeeze dry, to hurt;* it is an expansion of the word used previously. The prophet wants to emphasize that *God* did all this, that all the suffering to which the Messiah was subject originated with the Father. Regarding the suffering of the Messiah there seems to be no language strong enough to bring out the wholly unique character and the most fundamental cause of it.

When thou shalt make his soul an offering for sin, he shall see his seed. When it is said that His soul was offered, this means the same as saying that His soul was made a sacrifice. According to the biblical presentation, the soul, i.e., life, is in the blood. That is why Baalam cried out, "Let me die the death of the righteous!" The Savior offered Himself as a sacrifice for sin. Hence, it was an offer of great and infinite importance. A sin offering consisted of a perfect ram and was required when one had unknowingly sinned against God or had deliberately defrauded his fellow man. It was a sacrifice of satisfaction, it is in this sense that it is used here. As such it excludes all other sacrifices. God's wrath burned against sin, but because Christ offered Himself as a sin offering, this anger was removed. The threefold fruit of this perfect sacrifice now demands our attention.

He shall see his seed. The connection here is not temporal, such as *when* or *after* He had offered His soul as a sacrifice; is causal, not *after that* but *because of that.* The prophet had just used language derived from the Jewish sacrificial service. Here again he uses an expression that meant much more to an Israelite than to a Westerner. We might translate this phrase as: *He shall rejoice in having posterity.* In Israel, no greater blessing was imaginable than a numerous family. The next chapter is entirely based on this idea. What we find here is actually an unexpressed contrast. For the prophet has just said that He was *cut off* and *bruised,* so that it was logical that everyone would think that He would forever be deprived of the rich blessing of descendants. But this notion is emphatically contradicted. Although He was crushed, He would nevertheless see seed; indeed exactly *because of that*

He would rejoice in an abundant posterity. It is not necessary to point out that He would obtain this seed not in a generative but a federative way as the second Adam and representative Head of the covenant of grace (cf. Ps. 22:31).

As a second rich fruit of His sin offering, we read: *He shall prolong his days.* Just as desirable as a numerous family was the blessing of a long life. The word *prolong* therefore actually means *to cause to be long.* Israel was a people of this earth and had no clear concept of the things beyond death and the grave. What was most important to an Israelite was the temporal, not the eternal; the concrete and visible, not the invisible; the terrestrial, not the celestial; the present life, not the future life; this governed his entire view of life and the world. This must be kept in mind here, otherwise these words have little meaning. In spite of His shameful death, He will live long. The four most desirable things to a pious Jew mentioned in Ecclesiastes 6:3 are, remarkably enough, ascribed to the dead Messiah. If we keep this desired fourfold blessing in mind, a flood of light is cast on hundreds of texts in the Old Testament. We then can also understand the difference between Israel and the Church, as well as this beautiful chapter.

"The crown of glory blooms forever on the head of the great Son of David." *The pleasure of the Lord shall prosper in his hand.* This is the third glorious fruit of the death of Christ. *Pleasure* refers to the plan, the counsel of God to glorify Himself in the restoration of the entire creation from its fall, to destroy the works of the devil and to deliver His people from the greatest evil making them partakers of the greatest good. All of this lies, instrumentally, in the hand of the Messiah. How comforting this is! For how safe and assured it is in the hand of Him who is called the Mighty God! No devil or demon can snatch this plan from His hand! Christ, too, always works to materialize this plan, for we read that it prospers. Often it seems to us that it regresses or fails. This is because we do not give heed to the *hand* of Christ but look rather at the powerless hands of man. Sinful man indeed fails. Outside of God, sinners perish forever. But in the hand of our Mediator all things prosper, *happily* and *successfully* (Dutch version). He prospers in *wisdom,* for He is Wisdom personified; in *power* for He is the Mighty God. The words *proceed prosperously* (Dutch version) or *unhinderedly* are used of the unhindered flow of a stream. Just as a mountain stream can be stopped or dammed by nothing, so also Christ in the day of His coming again will break down all resistance and opposition. In 52:13 the same word is used where it is translated *deal prudently.* In Joshua 1:7, 8 it is used of strict adherence to the law. Christ will do this when He returns. The judgment of Israel is nothing but the application of the rule of the law to Israel. It is also used of Hezekiah, when he destroyed the brass serpent because He trusted in God and walked according to the law; he acted *courageously* (D.A.V.; KJV has *he prospered,* cf. II Kings 18:7). This word is full of instruction and makes us see that all of God's counsel must be seen Christologically. How much has been written and said in recent years about the counsel of God as though it were a *Gedankending,* an idea, a thing of the mind. All of Scripture, however, is Christocentric, it has Christ as its center. The same holds true of every doctrine. Whoever does not see this, simply does not understand half of Scripture, and must inevitably promote a dead orthodoxy which soon fills everyone with disgust.

Fruits of the Suffering and Death of the Savior

11. He shall see of the travail of his soul, and shall be satisfied: by his knowledge shall my righteous servant justify many for he shall bear their iniquities.

This verse mentions more fruits of the Savior's suffering. Thus far the converted children of Israel have spoken with indescribable sadness about their rejection of the Messiah, and their misery, as well as about the *manner* and the *reason* of His suffering and death. Now the Father Himself is introduced as the Speaker, as is evident from the words *my servant.* Naturally, the people could not speak of Him this way. A remarkable phenomenon is that from now on we no longer will find any mention of the *Servant of the Lord;* we do have references to the *servants of the Lord.* In 61:1-3 He is alluded to but not mentioned. On the other hand, there are many references to the *servants* (54:17; 56:6; 63:17; 65:8, 9, 13, 14, 15; 66:14). This is very significant. It tells us that with Christ's suffering and death His state as a servant has come to an end, and that through the *travail of his soul* many servants have come into being, who now serve Him. It is also very meaningful that this text speaks of the *travail* of His soul and not merely of His *work*. The words *labor, travail* and *work* are very different from each other. *Travail* is abnormal activity under abnormal circumstances, whereas *work* is normal activity under normal circumstances. The first Adam *worked* in the Garden of Eden, but he did not yet labor or travail. That he did only as the result and curse of sin. In heaven, where all the results of sin will have been removed, we will also work, but not travail. Here it is said that the second Adam *travailed,* that He painfully labored and toiled under the curse of sin. But because of His bearing the burden of the wrath of God, He will *see it* (Dutch version). See what? The answer cannot be anything else but His counsel, and the successful progress, the unfolding, the revelation and the completion of the plan and counsel of God. The Lord Jesus will rejoice in, and satisfy Himself with, the beholding of all God's Counsel. This will be the reward of the Father upon the travail of His soul. He cries in Psalm 22: "My praise shall be of thee in the great congregation (v. 22)." Presently He leads many children to glory, and at the presentation of the Church without spot and without wrinkle He will cry out in holy rapture: "Behold, I and the children thou gavest me!" Do we ever rejoice in the rejoicing of Christ?

By his knowledge shall my righteous servant justify many. This is yet another fruit of His death on the cross. What kind of knowledge is this text referring to? It is the same kind of knowledge as is mentioned in John 17:3 and Philippians 3:10. This knowledge includes faith and love, and results in salvation. In a typical Isaiahic play on words it is said that the Righteous One will make righteous. If He Himself were unrighteous, He would not be able to do so, for a stream never rises above its source. However, since He Himself is perfectly righteous, He is able to perform this miracle of grace by spreading the knowledge of Himself. He will *justify* many, i.e., absolve them of guilt and punishment and give them a child's right, an inheritance right to eternal life. He will not do so unto *all,* but in any case to *many.* For one day it will become a multitude no one can number.

For he shall bear their iniquities. This statement indicates the basis for the preceding. The word *bear,* which refers to the carrying of a heavy burden, and is also used in verse four, is never used for the carrying away of the guilt of sin as such. Another word is used for that idea. So it seems to us that we have no reference here to the carrying away of sin on the cross, which has frequently been mentioned before, but to His high-priestly carrying of our sins into the most holy place by high-priestly intercession. When the high priest went into the sanctuary to appear before God's countenance, he symbolically carried, after the shedding of blood, sinful Israel on his heart, just as he carried the twelve tribes symbolically in his breastplate. And this is what the Lord Jesus is doing now too for Israel and His Church. The future tense[1] of the verb is used to indicate the lasting and ever present power of this bearing. If He did not bear Israel and us on His great heart, no Jew or Gentile would become righteous at all. The next verse refers to the carrying away of sin.

The Messiah as Triumphant Victor

12. Therefore will I divide him a portion with the great, and he shall divide the spoil with the strong; because he hath poured out his soul unto death: and he was numbered with the transgressors; and he bare the sin of many, and made intercession for the transgressors.

This verse speaks of the final fruit and reward of the substitutionary death of Christ. His labor was heavy and His reward will be proportionately great. Christ is presented here as a mighty conqueror who has defeated all his enemies and now divides the spoil among his soldiers. Most expositors find here a reference to His spiritual triumphs over Satan, sin, death, the grave and hell. But this is chiefly a reference to His

---

[1] Bultema refers to the English translation here; Hebrew has no formal future tense as such. —ED.

victory over the antichristian world powers at the end of this present dispensation (cf. 63:1-6). The first clause is translated in many different ways, but the main thrust remains the same in all translations, i.e., that Christ after a great victory obtains rich spoils and great honor. The Father will give Him triumph, honor and riches. The same idea is repeated in different words: *He shall divide the spoil with the strong.* Which *strong* are referred to here? Are they the evil spirits, as some think, appealing to Colossians 2:15? Or are they mighty nations or kings or geniuses of the mind? We answer: they are all the powers that oppose Him (cf. chaps. 2, 14, 63; Eph. 1:21-22; 4:8; 6:10-17; Rev. 1:18). *Spoil* has nothing to do with street robbery, but with military spoils. *Because he hath poured out his soul unto death* indicates the reason why He received such great honor. His *soul* stands for His entire human nature and especially His body, because it is pointed out that He poured out Himself, emptied Himself, to the very last drop. Hence He poured out His soul, His life, unto death. Here we find a glorious twofold thought expressed. It speaks of both the *completeness* and the *voluntary aspect* of His sacrifice. This verse contains four reasons for His great victory over all ungodly powers of the future, and this is the first of them (cf. Philippians 2:5-10). The exaltation is beyond all measure since the humiliation was also beyond all measure.

The second reason for His exaltation is indicated in the words *he was numbered with the transgressors.* The words, transgressors, refers to insurrectionists, insurgents, rebels against legal authority. It was with this kind of scum the innocent Security allowed Himself to be numbered. They approached Him as if He were a heavily armed murderer; they chose a murderer in His stead; they crucified Him between two murderers, and they assigned Him a grave among the wicked rabble. This phrase seems to hint that the two malefactors who were crucified with Him were rebels against Roman authority.

And he bare the sin of many is the third reason for His glorious victory in the future. The piling up of words seems to indicate the prophet's fears that the people will not see the importance of the matter clearly. Hence he emphatically repeats the pronoun *he,* the same person who suffered so unspeakably. The word *bare* means to *take up, carry* and *carry away* sin. It is a different word than the one used in verse eleven. This word *bear* reminds one of the Baptist's statement: "Behold the Lamb of God that taketh away the sin of the world." It points out the substitutionary character of Christ's suffering. The word *many* contradicts not only Universal but also the doctrine of general redemption. God forgives the sins only of those whose debt is paid and whose spots are covered by His cleansing blood. Reconciliation and forgiveness are the result of satisfaction on the cross.

And made intercession for the transgressors. This is the fourth reason for His exaltation; it summarizes the entire final section. We need not take the meaning of the words *made intercession* in the narrow sense of intercession, but in the broad, general sense of *interceding for the purpose of removing guilt.* We must not limit these words to the Savior's prayer on the cross for the transgressors. That is evident from the fact that in the Hebrew the future tense[2] of the verb is used to indicate that this work is of an ongoing nature. He started it on the cross and continues it during this entire dispensation until there will no longer be any transgressors on earth. "Bless the Lord, O my soul: and all that is within me, bless His holy name!" We have seen that the description of the humiliated Christ lies between[3] the descriptions of His exaltation which is a glorious means to an even more glorious end.

[2]Bultema refers to the Hebrew imperfect which can be used for future action; the Hebrew imperfect by itself conveys only continuing action as he notes. The context suggests the future element. —ED.

[3]Bultema is thinking here of Isa. 52:13 which begins this servant song. —ED.

ISAIAH 54

He Shall See His Seed

> 1. Sing, O barren, thou that didst not bear; break forth into singing, and cry aloud, thou that didst not travail with child: for more are the children of the desolate than the children of the married wife, saith the LORD.

Many fail to see the connection between this and the preceding chapter. This chapter is connected with verse ten, i.e., with the expression *he shall see his seed.* Here we see that *seed* which Christ would obtain by His death on the cross of Golgotha. This entire chapter can be properly considered a continuation and further development of the preceding one.

The main thought of the chapter, as well as that of the entire second part of the book of Isaiah, is the reacceptance of Israel. These verses have been used as texts to prove the extension of the Church. But those who engage in glorifying the Church don't seem to realize that they are at the same time guilty of doing the Church a dishonor. If they were consistent, they would also have to compare the Church with a barren and despised woman, as she is depicted in the first verse. For the idea of Church extension, appeal is often made to Galatians 4:26, where the Apostle applies this text to the Jerusalem that is above. But this Jerusalem is by no means the same as the institutional Church. Nor has the Church ever been totally barren; but Israel has for over two thousand years. The Church has never been forsaken for a small moment (v. 7), for Christ promised to be with her until the end of the world. If we wish to explain a chapter like this as referring to the glory of the Church, we must of necessity run into all kinds of absurdities. But on the other hand, all the power and beauty of this figurative language can be fittingly explained as referring to Israel's future glory.

To understand this chapter correctly, it must further be observed that the entire presentation of Israel as a wife is based on the rich covenant relationship that exists between Israel as a nation and God. At the institution of this covenant with the people on Mt. Horeb this marriage was contracted from God's side out of free love; Israel responded to it with shameful adultery. Israel, as the wife of Jehovah, was *barren* and *unfaithful,* and for that reason He forsook her *for a small moment* (v. 7). This verse is an historical allusion to Sarah and Hannah. A barren woman in the Near East felt that her happiness was destroyed and therefore felt alone and miserable, often being ignored and despised. She considered a numerous offspring to be her glory. But one day the roles will be reversed for Israel, which as yet is barren, unfaithful, lonely and cast out. The lonely woman is here urged to rejoice greatly, as is evident from the three different expressions the prophet uses for rejoicing. The basis for this great joy will be the great number of children. They will be more in number than those of the *married woman.* The *desolate* and the *married* wife are juxtaposed here. *Desolate* actually means *destroyed,* and refers to the destruction of Jerusalem. The Lord will once more accept her and then as the formerly forsaken wife she will bear more children than she bore when she had not yet been forsaken. This exhortation to breaking forth into singing is comparable to the beautiful prophetic doxology of Hannah, recorded in I Samuel 2.

The Great Growth of Restored Israel

2. Enlarge the place of thy tent, and let them stretch forth the curtains of thine habitations: spare not, lengthen thy cords, and strengthen thy stakes;
3. For thou shalt break forth on the right hand and on the left; and thy seed shall inherit the Gentiles, and make the desolate cities to be inhabited.

Scripture contains numerous images derived from living in tents. Israel's ancestors lived in tents during the wanderings in the desert. But long after Israel no longer lived in tents, the use of the expression *tents* instead of *houses* continued (cf. I Kings 12:16; Song 1:5; cf. 33:20). Disassembling a tent in the end becomes the standing metaphor for death (Jer. 10:20; II Cor. 5:1; II Pet. 1:13), while on the other hand enlarging a tent and driving its stakes in deeply indicated constancy, prosperity and extension. The latter is found here. Since the children of the lonely woman will be so many, the dwelling place, the tent, must be enlarged. Tents, like our houses, were of various sizes. A lonely woman did not need a large tent, of course, but it is exactly such a forsaken woman who will receive a numerous offspring, and therefore her tent needs to be enlarged. The stakes around the tent, its area, the ropes and the curtains are mentioned by name. *Spare not,* the prophet adds casually and yet emphatically. It seems as if he already senses how narrow-minded Jewish particularism would attempt to hinder the prophesied extension. He uses no less than four similes regarding the enlargement of the tent, and one prohibition. As elsewhere, the commands stand for the certainty of their fulfillment.

Verse three contains the basis of the commands that are given. It lies in the enormous growth Israel will experience in that future day. In Israel, the expression *on the right hand and on the left* meant *in every direction.* Verse one already mentioned the multitude of children, but here this thought is further developed in even stronger language. The *seed,* repeatedly mentioned in connection with the patriarchs, and which the *Servant of the Lord* would see after His suffering, *shall inherit the Gentiles,* that is, will take possession of, have dominion over and rule. They will inhabit *the desolate cities* that have been in ruins from generation to generation. The Church does not have desolate cities, but Israel does. When as a theological student I expounded this text, I expressed the following comments, which rather reflect the general view of most commentators:

> If the question is asked when this promise will be fulfilled, the answer is that the actual, final fulfillment will not come until the coming of Christ, who Himself will annihilate all sin. But, already now for almost two thousand years, the triumphal march of the gospel to the four corners of the earth has begun; the Gentiles have been

disinherited; their destroyed cities have been taken, while the barren wildernesses of the earth have begun to bloom like a rose.

The exposition, regardless how beautiful it may sound, is totally wrong, since it robs Israel of her glorious future. Israel is the key and content of all prophetic predictions. Whoever loses sight of this fact does not do justice to these predictions.

The Fear, Shame, Reproach, and Confusion Taken Away

4. Fear not; for thou shalt not be ashamed: neither be thou confounded; for thou shalt not be put to shame: for thou shalt forget the shame of thy youth, and shalt not remember the reproach of thy widowhood any more.
5. For thy Maker is thine husband; the LORD of hosts is his name; and thy Redeemer the Holy One of Israel; The God of the whole earth shall he be called.
6. For the LORD hath called thee as a woman forsaken and grieved in spirit, and a wife of youth, when thou wast refused, saith thy God.

Whereas in verse one the lonely and barren woman was urged to sing joyfully here her fear is compensated. A woman in such a condition is easily subject to great fear. The Lord likes to see childlike fear in His people, but not slavish or childish fear, which fills the heart with anxiousness and concern and which expels love. And why does she need not fear? Because she will not be *put to shame.* As a barren woman she was despised by her husband and neighbors. But, as she was told already in the preceding verses, this will change; her seed will inherit the earth. Her Husband, Jehovah, lives! He will take care of her honor. God's people do not show much concern for *His* honor, but God Himself maintains *their* honor; He will bestow grace and *honor* on them. Israel's condition seems totally hopeless, but it is far from hopeless. *Thou shalt not be ashamed.* In Israel, an adulterous woman was publicly shamed, but here the woman is assured that she need not be confounded and that no blush of shame need color her cheeks, as her shame will not be made public by exposing her.

We take *the shame of thy youth* as a reference to Israel's unfaithfulness at the inauguration of the covenant of the law at Mt. Horeb and during her wanderings in the desert, while *the reproach of thy widowhood* refers to the periods of Israel's exile and banishment from the land and from the favor of the Lord. Those expositors who consider it a reference only to the Babylonian exile again have a far too narrow view of this grand chapter. For Israel is still dwelling as a barren, unfaithful and rejected people among the nations, outside of the holy land, full of shame and reproach. But the day is coming when Israel will *forget* even the shame and reproach of her earlier history. What grace this is! It is a grace that not only forgives and accepts again, but even causes the former shame to be forgotten. This tells us that Israel in the ages to come will not be vexed by the painful thought that as the wife of Jehovah, she had so shamefully forsaken her Maker and Husband. Not only Israel but Jehovah Himself will forgive and forget, for He has assured frequently that He will not *remember* Israel's sins.

Verse five positively indicates why she need not fear anything. He who created her, also married her. Again her Husband is mentioned with four glorious names, each of which expresses an inherent glory, but upon which we need not enlarge at this moment. A few remarks regarding the name *The God of the whole earth will suffice.* Here we see that Christ in the Kingdom of Peace will be acknowledged and glorified as the God of the whole earth, but that at the same time He will have a holy marriage relationship only with Israel. As the *Gaal* He will, with a drawn sword, maintain the rights of His wife and revenge the injustice done to her by the nations. Verse six depicts in the most tender language the entire history throughout the ages of Israel's sin, punishment and reacceptance. Not only does Jehovah pity the forsaken wife, but the most tender love for her re-emerges again.

A Small Moment and a Little Wrath

7. For a small moment have I forsaken thee; but with great mercies will I gather thee.
8. In a little wrath I hid my face from thee for a moment; but

with everlasting kindness will I have mercy on thee, saith the
LORD thy Redeemer.

Now Jehovah Himself is introduced as the Speaker.

The Creator remains Israel's Husband. She had never been
a real widow though people have thought so. Israel's total
rejection has been the foundation of most biblical
expositions and dogmatics in Christendom. Jehovah admits
here that He indeed had forsaken Israel, but it was only *for a
small moment* and *in a little wrath*. This is surprising
language, for how entirely different does Israel's rejection
appear to us. How totally different does Israel herself view
this rejection, according to the second part of chapter
sixty-three. God, however, has a different time table than we.
It is especially these expressions that seem to justify the
opinions of those who apply this chapter to the seventy-year
exile. The famous expositor Van der Palm, who sees this
chapter as referring to Israel's ultimate reacceptance, has
correctly refuted this view by saying:

> Why could we not call the present-day rejection of the
> Jews, regardless how long it has been, *a small moment* in
> comparison to the lasting and eternal love by which they
> will be gathered again unto God? — the more so since it is
> in the nature of our passions to consider even the longest
> time of grief as only a short moment once we are
> delivered, and years of suffering are frequently forgotten
> on account of one day of joy!

With great mercies will I gather thee. This statement is
deeper than the sea and higher than the mountains. If Israel's
great suffering is so small to God, how great then must be
that which *He* pleases to call *great!* At one time He lamented,
"But as a wife that committeth adultery, which taketh
strangers instead of her husband!" (Ezek. 16:32). But just as
Hosea accepted Gomer again after her shameful adulteries, so
will Jehovah accept His wife again. Does He not say through
Hosea: "And I will give her her vineyards from thence, and
the valley of Achor for a door of hope: and she shall sing
there, as in the days of her youth, and as in the day when she
came up out of the land of Egypt" (Hos. 2:15). In that day

Israel will call Him, *My Husband!* and no longer, *My Baal!* What a fullness of blessings still lies ahead for Israel as a nation! How much are those expositors missing who deny this comforting future of Israel! The word *gather* indicates the manner of reacceptance. Jehovah will cause His dispersed people to return and will gather them from wherever He has scattered them. He can do this as the mighty God of the hosts of angelic warriors (v. 5). He will send out His angels to gather His people from the four corners of the earth. He will accept her since as the Holy One of Israel He is the faithful God who makes His promises come true. He will be her *Gaal,* her *Redeemer.* The immaculately Holy One who cannot have anything to do with sin, wants to love this sinful people as His wife. "I will love them freely: for mine anger is turned away from him" (Hos. 14:4), and Israel will thank the Lord with these words, "I will praise thee: though thou wast angry with me, thine anger is turned away, and thou comfortedst me." Here we see unchanged love and faithfulness! This small *moment* and this little *wrath* have lasted for more than twenty-five hundred years already. They comprise the long and terrible history of Israel's blood and tears, but Jehovah speaks here as though all of this is nothing compared with the future joy of His *everlasting kindness.* And in spite of this, men dare to accuse Jehovah of being vengeful!

The Immovable Certainty of the Future Salvation

> 9. For this is as the waters of Noah unto me: for as I have sworn that the waters of Noah should no more go over the earth; so have I sworn that I would not be wroth with thee, nor rebuke thee.
> 10. For the mountains shall depart, and the hills be removed; but my kindness shall not depart from thee, neither shall the covenant of my peace be removed, saith the Lord that hath mercy on thee.

Here the Lord gives further proof and more assurances of the certainty of His love expressed in verses seven and eight, when He points out the historical example of the Flood, and more specifically the oath. He swore when making a covenant with Noah. It would be a tedious task, and not in keeping with the object of this commentary, if we were to go into a detailed comparison of the Flood of long ago with Israel's future reacceptance. The text does not demand this but rather forbids doing so, and indicates the actual *terium,* the third part of the comparison, when it mentions the *oath* which was spoken then in connection with Israel's restoration (Gen. 9:11). It is true that in Genesis 9:11 no specific mention is made of an oath, but the covenant God made with Noah presupposes an oath. At that time the Lord sware that He would never repeat the judgment of punishment in the form of a flood; here the Lord swears that He will never again be wroth with or rebuke Israel. The word *rebuke* actually means to *push forcefully, push away.* In this sense it is used in Zechariah 3:2 and Malachi 3:11. The correct meaning of this word is found especially in Psalm 104:7, where we read, "At thy rebuke they fled." There the Lord pushed the waters back so that they turned away. Likewise now the Lord will no longer push away His people into far countries. This is the sense that we must understand the words *wroth* and *rebuke.* Jehovah does not want to cast His people out of their land again, as He did in the past. Everyone knows that every rainbow in the cloud tells us that the covenant with Noah stands firm. And just as firm will be Israel's lasting peace, according to this word. The waters of His wrath will no more cover this people.

The correct interpretation of verse ten depends to some extent on how we interpret the little word *ki,* translated *for* here. Some take it in a concessive sense and translate it *although, even if this be the case, even if it were;* they do not see the departing of the mountains and the removal of the hills as a certain future fact, but only as a possibility or a probability. With others we take this word in a causative sense and view the statement as a prophecy that the mountains will depart (cf. Ps. 102:25-27; Hag. 2:6; Heb. 12:26-28). Jehovah is making a comparison here of what does and does not depart. We take the words *mountains* and *hills* literally and not as referring to proud nations, although, by way of application, this statement may be interpreted that way also. The mountains stand immovable, firm in floods and storms and are therefore the symbol of durability and imperishableness. And yet, when "he looketh on the earth, and it trembleth: he toucheth the hills, and they smoke." Earthquakes and tremors can make these proud colossi to tremble and to sink away and become deep valleys. Years ago this happened in China, Persia, Japan and other places. All these phenomena are but a pale example of what will happen at the Lord's return. Then, too, the mountains will melt away like hay and stubble, but God's tender mercy and the covenant of His peace will neither depart nor shake. The *covenant of peace* is the covenant of grace in its completed form as it will exist after Israel's restoration. Read and compare carefully 42:6; 49:8; 59:21; 61:8; Jer. 31:31-33; 32:40; 33:20-25; Ezek. 34:25-26; 37:26; Hos. 2:18.

Jehovah's Compassion with His Forsaken Wife

> 11. O thou afflicted, tossed with tempest, and not comforted, behold, I will lay thy stones with fair colours, and lay thy foundations with sapphires.
>
> 12. And I will make thy windows of agates, and thy gates of carbuncles, and all thy borders of pleasant stones.

After the solemn assurances of His faithfulness and love, the Lord addresses His forsaken wife directly. The words He speaks to her reflect His great compassion with her present miserable condition. First He calls her *afflicted,* i.e., miserable and oppressed. Does this not depict Israel's hopeless situation during the last two thousand years? She is deprived of her land, city and temple service and oppressed by Satan, sin, hell and the uncircumcised.

She is further called *tossed with tempest.* Imagine a weak woman on a lonely country road. She can hardly drag herself forward, for she is totally worn out and exhausted. But she is driven on by a heavy storm. Thunder and lightning keep her from resting. She must go on and on, without any respite. Israel's history could not have been depicted more strikingly. The storms of time, of persecution, of wars, revolutions, apostasy and destruction have driven this mysterious people on for centuries without end. The Jewish people are more restless than any other people in the world. As with an invisible hand the Jews are driven on to all other countries. They are seeking a place of rest but they will never find one except in the heart of Jehovah-Jesus.

And not comforted is the third name given here to Israel. No nation on earth had shown Israel help or comfort, while Jehovah Himself had hidden His face for a moment (v. 8). When God comforts, He pours His own compassion as a relieving balm into the grieving heart; that He had not done to Israel for many centuries. People can comfort only when they themselves have experienced God's truth in their own hearts. Unbelievers cannot comfort or be comforted themselves. Israel did and does have need of comfort, but she has not received any comfort from God or man during the ages of her dispersion.

After this threefold address the metaphor of a sad woman changes suddenly into that of a city. There are many who would rather call it "impalatable Eastern imagery." This sudden change is not as great to a Jew as it is to us; Scripture frequently presents a city as a woman. Also in Revelation seventeen and eighteen the presentation of Babylon, as the false Church, as a woman and a city constantly flow together, while the same is true of the glorified Church in Revelation twenty-one. The Lord presents Himself as the great Builder and Craftsman of the *city of the great King,* Jerusalem. In order to make the image of building a city very concrete in a truly Eastern manner, He mentions the kind of mortar and stones He wishes to use while He is building. For cement, He mentions a kind of powder with which women used to color their eyebrows. The custom to powder the eyes was and still is very common in the Near East. This must not be seen merely as a manifestation of pride and coquetry but also as a preventative and protective means against the heat of the sun, which was often too strong for tender eyes. This powder, which was in such great demand, the Lord will use as cement for the city of God. The sapphire on which the Lord will found Jerusalem is a hard stone of heavenly blue color.

Hence how solid and incomparably beautiful this foundation is going to be! It seems to us that God specifically wants to indicate the durability and beauty of His building. The tossing by a thunderstorm will make a place for the solidity of a firm city founded and built by God Himself; the present contempt will be replaced by the great beauty of this building made by God.

Verse twelve continues the description of the strength and beauty of the city. We would adhere to the wrong exegesis if we were to see and seek in this general and highly poetic description a precise indication of some spiritual background. We must admire this panorama in its royal glory as a whole and not analyze the separate parts as with a microscope. From of old there have been a great variety of explanations regarding the various precious stones mentioned here. The word *windows* literally means *suns;* we must keep something similar to this in mind here. The word *window* makes us think of the windows of a single house, while from the context it is clear that the prophet is referring to an entire city and not to a single building. With the Revised Version (ASV) we rather substitute the word *pinnacles, housetops,* and think of those parts that reflect the sunbeams so that from a distance they look like suns themselves. The Septuagint translates this word as *embrasures, loopholes, parapets.* These were built on top of a wall so that the sun made them look like many suns. If this is correct, then the word contains a hint of the safety of the city. The gates will be of *carbuncles,* which shine with a bright red glow and in the sunlight seem to be afire and to emanate sparks. Gates were a very important part of Near-Eastern cities; hence in the description they could not be omitted. *All the borders* of Israel will be aglitter from *pleasant stones,* which again refers to stones with a fiery red glow, most likely the bright red carbuncles. With this last phrase the prophet gives a brief resume of his description. The entire environment will be a joy to the eye. The entire city will be glorious to behold. The Church Father Ireneus was of the opinion, apparently on the basis of this description, that the new Jerusalem would be founded on one great carbuncle. He and thousands after him identified the glorified earthly Jerusalem with the glorified heavenly Jerusalem of Revelation twenty-one and twenty-two. What is depicted here is Israel's earthly glory, not the heavenly glory of the Church. The description thus far relates mainly to the external. In the following verse the prophet speaks of the internal spiritual beauty of the inhabitants.

The Inhabitants of Restored Jerusalem

13. And all thy children shall be taught of the LORD; and great shall be the peace of thy children.

14. In righteousness shall thou be established: thou shalt be far from oppression; for thou shalt not fear: and from terror; for it shall not come near thee.

The description of the beauty and glory of the city is continued here and now the spiritual beauty of the inhabitants is especially mentioned. Whereas the lonely woman in verse two was presented as living in a tent, she now lives in a beautiful city built by God's own hand. Her children — and she has many! — will *be taught of the Lord.* From a comparison with John 6:45 we may safely conclude that Jehovah-Jesus is referred to here. The word *taught* indicates a practical knowledge obtained by exercising and therefore means having become used to a certain thing, having become familiar with it, having learned to love it. In a complicated, involved way the beautiful thought is conveyed that the inhabitants of the city of God — for it is they who are meant here — have the Lord Jesus in their midst and will have intimate dealings with Him and enjoy His teachings. All of them will be pupils of Jehovah-Jesus. All the proud world cities of today will soon submit themselves to Jerusalem, the city of the great King. This is what the Lord Jesus will bring about at His coming. Everything is waiting for Him. "Beautiful for situation, the joy of the whole earth, is mount Zion, on the sides of the north, the city of the great King. *God is known in her palaces . . ."* Then the statement of Psalm 48:2, 3 will be fulfilled (cf. Mic. 4:1-4; Zech. 14:9). This does not, however, contradict the fact that now believers are taught of the Lord, have the Holy Spirit and by Him know all things that they must know to serve Him. The Church has the great privilege of living in the powers of the age to come.

The second thing said of the children is that their peace

will be great. This statement must be taken as a result of the *covenant of peace* in verse ten and as a gift of the King of Peace, Christ. The word *shalom* expresses physical and spiritual prosperity. It indicates salvation in the Old Testament sense of the word. In verse fourteen the prophet continues to describe the moral condition of the city's inhabitants. *In righteousness shalt thou be established.* The word *righteousness* refers to God's innate righteousness, not to His retributive or avenging righteousness; it is the revelation of His good and unchangeable will regarding His people. Jehovah is the Builder, Teacher and also the Judge of the city. By the revelation of His holy justice He upholds His people. Not only His throne, but also His people is founded on justice and righteousness as merited by Christ on the cross. Hence the third characteristic of these city dwellers is that they may enjoy the Lord's protection. In close connection with this it is further stated that they will be far removed from oppression, fear and terror. The reigning Christ will keep all enemies far from them so that His people can develop peacefully, freely and joyfully. The prophet piles one word atop the other to describe the peace and safety of the city of God. By centuries-long experience Israel has learned what it means to be oppressed by enemies and to be terrified. Hence the promise of verse fourteen is very comforting to this people that has been tormented for so long.

Israel's Complete Victory Over All Enemies

> 15. Behold, they shall surely gather together, but not by me: whosoever shall gather together against thee shall fall for thy sake.
> 16. Behold, I have created the smith that bloweth the coals in the fire, and that bringeth forth an instrument for his work; and I have created the waster to destroy.
> 17. No weapon that is formed against thee shall prosper; and every tongue that shall rise against thee in judgment thou shalt condemn. This is the heritage of the servants of the LORD, and their righteousness is of me, saith the LORD.

Verse fifteen is usually regarded as a vexing problem to expositors. This is mainly due to the word *goer,* which first of all means *leaving the road* to find shelter for the night; it also means *wandering from place to place as a stranger,* and finally *coming together and plotting together* as a horde with hostile intentions. In Psalm 140:2 this word is translated as *gathered together for war* and there is no doubt that here it means just that. The Septuagint and the Vulgate take it to mean the gathering of proselytes to Israel, but this is not the meaning here. This is clearly a reference to the final great advance against Israel as described in Ezekiel thirty-eight and thirty-nine and Zechariah 14:1-7 and in numerous places in the first part of Isaiah. The Lord says here that, although the enemies may once more plot together to battle against His people, this is not with His approval and that therefore they will not gain the victory over His people but will *fall.*

Important truths are related here concerning Israel's enemies. It is a characteristic trait of the entire book of Isaiah that it constantly points to the Creator of all things. Verse sixteen does so as well. As an indication of the greatness of God it is said that He created the *smith* and the *waster.* To explain these words as referring merely to a smith and his brother in arms, who is called to destroy, is a rather weak and meaningless exposition. Merely stating that God created the smith and the waster truly does not require the solemn and twice-repeated word *behold* for special emphasis and notice before it. We rather take it as a reference to the devil who *bloweth the coals in the fire* of Gog's hordes in the end time and who, according to Revelation 13:2, 16:13, and 19:20, in the days of the Great Tribulation blows the fire of hell of Satanic hatred against Christ as never before. The name *waster* fits him in a very special sense and the man of sin who works with the energy of Satan. It is not merely stated in a general sense here that God is the Creator of those who make and carry weapons in battle, but it conveys the glorious thought that He as the Creator is exalted even above the most powerful enemies of Israel. Verse seventeen enlarges upon the glorious idea expressed in verse sixteen. Weapons prepared against Israel will never strike their target. The centuries-long dispersion among and persecution by the nations is again the best commentary on this statement. No king or emperor, no pope or counsel have ever been able to combat Israel successfully. Every weapon against Israel has failed. No more than the fish could consume Jonah could the nations destroy the Jew. The *tongue,* kindled by the fire of hell, is an even more dangerous weapon than the sword. This weapon, too, has always been used against Israel, but sooner or later the slanderers have been damned themselves and will be damned and condemned by Israel in the judgment of the nations. For whom then are all the glorious promises enumerated in this chapter? For the *servants of the Lord,* who derive their *righteousness* from the *Servant of the Lord.*

ISAIAH 55

Kind Invitation to Salvation in Christ

> 1. Ho, every one that thirsteth, come ye to the waters, and he
> that hath no money; come ye, buy, and eat; yea, come, buy wine
> and milk without money and without price.
> 2. Wherefore do ye spend money for that which is not bread?
> and your labour for that which satisfieth not? hearken diligently
> unto me, and eat ye that which is good, and let your soul delight
> itself in fatness.
> 3. Incline your ear, and come unto me: hear, and your soul
> shall live; and I will make an everlasting covenant with you, even
> the sure mercies of David.

One could make an anthology of the prophet's words of
comfort as contained in this section and 40:1, 29-31; 41:10;
42:1-3; 44:22; 49:15; 53:1-12; 54:7, 10; 66:13, and say,
"This is the reason why Isaiah has been given the title of *the
Evangelist of the Old Covenant."* Yet these words of comfort
are misunderstood if they are applied to the Church and if
Israel is disregarded completely, for each of these beautiful
promises refer primarily and predominately to Israel.

Precious is the context in these last three chapters. In
chapter fifty-three we saw the cross of Christ; in fifty-four,
the *seed* that He saw upon the travail of His soul; here we
find the general invitation to the salvation which is in Christ
Jesus the Lord. The invitation is *general,* to all who thirst.
Nor is it said that they should have a spiritual thirst. All who
thirst after gold and honor and knowledge are included here.
Is there any man who does not thirst for one thing or
another? What is required of them? What conditions must
they meet? None. All they need to do is *come.* Whoever
thirsts must come to the source, the well, in order to drink
and quench his thirst. But there is not only water for that
satisfies only the thirsty. There is also food to *eat.* For the

little ones, the weak and the sick, there is *milk,* while there is also *wine* that gladdens the heart. All of these things can be *bought* without money and without the price of one's own merits.

In olden times silver was weighed to determine the sum that must be paid. That is what verse two is alluding to. Israel paid out her treasures for things that were worthless and left the soul empty. Today, instead of quenching their souls at the rich sacrificial meal of Christ, many squander everything, including their souls, to obtain the world, sin and Satan. This is why Jehovah-Jesus cries, *Hearken diligently unto me, and eat ye that which is good, and let your soul delight itself in fatness.* Here as well as in the following verse He strongly emphasizes *hearing and obeying Him.* Only then can the soul *delight itself in fatness.* The metaphor is derived from the variety of food at a sacrificial or festive meal. Both in the Old and New Testaments salvation in Christ is repeatedly compared to an abundant meal. So here we see that God not only wants us to eat our fill, but also that we *delight* ourselves in His salvation. The *everlasting covenant* is the same as the *covenant of peace* in the preceding chapter.

And what are the *sure mercies of David?* This is not merely a pious term for some other kind of bliss, but has a very definite historical and prophetic meaning. What is meant here are the covenant promises made at the inauguration of the Davidic covenant as recorded in II Samuel 7:12-17; 23:5; Psalm 89:1-4 and Psalm 110. Jehovah-Jesus promises here to fulfill the Davidic covenant and its firm promises of salvation in the way of obedience.

Christ the King, a Witness and Commander of the Nations

> 4. Behold, I have given him for a witness to the people, a leader and commander of the people.
> 5. Behold, thou shalt call a nation that thou knowest not, and nations that knew not thee shall run unto thee because of the LORD thy God, and for the Holy One of Israel; for he hath glorified thee.

Some expositors think these verses refer to David; others, to Cyrus. Hugo de Groot feels that Jeremiah is in view, but how this learned man arrived at this conclusion baffles us. As Barnes noted, he will no doubt forever be the only one to hold that opinion. It seems that he simply was determined to not see Christ anywhere in the prophets. But these words apply only to Christ and no one else. Proof is easily adduced: (1) The word *behold* always demands special attention and is very often used before Messianic predictions to call special attention to the Messiah (cf. 7:14; 42:1; Jer. 23:5; 33:14; Zech. 6:12). (2) The language used here is far too strong to refer to David, Cyrus or any other famous person. (3) The Lord Jesus is called *nagid,* leader. He is called this elsewhere as well. In Daniel 9:25 the word is emphatically applied to Messiah. In I Chronicles 9:20, 11:2 it is translated *ruler.* That is what the Lord Jesus is to all nations after His return. By *right,* He is this already; He will be this *actually* at His coming again. (4) In Jeremiah 30:9; Ezekiel 34:23-24; 37:24-25 and Hosea 3:5 the Lord Jesus is presented as the great King David. The word for *witness* has been translated as *ruler, monitor, testimony, lawgiver* and many other ways. The word *need* means witness, but in the sense of one who has the right to admonish and to speak out for the justice of the law against injustice (cf. Prov. 19:5, 9, where it is also translated *witness).* The word *witness* dictates His prophetic work at His Second Coming. The word *leader* points to His office as King. After His return the Lord Jesus will rule as the King of kings and Lord of lords. Meditate on Psalm 72 where He is so beautifully lauded as the King of the future. The word *commander* designates Him as the royal Lawgiver who will command and instruct all nations. The Lord Jesus will tear away the covering cast over all people (25:7), and afterwards He will cause them to walk in His light (2:1-4, 60:1-4). The greatest need of the world is such a *Witness, Leader* and *Commander.*

Verse five is a direct address to the Messiah regarding His conversion of all the nations of the earth. Nations whom He knew not, in the sense of loved not, and nations who in the past did not know Him, such as China, Japan, Africa and Australia, will *run* to Him and to His salvation. This comforting idea is greatly enlarged upon in 60:1-16. It is the continuous teaching of Scripture that one day all the nations will be converted to Christ, not by means of missions, but by means of the almighty Savior Himself. He can and will do it Himself after His return and after the judgment of the nations.

For he hath glorified thee. The Father will glorify the Son before the eyes of all nations when they come flowing to Him. Initially this took place at His resurrection and ascension (cf. 53:10; John 17:5; Acts 3:13). The Son glorifies the Father and the Father glorifies the Son.

The Call to Sinners to Come to Christ

> 6. Seek ye the LORD while he may be found, call ye upon him while he is near:
> 7. Let the wicked forsake his way, and the unrighteous man his thoughts: and let him return unto the LORD, and he will have mercy upon him; and to our God, for he will abundantly pardon.

When the prophet saw the heathen nations come running to salvation in Christ, he also called all the wicked in Israel to come to the Savior. He solemnly admonishes them to *seek* and to *call upon Him.* He urges them to make haste, for the time to find Him does not last forever and He is not always near. Just think of those who are already lost. The Lord wishes to be sought and called upon. He further admonishes the *wicked,* the proud, the evil one, to forsake his way. His way is not good; it is the broad way that ends in destruction. The *unrighteous man* is a criminal whose intent is to wreak havoc or to perpetrate some heinous crime. He is urged to forsake his *thoughts,* his *plans,* his evil intents. The wicked does not merely walk in an evil *way,* he *is* evil, and as a result he has evil *thoughts* regarding God, His Word, His Son and His service. After the wicked has been told what he must forsake, he is instructed what he must do. He must *return to the Lord;* Jehovah here means the Messiah. A precious encouragement of *mercy* and *abundant pardon* concludes this stirring call to conversion.

The Lord's Thoughts, Ways and Words

> 8. For my thoughts are not your thoughts, neither are your ways my ways, saith the LORD.

9. For as the heavens are higher than the earth, so are my ways higher than your ways, and my thoughts than your thoughts.

10. For as the rain cometh down, and the snow from heaven, and returneth not thither but watereth the earth, and maketh it bring forth and bud, that it may give seed to the sower, and bread to the eater:

11. So shall my word be that goeth forth out of my mouth: it shall not return unto me void, but it shall accomplish that which I please, and it shall prosper in the thing whereto I sent it.

Expositors by and large have had difficulty with the context in which these verses appear, but we obviously have here a contrast between the ways and thoughts of God and those of the people in the preceding verse, while at the same time, encouragement is given to come to Christ. It has just been said of the Messiah that He *forgives* abundantly and in this regard He is entirely different from the wicked people who are not forgiving but vengeful. These words are richly applied to all times and circumstances. The Lord's thoughts concerning the Messiah and Israel were totally different from Israel's, as we already saw in chapter fifty-three. The Lord's *ways* with Israel have run through water and fire until this very day. This is totally different from what the most pious people in Israel had imagined. The beautiful comparison of verse nine would only be spoiled if we were to explain it further. A crucified Messiah with heathen flowing to Him without first having been circumcised and free from the law were ideas that differed greatly from those of the Jews. Closely connected with this, the last two verses testify of the effective power of God's Word. *Rain* and *snow* descend from heaven and in that form never return there, but make the earth moist and fertile. Thus the Word does not return unto Him void. *Word* means specifically the promises concerning the crucified Christ to Israel, sinners and all nations, as were just indicated. The Word of the Lord will accomplish that which pleases God and it will be *prosperous* in its course and effect.

Israel's Restoration and Its Results

12. For ye shall go out with joy, and be led forth with peace:

the mountains and the hills shall break forth before you into singing, and all the trees of the field shall clap their hands.

13. Instead of the thorn shall come up the fir tree, and instead of the brier shall come up the myrtle tree: and it shall be to the LORD for a name, for an everlasting sign that shall not be cut off.

The causal conjunction *for* indicates a proof for the faithful fulfillment of God's Word which never returns to Him void. This is no less true of Israel's return from exile. Again we are dealing with the ultimate return and not the liberation from Babylon, since at that time nothing was seen of all the glory mentioned here. At that time Israel did not go out with joy and was not led forth with peace, for it was but a pitiful handful of hardly fifty thousand people. By far the majority of the Jews remained behind with the flesh pots of Babylon, and those that returned to the land of the fathers were engaged much more in mourning than in rejoicing. Only at the final great exodus will Israel have joy and peace after she finally has found her Messiah.

The reacceptance of Israel will be *life from the dead* (Rom. 11:15) for all of ravaged creation. The sighs of creation will be exchanged for glorious singing. When the afflicted Jews no longer weep but shout for joy, everything will shout with them. When the prodigal son had returned to the father, the latter said, *"Let us eat and be merry."* This is what God will say to the entire creation after Israel has returned from all nations, and with repentance has confessed her sin and accepted the Messiah. O that people might see that the whole world is in a state of ruin because of the fact that Israel as yet is not in a state of reconciliation with her God and King. Instead she is still in a state of hardening and blindness dispersed among the nations! What heartache, what misplaced zeal without knowledge would they save themselves if they were to see this on the basis of Scripture!

Only a foolish exegesis of verse thirteen can explain this verse in terms of the conversion of a sinner. If merely an application were derived of it to such a conversion we would keep silent, but to say that this is what the verse means is foolish because that clearly shows a lack of insight in the world-historical and eschatological significance of Israel. Whoever does not know Israel's far-reaching significance does not understand half of the prophetic Scriptures either, nor the signs of our troubled times in which everything is propelled toward the solution of the riddle of the ages. The people clapped their hands in joy when they suddenly saw their youthful King David (II Kings 11:12). In the same way all creation will rejoice when it sees its Sovereign King, the Lord Jesus Christ. And then what verse thirteen predicts will take place, not merely figuratively, but literally. The word *it* in verse thirteen refers to all the glory previously mentioned. This will be to the glorification of Jehovah-Jesus. The renewed creation will be a *sign* of His faithfulness, of the power of His blood, of His presence and of His reign.

ISAIAH 56

The Happy Times of Israel's Restoration

1. Thus saith the LORD, Keep ye judgment and do justice: for my salvation is near to come, and my righteousness to be revealed.

2. Blessed is the man that doeth this, and the son of man that layeth hold on it; that keepeth the sabbath from polluting it, and keepeth his hand from doing any evil.

3. Neither let the son of the stranger, that hath joined himself to the LORD, speak, saying, The LORD hath utterly separated me from his people: neither let the eunuch say, Behold, I am a dry tree.

4. For thus saith the Lord unto the eunuchs that keep my sabbaths, and choose the things that please me, and take hold of my covenant;

5. Even unto them will I give in mine house and within my walls a place and a name better than of sons and of daughters: I will give them an everlasting name, that shall not be cut off.

6. Also the sons of the stranger, that join themselves to the LORD, to serve him, and to love the name of the LORD, to be his servants, every one that keepeth the sabbath from polluting it, and taketh hold of my covenant;

7. Even them will I bring to my holy mountain, and make them joyful in my house of prayer: their burnt offerings and their sacrifices shall be accepted upon mine altar; for mine house shall be called an house of prayer for all people.

8. The Lord GOD which gathereth the outcasts of Israel saith, Yet will I gather others to him, beside those that are gathered unto him.

These verses can properly be considered an addendum to what was said before regarding Israel's restoration. There are indeed many expositors who claim that here Isaiah is giving practical admonitions to his contemporaries, but we find here an obviously continuing description of Israel's restoration and its far-reaching results. The coming again of the Lord is presupposed as an accomplished fact. Only in verse one is salvation presented as being near. In connection with this salvation, the audience is urged to lead godly lives, just as in the New Testament. The verse contains the word *righteousness* twice, at least in essence, once of the people and once of God. When this word is used of Israel, it can be translated in various ways such as: virtue, godly fear, uprightness, etc. Here the word has the meaning of practicing virtue and doing justice in accordance with the law. The two words *salvation* and *righteousness* taken together apply to the Messiah who will bring *salvation,* bliss, to the believers, and revenging justice to the wicked. At the same time, this avenging justice upon the wicked will be the rewarding righteousness to the godly.

This beatitude is not meant for the sabbatarian who presently keeps the sabbath. Seventh-day Adventism appropriates this word, it is true, but wholly without foundation. The beatitude applies to Israel to whom the sabbath is given, partially to the Israel of Isaiah's days, and partially to restored Israel. For it is clear from many texts in the prophets that just as Israel will have sacrifices and priests, feasts and pilgrimages, she will also have the sabbath after the return of the Lord, and observe it. According to this text, she will be *blessed* in doing so.

The *stranger,* the foreigner, who has joined himself to Jehovah-Jesus, will no longer feel himself separated by a wall from Israel, the Lord's people, as in the past. The eunuch, the castrated person, will no longer consider himself a dry tree. This is what he always was considered in the past, for such a person, like a bastard, Ammonite, or Moabite, was not allowed to attend the assembly of the Lord (Deut. 23:1). The idea here is that no one will be barred from holy Zion any more for external reasons, that restored Israel will not be narrow-minded but totally universal. Verses four and five state the conditions on which the eunuch will be treated better by God than the sons and daughters. A castrated person was even more despised in Israel than a barren one; now they not merely receive a place in the house of the Lord, but even in His heart. He will love them as His own children. Verse seven reveals the key to the secret, when it states, *My house shall be called an house of prayer for all people.* This text has appeared above the door of many a church, chapel, cloister and cell but it is no more appropriate above the door of a church than of that of a monastery. For there is not a single church building Jehovah can call *His house,* let alone a *house of prayer for all nations.* Verse eight informs us that God will gather Israel from all countries and cause the nations to flow to converted Israel. When one day all the ten tribes, led by His hand, will return, she will be a great multitude, but the Lord will gather even more, *others,* to Israel from among all nations.

The Final Great Invasion and Its Cause

> 9. All ye beasts of the field, come to devour, yea, all ye beasts in the forest.
> 10. His watchmen are blind: they are all ignorant, they are all dumb dogs, they cannot bark; sleeping, lying down, loving to slumber.
> 11. Yea, they are greedy dogs, which can never have enough, and they are shepherds that cannot understand: they all look to their own way, every one for his gain, from his quarter.
> 12. Come ye, say they, I will fetch wine and we will fill ourselves with strong drink; and to morrow shall be as this day, and much more abundant.

Most expositors see absolutely no connection between the preceding verses and these; we see a natural connection and contrast in them. Some are of the opinion that the nations, under the symbol of wild animals, are called to eat, that is to say, to share in, the salvation in Christ. That would constitute a beautiful contrast with the first two verses of the preceding chapter. We see it differently, that is, as a contrast between Israel's future glory as just described, and her coming misery at the final great and terrible invasion described in Ezekiel thirty-eight and thirty-nine. The proud and bloodthirsty nations are constantly compared in Scripture to wild beasts (9:12; Jer. 12:9; Dan. 7; Rev. 13).

The cause for this invasion is indicated in a few powerful statements. Certainly we may speak here of causes, for there will be a divine, a satanic and an international cause. But there will also be a Jewish cause for this invasion, and this is what is pointed out here. Israel will be like an unguarded flock, and what is an easier prey for predatory beasts than an unprotected flock whose shepherds are blind, ignorant, dumb and are sleeping or drunk, as they are depicted here?

ISAIAH 57

The Removal of the Righteous From Evil

> 1. The righteous perisheth, and no man layeth it to heart: and merciful men are taken away, none considering that the righteous is taken away from the evil to come.
> 2. He shall enter into peace: they shall rest in their beds, each one walking in his uprightness.

This chapter shows what becomes of a nation under the rule of apostate leaders. Expositors are not agreed on the time of which the prophet is speaking. One thing is clear to all: The period after the seventy-year exile cannot be meant, since there was no idolatry at that time as described here, nor a king as mentioned in verse nine. Moreover, this section obviously refers to a time of persecution, as the actual meaning of verse one compels us to believe. All in all we prefer to think of the reign of Manasseh, for the abominations that characterized the first period of this king are all found in this chapter. We know on the basis of II Kings 21:16 that Manasseh shed much innocent blood so that he caused Jerusalem's streets to run with it. The larger description in II Kings 21 and II Chronicles 33 may be compared with the first part of this chapter. It is quite probable that Isaiah lived a few years into the reign and fierce persecution of Manasseh; he was an eyewitness of the abominations of idolatry.

It is clear that Scripture wants us to view the persecution of those days as a type of the Great Tribulation that will come upon Israel during the reign of the man of sin. The first two verses of this chapter offer us an adumbration of the Rapture of the Church before the evil to come. We are *not* saying that the Rapture of the Church is clearly taught here, for we find this teaching only in the New Testament and particularly in the epistles of Paul. But just as the Old Testament is full of types and shadows of Christ, so it is also full of types regarding the Church and its Rapture. For at the removal of the Church the righteous will be taken away, before the evil to come. At that time, too, the remaining wicked will not take it to heart but continue in their wickedness. Then, too, the righteous will *enter into peace,* and have rest and relief (II Thess. 1:7) during the time when the judgments on earth will be executed with amazing rapidity upon the wicked. He took Enoch, Noah and Lot away from the evil to come, and He will soon do the same with the believing Church. The words *perish* and *take away* in verse one point to a violent and sudden death by persecution and torture, so that here we have an even more striking type of those who will be killed during the reign of the beast. The God-fearing people are described as *righteous* and *merciful,* compassionate and loving. This was a great calamity and it always will remain a calamity when the God-fearing and praying people with their prayers and admonitions, their example, talk, walk and kind deeds are taken away. This impoverishes the earth and should be taken to heart by those who remain behind; but that was not the case then and is not the case now, and will particularly not be the case during the reign of terror of the man of sin. The murdered children of God will awaken again, however, and return with Christ, for their sleeping is followed by a glorious reawakening.

The Wicked Summoned Before the Judge

3. But draw near hither, ye sons of the sorceress, the seed of the adulterer and the whore.

4. Against whom do ye sport yourselves? against whom make ye a wide mouth, and draw out the tongue? are ye not children of transgression, a seed of falsehood,

5. Enflaming yourselves with idols under every green tree, slaying the children in the valleys under the clifts of the rocks?

6. Among the smooth stones of the stream is thy portion; they, they are thy lot: even to them hast thou poured a drink offering, thou hast offered a meat-offering. Should I receive comfort in these?

The wicked are referred to with three different names. The designation *sons of the sorceress* means that with affection and devotion they venerated sorcery and witchcraft, cf. II Kings 21:3-7. The first part of verse four reproaches this wicked lot with their mockery of God, His Word and of His ambassadors. In cowardly ridicule and unabashed revulsion they opened their mouth wide and stuck their tongues out at God's servants, the prophets. They *sported* against them — made fun of them. Opening the mouth wide and sticking out the tongue were signs of the deepest contempt (Ps. 22:7, 13; 35:21; cf. II Chron. 36:16). With childlike affection they surrendered to the transgression of the law and to the lie, hence their name *children of transgression* and *seed of falsehood.*

According to the description of verse five they were enflamed with natural and spiritual whoredom, which at that time as well as now are closely related. The green canopy provided by the leaves of an oak stand was the most desired seat of idolatry as well as a place for the most despicable of sexual acts. No cost or trouble was too much for them to indulge in this sensual worship. They slaughtered their own children in honor of the fire god Moloch. They butchered them near brooks and under the clifts of rocks, that is in the dark valleys, clefts and caves in the rocks, possibly in deep places so that the cries and screams of the children could not be heard arousing protest and horror on the part of others.

Verse six is translated and interpreted in many different ways. It seems to us that Van der Palm, who translated and exposited Isaiah twice, understands this verse best when he translates as follows: "In barren valleys (you butcher) them who are your portion, them, them, your most precious possession! and at the same time you offer drink offerings and meat offerings! . . . Would I behold such things with impunity?" This reflects the spirit and contents very clearly and does justice to the context. The slaughtered children are called a *portion* and the *lot*, the most precious possession of parents. The cruelty and degeneracy of these sacrifices is magnified by adding that the sacrificers had the blatant courage to give these gods sacrificial wine and meat, and consume these things with them. The final phrase reflects the

Lord's loathing of these abominations. He will never acquiesce in these things or accept, tolerate and condone them. On the contrary, He will not let this pass unavenged but gird Himself for punishment. The eating of the *meat offering* contains the beautiful idea of the closest relationship between God and the sacrificer. Thus the abominable parents practiced the most intimate fellowship with the reprehensible god who had just burned their children while they filled the air with their heart rending screams. Would Jehovah, who was married to Israel, not be jealous on account of these things?

The Most Shameless Adultery

7. Upon a lofty and high mountain hast thou set thy bed: even thither wentest thou up to offer sacrifice.

8. Behind the doors also and the posts hast thou set up thy remembrance: for thou hast discovered thyself to another than me, and art gone up; thou hast enlarged thy bed, and made thee a covenant with them; thou lovedst their bed where thou sawest it.

9. And thou wentest to the king with ointment, and didst increase thy perfumes, and didst send thy messengers far off, and didst debase thyself even unto hell.

10. Thou are wearied in the greatness of thy way; yet saidst thou not, There is no hope: thou hast found the life of thy hand; therefore thou wast not grieved.

11. And of whom hast thou been afraid or feared, that thou hast lied, and hast not remembered me, nor laid it to thy heart? have not I held my peace even of old, and thou fearest me not?

12. I will declare thy righteousness, and thy works; for they shall not profit thee.

In Israel's opinion, the high hills and mountain tops were the most public places. According to the presentation of verse seven, the whoredom of Judah is compared to that of an adulteress who has become so impudent that she no longer commits her sins in secret but publicly and shamelessly. She acts without any restraint and refuses to blush with shame. In view of everyone at the foot of the mountain, she climbs up to the top, there to set up her bed and to bring her sacrifices.

Verse eight also speaks of the most brazen adultery, as it

was usually practiced in secret. She had painted deities and love symbols "for the instruction and slogans of her lovers" on all her doors and posts. Shamelessly she bared herself and enlarged her bed of fornication to many, and although she had a closer relationship with some, she nevertheless gave herself to many whoremongers. The picture of idolatry is so plastic and so terrible here that we need not enlarge upon it. Isaiah reminds us of the descriptions given by Ezekiel.

In verse nine Isaiah still has the image of an adulteress in mind, who, decked out in *ointment* and *perfume,* and in the apparel of a harlot, goes to the *king.* Who is meant by the *king.* The three oldest translations omit the word, but this is definitely incorrect. Some think it refers to the king of Egypt; others, to the king of Assyria, while still others take the word in a general sense as a collective name. Kelly, Gray, Gaebelein and Klein Haneveld think it refers to the Antichrist. The word *melech* is about the same as *moloch* and some expositors think it refers to this dreadful god. This agrees with the context, and it seems to us that this is what the word refers to primarily, but at the same time it may ultimately have reference to the Antichrist. For at that time Israel will accept him who comes in his own name (John 5:43) and make a covenant with him (Dan. 9:27) — a covenant with death — *and debase itself unto hell.* That which took place in Mannaseh's day was but a faint prelude to what will take place in the days of Antichrist. The relentless perseverence and obstinacy with which idolatry was practiced is presented in verse ten with the simile of a *weary traveler* after a long journey and of a sick person who denies all his maladies and sicknesses. The meaning is clear: Israel was on a long errant way, traveling toward hell, and was leprous from the top of her skull to the sole of her feet. But, she refused to admit it. In verse eleven, numerous accusations are made against Judah. Since Jehovah kept silent and did not immediately punish, His people showed no respect or fear of Him, forsaking and forgetting Him. The love of God is touching; it yearns for her love in return: *thou hast not . . . laid it to thy heart.* It is this, and nothing less, that God demands of His children. Without it, their *works* and *righteousness* avail nothing (v. 12).

The Vain Prayer of the Wicked

> 13a. When thou criest, let thy companies deliver thee; but the wind shall carry them all away; vanity shall take them: . . .

Punishment follows sin, as we see here again. The *Great Tribulation* will follow all the abominations described before. Hunger and sword at the destruction of Jerusalem were but a faint example and prelude of what will come upon Israel at the end of this dispensation. During that calamity Israel will cry, but the multitude of gods they have accumulated since the days of Manasseh will not send deliverance; the storm-wind of judgment will cause them to disappear as a fog and mist; the breath of the Almighty will take them away. All the gods of the earth will, in that day, be overcome by Him who then will be called *the God of all the earth*.

Promises for the Faithful Remnant

> 13b. but he that putteth his trust in me shall possess the land, and shall inherit my holy mountain;
> 14. And shall say, Cast ye up, cast ye up, prepare the way, take up the stumblingblock out of the way of my people.
> 15. For thus saith the high and lofty One that inhabiteth eternity, whose name is Holy; I dwell in the high and holy place, with him also that is of a contrite and humble spirit to revive the spirit of the humble, and to revive the heart of the contrite ones.

In the midst of the thundering threats of judgment, the tone suddenly changes. Now that the wicked with their gods have perished by the breath of His mouth, Jehovah in mercy turns His voice to the God-fearing remnant. Whoever puts his trust in Him *shall inherit the earth*. Psalm thirty-seven supplies a precious commentary on this statement. *Inheriting the holy mountain* means to have Canaan forever as one's portion, as an inheritance of the covenant.

Verse fourteen is a practical mandate for missions among the Jews. The nations have put many obstacles in the way for Israel. This *stumblingblock* is compared here to impassable roads which nearly prevent the exiles from returning to the land of their fathers. This is why the Lord wants to have the roads prepared and made passable.

The beautiful statement of verse fifteen intends to offer certainty for the promise of Israel's restoration. The people could easily get the idea that Jehovah was too high and exalted to be concerned with a little group of exiles and miserable sinners. This is why these words sound so lovely and beautiful to the God-fearing remnant. It is an inviting and encouraging word for all those who, crushed by their guilt, turn to Him. The Lord is *high and lofty*. All that is great in heaven and on earth is less than nothing and vanity compared to Him. Seated above the globe of the earth, He has absolute dominion over everything. He created and still supports all things. He *inhabits* eternity, He dwells on high and in holiness. What a dwelling place that is! He is elevated above the changes of time, place, and circumstances. But He has one more dwelling place. He also dwells with him *that is of a contrite and humble spirit*. This great God wants to take up His abode — not just pay a visit, but *dwell* — with him whose heart bleeds from burning grief over his transgressions. And for what purpose does He wish to do so? *To revive* him! Christ came to give life, indeed, abundant life. This exceeds the boldest human comprehension, but Christ reveals the secret of it to us. By His Word and Spirit He still does daily what this beautiful verse declares.

God's Deliverance After a Long Period of Silence

> 16. For I will not contend for ever, neither will I be always wroth: for the spirit should fail before me, and the souls which I have made.
> 17. For the iniquity of his covetousness was I wroth, and smote him: I hid me, and was wroth, and he went on frowardly in the way of his heart.
> 18. I have seen his ways, and will heal him: I will lead him also, and restore comforts unto him and to his mourners.
> 19. I create the fruit of the lips; Peace, peace to him that is far off, and to him that is near, saith the LORD; and I will heal him.
> 20. But the wicked are like the troubled sea, when it cannot rest, whose waters cast up mire and dirt.
> 21. There is no peace, saith my God, to the wicked.

Verse sixteen assumes that God will be *wroth* and *contend* with Israel for a very long time, and this has to be proved correct only too well by Israel's sad past. But no matter how long Israel's salvation tarries, one day the sun of her deliverance will dawn. If Jehovah were to contend forever with Israel, the Spirit of His people would be overwhelmed and the *souls* He created would perish, for no creature can stand the wrath of God. Hence we are told that Israel's so-called indestructibility does not lie in Israel, but in God only. The Lord was very angry with the accumulated unrighteousness of Israel. The Hebrew has: *the crime of their avarice,* which means that they committed their sins with *avarice, i.e.,* with a strong, burning desire. It was because of this burning desire to sin that Jehovah hid Himself from Israel. His *hiding* has lasted for almost two thousand years — since the *times of the Gentiles,* and this is the most significant fact of Israel's history. Israel constantly desires a sign, but God hides Himself (cf. 18:4; 45:15, 57:11; 64:1, 9, 12). Not until Christ's return will it be said to Israel: "Behold, here I am; behold, here I am." The Lord pounded Israel; for many centuries He hid Himself from and was angered by this stubborn people. Israel did not take it to heart, but went her own disobedient way according to the imaginations of her errant heart on paths of her own choosing (cf. 53:6). The Lord, however, sees His sheep wandering about among all the nations and He gives the glorious assurance: *I will heal him: I will lead him also.* The chief Shepherd, Christ, will seek His sheep and lead them to the lush pastures of the land of promise, to the mourning remnant (v. 18). He will *restore comforts.* In these verses, the Lord promises to give His remnant the following: (1) healing from the inflicted wounds. The *healing* in verse eighteen refers back to the *smiting* in verse seventeen; (2) *guidance* as the great Shepherd of His sheep; (3) *comforts* to the mourning. Those who do not mourn need no comfort; (4) *prayer and praise,* for this is what is meant with "fruit of the lips," which God promises to create; (5) an *abundance of peace,* as is evident from the repetition of *peace, peace.* This peace He wishes to give to those who are *far off,* the heathen, and to those who are *near,* Israel. Israel is bleeding from a thousand wounds and therefore the Lord repeats once more and very emphatically that He will *heal* Israel's wounds. The

Lord Jesus Christ will as the Sun of Righteousness have healing in His wings for all maladies and sicknesses (Mal. 4:2). The famous Mr. Vitringa who usually saw references to the Church in Revelation, the parables and the prophets, thinks that this chapter is referring to the deterioration of Rome's Church in the Middle Ages, but we have found that all these truths — the threatenings and promises — apply to Israel.

The final two verses contain a beautiful and easily understood application and admonition of the entire oracle of God contained in chapters forty-nine through fifty-seven (cf. 48:22). It almost seems as though we hear the noise of the angry, restless sea.

ISAIAH 58

The Wrong Manner of Fasting

1. Cry aloud, spare not, lift up thy voice like a trumpet, and shew my people their transgression, and the house of Jacob their sins.

2. Yet they seek me daily, and delight to know my ways, as a nation that did righteousness, and forsook not the ordinance of their God: they ask of me the ordinances of justice; they take delight in approaching to God.

3. Wherefore have we fasted, say they, and thou seest not? wherefore have we afflicted our soul, and thou takest no knowledge? Behold, in the day of your fast ye find pleasure, and exact all your labours.

4. Behold, ye fast for strife and debate, and to smite with the fist of wickedness: ye shall not fast as ye do this day, to make your voice to be heard on high.

5. Is it such a fast that I have chosen? a day for a man to afflict his soul? is it to bow down his head as a bulrush, and to spread sackcloth and ashes under him? wilt thou call this a fast, and an acceptable day to the LORD?

Isaiah is commanded to berate the sin of hypocritical religion. Organized religious life, formalism, the adherence to customs and forms, is always the greatest danger. It is having the form of godliness without the power of it, a body without a soul. There is possibly nothing more difficult for a religious leader than to point this sin out to his people. This is why the Lord here charges Isaiah so emphatically — and in him all His servants — to attack this sin loudly and clearly in its despicable character.

Verse two depicts the hypocritical existence of formalists. To all appearance they were a praying people and were of the opinion that everything was all right with them. Pharisaic formalism is also always very self-satisfied, orthodox and pious in its own estimation and easily imagines that God looks upon it in the same way. Hence, they ask God in amazement why He does not regard their *fasting*. It truly is a remarkable fact that all outward religion has always attached great importance to *fasting*. Heathendom in olden days tried to placate its gods and gain or regain their favor. The heathen Ninevites practised fasting (Jonah 3:5-9). Moses' law prescribed only one compulsory day of fasting a year, at the great day of atonement. The fasting on that day was not only a refraining from eating and drinking any food or drink but also a stopping of all joyful activities and of all sensual pleasures. "Then shalt thou grieve thine heart," was the Lord's command.

After the Babylonian exile, Jewish fasting greatly increased. Through the influence of emerging Phariseeism all kinds of days of remembrance and fasting were instituted (Zech. 7:5). Among all of the prophets, only in Joel 1:14 and 2:12 is there a call to a general day of fasting. According to the divine idea, fasting is no more than an aid to prayer, the constant calling upon God without any diversion. But, through the influence of man-instituted religion soon the means to an end became the end itself and the object and chief end of the entire religion. Separated from the spiritual condition of the heart fasting is no more than a vain show. This was the case with the people that Isaiah was speaking about. With a few strokes God denudes those hypocrites: (1) When they fast they find their *pleasure*. Even while fasting they pursued their pleasures. (2) *You exact all your labours.* This expression is difficult to understand. Apparently the main thought is that with all their pious fasting they were very strict in their demands of their servants. (3) Their fasting was attended by quarreling and arguing and angrily making a fist — strife that could be heard on high. It may be best to interpret the last phrase of verse four as the answering of prayer. Then it means that God says that all their strife makes it impossible for Him to answer their prayers. The voice of prayer is drowned out by the clamor of strife. In verse five the prophet once more engages in sarcasm. Calvin observed that this whole verse bristles with anger. Isaiah ridicules the misconception and falseness of fasting. The people thought that the object of fasting was self-torture and soul anguish and that it consisted in outward forms which could be seen and admired by others. How little these people knew their God! Self-vexation is never pleasing to God who wishes to deliver from all vexation.

True Fasting and Its Reward

> 6. Is not this the fast that I have chosen? to loose the bands of wickedness, to undo the heavy burdens, and to let the oppressed go free, and that ye break every yoke?
> 7. Is it not to deal thy bread to the hungry, and that thou bring the poor that are cast out to thy house? when thou seest the naked, that thou cover him; and that thou hide not thyself from thine own flesh?
> 8. Then shall thy light break forth as the morning, and thine health shall spring forth speedily: and thy righteousness shall go before thee; the glory of the LORD shall be thy rereward.
> 9. Then shalt thou call, and the LORD shall answer; thou shalt cry, and he shall say, Here I am. If thou take away from the midst of thee the yoke, the putting forth of the finger, and speaking vanity;
> 10. And if thou draw out thy soul to the hungry, and satisfy the afflicted soul; then shall thy light rise in obscurity, and thy darkness be as the noon day:
> 11. And the LORD shall guide thee continually, and satisfy thy soul in drought, and make fat thy bones: and thou shalt be like a watered garden, and like a spring of water, whose waters fail not.
> 12. And they that shall be of thee shall build the old waste places: thou shalt raise up the foundations of many generations; and thou shalt be called, The repairer of the breach, The restorer of paths to dwell in.

God states here what kind of fasting pleases Him. He is not concerned with forms but with what is good, with actions that are according to His holy will. He indicates that He wants all bands, all fetters, all chains, all yokes with which the people have shackled and caused the innocent to groan to be broken. He wants no abstinence from food and drink but from all oppression of the innocent. On the other hand, fasting that is pleasing to Him is when the people save their bread from their own mouths to give it to the hungry and when they give shelter to poor wanderers and fugitives, clothe the naked and do not withhold their tender care from their own family.

Such fasting is followed by the glorious reward of His retributive justice and by complete deliverance. Scripture frequently indicates that Israel would have obtained the privileges of the Kingdom of peace upon perfect obedience. Moreover we must not merely take Isaiah's call to conversion in a historical sense in his own day, but also in a prophetic sense. Immediately before the establishment of that kingdom a mighty call to conversion will go out to Israel, as was sent out by John the Baptist at the first coming of the Lord. So the Lord promises here: (1) *Light,* glorious morning light, which often is the metaphor used for the appearance of the Messiah, the Sun of Righteousness with healing in His wings. When He appears, all darkness of error and misery for Israel will pass away. (2) *Healing* from all maladies and miseries. The word *healing* indicates the binding up of deep wounds. In 1:6 Israel was described as an incurable patient, but one day the Lord will bind up and heal His people. (3) *Righteousness* will guide Israel as a guide and leader on her way and be her rereward. (4) The *glory* of Jehovah-Jesus will be their rereward. Here we have an historical allusion to Israel's army at the exodus from Egypt. (5) Then Israel's prayer will no longer go unanswered, as it is now, but will be heard immediately. Nor will He answer them with a few blessings, but with Himself saying, Behold, *Here I am* (cf. 65:1). Once more, however, she is reminded of the conditions for this salvation: removal of every *yoke,* every *putting forth of the finger,* all mockery and scorn (cf. Prov. 6:13) and all wicked acts and words must be put away and the hungry must be satisfied. Then the sun of Israel's salvation will dawn and her night of suffering will disappear. (6) He promises His people *constant guidance;* a *tender, safe* and *Almighty* guidance toward home. (7) *Satisfaction* of the soul. We must view this as Israel's returning to her homeland through a barren wilderness. (8) *Making the bones fat;* i.e., God will strengthen Israel in such a way that she can continue her homeward way quickly and ably. (9) *A watered garden* is a pleasure garden with many fruit trees, in which there are many little streams. (10) *A spring of water* is a source from which water constantly bubbles up. We must keep in mind that water is the type of all natural and spiritual blessings. (11) Israel's sons will rebuild the destroyed cities of Canaan. The old foundations, which for generations have been covered by rubble, will be built again. (12) Israel receives the new name of *repairer of breaches* and she is presented as one who is able to make dwelling places even of paths. Now let anyone attempt to explain all this of the Church!

The Sabbath for Israel

13. If thou turn away thy foot from the sabbath, from doing thy pleasure on my holy day; and call the sabbath a delight, the holy of the LORD, honourable; and shalt honour him, not doing thine own ways, nor finding thine own pleasure, nor speaking thine own words:

14. Then shalt thou delight thyself in the LORD; and I will cause thee to ride upon the high places of the earth, and feed thee with the heritage of Jacob thy father: for the mouth of the LORD hath spoken it.

This section actually belongs to the preceding verses, but it is not amiss to discuss these words on the sabbath separately. The sabbath was given to Israel and belongs to the people of this earth. It has been stated that the institution of the sabbath dates from creation, but Scripture emphatically teaches differently. The sabbath has been given to the people of the earth as a blessing of life upon the earth. Beside circumcision and Passover, the sabbath was one of the covenant signs between Jehovah and Israel. Whoever violated the sabbath was considered to break the covenant and as a covenant breaker was to be punished with death. There has never been anything similar for the Church. Sabbotanianism is blind indeed for not seeing this. If we are to keep the sabbath according to the Word of God, then we must also stone everyone who does not keep the sabbath. As far as the Law is concerned, it is a matter of either keeping it completely or not at all.

If we are not completely mistaken, we have here a clear proof that after the coming of the Sun of Righteousness to

Israel this people will still observe the sabbath. But they will do this no longer in a cold legalistic way, as before, nor for doing that which pleased the senses as baptized Christianity does; they will *delight themselves in the Lord*. The Lord will make Israel mighty and prosperous. She will *ride upon the high places of the earth,* which means she will conquer all her enemies (cf. Deut. 32:13; 33:29; Ps. 18:34; Isa. 37:24; Hab. 3:19). But Israel will not only be mighty and victorious over all her enemies, but she will also swim in a sea of abundance in Canaan, which then will be in the fullest sense of the word a land flowing with milk and honey. Canaan is called here the *heritage of Jacob thy father* to remind Israel of the fact that then the covenant promises will be fulfilled. Finally it is emphatically stated that the mouth of the Lord has spoken all of this. God is not a man that He should lie; "The promises the Lord has spoken remain eternally unbroken."

The law has been given to a *people* for a definite *time* and for a very specific *goal*. This people was Israel; the goal was *because of transgressions* (Gal. 3:19), while the time of the law ran *until the seed,* Christ, would have come. The Pharisees and scribes did not see this and that was one of the main reasons why they hated Christ's free interpretation of the sabbath. They thought that a sick person was not allowed ever to take medicine on the sabbath, nor that people were allowed to carry a handkerchief on the sabbath, nor even little nails in their sandals or shoes as this was considered carrying a burden. It is a remarkable fact that the fundamental concepts of the ten commandments return again and again in the New Testament, with the exception of the commandment regarding the sabbath, for not even a hint of it is to be found. In the New Testament we find no mention regarding the keeping of the sabbath, but rather a striking contrast when the Apostle in Galatians 4:10 and Colossians 2:16 argues against the keeping of the sabbath.

ISAIAH 59

The Cause of the Separation Between God and Israel

1. Behold, the LORD'S hand is not shortened, that it cannot save; neither his ear heavy, that it cannot hear.

2. But your iniquities have separated between you and your God, and your sins have hid his face from you, that he will not hear.

3. For your hands are defiled with blood, and your fingers with iniquity; your lips have spoken lies, your tongue hath muttered perverseness.

4. None calleth for justice, nor any pleadeth for truth: they trust in vanity, and speak lies; they conceive mischief, and bring forth iniquity.

5. They hatch cockatrice eggs, and weave the spider's web: he that eateth of their eggs dieth, and that which is crushed breaketh out into a viper.

6. Their webs shall not become garments, neither shall they cover themselves with their works: their works are works of iniquity, and the act of violence is in their hands.

7. Their feet run to evil, and they make haste, to shed innocent blood: their thoughts are thoughts of iniquity; wasting and destruction are in their paths.

8. The way of peace they know not; and there is no judgment in their goings: they have made them crooked paths: whosoever goeth therein shall not know peace.

This chapter is divided into three equal parts: Israel's sin; Israel's misery and confession and; thirdly, Israel's deliverance. These eight verses refers to Israel's sins. There were many people in Israel — and today there still are many — who were of the opinion that Jehovah was not able to deliver His captive people, or was not willing to do so. The first verses contradict this fallacy. The Lord can indeed deliver and He hears Israel cry; He is willing to deliver but Israel's *iniquities* make a separation between God and her. This is the terrible nature of sin — that it makes a separation between God and man and at the same time makes a bond between man, Satan and damnation. Sin is the correlation of eternal punishment. The iniquities which brought about this separation are listed, such as *murder, deceit, perverseness, injustice, lies.* The contrast between God's hand and their hands catches our attention. His mighty hand does not save them because their hands are covered with blood. It is their own fault that all hope of deliverance dissipates like smoke.

Isaiah's lively imagery is evident in verse five in two metaphors whereby he compares them to cockatrices and spiders, which hatch their eggs and weave their webs. The *cockatrice* was a very poisonous snake; he presents these people as poisonous and producing poisonous offspring. Those who participate in their devious designs are strikingly depicted as *eating their eggs,* for which they will have to pay with their lives. The crushing of these eggs can appropriately be interpreted as opposition against these evil plans. This opposition is depicted as totally futile, since the breaking of the eggs results only in the emergence of *vipers,* young snakes. Verse six is a further explanation of the weaving of spider's webs. No matter how finely the webs are spun, they are totally useless and worthless. The webs *will not become garments.* In France, the attempt was made once to make cloth of them, but that proved fruitless, just as Isaiah concludes. From this verse it is evident that by this product of spiders is meant the works of the wicked. But this material is not only totally useless; it is also a net with which to catch innocent flies. A spider is a very bloodthirsty creature and its web is small; it is one of the most terrible instruments in the world of insects. In certain webs we sometimes can see dozens of victims from which all the blood has been sucked out. A spider is the most remarkable little weaver that exists as it spins silken threads from its own body and with it weaves little webs of marvelous composition and symmetry.

All these verses show the greatest similarity to the sevenfold picture of man given in Romans 3:13-20.

Israel's Lament About Her Misery

9. Therefore is judgment far from us, neither doth judgment overtake us: we wait for light, but behold obscurity; for brightness, but we walk in darkness.

10. We grope for the wall like the blind and we grope as if we had no eyes: we stumble at noon day as in the night; we are in desolate places as dead men.

11. We roar all like bears, and mourn sore like doves: we look for judgment, but there is none; for salvation, but it is far off from us.

12. For our transgressions are multiplied before thee, and our sins testify against us: for our transgressions are with us; and as for our iniquities, we know them;

13. In transgressing and lying against the LORD, and departing away from our God, speaking oppression and revolt, conceiving and uttering from the heart words of falsehood.

14. And judgment is turned away backward, and justice standeth afar off: for truth is fallen in the street, and equity cannot enter.

15a. Yea, truth faileth; and he that departeth from evil maketh himself a prey:

The connection between these verses and the preceding ones is to be seen in part as that of cause and effect, and also as a contrast. Verses nine to eleven contain a stirring lament about Israel's misery voiced by the remnant in the end time; this misery is the result of the transgressions described before, which caused a separation between Israel and her God. In the remaining verses this remnant confesses its departure from God.

Israel's present misery is strikingly depicted in verses nine to eleven. Still, these words will obtain an even greater significance at the end time of the Great Tribulation. The misery is depicted as horrible, terrifying darkness and in its oppression the people anxiously await the light; but where-ever the afflicted people may cast their eyes, their justice or deliverance is nowhere to be seen. They are looking for a great *brightness,* the great light of Messianic deliverance from all their vexations, but everywhere there is fearful obscurity and black night. From 60:2 we know that darkness will cover the whole earth, but from other Scripture we know that at that time it will be especially for Israel a day of clouds and thick darkness (Jer. 30:5-7. Zech. 14:1-5). This almost palpable darkness and yearning for light cause Israel to compare herself to *the blind* who grope about in darkness for the wall; they stumble about as those whose eyes have been dug out. Their feet stumble, they bump themselves, they fall and lie flat and still like dead men. The expression *in desolate places* is translated in various ways. The Vulgate, Luther, Van Ess, Leeser, Kay and others translated it as *darkness* or *dark places* and that is undoubtedly correct and has always been accepted by the Jewish authorities. In that case, we have a parallel between the second and fourth clause and not between the third and fourth. According to this translation the Jews compare themselves to the dead who have descended into the graves or the realm of the dead. We note that the Septuagint has translated the expression as *they moan like dying people.* Many recent translations, however, have *the fat ones,* in the sense of the *prosperous* ones, or also the *fat,* i.e., fruitful places. The main idea remains the same in all translations however, i.e., that Israel is as the dead.

In their great affliction they roar like hungry bears. When in early spring the bears appear from their dens, after having hibernated all winter long, they make an eerie, hungry sound — this is the comparison.

Mourning sore like doves needs no further explanation when we remember that doves can produce a doleful sound. In her misery Israel keeps on looking for *judgment,* but the longed-for and much-desired Messianic salvation remains far away.

In verse thirteen Israel makes known in a very touching confession, which may be said to have the marks of being humble, upright and complete, the reason of her wretchedness. This confession is complete because she even bares the outgoings of her wicked heart before God. The causal connection between her sin and misery is once more emphasized in verse fourteen. Israel's *judgment,* or deliverance, tarries, because *truth is fallen in the street,* and justice finds no place. The virtuous person becomes the victim of the wrath of the evil ones.

What Jehovah-Jesus Does Upon Israel's Humble Confession

15b. . . . and the LORD saw it, and it displeased him that there was no judgment.

16. And he saw that there was no man, and wondered that there was no intercessor: therefore his arm brought salvation unto him; and his righteousness, it sustained him.

17. For he put on righteousness as a breastplate, and an helmet of salvation upon his head; and he put on the garments of vengeance for clothing, and was clad with zeal as a cloke.

18. According to their deeds, accordingly he will repay, fury to his adversaries, recompence to his enemies; to the islands he will repay recompence.

The division into verses could not have been more unfortunate than that in verse fifteen, as anyone can readily see. It would have been much better if a new chapter had started here. For then the glorious connection between Israel's humble confession and Jehovah's deliverance would have been much more obvious. Presently, this connection eludes most Bible readers. It is strikingly stated that Jehovah *saw* Israel's confession. Most expositors take the word *it* as referring to Israel's wicked conduct, but in fact it refers to the entire humble confession beginning at verse nine. Hence, *seeing* must not be taken in a bad sense, but in the favorable sense of God's pleasure, as He always does upon every humble confession. The supernaturalist Van der Palm and the totally modern Cheyne have sensed this better than orthodox expositors. God had indeed seen the whole history of Israel (18:3), but He looked with a merciful eye upon her humble confession and immediately went out as a warrior to deliver His people. In connection with this view we must not take the word *judgment* in verse fifteen in the sense of social justice as in verses eight and fourteen, but in the sense of a righteous defense of Israel's cause against her enemies, as is meant with the word *judgment* in verses nine and eleven. Nor must we take these verses in the sense of punishments God will carry out against Israel, for these are implied in verses nine to eleven, but in the sense of punishments God will inflict upon all Israel's enemies in the great day of His return, which is depicted in verse seventeen and mentioned emphatically in verse twenty. It is by no means redundant to remind ourselves once more that the past tense is again the normal prophetic *perfectum,* that is to say, a description of future things as though they already had taken place in the past. The view we advocate is justified by the context and the almost similar wording in 63:3-6, where the Messiah also goes out to avenge Israel's enemies. The Lord is presented here as being amazed, shocked that there was no *man* who stood in the gap for Israel as an intercessor. The word *intercessor* is not to be taken in its narrower sense but in the broader sense of representative, defender, who actually stood in the gap for Israel. Ezekiel 22:30 contains a good description of what is meant. The basic thought is that Jehovah-Jesus is filled with holy indignation at the fact that among all the nations and the powerful of this earth there is no one to be found who courageously takes up the cudgel for His miraculous people, which has been provoked and stepped on for so long. England, too, with all its seemingly condescending *Lords* does not take up the cudgel for Israel; it promises much, but it does nothing for the Jews. Only Christ's *arm* will bring about salvation for this oppressed people. As Israel's Champion He will descend with power and majesty from heaven. Verse seventeen describes the armor of this Warrior. He fastens *righteousness,* the righteous defense of His people, around Him as a breastplate, as a coat of mail; salvation is His *helmet;* vengeance His *garments; zeal* or jealousy for His beloved Israel, His *cloke.* In His burning anger He will everywhere avenge His and Israel's enemies according to their deeds. He will even recompence the *islands,* the European nations, according to their works. It seems that He has already begun doing this.

The Results of the Return of the Lord

19. So shall they fear the name of the LORD from the west, and his glory from the rising of the sun. When the enemy shall come in like a flood, the Spirit of the LORD shall lift up a standard against him.
20. And the Redeemer shall come to Zion, and unto them that turn from transgression in Jacob, saith the LORD.
21. As for me, this is my covenant with them, saith the

LORD; my spirit that is upon thee, and my words which I have put in thy mouth, shall not depart out of thy mouth, nor out of the mouth of thy seed, nor out of the mouth of thy seed's seed, saith the LORD, from henceforth and for ever.

The result of Christ's coming and judgment of the nations for the remnants of these nations will be that they will everywhere, in east and west, seeing the power and glory of Christ, *fear* Him and reverence and glorify Him with deepest respect. In short, a general conversion of the nations will take place after the return of Christ, but not before that, as so many seem to imagine. This will occur after the retribution and punishment of the nations for their hatred and persecution of the Jews, as we are emphatically taught here.

When the enemy shall come in like a flood, the Spirit of the Lord shall lift up a standard against him. This statement has been explained in various ways. The Septuagint and the Vulgate and almost all Roman Catholic expositors translate: "The anger of the Lord shall come like a wildly seething flood, swept along by the breath of the Lord." Henderson and Kay, on linguistic grounds, have conclusively proved that this translation is wrong, and that on the other hand the English Authorized Version, which here is the same as the Dutch Authorized Version, must be retained. The text speaks of the last great enemy of Israel. He is the same enemy as mentioned in Daniel 8:19, 23; 11:40-45. There he is depicted as a wily ruler who craftily carries out his plans and vehemently rages against the *holy nation* Israel and against the Messiah, but who will suddenly come to his end by the appearance of the Messiah, and will have no helper. This enemy is no one less than the future Assyrian whom we constantly met in the first part of Isaiah. This enemy will come *as a flood.* In keeping with the Hebrew manner of speaking, a great deliverance as well as a great calamity is compared to an overflowing stream. In 48:18 and 66:12 we find examples of the former; in 8:7, 8; 18:2 and Revelation 13:1 of the latter. When the unnamed enemy will threaten to flood Israel, the *Spirit of the Lord* will oppose him and lift up a banner against him. Several scholars translate this word as Jehovah's *breath* or *stormwind,* but not a single instance of the expression *Spirit of God* or *Spirit of the Lord* in Scripture has this meaning. The idea of a strong wind is expressed differently in Scripture — *ruach gedolah.* The Spirit of the Lord here means the *Spirit of judgment,* as it does in 4:4 (cf. II Thess. 2:8). This leads us to the result of the coming of the Lord, i.e., the activity of the Spirit. According to Revelation 22:17, this divine Person has a great interest in the coming of the Lord. He desires it and prays fervently for it, for the sake of Christ, of the Father, of the Church, and also of Himself. During and after the coming of the Lord He must do a great work against the enemy of Israel and for Israel, the nations, and the whole creation, both in judgment and in glorification (cf. 4:4; 11:2; 32:15; 44:3; 61:1; Ezek. 37: Joel 2:28; Zech. 10:10). According to verse twenty-one the Spirit of Christ will never depart from restored Israel *from henceforth and for ever.* This is a fruit of the covenant of grace, *saith the Lord,* even though men say otherwise.

Verse twenty mentions the *Gaal,* the Deliverer, by name. It is remarkable that Paul in Romans 11:26 says that the Deliverer comes out of Zion. That cannot be explained merely by the fact that he quotes the prophet by heart or because he follows the Septuagint, as Calvin claims, but because the Holy Spirit wants to indicate that first He comes *to* Zion and then comes *out of* Zion, Jerusalem. As mentioned before, the remnant is the recipient of salvation. Hence the four results of the Lord's return are very precious!

ISAIAH 60

The Light That Will Arise Upon Israel

1. Arise, shine; for thy light is come, and the glory of the LORD is risen upon thee.

2. For, behold, the darkness shall cover the earth, and gross darkness the people: but the LORD shall arise upon thee, and his glory shall be seen upon thee.

3. And the Gentiles shall come to thy light, and kings to the brightness of thy rising.

4. Lift up thine eyes round about, and see: all they gather themselves together, they come to thee: thy sons shall come from far, and thy daughters shall be nursed at thy side.

"The Lord urges His Church to rejoice in the salvation obtained for it by Christ" — so reads the superscription above this chapter (D.A.V.). Also the King James Version has written above it, "The Glory of the Church." The French translation of David Martin, too, has written above it, *"Accroissement de l'Eglise, Description mystique de ses biens spirituels,"* "The growth of the Church. A mystical description of its spiritual benefits." This has been the general idea of Protestantism for centuries. Apparently it followed Calvin in this regard who states: "Here it is specifically the oppressed Church which Isaiah in ecstasy addresses." At that time theologians had no better insight regarding the difference between Israel and the Church, nor in the word of prophecy, and for this reason we shall not be hard on these God-fearing people. But what must we say about those who still adhere to this antiquated idea that Israel literally receives only the curses in Scripture and the Church the spiritual blessings as described in this beautiful chapter; while in the meantime Protestantism has been rent into thousands of fragments and the fig tree, Israel, is budding, and the signs of the times are pointing to the national restoration of Israel? We can only say that this shows a great measure of blindness, unbelief, self-satisfaction, and stubborn prejudice. This fourfold accusation is almost too mild for this great foolishness and sin, which has had such detrimental results, and still has. We quote here with complete satisfaction what the famous expositors Van der Palm writes. In his introduction to this chapter he says:

> The prophecy contained in this chapter contains for the Israelite nation the most glorious prospects, the promises of being the very first in the rank of the nations, of the greatest happiness and prosperity, the most lasting and peaceful reign and all the glitter and glory which will emanate naturally from Jehovah's personal indwelling amongst His people. The tone, the style, and the expression of this prediction are so strong and lofty that we find here, if anywhere, vistas of future events, which, although unfulfilled as yet, will be ratified only in the last days by their results, and which will elevate Abraham's posterity, joined to the service of their and our Saviour, to the utmost glory. The attempts by some expositors to explain this divine oracle concerning the blessedness of the Israelites as taking place after the return from Babylon; and those of others to explain them wholly spiritually of the prosperity, growth and extension of the Christian Church during the first days of the New Testament, appear to us as unsatisfactory, since the former explanation must of necessity weaken the intended meaning of the words, and the letter violates *all sound, literal biblical exegesis.*

We have italicized the last words of this famous expositor, for this thought merits the attention of all of us. Van Hamelsveld and Klinkenberg, too, view this as the still future conversion of the Jews, although the latter speaks of the glorious state of the Church.

This promise applies to Israel, which must be seen as a poor prisoner in a dark dungeon, languishing in untold misery and woe and deprived of everything. They have robbed us of everything, Da Costa complained once — our country, our cities, our glorious name and the Church has robbed us of our promises. Does this not concern you, O Christians; where is there a grief like unto our grief? Imprisoned Israel herself groans: Our hope is gone, God has forgotten to be gracious unto us! But listen, suddenly a voice resounds in their ears in their dark dungeon: *Koemi, oeri! Arise, shine!* Let Israel shake off her shackles and bathe herself in the light of the Sun of Righteousness! At long last, after many centuries of waiting, Israel's sun has arisen, but, this time never to go down again. In nature, the sun is the source of life, power, growth, fruitfulness, beauty and joy. When after a long cold night the sun arises, darkness flees, the chilly mists evaporate and the birds sing their happy songs. All this the Sun of Righteousness will do in a much higher sense for Israel. This Light is called *thy light,* since it had been promised unto Israel from of old and had been waited for. It is further described as the *glory of the Lord,* the outward beauty and visible splendor of our Lord Jesus Christ in the day of His coming again. Whereas verse one tells us for whom and from whom this Light is, verse two tells us *when* and under what circumstances this Light comes to Israel. It had not arisen to this handful of fifty thousand people who sat down near the temple, weeping. This light will come when *darkness shall cover the earth* and *gross darkness the people,* i.e., at a time so dark as never before, which points to the terrible time of the Great Tribulation, when the nations of earth will be enveloped in a darkness greater than the Egyptian darkness. At that moment of the greatest misery Jehovah-Jesus will arise over Israel with healing in His wings. Then Israel's shackles will be broken and the doors of the prison thrown open; Israel will be pulled up from the pool of the wretchedness of her measureless misery.

What will be the fruit of this arisen Light? (1) The nations of the world will *see* the glory of Jehovah-Jesus. That the nations refuse to believe without seeing has been sufficiently proven after a history of almost two thousand years. The history of the nations is at the same time the history of unbelief. In His limitless mercy God will at long last show them the glory of His Son, so that they must either pay Him homage on their knees, or perish instantly. (2) The nations will not only see the Light of Christ, but will also, led by their kings, hasten to that light. Psalm 22:27ff and 86:9ff will be literally fulfilled. The believing Church will know that what it formerly sang in hollow sounds will prove to have been glorious prophecy. Israel sees the nations advance in stately parades from far and near to her land and her exalted King.

We realize immediately, however, that these and similar promises cannot be fulfilled as long as the seed of the Word only for one quarter makes roots downward and bears fruit upward, the weeds shoot up together with the wheat, unrighteousness is multiplied among all nations, faith becomes scarce upon the earth, there is but a small flock of cross-bearers and the great apostasy is visibly coming closer. In neither the past nor present has anything similar ever been seen. In this dispensation, in which these problems will continue, this promise of the conversion and enlightenment of the nations *cannot* be fulfilled; it can neither be fulfilled in eternity nor in heaven, so that we have no choice but to place the fulfillment of these and similar promises at the beginning of the millennium of peace (cf. Ps. 102:14-23).

The General March of the Nations to Zion

5. Then thou shalt see, and flow together, and thine heart shall fear, and be enlarged; because the abundance of the sea shall be converted unto thee, the forces of the Gentiles shall come unto thee.

6. The multitude of camels shall cover thee, the dromedaries of Midian and Ephah; all they from Sheba shall come: they shall bring gold and incense; and they shall shew forth the praises of the LORD.

7. All the flocks of Kedar shall be gathered together unto thee, the rams of Nebaioth shall minister unto thee: they shall come up with acceptance on mine altar, and I will glorify the house of my glory.

8. Who are these that fly as a cloud, and as the doves to their windows?

9. Surely the isles shall wait for me, and the ships of Tarshish first, to bring thy sons from far, their silver and their gold with them, unto the name of the LORD thy God, and to the Holy One of Israel, because he hath glorified thee.

Chapters 2:1-4 and 54:2 also speak of Zion's increase in population and her rule over the nations (cf. 44:5; 45:14;

49:7, 23; 52:15; 53:10; 55:5; 62:2; 66:12). One day every knee shall bow to the Lord Jesus Christ (45:23, 24). His judgment will be the light of the nations. Whoever blesses or swears will do so by His name (65:16).

Israel will be beside herself with amazement when after her restoration she will see the nations flow to her with their riches. The *fear* of the heart must be understood as surprise and amazement at such a sudden and great honor and glory. Then Israel's heart will be *enlarged,* something she never did before with respect to the *goim,* the nations. Until this very day Israel has something of Jonah's attitude toward Nineveh. But after her national conversion and restoration, her proud, dour and narrowminded heart will open up in love for the nations of the earth, which for many centuries have treated the Jews so shamefully. The *abundance of the sea* must be understood as the treasures of the sea of nations. Not until verse nine is there a reference to the actual sea. The *forces of the Gentiles* is a further explanation of the treasures which all the nations will pour into Israel's lap. Huge flocks of *fast camels* will cover the entire country. The *swift camels* (Dutch version) are dromedaries coming from *Midian* and *Ephah,* loaded with treasures. *Ephah* was a tribe of the Midianites (Gen. 25:4). These are mentioned here by way of example, as it is said that in times past they had many dromedaries. Sheba was a place in Fortunate Arabia which was rich in incense and gold. This area, too, like others mentioned here, are examples. Some expositors have thought that this reference to treasures of *incense* and *gold* contained a prophecy regarding the treasures the Wise Men laid at the feet of the Babe in Bethlehem; *myrrh* is also mentioned there. Myrrh indicated suffering, but suffering is a thing of the past when these treasures are brought to Israel and her King. The nations will not *show forth the praise of* the Jews, but of *the Lord.* They will be full of the praise of Zion's King, our precious Savior. The *Kedarenes* and the *Nabaioth* were descendants of Ishmael and are presented as being rich in cattle. In the boldest of metaphors the *rams,* which means the *kings,* are pictured as joyfully and willingly placing themselves upon the Lord's altar of thanksgiving. Truly it is no wonder that with such a willing people the house of the

Lord becomes glorious. While Israel sees the flow of nations approaching from one side, she suddenly sees great multitudes, which come flying like doves in the sky, from another direction. There can be no doubt that this is a reference to aircraft, which at that time will probably be the means of transportation *par excellence.* The isles, Europe and America, are then waiting for King Jesus and the excellent ships of Tarshish will be ready first to carry the Jews, the ten tribes, back to their country. The *silver and the gold* of the Jews comes along to Zion and will be sanctified to the Lord Jesus out of gratitude for all He has done for Israel.

The text speaks of a glory for Israel and the nations such as has never been seen before and never will be seen until the Lord Jesus Himself comes from heaven to materialize all these things.

The Inexpressible Splendor of Reborn Zion

10. And the sons of strangers shall build up thy walls, and their kings shall minister unto thee: for in my wrath I smote thee, but in my favour have I had mercy on thee.

11. Therefore thy gates shall be open continually; they shall not be shut day nor night; that men may bring unto thee the forces of the Gentiles, and that their kings may be brought.

12. For the nation and kingdom that will not serve thee shall perish; yea, those nations shall be utterly wasted.

13. The glory of Lebanon shall come unto thee, the fir tree, the pine tree, and the box together, to beautify the place of my sanctuary and I will make the place of my feet glorious.

14. The sons also of them that afflicted thee shall come bending unto thee; and all they that despised thee shall bow themselves down at the soles of thy feet; and they shall call thee The city of the LORD, The Zion of the Holy One of Israel.

15. Whereas thou hast been forsaken and hated, so that no man went through thee, I will make thee an eternal excellency, a joy of many generations.

16. Thou shalt also suck the milk of the Gentiles, and shalt suck the breast of kings: and thou shalt know that I the LORD am thy Saviour and thy Redeemer, the mighty One of Jacob.

17. For brass I will bring gold, and for iron I will bring silver, and for wood brass, and for stones iron: I will also make thy officers peace, and thine exactors righteousness.

18. Violence shall no more be heard in thy land, wasting nor destruction within thy borders; but thou shalt call thy walls Salvation, and thy gates Praise.

19. The sun shall no more be thy light by day; neither for brightness shall the moon give light unto thee: but the LORD shall be unto thee an everlasting light, and thy God thy glory.

20. Thy sun shall no more go down; neither shall thy moon withdraw itself: for the LORD shall be thine everlasting light, and the days of thy mourning shall be ended.

21. Thy people also shall be all righteous: they shall inherit the land for ever, the branch of my planting, the work of my hands, that I may be glorified.

22. A little one shall become a thousand, and a small one a strong nation: I the LORD will hasten it in his time.

When we fully realize that all this glory concerns Israel and the nations, and not the Church or heaven, and that this predicted glory will not be fulfilled in this dispensation, but will dawn at and by the coming again of the Lord Jesus Christ, then these promises are very simple and even the simplest reader of Scripture can have no difficulty with them. Since all these verses as well as the following chapters mainly cover the same subject, we can naturally be very brief in our exposition. Verse ten speaks of Israel's great *honor,* for even the *kings* of the nations will serve the people they once oppressed. Zion is the mistress, the queen of the nations, and Jerusalem the capital of the nations. Jerusalem, which in the past had so long and so repeatedly been trampled down by the Gentiles is now completely safe and at rest, for her gates are open day and night. There is another reason, however, why her gates will never be shut. It is because the flow of the kings and cultures of the nations will be constant towards the holy city, which will be the focus of all nations. Woe unto the nation and the kingdom that will refuse to show Israel the honor it owes her. By the Almighty hand of King Jesus the opposers are utterly destroyed. Even the kings of foreigners will take off their crowns and cast them at the feet of Israel and her King. All the beauty of the magnificent trees of Lebanon will beautify the great temple at Jerusalem and the throne of Jehovah-Jesus (cf. Ezek. 40 - 48). The erstwhile oppressors and slanderers of the Jews will in that day fall at the feet of the holy nation and kiss the impression of their feet and call them *the city of Jehovah-Jesus,* the *Zion of the Holy One of Israel.*

No one dares to deny that until this day Israel is *forsaken* and *hated.* Why then do people not believe that one day this will be *past tense* as God says here, and that He will make Israel an eternal *excellency* and *joy?* Just as a suckling child sucks its strength and life from its mother, so restored Israel will gladly receive all the treasures of culture from the nations. A preview of this is seen in the reign of Solomon (I Kings 10:24-27; II Chron. 1:15; 9:20-27), when his treasures were already so immeasurable that silver was hardly appreciated. The *officers,* magistrates and the *exactors* — the rulers and administrators — will be peaceable and just. All violence, disturbance and destruction will be far away; everything will breathe justice and peace. The walls are called *Salvation,* and the gates *Praise* (cf. 26:1). While Israel has been in darkness for many centuries, the Lord Jesus Himself will be her *everlasting light* and her *glory* (cf. 2:2). What a contrast! In the past Israel languished, as a prisoner in a dark dungeon (49:9), and hoped for light (59:9), but in that day she will have an *everlasting light, and the days of her mourning* will have ended. The band of righteousness will be around the entire nation and the bond of love and of holiness will tie her together, and all this will be to the honor of King Jesus (v. 16), and to His glorification (v. 21). *A little one shall become a thousand* is an expression that points to the much desired glory of fruitfulness which was correlated with power and glory in the mind of Israel. Finally, the assurance is given that God *in his time* will materialize this salvation for Israel. He has already been waiting for many centuries, but once He begins to deliver Israel, He will do so speedily.

ISAIAH 61

The Program of the Lord Jesus

1. The Spirit of the Lord GOD is upon me; because the LORD hath anointed me to preach good tidings unto the meek; he hath sent me to bind up the brokenhearted, to proclaim liberty to the captives, and the opening of the prison to them that are bound;
2. To proclaim the acceptable year of the LORD, and the day of vengeance of our God; to comfort all that mourn;
3. To appoint unto them that mourn in Zion, to give unto them beauty for ashes, the oil of joy for mourning, the garment of praise for the spirit of heaviness; that they might be called trees of righteousness, the planting of the LORD, that he might be glorified.

We might call this the proclamation of King Jesus, for the word *proclaim* in verse two refers to the publication of a general proclamation. These verses are very rich in content. The famous preacher Spurgeon wrote a valuable booklet on it, entitled, *The Comforter of the Mourning.* We doubt, however, whether this great and extremely practical preacher did see the connection and the full scope of these words for Israel and the nations of the world. For he explains everything in terms of the present work of the Lord for His Church. On the basis of Luke 4:17-20 we can admit that this glorious manifesto of King Messiah also allows for this application, but from the entire preceding and following context it is sufficiently apparent that these words do not so much apply to the humiliated and rejected Messiah as they do to the exalted and glorified Messiah; that they are not meant for the Church, but for captive Israel, those that mourn in Zion; and that they are not applicable to this time, but to the day of His return, when He will fully manifest His anointing and threefold office and implement and carry out this wholly unique program before the entire world. Then, and not before that time, the year of jubilee, here called *the acceptable year of the Lord,* will have arrived. When the Savior was reading these words in the synagogue at Nazareth, He suddenly stopped, rolled up the scroll, and gave it back to the minister. How strange, to stop reading in the middle of a full sentence, to close the book and to lay it aside. At His first coming He was not sent to introduce the *day of vengeance,* nor *to comfort all who mourned* and to carry out what is written in verse three. The Church does not have waste places, as mentioned in verse four and Israel did not rebuild the *old waste places* at Christ's first coming. Not until seventy years after Christ was her country totally laid waste. But when Christ will have come back, then Israel's cities will have laid waste *for many generations.* Foreign nations will be Israel's shepherds, farmers and vinedressers and Zion's land and people will shine in unlimited glory. In contrast to the limited, symbolical priesthood of the Old Testament, all Jews will be called *the priests of Jehovah* by the nations (v. 6). In Israel, priests were exempted from field work, hence the strangers will do all the work for Israel, which is a *priestly kingdom* and just as the priests ate of the tithes of the people, so all of Israel will eat the *riches of the Gentiles.* In the preceding chapter all the nations of the earth carried their treasures within Jerusalem's walls.

It is certain that justice is not done to this prophecy if we explain it merely spiritually as do Spurgeon, Sikkel and Macduff, although we gladly admit once more that on the basis of Luke 4:17-20 we can also draw rich instruction and comfort in that sense from it. At His first coming, the Lord Jesus was *anointed* and *sent* to bind up the brokenhearted and proclaim liberty. This is why the Lord Jesus could say, "This day is this scripture fulfilled in your ears." *The year of the good pleasure of the Lord* (Dutch version) is, as we already noted the culmination of the year of jubilee. This was the year of *rest, peace, liberty, joy, satisfaction* and *abundance.* The state of Paradise had then as it were, returned. This *year* finds its materialization in the Kingdom of Peace, while the day of *vengeance* described in 63:1-6, refers to the time of the Great Tribulation (Rev. 6-19). This day is placed between *the acceptable year* and the *comforting of all who mourn* as the means to lead to this glorious goal. *Them that mourn in Zion* are presented here as bound in prison where they mourn, of which *ashes* is the symbol. The Messiah is *anointed* and *sent* by the Father to give them *beauty* or, as Lowth translates, *a beautiful crown; oil of joy* — festive ointment, fragrant fluid — for mourning, and the *garment of praise,* i.e., festive clothing, for the spirit of heaviness. The *oak trees* (Dutch version) are the converted Jews. They are then the oak trees *of righteousness* in contrast with the *oak trees of unrighteousness* in 1:29. The object of all of this is the glorification of Christ (cf. 60:21).

Israel as a Restored and Glorified Nation

4. And they shall build the old wastes, they shall raise up the former desolations, and they shall repair the waste cities, the desolations of many generations.
5. And strangers shall stand and feed your flocks, and the sons of the alien shall be your plowmen and your vinedressers.
6. But ye shall be named the Priests of the LORD: men shall call you the Ministers of our God: ye shall eat the riches of the Gentiles, and in their glory shall ye boast yourselves.
7. For your shame ye shall have double; and for confusion they shall rejoice in their portion: therefore in their land they shall possess the double: everlasting joy shall be unto them.
8. For I the LORD love judgment, I hate robbery for burnt offerings; and I will direct their work in truth, and I will make an everlasting covenant with them.
9. And their seed shall be known among the Gentiles, and their offspring among the people: all that see them shall acknowledge them, that they are the seed which the LORD hath blessed.

This section is very much like the preceding chapter and must be considered as a direct result of the carrying out of the Messianic program discussed before. Here we find a description of Israel's relationship to the past (v. 4) to the aliens (v. 5), to Jehovah (v. 6) and to the provided salvation (v. 7). In the past Israel had sinned doubly and therefore had received double *shame* from the hand of the Lord. But after the double sin and the double punishment the beloved nation will also have double joy and glory. Israel's sun will never go down again. It never escapes our attention in Isaiah that in this connection we are constantly reminded of the everlasting duration of Israel's salvation (cf. 60:15, 19, 21; 61:7, 8). Israel's sun cannot set since it is not the sun of nature but the Sun of Righteousness, Christ, that would be an *everlasting* light (60:20). Since the entire world has become tributary to Israel which is now a nation of only righteous people and priests, the redeemed nation will bathe in the light of His love. The future glory of Israel can already be concluded from the fact that the King of Israel will be in the midst of them with His light and joyful sound.

The connection of verse eight with the rest has not always been correctly understood. The connection is the basis for the double and endless joy in verse seven. Israel's bliss is founded on God's judgment. This is the continuous teaching of Isaiah (1:27) and of the entire Scripture. "How blessed is the man who has all his sins forgiven." Christ satisfied God's justice and on this unshakable foundation God grants us and Israel grace. It is also according to His inviolable justice that in the history of mankind there is a law of compensation, a law of retribution. Whereas Israel for many centuries had suffered shame, now Israel receives double joy. The people who are now still more miserable than any other nation will then be more glorious than all other nations.

I hate robbery for burnt offerings. It cannot be denied that this is a difficult expression. Jehovah's hatred is contrasted here with His love of righteousness. His hatred of those who oppress His people is as great as His love of justice. It seems to us that this idea has been beautifully expressed by Paul with respect to the Church in II Thessalonians 1:6, 7. For many centuries, people have robbed and plundered His people Israel, and that in the name of Jesus and the honor of God. This is apparently what the Lord means here. Then the meaning of this statement is: "Although people offered as a burnt sacrifice to Me that which they robbed and stole from My people, I nevertheless hate that kind of sacrifice." It may be that people have persecuted Israel because they considered them to be murderers of Christ, but God declares here that He hates and despises all such religiosity. The word *work* in verse eight must be taken in the sense of *reward,* as in 40:10;

62:11. God in His faithfulness wants to reward Israel for all her labor and trouble. This will be the result of the Lord's covenant of peace with Israel (cf. 28:18; 42:6; 49:8; 55:3).

Verse nine declares that Israel will be known and loved among the nations. Verse six stated that the nations would *call* the restored Jews priests of the Lord, i.e., they would publicly acknowledge them as the holy servants of the Lord. The God-fearing people in Israel thought much of their priests in olden days. These priests still had an aura of holiness during the time when Israel had backslidden. Thus one day the nations who will be saved will consider the Jews as the servants of God who have been blessed and sanctified by Him. They will have the greatest esteem for them and no longer oppress them.

A Song of Praise Concerning All the Blessings Given

> 10. I will greatly rejoice in the LORD, my soul shall be joyful in my God; for he hath clothed me with the garments of salvation, he hath covered me with the robe of righteousness, as a bridegroom decketh himself with ornaments, and as a bride adorneth herself with her jewels.
> 11. For as the earth bringeth forth her bud, and as the garden causeth the things that are sown in it to spring forth; so the Lord GOD will cause righteousness and praise to spring forth before all the nations.

When Isaiah looks at the whole *salvation* that one day will be given his wretched and poor people, a song of exultation wells up in his noble heart, a song that at the same time is a prophecy and that one day will be taken up by the whole redeemed nation. For a correct understanding of a statement like this, we must realize that in those days beautiful clothes were the sign of *riches, joy* and *honor.* Since the Lord would give all these things to Israel, the prophet who identified himself so closely with his people feels as though he himself has been clothed with the most beautiful garments. They are the *garments of salvation,* of bliss and redemption by the Messiah from all calamities and death itself. The *robe of righteousness* is not a reference to justification, for that is already implied in the first expression, but to that which is added to salvation, i.e., the righteous retribution of the reward of grace. The priests of the Lord in verse six also have priestly attire of *white, purple, heavenly blue,* and *gold. Purple* pointed to blood, *white* to purity, *gold* to righteousness of faith and *heavenly blue* to heaven. The adornment of the bride points to great sparkling joy and lovely beauty – a mighty contrast with the misery of verse three (cf. Jeremiah 2:32; Revelation 21:2 on the meaning of bridal adornment).

The prophet rejoices not only in the ecstatic happiness of Israel, but also in the renewing of the whole earth. At the time of Israel's national and territorial restoration the earth will never again see blighted crops or failing harvest. Every field will yield its crops and every garden will cause its seed to sprout. In the same manner, the Lord will reveal His *righteousness* in Christ to all nations, and His *praise* in the sight of all the nations of the earth.

ISAIAH 62

1. For Zion's sake will I not hold my peace, and for Jerusalem's sake I will not rest, until the righteousness thereof go forth as brightness, and the salvation thereof as a lamp that burneth.

2. And the Gentiles shall see thy righteousness, and all kings thy glory: and thou shalt be called by a new name, which the mouth of the LORD shall name.

3. Thou shalt also be a crown of glory in the hand of the LORD, and a royal diadem in the hand of thy God.

This chapter still deals with the same subject and refers to the same time as the preceding. The prophet does not predict here the glorious state of the Church but of Israel during the millennium of peace. Who is the speaker? Various answers have been given to this question: God, the Church, the preachers, Isaiah, Christ. The last is correct. The same one who spoke in 61:1-3 is speaking here, and it is He alone who has placed watchmen on the walls of Zion and who can give the commands of this chapter. Zion occupies a central place in the heart of Christ. He came to Israel once and wept over Jerusalem once. When people murdered Him, He prayed for them. Here He says that He will not hold His peace with regard to Zion. Psalm 121 is the true commentary on this statement. The One who is more than Boaz will not rest *until* Zion's *righteousness* will manifest itself publicly as *brightness,* and her *salvation,* her bliss, her fullness of happiness, as a *burning lamp.* He wishes to be sunlight and a brightly burning lamp to His earthly people. In Psalm 132:17 the Father says, "I have ordained a lamp for mine anointed." He Himself, the Sun of Righteousness, will be Israel's *righteousness* and her *salvation.* The *new name* is not known to us, unless the names of verse four are meant (cf. 65:15). The nations will behold Israel's glorious righteousness and the kings her brightness and glory. Jehovah-Jesus will consider Israel His crown of glory and the Father will place Israel on Christ's head like a glimmering royal diadem. In that day Christ will have many diadems (Rev. 19:12).

The Marriage Relationship Between God and Israel Restored

> 4. Thou shalt no more be termed Forsaken; neither shall thy land any more be termed Desolate: but thou shalt be called Hephzibah, and thy land Beulah: for the LORD delighteth in thee, and thy land shall be married.
> 5. For as a young man marrieth a virgin, so shall thy sons marry thee: and as the bridegroom rejoiceth over the bride, so shall thy God rejoice over thee.

Verse four presents a sharp contrast between the new glory of Israel and its former wretchedness. It is regrettable that the four Hebrew names, two of which mean destruction and two the glory and restored relationship between God and Israel, have not been left untranslated here. As elsewhere, the two ideas of city and wife run together again. The English translators have, very inconsistently, translated the first two but not the last two names. The original names contain the most beautiful sounds. Zion will no more be called *Azubah,* forsaken, lonely woman (cf. 54:1-4). Canaan will no longer be called what it is called now, *Shammah,* destruction. This name has been given it for almost twenty centuries by the nations. On the contrary, from henceforth Zion will bear the name of *Hephzibah.* This was the name of Hezekiah's wife, and means *My desire is toward her,* or *my very dearest one, my most beloved one.* This name alone speaks volumes concerning Israel's future glory and God's grace. For Christ, who was nailed to the accursed cross at one time speaks here of His desire toward His erstwhile murderers. And Israel's land will be called *Beulah,* Married One. The country which for so many centuries was trodden under foot and robbed bare by the nations will one day bloom as a rose. The Lord also loves this land and when He remarries Israel He will also, in community of property, marry the land. Christianity may sweetly sing, *Sweet Beulah Land!* but how little is the glorious fact understood that the country and the people of

Israel belong together. Verse five explains the marriage further. As a bridegroom rejoices over his bride, so God will rejoice over Israel.

The Watchmen on Israel's Walls

6. I have set watchmen upon thy walls, O Jerusalem, which shall never hold their peace day nor night: ye that make mention of the LORD, keep not silence.
7. And give him no rest, till he establish, and till he make Jerusalem a praise in the earth.

This text is to be compared with 21:6-9. Like all ancient cities, Jerusalem had walls for her protection; on the walls there were towers, and in those towers watchmen to guard the city. The protection of the city depended for the most part on them. This must be kept in mind here. *Watchmen* does not mean ministers, but prophets, priests and kings and in a spiritual sense all those who love and seek the peace of Jerusalem. The latter idea is suggested by the exclamation: *Ye that make mention of the LORD.* Since the Lord Himself does not keep silence for Zion's sake, but as the great and only High Priest in heaven prays for Israel, He also demands that all those who pray — this is what is meant in the phrase — will make God remember Jerusalem by their prayers. In their supplications for Israel they will make Jehovah remember His unfailing promises. This kind of prayer will not admit of any keeping silence on their part. The first part of verse seven says, *Give him no rest,* or *peace.* There is a threefold rich thought: (1) The Lord Himself does not rest with regard to Zion; (2) He does not want His petitioners to keep silence in their prayers for Israel; (3) and He does not want His people to leave Him alone concerning Israel's deliverance. He, and those who turn to Him in prayer, will allow themselves no rest *till he establish* His Word and His Kingdom, and *make Jerusalem a praise in the earth.* Jerusalem will be the shining focal point and uniting point of all nations and the royal residence of the King of Israel who at the same time is the King of all the earth. But, alas, how little do those who do pray, pray for Israel's future restoration!

A Significant Oath of the Lord

> 8. The LORD hath sworn by his right hand, and by the arm of
> his strength, Surely I will no more give thy corn to be meat for
> thine enemies; and the sons of the stranger shall not drink thy
> wine, for the which thou hast laboured:
> 9. But they that have gathered it shall eat it, and praise the
> LORD; and they that have brought it together shall drink it in the
> courts of my holiness.

The Lord has often sworn an oath in connection with
Israel's restoration. He can swear by no one higher than
Himself and therefore He does so (Heb. 6:13); He also swears
His strong *right hand,* which He will reveal and use for the
complete deliverance of His people. He promises with an
oath, which among people is the end of all contradiction
(unfortunately among Christian people not as far as God's
oaths over Israel are concerned!), that He will give Israel a
lasting peace and abundance. When the Lord swears by the
arm of His strength, He promises salvation and peace in a
very striking form. He will no longer give the lush corn that
grows on Israel's married land, which will then be the pride
of the world, as food to Israel's enemies; neither the wine or
grape juice that grew on the mountaintop and was prepared
by Israel. In contrast with what often took place in Israel's
past, those that gather the harvest will also eat it. They will
sing a harvest song of thanksgiving to the honor of Israel's
God. We have to keep in mind what was said in 61:5
concerning the *vinedressers.* From this abundant harvest of
sweet juice, which will not contain any stupefying elements,
a festive banquet will be held in the courts of the Lord's
sanctuary (cf. Ezek. 45:15-25; 46:14, 20). At the same time
the oath says that no devastations of war will strike Israel any
more.

All Obstacles to Israel's Restoration Removed

> 10. Go through, go through the gates; prepare ye the way of
> the people; cast up, cast up the highway; gather out the stones; lift
> up a standard for the people.

11. Behold, the LORD hath proclaimed unto the end of the world, Say ye to the daughter of Zion, Behold, thy salvation cometh; behold his reward is with him, and his work before him.

12. And they shall call them, The holy people, The redeemed of the LORD: and thou shalt be called, Sought out, a city not forsaken.

Verse ten contains a similar command for removing all obstacles to that of 40:3 and 57:14. We must imagine Jerusalem's gates as standing open to receive the people, while the people themselves in stately caravans approach the holy city; the roads are uneven, bumpy, and impassable so that the pilgrims can hardly make any progress. In view of this, the people within the city are called upon to hasten to the aid of the approaching pilgrims, so that nothing may slow down their hurried march toward the city of God. They can help the approaching pilgrims by removing the stones and filling the holes in the roads. This command is again of the greatest practical importance to all who love Israel for the Lord's sake. The mission among the Jews is hardly a century old and may be called a very serious sign of the times in the light of this and similar statements. It is nothing short of a preparation of the way to Israel's complete reacceptance. The lifting up of a *standard* among the nations may be called, on the basis of 11:10, 18:3, and other places, the preaching of Christ among the nations, a mission to the heathen. We have no doubt that here we find in Old Testament form a divine injunction to engage in missions to the heathen with a view to and as a preparation for the restoration of Israel. With a prophetic *perfectum* it is further stated that God will proclaim to Israel from the ends of the world, *Behold, thy salvation* (and Savior) *cometh*. Christ Himself is meant as the Savior of Israel, as is also evident from the following words: *His reward is with him, and his work before Him*. In light of this verse the premillennial mission among the heathen is a sign of the times, for it proclaims everywhere that the Lord Jesus is coming as the Savior of Israel. Verse twelve shows again the high esteem and honor Israel will obtain from the nations. All nations will seek Israel; she is named *Sought out*.

ISAIAH 63

The Vision of the Downfall of the World Powers

1. Who is this that cometh from Edom, with dyed garments from Bozrah? this that is glorious in his apparel, travelling in the greatness of his strength? I that speak in righteousness, mighty to save.

2. Wherefore art thou red in thine apparel, and thy garments like him that treadeth in the winefat.

3. I have trodden the winepress alone; and of the people there was none with me: for I will tread them in mine anger, and trample them in my fury; and their blood shall be sprinkled upon my garments, and I will stain all my raiment.

4. For the day of vengeance is in mine heart, and the year of my redeemed is come.

5. And I looked, and there was none to help; and I wondered that there was none to uphold: therefore mine own arm brought salvation unto me; and my fury, it upheld me.

6. And I will tread down the people in mine anger, and make them drunk in my fury, and I will bring down their strength to the earth.

The result of the Lord's coming was indicated in the last verse of the preceding chapter; here in a dialogue between Christ and the prophet what the result will be for *Edom,* is described which is mentioned here as the representative of all anti-christian, anti-Semitic nations. It is almost inconceivable how anyone could ever get the idea that here we find a reference to Christ's suffering. This is a typical example of Scripture exegesis that goes by the sound of words. Only the color of blood and the treading of the winepress give this idea. But when Christ suffered, He did not press, but was pressed in the winepress of God's anger. At the time of His return to judge the nations He will tread the winepress Himself (cf. Rev. 14:20 and 19:11-21).

On the road from Edom and Bozrah, the capital of Edom, the prophet sees a fearful warrior approaching with forceful and rapid strides. His war raiment is colored red and drips with the blood of his enemies. Full of amazement the prophet asks who it is who is marching onward in his magnificent armor and with such strength. Many would answer that it was Judas the Maccabee, but there is a better answer. The Warrior answers that He is the one who not only *speaks in righteousness,* in the sense of teaching and predicting, but that He is also mighty to do what He has promised, to avenge His people upon their enemies and to deliver His people. The Warrior makes Himself known as Israel's mighty Deliverer.

The prophet asks further why His apparel is so red with blood, as of one who has trodden the winepress; He answers that He has trodden the winepress of God's anger. He has not trodden grapes but the *nations.* He has trodden them in His anger and trampled them in His fury, and their *strength,* their life blood has dirtied and sprinkled His garments. All alone, He has attacked and beaten this great army of all nations. The angels and saints, who will judge the world with Him, have no power except through their Creator and Lord. In verse four He gives His reason for trampling the nations: The *day of vengeance* was in His *heart,* and the *year* of His redeemed had come. A beautiful order and time measure is contained in this brief statement: first the brief day of vengeance — the seven years of the Great Tribulation, and after that the *year* of jubilee for His redeemed. There is but a moment in His wrath, and then eternal life in His favor. With this judgment, Christ carries out His program as indicated in 61:1-3. The *day of vengeance* is not the final goal of His Coming again, but the year of His redeemed. In spite of this fact however, all Roman Catholic and Protestant churches testify that the actual goal, if not the only one, of Christ's return lies in the judgment. Nothing pleases the heart of the believer more than the thought that the Lord Jesus is coming again as Savior, to give complete salvation from all the results of sins. On Golgotha He delivered from the guilt and punishment of sin; from the power of sin He delivers us every day; from all the results of sin He will deliver us, and Israel, at His Second Coming. In highly poetic language, He declares in verses five and six that He alone is the great Judge of the nations.

A Song of Praise for God's Rich Mercy

> 7. I will mention the lovingkindnesses of the LORD, and the praises of the LORD, according to all that the LORD hath bestowed on us, and the great goodness toward the house of Israel, which he hath bestowed on them according to his mercies, and according to the multitude of his lovingkindnesses.
> 8. For he said, Surely they are my people, children that will not lie: so he was their Savior.
> 9. In all their affliction he was afflicted, and the angel of his presence saved them: in his love and in his pity he redeemed them; and he bare them, and carried them all the days of old.

Clarity would be served if a new chapter were begun here and continued with the next, for from here to the end of the next chapter we find one long and touching confession and prayer by the remnant of the end time. Gaebelein says of it, "This is one of the greatest prayers in the Bible," and with him, and others, we are convinced that the prophet himself first prayed this prayer by the Spirit of Christ. This stirring prayer can be appropriately compared with the penitent prayer and confession of Daniel nine. As there, this prayer can be divided into thanksgiving, confession and supplication. In these three verses, the prophet, as the mouthpiece of the Lord's servants (v. 17) breaks into a song of praise for the great blessings of God bestowed upon the Jewish nation in the past. He offers the *manifold praises* of Jehovah-Jesus in the most powerful words. No human words strong enough to express the multitude of God's mercies toward Israel.

The Lord said of Israel, *Surely they are my people, children that will not lie.* This statement is deeper than the abysses and higher than the heavens. We only mention: (1) The Jews *are* God's people and do not have to become so after a long period of striving. (2) The Lord Himself declares that He recognizes them as such. (3) Over against Israel's enemies and the devil and the powers of hell, the Lord acknowledges that Israel is His people. And He still says *surely* even today to them who self-satisfiedly claim that Israel has had her time and that the Church has come in Israel's place. *Are* does not mean *were.* (4) He calls the Jews *children;* the Jewish people are a nation of covenant children and *children* of the Kingdom. This is why the remnant calls out twice in verse sixteen: *Thou art our Father!* (5) The most remarkable thing is that He calls them children *that will not lie.* The Hebrew word for *lie* contains even more than our word. It was applied to a fountain, pit or brook that contained no water any more and so disappointed the thirsty person, and to a fruit tree that no longer yielded any fruit (Hab. 3:17). With this one significant word, the Lord meant to say that His people will not deceive and disappoint Him; they will not degenerate nor be unfruitful or deny Him. In amazement the question has been asked how God can say this of the deceitful and apostate Jewish nation. To answer this question it can be said that the Lord is not considering the actual *condition* of His people but their state according to His will and decree. Whatever falls away in Israel, the nation as a nation does not fall away or degenerate, and although presently she may be like a dormant tree in winter, the tree will bud again; they may be like unto dead men's bones but will become alive again, filled with the Spirit. Calvin did not understand a word of this verse, for he derives from it the main idea and conclusion that God was *grievously disappointed.* Thus, as expressed in this glorious word *surely,* Jehovah has become a *Savior* unto them. Israel did succumb to the power of Satan and sin, but the unchangeable and faithful Jehovah became a *Savior* unto them, a Redeemer, a Helper, not only from Egypt and Babylon, but also from the hostile forces of the future.

Verse nine also breathes tender love. *In all their affliction he was afflicted.* How unfathomable this statement is! According to this word, every pogrom in Russia, Hungary, and Poland grieves His sympathetic heart. The *angel of his presence* is the Messiah, in whom God's favorable countenance beamed forth to the Jews. The Son is the image of the invisible God (II Cor. 4:4, Phil. 2:6, Col. 1:15, Heb. 1:3). Whoever sees Him sees the Father. Calvin sees in this angel merely a serving angel. But of this Angel it is said that

He by His *love* and *pity* saved Israel; this can hardly be said of a created angel. It is the Christ who is meant here.

Humble Confession

> 10. But they rebelled, and vexed his holy Spirit: therefore he was turned to be their enemy, and he fought against them.
>
> 11. Then he remembered the days of old, Moses, and his people, saying, Where is he that brought them up out of the sea with the shepherd of his flock? where is he that put his holy Spirit within him?
>
> 12. That led them by the right hand of Moses with his glorious arm, dividing the water before them, to make himself an everlasting name?
>
> 13. That led them through the deep, as an horse in the wilderness, that they should not stumble?
>
> 14. As a beast goeth down into the valley, the Spirit of the LORD caused him to rest: so didst thou lead thy people, to make thyself a glorious name.

Israel's unfaithfulness sadly contrasts with this unfathomable and never failing love of God. Israel has been rebellious for centuries — to this very day. They *vexed his holy Spirit*. Like the Savior's anguish, this, too, is a word of incomprehensible depth. We protest, however, against all attempts to ignore and minimize this word, as so many expositors have done. It is irrefutable that these words represent a fearful reality, but this rock is too high and unassailable to our mind. It is a statement that cannot be comprehended and defined, but must be believed, admired and contemplated.

Therefore, because they vexed His Spirit, *he was turned to be their enemy.* It is terrible when Christ, the greatest Friend of sinners, *turns* into their *enemy* as has happened to Israel. He *Himself* fought against them. The Sennacheribs, Esar-haddons, Shalmanesers, Nebuchadnezzars and Tituses were but rods in His hand and of His wrath, the instruments of His anger. In His anger He has hid His face from Israel for many centuries already, calling them *Lo-Ammi* — not-My-people. *Where is he?* Israel has cried for many hundreds of years — He who once led Israel through the Red Sea, who once put His *holy Spirit* in the midst of Israel. In these verses we find a precious proof of the holy Trinity: the Savior, the Holy Spirit and the Angel of *his* (the Father's) presence. Jehovah's faithful guidance of Israel is beautifully described: *as an horse in the wilderness* — the level steppe. A horse has no sure footing on mountains and rocks, but on level plains it can safely run forward without stumbling. As a beast *goeth down into the valley* to drink and to lie down underneath the trees near a stream, so God gave rest to Israel after her forty-year wanderings. The purpose of this faithful and loving guidance of God is indicated in verses twelve and fourteen; He would make Himself an *everlasting* and *glorious* name, hence God's Self-glorification is in view. One day this will be fulfilled (Phil. 2:10, 11).

A Heartrending Supplication

15. Look down from heaven, and behold from the habitation of thy holiness and of thy glory: where is thy zeal and thy strength, the sounding of thy bowels and of thy mercies toward me? are they restrained?

16. Doubtless thou art our father, though Abraham be ignorant of us, and Israel acknowledge us not: thou, O LORD, art our father, our redeemer; thy name is from everlasting.

17. O LORD, why hast thou made us to err from thy ways, and hardened our heart from thy fear? Return for thy servants' sake, the tribes of thine inheritance.

18. The people of thy holiness have possessed it but a little while: our adversaries have trodden down thy sanctuary.

19. We are thine: thou never barest rule over them; they were not called by thy name.

In order to understand this suppliant prayer correctly, we must realize that it will be prayed in the end time, the time of the Great Tribulation by the faithful remnant, shortly before the manifestation of the Lord Jesus with His saints for the deliverance of Israel (Zech. 14:1-5). Many penitential Psalms depict this remnant at prayer. Nehemiah's prayer is an example of the heartrending lamentation to God in that day (Neh. 1:4-11; cf. 9:4-38). This remnant, oppressed by the powers of hell, will then be totally helpless and flee to God making an appeal to His ancient and most inward mercy, called the *sounding of thy bowels.* By saying, *thou art our father,* they appeal to the close relationship between God and Israel, while they no longer have any carnal claim to Abraham or Jacob. In verse seventeen they confess that according to the righteous justice of God they are subject to the judgment of blindness and hardening of the heart. There are those who try to argue this terrible fact away or to soften it, but this is a vain effort (cf. 6:9-10; 13:4; Mark 4:12; Luke 8:10; John 12:40; Acts 28:26; Rom. 11:8). Israel confesses this in the form of a question and in faith holds fast to Israel as God's *holy nation,* which has possessed her land and sanctuary *but a little while,* and has become *Lo-Ammi.* This prayer will not remain unanswered (see 65:1).

ISAIAH 64

A Prayer for the Coming of the Messiah

1. Oh that thou wouldest rend the heavens, that thou wouldest come down, that the mountains might flow down at thy presence.

2. As when the melting fire burneth, the fire causeth the waters to boil, to make thy name known to thine adversaries, that the nations may tremble at thy presence!

3. When thou didst terrible things which we looked not for, thou camest down, the mountains flowed down at thy presence.

The prayer increases in passionate fervor and presses closer in upon God. Whereas earlier it was said, *Look down from heaven, and behold,* the suppliants now are no longer content with that and desire that the Lord Himself come down to deliver His people. In times of self-satisfaction and indolent security one can be satisfied with the rich blessings of the Lord, but in days of persecution and anxiety the loving heart is not satisfied and voices one's burning desire in ardent supplication that the Lord Himself may come down unto salvation. This prayer is called the Advent Prayer of the Old Church, and it is generally imagined that the first Christmas was the fulfillment of it. It is true that at that time the heavens were rent and the Lord came down, but the *mountains* did not flow down at His presence nor did He cause the nations to tremble before His countenance. The majority of the Jewish people did not acknowledge Him as the Messiah. On the contrary, His coming caused many to be without hope for many centuries. This is not so much a prayer of ancient God-fearing Israel, even though the pious Israelites in those days undoubtedly often poured out their hearts in this manner; it is rather the prayer of the faithful remnant of the Jews in the end time, who in their bitter grief longingly look forward to the descent of the Messiah, who exactly at that moment, when the need is greatest, will indeed come to them (Zech. 14:1-5). They do not expect the Messiah the way we do now. We expect Him to take us up in the air; Israel expects Him to descend to them, which He will do. We expect His coming purely in grace as the Savior; Israel expects Him as the terrible Law-Giver and Judge who once appeared like lightning on Sinai causing the earth to tremble and Israel to fear. It is clear that these verses allude to God's coming down on Horeb.

The Blessing of Waiting for the Lord

> 4. For since the beginning of the world men have not heard, nor perceived by the ear, neither hath the eye seen, O God, beside thee, what he hath prepared for him that waiteth for him.
>
> 5a. Thou meetest him that rejoiceth and worketh righteousness, those that remember thee in thy ways:

In I Corinthians 2:9 the Apostle does not merely mean to quote verse four but derives from it a totally different thought. The Holy Spirit, as the great Author, can Himself know how He wishes to quote and apply His own words. Paul is not thinking of *waiting* for the Messiah but of *loving* Him, as the mystical body of Christ does. This is why he says, "But God hath revealed them unto us by his Spirit." Hence the Holy Spirit purposely avoids the word *wait* there, for the mystery of the Church has already been revealed by the Holy Spirit. There is, however, a special blessing connected with *waiting for the Lord*. Men, even church-going men, would rather *work* than *wait*. They also love legalism more than the holiness of waiting. Church leaders of today think waiting for the Lord is foolish dreaming. They consider it all right for old God-fearing people but not for modern man. They may also call it pessimism; Scripture says, *Rejoice in hope!* God *meets him who rejoices,* who *works righteousness* while he waits. According to God, waiting and working go hand in hand. And, according to these words, prayer and walking in God's ways go hand in hand with waiting for Christ. *Remember thee* suggests a prayerful life, as in 62:6. Nothing results in more blessing for our spiritual life than this kind of waiting. "Wait for the Lord, ye that fear Him!"

A Holy Sense of Solidarity

5b. . . . behold, thou art wroth; for we have sinned: in those is continuance, and we shall be saved.

6. But we are all as an unclean thing, and all our righteousnesses are as filthy rags; and we all do fade as a leaf; and our iniquities, like the wind, have taken us away.

7. And there is none that calleth upon thy name, that stirreth up himself to take hold of thee: for thou hast hid thy face from us, and hast consumed us, because of our iniquities.

8. But now, O LORD, thou art our father; we are the clay, and thou our potter; and we all are the work of thy hand.

9. Be not wroth very sore, O LORD, neither remember iniquity for ever: behold, see, we beseech thee, we are all thy people.

10. Thy holy cities are a wilderness, Zion is a wilderness, Jerusalem a desolation.

11. Our holy and our beautiful house, where our fathers praised thee, is burned up with fire: and all our pleasant things are laid waste.

12. Wilt thou refrain thyself for these things, O LORD? wilt thou hold thy peace, and afflict us very sore?

In those is continuance is an expression that refers back to the *ways* of God. The meaning of the second part of verse five is this: Israel would have been saved forever if the people had walked in obedience to God's ways. Thereupon verse six gives the assurance that Israel had not piously walked in the old ways. On the contrary, they were all as an *unclean thing,* as someone who according to God's law might not appear before Him. Even the most virtuous works, let alone the evil ones, were as the polluted garment of an unclean person. In quickly changing metaphors the supplicant compares himself and his people to a withered leaf that is blown away by the wind. Misdeeds always have a withering and killing effect; the image is very apt in portraying Israel's barrenness and wanderings. Because of her own misdeeds Israel must wander about as a dry leaf among the nations. Sin drags Israel and many others toward destruction.

Verse seven mentions *prayerlessness.* Scriptural prayer is seizing God and wrestling with Him (27:5; 56:2; Gen. 32:27,28; Hos. 12:4). Israel is too indolent to wrestle with God, which is an old malady that is not unknown among us either, but claims many victims. James says, "You have not because you do not pray," and this Israel has experienced until this very day. Of course, Israel does pray to the Father, but no one comes to the Father but by the Son. "He who does not honour the Father, honours not the Son either." During the *times of the Gentiles* God hides His face from Israel and He causes Israel to melt because of her iniquities.

Notwithstanding its sin and guilt, the remnant, of which the prophet is the unfailing mouthpiece, still holds fast to the solid covenant relationship between God and Israel. Will not God as the Father have mercy upon His children and take their weakness into account? Verse eight expresses a twofold relationship: the intimate relationship between a father and his children, and the exalted relationship to the absolute sovereignty of God. He had the right and the power to knead and form Israel as moist clay. The metaphor of a potter often serves to sovereignty in Scripture.

The thought of solidarity or togetherness in common guilt is remarkable here. Although the prophet Isaiah was a man of tender godliness and there will always be some seven thousand God-fearing people left even in the darkest of times, the prophet nevertheless includes himself and his fellow believers in the corrupt mass, saying, *We all are as an unclean thing, we all fade as a leaf.* On the other hand, he continues to hold on to the entire nation, saying, *We are all thy people.* In the prayers of Jeremiah, Ezra, Nehemiah and Daniel we find the same solidarity. Verse eleven is used by the critics as an argument for the supposition that an unknown author during or after the exile wrote the second part of Isaiah. This shows how little these men have penetrated the spirit of this prophecy. They forever base their explanation on the past and seem to be unable to think of the present or future state of Israel. On God's *holding* His *peace* (cf. 42:14; 57:11; 63:15-19). God acts as though He were deaf to Jacob's lamentations during the *times of the Gentiles.* As soon as that period has passed, this will change immediately.

ISAIAH 65

God's Willingness to Help

> 1. I am sought of them that asked not for me; I am found of them that sought me not: I said, Behold me, behold me, unto a nation that was not called by my name.
> 2. I have spread out my hands all the day unto a rebellious people, which walketh in a way that was not good, after their own thoughts;

The two chapters still remaining contain the divine answer to the preceding prayer. Because of a mistaken interpretation of the New Testament quotations from this chapter in general and by a wrong appeal to Romans 10:20, 21 in particular, these two verses have been cited to prove the theory of Israel's complete rejection and the substitution of the Church for Israel. But neither here nor there, nor in the entire Scripture, is there anything to warrant this; on the contrary, this idea is contradicted everywhere.

The beautiful argument God uses here is usually overlooked. In response to the heartrending complaint about God's long-lasting silence, Israel is told that she must not think that He is not ready to reveal and give Himself to the sinner. Even to the uncircumcised, the unclean dogs of the heathen, He has given Himself, saying, *Behold, here am I.* The repetition points out that He has completely given Himself. Would He then not give Himself to Israel? If He even gives Himself to heathen who do not ask for Him, how much more will He give Himself to His covenant people when they seek Him wholeheartedly. His willingness to accept Israel was so great that all day long He *spread* out His hands to this rebellious people, just like a loving father does to receive his child with open arms. *Spreading out* of the hands was a sign of a loving, urgent invitation (Prov. 1:24). The object of these two verses is to show God's willingness to re-accept Israel. The argument moves from the lesser to the greater. If He does not reject but accept the heathen who are estranged from Him, and if He continues kindly to invite rebellious Israel, how much more willing must He then be to accept again in mercy His people who turn to Him in repentance.

The Apostate Will Perish

3. A people that provoketh me to anger continually to my face; that sacrificeth in gardens, and burneth incense upon altars of brick;

4. Which remain among the graves, and lodge in the monuments, which eat swine's flesh, and broth of abominable things is in their vessels;

5. Which say, Stand by thyself, come not near to me; for I am holier than thou. These are a smoke in my nose, a fire that burneth all the day.

6. Behold, it is written before me: I will not keep silence, but will recompense, even recompense into their bosom,

7. Your iniquities, and the iniquities of your fathers together, saith the LORD, which have burned incense upon the mountains, and blasphemed me upon the hills: therefore will I measure their former work into their bosom.

Expositors have never been able to identify the sins mentioned here in Israel's past; it is no wonder, for the prophetic vision reaches again to the tumultuous end time, when God will *hasten* the promised threats and deliverances (60:22). The greatest part of the last book of the Bible deals with this perilous period; it must not surprise us that the prophet returns to this subject again and again. The culmination point of Israel's apostasy is described here. The partly restored but still unconverted Israelite nation continually provokes God to His face by the most abominable idolatry in gardens (1:29) and on altars of tile or baked brick which God had commanded to be made of unhewn stones (Exod. 20:24, 25). They were sitting among the graves to call up the *dead;* they thought that burial grounds were eminent places to learn the future from the spirits of the departed. They lodged with those *who are kept* (Dutch version). We must remember that the dead were buried in caves and grottos where the charmers spent the night.

To eat swine's flesh was forbidden by the law (Lev. 11:7). During the time of the Maccabees the Jews would rather have died than do it. They also had unholy, abominable drink in their vessels. While doing all these things, they even boasted of their imagined holiness. Their talk bore the stamp of true Phariseeism. They considered themselves deeply initiated and others profane. The anger of God burns against this evil lot. The Lord will not passively view these abominations but mete out righteous retribution. There is nothing He lets go unrewarded or unpunished.

The God-fearing Remnant and the Apostate

8. Thus saith the LORD, As the new wine is found in the cluster, and one saith, Destroy it not; for a blessing is in it: so will I do for my servants' sakes, that I may not destroy them all.

9. And I will bring forth a seed out of Jacob, and out of Judah an inheritor of my mountains: and mine elect shall inherit it, and my servants shall dwell there.

10. And Sharon shall be a fold of flocks, and the valley of Achor a place for the herds to lie down in, for my people that have sought me.

11. But ye are they that forsake the LORD, that forget my holy mountain, that prepare a table for that troop, and that furnish the drink offering unto that number.

12. Therefore will I number you to the sword, and ye shall all bow down to the slaughter: because when I called, ye did not answer; when I spake, ye did not hear; but did evil before mine eyes, and did choose that wherein I delighted not.

The entire prophecy of Isaiah is one continuous *weal* for the God-fearing and one continuous *woe* for the wicked. It will be well with the God-fearing remnant that turns to Him in repentance. Isaiah depicts the character of the remnant in the simple but significant image of a *cluster of grapes.* The God-provoking sins and the burning and smoking wrath of God might easily lead one to think that no one in Israel would be saved. With this metaphor Isaiah illustrates that this is not the case at all. We see a vinedresser standing before a vine that is very dry and deserves to be uprooted. He examines it more closely and then his eye suddenly discovers a cluster of good grapes in which there is juice. Do not hew the trunk down, he cries to his servant, for it still contains a *blessing,* some fruit. In the same manner, for the same reason and with the same purpose in mind, the Lord will *not destroy them all* for the sake of His servants. If the Church had clearly understood this simple example, then, it would not have dared to teach Israel's total rejection. Even as He would have saved Sodom for the sake of five righteous people, so He will spare Israel, His vine, for the sake of His *servants,* the cluster of good grapes (cf. Zech. 13:8). He will cause Jacob to bring forth a new *seed,* sanctified to God, and Judah will bring forth a generation of inheritors to occupy His mountains, His land; His elect servants will dwell there in safety and peace. According to Isaiah's presentation, we must view the *servants* of the Lord in close connection with the *Servant of the Lord,* for after this *Servant* as the crucified *Servant* is exalted in 53:12, we no longer hear about Him, but we do hear about His *servants. Sharon* was a fertile strip of ground bordering the Mediterannean Sea and famous for its lush pastures. At the restoration and renewal of all things, when the world's population will mainly be engaged in agriculture, this fertile pasture land of Sharon will revive again. The *valley of Achor* was near Jericho and has obtained a sad name on account of the history of Achan. Since Israel stoned Achan there, and he was covered with stones, it seems that this valley was stony and barren and a place of abhorrence, which Israel wanted to avoid. But at the restoration of all things, as a fruit of Israel's restoration, God will make Achor a *door of hope.* The place of disappointment, judgment, banishment, trouble and unfruitfulness will again become a place of rich blessings, of which the words *a place for the herds to lie down in* serves as image and example. This expression may be compared with the beautiful description of Hosea 2:13-22. For whom will these rich benefits be? For those who have *sought* Him, His servants, the remnant, which in the preceding two chapters sought Him earnestly in prayer.

The forsakers of God, the apostates, who have forgotten the land of the fathers and felt at home in the dispersion will bow down to the slaughter. All expositors agree that the translation of verse eleven is rather unfortunate. It would have been better to leave the words *gad* and *meni,* now translated into *troop* and *number,* in the Hebrew, since a pair of idols is meant. The thought of expositors is nearly unanimous that *Gad* refers to a goddess of fortune like the *Fortuna* of the Romans, from which our word fortune has been derived, and that *Meni* stands for fate. It is noteworthy that the Jews of today on the one hand honor the fortune of commerce, of sports, and of speculation, and on the other hand are adherents of pantheism and evolutionism, in which the blind fate of natural laws dominates; metaphorically stated, they offer food and drink to *Gad* and *Meni.* These apostate people perish in the day of Jacob's tribulation in the end time.

Contrast Between the Salvation of the Remnant and the Adversity of the Apostate

13. Therefore thus saith the Lord GOD, Behold, my servants shall eat, but ye shall be hungry: behold, my servants shall drink, but ye shall be thirsty: behold, my servants shall rejoice, but ye shall be ashamed:
14. Behold, my servants shall sing for joy of heart, but ye shall cry for sorrow of heart, and shall howl for vexation of spirit.
15. And ye shall leave your name for a curse unto my chosen: for the Lord GOD shall slay thee, and call his servants by another name:
16. That he who blesseth himself in the earth shall bless himself in the God of truth; and he that sweareth in the earth shall swear by the God of truth; because the former troubles are forgotten, and because they are hid from mine eyes.

Now in five contrasts the prophet presents the calamity that befalls the apostate and the happiness God's faithful servants will experience. The Lord's servants will *eat* and *drink,* which here stands for all temporal happiness and enjoyment, while the apostate will hunger and thirst; the Lord's servants are made to *rejoice,* but the apostate will be *ashamed;* God's servants will *sing for joy* from the bottom of their hearts, but the apostate will *cry for sorrow of heart* and *howl for vexation of spirit;* the faithful servants will be called by *another name,* while the apostate rebels will be slain and leave their name for a curse to the elect of God. Their name will be left as a symbol of God's judgments, while the chosen remnant will *forget* their *former afflictions.* How precious this is! Restored Israel will not be vexed with remorse, indeed not even with painful memories of her murder of the Messiah. Israel's deliverance will be complete. God removes not only sin but even its red scars. The result of Israel's reacceptance is indicated in verse sixteen by the word *that.* Whoever blesses himself on earth, i.e., calls himself blessed, and whoever swears, will do so from hence forward in the name of Israel's true and faithful God. Israel will forget not only her former afflictions, but even her sin and guilt will be covered before God's all-seeing eye by the precious blood of covering. The precious blood of the Lamb covers completely even from God's omniscient penetrating eye.

The Renewed Creation

17. For, behold, I create new heavens and a new earth: and the former shall not be remembered, nor come into mind.

18. But be ye glad and rejoice for ever in that which I create: for, behold, I create Jerusalem a rejoicing, and her people a joy.

19. And I will rejoice in Jerusalem, and joy in my people: and the voice of weeping shall be no more heard in her, nor the voice of crying.

20. There shall be no more thence an infant of days, nor an old man that hath not filled his days: for the child shall die an hundred years old; but the sinner being an hundred years old shall be accursed.

21. And they shall build houses, and inhabit them; and they shall plant vineyards, and eat the fruit of them.

22. They shall not build, and another inhabit; they shall not plant, and another eat: for as the days of a tree are the days of my people, and mine elect shall long enjoy the work of their hands.

23. They shall not labour in vain, nor bring forth for trouble; for they are the seed of the blessed of the LORD, and their offspring with them.

24. And it shall come to pass, that before they call, I will answer; and while they are yet speaking, I will hear.

25. The wolf and the lamb shall feed together, and the lion shall eat straw like the bullock: and dust shall be the serpent's meat. They shall not hurt nor destroy in all my holy mountain, saith the Lord.

There will be *new heavens* and a *new earth,* which are conformable to the original creation and to the earthly and heavenly people of the Lord. Correspondingly, the Kingdom of Peace will have a double aspect. Since this is little understood, we shall briefly say a few words about it.

People often scorn this teaching and its adherents, but it is a very comforting doctrine. It has pleased God to let all the prophets speak about it, even though it is true that its duration is not revealed until near the end of the book of Revelation. When we speak of the double aspect, we mean its earthly and its heavenly aspect. The dimensions of this Kingdom encompass both heaven and earth (Ps. 8; Dan. 7:13-14; Eph. 1:10).

1. There will be a kingdom of the *Son* and a Kingdom of the Father (Matt. 13:41, 43; cf. Eph. 5:5). The realm of the former is the *earth;* the sphere of the latter is *heaven.*

2. There will be a glorified earthly people and a glorified heavenly people. Israel is the earthly people, who will then be converted (Deut. 30:1-9; Rom. 11; Heb. 8:8-13; Isa. 2, 11; 59:20, restored and unified, Jer. 3:18; 50:4-5; Ezek. 37; Hos. 2:21-23; Zech. 8:19-21; 10:6). The heavenly people are the glorified Church, which will reign with Christ (II Tim. 2:12; Rev. 20:6).

3. There will be two Jerusalems, an earthly one in Palestine and a heavenly one in the celestial regions; though descended from the third heaven, it is nevertheless not on earth. It will be above the earth, so that its light illuminates the earth. Regarding this glorified earthly Jerusalem, see 2:3; 60; Psalm 48:2; Jer. 3:17; Micah 4:1-4; Zechariah 8. This Jerusalem will have a new name: *Jehovah Shammah,* The Lord is there, and it will be the center of the law for the entire world (2:1-3; 6; 7; Mic. 4:1-2; Zech. 8). The former city of prophet killers will then have inhabitants who will all be holy (1:26, 27; 4:3; Obad. 17; Zech. 13:9; 14:20, 21). The nations of the earth go up to it annually to worship Jehovah (56:7, 60:11-14, Zech. 14:16). The heavenly Jerusalem is described in Revelation 21.

4. There will be two seats of government and two persons who reign. Strictly speaking Christ rules everything and everyone from the celestial regions (Ps. 8; Eph. 1:10; Dan.

7:13-14; Rev. 21-22:1-5). In Jerusalem on earth a viceregent of Christ will reign, however; that may very well be the resurrected David (Ezek. 37:24; 45; 46:1-2; Hos. 3:4-5; Zech. 6:13). The Lord's law and word will go forth by this viceregent's agency from Jerusalem (2:1-4, Micah 4:1-4). We must not think, however, that Christ will never show His glory; He will constantly manifest it to Jerusalem and all the nations.

After these general remarks concerning the double aspect of the thousand-year Kingdom of Peace, we shall briefly touch on the main aspects of this Kingdom: (1) It will be a new creation or recreation; so that we may conclude that there will be an entirely new order of existence for all things; as a consequence we may not place the fulfillment of these words in the present dispensation. It will be so brilliantly new and excellent that *the former things will not enter the heart or mind.* Now men's hearts are full of politics and criticism, war and peace conference, revolution and rebellion, alcoholism and prohibition, service of Bacchus and Venus, atheism and evolution, religion and churchism, black, white and yellow slavery, adultery and theft, train and mine accidents — all these things will not be remembered any more. It will almost be unbelievable that these things existed in former ages. (2) The citizens of this Kingdom will be *glad* and rejoice forever. The voice of weeping and crying will no longer be heard. This is especially true of Israel, the nation that has such a long and extremely sad history. (3) *Jerusalem* will be the shining center, the capital and royal city of this glorious Kingdom of Peace. We have seen that all nations will *run* to it (55:5, 60:3). The seat of the central government of the world will be there. The city represents the zenith of beauty, the shining pinnacle of the new culture of the nations; the high point of the nations' longing and striving; the focus of bliss and peace, unity and rest. It will be the chief end and culmination point of God's ways with men on earth. (4) The Lord Jesus will rejoice in Jerusalem's glory. At His first coming this Precious One wept over Jerusalem's stubborn unbelief and apostasy, but in that day His joy over it will be complete. It would, moreover, be unreasonable to think that His tears over Jerusalem were the last thing we heard of it. But this is not so; rather His rejoicing in it will be the last thing. (5) *Death* will no longer be, as it now is, the rule but the great exception. Little children and converted people no longer will die, but only the unconverted. Whoever dies at the age of one hundred years will be considered to have died as a lad or young man, and it will be seen not only as an early death but also as an exceptional case and as proof that as an unconverted person he was struck with a curse. The believers will reach the age of a tree, the entire one thousand years as before the Flood. After that they will undoubtedly be changed in a moment and be showered with the full glory of God. (6) The inhabitants will *work* — plant, build, harvest — but no longer toil, let alone labor in vain, as had once been threatened and had happened in the past (Lev. 26:16-20; Deut. 28:30, 33, 51). There is nothing more disappointing and grievous to an agricultural population than to see an enemy eat its harvest while the sowers themselves starve. God will not need to send an enemy into the land to punish Israel, for the *seed of evildoers* (1:4) have by the power of grace become *the seed of the blessed of the Lord,* children who in practical life will not *lie* any more (63:8). (7) There will be an immediate answering of prayer in contrast with Israel's ages-long groaning and God's silence. (8) All will be peace in the animal kingdom. Not only the nature but also the bodily form of wild animals will be changed considerably. Expositors vie with each other in saying that this must not be taken literally; but why not? The serpent's eating of dust is mentioned as a single example that the curse of the fall has not been completely removed (Gen. 3:14).

ISAIAH 66

1. Thus saith the LORD, The heaven is my throne, and the earth is my footstool: where is the house that ye build unto me? and where is the place of my rest?

2. For all those things hath mine hand made, and all those things have been, saith the LORD: but to this man will I look, even to him that is poor and of a contrite spirit, and trembleth at my word.

3. He that killeth an ox is as if he slew a man; he that sacrificeth a lamb, as if he cut off a dog's neck; he that offereth an oblation, as if he offered swine's blood; he that burneth incense, as if he blessed an idol. Yea, they have chosen their own ways, and their soul delighteth in their abominations.

4. I also will choose their delusions, and will bring their fears upon them; because when I called, none did answer; when I spake, they did not hear: but they did evil before mine eyes, and chose that in which I delighted not.

5. Hear the word of the LORD, ye that tremble at his word; Your brethren that hated you, that cast you out for my name's sake, said, Let the LORD be glorified: but he shall appear to your joy, and they shall be ashamed.

6. A voice of noise from the city, a voice from the temple, a voice of the LORD that rendereth recompense to his enemies.

The Lord's answer to the praying remnant continues. The Lord had said that He would rejoice in His city and His people during the Kingdom of Peace. This might easily lead one to conclude that He was like a shortsighted and limited man; to guard against this misconception He says that He will establish His throne in the heavens and that the earth will be to Him, i.e., Jehovah-Jesus, as a footstool. The grand presentation is derived from the sitting of an earthly monarch on his high throne with a footstool under his feet. The whole earth is compared with such a footstool. But just as a king by his presence connects his throne and his footstool, so the Lord Jesus in that day will connect heaven and earth. And since He is so high and exalted, there is no house big enough to contain Him.

Nevertheless, the Jews after their initial restoration will have the illusion that they can build a house for Jehovah in which He wishes to live as in the days of old, and as in former days that they will also bring sacrifices to Him. This interpretation contains some difficulties, but by no means as many as other interpretations. This is not a description of the time before, during, or after the exile, nor of the new dispensation. Each of these views is fraught with a violation of the words, while the suggestion above sheds new light on almost every word. The famous expositor Van der Palm says:

> As far as we are concerned we are unable to explain the first part, contained in the first six verses, in any other way than of the state of the Jews during the time of their rejection in the period of the New Testament, as they, being without temple, and without an altar ministry (vv. 1-3) experience the reward of their actions and enmity against God.

Yet it seems to us that the least forced interpretation of verse three is that the Jews in unbelief have built a temple and have sacrificed in it. Thereupon God declares first of all that by His omnipotence He has brought forth heaven and earth and hence cannot be restricted to a house. Secondly He declares to the Christ-rejecting Jews that He looks with pleasure only on those who are *poor* and of a *contrite* spirit and who *tremble* at His *Word;* this is exactly what the apostate do not do. As a result their offers are an abomination. He who kills an ox is just as abominable as he who kills a man. Whoever sacrifices a lamb while rejecting the Lamb of God is just as abominable to Him as offering Him the most unclean animal, a dog for example as some heathen nations offer their gods. Whoever, as a rejecter of Christ, offers Him an oblation is considered by Him as one who offers *swine's blood.* Together with a dog, a swine was one of the most unclean animals. He views him as an idolator who burns incense to Him in this state of unbelief. Some are of the incorrect opinion that hypocrisy in religion is condemned here. So they read the text as, "He who kills an ox slays *at the same time* a man," etc. Proverbs 1:24-27 sheds inerrant light on verse four. *I also will choose their delusions* means that God will take pleasure in their grief as a result of their disobedience to the Messiah. "He who is disobedient to the Son shall not see life, but the wrath of God remains on him." These unbelieving Jews also hate their brothers according to the flesh, i.e., those Jews who do expect the Messiah — the praying remnant — and they cast them out because they hold fast to the Messianic promise. They derisively cry, *Let the Lord be glorified!* They speak mockingly of the return of Christ as if to say that He then should manifest Himself gloriously. Soon the Lord will appear to the joy of those outcasts who wait for Him, and to the shame and destruction of these wicked people (v. 5). The sudden coming of the Lord is described in verse six. The citizens of Jerusalem cry out in terror; the apostate servants of the temple who trample the blood of Christ emit screams of anguish; and the thundering voice of Jehovah-Jesus resounds above the din. That the unbelieving Jews will rebuild a temple is evident from Daniel 8:11-13; 9:27; Matthew 24:15; II Thessalonians 2:3-4 and Revelation 11:1,2.

Israel's Sudden and Complete Restoration

7. Before she travailed, she brought forth; before her pain came, she was delivered of a man child.

8. Who hath heard such a thing? who hath seen such things? Shall the earth be made to bring forth in one day? or shall a nation be born at once? for as soon as Zion travailed, she brought forth her children.

9. Shall I bring to the birth, and not cause to bring forth? saith the LORD: shall I cause to bring forth, and shut the womb? saith thy God.

10. Rejoice ye with Jerusalem, and be glad with her, all ye that love her: rejoice for joy with her, all ye that love her: rejoice for joy with her, all ye that mourn for her.

11. That ye may suck, and be satisfied with the breasts of her consolations; that ye may milk out, and be delighted with the abundance of her glory.

12. For thus saith the LORD, Behold, I will extend peace to her like a river, and the glory of the Gentiles like a flowing stream: then shall ye suck, ye shall be borne upon her sides, and be dandled upon her knees.

13. As one whom his mother comforteth, so will I comfort

you; and ye shall be comforted in Jerusalem.

14. And when ye see this, your heart shall rejoice, and your bones shall flourish like an herb: and the hand of the LORD shall be known toward his servants, and his indignation toward his enemies.

These verses describe the re-acceptance of Israel, which will be the symbol of life from death unto the whole world (Rom. 11:15) and that as the result of Christ's return. The words are entirely simple, if we correctly understand the underlying metaphor. Zion has been re-accepted as the wife of Jehovah (cf. 54:1-4; Hos. 3). This re-accepted wife is suddenly delivered *of a man child* even before the pains of travail come upon her. This little child, however — and this is something unheard of — is nothing less than the entire country and nation of Israel reborn by the coming of the Savior. It is true, Zion had had labor pains in the Great Tribulation, but this miracle child was suddenly born on Mt. Olivet by the coming of the Lord and His Church. In verse nine the Lord Himself explains this great wonder when He points out that He makes fruitful and *opens the womb.* Would He, as the Husband of Zion, the Source of life, not Himself generate and thereby deny Himself the high honor of a numerous offspring? Thus, Israel's restoration is explained as a supernatural event, a result of the marriage covenant between God and Israel and of His honor and creative power. In verse ten all those who *love* Zion, including the angels and the glorified Church, are enjoined to rejoice in her glory. The image of a woman, now a nursing mother, is continued in verse eleven. Those who love Zion are urged to quench themselves at her breasts with genuine milk. We Westerners would rather not use such imagery any longer, but Eastern people love it (cf. 60:4). The metaphor is explained in the first part of verse twelve and continued and extended in the second part. Mother Zion not only bears and nurses her children; she also carries, hugs and dandles them.

Verse thirteen is uniquely beautiful and tender. Jehovah promises to comfort Israel as a loving and caring mother comforts her child. He, Jehovah Himself, will comfort Zion. Indeed there is none other in heaven or on earth who can comfort this people but He who prayed for them on the cross and wanted to gather them under His wings like a hen gathers her chicks. He will yet do so tenderly and lovingly, like a mother; He will do so after His coming again to Jerusalem. We may be sure that when He comforts Israel in the future He will do no half-job, since the first part of verse fourteen emphasizes that His comforting will be complete. In that day the great contrast between the Lord's friends and enemies will be clearer than ever before (cf. Mal. 3:18; 4:1, 2).

The Great Tribulation of the Wicked

> 15. For, behold, the LORD will come with fire, and with his chariots like a whirlwind, to render his anger with fury, and his rebuke with flames of fire.
> 16. For by fire and by his sword will the LORD plead with all flesh: and the slain of the LORD shall be many.
> 17. They that sanctify themselves, and purify themselves in the gardens behind one tree in the midst, eating swine's flesh, and the abomination, and the mouse, shall be consumed together, saith the LORD.
> 18a. For I know their works and their thoughts: . . .

The last chapter can be divided into four parts; this section is the third. Once again the glory of restored Israel is contrasted with the judgment of the wicked. *Fire* is frequently used in connections with the Lord's coming for judgment (Ps. 50:3; 97:3; Hab. 3:5; II Thes. 1:8; Heb. 10:27; II Pet. 3:7). Together with *fire* five more means of judgment are mentioned, i.e., *chariots* of clouds, *whirlwind, rebuke, flames of fire,* (lightnings), and the *sword* of war. All the elements of nature serve Him as weapons and instruments of destruction; it is no wonder that His *slain* are many. Revelation 9:18 states that one-third of mankind will be killed. The cities of the nations will *fall* (Rev. 16:19).

On whom will the Lord Jesus pour out His fiery wrath? They are the same people as mentioned in verses three and four. They are described here as people who (1) *purify themselves.* But they do so in their own manner and not as God demands. God's way of purification, the blood of the Lamb, is rejected by them. Only at Golgotha will God cleanse the sinner by the blood of His Lamb. (2) These apostate people are said to follow a mysterious enemy, whose name is not mentioned, but of whom it is said in a complicated way that (a) he is *one* out of many, a special enemy, an enemy in the extreme. (b) He is an example in self-cleansing and so also in rejecting Christ's blood. (c) He has great influence on his followers for they all follow him. (d) He exalts himself greatly, for he is in the *midst.* That was, and is, and always will be, Christ's place. Christ was in the midst as one who served, in the midst on the cross, in their midst after the resurrection, in the midst of the throne and of the angels and saints, and one day He will also reign in the midst of His enemies. Hence this unnamed enemy wants to take Christ's place. (e) Finally it may be noted of this enemy that he together with his apostate followers will be struck by Christ's coming for judgment. All these sparse and yet significant indications point to no one else but the Antichrist, Christ's great enemy in the end time. The apostate, who lives by the principle of self-purification, self-salvation, wallows meanwhile in the basest of uncleanness – eats *swine's flesh,* unmentionable *abomination,* and *mice,* which were eaten as a delicacy by the Romans and other heathen people and were used by others as idolatrous sacrifices. Mice as well as swine were unclean animals and if by *abomination* is meant creeping animals, then the former are an abomination as well, according to the law. Antichrist, whose name is not mentioned because of a certain abhorrence, will, together with his entire God-forsaking horde and with his *works* and *thoughts,* his Satanic activities and devices, be consumed by the fire of judgment.

18b. ... it shall come, that I will gather all nations and tongues; and they shall come, and see my glory.

19. And I will set a sign among them, and I will send those that escape of them unto the nations, to Tarshish, Pul, and Lud, that draw the bow, to Tubal, and Javan, to the isles afar off, that have not heard my fame, neither have seen my glory; and they shall declare my glory among the Gentiles.

20. And they shall bring all your brethren for an offering unto the LORD out of all nations upon horses, and in chariots, and in litters, and upon mules, and upon swift beasts, to my holy mountain Jerusalem, saith the LORD, as the children of Israel bring an offering in a clean vessel into the house of the LORD.

21. And I will also take of them for priests and for Levites, saith the LORD.

22. For as the new heavens and the new earth, which I will make, shall remain before me, saith the LORD, so shall your seed and your name remain.

23. And it shall come to pass, that from one new moon to another, and from one sabbath to another, shall all flesh come to worship before me, saith the LORD.

24. And they shall go forth, and look upon the carcases of the men that have transgressed against me: for their worm shall not die, neither shall their fire be quenched; and they shall be an abhorring unto all flesh.

We have now come to the fourth part of this chapter, which at the same time is the last part of this great prophecy. We may appropriately call these verses a fitting conclusion to the entire book. The four main topics, which we met again and again, are once more depicted in brief but bold strokes: Israel, the conversion of the nations, the renewal of the entire creation, and the destruction of all the wicked. Verse eighteen tells us that God will gather all nations for the purpose of showing them His glory. None else but Christ is the image and the glory of God.

God says that He will set a *sign* among the nations. This sign is the same as the *sign of the Son of man* (Mat. 24:30), which is called elsewhere in Isaiah a *banner* or *ensign*. Beside this general signal to gather, God will also send emissaries — people who have escaped the judgment — to the most distant nations which as yet have not heard the fame of the returned Christ nor seen His glory; these envoys will declare the glory of King Jesus. By these escapees are meant, of course, the chosen remnant, which have been suddenly converted, like Paul before them, by the appearance of Christ. They are sent to *Tarshish* (Spain, France and Italy) to *Pul* (a region in Africa) and to *Lud,* which according to some is the same as Lydia, though it seems preferable to take *Pul* and *Lud* together for all of Africa. Tubal was a son of Japheth, whose descendants settled in north-eastern Europe or Russia and *Javan* is the biblical name for Greece. These names point to western and eastern Europe and Africa as the regions where the converted Jews will be sent. But North and

South America and Australia are not excluded for they are referred to by the words *the isles afar off.* This even includes Japan, China and India.

What will these Jews preach? The gospel of the Kingdom, which was initiated by John the Baptist and the Lord Jesus and which preaching is continued today. Repent or perish, they will cry; kiss the returned Son who is enthroned in Zion lest you be struck by His immediate and swift judgments. Such preaching will resemble that of Jonah who, having himself escaped judgment, had to warn others about judgment. And what will be the result of this preaching? Verse twenty tells us that nations will one day, like Nineveh, believe the preaching and turn to King Jesus and as a sign of their genuine conversion terminate their hatred of the dispersed Jews and bring them as an offering to Jerusalem to the honor of Zion's exalted King. The description of the various animals means that they will make use of the best means of transportation to bring the dispersed Jews speedily to Jerusalem where they may pay homage to their King. In addition, the Lord wishes to use some of those gathered-up Jews as priests and Levites in the new and great house of the Lord as is so extensively described by Ezekiel. If Israel should fear that this joy would be of short duration, since in the past Jerusalem had been so often and for so long trampled down, then the assurance of verse twenty-two will put them perfectly at ease. As permanent as heaven and earth, so permanent will Israel and her seed be; she will be eternally secure. This is the continuous teaching of Isaiah and all the prophets. As beautifully as the new creation will be adorned, so beautifully will Israel, though formerly long despised, shine in her beauty above all the nations as Christ's jewel among the saved.

Not only Israel will then be converted, but all nations will bow before Him. Psalm sixty-seven will be fulfilled, and many other Psalms as well. *All flesh will come to Thee* sang the God-fearing people, and Isaiah in verse twenty-three records its fulfillment. Jehovah-Jesus is the *confidence of all the ends of the earth,* and His footsteps (paths) drop fatness (Ps. 65:11). The Jewish *sabbath* will be observed by Israel and all the nations, and the whole world will have to order its religion according to the worship service of once despised Jewry.

Isaiah concludes with an absolute antithesis, however, as does Malachi, the last prophet of the Old Testament. The nations that have been saved and at regular intervals go up to Jerusalem to offer the Lord Jesus their homage will even in the neighborhood of Jerusalem see a warning and shocking sight; they view the corpses of the apostates, in the valley of Topheth, who have rebelled against Jehovah-Jesus and been struck down by His holy wrath. Apparently from the rim of an abyss the holy pilgrims can see the corpses whose worm shall not die and whose fire will not be quenched (cf. Mark 9:44-46). Jehovah has a purpose with this abhorrent sight. He wants this to be an *abhorring* unto all the nations. He wants the nations, among whom there will still be the few unconverted who have only feigned subjecting themselves to Him, to have a deep impression of His holiness and of the horribleness of sin and rebellion against His authority. This is the grand and sublime ending of the book of the prophet Isaiah who undoubtedly one day will occupy a glorious place in the Kingdom of the Messiah. May all who read this share one day in the glory of that Kingdom and not in the horrors of the lake of fire!